Why I love Paris

By Catherine Le Nevez

Paris' grandeur is inspiring but what I love most about the city is its intimacy. Its *quartiers* are like a patchwork of villages, and while it's one of the world's major metropolises – with all of the culture and facilities that go with it – there's a real sense of community at the local shops, markets and cafes that hasn't changed since my childhood. Yet because every little 'village' has its own evolving character, I'm constantly discovering and rediscovering hidden corners of the city.

For more about our authors, see p432.

Top: Jardin des Tuileries (p115) in autumn

Paris' Top 16

PETER LANGER / CORBIS ©

Eiffel Tower *(p78)*

1 No one could imagine Paris today without its signature spire. But Gustave Eiffel only constructed this graceful tower – then the world's tallest, at 320m – as a temporary exhibit for the 1889 Exposition Universelle. Luckily, its popularity assured its survival beyond the World Fair and its elegant art nouveau webbed-metal design has become the defining fixture of the city's skyline. Head here at dusk for the best day and night views of the glittering city, and toast making it to the top at the sparkling-new champagne bar.

⊙ ***Eiffel Tower & Western Paris***

Musée Rodin *(p230)*

2 The lovely Musée Rodin is the most romantic of Paris' museums. Auguste Rodin's former workshop and showroom, the 1730-built Hôtel Biron, is filled with Rodin's own sculptural masterpieces like the marble monument to love, *The Kiss*, as well as creations by his muse and protégé, sculptor Camille Claudel, and other artists whose works Rodin collected, including Van Gogh and Renoir. But the real treat is the mansion's rambling, scented sculpture garden, which provides an entrancing setting for contemplating works like *The Thinker*. BELOW: AUGUSTE RODIN'S SCULPTURE, *THE KISS*

⊙ ***St-Germain & Les Invalides***

PETER BARRITT / CORBIS ©

3

DALLAS AND JOHN HEATON / CORBIS ©

Louvre (p103)

3 The *Mona Lisa* and the *Venus de Milo* are just two of the priceless treasures resplendently housed inside this fortress turned royal palace turned France's first national museum. Stretching a whopping 700m along the Seine, the world's biggest museum can seem overwhelming, but there are plenty of ways to experience it, even if you don't have nine months to glance at every artwork and artefact here. One of the best is its thematic trails – from the 'Art of Eating' to 'Love in the Louvre'. TOP LEFT: STAIRS INSIDE THE LOUVRE'S GLASS PYRAMID, DESIGNED BY IM PEI

Louvre & Les Halles

Arc de Triomphe (p90)

4 If anything rivals the Eiffel Tower as the symbol of Paris, it's this magnificent 1836-built monument to Napoleon's 1805 victory at Austerlitz, which he commissioned the following year. The intricately sculpted triumphal arch stands sentinel in the centre of the Étoile (star), the world's largest roundabout – just be sure to use the pedestrian tunnels below ground to reach it! Some of the best vistas in Paris radiate from the top, including swooping views along the luxury shop-lined Champs-Élysées, Paris' most glamorous avenue.

Champs-Élysées & Grands Boulevards

Basilique du Sacré-Cœur (p131)

5 Sacré-Cœur is a place of pilgrimage in more ways than one. Follow the staircased, ivy-clad streets up the hill of the fabled artists' neighbourhood of Montmartre to a funicular gliding up to the white domes of Basilique du Sacré-Cœur (Sacred Heart Basilica). The chapel-lined basilica – featuring the shimmering apse mosaic *Christ in Majesty* – crowns the 130m-high Butte de Montmartre (Montmartre Hill). Its lofty position provides dizzying vistas across Paris from the basilica's front steps and, above all, from up inside its main dome.

Montmartre & Northern Paris

Centre Pompidou *(p111)*

6 The primary-coloured, inside-out building houses France's national modern and contemporary art museum, the Musée National d'Art Moderne (MNAM), containing works from 1905 through to the present day, including a fabulous Matisse collection. And the centre's cutting-edge cultural offerings include temporary exhibition spaces, a public library, cinemas and entertainment venues. Topping it off is the spectacular panorama radiating from the roof.
BELOW: CENTRE POMPIDOU DESIGNED BY R PIANO, R ROGERS AND G FRANCHINI

Louvre & Les Halles

Notre Dame *(p196)*

7 A vision of stained glass rose windows, flying buttresses and frightening gargoyles, Paris' glorious cathedral on the larger of the two inner-city islands is the city's geographic and spiritual heart. This gothic wonder took nearly 200 years to build, but would have been demolished following damage during the French Revolution had it not been for the popularity of Victor Hugo's timely novel, *The Hunchback of Notre Dame*, which sparked a petition to save it. Climb its 422 spiralling steps for magic rooftop views.

The Islands

6

IZZET KERIBAR / GETTY IMAGES ©

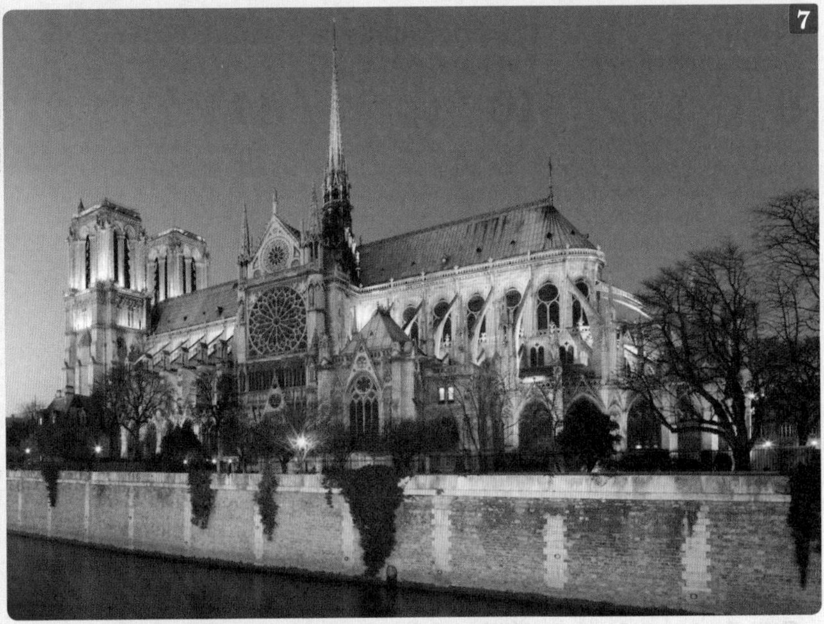

JUMPER / GETTY IMAGES ©

IZZET KERIBAR / GETTY IMAGES©

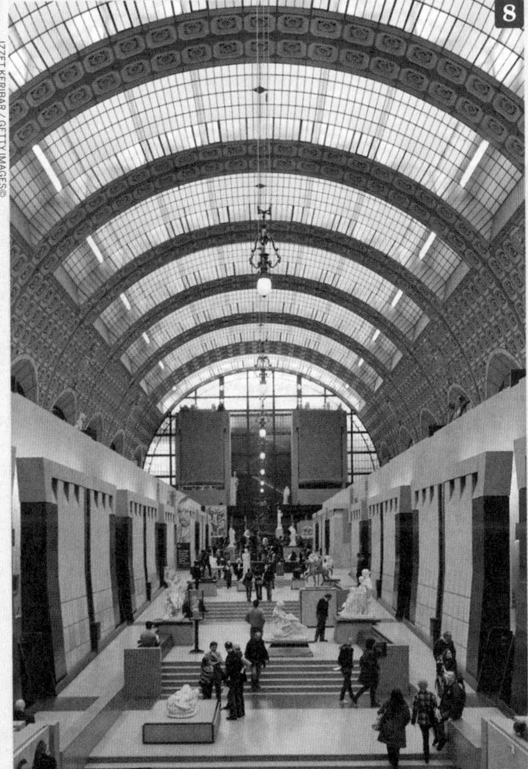

Musée d'Orsay *(p224)*

8 The Musée d'Orsay's celebrated canvases by impressionist and post-impressionist masters including Renoir, Gaugin, Cézanne, Sisley, Manet, Monet, Degas and Toulouse-Lautrec might not have changed, but magnificent renovations at the Musée d'Orsay now make them appear as if they're hung in an intimate home. The grand former railway station (the Gare d'Orsay) housing the museum is still an exemplar of art nouveau architecture, of course, but France's treasured national collection of masterpieces from 1848 to 1914 are now – more than ever – the star of the show.

St-Germain & Les Invalides

Jardin du Luxembourg *(p228)*

9 The Jardin du Luxembourg offers a snapshot of Parisian life. Couples stroll through the chestnut groves. Children chase wooden sailboats around the octagonal pond and laugh at the antics of engaging marionettes. Old men play rapid-fire chess with cherished pieces at weathered tables. Students pore over books between lectures. Office workers snatch some sunshine, lounging in sage-green metal chairs. Musicians strike up in the bandstand. Joggers loop past stately statues. And friends meet and make plans to meet again.

St-Germain & Les Invalides

Cimetière du Père Lachaise *(p154)*

10 Paris is a collection of villages and these sprawling hectares of cobbled lanes and elaborate tombs, with a population (as it were) of over one million, qualifies as one in its own right. The world's most visited cemetery was founded in 1804, and initially attracted few funerals because of its distance from the city centre. The authorities responded by exhuming famous remains and resettling them here. Their marketing ploy worked and Cimetière du Père Lachaise has been Paris' most fashionable final address ever since.

Le Marais & Ménilmontant

Musée National du Moyen Âge *(p206)*

11 Medieval weapons, suits of armour, furnishings, and gold, ivory and enamel *objets d'art* aren't the only reasons to visit France's national museum of the Middle Ages. Nor are the sublime series of late-15th-century tapestries *The Lady with the Unicorn*, nor the gardens planted with flowers, herbs and shrubs that appear in masterpieces hanging throughout the museum (including the Unicorn Forest). Here you can see both France's finest civil medieval building, the Hôtel de Cluny, and the remains of Gallo-Roman baths dating to AD 200.

Latin Quarter

9

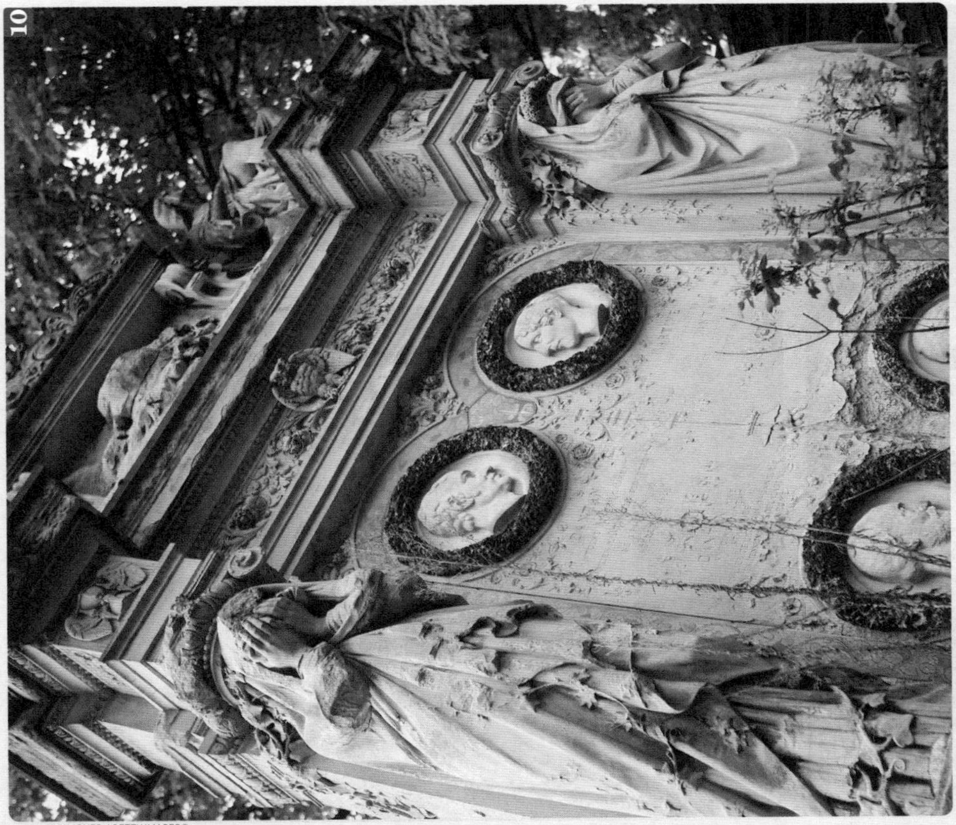

10

11

GLENN BEANLAND / GETTY IMAGES ©

Canal St-Martin

(p136)

12 Bordered by shaded towpaths and traversed by iron footbridges, the charming, 4.5km-long Canal St-Martin was slated to be concreted over when barge transportation declined until local residents rallied to save it. The quaint setting lured artists, designers and students, who set up artists' collectives, vintage and offbeat boutiques and a bevy of neo-retro cafes and bars. Enduring maritime legacies include old swing bridges that still pivot 90 degrees when boats pass through the canal's double-locks, and a canal cruise is the best way to experience Paris' lesser-known waterway.

Montmartre & Northern Paris

13

Stylish Shopping *(p57)*

13 Paris, like any major city, has its international chains (including icons that originated here). But what really sets Parisian shopping apart is its incredible array of specialist shops. Candles from the world's oldest candle maker, pigments from the art supply shop that developed 'Klein blue' with the artist, soft leather handbags made in the hip Haut Marais, green-metal *bouquiniste* (secondhand bookshop) stalls lining the banks of the Seine and fashions displayed beneath the stained-glass dome of *grande dame* department store Galeries Lafayette are just some of the goodies in store. LEFT: DOME OF GALERIES LAFAYETTE (P99).

Shopping

Versailles *(p267)*

14 No wonder revolutionaries massacred the Château de Versailles palace guard and dragged King Louis XVI and his queen Marie Antoinette back to Paris. This monumental, 700-room palace and sprawling estate – with its fountained gardens, ponds and canals – could not have been in starker contrast to taxpayers' average living conditions at the time. A Unesco World Heritage-listed wonder, Versailles is easily reached from central Paris; try to time your visit to catch musical fountain displays and equestrian shows.

Day Trips from Paris

Street Markets *(p58)*

15 Stall after stall of Camembert, Cantal and Roquefort cheeses, punnets of raspberries, baguettes, tomatoes, pigs' trotters, horsemeat sausages, spit-roasted chickens, glass bottles of olives and olive oils, quail eggs, duck eggs, boxes of chanterelle mushrooms and knobbly truffles, long-clawed langoustines and prickly sea urchins on beds of crushed ice – along with belts, boots, wallets, cheap socks, chic hats, colourful scarves, striped t-shirts, wicker baskets, wind-up toys, buckets of flowers... Paris' street markets, such as the wonderful Marché Bastille, are a feast for the senses.

RIGHT: SEAFOOD, RUE MOUFFETARD STREET MARKET (P217)

Shopping

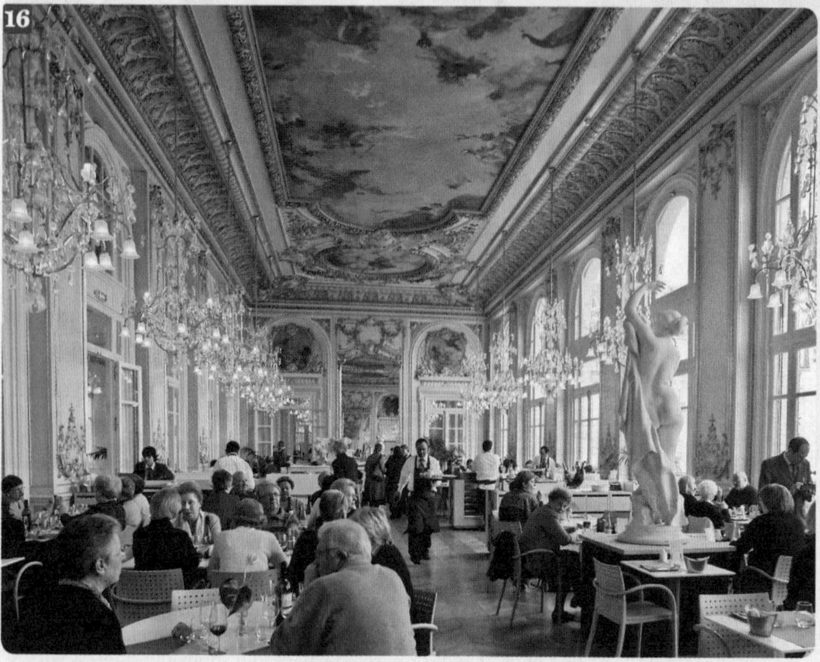

16

Parisian Dining *(p42)*

16 There's a reason that boxes of leftovers aren't done in Paris, and it has nothing to do with portion sizes. Whether you're at an unchanged-in-decades neighbourhood haunt, a beautiful art nouveau brasserie, a smart, switched-on neobistro or a fêted haute cuisine establishment helmed by a legendary chef, the food and the dining experience are considered inseparable. France pioneered what is still the most influential style of cooking in the Western world and Paris is its showcase *par excellence*. Do as Parisians do and savour every moment.

ABOVE: RESTAURANT MUSÉE D'ORSAY (P225)

Eating

What's New

Future Forum

Since Paris' historic wholesale markets shifted out of the city centre in the 1970s, their replacement, the banal Forum des Halles shopping mall, has been a source of civic shame. But a rainforest-inspired giant glass canopy and lush, landscaped meadow-like gardens atop the subterranean mall (itself receiving a facelift) are set to restore Parisian pride from 2013 on, with final completion in 2016. (p117)

Louvre Flying Carpet

The interior courtyard of the Louvre's Cour Visconti, housing the new Islamic art galleries, was crowned by a shimmering gold 'flying carpet' roof in late 2012. (p103)

Notre Dame Bells

As part of 2013's celebrations for the 850th anniversary since Notre Dame's construction began, some of the cathedral's worn bells are being melted down to create nine new bells replicating the original medieval chimes. (p196)

Musée Picasso Reopening

From summer 2013, after four years of renovations, the Musée Picasso, housed inside a beautiful 17th-century Marais mansion, once again displays thousands of the master's works from summer 2013. (p158)

Fashion Museum Revamp

Yet another long-awaited 2013 reopening following renovations is Paris' fashion museum, the Musée Galliera de la Mode de la Ville de Paris, fittingly housed in a lavish Italianate palace. (p82)

Burger Mania

The burger trend sweeping Paris is, unsurprisingly, *très* gourmet. Recent openings include buzzing Blend, serving burgers with house-baked brioche buns, homemade ketchup and hand-cut meat. (p121)

Minipalais

Art nouveau architecture, artist studio ambience and all-day dining on fare like truffled duck breast and foie gras burgers make the Grand Palais' new restaurant a maxipleasure. (p95)

Bus Palladium Redux

It swung in the '60s and now mythical Pigalle club Bus Palladium is rolling on again with rock, electro and funk nights, acoustic concerts and a vintage-cool restaurant. (p148)

Pic's Parisian Debut

France's only triple-Michelin-starred female chef, Anne-Sophie Pic, is preparing to open at 20 rue du Louvre, 1er: watch this space. (www.anne-sophie-pic.com)

For more recommendations and reviews, see **lonelyplanet.com/paris**

Need to Know

Currency
Euro (€)

Language
French

Visas
No restrictions for EU citizens. Generally not required for most other nationalities for stays of up to 90 days.

Money
ATMs widely available. Visa and MasterCard accepted in most hotels, shops and restaurants; fewer establishments accept American Express.

Mobile Phones
Check with your provider before you leave about roaming costs and/or ensuring your phone's unlocked to use a French SIM card (available cheaply in Paris).

Time
Central European Time (GMT/UTC plus one hour).

Tourist Information
Paris Convention & Visitors Bureau (☎08 92 68 30 00; www.parisinfo.com; 25-27 rue des Pyramides, 1er; ⏲9am-7pm; MPyramides). Main branch.

Your Daily Budget

Budget under €80
- Dorm beds €25–35
- Excellent self-catering supermarkets and markets
- Inexpensive public transport, standby theatre tickets

Midrange €80–200
- Double room €110–200
- Two-course dinner with glass of wine €20–40
- Affordable museums

Top end over €200
- Historic luxury hotels
- Gastronomic restaurants
- Designer boutiques

Advance Planning

Two months before Book your accommodation, organise opera, ballet or cabaret tickets and make reservations for high-end/popular restaurants.

Two weeks before Sign up for a free, local-led tour, book a sight-seeing balloon 'flight' and start narrowing down your choice of museums, pre-purchasing tickets online where possible.

Two days before Pack your comfiest shoes!

Useful Websites

- **Lonely Planet** (www.lonelyplanet.com/paris) Destination information, bookings, traveller forum and more.
- **Paris Info** (www.parisinfo.com) Comprehensive tourist-authority website with updated What's On section.
- **Secrets of Paris** (www.secretsofparis.com) Loads of resources and reviews.
- **Paris By Mouth** (http://parisbymouth.com) Foodie heaven.
- **My Little Paris** (www.mylittleparis.com) Little-known local treasures.

WHEN TO GO

Spring and autumn are ideal times to visit. Summer is the main tourist season, but some businesses close during August. Sights are quieter and prices lower during winter.

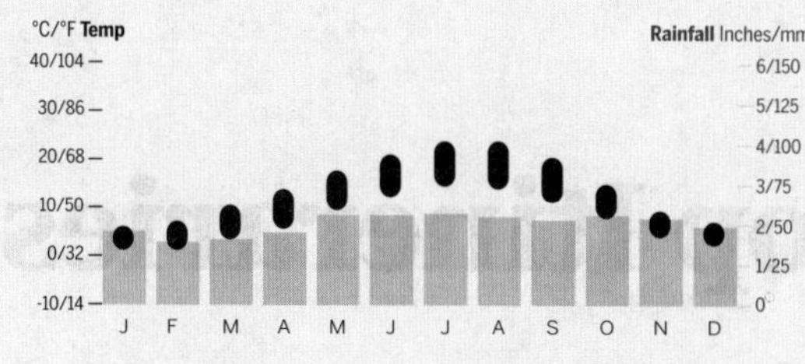

Arriving in Paris

Charles de Gaulle Airport trains (RER), buses, night buses and private door-to-door shuttles to the city centre €9-15, plus private door-to-door shuttles €26-42; taxi around €50 to €65.

Orly Airport Trains (Orlyval then RER), buses, night buses and private door-to-door shuttles to the city centre €7-15, plus private door-to-door shuttles €26-42; taxi around €40 to €50.

Beauvais Airport Buses (€15) to Porte Maillot then metro (€1.70); taxi from €140 (day) and €180 (night and all day Sunday).

Gare du Nord Train Station Within central Paris; served by metro (€1.70).

For much more on **arrival,** see p338

Getting Around

Walking is a pleasure in Paris, but the city also has one of the most efficient and inexpensive public transport systems in the world, making getting around a breeze.

➡ **Metro & RER** The fastest way to get around. Runs from about 5.20am to 1.15am (around 2.15am on Friday and Saturday nights), depending on the line.

➡ **Bicycle** Virtually free pick-up, drop-off Vélib' bikes operate across 1800 stations citywide.

➡ **Bus** Good for parents with prams/strollers and people with limited mobility.

➡ **Boat** The Batobus is a handy hop-on, hop-off service stopping at eight key destinations along the Seine.

For much more on **getting around,** see p340

Sleeping

Paris has a wealth of accommodation, but it's often *complet* (full) well in advance. Reservations are recommended any time of year, and are essential during the warmer months (April to October) and all public and school holidays. Accommodation outside central Paris is marginally cheaper than within the city itself, but it's almost always a false economy, as travelling into the city takes time and money. Try to choose somewhere within Paris' 20 *arrondissements* (city districts).

Useful Websites

➡ **Paris Hotel** (www.hotels-paris.fr) Well-organised site with lots of user reviews.

➡ **Paris Hotel Service** (www.parishotelservice.com) Specialises in boutique gems.

➡ **Paris Hotels** (www.parishotels.com) Loads of options and locations.

➡ **Lonely Planet** (www.lonelyplanet.com/hotels) Reviews of Lonely Planet's top choices.

For much more on **sleeping,** see p282

TIPPING

A tip on tipping: a service charge is already included in prices under French law, meaning that tipping is generally neither expected nor necessary in Paris. If service is particularly good, however, you might want to tip five to 10 percent in restaurants. It's customary to round taxi fares up to the nearest euro. For more information, see p349.

Top Itineraries

Day One

Louvre & Les Halles (p101)

Start your day with a stroll through the elegant **Jardin des Tuileries**, stopping to view Monet's enormous *Waterlilies* at the **Musée de l'Orangerie** and/or photography exhibits at the **Jeu de Paume**. IM Pei's glass pyramid is your compass point to enter the labyrinthine **Louvre**.

Lunch The Louvre's nine cafes and restaurants include Café Marly (p123).

Louvre & Les Halles (p101)

Visiting the world's largest museum could easily consume a full day but once you've had your fill, take a well-earned break browsing the colonnaded arcades of the exquisite **Jardin du Palais Royal**, and visiting the beautiful church **Église St-Eustache**. Tap into the soul of the former Les Halles wholesale markets along back-street legacies like the former oyster market, **rue Montorgueil**. Linger for a drink on **rue Montmartre**, then head to the late-opening **Centre Pompidou** for modern and contemporary art and amazing rooftop views.

Dinner Frenchie (p118) and Verjus (p119) offer walk-in wine-bar dining.

Le Marais & Ménilmontant (p152)

There's a wealth to see in the Marais by day, but the neighbourhood really comes into its own at night, with a cornucopia of hip bars and clubs.

Day Two

Champs-Élysées & Grands Boulevards (p88)

Climb the mighty **Arc de Triomphe** for a pinch-yourself Parisian panorama. Promenade down Paris' most glamorous avenue, the **Champs-Élysées**, and give your credit card a workout in the **Triangle d'Or**, **Galeries Lafayette** or **place de la Madeleine** before catching edgy art exhibitions at **La Pinacothèque**.

Lunch Café Branly (p85): casual yet classy, with ringside Tower views.

Eiffel Tower & Western Paris (p76)

Check out indigenous art as well as the awesome architecture of the **Musée du Quai Branly**. This cultural neighbourhood is also home to the world's largest Monet collection at the **Musée Marmottan-Monet**, contemporary installations at the **Palais de Tokyo**, and Asian treasures at the **Musée Guimet**. Sunset is the best time to ascend the **Eiffel Tower**, to experience both the dizzying views during daylight and then the glittering *la ville lumière* (the City of Light) by night.

Dinner Fabulous bistro fare at Firmin Le Barbier (p84).

Montparnasse & Southern Paris (p250)

Detour for a drink at a historic Montparnasse brasserie like **Le Select** or continue straight down the Seine to party aboard floating nightclubs like **Le Batofar**.

Day Three

The Islands (p194)

Starting your day at the city's most visited sight, **Notre Dame**, gives you the best chance of beating the crowds. In addition to its stained-glass interior, allow around an hour to visit the top and another to explore the archaeological **crypt**. For even more beautiful stained-glasswork, don't miss nearby **Ste-Chapelle**. Cross the **Pont St-Louis** to buy a **Berthillon** ice cream before browsing the Île St-Louis' enchanting boutiques.

Lunch Market-fresh fare at 'old friend' Mon Vieil Ami (p202).

St-Germain & Les Invalides (p222)

Swoon over impressionist masterpieces in the magnificent **Musée d'Orsay**, scout out the backstreet boutiques and storied shops of St-Germain, sip coffee on the terrace of literary cafes like **Les Deux Magots** and laze in the lovely **Jardin du Luxembourg**, the city's most popular park.

Dinner French classics in the art nouveau jewel Bouillon Racine (p235).

Latin Quarter (p204)

Scour the shelves of late-night bookshops like the fabled **Shakespeare & Company**, then join Parisian students and academics in the Latin Quarter's bars, cafes and pubs on **rue Mouffetard** or hit a jazz club like **Café Universel**.

Day Four

Montmartre & Northern Paris (p129)

Montmartre's slinking streets and steep staircases lined with crooked ivy-clad buildings are enchanting to meander in the early morning when tourists are few. Head to the hilltop **Sacré-Cœur** basilica, then brush up on the area's fabled history at the **Musée de Montmartre**.

Lunch Locals' favourite Le Miroir (p139) offers top lunch *menu* specials.

Montmartre & Northern Paris (p129)

Stroll the shaded towpaths of cafe-lined **Canal St-Martin**, and visit the futuristic **Parc de la Villette**, the kid-friendly **Cité des Sciences** museum and the instrument-filled **Musée de la Musique**, within the **Cité de la Musique**. Sailing schedules permitting, hop on a **canal cruise** to Bastille.

Dinner Modern French culinary magic at Septime (p184).

Bastille & Eastern Paris (p181)

The Bastille neighbourhood calls for a cafe crawl: classics include the cherry-red **Le Pure Café** and absinthe specialist **La Fée Verte**. Salsa your socks off at the 1936 dance hall **Le Balajo** on nightlife strip **rue de Lappe** or catch electro, funk and hip hop at **La Scène Bastille**.

If You Like...

Markets

Marché Bastille Excellent open-air market in the city. (p186)

Marché d'Aligre Wonderfully chaotic market street with all the staples of French cuisine. (p186)

Marché St-Quentin Covered market dating back to 1866. (p144)

Marché aux Enfants Rouges Nothing beats this glorious maze of food stalls in the Marais with ready-to-eat dishes from around the globe. (p168)

Marché aux Fleurs Fragrant flower market. (p203)

Marché Raspail Especially popular for its fabulous Sunday organic market. (p242)

Marché aux Puces de St-Ouen Europe's largest flea market, with over 2500 stalls. (p149)

Rue Mouffetard Atmospheric commercial street with food shops and stalls galore. (p217)

Churches

Église St-Eustache Architecturally magnificent and musically outstanding, this church has sent souls soaring for centuries. (p113)

Cathédrale de Notre Dame de Paris The city's mighty cathedral is without equal. (p196)

Basilique du Sacré-Cœur Paris' landmark basilica lords over Montmartre. (p131)

Église de Ste-Marie Madeleine Neoclassical landmark in western Paris. (p93)

RUSSELL MOUNTFORD / GETTY IMAGES ©

Marché Bastille (p186)

Église St-Pierre Where the Jesuit order was founded. (p134)

Ste-Chapelle Classical concerts provide the perfect opportunity to truly appreciate Ste-Chapelle's beauty. (p202)

Basilique de St-Denis France's first major Gothic structure and still one of its finest. (p138)

Église St-Germain des Prés Built in the 11th century, this is Paris' oldest church. (p234)

Église St-Sulpice Frescoes by Delacroix and a starring role in *The Da Vinci Code*. (p232)

Cathédrale Notre Dame – Chartres Renowned for its brilliant blue stained glass. (p277)

Romance

Jardin du Palais Royal With its arcaded galleries and gravel walkways embraced by the neoclassical Palais Royal, there is no urban garden more elegant or romantic. (p115)

Le Grand Véfour Savour the romance of 18th-century Paris in one the world's most beautiful restaurants. (p121)

The Islands Paris' little islands harbour a trove of hidden romantic spots. (p194)

Eiffel Tower There's a reason the top platform sees up to three marriage proposals an hour. (p78)

Canal St-Martin Stroll the shaded towpaths or sit on the banks and watch the boats float by. (p136)

Place St-Sulpice The *place* (square) in front of Église St-Sulpice is an enchanting spot to linger. (p232)

Musée Rodin Swoon over Rodin's marble monument to love, *The Kiss*, and stroll the museum's rose-clambered, sculpture-filled garden. (p230)

Le Pradey With its deep red walls, frilly bedspread and heart-shaped door frame, the themed Moulin Rouge room at this design hotel is pure romance. (p286)

Pont de l'Archevêché Padlocks chained to city bridges such as Pont de l'Archevêché symbolise eternal love to the couples who attach them (if not to city authorities). (p207)

Literature

Maison de Victor Hugo Visit the elegant home of celebrated novelist and poet Victor Hugo overlooking one of Paris' most sublime city squares. (p157)

Maison de Balzac The novelist's residence/writing studio from 1840–47 is a charmer. (p83)

St-Germain literary addresses Take a literary loop walking tour through this fabled part of the Left Bank. (p233)

Latin Quarter literary addresses The Latin Quarter is scattered with seminal literary addresses. (p209)

Montparnasse literary addresses Writers, artists and political exiles flocked to Montparnasse's brasseries in its early 20th century heyday. (p252)

Shakespeare & Company Attend a reading by established and emerging authors, curl up in the reading library or browse the shelves of this magical bookshop/writers' hub. (p216)

Bibliothèque Nationale de France France's national library frequently mounts literary exhibitions. (p254)

For more top Paris spots, see the following:

- ➡ Museums & Galleries (p38)
- ➡ Eating (p42)
- ➡ Drinking & Nightlife (p51)
- ➡ Shopping (p57)
- ➡ Entertainment (p62)
- ➡ Gay & Lesbian (p68)
- ➡ Sports & Activities (p70)

Panoramas

Eiffel Tower Each of Paris' landmark tower's three viewing platforms offer a different perspective of the city. (p78)

Tour Montparnasse The views over Paris are the redeeming feature of this otherwise soulless skyscraper. (p252)

Galeries Lafayette Some of the best free views of the city are from the top of this grand department store. (p99)

Parc de Belleville Climb to the top of the hill in this little-known Belleville park to savour some of the best views of the city. (p157)

Arc de Triomphe Swooping views along the Champs-Élysées. (p90)

Centre Pompidou Although only six storeys high, the rooftop views across low-rise Paris are phenomenal. (p111)

Le Ballon Air de Paris Airborne views over the city don't come better than from the skyhigh perspective of a hot-air balloon. (p254)

Palais de Chaillot Front-row Eiffel Tower views. (p81)

Grande Arche Great views of the Arc de Triomphe extend from La Défense's own arch. (p84)

Basilique du Sacré-Cœur The views from Sacré Cœur's steps are superb and just get better once you climb up inside its central dome. (p131)

Art Nouveau

Eiffel Tower The graceful latticed metalwork of Paris' 'iron lady' is art nouveau architecture at its best. (p78)

Abbesses metro entrance Hector Guimard's finest remaining glass-canopied metro entrance, illuminated by twin lamps. (p137)

Musée d'Orsay The 1900-built former railway station housing this monumental museum justifies a visit alone. (p224)

Le Train Bleu Resplendent restaurant inside the Gare de Lyon. (p190)

Musée Carnavalet Fouquet's stunning art nouveau jewellery shop from rue Royale inside the city's leading history museum is a real treat. (p156)

Galeries Lafayette Glorious department store topped by a stunning stained-glass dome. (p99)

Marché du Temple This old art nouveau covered market will once again become the hub of local Marais life when it reopens as a cutting-edge cultural centre. (p161)

Bofinger Nothing quite so tasty as dining between art nouveau brass, glass and mirrors in Paris' oldest brasserie. (p165)

Modern & Contemporary Architecture

Centre Pompidou Designed inside-out by Renzo Piano and Richard Rogers in the 1970s, Paris' premier cultural centre is still cutting-edge today. (p111)

La Défense The only place in the city to see a forest of skyscrapers. (p83)

Musée du Quai Branly Striking Seine-side museum designed by Jean Nouvel. (p80)

Institut du Monde Arabe The building that established Nouvel's reputation blends modern and traditional Arab elements with Western influences. (p210)

Fondation Cartier Pour l'Art Contemporain Stunning contemporary art space courtesy of Nouvel. (p252)

Fondation Louis Vuitton pour la Création This Frank Gehry-designed fine arts centre, topped by a giant glass 'cloud', is expected to open in late 2013. (p86)

Louvre glass pyramid Egypt's original pyramid builders couldn't have imagined this. (p103)

Bibliothèque Nationale de France The national library's four towers are shaped like half-open books. (p254)

Cité de l'Architecture et du Patrimoine Inside the 1937-built Palais du Chaillot, the exhibits not only cover Paris' architectural past and present but also its future. (p81)

Parks & Gardens

Jardin du Luxembourg Paris' most popular inner-city oasis. (p228)

Jardin des Tuileries Meet Monet and revel in Paris at its symmetrical best. (p115)

Promenade Plantée The world's first elevated park, atop a disused 19th-century railway viaduct. (p183)

Maison de Claude Monet The flower-filled gardens surrounding Monet's former home take on a palette of hues come spring. (p280)

Parc de la Villette Canal-side 35-hectare pavilion-filled 'park of the future' with state-of-the-art facilities for kids and adults. (p133)

Parc des Buttes-Chaumont Hilly, forested haven in northern Paris. (p138)

Versailles Designed by André Le Nôtre, the château's gardens are fit for a king. (p267)

Jardin des Plantes The city's beautiful botanic gardens shelter rare plants and greenhouses. (p207)

Bois de Vincennes Paris' eastern woods were once royal hunting grounds. (p187)

Bois de Boulogne Explore Paris' western woods by rowboat or bicycle. (p86)

French Revolution-Era History

Place de la Bastille Site of the former prison stormed on 14 July 1789, mobilising the Revolution. (p183)

Versailles The October 1789 March on Versailles forced the royal family to leave the château. (p267)

Conciergerie Louis XVI's queen Marie Antoinette was one of the aristocratic prisoners tried and imprisoned here. (p201)

Place de la Concorde Louis XVI and Marie Antoinette, were among thousands guillotined where the obelisk now stands. (p92)

Chapelle Expiatoire Original burial grounds of Louis XVI and Marie Antoinette. (p94)

RELAXIMAGES / CORBIS ©

(Top) Obelisk, Place de la Concorde (p92)
(Bottom) Bronze statue in front of Château de Versailles (p267)

BRUCE BI / GETTY IMAGES ©

Parc du Champ de Mars This former military training ground was the site of revolutionary festivals. (p81)

Musée Carnavalet Paris' history museum offers a comprehensive overview of this pivotal time in the city's history. (p156)

Concorde metro station Ceramic tiles spell out the text of the Declaration of the Rights of Man and of the Citizen, setting forth the principles of the French Revolution. (p332)

Caveau de la Huchette Long a swinging jazz club, this cellar was used as a courtroom and torture chamber during the Revolution. (p216)

Medieval History

Marais The Marais' medieval streets largely escaped Baron Haussmann's reformation. (p159)

Notre Dame Constructed between 1163 and the early 14th century. (p196)

Louvre Immense fort-turned-palace-turned-museum, constructed 1190–1202. (p103)

Ste-Chapelle Consecrated in 1248. (p202)

Sorbonne University founded in 1253. (p208)

Musée National du Moyen Âge Partly housed in the 15th-century Hôtel de Cluny, Paris' finest civil medieval building. (p206)

Basilique de St-Denis Work on this Gothic wonder started around 1136. (p138)

Cathédrale Notre Dame – Chartres France's best-preserved medieval cathedral, built in the 13th century. (p277)

Château de Vincennes The only medieval castle in Paris. (p187)

Month by Month

TOP EVENTS

Paris Plages, July

Banlieues Bleues, March

Bastille Day, July

Rock en Seine, August

Nuit Blanche, October

January

The frosty first month of the year isn't the most festive in Paris, and turn-of-the-new-year celebrations have been subdued in recent years, but fashion shows brighten the mood.

Louis XVI Commemorative Mass

On the Sunday closest to 21 January, royalists and right-wingers attend a mass at the Chapelle Expiatoire (www.monuments-nationaux.fr) marking the execution by guillotine of King Louis XVI in 1793.

Fashion Week

Prêt-à-porter (www.pretparis.com), the ready-to-wear fashion salon held twice a year (in late January and in September), is a must for fashion buffs, who flock to the Parc des Expositions at Porte de Versailles in the 15e.

Chinese New Year

Paris' largest lantern-lit festivities and dragon parades take place in the city's main Chinatown in the 13e in late January or early February.

February

Food and wine are celebrated with gusto throughout the year, but the biggie is February's Salon International de l'Agriculture.

Salon International de l'Agriculture

A 10-day international agricultural fair (www.salon-agriculture.com) with produce and animals from all over France turned into starter and main-course fare at the Parc des Expositions at Porte de Versailles, 15e from late February to early March.

March

As the winter chill starts to thaw, blooms appear in Paris' parks and gardens, leaves start greening the city's avenues and festivities begin to flourish.

Banlieues Bleues

Big-name acts perform during the 'Suburban Blues' jazz, blues and R&B festival (www.banlieuesbleues.org) from mid-March to mid-April in Paris' northern suburbs.

Salon du Livre

France's largest international book fair (www.salondulivreparis.com) takes place in mid-March at the Parc des Expositions at Porte de Versailles, 15e.

Printemps du Cinéma

Selected cinemas across Paris offer film-goers a unique entry fee of €3.50 over three days sometime around 21 March (www.printempsducinema.com).

April

Sinatra sang about April in Paris, and the month sees the city's 'charm of spring' in full swing, with chestnuts blossoming and cafe terraces coming into their own.

Foire du Trône

Dating back some 1000 years (!), this huge funfair (www.foiredutrone.com) is held on the Pelouse de Reuilly of the Bois de Vincennes from around early April to late May.

Marathon International de Paris

On your marks... The Paris International Marathon (www.parismarathon.com), usually held on the second Sunday of April, starts on the av des Champs-Élysées, 8e, and finishes on av Foch, 16e, attracting more than 40,000 runners from over 100 countries.

Foire de Paris

Gadgets, widgets, food and wine feature at this huge contemporary-living fair (www.foiredeparis.fr), held from late April to early May at the Parc des Expositions at Porte de Versailles, 15e.

May

The temperate month of May has the most public holidays of any month in France. Watch out for closures, particularly on May Day (1 May).

La Nuit Européenne des Musées

Key museums across Paris stay open late for the European Museums Night (www.nuitdesmusees.culture.fr), on one Saturday/Sunday in mid-May.

La Course des Garçons de Café

Waiters have raced through central Paris balancing a glass and bottle on a tray since the early 20th century, and there are now nearly 800 similar annual events worldwide (www.waitersrace.com).

Art St-Germain des Prés

Some 70 galleries in the 6e come together in late May to showcase their top artists (www.artsaintgermaindespres.com).

Portes Ouvertes des Ateliers d'Artistes de Belleville

More than 200 painters, sculptors and other artists in Belleville in the 10e open their studio doors to visitors over four days (Friday to Monday) in late May (www.ateliers-artistes-belleville.org).

French Open

The glitzy Internationaux de France de Tennis Grand Slam hits up from late May to early June at Stade Roland Garros (www.rolandgarros.com) at the Bois de Boulogne, 16e.

June

Paris is positively jumping in June, thanks to warm temperatures and long daylight hours. Come evening, twilight lingering until nearly 11pm is the stuff of midsummer night dreams.

Festival de Saint Denis

Book ahead for this prestigious cycle of classical music concerts at the Basilique de St-Denis (www.festival-saint-denis.com) and nearby venues held throughout the month.

Fête de la Musique

This national music festival (http://fetedelamusique.culture.fr) welcomes in summer on the solstice (21 June) with staged and impromptu live performances of jazz, reggae, classical and more, all over the city.

Gay Pride March

Late June's colourful Saturday-afternoon Marche des Fiertés (www.gaypride.fr) through the Marais to Bastille celebrates Gay Pride Day with over-the-top floats and outrageous costumes.

Paris Jazz Festival

Free jazz concerts swing every Saturday and Sunday afternoon in June and July in the Parc Floral de Paris (www.parisjazzfestival.paris.fr); park entry for adults/under 25s of €5/3 applies.

La Goutte d'Or en Fête

Algerian raï reggae and rap feature at this week-long world-music festival (www.gouttedorenfete.org) on place Léon, 18e in late June.

July

Sand and pebble 'beaches' – complete with sun beds, umbrellas, atomisers, lounge chairs and palm trees – line the banks of the Seine during the Parisian summer.

Paris Cinéma

Rare and restored films screen in selected cinemas city-wide during this 12-day festival (www.pariscinema.org) in the first half of July.

Bastille Day (14 July)

Paris celebrates France's national day with a military parade along av des Champs-Élysées accompanied by a fly-past of fighter aircraft and helicopters, and *feux d'artifice* (fireworks) above the Champ de Mars by night.

Paris Plages

From mid-July to mid-August, 'Paris Beaches' take over the Right Bank from the Pont Neuf, 1er to the Pont de Sully, 4e; and the Rotonde de la Villette to Rue de Crimée, 19e.

Tour de France

The last of 21 stages of this legendary, 3500km-long cycling event (www.letour.fr) finishes with a dash up av des Champs-Élysées on the third or fourth Sunday of July.

August

Parisians desert the city during the summer swelter when, despite an influx of tourists, many restaurants and shops shut. It's a prime time to cycle, with far less traffic on the roads.

Rock en Seine

Headlining acts rock the Domaine National de St-Cloud on the city's southwestern edge at this popular music festival (www.rockenseine.com).

Cinéma au Clair de Lune

Themed film screenings take place under the stars around town during Paris' free 'moonlight cinema' (www.forumdesimages.fr).

(Top) Nuit Blanche revellers
(Bottom) Cadel Evans, Tour de France

September

Tourists leave and Parisians come home: *la rentrée* marks residents' return to work and study after the summer break. Cultural life shifts into top gear and the weather is at its blue-skied best.

Jazz à La Villette

This super two-week jazz festival (www.jazzalavillette.com) in the first half of September has sessions in Parc de la Villette, at the Cité de la Musique and in surrounding bars.

Festival d'Automne

Painting, music, dance and theatre take place at venues throughout the city from mid-September to late December as part of the long-running Autumn Festival of arts (www.festival-automne.com).

Journées Européennes du Patrimoine

The third weekend in September sees Paris open the doors of otherwise-off-limits buildings – such as embassies, government ministries, corporate offices and the Palais de l'Élysée – during European Heritage Days (www.journeesdupatrimoine.culture.fr).

Techno parade

Part of the annual Rendez-vous Électroniques (Electronic Meeting) festival (www.technoparade.fr), on the third Saturday of September floats carrying musicians and DJs start and end a spin around the Marais at place de la Bastille, 12e.

October

October heralds an autumnal kaleidoscope in the city's parks and gardens. Expect bright, crisp days and cool, clear nights, and excellent cultural offerings.

Nuit Blanche

From sundown until sunrise on the first Saturday and Sunday of October, museums and recreational facilities like swimming pools stay open, along with bars and clubs, for one 'White Night' (ie 'All Nighter').

Fête des Vendanges de Montmartre

The grape harvest from the Clos Montmartre in early October is followed by five days of festivities including a parade (www.fetedesvendangesdemontmartre.com).

Foire Internationale d'Art Contemporain

Scores of galleries are represented at the contemporary art fair known as FIAC (www.fiac.com), held over four days in late October at venues including the Grand Palais.

November

Dark, chilly days and long cold nights see Parisians take refuge indoors: the opera and ballet seasons are going strong and there are plenty of cosy bistros and bars.

Africolor

From mid-November to late December, this six-week-long African music festival (www.africolor.com) is primarily held in surrounding suburbs, such as St-Denis, St-Ouen and Montreuil.

December

Twinkling fairylights, brightly decorated Christmas trees and shop windows, and outdoor ice skating rinks make December a magical month to be in the City of Light.

Jumping International de Paris

Celebrated showjumpers complete at the Palais Omnisports de Paris-Bercy, 12e in early December as part of the Salon du Cheval (Horse Fair; www.salon-cheval.com) at the Parc des Expositions at Porte de Versailles, 15e.

Christmas Eve Mass

Mass is celebrated at midnight on Christmas Eve at many Paris churches, including Notre Dame – arrive by 11pm to find a place.

New Year's Eve

Bd St-Michel (5e), place de la Bastille (11e), the Eiffel Tower (7e) and, above all, av des Champs-Élysées (8e) are the places to be to welcome in the New Year.

With Kids

Paris is extraordinarily kid-friendly and we're not just talking Disneyland: children are welcome participants in many aspects of social life in France, including visiting museums and eating out. If you're on a family trip, you'll find no shortage of things to do.

ATLANTIDE PHOTOTRAVEL / CORBIS ©

Cité des Sciences (p136)

Kid-Friendly Museums

Cité des Sciences

If you only have time for one museum, make it the city's interactive science museum. Book sessions in advance to avoid grappling with gravely disappointed kids.

Musée National d'Histoire Naturelle

No space is better designed for children (six to 12 years) than the inventive Galerie des Enfants inside the Grande Galerie de l'Evolution of Paris' first-class Natural History Museum.

Palais de la Découverte

The permanent collection of this highly-regarded science museum in the 8e, around since 1937, is a perfect mix of interactive exhibits and serious information. Its temporary exhibitions are outstanding and older children (over 10 years) are fascinated by the science-experiment *ateliers* (workshops).

Musée des Égouts de Paris

Romping through sewage tunnels, learning what happens when you flush a loo in Paris and spotting rats is all part of the kid-cool experience at this quirky museum.

Les Catacombes

Older kids (12 years) generally get a kick out of Paris' most gruesome and macabre sight, but be warned: guided tours of this underground cemetery packed with more skulls than you can imagine is not for the fainthearted, young or old.

Hands-On Activities

Crafty Happenings at Musée du Quai Branly

Mask-making, boomerang-throwing and experimenting with traditional instruments: the *ateliers* at this Seine-side museum devoted to Africa, Asian and Oceanic art and culture are diverse and creative.

Music at Cité de la Musique

Concerts, shows and workshops (discovery, percussion, guitar, Javanese gamelan, drums and so on) form part of the

NOT FOR PARENTS

For an insight into Paris aimed directly at kids, pick up a copy of Lonely Planet's *Not for Parents: Paris*. Perfect for children aged eight and up, it opens up a world of intriguing stories and fascinating facts about Paris' people, places, history and culture.

world-music repertoire at the City of Music in Parc de la Villette.

Perfume Making

Little girls can concoct their own scents with a professional *nez* (nose) at L'Artisan Parfumeur and Le Studio des Parfums in the Marais.

Art Attack

Centre Pompidou

The Georges Pompidou National Centre of Art and Culture has a packed agenda: modern-art exhibitions in the Galerie des Enfants, workshops solo or *en famille* (three to 12 years) and teen events in Studio 13/16 (13 to 16 years).

Musée en Herbe

This thoughtful art museum features a different modern artist every year, has an excellent bookshop for children's art titles and hosts art workshops (two to 12 years).

Palais de Tokyo

As if the interactive installations and art works in the main exhibition are not enough, this contemporary art space near the Eiffel Tower hosts art workshops (three to 10 years).

Animal Mad

Equestrian Shows at Versailles

The world-class equestrian shows at Château de Versailles are mesmerising and magical – combine with a visit of the beautiful stables.

Sharks at Cinéaqua

It won't be the best aquarium you ever visit, but Cinéaqua by the Jardins du Trocadéro has a shark tank, 500-odd different species of fish and a cinema screening ocean-themed films and documentaries.

Ménagerie du Jardin des Plantes

The collection of animals in the Jardin des Plantes includes snow panthers and pandas, and the snake and monkey houses built in 1926 and 1936 are beautiful examples of art deco. Combine the menagerie with the neighbouring Natural History Museum.

Parks & Outdoor Capers

Sailboats in Jardin du Luxembourg

Playgrounds, puppet shows, pony rides, chess and an old-fashioned carousel: this mythical city park has pandered to children forever. But for impossible romantics it is the vintage toy sailboats to rent and sail that is the real heart-stealer. Kids, get set to vie with Dad for a turn at the helm.

Jardin des Tuileries

A great combo with the neighbouring Louvre, this Seine-side park stages kid's activities on Wednesday and weekends, and hosts a summertime amusement park.

Parc Floral de Paris

Easily the best playground in Paris, especially for kids over eight years: outdoor concerts, puppet shows and giant climbing webs, 30m-high slides and a zip line, among other high energy-burning attractions.

Jardin d'Acclimatation

This enormous green area with cycling paths, forest, lakes and ponds in the Bois de Boulogne is a family must. Renting a *pedalo* (paddleboat) – bring a picnic – is a lovely warm weather treat and every child loves the faster-paced amusement park.

RANDY FARIS / CORBIS ©

(Top) Sailboats at Grand Bassin (p228), Jardin du Luxembourg

(Bottom Left) Boy looking at gargoyle

Locks on Canal St-Martin

Watching canal boats navigate the many locks is fascinating and free.

Promenade Plantée

Parisian traffic can be trying and terrifying – take a stroll (or inline skate) on the quiet side along this peaceful 4.5km-long pedestrian walkway atop a disused railway viaduct.

An Afternoon at the Theatre

The city's diverse theatre scene stages bags of *spectacles* (shows), *théâtre classique* (classical theatre) and other performances for kids, some in English; weekly entertainment mag *Pariscope* (€0.40) lists what's on, including **puppet shows** for kids in Jardin du Luxembourg, Jardin d'Acclimatation, Parc Floral de Paris and Parc du Champ du Mars.

Easy Dining

Pink Flamingo Pizza Picnic

Where else are you sent away with a pink balloon when you order? Kids adore take away pizzeria Pink Flamingo with outlets on Canal St-Martin and in the Marais.

Hand-pulled noodles at Les Pâtes Vivantes

Watching nimble-fingered chefs pull traditional Chinese noodles by hand at Les Pâtes Vivantes in the 5e and 9e is spellbinding.

Le Clown Bar

Parisian children have been piling into this circus-themed cafe in the Marais for decades, before or after a performance at the neighbouring circus. Its wall and ceiling paintings are magical, and its children's lunch *menu is* just what the doctor ordered.

Le Jardin des Pâtes

What child does not like pasta? This Left-Bank address, footsteps from the Jardin des Plantes, cooks up some of the city's most creative and tastiest pasta.

Lunch at La Coupole

The historic 1927 setting might not overimpress kids, but the lavish children's *menu* and game-filled notebooks to entertain certainly will.

Take a Dip at Chalet Savoyard

Nothing provides as much gastronomic entertainment for kids as a bubbling pot of cheese, a basket of bread and a fondue fork. Head for this spacious place in the Bastille area.

Best Crêpes in Town

The best bit about the Breizh Café on one of the trendiest streets in the Marais is the Breton cider parents can sip while kids tuck into some of the best savoury and sweet crêpes in Paris.

Rainy Day Ideas

Magic Shows Afloat

Moored on the Seine in the Latin Quarter is theatre-boat *Métamorphosis*, host to Sunday magic shows.

Cirque d'Hiver

Children have laughed at clowns and been mesmerised by trapeze artists at this circus in the Marais since 1852.

Like a Local

Paris is the world's most visited city, but it's not just an urban resort. The city has the highest population density of any European capital, and its parks and cafes are its communal living and dining rooms, while neighbourhood shops and markets are cornerstones of local life.

CARLOS SANCHEZ PEREYRA / JAI / CORBIS ©

Cycling through the Marais

Drinking Like a Local

Paris' high concentration of city dwellers is why most bars and cafes close around 2am, due to noise restrictions, and why nightclubs in the inner-city are few.

In Paris, meals are almost always washed down with wine, which often costs less than bottled water. In general alcohol is something to be savoured rather than as a means of intoxication. Parisians tend to go to bars with groups of friends, so you may find there's less mingling than in British-style pubs. For the low-down on clubbing Parisian-style, see p55.

Dining Like a Local

Parisians are obsessed with talking about, shopping for, preparing and, above all, eating food. Quality trumps quantity, which is reflected by small, specialist gourmet food shops that not only survive but thrive. It's also reflected by portion sizes, which, although they may often be smaller than in other countries, are exquisite – and delicious.

Sunday lunch is traditionally France's main meal of the week, but brunch has become a trendy fixture on the weekend's social calendar. Numerous cafes and bars serve Sunday brunch from around noon, stretching out to about 4pm. Prebooking is recommended for popular venues; many places serve brunch on Saturdays too.

Conversing Like a Local

Food aside, conversations between locals often revolve around philosophy, art, and sports such as rugby, football, cycling and tennis. Talking about money (salaries or spending outlays, for example) is generally taboo in public. For a witty – and very accurate – insight into Parisian interaction, get hold of a copy of Olivier Magny's book *Stuff Parisians Like* (2011), or check out the blog that inspired it (www.o-chateau.com/stuff-parisians-like).

Debating Like a Local

Grappling with concepts such as existentialism is required for Parisians to pass the *baccalauréat* (school certificate) – hence the popularity of *philocafés* (philosophy cafes), where wide-ranging, brain-teasing discussions like 'what is a fact?' take place. The original (and arguably best), the Marais' Café des Phares (p170), was established by late philosopher and Sorbonne professor Marc Sautet (1947–98). Most *philocafé* sessions are in French, but there's a popular English-language version at St-Germain des Prés' Café de Flore (p243) on the first Wednesday of every month from 7pm to 9pm. Entry's free but you need to buy a drink. To sign up, visit www.philosophy.meetup.com/274.

Dressing Like a Local

It's nearly impossible to overdress in this fashion-conscious city. Parisians have a finely tuned sense of aesthetics, and take meticulous care in their presentation. You'll never see a Parisian leave their apartment with just-out-of-the-shower wet hair, wearing running shoes with a business suit or a jumper tied around the waist (rather than the shoulders). Parisians favour style over fashion, mixing basics from chain stores like H&M with designer pieces, vintage finds (see p57 for some of the best) and well-chosen accessories. Even Parisian dogs are fashionably outfitted, with some shops selling nothing but doggie wear.

Getting Around Like a Local

Navigation

A few pointers to help navigate the city: street numbers notated *bis* (twice), *ter* (thrice) or *quater* (four times) are similar to the English a, b etc. If you're entering an apartment building, you'll generally need the alphanumeric *digicode* (entry code) to open the door. Once inside, apartments are usually unmarked, without any apartment numbers or even occupants' names. To know which door to knock on, you're likely to be given cryptic directions like *cinquième étage, premier à gauche* (5th floor, first on the left) or *troisième étage, droite droite* (3rd floor, turn right twice). In all buildings, the 1st floor is the floor above the *rez-de-chaussée* (ground floor).

NEED TO KNOW

Paris is divided into 20 *arrondissements* (city districts), which spiral clockwise like a snail shell from the centre, and *arrondissement* numbers (1er, 2e etc) form an integral part of all Parisian addresses (including in this book). Each has its own personality, but it's the *quartiers* (quarters, ie neighbourhoods), which often overlap *arrondissement* boundaries, that give Paris its village atmosphere.

Transport

Parisians of all walks of life – from students to celebrity chefs – use the metro. If you're here for a week or more, get a Navigo pass (p341) to save money and zip through the turnstiles without queuing for tickets.

Virtually free Vélib' bikes (p341) have been hugely popular since they were introduced several years ago – fashionable Parisians who previously wouldn't have been seen dead behind handlebars now flit everywhere on these pearly-grey machines.

In the wake of this success, in late 2011, Paris launched the world's first electric-car-share program, Autolib' (p343). But this is one instance where you might not want to follow the locals' lead – negotiating the city's unlaned roundabouts, one-way streets and scooters and cyclists that appear from nowhere can be a nerve-wracking experience for the uninitiated. (Note too that Parisian drivers frequently ignore green pedestrian lights – take care crossing roads!)

If you'd rather let someone else drive, regular buses are a cheap and much more local alternative to tourist buses. Scenic bus routes include lines 21 and 27 (Opéra–Panthéon), line 29 (Opéra–Gare de Lyon), line 47 (Centre Pompidou–Gobelins), line 63 (Musée d'Orsay–Trocadéro), line 73 (Concorde–Arc de Triomphe) and line 82 (Montparnasse–Eiffel Tower). See p342 for ticket info.

Thanks to (generally) clement weather and (generally) flat terrain, locals – even police officers – often whizz around the city on inline skates. Paris is also home to the world's largest mass-skate, Pari Roller – see p264.

For Free

Paris might be home to haute couture, haute cuisine and historic luxury hotels, but if you're still waiting for your lottery numbers to come up, don't despair. There's a wealth of ways to soak up the French capital without spending a centime (or scarcely any, at least).

MICK ROESSLER / CORBIS ©

Cathédrale de Notre Dame de Paris (p196)

Free Museums

If you can, time your trip to be here on the first Sunday of the month when you can visit the musées nationaux (www.rmn.fr) for free, as well as a handful of monuments (some during certain months only).

European citizens under 26 get free entry to national museums and monuments, so don't buy a Paris Museum Pass if you qualify.

At any time, you can visit the permanent collections of selected musées *municipaux* (www.paris.fr) for free.

Temporary exhibitions at both national and city museums always incur a separate admission fee. Some museums also have reduced entry at various times of the day or week.

National Museum & Monument Free Days

The museums and monuments offering free admission on the first Sunday of the month are:

- Arc de Triomphe (November to March only)
- Basilique de St-Denis (November to March only)
- Château de Fontainebleau
- Cité de l'Architecture et du Patrimoine
- Cité Nationale de l'Histoire de l'Immigration
- Conciergerie (November to March only)
- Musée d'Art et d'Histoire
- Musée de la Chasse et de la Nature
- Musée de l'Assistance Publique-Hôpitaux de Paris
- Musée de l'Orangerie
- Musée des Impressionismes Giverny
- Musée d'Orsay
- Musée du Louvre
- Musée du Quai Branly
- Musée Guimet des Arts Asiatiques
- Musée Ernest Hébert
- Musée National d'Art Moderne (within the Centre Pompidou)
- Musée National du Moyen Âge (aka Musée de Cluny)
- Musée National du Sport
- Musée National Eugène Delacroix

- Musée National Gustave Moreau
- Musée Rodin
- Panthéon (November to March only)
- Ste-Chapelle (November to March only)
- Tours de Notre Dame (November to March only)

Other Free Museums

Other freebies include Paris' fascinating town-planning and architectural centre, the Pavillon de l'Arsenal, and the Musée du Parfum, which are free every day year round.

Admission to the Maison Européenne de la Photographie is free from 5pm to 8pm every Wednesday evening.

Free Churches

Some of the city's most magnificent buildings are its churches and other places of worship. Not only exceptional architecturally and historically, they contain exquisite art, artefacts and other priceless treasures. And best of all, entry to general areas within them is, in most cases, free.

Do bear in mind that although many of Paris' places of worship are also major tourist attractions, Parisians come here to pray and celebrate significant events on religious calendars as part of their daily lives. Be respectful, keep noise to a minimum, obey photography rules (check signs), dress appropriately, and try to avoid key times (eg Mass) if you're sightseeing only.

Free Cemeteries

Paris' celebrity-filled cemeteries, including the three largest – Père Lachaise, Cimetière de Montmartre and Cimetière du Montparnasse – are free to wander.

Free Entertainment

Concerts, DJ sets and recitals regularly take place for free (or the cost of a drink) at venues throughout the city.

Busking musicians and performers entertain crowds on Paris' streets, squares and even aboard the metro – top spots to catch them are listed on p66.

Free Literary Events

This literary-minded city is an inspired place to catch a reading, author signing or writing workshop. English-language bookshops such as Shakespeare & Company and Abbey Bookshop have details of literary events throughout the year, many of which are held at the shops themselves.

Free Fashion Shows

Reserve ahead to attend free weekly fashion shows at the flagship store of Galeries Lafayette (p99). While you're here, don't miss one of the best free views over the Parisian skyline from Galeries Lafayette's rooftop.

Free Festivals

Loads of Paris' festivals and events are free, such as the summertime Paris Plages riverside beaches. See p26 for details.

Getting Around For Free

Walking

Paris is an eminently walkable city, with beautiful parks and gardens, awe-inspiring architecture, markets and shops (well, window shopping never goes out of style) to check out along the way.

For a free walking tour, contact Paris Greeter (p344) in advance for a personalised excursion led by a resident volunteer.

Cycling (Almost Free)

If you'd rather free-wheel around Paris, the Vélib' (p341) system costs next-to-nothing for a day's subscription, and the first 30 minutes of each bike rental is free.

NEED TO KNOW

Paris has 400 free wi-fi points (some time-limited) at popular locations including parks, libraries, local town halls and tourist hotspots. Locations are mapped at www.paris.fr.

Consider investing in a transport (p341) or museum (p345) pass.

Theatre tickets are sold for half price on the day of performance (p63).

Paris' parks are perfect for picnics made from market fare.

Musée du Quai Branly (p80), designed by Jean Nouvel

Museums & Galleries

If there's one thing that rivals a Parisian's obsession with food, it's art. Over 200 museums pepper the city, and whether you prefer the classicism of the Louvre, the impressionists of the Orsay or detailed exhibits of French military history, you can always be sure to find something new just around the corner.

Paris Museum Pass

If you think you'll be visiting more than two or three museums and monuments while in Paris, the single most important investment you can make during your trip is the Paris Museum Pass. The pass (p345) is valid for entry to some 38 venues in the city – including the Louvre, Centre Pompidou, Musée d'Orsay and the Musée Rodin (but not the Eiffel Tower). It will get you into another 22 places outside the city, including the châteaux at Versailles and Fontainebleau and the Basilique de St-Denis.

One of the best features of the pass is that you can bypass the *lonnng* ticket queues at major attractions. But be warned, the pass is valid for a certain number of days, not hours, so if you activate a two-day pass late Friday afternoon, for instance, you will only be able to use it for a full day on Saturday. Also keep in mind that most museums are closed on either Monday or Tuesday, so think twice before you activate a pass on a Sunday.

The Paris Museum Pass is conveniently available online, as well as at participating museums, tourist desks at the airports, branches of the Paris Convention & Visitors Bureau, Fnac outlets and major metro stations. European citizens under 26 and children under 18 get free entry to national museums and monuments, so *don't* buy this pass if you qualify.

For Free

Municipal museums in Paris (eg Musée Carnavalet) are all free; many other museums have one free day (p36) per month (generally the 1st Sunday of the month). Note that temporary exhibits always charge a separate admission fee, even at free museums.

Performances

Many museums host excellent musical concerts and performances, with schedules that generally run from September to May. Some of the top venues include:

Musée du Louvre (p103) A series of lunchtime and evening classical concerts throughout the week.

Musée d'Orsay (p224) Chamber music every Tuesday at 12.30pm, plus various evening classical performances.

Musée du Quai Branly (p80) Folk performances of theatre, dance and music from around the world.

Musée National du Moyen Âge (p206) Medieval music performances once a week.

Centre Pompidou (p111) Film screenings and avant-garde dance and music performances.

Le 104 (p136) A veritable potpourri of everything from circus and magic to afternoon breakdancing.

Workshops

If you have kids in tow, make sure you check out the day's workshops (*ateliers*). Although these are often in French, most activities involve hands-on creation, so children should enjoy themselves despite the language barrier. At major museums (eg Centre Pompidou), it's best to sign up in advance. For a list of the most popular museum workshops, see p30.

Dining

Although there are plenty of tourist cafeterias to be found in Paris, the dining options in museums are generally pretty good – some are desinations in and of themselves. Even if you're not out sightseeing, consider a meal at one of the following:

Café Marly (p123) Views of the Louvre pyramid are what it's all about here.

NEED TO KNOW

Tickets

➡ Consider booking online to avoid queues where possible (eg Musée d'Orsay, Centre Pompidou), but make sure you have a way to print out the tickets. Alternatively, in many cases you can download the tickets onto a smart phone (eg BlackBerry, iPhone), but check first before you make a purchase. Also ensure you can download more than one ticket onto your phone if need be.

➡ If you can't book online, keep an eye out for automated machines at museum entrances, which generally have shorter queues. Note that North American credit cards (ie cards without an embedded smart chip) won't work in these machines.

➡ City museums (eg Musée Carnavalet, Petit Palais, Musée Cognacq-Jay) are free.

➡ Temporary exhibits always have a separate admission fee, even at free museums.

➡ Ask if you qualify for a reduced-price ticket (*tarif réduit*): students, seniors and children generally get discounts or free admission.

Opening Hours

➡ Most museums are closed on either Monday or Tuesday – it is vital that you verify opening days before drawing up the day's schedule.

➡ General opening hours are from 10am to 6pm, though all museums shut their gates between 30 minutes and an hour before their actual closing times. Thus, if a museum is listed in this guide as closing at 6pm, make sure you get there before 5pm.

➡ Major museums are often open one or two nights a week, which is an excellent time to visit as there are fewer visitors.

TIPS FOR AVOIDING MUSEUM FATIGUE

➡ Wear comfortable shoes and make use of the cloakrooms.

➡ Sit down as often as you can; standing still and walking slowly promote tiredness.

➡ Reflecting on the material and forming associations with it causes information to move from your short- to long-term memory; your experiences will thus amount to more than a series of visual 'bites'.

➡ Studies suggest that museum-goers spend no more than 10 seconds viewing an exhibit and another 10 seconds reading the label as they try to take in as much as they can. To avoid this, choose a particular period or section to focus on, or join a guided tour of the highlights.

Les Ombres (p85) & **Café Branly** (p85) Ringside seats for the Eiffel Tower at these two dining options at the Musée du Quai Branly.

Tokyo Eat (p85) Hip fusion food in the Palais du Tokyo.

Minipalais (p95) Gorgeous terrace and modern French cuisine in the Grand Palais.

Le Cristal Room (p85) Baccarat crystal meets Philippe Starck design in this plush Galerie-Musée Baccarat stunner.

Musée Jacquemart-André (p135) Lunch or tea in the sumptuous dining room of a 19th-century mansion.

Museums & Galleries by Neighbourhood

➡ **Eiffel Tower & Western Paris** (p76) The largest concentration of museums in Paris, from the Quai Branly to Musée Marmottan Monet.

➡ **Louvre & Les Halles** (p101) The Louvre, Centre Pompidou, Musée de l'Orangerie and others.

➡ **Champs-Élysées & Grands Boulevards** (p88) Grand Palais, La Pinacothèque, Petit Palais and others.

➡ **Montmartre & Northern Paris** (p129) Musée Jacquemart-André, Cité des Sciences, Le 104 and others.

➡ **St-Germain & Les Invalides** (p222) Musée d'Orsay, Musée Rodin & others.

➡ **Latin Quarter** (p204) Musée National du Moyen Âge, Musée National d'Histoire Naturelle, Institut du Monde Arabe.

➡ **Le Marais & Ménilmontant** (p152) Musée Picasso, Musée Carnavalet and others.

➡ **Bastille & Eastern Paris** (p181) Cinémathèque Française and others.

➡ **Montparnasse & Southern Paris** (p250) Fondation Cartier and others.

Lonely Planet's Top Choices

Musée du Louvre (p103) The one museum you just can't miss.

Musée d'Orsay (p224) Monet, Van Gogh and company.

Centre Pompidou (p111) One of the top modern art museums in Europe.

Musée Rodin (p230) Superb collection of Rodin's masterpieces in an intimate setting.

Musée Picasso (p158) An incomparable overview of Picasso's work and life (reopening summer 2013).

Best Modern Art Museums & Installations

Grand Palais (p93)

Palais de Tokyo (p81)

Jeu du Paume (p115)

Musée Européenne de la Photographie (p160)

Musée d'Art Moderne de la Ville de Paris (p82)

Le 104 (p136)

Best Unsung Museums

La Pinacothèque (p94)

Cité de l'Architecture et du Patrimoine (p81)

Musée Jacquemart-André (p135)

Musée Dapper (p81)

Best History Museums

Musée National du Moyen Âge (p206)

Musée Carnavalet (p156)

Musée de l'Armée (p231)

Musée de Montmartre (p134)

Musée d'Art et Histoire (p139)

Best Museums for Non-European Art

Musée du Quai Branly (p80)

Musée Guimet (p83)

Institut du Monde Arabe (p210)

Musée Cernuschi (p136)

Best Small Museums

Musée de l'Orangerie (p84)

Musée Maillol-Fondation Dina Vierny (p235)

Cinémathèque Française (p183)

Musée National Gustave Moreau (p94)

Musée de la Vie Romantique (p134)

Best Quirky Museums

Musée de l'Erotisme (p135)

Musée du Parfum (p94)

Musée de la Poste (p253)

Musée de l'Évantail (p138)

Galerie-Musée Baccarat (p82)

Best Science Museums

Cité des Sciences (p136)

Musée National d'Histoire Naturelle (p207)

Palais de la Découverte (p93)

Musée des Arts et Métiers (p158)

Best Residence Museums

Musée National Eugène Delacroix (p232)

Musée Bourdelle (p252)

Musée Cognacq-Jay (p157)

Musée Nissim de Camondo (p135)

Maison de Victor Hugo (p157)

Best Fashion Museums

Fondation Pierre Bergé-Yves Saint Laurent (p82)

Musée Galliera de la Mode de la Ville de Paris (p82)

Musée de la Mode et du Textile (p114)

Macarons at Angelina (p122)

Eating

Some cities rally around the local sports teams, but in Paris, they rally around la table – and everything on it. Pistachio macarons, shots of tomato consommé, decadent bœuf bourguignon, a gooey wedge of Camembert running onto the cheese plate: food is not fuel here, it's the reason you get up in the morning.

Minipalais (p95)

Types of Restaurants

BISTROS

A bistro (or *bistrot*) is a small or moderately sized neighbourhood restaurant that serves French standards, such as duck confit or *steak-frites*. The setting is usually casual; if you're looking for a traditional French meal, a bistro is the place to start. On that note, remember that you should not come to a bistro and expect haute-cuisine service; most simply do not have the staff to cater to a diner's every whim.

NEOBISTROS

Neobistros offer some of the most exciting dining options in Paris today. Generally small and relatively informal, they're run by young, talented chefs who aren't afraid to experiment and push the envelope of traditional French fare. The focus is on quality products and market-driven cuisine, hence choices are often limited to two or three dishes per course.

CAVES À MANGER & WINE BARS

Picture a tiny wine shop that's plonked down a couple of tables in the middle of the store – this is the *cave à manger* at its most basic. The focus is on sampling wine; the style of cuisine, while often excellent, can be wildly different. Some places serve nothing more than plates of cheese and charcuterie alongside simple meals made in an overworked toaster oven; others are full-on gastronomic destinations with a talented chef running the kitchen.

The difference between a *cave à manger* and a wine bar is that a *cave à manger* probably won't have a liquor licence, so

NEED TO KNOW

Price Ranges

The symbols below indicate the cost for a two-course meal at the restaurant in question.

€	under €20
€€	€20-40
€€€	more than €40

Prix-Fixe Menus

In addition to the *carte* (menu), most Parisian restaurants offer daily *formules* or *menus* (prix-fixe menus), which typically include two- to four-course meals. In some cases, particularly at market-driven neobistros, there is no *carte* – only a selection of *menus*.

Lunch *menus* are often a fantastic deal and allow you to enjoy haute cuisine at very affordable prices. In this guide, when we list the price for a lunch *menu*, it generally corresponds to a two-course meal served Monday to Friday. The price for a dinner *menu* generally corresponds to a three-course meal, available every day.

Opening Hours

Restaurants generally open from noon to 2pm for lunch and from 7.30pm to 10.30pm for dinner. If you want to avoid the rush, remember that the peak Parisian dining times are 1pm and 9pm.

During the week, most restaurants shut for a full day (usually Sunday) and sometimes an additional afternoon. August is the peak holiday month and many places are consequently closed during this time.

Tipping

A *pourboire* (tip) on top of the bill is not necessary as service is always included. But it is not uncommon to round up the bill if you were pleased with your waiter or waitress.

Paying the Bill

Trying to get *l'addition* (the bill) can be maddeningly slow in many cases. Do not take this personally. The French consider it rude to bring the bill immediately – you have to be persistent when it comes to getting your server's attention.

WILL SALTER / GETTY IMAGES ©

Top: Cheese selection on rue St-Louis en l'Île

Left: Bread in a shop window, Belleville

Eating by Neighbourhood

Seine

Montmartre & Northern Paris Neobistros, wine bars and world cuisine (p139)

Champs-Élysées & Grands Boulevards Big-name chefs, backstreet bistros (p94)

Louvre & Les Halles Trendy restaurants on the rise (p118)

Le Marais & Ménilmontant Premier foodie destination (p161)

Eiffel Tower & Western Paris Gastronomic palaces and museum restaurants (p84)

Eiffel Tower

The Islands Unspectacular dining options but gorgeous setting (p202)

St-Germain & Les Invalides Chic cafes, haute cuisine (p235)

Bastille & Eastern Paris Balances tradition and innovation (p184)

Latin Quarter Cheap eats and Left Bank treasures (p209)

Montparnasse & Southern Paris Historic brasseries and hip eateries (p256)

you can't just drop by for a drink; food, no matter how small the dish, must be ordered with the wine.

CRÊPERIES

A classic Parisian stereotype is the street crêpe made to order, slathered with Nutella and folded up in a triangular wedge (ideally with the Eiffel Tower or Notre Dame looming in the background). Crêpes can be so much more than this, however, as a trip to any authentic *crêperie* will reveal. Savoury crêpes, known as *galettes*, are made with buckwheat flour; dessert crêpes are made with white flour – usually you order one of each accompanied by a bowl of cider.

GASTRONOMIC

Alain Ducasse, Pierre Gagnaire, Alain Passard, Pascal Barbot... Paris has one of the highest concentrations of culinary magicians in the world. Designed to amaze your every sense, many of these *grands restaurants* are once-in-a-lifetime destinations – even for Parisians – so do your homework and make sure you reserve well in advance.

BRASSERIES

Unlike the vast majority of restaurants in Paris, brasseries – which can look very much like cafes – serve full meals from morning till 11pm or even later. They are larger than bistros and slightly more upscale. The brasserie, which means 'brewery' in French, originated in Alsace; their featured dishes often include *choucroute* (sauerkraut) and sausages.

CAFES

Cafes are an important focal point for social life in Paris, and sitting in a cafe to read, write, talk with friends or just daydream is an integral part of many people's daily life.

The main focus, of course, is drinking (coffee by day, alcohol by night) and only basic food is available at most cafes. Nevertheless, they serve both lunch and dinner and generally offer the least expensive sit-down meals available.

Specialities

Many people in Paris buy at least some of their food from a series of small neighbourhood shops, each with its own speciality. Having to go to a series of shops and stand in several queues to fill the fridge (or assemble a picnic) may seem a waste of time, but the whole ritual is an important part of the way many Parisians live their daily lives.

BOULANGERIES

Few things in Paris are as tantalising as the smell of just-baked buttery croissants wafting out of an open *boulangerie* (bakery) door. With roughly 1200 bakeries in Paris – or 11.5 per sq km – you'll likely find yourself inside one at some point during your stay. And, as you'll notice in the extravagant display windows, bakeries bake much more than baguettes: they also sell croissants, chocolate éclairs, quiches, pizzas and an astounding array of pastries and cakes that you've likely never even heard of before.

If it's the bread you're after, try to familiarise yourself with the varieties on sale while you're standing in the queue – not all baguettes are created equal. Most Parsians today will ask for a *baguette tradition* (traditional-style baguette), which is considerably better than the standard baguette. Other breads you'll see include *boules* (round loaves), *pavés* (flattened rectangular loaves), and *ficelles* (skinny loaves that are half the weight of a baguette).

PATISSERIES & CHOCOLATIERS

Patisseries (pastry shops) are similar to bakeries, but generally up a notch on the sophistication scale. Although they sell different varieties of pastries and cakes, each one is often known for a particular speciality – Ladurée and Pierre Hermé do *macarons*, Gérard Mulot does cakes and *tartes*, and so on. A *chocolatier* specialises in chocolates, generally sold in 100g increments and available in over a dozen mouthwatering flavours: pistachio, lavender, ginger, orange...

FROMAGERIES

'How can you govern a country that has 246 types of cheese?', Charles de Gaulle once quipped. A more relevant question for nonFrenchies: How do you come to grips with a shop that sells 246 types of cheese? Whether you want a hard goat's cheese, creamy Époisses or mouldy Roquefort, the *fromagerie* is the place for unpasteurised goodness. For more details on the different types of French cheese, see p150.

BOUCHERIES

The neighbourhood butcher's shop is a common fixture in Paris; short-term visitors will be most interested in checking them out for their selection of *charcuterie* (prepared meats; usually pork, sometimes poultry), such as pâtés, terrines, *saucissons* (salami) and *rillettes* (meat spreads).

TRAITEURS

Similar to a deli, the *traiteur* specialises in prepared dishes – in its earliest form, this was the origin of the modern-day restaurant. Like at the *boucherie* you'll find a selection of charcuterie, however you'll also find a variety of salads, baked goods (eg quiches) and sometimes sandwiches.

MARCHÉS

Even in the supermarket age, open-air and covered markets (*marchés alimentaires*) are a staple of Parsian life. Here you'll find all the French culinary specialities in the same place, in addition to fresh fruit and vegetables. At last count there were 82 food markets in the city. Most are open twice weekly from 8.30am to 1pm, though covered markets keep general shop hours, reopening around 4pm.

CAVISTES

Neighbourhood wine shops (*cavistes*) are another typically French establishment. Although foreigners may find French wine intimidating – for starters, wines are classified by region, not grape variety, which undermines a basic level of familiarity for many – *cavistes* staff are generally eager to share their knowledge and passion.

If you're interested in sampling French wine paired with a good meal, your best bet is to visit a *bar à vin* (wine bar) or a *cave à manger* – a *caviste* that serves meals in addition to selling wine.

Vegetarians & Vegans

Vegetarians and vegans make up a small minority in a country where *viande* (meat) once also meant 'food', and they are not particularly well catered for. Specialist vegetarian restaurants are few and far between in Paris, and it's safe to say that vegetarians will still be met with looks of bewilderment at some traditional bistros. On the up side, more and more modern places are offering vegetarian choices on their set *menus*; another good bet is non-French cuisine. See www.happycow.net for a decent guide to veggie options in Paris.

Also consider self-catering – the health-food supermarket **Naturalia** (www.naturalia.fr) has branches throughout the city.

Cooking Classes

What better place to discover the secrets of *la cuisine française* than in Paris, the capital of gastronomy? Courses are available at different levels and durations.

Les Coulisses du Chef (www.coursdecuisineparis.com) Popular courses for beginners.

Cook'n With Class Map p398 (www.cooknwithclass.com) Seven international chefs, small classes and a Montmartre location.

La Cuisine Paris Map p416 (www.lacuisineparis.com) A variety of courses from bread and pastries to market classes and 'foodie walks'.

NATURAL WINE

The latest trend to hit the culinary world, *les vins naturels* (natural wines) have a fuzzy definition – no one really agrees on the details – but the general idea is that they are made with as little human interference possible. Quick translation? Natural wines contain little or no sulphites, which are added as a preservative in most wines. The good news is that this gives natural wines a much more unique personality (or *terroir*, as the French say), the bad news is that the wines can also be more unpredictable. See the website www.morethanorganic.com.

La Cuisine de Bertrand (www.lacuisinedebertrand.com) Learn traditional French cooking in Bertrand's Versailles home.

École Le Cordon Bleu (www.cordonbleu.edu) One of the world's foremost culinary arts schools.

Patricia Wells (www.patriciawells.com) Five-day moveable feast from the former *International Herald Tribune* food critic.

Pastries and croissants in a patisserie

Supper Clubs

Half restaurant, half mystery dinner party, supper clubs aren't quite as big in Paris as they are in London and New York. They still exist though, and while it's unlikely you'll meet any Parisians at these affairs, they're a good way to connect with fellow travellers from around the globe.

http://newfriendstable.blogspot.com Supper club with tables in Paris and London.

www.lunchintheloft.com Another way of having lunch in the City of Light.

www.jim-haynes.com The original Paris supper club.

Paris Food Bloggers & Useful Websites

Le Fooding (www.lefooding.com) The French movement that's giving Michelin a run for their money as the last word on culinary greatness. Their mission is to shake up the ossified establishment, so expect a good balance between quirky, under-the-radar reviews and truly fine dining (the latter is tagged as *fais-moi mal!* – hurt me, baby!). In French (mostly).

Resto de Paris (www.resto-de-paris.com) Penned by Aude, a journalist for the French weekly *Le Nouvel Obs* and a dedicated restaurant reviewer. In French.

La Fourchette (www.thefork.com) Website offering user reviews and great deals of up to 50% off in restaurants in Paris.

Paris by Mouth (www.parisbymouth.com) Capital dining and drinking; one-stop surf for deciding where to eat and snagging a table in advance.

David Lebovitz (www.davidlebovitz.com) Former San Francisco Bay Area pastry chef who relocated to Paris in 2004.

Paris Kitchen (www.theparískitchen.com) Insightful tidbits on French dining from a name-dropping Southerner turned Parisian.

Reservations

While you can generally find a free table for lunch at midrange restaurants, it is always advisable to book in advance for dinner. Reservations are absolutely mandatory for top-end restaurants, lunch or dinner – sometimes up to one or two months in advance.

Top: Les Deux Magots (p242)

Middle: Parisian gastronomy

Bottom: Display of French cakes

Lonely Planet's Top Choices

Septime (p184) The new beacon of modern cuisine.

Au Passage (p161) Creative bistro fare and back-alley simplicity combine for a devastating one-two punch.

L'AOC (p209) Nothing but the finest ingredients and wines.

Derrière (p161) Cheeky apartment-style venue for a sophisticated home-cookin' feel. Ping-pong table included.

Vivant (p142) Where else will you get to dine in a century-old exotic bird shop?

Bouillon Racine (p235) An art nouveau jewel with traditional French fare.

Best Neobistros

Chatomat (p162)

Jadis (p256)

L'Office (p142)

Le Dauphin (p161)

La Gazzetta (p185)

L'Agrume (p210)

Best Traditional French

Le Pantruche (p139)

Aux Deux Amis (p168)

Le Coupe-Chou (p210)

Frenchie (p118)

Polidor (p236)

Philou (p143)

Best Wine Bars & Caves à Manger

Racines (p121)

Le Verre Volé (p143)

Verjus Bar à Vin (p119)

Le Siffleur de Ballons (p184)

Frenchie (p118)

Les Pipos (p211)

Best By Budget

€

La Grande Épicerie Le Comptoir Picnic (p240)

Candelaria (p162)

40/60 (p186)

Kunitoraya (p118)

Mama Shelter (p186)

Le Coquelicot (p140)

€€

Verjus (p119)

Spring (p119)

Eat Intuition (p185)

Bistrot Les Papilles (p211)

Cul de Poule (p139)

Les Cocottes (p240)

€€€

L'Astrance (p85)

Chateaubriand (p161)

Ze Kitchen Galerie (p235)

Yam'Tcha (p120)

L'Arpège (p240)

Makoto Aoki (p95)

Best Patisseries

Ladurée (p95)

La Pâtisserie des Rêves (p242)

Arnaud Delmontel (p140)

Dardonville (p275)

Best Boulangeries

Poilâne (p239)

Boulangerie Bazin (p185)

Besnier (p240)

Du Pain et des Idées (p143)

Boulangerie Pâtisserie du Grand Richelieu (p120)

Boulangerie Bruno Solques (p211)

Best Views

Les Ombres (p85)

Café Marly (p123)

Lafayette Café (p96)

La Tour d'Argent (p210)

58 Tour Eiffel (p85)

Best Markets

Marché d'Aligre (p186)

Marché Bastille (p186)

Marché aux Enfants Rouges (p168)

Marché Edgar Quinet (p258)

Best Global

Krishna Bhavan (p143)

Restaurant du Palais Royal (p120)

La Mosquée de Paris (p211)

Waly Fay (p185)

Nanashi (p162)

Kootchi (p213)

Best Sunday Night Bites

Le Petit Trianon (p140)

Minipalais (p95)

Kaï (p119)

Chez Paul (p259)

Best Crêperies

Breizh Café (p166)

Crêperie Josselin (p259)

Mamie Tevennec (p186)

Crêperie Plougastel (p259)

Best Organic

SuperNature (p96)

Le Jardin des Pâtes (p211)

Le Puits de Légumes (p213)

Soya Cantine Bio (p163)

Bioboa (p121)

Zuzu's Petals (p144)

Best Seafood

La Mascotte (p140)

La Cabane à Huîtres (p256)

L'Écailler du Bistrot (p185)

Le Dôme (p256)

Chez Michel (p142)

La Cagouille (p257)

Best Italian

Casa Bini (p237)

Caffè dei Cioppi (p185)

Pozzetto (p166)

Le Cherche Midi (p238)

Caffè (p95)

Best Terraces

Restaurant du Palais Royal (p120)

Le Saut du Loup (p119)

L'Été en Pente Douce (p140)

Le Comptoir du Panthéon (p212)

La Salle à Manger (p213)

La Sardine (p144)

Best Kids

Le Clown Bar (p166)

Pink Flamingo (p167)

La Tropicale (p260)

Grom (p237)

Best Hip Lunches

Cantine Merci (p163)

Le Baba Bourgeois (p214)

KGB (p238)

Tokyo Eat (p85)

Hotel Amour (p141)

Best Retro Bistros

Bistrot Paul Bert (p185)

Le Petit Pontoise (p211)

Aux Deux Amis (p168)

Bistrot des Faubourgs (p143)

Le Petit Trianon (p140)

Chez Paul (p186)

Best African

Waly Fay (p185)

Jambo (p144)

Entoto (p259)

Nouveau Paris-Dakar (p96)

Le Mono (p141)

À La Banane Ivoirienne (p189)

Best North African

La Mosquée de Paris (p211)

404 (p163)

Mansouria (p186)

Le Souk (p188)

Best Asian

Nanashi (p162)

Kootchi (p213)

Pho 14 (p259)

Sichuan Panda (Galeries Lafayette) (p96)

Les Pâtes Vivantes (p97)

Sawadee (p257)

Best Burgers

Blend (p121)

Aubrac Corner (p95)

Beef Club (p118)

Best Veggie

Krishna Bhavan (p143)

Bob's Juice Bar (p143)

Rose Bakery (p163)

Jardin des Voluptés (p143)

Au Grain de Folie (p141)

Cocktail at the Experimental Cocktail Club (p123)

Drinking & Nightlife

For Parisians, drinking and eating go together like wine and cheese, and the line between a cafe, salon de thé (tearoom), bistro, brasserie, bar, and even bar à vins (wine bar) is blurred, while the line between drinking and clubbing is often nonexistent – a cafe that's quiet midafternoon might have DJ sets in the evening and dancing later on.

NEED TO KNOW

Tiered Pricing

Drinking in Paris essentially means paying the rent for the space you take up. So it costs more sitting at tables than standing at the counter, more for coveted terrace seats, more on a fancy square than a backstreet, more in the 8e than in the 18e.

Average Costs

A glass of wine starts from €3 or €4, a cocktail costs €10 to €15 and a *demi* (half-pint) of beer is between €3 and €5. In clubs and chic bars, prices can be easily double this. Admission to clubs is free to around €20; entry is often cheaper before 1am.

Happy 'Hour'

Most mainstream bars and international-styled pubs have a 'happy hour' – called just that (no French translation) – which ushers in reduced-price drinks for a good two or three hours, usually from around 5pm to 9pm.

Closing Times

Closing time for cafes and bars tends to be 2am, though some have licences until dawn. Club hours vary depending on the venue, day and event.

Top Tips

➡ Arrive early: come 10pm many cafes apply a pricier *tarif de nuit* (night rate).

➡ Although most places serve at least light meals (often full menus), it's normally fine to order a coffee or alcohol if you're not dining.

➡ The French rarely go wild-drunk and tend to frown upon it.

Coffee Decoded

➡ **Un café** A single shot of espresso.

➡ **Un café allongé** An espresso lengthened with hot water (usually, but not always, served separately).

➡ **Un café au lait** A coffee with milk.

➡ **Un café crème** A shot of espresso lengthened with steamed milk (closest thing to a caffè latte).

➡ **Un double** A double shot of espresso.

➡ **Une noisette** A shot of espresso with a spot of milk.

Wine tasting at a Parisian market

Drinking

Drinking in Paris, as Parisians do, means anything from downing a coffee at a zinc counter with locals, getting a fruit juice vitamin fix or sipping Japanese *gyokuro* (green tea) in a sleek *salon de thé*, to meeting friends after work for *une verre* ('a glass'), savouring a cheese and/or charcuterie platter over a glass of sauvignon on a pavement terrace, debating existentialism over an early-evening *apéritif* (pre-dinner drink) in the same literary cafes as Sartre and Simone did, dancing on tables to bossa nova beats, or swilling martinis on a dark leather couch while listening to jazz or partying aboard floating clubs on the Seine...and much, much more.

COFFEE, TEA & HOT CHOCOLATE

Coffee has always been Parisians' drink of choice to kick-start the day. But surprisingly in this quality-conscious city, it's nowhere near the gold standard set by neighbouring Italy, although there are some notable exceptions where you'll find the perfect accompanient to your buttery breakfast croissant.

Surprisingly too, tea – traditionally more strongly associated with France's western neighbours, the UK and Ireland – is extremely popular in Paris. Tearooms continue to proliferate throughout the city, and there's even a tea museum within the original Marais branch of **Mariage Frères** (p171).

For decadently rich hot chocolate, *the crème de la crème* is venerable tearoom Angelina (p122), whose new branches

HUW JONES / GETTY IMAGES ©

Top: Lizard Lounge (p170)
Right: Mariage Frères (p171)

JOEL SAGET / AFP / GETTY IMAGES ©

Drinking by Neighbourhood

include Galeries Lafayette (p96), the Musée du Luxembourg and two at Versailles, including one inside the château.

WINE

Wine is easily the most popular beverage in Paris (house wine invariably costs less than bottled water). Of France's dozens of wine-producing regions, the principal ones are Burgundy, Bordeaux, the Rhône and the Loire valleys, Champagne, Languedoc, Provence and Alsace. Wines are generally named after the location of the vineyard rather than the grape varietal. Organic and biodynamic wines (p47) are becoming popular. The best wines are Appellation d'Origine Contrôlée (AOC), meaning they meet stringent regulations governing where, how and under what conditions they're grown, fermented and bottled. For the best wine bars, where the food is the main attraction, see p49.

BEER

Beer isn't traditionally popular in France – the country ranks 64th for beer consumption per capita, yet 16th for alcohol overall. The main French beer you're likely to encounter is Strasbourg-brewed Kronenbourg 1664 (5.5%) premium larger. There are, however, a handful of pubs producing their own microbrews.

Nightlife

Paris' residential make up means nightclubs aren't ubiquitous. Lacking a mainstream scene, clubbing here tends to be underground and extremely mobile, making blogs, forums and websites the savviest means of keeping apace with what's happening. The best DJs and their followings have short stints in a certain venue before moving on, and the scene's hippest *soirées clubbing* (clubbing events) float between venues – including the city's many dance-driven bars.

But the beat is strong. Electronic music is of particularly high quality in Paris' clubs, with some excellent local house and techno. Funk and groove have given the whimsical predominance of dark minimal sounds a good pounding, and the Latin scene is huge; salsa dancing and Latino music nights pack out plenty of clubs. R 'n' B and hip-hop pickings are decent, if less represented than many other European capitals. Look for flyers at cafes, bars and music shops or check the websites listed in this section. For live music, see p62.

CLUBBING WEBSITES

Track tomorrow's cool soirée with these finger-on-the-pulse Parisian nightlife links.

- **Gogo Paris** (www.gogoparis.com)
- **Paris DJs** (www.parisdjs.com)
- **Nova Planet** (www.novaplanet.com)
- **Paris Bouge** (www.parisbouge.com)
- **Parissi** (www.parissi.com)
- **Tribu de Nuit** (www.tribudenuit.com)
- **Le Figaro Scope** (www.figaroscope.fr) Great search tool for concerts by *arrondissement* – click on the map.
- **France Techno** (www.france-techno.fr)

CLUBBING IN PARIS: BEFORE, AFTER AND AFTER D'AFTERS

Seasoned Parisian clubbers, who tend to have a finely tuned sense of the absurd, split their night into three parts. First, *la before* – drinks in a bar that has a DJ playing. Second, they head to a club for *la soirée*, which rarely kicks off before 1am or 2am. When the party continues (or begins) at around 5am and goes until midday, it's *l'after*. Invariably, though, given the lack of any clear-cut distinction between Parisian bars and clubs, the before and after can easily blend into one without any real 'during'. *After d'afters*, meanwhile, kicks off in bars and clubs on Sunday afternoons and evenings, with a mix of strung-out hardcore clubbers pressing on amid those looking for a party that doesn't take place in the middle of the night.

Le Batofar (p262) on quai François Mauriac

Lonely Planet's Top Choices

Cinéma Café Merci (p168) Retro cafe lined with black-and-white photos of silver screen stars.

Le Baron Rouge (p190) Wonderfully convivial barrel-filled wine bar.

Experimental Cocktail Club (p123) Parisian style blends with New York street cred.

Le Rex Club (p125) Mythical house and techno club with a phenomenal sound system.

Le Batofar (p262) Red-metal tugboat with a rooftop bar and portholed club beneath.

Kong (p124) Seine views stretch from this Philippe Starck–designed stunner.

Best Coffee

La Caféthèque (p171)

Kooka Boora (p146)

Pozzetto (p166)

Merce and the Muse (p171)

Best Tearooms

Mariage Frères (p171)

Kilàli (p244)

La Mosquée de Paris (p211)

Le Loir dans La Théière (p171)

Best Cocktails

Harry's New York Bar (p124)

Panic Room (p168)

Mojito Lab (p191)

Jefrey's (p124)

Le Rosebud (p261)

Cubana Café (p243)

Best Nightclubs

ShowCase (p97)

La Machine du Moulin Rouge (p147)

Bus Palladium (p148)

Social Club (p125)

Le Nouveau Casino (p169)

La Dame de Canton (p262)

Best DJ Bars

Café Chéri(e) (p147)

Café Charbon (p169)

L'Alimentation Générale (p170)

La Mezzanine (p243)

Best Wine Bars

Taverne Henri IV (p203)

Tandem (p261)

Au Sauvignon (p242)

Café de la Nouvelle Mairie (p214)

Best Pubs

Charlie Birdy (p97)

Le 10 (p244)

Le Pub St-Hilaire (p214)

Frog & British Library (p261)

Brasserie O'Neil (p243)

Best Pavement Terraces

Les Deux Magots (p242)

Chez Prune (p146)

Les Etages St-Germain (p243)

Le Barav (p168)

Café Delmas (p214)

Le Square (p240)

Best Classic Cafes

Le Pure Café (p190)

Pause Café (p191)

L'Atmosphère (p146)

Le Verre À Pied (p214)

Best Backstreet Bars

La Fée Verte (p190)

Café de la Plage (p191)

Café La Fusée (p125)

Chez Jeannette (p146)

Swinging Londress (p146)

La Folie en Tête (p262)

Le Bon Marché (p245)

Shopping

Paris has it all: broad boulevards lined with international chains, luxury avenues studded with designer fashion houses, famous grands magasins *(department stores) and fabulous markets. But the real charm of Parisian shopping lies in strolling through the backstreets, where tiny speciality shops and quirky boutiques selling everything from strawberry-scented Wellington boots to heaven-scented candles are wedged between cafes, galleries and churches.*

NEED TO KNOW

Opening Hours

Shops generally open between 10am and 7pm Monday to Saturday. Smaller shops often shut all day on Monday and/or may close from noon to around 2pm for lunch. Many larger stores hold *nocturnes* (late-night shopping), usually on Thursday, until around 10pm. For Sunday shopping, the Champs-Élysées, Montmartre and Le Marais are liveliest.

Sales

Paris' twice-yearly *soldes* (sales) usually last around six weeks, starting in mid-January and again in mid-June.

Tax Refunds

Non-EU residents may be eligible for a TVA (VAT; sales tax) refund (p348).

Top Shopping Tips

- The most exclusive designer boutiques require customers to buzz to get in – don't be shy about ringing the bell.
- Particularly in smaller shops, shopkeepers may not like you touching the merchandise until invited to do so.
- Clothing sizes aren't standardised among European countries – head to a *cabine d'essayage* (fitting room) or www.onlineconversion.com/clothing.
- If you're happy browsing, tell sales staff '*Je regarde*' – 'I'm just looking'.
- Practically all shops offer free (and very beautiful) gift wrapping – ask for *un paquet cadeau*.
- A *ticket de caisse* (receipt) is essential for returning/exchanging an item (within one month of purchase).
- Bargaining is only acceptable at flea markets.

Fashion

Fashion shopping is Paris' forte. Yet although its well-groomed residents make the city at times look and feel like a giant catwalk, fashion here is about style and quality first and foremost, rather than status or brand names. A good place to get an overview of Paris fashion is at department stores like Le Bon Marché (p245), Galeries Lafayette (p99) and Le Printemps (p99).

Shopping in Paris

FASHION SHOWS

Although tickets for Paris' famed haute couture and prêt-à-porter (ready-to-wear) fashion shows are scarce, you can see some runway action: reserve ahead to attend free weekly fashion shows at Galeries Lafayette (p99).

DRESSING FOR LESS

Parisian fashion doesn't have to break the bank: there are fantastic bargains at vintage and secondhand boutiques (generally, the more upmarket the area, the better quality the cast-offs), along with outlet shops selling previous seasons' collections, surpluses and seconds by name-brand designers.

Arcades

Dating from the 19th century, Paris' glass-roofed covered passages are treasure chests of small, exquisite boutiques. Take a walk (p116) through some of the Right Bank's best-preserved arcades.

Markets

Nowhere encapsulates Paris' village atmosphere more than its markets. Not simply places to shop, the city's street markets (p22) are social gatherings for the entire neighbourhood.

Nearly every little quarter has its own street market at least once a week (never Mondays), where tarpaulin-topped trestle tables bow beneath fresh, cooked and preserved delicacies. *Marchés biologiques* (organic markets) are increasingly sprouting up across Paris. Many street markets

STEPHANE CARDINALE / PEOPLE AVENUE / CORBIS ©

Top: Chanel show, Fashion Week (p26)

Right: Designer accessories, Stella McCartney boutique (p115)

HUFTON + CROW / VIEW / CORBIS ©

Shopping by Neighbourhood

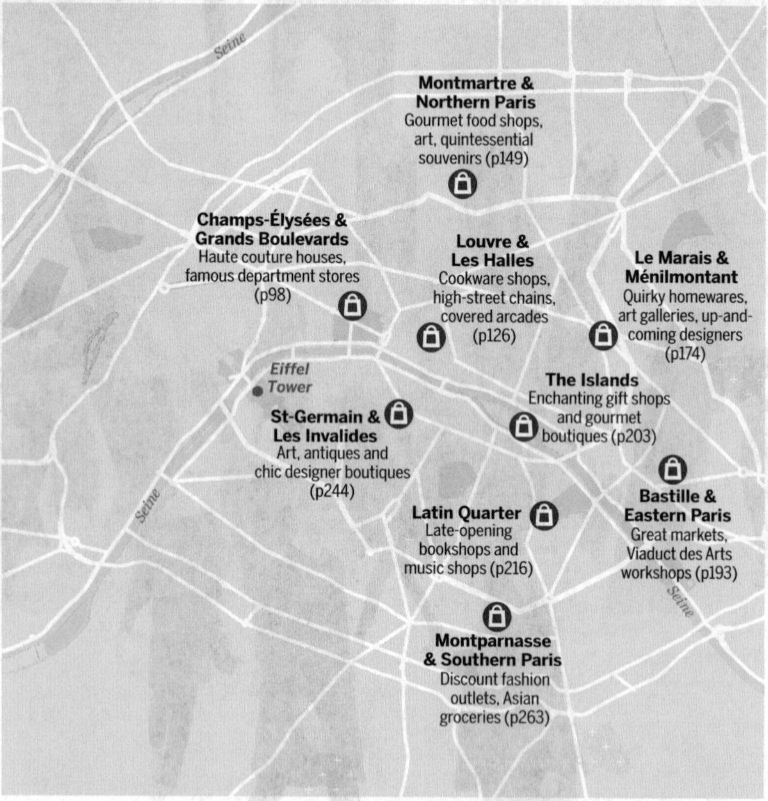

Seine

Montmartre & Northern Paris
Gourmet food shops, art, quintessential souvenirs (p149)

Champs-Élysées & Grands Boulevards
Haute couture houses, famous department stores (p98)

Louvre & Les Halles
Cookware shops, high-street chains, covered arcades (p126)

Le Marais & Ménilmontant
Quirky homewares, art galleries, up-and-coming designers (p174)

Eiffel Tower

The Islands
Enchanting gift shops and gourmet boutiques (p203)

St-Germain & Les Invalides
Art, antiques and chic designer boutiques (p244)

Bastille & Eastern Paris
Great markets, Viaduct des Arts workshops (p193)

Latin Quarter
Late-opening bookshops and music shops (p216)

Montparnasse & Southern Paris
Discount fashion outlets, Asian groceries (p263)

also sell clothes, accessories, homewares and more.

Bric-a-brac, antiques, retro clothing, jewellery, cheap brand-name clothing, footwear, African carvings, DVDs, electronic items and much more are laid out at the city's flea markets. Watch out for pickpockets!

The website www.paris.fr (in French) lists every market by *arrondissement*, including speciality markets such as flower markets.

Gourmet Goods

Food, wine and tea shops make for mouthwatering shopping. Pastries may not keep, but patisserie items you can take home (customs regulations permitting) include light-as-air *macarons*. Other specialty items include honey, mustard, truffles, foie gras, chocolates, jams, preserves and cheese.

Art, Antiques & Homewares

From venerable antique dealers to edgy art galleries, there are a wealth of places in this artistic city to browse and buy one-off conversation pieces and collectibles. Paris also has some unique home and garden shops selling colourful, quirky innovations to brighten your living and/or working environment.

Books

Paris' literary heritage has inspired atmospheric bookshops, including many English-language bookshops that are a magnet for writers and host readings, workshops and other literary events. *Bandes dessinées* (comics), known as *le neuvième art* (the ninth art), are big business in France, with dozens of specialist shops.

Lonely Planet's Top Choices

Didier Ludot (p126) Couture creations of yesteryear including the timeless little black dress.

E Dehillerin (p126) Paris' professional chefs stock up at this cookware shop c 1820.

Village St-Paul (p177) Artisan boutiques and galleries tucked within a 14th-century walled garden.

La Grande Épicerie de Paris (p245) Glorious food emporium.

Adam Montparnasse (p263) Historic art supply shop with paints, canvases and paraphernalia galore.

Shakespeare & Company (p216) A 'wonderland of books', as Henry Miller described it.

Best Concept Stores

Merci (p174)

Colette (p126)

Lieu Commun (p174)

Hermès (p246)

Best Fashion

Best Multidesigner Fashion Boutiques

L'Éclaireur (p177)

Trésor (p175)

Abou d'Abi Bazar (p177)

La Citadelle (p149)

Green in the City (p177)

Shine (p178)

Best Accessories & Handbags

JB Guanti (p247)

A La Recherche De Jane (p247)

Losco (p177)

Alexandra Sojfer (p246)

Jamin Puech (p127)

Pauline Pin (p175)

Best Vintage & Recycled Fashion

Andrea Crews (p174)

Violette et Léonie (p175)

Made in Used (p177)

Room Service (p126)

Le Dépôt-Vente de Buci (p245)

Ragtime (p245)

Best Kids' Fashion & Accessories

Grand Bonton (p174)

Galeries Lafayette (p99)

By Sophie (p174)

Le Petit Bazar (p264)

Lin et Cie (p247)

Best Perfume

Guerlain (p98)

Séphora (p98)

L'Artisan Parfumeur (p176)

Fragonard (p176)

Frédéric Malle (p246)

Le Studio des Parfums (p176)

Best Gourmet Shops

Best Food Shops

Place de la Madeleine (p99)

Comptoir de la Gastronomie (p127)

Fromagerie Alléosse (p150)

Maison Georges Larnicol (p176)

La Petite Scierie (p203)

Première Pression Provence (p203)

Best Drink Shops

La Dernière Goutte (p247)

Les Caves Augé (p98)

Lucien Legrand Filles & Fils (p128)

Mariage Frères (p52)

Cave St-Sulpice (p247)

Julien Caviste (p178)

Best Home & Garden

Fermob (p193)

Deyrolle (p246)

Le Bain Rose (p247)

Cire Trudon (p245)

Flamant Home Interiors (p248)

Bercy Village (p193)

Best Bookshops

Abbey Bookshop (p218)

Librairie Ulysse (p203)

Librairie Gourmande (p127)

Galignani (p127)

I Love my Blender (p175)

Best Art & Antiques

Viaduc des Arts (p193)

Carré Rive Gauche (p246)

La Maison de Poupée (p245)

Hôtel Drouot (p100)

Atelier d'Autrefois (p179)

Marché aux Puces de St-Ouen (p149)

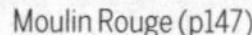

Moulin Rouge (p147)

Entertainment

Catching a performance in Paris is a treat. French and international opera, ballet and theatre companies and cabaret dancers take to the stage in venues of mythical proportion, and a flurry of young, passionate, highly creative musicians, theatre aficionados and artists make the city's fascinating fringe art scene what it is.

French singer Nicola Sirkis performs at Le Bataclan (p173)

Cabarets

Whirling lines of feather-boa-clad, high-kicking dancers at grand-scale cabarets like the can-can creator, the Moulin Rouge, are a quintessential fixture on Paris' entertainment scene – for everyone but Parisians. Still, the dazzling sets, costumes and dancing guarantee an entertaining evening (or matinee).

Tickets to these spectacles start from around €90 (from €130 with lunch, from €150 with dinner), and usually include a half-bottle of champagne. Advance reservations are essential.

Music

Festivals for just about every music genre going ensure that everyone gets to listen in. Street music is a constant in this busker-filled city, with summer adding a soul-stirring string of open-air concerts along the Seine and in city parks to the year-round hum of accordion players.

Of the surfeit of various French-language freebies, easy to pick up on the street and great for a gander between metro stops, **A Nous Paris** (www.anous.fr/paris) is among the most informed and posts its entire magazine online. Pocket-sized booklet **LYLO** (www.lylo.fr), short for Les Yeux, Les Oreilles (meaning 'eyes and ears'), is freely available at bars and cafes, and offers a fortnightly low-down on the live music, concert and clubbing scene. Flyers, schedules and programs for cultural events float around the ticket-office areas in Fnac.

NEED TO KNOW

Listings

Paris' top two listings guides *Pariscope* (€0.40) and **L'Officiel des Spectacles** (www.offi.fr; €0.35), both in French, are available from newsstands on Wednesdays, and are crammed with everything that's on in the capital.

Tickets

Purchase concert, theatre and other cultural and sporting event tickets at the *billeteries* (ticket offices) or by phone or online from **Fnac** (☎08 92 68 36 22; www.fnactickets.com) and **Virgin Megastore** (place Raoul Dautry, ⏰7am-8.30pm Mon-Thu, to 9pm Fri, 8am-8pm Sat; Ⓜ Montparnasse Bienvenüe). Tickets generally can't be returned or exchanged unless a performance is cancelled.

Other ticket agencies:

Agence Marivaux (☎01 42 97 46 70; 7 rue de Marivaux, 2e; ⏰11am-7.30pm Mon-Fri, noon-4pm Sat; Ⓜ Richelieu Drouot)

Agence Perrossier & SOS Théâtres (☎01 42 60 58 31, 01 42 60 26 87; www.agencedetheatresdeparis.fr; 6 place de la Madeleine, 8e; ⏰10am-7pm Mon-Sat; Ⓜ Madeleine)

Discount Tickets

On the day of performance, theatre, opera and ballet tickets are sold for half price (plus €3 commission) at the following kiosks:

Kiosque Théâtre Madeleine (p98)

Kiosque Théâtre Ternes (www.kiosquetheatre.com; place des Ternes, 8e; ⏰12.30-8pm Tue-Sat, to 4pm Sun; Ⓜ Ternes)

Kiosque Théâtre Montparnasse (www.kiosquetheatre.com; Parvis Montparnasse, 15e; ⏰12.30-8pm Tue-Sat, to 4pm Sun; Ⓜ Montparnasse Bienvenüe)

Alternatively buy discount tickets online at www.billetreduc.com, www.ticketac.com and www.webguichet.com.

JAZZ & BLUES

Paris became Europe's most important jazz centre after WWII and the city's best clubs and cellars still lure international stars to this day.

ALESHKOVSKY MITYA / ITAR-TASS PHOTO / CORBIS

Top: Palais Garnier (p92)

Left: National Opera ballet soloist Charline Giezendanner performing a scene from La Source ballet by L Minkus and L Delibes

Admission generally ranges from free to around €25 depending on the artist, time and venue.

Download podcasts, tunes, concert information and all that jazz to listen to on your iPod from Paris' jazz radio station, **TFS** (89.9 MHz FM; www.tsfjazz.com).

FRENCH CHANSONS

While *chanson* literally means 'song' in French, it also specifically refers to a style of heartfelt, lyric-driven music typified by Édith Piaf, Maurice Chevalier, Charles Aznavour et al. You'll come across some stirring live covers of their most famous songs at traditional venues. Contemporary twists on the genre include the fusion of dance beats with traditional *chanson* melodies. The term also covers intimate cabarets such as Montmartre's Au Lapin Agile (p148).

Admission generally ranges from free to around €25 depending on the artist, time and venue.

ROCK, POP & INDIE

Palais Omnisports de Paris-Bercy (p193) **Stade de France** (☎08 92 39 01 00; www.stadefrance.com; rue Francis de Pressensé, ZAC du Cornillon Nord, St-Denis La Plaine; Ⓜ St-Denis-Porte de Paris) and **Le Zénith** (Map p400; ☎01 55 80 09 38, 08 90 71 02 07; www.le-zenith.com; 211 av Jean Jaurès, 19e; Ⓜ Porte de Pantin) in Parc de la Villette are the largest venues but also the most impersonal; it's the smaller concert halls with real history and charm that most fans favour. Check http://gigsinparis.com for listings.

CLASSICAL MUSIC

The city hosts dozens of orchestral, organ and chamber-music concerts each week. In addition to theatres and concert halls, Paris' beautiful, centuries-old stone churches have magnificent acoustics and provide a meditative backdrop for classical music concerts. Posters outside churches advertise upcoming events with ticket information, or visit www.ampconcerts.com, where you can make online reservations. Tickets cost around €23 to €30.

The Jean Nouvel–designed 2400-seat concert hall the Philharmonie de Paris is expected to open in the Parc de la Villette in early 2014.

WORLD & LATINO

Sono mondiale (world music) has a huge following in Paris, where everything – from Algerian *raï* and other North African music to Senegalese *mbalax* and West Indian *zouk* – goes at clubs. Latino music, especially Cuban salsa, has been overwhelmingly popular over the past decade or so. Many concert and clubbing venues have salsa classes.

ÉDITH PIAF

Allegedly born in a Belleville gutter in 1915, Édith Gassion was dubbed *la môme piaf* (urchin sparrow) by her first employer, Louis Leplée, who introduced her to Paris' cabarets.

After Leplée's murder, ex-French Legionnaire Raymond Asso liberated her from her hustler friends and inspired her first big hit, *'Mon Légionnaire'* ('My Legionnaire') in 1937.

Although seriously injured in a car accident in 1951, Piaf continued to take the world stage despite her declining health, and recorded some of her best-known songs such as *'Je ne Regrette Rien'* ('I regret nothing'). She died in 1963 and is buried at Cimetière Père Lachaise (p154).

Cinema

The film-lover's ultimate city, Paris has some wonderful movie houses to catch new flicks, avant-garde cinema and priceless classics.

Foreign films (including English-language films) screened in their original language with French subtitles are labelled 'VO' (*version originale*). Films labelled 'VF' (*version française*) are dubbed in French.

Pariscope and *L'Officiel des Spectacles* list the full crop of Paris' cinematic pickings and screening times; online check out http://cinema.leparisien.fr or www.allocine.com.

First-run tickets cost around €10 for adults (€13 for 3D). Students, under 18s and over 60s get discounted tickets (usually about €7.20 or €10.20 for 3D) every night except Friday, and all day Saturday and on Sunday matinées. There are across-the-board discounts on Wednesday.

Opera & Ballet

France's Opéra National de Paris and Ballet de l'Opéra National de Paris, perform at Paris' two opera houses, the Palais Garnier and Opéra Bastille. The season runs between September and July.

Theatre

The majority of theatre productions in Paris, including those originally written in other languages, are – naturally enough – performed in French. Only very occasionally do English-speaking troupes play at smaller venues in and around town. Consult *Pariscope* or *L'Officiel des Spectacles* for details.

COMEDY

An outfit called **Laughing & Music Matters** (☎01 53 19 98 88; www.anythingmatters.com), with no fixed address, presents some of the best English-language laugh-fests in town, with both local and imported talent.

Buskers in Paris

Paris' gaggle of clowns, mime artists, living statues, acrobats, roller-bladers, buskers and other street entertainers can be loads of fun and cost substantially less than a theatre ticket (a few coins in the hat is appreciated). Some excellent musicians perform in the long echo-filled corridors of the metro, a highly prized privilege that artists audition for. Outside, you can be sure of a good show at the following:

➡ **Place Georges Pompidou, 4e** The huge square in front of the Centre Pompidou.

➡ **Pont St-Louis, 4e** The bridge linking Paris' two islands (best enjoyed with Berthillon ice cream in hand).

➡ **Pont au Double, 4e** The pedestrian bridge linking Notre Dame with the Left Bank.

➡ **Place Jean du Bellay, 1e** Musicians and fire-eaters near the Fontaine des Innocents.

➡ **Parc de la Villette, 19e** African drummers at the weekend.

➡ **Place du Tertre, Montmartre, 18e** Montmartre's original main square wins hands down as Paris' busiest busker stage.

Caveau de la Huchette (p216)

Entertainment By Neighbourhood

➡ **Eiffel Tower & Western Paris (p87)** Entertainment options are limited in this refined residential area.

➡ **Champs-Élyées & Grands Boulevards (p97)** Famous revues and Paris' palatial 1875-built opera house take top billing here.

➡ **Louvre & Les Halles (p125)** Swinging jazz clubs, centuries-old theatres and cinemas mix it up with pumping nightclubs.

➡ **Montmartre & Northern Paris (p147)** Show-stopping cabarets, mythologised concert halls and cutting-edge cultural centres scatter throughout Paris' northern quarters.

➡ **Le Marais & Ménilmontant (p173)** Rockin' live music venues, gay and lesbian clubs, DJs hitting the decks and old-style *chansons*.

➡ **Bastille & Eastern Paris (p192)** Salsa dancing, old-time tea dancing, and France's national cinema institute are big drawcards.

➡ **The Islands (p194)** Church concerts and street entertainers are the only entertainment options on Paris' islands.

➡ **Latin Quarter (p215)** Swing bands, cinema retrospectives and jam sessions are among the Latin Quarter's offerings.

➡ **St-Germain & Les Invalides (p244)** Atmospheric cinemas, cultural centres and theatres inhabit this chic, sophisticated neighbourhood.

➡ **Montparnasse & Southern Paris (p262)** Some of this area's most happening venues are aboard boats moored on the Seine.

Lonely Planet's Top Choices

Palais Garnier (p97) Paris' premier, palatial opera house is an artistic inspiration.

Point Éphemère (p148) Ubercool cultural centre on the banks of Canal St-Martin.

Moulin Rouge (p147) The can-can creator razzle-dazzles with spectacular sets, costumes and choreography.

La Flèche d'Or (p192) Former railway station club renowned for unearthing prodigious new talent.

Café Universel (p215) Brilliant jazz club showcasing a diverse range of styles.

Best Cinema

La Pagode Cinema (p244)

Cinémathèque Française (p192)

Le Champo (p216)

Le Grand Rex (p127)

Best Live Music

Best Jazz Clubs

Le Caveau des Oubliettes (p216)

New Morning (p149)

Le Baiser Salé (p124)

Sunset & Sunside (p124)

Le Petit Journal St-Michel (p216)

Le Caveau de la Huchette (p216)

Best Rock, Pop & Indie

Le Motel (p192)

Alhambra (p149)

Le Bataclan (p173)

L'Olympia (p98)

La Cigale (p148)

Le Divan Du Monde (p148)

Best French Chansons

Au Limonaire (p98)

Le Vieux Belleville (p174)

Au Lapin Agile (p148)

Chez Louisette (p146)

Best Classical

Salle Pleyel (p98)

Ste-Chapelle (p202)

Église de Ste-Marie Madeleine (p93)

Église St-Eustache (p113)

Cité de la Musique (p149)

Best World & Latino

La Favela Chic (p173)

Cabaret Sauvage (p148)

La Java (p173)

Olympic Café (p147)

Satellit Café (p173)

La Chapelle des Lombards (p193)

Best Cultural Centres

Centre Pompidou (p111)

La Bellevilloise (p174)

Le 104 (p149)

L'Entrepôt (p262)

Le Lucernaire (p244)

Best Theatre, Opera & Dance

Comédie Française (p125)

Opera Bastille (p192)

Opéra Comique (p126)

Théâtre du Châtelet (p126)

Théâtre de la Ville (p126)

Théâtre Le Point Virgule (p173)

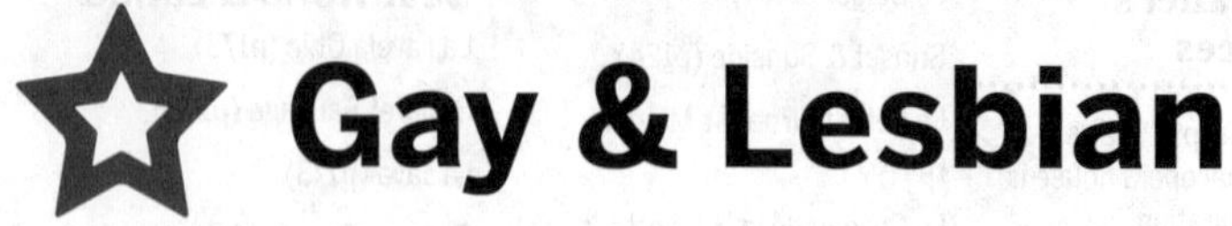

Gay & Lesbian

The city known as 'gay Paree' lives up to its name. Paris is so open in fact that there's less of a defined 'scene' here than other cities where it's more underground. While the Marais is the mainstay of gay and lesbian nightlife, you'll find venues right throughout the city attracting a mixed crowd.

Drinking & Nightlife

The Marais, especially the areas around the intersection of rue Ste-Croix de la Bretonnerie and rue des Archives, and eastwards to rue Vieille du Temple, has been Paris' main centre of gay nightlife for some three decades and is still the epicentre of gay and lesbian life in Paris. There are also a few bars and clubs within walking distance of bd de Sébastopol. The lesbian scene is less prominent than its gay counterpart, and centres around a few cafés and bars in Le Marais, particularly along rue des Écouffes. Bars and clubs are generally all gay- and lesbian-friendly.

Gay & Lesbian Publications

Guidebooks listing pubs, restaurants, clubs, beaches, saunas, sex shops and cruising areas are available from Les Mots à la Bouche (p180) bookshop in Le Marais. One of the best is the comprehensive French-language guide **Le Petit Futé Paris Gay et Lesbien** (www.petitfute.com), which goes well beyond just hedonistic pursuits.

Of the gay and lesbian mags, **Têtu** (www.tetu.com; €5) is a popular and widely circulated glossy monthly available at newsstands everywhere. Be on the lookout for bimonthly freebies such as **2X** (www.2xparis.fr) and **Mâles-a-Bars** (www.males-a-bars.com), which have interviews, articles and listings of gay clubs, bars, associations and personal classifieds. You'll find them stacked up at most gay venues. The monthly *Lesbia Magazine* (€4.20), established in 1983, looks at lesbian women's issues and gives a rundown of what's happening around the country. Also for women, **La Dixième Muse** (www.ladixiememuse.com; €4.50) is more culturally oriented.

Organisations & Resources

Most of France's major gay organisations are based in Paris. For a complete list, pick up a copy of *Genres,* a listing of gay, lesbian, bisexual and transsexual organisations, at the Centre Gai et Lesbien de Paris Île de France or download it from its website.

Centre Gai et Lesbien de Paris Île de France (CGL; ☎01 43 57 21 47; www.centrelgbtparis.org; 61-63 rue Beaubourg, 3e; ⏰6-8pm Mon, 3.30-8pm Tue-Thu, 1-8pm Fri & Sat; Ⓜ Rambuteau or Arts et Métiers) Gay and lesbian travellers' single best source of information in Paris, with a large library of books and periodicals and a sociable bar.

Écoute Gaie (☎08 10 81 10 57; http://ecoute-gaie.france.qrd.org; ⏰6-10pm Mon-Fri) Established in 1982, this is the oldest hotline for gays and lesbians in Paris.

Association des Médecins Gais (AMG; ☎01 48 05 81 71; www.medecins-gays.org) The Association of Gay Doctors deals with gay-related health issues. Telephone advice on physical-health issues is available from 6pm to 8pm on Wednesday and 2pm to 4pm on Saturday. For counselling, call between 8.30pm and 10.30pm on Thursday.

SOS Homophobie (☎08 10 10 81 35, 01 48 06 42 41; www.sos-homophobie.org; ⏰6-10pm Mon-Fri, 8-10pm Tue-Thu, 2-4pm Sat, 6-8pm Sun) This hotline takes anonymous calls concerning discriminatory acts against gays and lesbians.

Act Up Paris (www.actupparis.org) Politically oriented association known for its 'outings' of the not-always rich and famous and other extreme actions.

Lonely Planet's Top Choices

Open Café (p172) The wide, white-seated terrace is prime for talent-watching.

Scream Club (p172) Saturday night's the night at 'Paris' biggest gay party'.

3W Kafé (p173) Men are welcome but rare at this sleek lesbian lounge.

Queen (p97) Don't miss disco night!

La Champmeslé (p125) Cabaret nights, fortune-telling and art exhibitions attract an older lesbian crowd.

Le Tango (p173) Historic 1930s dancehall hosting legendary gay tea dances.

Best Choices for a Weekend in Le Marais

Place des Vosges (p157) Charming city square.

Pozzetto (p166) Ice cream from heaven.

Cimetière du Père Lachaise (p154) Oscar Wilde's winged-angel-topped tomb is a highlight.

Derrière (p161) Play ping pong between courses at this stellar restaurant.

Café Baroc (p170) Fab flavoured beer and, if you're in luck, '80s tunes.

My E-Case (p175) Irresistibly sexy Smartphone covers.

Best Party Spots Beyond Le Marais

Ménilmontant (p173) Edgy urban cool.

Pigalle (p147) More than just the Moulin Rouge...

Champs-Élysées (p97) Glam bars and clubs.

Bastille (p192) Lively local vibe.

Canal St-Martin (p147) Arty, indie venues.

NEED TO KNOW

Useful Websites

➡ **Spartacus International Gay Guide** (www.spartacus-world.com) Gay travel guide with solid recommendations for gay-friendly accommodation in particular.

➡ **CitéGay** (www.citegay.com) One of the best all-inclusive gay sites, with a heavily political agenda.

➡ **Dyke Planet** (www.dykeplanet.com) Loads of recommendations for gay women.

➡ **La France Gaie & Lesbienne** (www.france.qrd.org) 'Queer resources directory' for gays and lesbians, covering cinema, music, art and much more.

➡ **Paris Gay** (www.paris-gay.com) Bang-up-to-date overview of clubbing and other events in the French capital.

➡ **Ze Girlz** (www.zegirlz.com) Gals' site with podcasts, Q&As, forums and news.

Sports & Activities

Hot, sticky sports and ice-cool Parisians seemingly don't go together. Au contraire: not only are Parisians mad about watching sport, they play it too. But they wouldn't be seen dead walking down the street in their tracksuit.

Spectator Sport

Paris hosts a great variety of sporting events throughout the year, from the French Open (p87) to local football matches. There are a handful of stadiums in and around the city; for upcoming events, follow the What's On link at http://en.parisinfo.com. Better yet, if you can read French, sports daily **L'Équipe** (www.lequipe.fr) will provide more depth. Local teams include Paris Saint-Germain (football; www.psg.fr) and the pink-clad Stade Français Paris (rugby; www.stade.fr).

Cycling

Everyone knows that the Tour de France races up the Champs-Élysées at the end of July every year, but you don't need Cadel Evans' leg muscles to enjoy Paris on two wheels. Between Vélib' (p341; the Paris bike-share scheme) and the hundreds of kilometres of urban bike paths, cycling around the city has never been easier. Sign up for one of the great city bike tours (p343) or hire a bike (p341) yourself. Some streets are closed to vehicle traffic on Sundays – great news for cyclists!

Skating

The next most popular activity after cycling has to be skating, whether on the street or on ice. Rent a pair of inline skates at Nomades (p180) and join the Friday evening skate (Pari Roller; p264) that streaks through the Paris streets, or join the more laid-back Sunday afternoon skate (Rollers & Coquillages; p180).

During the winter holidays several temporary outdoor rinks are installed around Paris – the most famous are located in front of the Hôtel de Ville (p157) and on the 1st floor of the Eiffel Tower (p78). See www.paris.fr for other locations.

Hammams & Spas

Whether you want to hobnob with the stars at a *spa de luxe* or get a *savon noir* (black soap) exfoliation at the neighbourhood *hammam* (Turkish steambath), Paris has spaces to suit every whim. Spoil yourself.

Boules

Don't be surprised to see groups of earnest Parisians playing *boules* (France's most popular traditional game, similar to lawn bowls) in the Jardin du Luxembourg and other parks and squares with suitably flat, shady patches of gravel. The Arènes de Lutèce *boulodrome* (p208) in a 2nd-century Roman amphitheatre in the Latin Quarter is a fabulous spot to absorb the scene. There are usually places to play at Paris Plages (p26).

Lonely Planet's Top Choices

Bike tours (p343) See the sights of Paris on two wheels.

Hammam de la Mosquée de Paris (p218) Sweat your cares away in this gorgeous traditional *hammam*.

Rollers & Coquillages Ramble (p180) Sunday-afternoon skate through the Paris streets.

Stade de France (p65) Catch Les Bleus in an international friendly.

Vélib' (p341) A handy way to get around town with much better scenery than the metro.

Best Venues for Spectator Sports

Parc des Princes (p87)

Palais Omnisports de Paris-Bercy (p193)

Stade Roland Garros (p87)

Hippodrome d'Auteuil (p87)

Best Spas & Hammams

Les Bains du Marais (p180)

Hammam Medina (p151)

Russie Blanche (p100)

Best Parks For Sports & Activities

Bois de Boulogne (p86)

Bois de Vincennes (p187)

Jardin du Luxembourg (p228)

Parc des Buttes-Chaumont (p138)

Parc de la Villette (p133)

Best for Skating

Pari Roller (p264)

Nomades (p180)

Hôtel de Ville (p157)

Eiffel Tower (p78)

Best for Swimming

Piscine Joséphine Baker (p264)

Piscine de la Butte Aux Cailles (p265)

Aquaboulevard (p265)

Piscine Pontoise (p219)

Piscine Keller (p265)

NEED TO KNOW

Where Can I Find...

The best single source of information on participatory sports in Paris can be found online at the city hall's website www.paris.fr (in French). Follow the Practiquer un sport link in the Paris Loisirs menu for info on everything from skating and badminton (currently the hottest sport around) to stadiums and equipment rental. *Mairies* (town halls) in every *arrondissement* also have information on sports in their own patch. For an abbreviated version in English, head to http://en.parisinfo.com and follow the Well Being link in the Practical Paris menu.

Tickets

Tickets for big events can generally be purchased through the venue's website. In most cases you'll need to book in advance, so this is best done before you leave home. If you want to try your luck, however, head to the box office at the nearest Fnac store (www.fnac.com, follow the Magasins link to locate a branch), which should have a schedule of upcoming events.

Swimming

If you want to go swimming at your hotel or in a public pool, you'll need to don a *bonnet de bain* (bathing cap) – even if you don't have any hair. They are generally sold at most pools. Men are required to wear skin-tight trunks (Speedos); loose-fitting shorts are not allowed.

Explore Paris

PARIS
TOP SIGHTS

Neighbourhoods at a Glance

❶ Eiffel Tower & Western Paris (p76)

Home to *very* well-heeled Parisians, this *grande dame* of a neighbourhood is where you can get up close and personal with the city's symbolic tower as well as striking new architecture in the high-rise business district of La Défense just outside the *Périphérique* (ring road) encircling central Paris.

❷ Champs-Élysées & Grands Boulevards (p88)

Baron Haussmann reshaped the Parisian cityscape around the Arc de Triomphe, from which 12 avenues radiate, including the Champs-Élysées. To its east are gourmet shops garlanding the Église de la Madeleine, the Palais Garnier opera house and the Grands Boulevards' department stores.

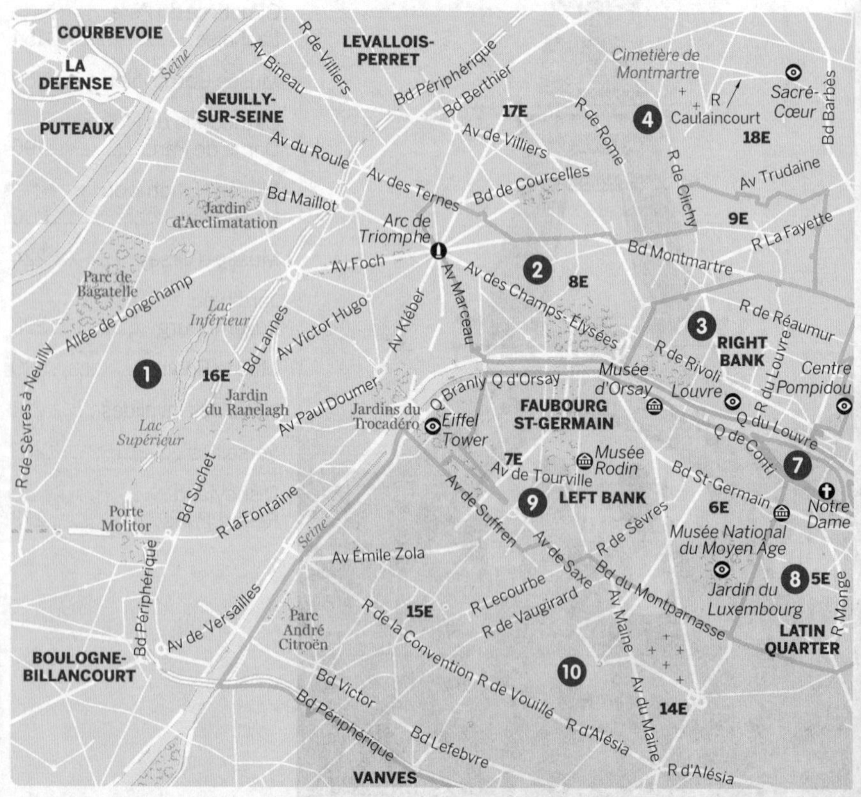

❸ Louvre & Les Halles (p101)

Paris' splendid line of monuments, the *axe historique* (historic axis; also called the grand axis), passes through the Tuileries gardens before reaching IM Pei's glass pyramid at the entrance to the world's largest museum, the Louvre. Nearby, the Forum des Halles shopping precinct is undergoing a much-welcomed makeover.

❹ Montmartre & Northern Paris (p129)

Montmartre's lofty views, wine-producing vines and hidden village squares have lured painters from the 19th century and onwards. Crowned by Basilique du Sacré-Cœur, Montmartre is the city's steepest quarter, and its slinking streets lined with crooked ivy-clad buildings retain a fairy-tale charm.

❺ Le Marais & Ménilmontant (p152)

Funky bars and restaurants, emerging designers' boutiques and the city's thriving gay and Jewish communities all squeeze into Le Marais' warren of narrow medieval laneways, while neighbouring Ménilmontant has some of the city's hippest nightlife.

❻ Bastille & Eastern Paris (p181)

Fabulous markets, intimate bistros, and a disused 19th-century railway viaduct with artist studios below and a four-storey-high park (Promenade Plantée) on top make this area a place to discover the Parisians' Paris.

❼ The Islands (p194)

Paris' geographic and historic heart is here in the Seine. The larger of the two inner-city islands, the Île de la Cité, is dominated by Notre Dame. Serene little Île St-Louis is graced with elegant apartments and hotels and charming eateries and boutiques.

❽ Latin Quarter (p204)

The hub of academic life in Paris, the Latin Quarter centres on the Sorbonne's main university campus. It harbours some fine museums and churches, and Paris' beautiful art deco mosque and botanic gardens.

❾ St-Germain & Les Invalides (p222)

Literary lovers, antique collectors and fashionistas flock to this mythological part of Paris, where presences of legendary writers such as Sartre, de Beauvoir and Hemingway still linger. And chic boutiques abound.

❿ Montparnasse & Southern Paris (p250)

Montparnasse has brasseries from its mid-20th-century heyday and re-energised backstreets buzzing with local life, while Paris' largest Chinatown is filled with Asian grocers and eateries.

Eiffel Tower & Western Paris

EIFFEL TOWER & 16E | LA DÉFENSE

Neighbourhood Top Five

❶ Ascend the **Eiffel Tower** (p78) at dusk and watch the lights blink on across Paris.

❷ Find inspiration in the traditional art on display at the **Musée du Quai Branly** (p80).

❸ Wander past cathedral portals, gargoyles and intricate scale models at the **Cité de l'Architecture et du Patrimoine** (p81).

❹ Explore the **Bois de Boulogne** (p86): from bike rides, rowboats and horse races to a landmark amusement park.

❺ Take a trip out to the **Musée Marmottan Monet** (p84) to see the world's largest collection of Monet canvases.

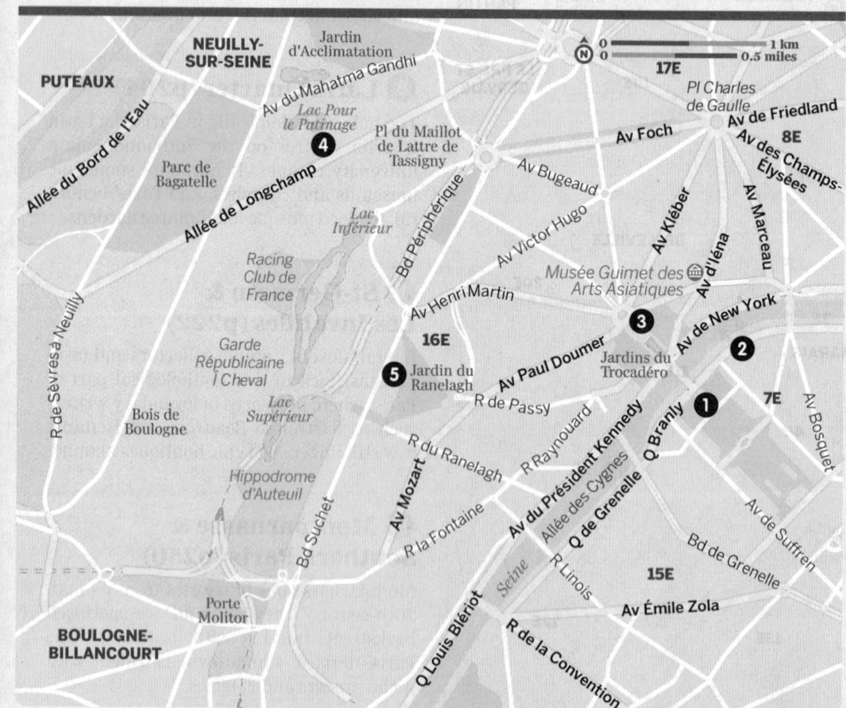

For more detail of this area, see Map p382 ➡

Explore: Eiffel Tower & Western Paris

With its hourly sparkles that illuminate the evening skyline, the Eiffel Tower needs no introduction. Ascending to its viewing platforms will offer you a panorama over the whole of Paris, with the prestigious neighbourhood of Passy (the 16e *arrondissement*) stretching out along the far banks of the Seine to the west.

Passy is home to some fabulous museums, and culture vultures will certainly be busy. There's the Musée Marmottan-Monet, with the world's largest collection of Monet paintings; the hip Palais de Tokyo, with modern art installations; the Musée Guimet, France's standout Asian art museum; the underrated Cité de l'Architecture et du Patrimoine, with captivating sculptures and murals; and a host of smaller collections devoted to fashion, crystal, wine and even sub-Saharan art. On the Left Bank is the prominent Musée du Quai Branly, introducing indigenous art and culture from outside Europe, while at the city's western edge is the leafy refuge of the Bois de Boulogne. Beyond this lies the business district of La Défense.

Local Life

➡ **Museum hopping** Parisians flock to this part of town for the museums: there are over 10 in the 16e alone.

➡ **Green space** The leafy Bois de Boulogne (p86) is where city-dwellers head to escape the concrete, whether on bikes, skates, or by *footing* (jogging).

➡ **Daily commute** Over 150,000 people squeeze onboard the morning trains to La Défense (p83), the city's business district. But there's more here than just office space.

Getting There & Away

➡ **Metro** Line 6 runs south from Charles de Gaulle–Étoile past the Eiffel Tower (views are superb from the elevated section); line 9 runs southwest from the Champs-Élysées.

➡ **RER** RER A runs west to La Défense; RER C runs east–west along the Left Bank, with a stop at the Eiffel Tower.

➡ **Bus** One of Paris' most scenic bus routes, bus 69 runs from the Champ du Mars (Eiffel Tower) along the Left Bank, crosses the Seine at the Louvre, and then continues east to Père Lachaise.

➡ **Bicycle** A convenient Vélib' station is located in front of the Musée du Quai Branly.

➡ **Boat** Eiffel Tower

Lonely Planet's Top Tip

Although there are some excellent top-end restaurants in the 16e, there isn't a whole lot of choice overall. If you're out sightseeing during the day, your best bet is generally to grab lunch at the sight itself; it'll save you both time and hassle.

Best Places to Eat

➡ Firmin Le Barbier (p84)

➡ Tokyo Eat (p85)

➡ L'Astrance (p85)

➡ 58 Tour Eiffel (p85)

➡ Les Ombres (p85)

For reviews, see p84 ➡

Best Museums

➡ Musée du Quai Branly (p80)

➡ Cité de l'Architecture et du Patrimoine (p81)

➡ Musée Marmottan Monet (p84)

➡ Musée Guimet des Arts Asiatiques (p83)

➡ Musée Dapper (p81)

➡ Palais de Tokyo (p81)

For reviews, see p81 ➡

Best Sports & Activities

➡ Bike rides in the Bois de Boulogne (p86)

➡ Roland Garros (p87)

➡ Hippodrome d'Auteuil (p87)

➡ Parc des Princes (p87)

For reviews, see p87 

GLENN BEANLAND / GETTY IMAGES ©

TOP SIGHTS
EIFFEL TOWER

There are many ways to experience the Eiffel Tower, from an evening ascent amid the lights to a meal in one of its two restaurants, and even though some 6.7 million people come annually, few would dispute the fact that each visit is unique. Like many Parisian icons, it has gone from being roundly criticised by city residents to much loved – though the transformation didn't take place overnight.

Named after its designer, Gustave Eiffel, the Tour Eiffel was built for the 1889 Exposition Universelle (World Fair), marking the centenary of the French Revolution. It took 300 workers, 2.5 million rivets and two years of nonstop labour to assemble, and upon completion the tower became the tallest man-made structure in the world (324m or 1063ft) – a record held until the completion of the Chrysler Building in New York (1930). A symbol of the modern age, it faced massive opposition from Paris' artistic and literary elite, and the 'metal asparagus', as some Parisians snidely called it, was originally slated to be torn down in 1909 – spared only because it proved an ideal platform for the transmitting antennas needed for the newfangled science of radiotelegraphy.

The tower has three platforms, around which visits are organised. You can either ascend to the first two floors or go all the way to the top. Visits are usually top to bottom.

Top Floor

Views from the top floor (276m) can stretch up to 60km on a clear day, though at this height the panoramas are more sweeping than detailed. Celebrate your ascent with a glass of bubbly from the champagne bar while you try to pick out

DON'T MISS

- Views from the 2nd Floor
- The Champagne Bar on the Top Floor

PRACTICALITIES

- Map p382
- 01 44 11 23 23
- www.tour-eiffel.fr
- lift to 3rd fl adult/12-24yr/4-12yr €14/12.50/9.50, lift to 2nd fl €8.50/7/4, stairs to 2nd fl €5/3.50/3
- lifts & stairs 9am-midnight mid-Jun–Aug, lifts 9.30am-11pm, stairs 9.30am-6pm Sep–mid-June
- M Champ de Mars–Tour Eiffel or Bir Hakeim

the monuments below, or check out Gustave Eiffel's restored top-level office, where lifelike wax models of Eiffel and his daughter greet Thomas Edison.

In order to access the top floor, you'll need to take a separate lift on the 2nd level. Note that it will close in the event of heavy wind.

2nd Floor

Views from the 2nd floor (115m) are generally considered to be the best, as they are impressively high but still close enough to see the details of the city below. Telescopes and panoramic maps placed around the tower pinpoint locations in Paris and beyond. Other sights to look out for include the story windows, which give a nuts-and-bolts overview of the lifts' mechanics, and the vision well, which allows you to gaze down (and down, and d-o-w-n) through glass panels to the ground. Also up here is the Michelin-starred restaurant Jules Verne, now run by Alain Ducasse.

1st Floor

The 1st floor (57m), which should be finishing the tail end of a massive redevelopment project by the time you read this, has the most space but the least impressive views, which makes it a prime location for its new museum-like layout. Glass floors, interactive history exhibits, and an immersion film are some of the new features that you can expect to find as you learn more about the tower's ingenious design.

If you're visiting Paris during the winter holidays, definitely check to see if the ice-skating rink has been set up here; it's usually open from mid-December to mid-January and is free for visitors (skates included). Also on this level is the restaurant 58 Tour Eiffel and simpler dining options.

Ticket Purchases & Queueing Strategies

Highly recommended is the online booking system that allows you to buy your tickets in advance, thus avoiding the monumental queues at the ticket office. Note that you need to be able to print out your tickets to use this service or have your ticket on a smartphone screen (eg Blackberry or iPhone) that can be read by the scanner at the entrance. If you can't reserve your tickets ahead of time, expect waits of well over an hour in high season.

Another option for avoiding long queues (and for working off that last meal) is to take the stairs. These are accessed at the south pillar: the climb consists of 360 steps to the 1st level and another 360 steps to the 2nd pillar. You cannot reserve stair tickets online.

Finally, if you have reservations for either restaurant, you are granted direct access to the lifts.

NIGHTLY SPARKLES

Every hour on the hour, the entire tower sparkles for five minutes with 20,000 gold-toned lights. First installed for Paris' millennium celebration in 2000, it took 25 mountain climbers five months to install the current bulbs and 40km of electrical cords. For the best view of the light show, head across the Seine to the Jardins du Trocadéro.

Slapping a fresh coat of paint on the Tower is no easy feat – it takes a 25-person team 18 months to complete the task. Originally painted red, it's had six different colours throughout its lifetime, including yellow!

MAN ON A WIRE

In 1989 tightrope artist Philippe Petit walked up an inclined 700m cable across the Seine, from the Palais Chaillot to the Eiffel Tower's 2nd level. The act, performed before an audience of 250,000 people, was held to commemorate the French Republic's bicentennial.

TOP SIGHTS
MUSÉE DU QUAI BRANLY

A tribute to the incredible diversity of human culture, the Musée du Quai Branly presents an overview of indigenous and folk art from around the world.

Divided into four main sections, the museum showcases an impressive array of masks, carvings, weapons, jewellery and more, all displayed in a refreshingly unique interior without rooms or high walls.

The **Oceania section,** features some remarkable carvings from Papua New Guinea and the surrounding islands, including a series of facade masks, daggers, jewellery, hair pieces and several ancestor skulls. Other cultures well represented here include Maori and Australian Aboriginal Torres Strait Islander.

The **Asian collection** includes clothing, jewellery and textiles from ethnic minorities from India to Vietnam, though one of the most striking articles on display is an Evenk shaman cloak from eastern Siberia. Also worth looking for are the intricate cured-leather Chinese shadow puppets and the Tibetan *thangkas* (Buddhist paintings on silk scrolls).

The **Africa collection** is particularly strong on musical instruments and masks, but there are some other unusual pieces here, such as the life-sized 11th-century sculpture of a hermaphrodite (Mali), which greets visitors with a raised arm. One of the more notable masks on display is a Krou mask from the Ivory Coast, which is said to have influenced Picasso.

Look for highlights from the great civilisations in the **Americas collection** – the Mayas, Aztecs and Incas – as well as objects from lesser-known peoples, such as the grizzly totem pole (Tsimshian) or the crazily expressive Kiiappaat masks (Greenland).

DON'T MISS

- The Papua New Guinea Collection, Oceania
- The Evenk Shaman Cloak, Asia
- The Soninke Hermaphrodite, Africa
- The Grizzly Totem Pole, Americas

PRACTICALITIES

- Map p382
- www.quaibranly.fr
- 37 quai Branly, 7e
- adult/child €8.50/free
- 11am-7pm Tue, Wed & Sun, to 9pm Thu-Sat
- M Pont de l'Alma or Alma-Marceau

SIGHTS

Eiffel Tower & 16e

EIFFEL TOWER LANDMARK

See p78.

MUSÉE DU QUAI BRANLY ART MUSEUM

See p80.

PARC DU CHAMP DE MARS PARK

Map p382 (ⓂChamp de Mars–Tour Eiffel or École Militaire) Running southeast from the Eiffel Tower, the grassy Champ de Mars was originally used as a parade ground for the cadets of the 18th-century **École Militaire** (Military Academy; Map p382), the vast, French-classical building at the south-eastern end of the park, which counts none other than Napoleon Bonaparte among its graduates. The wonderful steel-and-etched glass **Wall for Peace memorial** (2000) facing the academy and the statue of Maréchal Joffre (1870–1931) are by Clara Halter.

Today it's the ideal spot for a summer picnic. Pick up some bread, cheese and wine on nearby rue Cler (about a 20-minute walk) and you're all set to enjoy one of the most memorable meals in Paris. Also here are puppet shows (p87).

MUSÉE DAPPER ART MUSEUM

Map p382 (www.dapper.com.fr; 35 rue Paul Valéry, 16e; adult/senior/under 26yr €6/4/free; ⌚11am-7pm, closed Tue & Thu; ⓂVictor Hugo) Focused on African and Caribbean art, this jewel of a museum is an invitation to leave Paris behind for an hour or two. Although exhibits rotate throughout the year, expect to find a superb collection of ritual and festival masks and costumes accompanied by several video presentations in each room. The ever-active auditorium sponsors cultural events year-round, from concerts to storytelling and films.

PALAIS DE TOKYO ART MUSEUM

Map p382 (www.palaisdetokyo.com; 13 av du Président Wilson, 16e; adult/18-25yr/under 18yr €8/6/free; ⌚noon-midnight Tue-Sun; ⓂIéna) The Tokyo Palace, created for the 1937 Exposition Universelle and now a contemporary art space, has no permanent collection. Instead its shell-like interior of polished concrete and steel is the stark backdrop for rotating, interactive art

TOP SIGHTS CITÉ DE L'ARCHITECTURE ET DU PATRIMOINE

In the eastern wing of the **Palais de Chaillot** (17 place du Trocadéro et du 11 Novembre, 16e; ⓂTrocadéro), directly across from the Eiffel Tower, is this standout museum devoted to French architecture and heritage. The burgundy walls and skylit rooms here showcase 350 plaster casts taken from the country's greatest monuments, a collection whose seeds were sown following the desecration of many buildings during the French Revolution.

Some of the original details from which the casts were made, such as sculptures from the Reims Cathedral, were later destroyed in the wars that followed. Although not in situ, wandering through such a magnificent collection of church portals, gargoyles, and saints and sinners from around France is an incomparable experience for anyone interested in the elemental stories that craftsmen chose to preserve in stone.

On display on the upper floors are reproduced murals and stained-glass windows from some of France's most important monuments, which are arranged in an intriguing labyrinthine layout. One of the most beautiful reproductions in this section is the Cathédrale of St-Etienne cupola.

DON'T MISS...

- The Casts Gallery
- The Murals & Stained Glass Galleries
- The Cathédrale of St-Étienne Cupola

PRACTICALITIES

- Map p382
- www.citechaillot.fr
- 1 place du Trocadéro et du 11 Novembre, 16e
- adult/18-25yr/under 18yr €8/5/free
- ⌚11am-7pm Wed-Mon, to 9pm Thu
- ⓂTrocadéro

installations (the rooftop, for example, has been the setting for attention-getting projects like the transient Hotel Everland and the see-through restaurant Nomiya). Exhibition space was tripled in 2012.

FREE **MUSÉE D'ART MODERNE DE LA VILLE DE PARIS** ART MUSEUM

Map p382 (www.mam.paris.fr; 11 av du Président Wilson, 16e; permanent collections free; ⌚10am-6pm Tue-Sun, to 10pm Thu; Ⓜléna) The permanent collection at the city's modern-art museum displays works representative of virtually just about every major artistic movement of the 20th and nascent 21st centuries: Fauvism, cubism, Dadaism, and so on up through to video installations. While the museum merits a wander – you'll find stunning works by Modigliani, Matisse, Braque and Soutine here – the permanent collection is not quite at the level of the Centre Pompidou.

There is one jewel of a room though, containing several gorgeous canvases from Dufy and Bonnard. The main reason for a trip here is to check out one of the cutting-edge temporary exhibits.

FONDATION PIERRE BERGÉ YVES SAINT LAURENT FASHION MUSEUM

Map p382 (www.fondation-pb-ysl.net; 3 rue Léonce Reynaud, 16e; adult/10-25yr & senior €7/5; ⌚11am-6pm Tue-Sun; ⓂAlma-Marceau) This foundation dedicated to preserving the work of the *haute couture* legend organises two to three temporary exhibits (not necessarily related to YSL) per year, with an emphasis on fashion and art.

LA COLLINE DES MUSÉES PASS

This five-day museum pass is valid for the Cité de l'Architecture et du Patrimoine, Palais de Tokyo, Musée Quai Branly and Musée d'Art Moderne de la Ville de Paris, all four of which are within walking distance of the Eiffel Tower. It offers reduced admission to the second and third museums and free admission to the fourth, including temporary exhibitions, no matter what order you visit them in. Download the pass at www.lacollinedesmusees.com.

MUSÉE GALLIERA DE LA MODE DE LA VILLE DE PARIS FASHION MUSEUM

Map p382 (www.galliera.paris.fr; 10 av Pierre 1er de Serbie, 16e; ⌚10am-6pm Tue-Sun; Ⓜléna) Paris' Fashion Museum, housed in the 19th-century Palais Galliera, warehouses some 100,000 outfits and accessories – from canes and umbrellas to fans and gloves – from the 18th century to the present day. The sumptuous Italianate palace and gardens dating from the mid-19th century are worth a visit in themselves. The museum has been undergoing renovations since 2009, but should be open by the time you read this.

CINÉAQUA AQUARIUM

Map p382 (www.cineaqua.com; av des Nations Unies, 16e; adult/child €20/13; ⌚10am-7pm; ⓂTrocadéro) On the eastern side of the Jardins du Trocadéro is Paris' largest aquarium. It's not the best you'll ever see, but it is a decent rainy-day destination for families, with a shark tank and some 500 species of fish on display. There are also, somewhat oddly, three cinemas inside (only one of which shows ocean-related films), though non-French-speaking kids will need to be old enough to read subtitles, as almost everything is dubbed into French.

GALERIE-MUSÉE BACCARAT CRYSTAL MUSEUM

Map p382 (www.baccarat.com; 11 place des États-Unis, 16e; adult/18-25yr/under 18yr €5/3.50/free; ⌚10am-6.30pm Mon & Wed-Sat; ⓂBoissière or Kléber) Showcasing 1000 stunning pieces of crystal, many of them custom-made for princes and dictators of former colonies, this flashy museum is at home in its striking new rococo-style premises designed by Philippe Starck in the ritzy 16e. It is also home to a superb restaurant called – what else? – Le Cristal Room.

MUSÉE DE LA MARINE NAVAL MUSEUM

Map p382 (Maritime Museum; www.musee-marine.fr; 17 place du Trocadéro et du 11 Novembre, 16e; adult/18-25yr/under 18yr €7/5/free; ⌚11am-6pm Wed-Mon, to 7pm Sat & Sun; ⓂTrocadéro) Located in the western wing of the Palais de Chaillot, the Maritime Museum examines France's naval adventures from the 17th century until today and boasts one of the world's finest collections of model ships, as well as ancient figureheads, compasses, sextants, telescopes and paintings.

Also located in this wing is **Musée de l'Homme** (Museum of Humankind; Map p382;

TOP SIGHTS
MUSÉE GUIMET DES ARTS ASIATIQUES

France's foremost Asian arts museum, the Musée Guimet has a superb collection of sculptures, paintings and religious articles that originated in the vast stretch of land between Afghanistan and Japan. In fact, it's possible to observe the gradual transmission of both Buddhism and artistic styles along the Silk Road in some of the museum's pieces, from the 1st-century Gandhara Buddhas from Afghanistan and Pakistan to the later Central Asian, Chinese and Japanese Buddhist sculptures and art.

Other strong points of the museum include the Southeast Asian statuary on the ground floor (which has the world's largest collection of Khmer artefacts outside Cambodia), the Nepalese and Tibetan bronzes and mandalas, and the vast China collection, which encompasses everything from ink paintings and calligraphy to funerary statuary and early bronzes.

Part of the collection, comprised of Buddhist paintings and sculptures, is housed in the nearby **Galeries du Panthéon Bouddhique du Japon et de la Chine** (Map p382; 19 av d'Iéna, 16e). Don't miss the wonderful Japanese garden here.

DON'T MISS...

- Afghan Collection
- The Southeast Asian Statuary
- China Collection
- The Galeries du Panthéon Bouddhique

PRACTICALITIES

- Map p382
- www.museeguimet.fr
- 6 place d'Iéna, 16e
- adult/18-25yr €7.50/5.50
- 10am-6pm Wed-Mon
- M Iéna

www.mnhn.fr), which is closed for renovations until 2015.

MUSÉE DU VIN WINE MUSEUM

Map p382 (01 45 25 63 26; www.museeduvinparis.com; 5 sq Charles Dickens, 16e; adult/child €12/free; 10am-6pm Tue-Sun; M Passy) The not-so-comprehensive Wine Museum, headquarters of the prestigious International Federation of Wine Brotherhoods, introduces visitors to the fine art of viticulture with various mock-ups and displays of tools. Admission includes a glass of wine at the end of the visit. Entry is free if you have lunch at the attached restaurant.

FLAME OF LIBERTY MEMORIAL MONUMENT

Map p382 (M Alma-Marceau) This bronze sculpture, a replica of the one topping the Statue of Liberty, was placed here in 1987 on the centenary of the launch of the *International Herald Tribune*, as a symbol of friendship between France and the USA. On 31 August 1997 in the place d'Alma underpass, Diana, Princess of Wales, was killed in a devastating car accident along with her companion, Dodi Fayed, and their chauffeur, Henri Paul. The sculpture is located on the place de l'Alma, near the end of the Pont de l'Alma bridge.

FREE **MAISON DE BALZAC** MUSEUM

Map p382 (www.balzac.paris.fr; 47 rue Raynouard, 16e; permanent collection free; 10am-6pm Tue-Sun; M Passy or Avenue Président Kennedy) This pretty, three-storey spa house in Passy, about 800m southwest of the Jardins du Trocadéro, is where the realist novelist Honoré de Balzac (1799–1850) lived and worked from 1840 to 1847, editing the entire *Comédie Humaine* and writing various books. There's lots of memorabilia, letters, prints and portraits; it's probably for die-hard Balzac fans only.

La Défense

LA DÉFENSE NEIGHBOURHOOD

(M La Défense) Architecture buffs will have a field day in Paris' business district, located in the western suburbs. Begun in the 1950s, today La Défense counts more than 100 buildings, including the headquarters of three-quarters of France's largest corporations, and showcases extraordinary monumental art. Strict zoning regulations in the city centre means that this is the only place in Paris where you'll see skyscrapers.

GRANDE ARCHE DE LA DÉFENSE LANDMARK
(1 Parvis de la Défense; Ⓜ La Défense) La Défense's landmark edifice is the white marble Grande Arche, a striking cube-like structure that was built in the 1980s and is now home to government and business offices. The arch marks the western end of the Axe Historique (Historic Axis), though Danish architect Johan-Otto von Sprekelsen deliberately placed the Grande Arche fractionally out of alignment.

Access to the roof has been suspended indefinitely for security reasons.

MUSÉE DE LA DÉFENSE HISTORY MUSEUM
(www.ladefense.fr; 15 place de la Défense; 10am-6pm Sun-Fri, to 7pm Sat; Ⓜ La Défense) This museum provides a good overview of the area through drawings, architectural plans and scale models. Pick up tourist info and maps on the ground floor.

The 16e *arrondissement* is best known for its monuments and museums and, conveniently, there are a number of good restaurants located in the sights themselves. Around the Eiffel Tower you can grab picnic supplies at rue Cler or choose from the restaurants on rue de Monttessuy. And, for a truly memorable experience, you can even dine in the icon itself.

TOP CHOICE **FIRMIN LE BARBIER** BISTRO €€
Map p382 (01 45 51 21 55; www.firminlebarbier.fr; 20 rue de Monttessuy, 7e; mains €22; lunch Sun only, dinner Tue-Sun; Ⓜ Pont de l'Alma) This discreet brick-walled bistro was opened by a retired surgeon turned gourmet, and his passion for a good meal is apparent in everything from the personable service to the wine list. The menu is traditional French (sirloin steak with polenta, decadent bœuf bourguignon), while the modern interior is bright and cheery and even benefits from an open kitchen – a rarity in smaller Parisian restaurants.

TOP SIGHTS
MUSÉE MARMOTTAN MONET

Housed in the duc de Valmy's former hunting lodge (well, let's call it a mansion), this intimate museum houses the world's largest collection of Monet paintings and sketches. It begins with paintings such as the seminal *Impression Soleil Levant* (1873) and *Promenade près d'Argenteuil* (1875), passing through numerous water-lily studies, before moving on to the rest of the collection, which is considerably more abstract and dates to the early 1900s. Some of the masterpieces to look out for include: *La Barque* (1887), *Cathédrale de Rouen* (1892), *Londres, le Parlement* (1901) and the various *Nymphéas.* (Many of the Nymphéas series were smaller studies for works now on display in the **Musée de l'Orangerie** (Map p388; www.musee-orangerie.fr; Quai des Tuileries & rue de Rivoli; adult/child €7.50/5.50; 7am-7.30pm, 9pm or 11pm; Ⓜ Tuileries or Concorde).

Temporary exhibitions, included in the admission price and always excellent, are generally shown either in the basement or on the 1st floor. Also on display are a handful of canvases by Renoir, Pissarro, Gauguin and Morisot, and a collection of 15th- and 16th-century illuminations, which are quite lovely if somewhat out of place.

DON'T MISS...

- *Impression Soleil Levant*
- *Promenade près d'Argenteuil*
- *Londres, le Parlement*

PRACTICALITIES

- Map p382
- 01 44 96 50 33
- www.marmottan.com
- 2 rue Louis Boilly, 16e
- adult/7-25yr €10/5
- 10am-6pm Tue-Sun, to 9pm Thu
- Ⓜ La Muette

The good news: it's a five-minute walk from the Eiffel Tower. The bad: it doesn't seat many more than 20 people – be sure to reserve.

TOP CHOICE **TOKYO EAT** FUSION €€

Map p382 (☎01 47 20 00 29; www.palaisdetokyo.com; 13 av du Président Wilson, 16e; lunch menu €20, mains €12-28; ⊙noon-1am Tue-Sun; Ⓜléna) Certainly the funkiest dining option in the otherwise sedate west, Tokyo Eat is the artsy canteen attached to the modern-art museum Palais de Tokyo. Much like the museum itself, the setting is very industrially chic, with colourful flying saucers hovering above the tables and changing art exhibits in the street-facing windows.

The cuisine is unpredictable and fun – expect anything from chicken curry with fruit served on a banana leaf to pan-fried lamb chops with edamame beans, confit of aubergine and peanut sauce. In summer, diners usually decamp to the terrace located down the main staircase east of the main entrance. DJs sometimes hit the decks at night.

L'ASTRANCE GASTRONOMIC €€€

Map p382 (☎01 40 50 84 40; 4 rue Beethoven, 16e; lunch/dinner menus €70/210; ⊙Tue-Fri; ⓂPassy) It's been over a decade now since Pascal Barbot's dazzling cuisine at the three-star L'Astrance made its debut, but it has shown no signs of losing its cutting edge. Look beyond the complicated descriptions on the menu – what you should expect are teasers of taste that you never even knew existed, and a presentation that is an art unto itself.

A culinary experience unique to Paris, you'll need to reserve two months in advance (one month for lunch).

58 TOUR EIFFEL BRASSERIE €€

Map p382 (☎01 45 55 20 04; www.restaurants-toureiffel.com; 1st level, Champ de Mars, 7e; lunch menu €18 & €23, dinner menu €67-150; ⊙11.30am-4.30pm & 6.30-11pm; ⓂChamp de Mars–Tour Eiffel or Bir Hakeim) If you're intrigued by the idea of a meal in the Tower, the 58 Tour Eiffel is a pretty good choice. It may not be the caviar and black truffles of **Jules Verne** (Map p382; ☎01 45 55 61 44; Champ de Mars; ⊙lunch & dinner; ⓂChamp de Mars-Tour Eiffel or Bir Hakeim) on the 2nd level, but Alain Ducasse did sign off on the menu, ensuring that this is much more than just another tourist cafeteria.

LOCAL KNOWLEDGE

THE ART OF LA DÉFENSE

More than just office space, La Défense is also an open-air art gallery. Calder, Miró, Agam, César and Torricini are among the international artists behind the colourful and often surprising sculptures and murals that pepper the central 1km-long promenade. Pick up a detailed map at the Espace-Info information centre at the Musée de la Défense.

For lunch, go first to the restaurant's outside kiosk (near the north pillar); for dinner, reserve online or by telephone.

LES OMBRES MODERN FRENCH €€€

Map p382 (☎01 47 53 68 00; www.lesombres-restaurant.com; 27 quai Branly, 7e; lunch €26-38, dinner €65; ⊙daily; ⓂPont de l'Alma or léna) Paris gained not only a museum in the Musée du Quai Branly but also this glass-enclosed rooftop restaurant on the 5th floor. Named the 'Shadows' for the patterns cast by the Eiffel Tower's webbed ironwork, the dramatic views are complemented by the kitchen's creations, such as *gambas* (prawns) with black rice and fennel, or sea bream in a parmesan crust.

Stop by between 3pm and 5pm to sample pastry chef Pascal Chanceau's decadent afternoon-tea menu, or in the evening when the tower is all a glitter.

CAFÉ BRANLY CAFE €€

Map p382 (27 quai Branly, 7e; mains €12-19; ⊙9.30am-6pm Tue, Wed & Sun, to 8pm Thu, Fri & Sat; ⓂPont de l'Alma or léna) This casual spot at the Musée du Quai Branly has ringside views of the Eiffel Tower and quality cafe fare (foie gras salad, XL *croque monsieur*). The setting is fantastic and the meals a cut above the nearby brasseries. It's open all afternoon, but past 3.30pm it's more cafe than restaurant.

LE CRISTAL ROOM MODERN FRENCH €€€

Map p382 (☎01 40 22 11 10; www.baccarat.com; 11 place des États-Unis, 16e; mains €39-42, menus €29-55 (lunch only) & €109; ⊙lunch & dinner Mon-Sat; Ⓜléna) Located on the first floor of the Galerie-Musée Baccarat, this stunner of a venue features interiors conceived by the overemployed Philippe Starck: mirrors, crystal and even a black chandelier. The menu by Guy Martin is excellent but

BOIS DE BOULOGNE

The 845-hectare Bois de Boulogne owes its informal layout to Baron Haussmann, who, inspired by London's Hyde Park, planted 400,000 trees here in the 19th century. Along with various gardens and other sights, the park has 15km of cycle paths and 28km of bridle paths through 125 hectares of forested land.

Be warned that the area becomes a distinctly adult playground after dark, especially along the Allée de Longchamp running northeast from Étang des Réservoirs (Reservoirs Pond), where all kinds of prostitutes cruise for clients.

The Bois de Boulogne is served by metro lines 1 (Porte Maillot, Les Sablons), 2 (Porte Dauphine), 9 (Michel-Ange-Auteuil) and 10 (Michel-Ange-Auteuil, Porte d'Auteuil), and the RER C (Avenue Foch, Avenue Henri Martin). Vélib' stations are found near most of the park entrances, but not within the park itself.

Paris Cycles (01 47 47 76 50; per hr €5; 10am-7pm mid-Apr–mid-Oct) If you're longing to cruise through the park on two wheels but can't get your hands on a Vélib', fret not. Bicycles can be hired at two locations in the Bois de Boulogne: on av du Mahatma Gandhi, across from the Porte Sablons entrance to the Jardin d'Acclimatation, and near the Pavillon Royal (av Foch) at the northern end of Lac Inférieur.

Jardin d'Acclimatation (Map p382; www.jardindacclimatation.fr; av du Mahatma Gandhi; admission €2.90, activity tickets €2.90, under 3yr free; 10am-7pm Apr-Sep, to 6pm Oct-Mar; M Les Sablons) Families with young kids flock to this great amusement park with puppet shows, boat rides, a small water park, pony rides, art exhibits and sometimes special movies. Most activities cost extra.

Row boats (Map p382; per hr €15; 10am-6pm mid-Mar–mid-Oct; M Av Henri Martin) Boats can be hired at Lac Inférieur, the largest of the Bois' lakes and ponds.

Parc de Bagatelle (adult/child €5/free; 9.30am-5pm, to 8pm in summer; M Porte Maillot) These enclosed gardens, originally designed as the result of a wager between Marie Antoinette and the Count of Artois, surround the 18th-century **Château de Bagatelle** (rue de Sèvres à Neuilly; adult/child €6/free; tour 3pm Sat & Sun Apr-Oct). There are areas dedicated to irises (which bloom in May), roses (June to October) and water lilies (August).

Pré Catelan (Catelan Meadow; 9.30am-5pm, to 8pm in summer; M Ranelagh) This garden area at the Parc de Bagatelle includes the Jardin Shakespeare, in which plants, flowers and trees mentioned in Shakespeare's plays are cultivated.

Jardin des Serres d'Auteuil (av de la Porte d'Auteuil; 9.30am-5pm, to 8pm summer; M Porte d'Auteuil) Located at the southeastern end of the Bois de Boulogne, these impressive conservatories (opened 1898) house a large collection of tropical plants.

Tenniseum-Musée de Roland Garros (www.fft.fr; 2 av Gordon Bennett; adult/child €7.50/4, with stadium visit €15/10; 10am-6pm Tue-Sun; M Porte d'Auteuil) The world's most extravagant tennis museum traces the sport's 500-year history through paintings, sculptures and posters. Tours of the stadium take place at 11am and 3pm in English; reservations are required.

Fondation Louis Vuitton pour la Création (Map p382; www.fondationlouisvuitton.fr) Designed by Frank Gehry, this fine-arts centre is expected to open sometime in 2013. It's located just south of the Jardin d'Acclimatation.

expensive. Note that you will need to book well in advance.

LE PETIT RÉTRO — BISTRO €€

Map p382 (01 44 05 06 05; www.petitretro.fr; 5 rue Mesnil, 16e; mains €15-29, menus €25 (lunch only), €30 & €35; lunch & dinner to 10.30pm Mon-Fri; M Victor Hugo) From the gorgeous 'Petit Rétro' emblazoned on the zinc bar to the art nouveau folk tiles, this is a classy old-style bistro. It serves up classic French fare year-round, such as blood sausage with apples and honey and *blanquette de veau* (veal in a butter and cream sauce).

BERT'S — CAFE €

Map p382 (www.berts.com; 4 av du Président Wilson, 16e; sandwiches €5.50-7, salads €7-8.50; 8am-9pm; ; M Alma-Marceau) Elsewhere this modern cafe chain with worn leather couches and comfy armchairs might not stand out, but in this part of town it's a good address to have on hand – not least because it's open daily. Sandwiches are served on organic bread and there are plenty of veggie options available.

MARCHÉ PRÉSIDENT WILSON MARKET

Map p382 (av du Président Wilson, 16e; ⏲7am-2.30pm Wed & Sat; Ⓜléna or Alma-Marceau) This open-air market is the most convenient in the neighbourhood.

ENTERTAINMENT

MARIONNETTES DU CHAMP DE MARS PUPPET SHOWS

Map p382 (☎01 48 56 01 44; allée du Général Margueritte, 7e; admission €3.50; ⓂÉcole Militaire) For time-honoured French entertainment, take the kids to see one of the puppet shows held in a Napoleon III–style puppet theatre on the Champ de Mars. Show times are 3.15pm and 4.15pm on Wednesdays, Saturdays and Sundays. Everything is in French, of course, but the performances are amusing all the same.

SPORTS & ACTIVITIES

STADE ROLAND GARROS TENNIS

(www.billetterie.fft.fr; 2 av Gordon Bennett, Bois de Boulogne; ⓂPorte d'Auteuil) By far the glitziest annual sporting event in Paris is the French Open, held on clay at the 16,500-seat Stade Roland Garros from late May to mid-June. Tickets are like gold dust; they go on sale mid-December and bookings must be made by March. They are only available online or via mail.

If the sound of feet sliding across clay is music to your ears, check out the Tenniseum (Tennis Museum) in the Bois de Boulogne. A new stadium is currently undergoing construction nearby; it's expected to open in 2016.

HIPPODROME D'AUTEUIL HORSE RACING

Map p382 (www.france-galop.com; Champ de Courses d'Auteuil, Bois de Boulogne; admission adult/child €3/free; ⓂPorte d'Auteuil) One of two horse-racing tracks in the Bois de Boulogne, the Hippodrome d'Auteuil is host to steeplechases from four to six times a month from March to late June and early September to early December. The excitement of the race and the elegance of the steeds makes this a popular activity with children as well.

PARC DES PRINCES FOOTBALL

(www.leparcdesprinces.fr; 24 rue du Commandant Guilbaud, 16e; ⏲box office 9am-7pm Mon-Fri & 3hr before match; ⓂPorte de St-Cloud) The city's top-division football team, **Paris-St-Germain** (www.psg.fr) wears red and blue and plays its home games at this 48,500-seat stadium.

Champs-Élysées & Grands Boulevards

CHAMPS-ÉLYSÉES | GRANDS BOULEVARDS

Neighbourhood Top Five

1. Climb the **Arc de Triomphe** (p90) to survey the *axe historique*, which extends from the Louvre to La Défense.

2. View a performance or tour the opulent 19th-century **Palais Garnier opera house** (p97).

3. Go on a *haute couture* treasure hunt in the Triangle d'Or (p99) or **Galeries Lafayette** (p99).

4. Take in the excellent art exhibits at the **Grand Palais** (p93) or **La Pinacothèque** (p94).

5. Stroll the over-the-top **Champs-Élysées** (p92) – you can't leave Paris without doing it once.

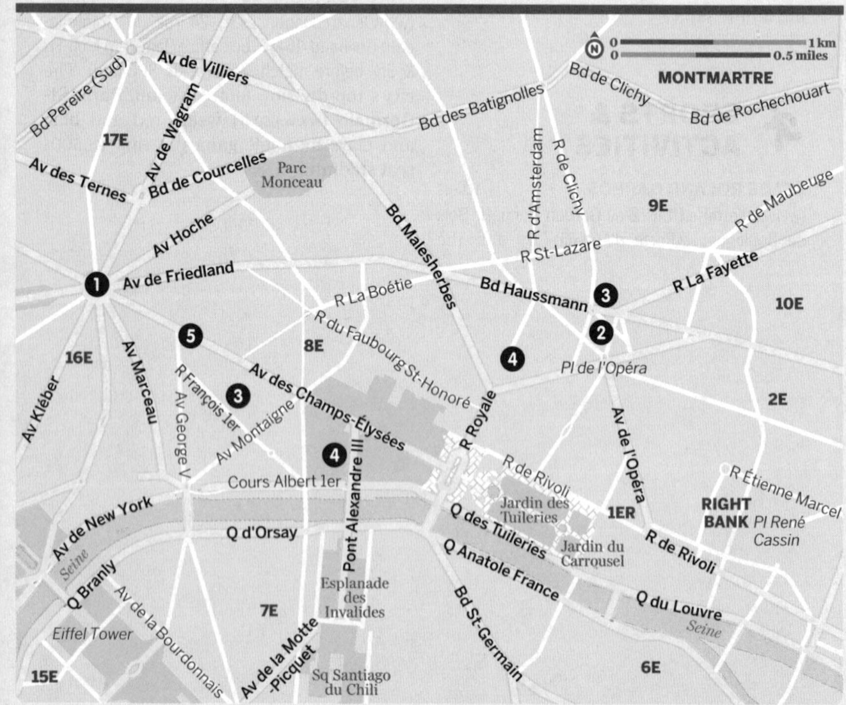

For more detail of this area, see Map p384 and p386

Explore: Champs-Élysées & Grands Boulevards

Western Paris is grandiose in layout and it's possible to play an epically proportioned game of connect the dots here. The main landmarks – the Arc de Triomphe, place de la Concorde, place de la Madeleine and the Opéra – are all joined by majestic boulevards, each lined with harmonious rows of Haussmann-era buildings.

Monumental vistas won't keep your eyes occupied for long, however, and many will soon find their gaze slipping to the display windows of the luxury shops that fill the streets. Dior, Chanel, Louis Vuitton – fans of *haute couture* will find themselves pulled increasingly southward into the famed Triangle d'Or (Golden Triangle), which lies just below the Champs-Élysées. Further east along the Grands Boulevards are the historic *grands magasins* (department stores) like Le Printemps and Galeries Lafayette, which will appeal to shoppers more interested in a broader overview of French fashion.

If shopping is not your thing, don't despair. The vestiges of the 1900 World's Fair – the Grand Palais and Petit Palais (along with the bridge Pont Alexandre III) – play host to a variety of excellent exhibits, which range from contemporary art to a family-friendly science museum.

Entertainment, too, has a strong tradition along the Grands Boulevards, the most notable venue being the Palais Garnier. While non-French speakers will want to skip the theatres along the Grands Boulevards, there are plenty of other music venues – from classical to rock – that require no language skills to appreciate.

Local Life

- **Shopping** *Haute couture* shops (p99) and elegant department stores (p98) are this district's raison d'être.
- **Wine** Just north of the Grands Boulevards metro stop are a handful of casual restaurant–wine bars, like Autour d'un Verre (p96).
- **Art** La Pinacothèque (p94) is the latest museum to take the city by storm.

Getting There & Away

- **Metro** Line 1, which follows the Champs-Élysées below ground, is the most useful, followed by lines 8 and 9, which serve the Grands Boulevards.
- **RER** RER A stops at Auber (Opéra) and Charles de Gaulle-Étoile.
- **Bicycle** Bike-hire stations line the upper part of the Champs-Élysées.
- **Boat** Champs-Élysées

Lonely Planet's Top Tip

Haute cuisine – and haute prices – are the rule in the 8e, but if you choose to eat at one of the finer restaurants for lunch on a weekday, you'll save a bundle and still get to treat your tastebuds to an extraordinary meal. Make sure to reserve.

Best Places to Eat

- Le Hide (p94)
- Makoto Aoki (p95)
- Le Boudoir (p95)
- Le J'Go (p96)
- SuperNature (p96)

For reviews, see p94

Best Entertainment

- Palais Garnier (p97)
- Au Limonaire (p98)
- L'Olympia (p98)
- Salle Pleyel (p98)

For reviews, see p97

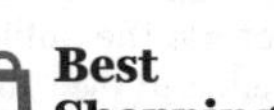

Best Shopping

- Galeries Lafayette (p99)
- Le Printemps (p99)
- Triangle d'Or (p99)
- Place de la Madeleine (p99)

For reviews, see p98

TOP SIGHTS
ARC DE TRIOMPHE

MILES ERTMAN / ALL CANADA PHOTOS / CORBIS ©

Napoleon's armies never did march through the Arc de Triomphe showered in honour, but the monument has nonetheless come to stand as the very symbol of French patriotism. The Tomb of the Unknown Soldier and the names of the numerous generals engraved onto the arch's inner walls pay homage to those who have fought and died for France. It's not for nationalistic sentiments, however, that so many visitors huff up the narrow, spiralling staircase every day. Rather it's the sublime panoramas from the top, which extend out over the Paris skyline, that make the arch such a notable attraction.

The arch was first commissioned in 1806 in the style of a Roman triumphal arch, following Napoleon's victory at Austerlitz the year before. At the time, the victory seemed like a watershed moment that confirmed the tactical supremacy of the French army, but a mere decade later, Napoleon had already fallen from power and his empire had crumbled. The Arc de Triomphe, however, was never fully abandoned – simply laying the foundations, after all, had taken an entire two years – and in 1836, after a series of starts and stops under the restored monarchy, the project was finally completed. In 1840 Napoleon's remains were returned to France and passed under the arch before being interred at Invalides.

DON'T MISS

- The Tomb of the Unknown Soldier
- The Multimedia Exhibit
- The Viewing Platform

PRACTICALITIES

- Map p384
- www.monuments-nationaux.fr
- place Charles de Gaulle
- adult/18-25yr €9.50/6
- 10am-10.30pm, to 11pm Apr-Sep
- M Charles de Gaulle–Étoile

Beneath the Arch

At ground level lies the Tomb of the Unknown Soldier. Honouring the 1.3 million French soldiers who lost their lives in WWI, the Unknown Soldier was laid to rest in 1921, beneath an eternal flame which is rekindled daily at 6.30pm.

Also here are a number of bronze plaques laid into the ground. Take the time to try and decipher some: these mark significant moments in modern French history, such as the proclamation of the Third French Republic (4 September 1870) or the return of Alsace and Lorraine to French rule (11 November 1918). The most notable plaque is the text from Charles de Gaulle's famous London broadcast on 18 June 1940, which sparked the French Resistance to life: 'Believe me, I who am speaking to you with full knowledge of the facts, and who tell you that nothing is lost for France. The same means that overcame us can bring us victory one day. For France is not alone! She is not alone!'

The Sculptures

The arch is adorned with four main sculptures, six panels in relief, and a frieze running beneath the top. Each was designed by a different artist; the most famous sculpture is the one to the right as you approach from the Champs-Élysées: *La Marseillaise* (Departure of the Volunteers of 1792). Sculpted by François Rude, it depicts soldiers of all ages gathering beneath the wings of victory, en route to drive back the invading armies of Prussia and Austria. The higher panels depict a series of important victories for the Revolutionary and imperial French armies, from Egypt to Austerlitz, while the detailed frieze is divided into two sections: the *Departure of the Armies* and the *Return of the Armies*. Don't miss the multimedia section beneath the viewing platform, which provides more detail and historical background for each of the sculptures.

Viewing Platform

Climb the 284 steps up to the viewing platform at the top of the 50m-high arch and you'll be suitably rewarded with magnificent panoramas over western Paris. From here, a dozen broad avenues – many of them named after Napoleonic victories and illustrious generals – radiate out towards every compass point. The Arc de Triomphe is the highest point in the line of monuments known as the *axe historique* (historic axis; also called the grand axis); it offers views that swoop east down the Champs-Élysées to the gold-tipped obelisk at place de la Concorde (and beyond to the Louvre's glass pyramid), and west to the skyscraper district of La Défense, where the colossal Grande Arche marks the *axe*'s western terminus.

ARCH ACROBATICS

On 7 August 1919, three weeks after the World War I victory parade, Charles Godefroy flew a biplane through the arch (14.5m wide) to honour the French pilots who had fought in the war. It was no easy feat: Jean Navarre, the pilot originally chosen to perform the flight, crashed his plane while practising and died.

Tickets to the Arc de Triomphe viewing platform are sold in the underground passageway that surfaces on the even-numbered side of av des Champs-Élysées. It is the only sane way to get to the base of the arch and is *not* linked to nearby metro tunnels.

BASTILLE DAY CELEBRATION

The military parade commemorating France's national Bastille Day (14 July) kicks off from the arch (adorned by a billowing tricolour).

SIGHTS

Champs-Élysées

ARC DE TRIOMPHE LANDMARK
See p90.

AVENUE DES CHAMPS-ÉLYSÉES LANDMARK
Map p384 (MCharles de Gaulle–Étoile, George V, Franklin D Roosevelt or Champs-Élysées-Clemenceau) If the Eiffel Tower is Paris, then the Champs-Élysées is la belle France in all its grandeur and glamour. First laid out in the 17th century, the broad avenue today is where presidents and soldiers strut their stuff on Bastille Day, the Tour de France holds its final sprint and, most importantly, where the country parties when it has a reason to celebrate.

It's also one of the globe's most sought-after addresses, which you'll undoubtedly notice as you stroll down the avenue: many of the world's biggest brands have opened up showrooms here looking to promote their prestige. Part of the *axe historique*, the Champs-Élysées links place de la Concorde with the Arc de Triomphe.

PLACE DE LA CONCORDE CITY SQUARE
Map p384 (MConcorde) With is majestic vistas in just about every direction – the Arc de Triomphe, the Assemblée Nationale (the lower house of Parliament) and even a rare swath of open sky above – place de la Concorde is one of Paris' most impressive squares. It was first laid out in 1755 and originally named after King Louis XV; however, its associations with royalty meant that it would eventually go on to take centre stage during the Revolution.

Louis XVI was the first to be guillotined here in 1793; during the next two years, 1343 more people, including Marie Antoinette, Danton and Robespierre, all lost their heads here as well. The square was given its present name after the Reign of Terror in the hope that it would become a place of peace and harmony. In the centre, atop the site of one of the former guillotines, stands a 3300-year-old Egyptian obelisk engraved with hieroglyphics. It originally stood in the Temple of Ramses at Thebes (now Luxor) and was presented to France in 1831. The corners of the square are marked by eight statues representing what were once the largest cities in France.

TOP SIGHTS PALAIS GARNIER

Few other Paris monuments have provided artistic inspiration in the way that the Palais Garnier has. From Degas' ballerinas to Gaston Leroux' Phantom and Chagall's ceiling, the layers of myth painted on gradually over the decades have bestowed a particular air of mystery and drama to its ornate interior. Designed in 1860 by Charles Garnier (then an unknown 35-year-old architect), the opera house was part of Baron Haussmann's massive urban renovation project.

The opera is open to visitors during the day, and the building is a fascinating place to explore if you're not already taking in a show here. Highlights include the opulent Grand Staircase, the library-museum (1st floor) and the horseshoe-shaped auditorium (2nd floor), with its extravagant gilded interior and red velvet seats. Above the massive chandelier is Chagall's gorgeous ceiling mural (1964), which depicts scenes from 14 operas.

Visits are generally unguided, though three days a week you can reserve a spot on an English-language guided tour. Staff advise showing up at least 30 minutes ahead of time. Check the website for updated schedules.

DON'T MISS...

- Grand Staircase
- Library-Museum
- Chagall's Ceiling

PRACTICALITIES

- Map p386
- www.operadeparis.fr
- cnr rues Scribe & Auber
- unguided tour adult/10-25yr/under 10yr €9/6/free, guided tour adult/10-25yr/under 10yr €13.50/9.50/6.50
- 10am-4.30pm
- MOpéra

GRAND PALAIS ART GALLERY

Map p384 (www.grandpalais.fr; 3 av du Général Eisenhower; adult/13-25yr/under 13yr €12/8/free; ⌚10am-10pm Wed-Mon, to 8pm Thu; Ⓜ Champs-Élysées Clemenceau) Erected for the 1900 Exposition Universelle (World's Fair), the Grand Palais today houses several exhibition spaces and a restaurant (Minipalais) beneath its huge 8.5-ton art nouveau glass roof. Some of Paris' biggest shows (Renoir, Chagall, Turner) are held in the Galeries Nationales, lasting three to four months.

Other exhibit spaces include the imaginative Nef – which plays host to concerts, art installations, a seasonal amusement park and horse shows – and several other minor galleries. Renovations are ongoing and the monument will continue to develop its layout in the coming years, though it will remain open. Hours, prices and the exhibit dates vary significantly for all galleries. Those listed here generally apply to the Galeries Nationales, but be sure to always check the website for exact details. Reserving a ticket online for any show is strongly advised.

FREE PETIT PALAIS ART MUSEUM

Map p384 (www.petitpalais.paris.fr; av Winston Churchill; permanent collections free; ⌚10am-6pm Tue-Sun; Ⓜ Champs-Élysées-Clemenceau) Like the Grand Palais opposite, this architectural stunner was also built for the 1900 Exposition Universelle, and is home to the Paris municipality's Museum of Fine Arts. It specialises in medieval and Renaissance objets d'art such as porcelain and clocks, tapestries, drawings and 19th-century French painting and sculpture. There are also paintings here by such artists as Rembrandt, Colbert and Cézanne.

PALAIS DE LA DÉCOUVERTE SCIENCE MUSEUM

Map p384 (www.palais-decouverte.fr; av Franklin D Roosevelt, 8e; adult/senior & 6-25yr/under 6yr €8/6/free; ⌚9.30am-6pm Tue-Sat, 10am-7pm Sun; Ⓜ Champs-Élysées-Clemenceau) Attached to the Grand Palais, this children's science museum has excellent temporary exhibits (eg moving lifelike dinosaurs) as well as a hands-on, interactive permanent collection focusing on astronomy, biology, physics and the like. Some of the older exhibits have French-only explanations, but overall this is a dependable family outing.

LOCAL KNOWLEDGE

THE UNSUNG MUSEUMS OF PARIS

Marc Restellini, director of the excellent La Pinacothèque (p94), filled us in on his favourite art museums in Paris.

Musée d'Art Moderne de la Ville de Paris (p82)

An intelligent museum with high-quality, original exhibits, it carries out its mission as a modern-art museum with courage.

Musée Dapper (p81)

The greatest collection of African art in the world, imbued with a magical setting. It's a small museum, but when you leave it's as if returning from an incredible journey.

Musée Jacquemart-André (p135)

The second major private museum in Paris along with La Pinacothèque, it stages real art-history exhibits that are both original and daring.

FREE LOUIS VUITTON ESPACE CULTUREL GALLERY

Map p384 (☎01 53 57 52 03; www.louisvuitton.com/espaceculturel; 60 rue de Bassano, 8e; admission free; ⌚noon-7pm Mon-Sat, 11am-7pm Sun; Ⓜ George V) At the top of Louis Vuitton's flagship store is this contemporary art gallery with changing exhibits throughout the year. The main entrance is off a side street, but you can also reach it via the mammoth flagship store, which, of course, is something of a sight in itself.

⊙ Grands Boulevards

PLACE DE LA MADELEINE CITY SQUARE

Map p386 (Ⓜ Madeleine) Ringed by fine-food shops, place de la Madeleine is named after the 19th-century neoclassical church at its centre, the **Église de la Madeleine** (Church of St Mary Magdalene; Map p386; www.eglise-lamadeleine.com; ⌚9.30am-7pm). Constructed in the style of a Greek temple, what is now called 'La Madeleine' was consecrated in 1842 after almost a century of design changes and construction delays.

The staircase on the south side affords one of the city's most Parisian panoramas: down rue Royale to place de la Concorde and its obelisk and across the Seine to the Assemblée Nationale. The gold dome of the Invalides appears in the background.

The church is a popular venue for classical-music concerts (some free); check the posters outside or the website for dates. Paris' cheapest belle époque attraction is the public toilet on the church's east side, which dates from 1905.

LA PINACOTHÈQUE ART MUSEUM

Map p386 (www.pinacotheque.com; 28 place de la Madeleine, 8e; adult/12-25yr/under 12yr €10/8/free; ⌚10.30am-6pm, to 9pm Wed & Fri; Ⓜ Madeleine) The top private museum in Paris, La Pinacothèque organises three to four major exhibits per year. Its nonlinear approach to art history, with exhibits that range from Mayan masks to retrospectives covering the work of artists such as Edvard Munch, has shaken up the otherwise rigid Paris art world and won over residents used to more formal presentations elsewhere.

Although the focus here is primarily on temporary exhibits, make sure to visit the permanent collection as well. Displayed thematically, it presents artwork rarely seen side by side in most other museums.

CHAPELLE EXPIATOIRE CHAPEL

Map p386 (www.monuments-nationaux.fr; square Louis XVI, 8e; adult/18-25yr/under 18yr €5.50/4/free; ⌚1-5pm Thu-Sat; Ⓜ St-Augustin) The austere, neoclassical Atonement Chapel, opposite 36 rue Pasquier, sits atop the section of a cemetery where Louis XVI, Marie Antoinette and many other victims of the Reign of Terror were buried after their executions in 1793. It was erected by Louis' brother, the restored Bourbon king Louis XVIII, in 1815. Two years later the royal bones were removed to the Basilique de St-Denis.

MUSÉE NATIONAL GUSTAVE MOREAU ART MUSEUM

Map p386 (www.musee-moreau.fr; 14 rue de La Rochefoucauld, 9e; adult/18-25yr €5/3; ⌚10am-12.45pm & 2-5.15pm Mon, Wed & Thu, 10am-5.15pm Fri-Sun; Ⓜ Trinité) Dedicated to the work of symbolist painter Gustave Moreau, this two-storey museum is housed in his former studio and crammed with 4800 of his paintings, drawings and sketches. Although symbolism received more attention as a literary movement in France (Baudelaire, Verlaine, Rimbaud), his fellow painters abroad included such notables as Klimt and Munch.

One particular highlight here is *La Licorne* (The Unicorn), inspired by *La Dame à la Licorne* (The Lady with the Unicorn) cycle of tapestries in the Musée National du Moyen Âge. Reduced admission is granted with a ticket from the Palais Garnier or Musée d'Orsay.

FREE **MUSÉE DU PARFUM** PERFUME MUSEUM

Map p386 (www.fragonard.com; 9 rue Scribe, 2e; ⌚9am-6pm Mon-Sat, to 5pm Sun; Ⓜ Opéra) If the art of perfume-making entices, stop by this collection of copper distillery vats and antique flacons and test your nose on a few basic scents. It's run by the parfumerie Fragonard and located in a beautiful old *hôtel particulier* (private mansion); free guided visits are available in multiple languages. A separate wing is a short distance south in the **Théâtre-Musée des Capucines** (Map p386; 39 blvd des Capucines; ⌚9am-6pm Mon-Sat; Ⓜ Opéra).

MUSÉE GRÉVIN WAX MUSEUM

Map p386 (www.grevin.com; 10 bd Montmartre; adult/6-14yr €21.50/14; ⌚10am-6.30pm; Ⓜ Grands Boulevards) This large waxworks museum inside the passage Jouffroy boasts an impressive 300 wax figures. They largely look more like caricatures than characters, but where else do you get to see Marilyn Monroe, Charles de Gaulle and Spiderman face to face, or the original death masks of some of the French Revolution leaders?

EATING

The area around the Champs-Élysées is known for its big-name chefs (Alain Ducasse, Pierre Gagnaire) and culinary icons (Taillevent), but there are a few under-the-radar restaurants here too, where the Parisians who live and work in the area actually dine on a regular basis. For a more diverse selection, head east to the Grands Boulevards, where you'll find everything from hole-in-the-wall wine bars to organic cafes.

Champs-Élysées

LE HIDE TRADITIONAL FRENCH €€

Map p384 (☎01 45 74 15 81; www.lehide.fr; 10 rue du Général Lanrezac, 17e; menus €24 & €30;

⌚lunch Mon-Fri, dinner Mon-Sat; Ⓜ Charles de Gaulle–Étoile) A reader favourite, Le Hide is a tiny neighbourhood bistro serving scrumptious traditional French fare: snails, baked shoulder of lamb with pumpkin purée or monkfish in lemon butter. Unsurprisingly, this place fills up faster than you can scamper down the steps at the nearby Arc de Triomphe. Reserve well in advance.

TOP CHOICE LADURÉE PATISSERIE €

Map p384 (www.laduree.fr; 75 av des Champs-Élysées, 8e; pastries from €1.50; ⌚7.30am-11pm; Ⓜ George V) One of the oldest patisseries in Paris, Ladurée has been around since 1862 and was the original creator of the lighter-than-air *macaron*. The tearoom here is the classiest spot to indulge your sweet tooth on the Champs Élysées; alternatively, pick up some pastries to go – from croissants to its trademark *macarons*, it's all quite heavenly. Your only problem is trying to choose.

MAKOTO AOKI TRADITIONAL FRENCH €€€

Map p384 (☎01 43 59 29 24; 19 rue Jean Mermoz, 8e; lunch menu €22, mains €34-38; ⌚lunch Mon-Fri, dinner Mon-Sat; Ⓜ Franklin D Roosevelt) In an *arrondissement* known for grandiose dining rooms and superstar chefs who are often elsewhere, this intimate neighbourhood favourite is a real find. Don't let the name confuse you – the chef, although Japanese, is an *haute cuisine* perfectionist who trained with Alain Senderens and Lucas Carton. Lunch might include an extravagant bacon-morel brioche; dinner a heavenly risotto with John Dory or truffles.

LE BOUDOIR TRADITIONAL FRENCH €€€

Map p384 (☎01 43 59 25 29; www.boudoirparis.fr; 25 rue du Colisée, 8e; lunch menu €25, mains €25-29; ⌚lunch Mon-Fri, dinner Tue-Sat; Ⓜ St-Philippe du Roule or Franklin D Roosevelt) Spread across two floors, the quirky salons here – Marie Antoinette, Palme d'Or, le Fumoir – are individual works of art with a style that befits the name. Expect classy bistro fare (quail stuffed with dried fruit and foie gras, chateaubriand steak with chestnut purée) prepared by chef Arnaud Nicolas, a recipient of France's top culinary honour.

AUBRAC CORNER BURGERS €

Map p384 (www.aubrac-corner.com; 37 rue Marbeuf, 8e; sandwiches from €5.20, burgers from €9.20; ⌚7.30am-6.30pm Mon-Sat; Ⓜ Franklin D Roosevelt) Burgers? On the Champs-Élysées? It might not sound all that French, but rest assured, this isn't fast food – it's actually the gourmet deli of a famous steakhouse. The burgers come with bowls of fries or *aligot* (mashed potatoes with melted cheese); take it all downstairs into the hidden wine cellar, a welcome refuge from the nonstop commotion outside.

After lunch, browse the deli for jars of foie gras, Laguiole (the special *aligot* cheese) and other gastronomic treats.

CAFFÈ ITALIAN €€€

Map p384 (☎01 53 75 42 00; 9 rue du Colisée, 8e; lunch menu €29, mains €16-36; ⌚lunch Mon-Fri, dinner Mon-Sat; Ⓜ Franklin D Roosevelt) Caffè is supposed to evoke 1950s Milan, but if that doesn't mean much to you designwise, no matter: all you need to know is that it's got an interior that's seductive enough to pull in a few stars. In keeping with the spirit of the place, desserts come first on the menu, providing a teasing thrill of the pleasure to come.

MINIPALAIS MODERN FRENCH €€€

Map p384 (☎01 42 56 42 42; www.minipalais.com; av Winston Churchill, 8e; lunch menu €28, mains €15-35; ⌚10am-1am; Ⓜ Champs-Élysées Clemenceau or Invalides) Set inside the fabulous Grand Palais, the Minipalais resembles an artist's studio on a colossal scale, with unvarnished hardwood floors, industrial lights suspended from ceiling beams and a handful of plaster casts on display. Its sizzling success, however, means that the crowd is anything but bohemian; dress to impress for a taste of the lauded modern cuisine.

COJEAN SANDWICH BAR €

Map p384 (www.cojean.fr; 25 rue Washington, 8e; salads €4.80-7, sandwiches €5-6; ⌚Mon-Fri 10am-4pm; Wi-Fi; Ⓜ George V) Cojean is one of the places that redefined the Parisian idea of a quick lunch. Where are those buttered baguettes with processed ham, hi-cal saucisson and chicken slathered in mayonnaise? Gone, gone and gone. Instead you get a Champs-Élysées chic interior and health-conscious fare (salads, quiches, soups) that probably would have met with bewildered looks a mere decade ago.

Grands Boulevards

LE J'GO REGIONAL CUISINE €€

Map p386 (☎01 40 22 09 09; www.lejgo.com; 4 rue Drouot, 9e; menus lunch/dinner €16/35; ⊙Mon-Sat; ⓂRichelieu Drouot) This contemporary Toulouse-style bistro is meant to magic you away to southwestern France for a spell (perfect on a grey Parisian day). Its bright yellow walls are decorated with bullfighting posters and the flavourful regional cooking is based around the rotisserie – not to mention other Gascogne standards like cassoulet and foie gras.

For the full experience, it's best to go in a small group with time to spare: the roasting takes a minimum 20 minutes, which gives you the opportunity to sample its choice selection of sunny southern wines.

SUPERNATURE ORGANIC €

Map p386 (☎01 47 70 21 03; www.super-nature.fr; 12 rue de Trévise, 9e; mains €13, menu €15.80; ⊙lunch Mon-Fri, brunch Sun; ⓂCadet or Grands Boulevards) A funky organic cafe, Supernature has some clever creations on the menu, like curried split-pea soup and a cantaloupe, pumpkin seed and feta salad. Though there are plenty of veggie options available, it's not all legumes – this is France after all – and you can still order a healthy cheeseburger with sprouts if so inclined.

A takeaway branch two doors down (at no 8) serves sandwiches, salads and thick slices of sweet potato and gorgonzola quiche.

AUTOUR D'UN VERRE WINE BAR €€

Map p386 (☎01 48 24 43 74; 21 rue de Trévise, 9e; menu lunch/dinner €16/23; ⊙lunch Mon-Fri, dinner Tue-Sat; ⓂCadet or Grands Boulevards) You'd be forgiven for thinking that Autour d'un Verre is one of those pop-up restaurants: aside from the fact that there's an open kitchen in the back, it doesn't appear to have been renovated since the 1950s. But that's all part of its undercover appeal – and after a few glasses of Clos du Tue-Boeuf, who cares about decoration anyway?

To be clear, the reason most folks find this place is for the superb selection of natural wines; the homestyle French cuisine is almost an afterthought.

CHEZ PLUME ROTISSERIE €

Map p386 (6 rue des Martyrs, 9e; dishes €4.50-8.50; ⊙10am-3pm Tue-Sun, 5.30-8.30pm Tue-Sat; ⓂNotre Dame de Lorette) This gourmet rotisserie specialises in free-range chickens from southwest France, prepared in a variety of fashions: simply roasted, as a crumble, or even in a quiche or sandwich. It's wonderfully casual: add a side or two (potatoes, polenta, seasonal veggies) and pull up a counter seat.

CASA OLYMPE GASTRONOMIC €€€

Map p386 (☎01 42 85 26 01; www.casaolympe.com; 48 rue St-Georges, 9e; mains €29-34, menu lunch & dinner €48; ⊙lunch Mon-Fri, dinner Mon-Sat; ⓂSt-Georges) This very smart restaurant run by Olympe Versini, who earned her first Michelin star at the age of 29, serves excellent and rather inventive dishes (swordfish with almonds, millefeuille of spiced venison) in surprisingly ample sizes.

GALERIES LAFAYETTE CAFE €€

Map p386 (40 bd Haussmann, 9e; ⊙9.30am-8pm Mon-Sat, to 9pm Thu; ⓂAuber or Chaussée d'Antin) You don't have to be a bag-toting fashionista to appreciate the dining options in Galeries Lafayette: this is arguably the best place to eat in the Opéra neighbourhood. Whether you're after a plush cafe, a healthy lunch, or dinner with a view over Paris, the main store caters to all – including aficionados of Sichuanese peppercorns.

Top picks include Angélina and the champagne bar on the 1st floor, Lafayette Organic (soups, salads and sandwiches) on the 3rd floor, Sichuan Panda on the 6th floor and the **rooftop restaurant** (⊙May-Oct).

LE ZINC DES CAVISTES BAR, CAFE €

Map p386 (☎01 47 70 88 64; 5 rue du Faubourg Montmartre, 9e; lunch menu €16, mains €11-19; ⊙8am-10.30pm; ⓂGrands Boulevards) Don't tell the masses standing dutifully in the Chartier queue that there's a much better restaurant right next door – your formerly friendly waiter will probably run off screaming. A local favourite, Le Zinc des Cavistes is as good for a full-blown meal (duck confit, salads) as it is for sampling new vintages.

NOUVEAU PARIS-DAKAR SENEGALESE €€

Map p386 (☎01 42 46 12 30; www.lenouveauparis-dakar.com; 11 rue de Montyon, 9e; mains €14-22, menus €10.90 (lunch only) & €25-40; ⊙lunch Mon-Thu, Sat & Sun, dinner daily; ⓂGrands Boulevards) This is a little bit of Senegal in Paris, with Mamadou still reigning as the King of Dakar. Specialities here include *yassa* (chicken or fish marinated in lime juice and onion sauce) and *maffé Cap Vert* (lamb in peanut sauce). Live African music some nights.

PREGO ITALIAN €

Map p386 (☎01 44 83 97 07; www.leprego.fr; 8 rue de la Boule Rouge, 9e; lunch menu €13.50, mains €9.50-16; ⏰lunch & dinner Mon-Fri, dinner only Sat; Ⓜ Cadet or Grands Boulevards) Prego is a hugely popular two-in-one address, with the intimate and refined trattoria side on rue de la Boule Rouge and the more allegro **pizzeria** (☎01 47 70 53 38; ⏰lunch & dinner Tue-Fri, dinner only Sat) entered via the back door at 15 rue de Trévise. Good selection of Italian wines.

LES PÂTES VIVANTES CHINESE €

Map p386 (46 du Faubourg Montmartre, 9e; noodles €9.50-12; ⏰Mon-Sat; Ⓜ Le Peletier) This is one of the only spots in Paris for *là miàn* (hand-pulled noodles) made to order in the age-old northern Chinese tradition. It packs in a crowd, so arrive early to stake out a table on the ground floor and watch as the nimble noodle maker works his magic.

COJEAN SANDWICH BAR €

Map p386 (www.cojean.fr; 64 bd Haussmann, 9e; salads €4.80-7, sandwiches €5-6; ⏰9.35am-8pm Mon-Sat ; 📶; Ⓜ Havre Caumartin) This handy Cojean branch is located in the basement of Le Printemps de la Mode department store.

DRINKING & NIGHTLIFE

Champs-Élysées

CHARLIE BIRDY PUB

Map p384 (124 rue de la Boétie, 8e; ⏰noon-5am; Ⓜ Franklin D Roosevelt) This kick-back brick-walled pub just off the Champs-Élysées is easily the most inviting spot in the neighbourhood for a drink. The usual array of bar food is served; DJs hit the decks on weekend nights.

QUEEN CLUB

Map p384 (☎01 53 89 08 90; www.queen.fr; 102 av des Champs-Élysées, 8e; admission €20; ⏰11.30pm-10am; Ⓜ George V) Once the king (as it were) of gay discos in Paris, Le Queen now reigns supreme with a very mixed crowd, though it still has a mostly gay Disco Queen on Monday. While right on the Champs-Élysées, it's not as difficult to get into as it used to be – and not nearly as inaccessible as the other nearby clubs.

SHOWCASE CLUB

Map p384 (www.showcase.fr; Port des Champs Élysées, 8e; ⏰11.30pm-dawn Fri & Sat; Ⓜ Invalides or Champs-Élysées-Clemenceau) This gigantic electro club has solved the neighbour-versus-noise problem that haunts so many other Parisian nightlife spots: it's secreted away beneath a bridge alongside the Seine. Unlike many of the other exclusive backstreet clubs along the Champs, the Showcase can pack 'em in (up to 1500 clubbers) and is less stringent about its door policy, though you'll still want to look like a star.

Grands Boulevards

FOLIE'S CAFÉ CAFE

Map p386 (16 rue Geoffroy Marie, 9e; ⏰8am-1am; 📶; Ⓜ Cadet or Grands Boulevards) A reliable spot for smoothies, cocktails, cafes au lait and simple bistro fare.

O'SULLIVAN'S PUB

Map p386 (1 bd Montmartre, 2e; ⏰noon-5am Sun-Thu, to 7am Fri & Sat; 📶; Ⓜ Grands Boulevards) This looks like just another supermarket-chain Irish pub, but O'Sullivan's is so much more. The spacious surrounds are always packed for big sporting events, plus concerts (jazz, rock, pop, Irish music) on Thursdays and DJs at the weekend.

AU GÉNÉRAL LA FAYETTE BRASSERIE

Map p386 (52 rue La Fayette, 9e; ⏰10am-3am; Ⓜ Le Peletier) With its archetypal belle époque decor and special beers on offer, this old-style brasserie is a dependable stop for an afternoon coffee or evening drink.

ENTERTAINMENT

PALAIS GARNIER OPERA

Map p386 (☎08 92 89 90 90; www.operadeparis.fr; place de l'Opéra, 9e; Ⓜ Opéra) The city's original opera house is smaller than its Bastille counterpart, but boasts perfect acoustics. Due to its odd shape, however, some seats have limited or no visibility. Ticket prices and conditions (including last-minute discounts) are available at the **box office** (cnr rues Scribe & Auber; ⏲2.30-6.30pm Mon-Sat).

AU LIMONAIRE LIVE MUSIC

Map p386 (☎01 45 23 33 33; http://limonaire.free.fr; 18 cité Bergère, 9e; ⏲7pm-midnight; Ⓜ Grands Boulevards) This little wine bar is one of the best places to listen to traditional French *chansons* and local singer-songwriters. Performances begin at 10pm Tuesday to Saturday and 7pm on Sunday. Entry is free, the wine is good and dinner is served (plat du jour €7). Reservations are recommended if you plan on dining.

L'OLYMPIA LIVE MUSIC

Map p386 (☎08 92 68 33 68; www.olympiahall.com; 28 bd des Capucines, 9e; Ⓜ Opéra) The Olympia was opened by the founder of the Moulin Rouge in 1888 and is said to be the oldest concert hall in Paris. It has hosted all the big names over the years, from Édith Piaf to Jimi Hendrix and Jeff Buckley, though it's small enough to put on a fairly intimate show.

SALLE PLEYEL CLASSICAL

Map p384 (☎01 42 56 13 13; www.sallepleyel.fr; 252 rue du Faubourg St-Honoré, 8e; ⏲box office noon-7pm Mon-Sat, to 8pm on day of performance; Ⓜ Ternes) This highly regarded hall dating from the 1920s hosts many of Paris' finest classical-music recitals and concerts, including those by the celebrated **Orchestre de Paris** (www.orchestredeparis.com).

CRAZY HORSE CABARET

Map p384 (☎01 47 23 32 32; www.lecrazyhorseparis.com; 12 av George V, 8e; Ⓜ Alma-Marceau) This popular cabaret, whose dressing (or, rather, undressing) rooms were featured in Woody Allen's film *What's New Pussycat?* (1965), now promotes fine art – abstract 1960s patterns appear superimposed on the female nude form.

KIOSQUE THÉÂTRE MADELEINE DISCOUNT TICKETS

Map p386 (opposite 15 place de la Madeleine, 8e; ⏲12.30-8pm Tue-Sat, to 4pm Sun; Ⓜ Madeleine) Pick up half-price tickets for same-day performances of ballet, opera and music at this outdoor kiosk. Grab a copy of *Pariscope* from a newsstand to help you choose what you want to see, then make your request. Figure on paying €24 on average, though it can go cheaper.

SHOPPING

Global chains line the Champs-Élysées, but it's the luxury fashion houses in the Triangle d'Or that have made Paris famous. The area around Opéra and the Grands Boulevards is where you'll find department stores such as Galeries Lafayette.

GUERLAIN PERFUME

Map p384 (www.guerlain.com; 68 av des Champs-Élysées, 8e; ⏲10.30am-8pm Mon-Sat, noon-7pm Sun; Ⓜ Franklin D Roosevelt) Guerlain is Paris' most famous parfumerie, and its shop (dating from 1912) is one of the most beautiful in the city. With its shimmering mirror and marble art-deco interior, it's a reminder of the former glory of the Champs-Élysées. To experience total indulgence during your stay, make an appointment at its decadent **spa** (☎01 45 62 11 21).

SÉPHORA PERFUME

Map p384 (www.sephora.com; 70-72 av des Champs-Élysées, 8e; ⏲10am-midnight; Ⓜ Franklin D Roosevelt) Séphora's flagship store features more than 12,000 fragrances and cosmetics for your sampling pleasure. You can easily spend hours in here and will invariably come out with bags of stuff (and maybe a headache from all the scent in the atmosphere).

LES CAVES AUGÉ FOOD, DRINK

Map p384 (www.cavesauge.com; 116 bd Haussmann, 8e; ⏲Mon-Sat; Ⓜ St-Augustin) Founded in 1850, this fantastic wine shop with bottles stacked in every conceivable nook and cranny should be your first choice if you trust the taste of Marcel Proust, who was a regular customer. The shop organises tastings every other Saturday (see website), where you can meet local winemakers from different regions.

CHLOÉ FASHION

Map p384 (54 rue du Faubourg St-Honoré, 8e; ⏲Mon-Sat; Ⓜ Champs-Élysées-Clemenceau) Bold prints, bohemian layers and uneven hemlines have given street cred to this 1950s-established Parisian label.

LANCEL ACCESSORIES

Map p384 (127 av des Champs-Élysées, 8e; ⏲daily; Ⓜ Charles de Gaulle–Étoile) Open racks of luscious totes fill this handbag designer's gleaming premises.

GALERIES LAFAYETTE DEPARTMENT STORE

Map p386 (www.galerieslafayette.com; 40 bd Haussmann, 9e; ⌚9.30am-8pm Mon-Sat, to 9pm Thu; Ⓜ Auber or Chaussée d'Antin) Probably the best known of the big Parisian department stores, Galeries Lafayette is spread across three buildings: the main store (the historic dome of which just turned 100 in 2012), the men's store and the home-design store.

You can check out modern art in the **gallery** (1st fl; ⌚11am-7pm Mon-Sat), take in a **fashion show** (☎bookings 01 42 82 30 25; ⌚Mar-Jul & Sep-Dec) at 3pm on Fridays, or ascend to the rooftop for a windswept Parisian panorama (free). When your legs need a break, head to one of the many restaurants and cafes (p96) inside.

LE PRINTEMPS DEPARTMENT STORE

Map p386 (www.printemps.com; 64 bd Haussmann, 9e; ⌚9.35am-8pm Mon-Sat, to 10pm Thu; Ⓜ Havre Caumartin) This is actually three separate stores – Le Printemps de la Mode (women's fashion), Le Printemps de l'Homme (for men) and Le Printemps de la Beauté et Maison (for beauty and household goods) – offering a staggering display of perfume, cosmetics and accessories, as well as established and up-and-coming designer wear.

PLACE DE LA MADELEINE FOOD, DRINK

Map p386 (place de la Madeleine, 8e; Ⓜ Madeleine) Ultragourmet food shops are the treat here; if you feel your knees start to go all wobbly in front of a display window, you know you're in the right place. The most notable names include truffle dealers La Maison de la Truffe; luxury food shop Hédiard; mustard specialist Boutique Maille; and Paris' most famous caterer, Fauchon, selling incredibly mouth-watering delicacies, from foie gras to jams, chocolates and pastries.

ERES FASHION, ACCESSORIES

Map p386 (www.eres.fr; 2 rue Tronchet, 8e; ⌚Mon-Sat; Ⓜ Madeleine) You will pay an arm and a leg for a swimsuit here, but anyone who has despaired of buying one in the past will understand why these have become a must-have item for those in the know. The stunning swimsuits are cut to suit all shapes and sizes, with bikini tops and bottoms sold separately. It also stocks magnificent lingerie.

LAFAYETTE GOURMET FOOD, DRINK

Map p386 (40 bd Haussmann, 9e; ⌚8.30am-9.30pm Mon-Sat; Ⓜ Auber or Chaussée d'Antin) On the 1st floor of the Galeries Lafayette men's store is Lafayette Gourmet, an entire

HISTORIC HAUTE COUTURE

A stroll around the legendary Triangle d'Or (av Montaigne and av George V; Ⓜ George V) and along rue du Faubourg St-Honoré (Ⓜ Concorde), all in the 8e, constitutes the walk of fame of top French fashion. Rubbing shoulders with the world's top international designers are Paris' most influential French fashion houses:

Chanel (Map p384; www.chanel.com; 42 av Montaigne, 8e; Ⓜ George V) Box jackets and little black dresses, chic ever since their first appearance in the 1920s.

Christian Dior (Map p384; www.dior.com; 30 av Montaigne, 8e; Ⓜ George V) Post-WWII, Dior's creations dictated style, re-establishing Paris as the world fashion capital.

Givenchy (Map p384; www.givenchy.com; 3 av George V, 8e; Ⓜ George V) The first to present a luxurious collection of women's prêt-à-porter.

Hermès (Map p384; www.hermes.com; 24 rue du Faubourg St-Honoré, 8e; Ⓜ Concorde) Founded in 1837 by a saddle-maker, its famous scarves are *the* fashion accessory.

Jean-Paul Gaultier (Map p384; www.jeanpaulgaultier.com; 44 av George V, 8e; Ⓜ George V) A shy kid from the Paris suburbs, JPG morphed into the enfant terrible of the fashion world with his granny's corsets, men dressed in skirts and Madonna's conical bra.

Lanvin (Map p384; www.lanvin.com; 22 rue du Faubourg St Honoré, 8e; Ⓜ Concorde) One of Paris' oldest fashion houses, established in 1909.

Louis Vuitton (Map p384; www.vuitton.com; 101 av des Champs-Élysées, 8e; Ⓜ George V) Take home an authentic canvas bag with the 'LV' monogram.

Yves Saint Laurent (Map p384; www.ysl.com; 38 rue du Faubourg St-Honoré, 8e; Ⓜ Concorde) One of the top Parisian designers from the 1960s on, YSL was the first to incorporate non-European styles into his work.

floor dedicated to the art of pleasing the palate. You'll find perfect pastries, chocolates, fondants, cheeses, pâté, organic muffins, you name it. There's also an excellent wine shop with a very affordable selection.

HÉDIARD FOOD, DRINK

Map p386 (21 place de la Madeleine, 8e; ⏰9am-9pm Mon-Sat; Ⓜ Madeleine) This famous luxury food shop established in 1854 consists of two adjacent sections selling prepared dishes, teas, coffees, jams, wines, pastries, fruits, vegetables and so on, as well as a **restaurant** (☎01 43 12 88 99), where tea is served from 3pm to 6pm.

HÔTEL DROUOT ART, ANTIQUES

Map p386 (www.drouot.com; 7-9 rue Drouot, 9e; ⏰11am-6pm; Ⓜ Richelieu Drouot) Selling everything from antiques and jewellery to rare books and art, Paris' most established auction house has been in business for more than a century. Viewings are from 11am to 6pm the day before and from 11am to noon the morning of the auction.

If you plan on stopping by, make sure you pick up a copy of the weekly catalog **Gazette de l'Hôtel Drouot** (www.gazette-drouot.com), available at the auction house and selected newsstands on Friday.

SPORTS & ACTIVITIES

RUSSIE BLANCHE SPA

Map p384 (☎01 40 70 16 49; www.russieblanche.com; 6 rue de la Renaissance, 8e; 1hr massage €85; ⏰11am-7.30pm Mon-Sat, to 9pm Thu & Fri; Ⓜ Alma-Marceau) The creation of former Russian model Julia Lemigova, this exclusive spa unwinds wound-up city slickers with detox and de-stress massages using natural and essential oils.

Louvre & Les Halles

Neighbourhood Top Five

❶ Get lost in the world of art at the world's largest museum, the palatial **Musée du Louvre** (p103); jostle for camera space before *Mona Lisa* and break your visit with lunch in Paris' most talked-about kitchens.

❷ Contemporary art and architecture, family fun and culture is the essence of the **Centre Pompidou** (p111).

❸ Feast on exquisite sacred art and soulful music in Paris' most beautiful church, **Église St-Eustache** (p113).

❹ Meet Monet and revel in Paris at its symmetrical best in **Jardin des Tuileries** (p115).

❺ Browse designer boutiques beneath the arcaded galleries of **Jardin du Palais Royal** (p115).

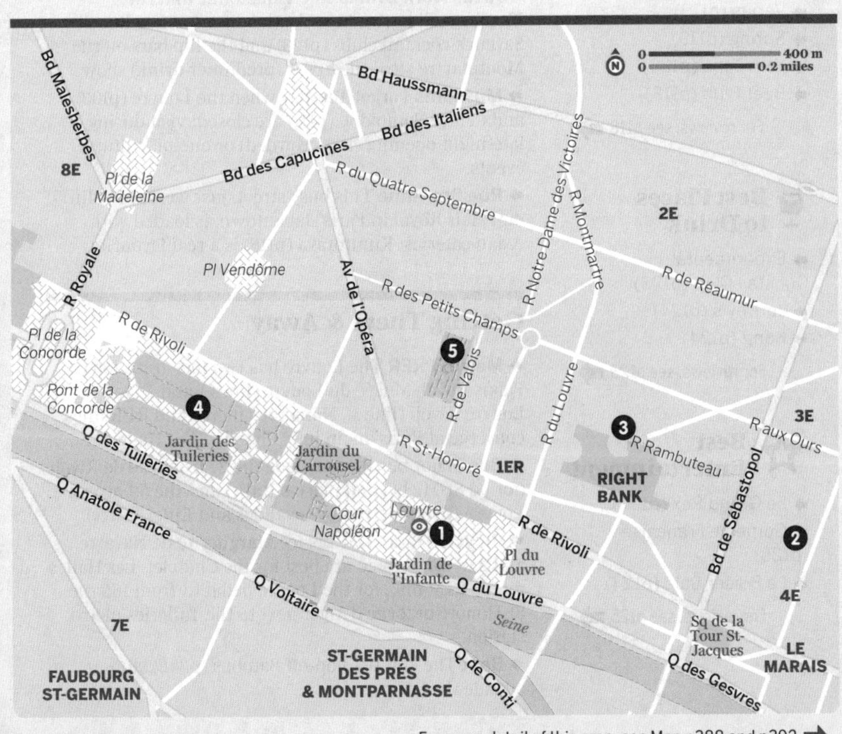

For more detail of this area, see Map p388 and p392 ➡

Lonely Planet's Top Tip

Some of Paris' top tables are here, but you need to book in advance: up to two months ahead for a table at **Frenchie** (p118), a week before at **Yam'Tcha** (p120) and **Verjus** (p119; walk-ins often work Monday to Wednesday), and a couple of days ahead for dinner at **Spring** (p119; lunchtime is generally less busy). Otherwise, three of the four addresses have neighbouring wine bars where you simply rock up and wait for a table to feast on lighter creations cooked up by the same, talented restaurant chef.

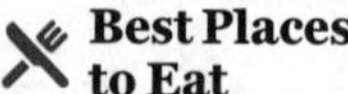

Best Places to Eat

- Frenchie (p118)
- Verjus (p119)
- Spring (p119)
- Yam'Tcha (p120)
- Beef Club (p118)

For reviews, see p118

Best Places to Drink

- Experimental Cocktail Club (p123)
- Jeffrey's (p124)
- Kong (p124)

For reviews, see p123

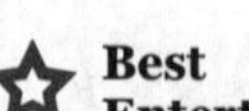

Best Entertainment

- Le Grand Rex (p127)
- Comedie Française (p125)
- Le Baiser Salé (p124)

For reviews, see p125

Explore: Louvre & Les Halles

The banks of the Seine make an enchanting starting point. Explore westwards along quai des Tuileries, past the sculptures and green lawns, pools and fountains of Jardin des Tuileries, to the Musée de l'Orangerie and Jeu du Paume. Continue on foot north to ritzy place Vendôme, then loop back east along shop-chic rue St-Honoré to Palais Royal.

Set aside at least a day (or more) for the Musée du Louvre. Combine the often intimidating art gallery with a long lunch or a picnic and stroll around the designer galleries and manicured gardens of Jardin du Palais Royal. Serious theatre lovers could indulge in an evening performance at the Comédie Française.

Cross rue du Louvre into Les Halles and the timeless sophistication of the Louvre area disappears into bright lights, painted ladies and swinging jazz clubs. Day and night the mainly pedestrian zone between the Centre Pompidou and Forum des Halles is packed with people, just as it was for the 850-odd years when Paris' main *halles* (marketplace) for foodstuffs was here.

Local Life

- **After Work Drinks** Rue Tiquetonne and rue Montorgueil have a hip selection of cafe-bars. Rue St-Saveur's cocktail clubs (p123) and the hip bars on rue Montmartre steal the *apéro* (predinner drink) show.
- **Museums** Forget Tuesday when the Louvre (p103) and Centre Pompidou (p111) are closed; visit during late-night opening (less crowded) or one-off cultural events.
- **Rue Ste-Anne** This busy street, just west of Jardin du Palais Royal in Paris' Japantown, is loaded with Asian eateries; Kunitoraya (p118) is a real favourite.

Getting There & Away

- **Metro & RER** The Louvre has two metro stations: Palais Royal–Musée du Louvre (lines 1 and 7) and Louvre Rivoli (line 1). Numerous metro and RER lines converge at Paris' main hub, Châtelet–Les Halles.
- **Bus** Major bus lines include the 27 from rue de Rivoli (for bd St-Michel and place d'Italie) and the 69 near the Louvre Rivoli metro (for Invalides and Eiffel Tower).
- **Bicycle** Stations at 1 place Marguerite de Navarre and 2 ue de Turbigo are best for the Châtelet–Les Halles metro/RER hub; for the Louvre pedal to/from 165 rue St-Honoré or 2 rue d'Alger next to the Tuileries metro station.
- **Boat** The hop-on, hop-off Batobus (p342) stops outside the Louvre

GEOFF STRINGER / GETTY IMAGES ©

TOP SIGHTS
THE LOUVRE

Few art galleries are as prized or daunting as the Musée du Louvre, Paris' pièce de résistance that no first-time visitor to the city can ignore. This is, after all, the world's largest museum. Showcase to 35,000 works of art, it would take nine months to glance at every piece, rendering advance planning essential.

Works of art from Europe form the permanent exhibition, alongside priceless collections of Assyrian, Etruscan, Greek, Coptic and Islamic art and antiquities. Yet the essential raison d'être of the Louvre is the presentation of Western art from the Middle Ages to the mid-19th century.

Palais du Louvre

Philippe-Auguste had this vast fortress built on the Seine's right bank (constructed 1190–1202). In the 16th century it became a royal residence and after the Revolution, in 1793, it was turned into a national museum. Its booty was no more than 2500 paintings and objets d'art.

Over the centuries French governments amassed the paintings, sculptures and artefacts displayed today. The 'Grand Louvre' project inaugurated by the late President Mitterrand in 1989 doubled the museum's exhibition space, and both new and renovated galleries have since opened devoted to objets d'art such as the crown jewels of Louis XV (Room 66, 1st floor, Denon). The official opening, at the end of 2012, of new Islamic art galleries in the restored **Cour Visconti** was a moment of national pride for French art and architecture lovers. The interior courtyard, unkempt and abandoned for years, has been topped with an elegant, shimmering gold 'flying carpet' roof, evocative of a veil fluttering in the wind, designed by Italian architects Mario Bellini and Rudy Ricciotti.

DON'T MISS

- *Mona Lisa*
- *Venus de Milo*
- *Winged Victory of Samothrace*

PRACTICALITIES

- Map p388
- ☎01 40 20 53 17
- www.louvre.fr
- Rue de Rivoli & Quai des Tuileries, 1er
- permanent/temporary collection €11/12, both €15, under 18yr free
- ⏲9am-6pm Mon, Thu, Sat & Sun, to 9.45pm Wed & Fri
- MPalais Royal–Musée du Louvre

OUT TO LUNCH

Tickets to the Louvre are valid for the whole day, meaning you can nip out for lunch – the best way to avoid Louvre fatigue if you're there all day. Pay the price for an exquisite and romantic, Paris-perfect view at Café Marly (p123) or Le Saut du Loup (p119) or opt for a 19th-century passage at Le Véro Dodat (p122). For speed and good value, try Cojean (p123) or Spring Épicerie (p119), and for serious gourmets, Spring (p119) and Kaï (p119) are a five-minute walk away.

French kings only ever wore their crowns once – at their coronation. Lined with embroidered satin and topped with openwork arches and a fleur-de-lis, Louis XV's 1722-crafted crown (Room 66, 1st floor, Denon) was originally adorned with pearls, sapphires, rubies, topazes, emeralds and diamonds (replaced in 1729 with paste imitations seen today).

Antiquity to Renaissance

The palace rambles through three wings: the **Sully Wing** creates the four sides of the **Cour Carrée** (literally 'square courtyard') at the eastern end of the complex; the **Denon Wing** stretches 800m along the Seine to the south; and the northern **Richelieu Wing** skirts rue de Rivoli.

One of the most famous works from antiquity is the cross-legged *Seated Scribe* (Room 22, 1st floor, Sully), a painted limestone statue with rock-crystal inlaid eyes dating to c2620–2500 BC. Measuring 53.7cm tall, the unknown figure is depicted holding a papyrus scroll in his left hand; he's thought to have been holding a brush in his right hand that has since disappeared. Equally compelling is the *Code of Hammurabi* (Room 3, ground floor, Richelieu), and armless duo **Venus de Milo** (Room 16, ground floor, Sully) and **Winged Victory of Samothrace** (top of Daru staircase, 1st floor, Denon).

The eastern side of the Sully Wing's ground and 1st floors house the Louvre's astonishing cache of Pharaonic Egyptian treasures. Don't miss the mummy of a man from the Ptolemaic period (Room 15, ground floor, Sully) and the funerary figurine of pharaoh Ramesses IV (Room 13, ground floor, Sully). From the Renaissance, Michelangelo's marble masterpiece *The Dying Slave* (Room 4, ground floor, Denon) and works by Raphael, Botticelli and Titian (1st floor, Denon) draw big crowds.

Mona Lisa

Easily the Louvre's most admired work (and world's most famous painting) is Leonardo da Vinci's *La Joconde* (in French; *La Gioconda* in Italian), the lady with that enigmatic smile known as *Mona Lisa* (Room 6, 1st floor, Denon). For centuries admirers speculated on everything from the possibility that the subject was mourning the death of a loved one to the possibility that she might have been in love or in bed with her portraitist.

Mona (*monna* in Italian) is a contraction of *madonna,* and Gioconda is the feminine form of the surname Giocondo. Canadian scientists used infrared technology to peer through paint layers and confirm *Mona Lisa's* identity as Lisa Gherardini (1479–1542?), wife of Florentine merchant Francesco de Giocondo. Scientists also discovered her dress was covered in a transparent gauze veil typically worn in early-16th-century Italy by pregnant or new mothers; it's surmised that the work was painted to commemorate the birth of her second son around 1503, when she was aged about 24.

LOUVRE

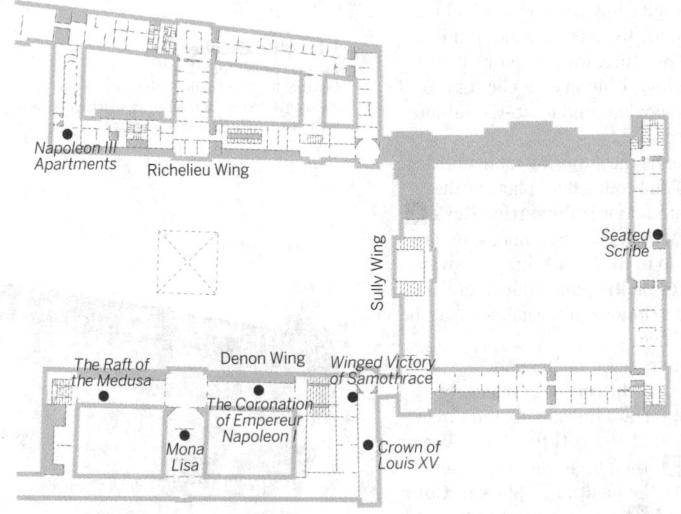

First Floor

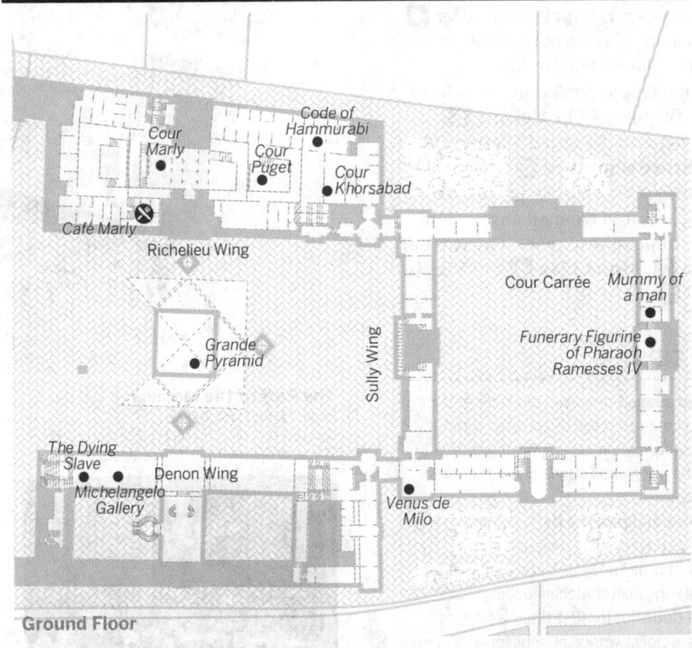

Ground Floor

TOP SIGHTS
THE LOUVRE

A HALF-DAY TOUR

Successfully visiting the Louvre is a fine art. Its complex labyrinth of galleries and staircases spiralling three wings and four floors renders discovery a snakes-and-ladders experience. Initiate yourself with this three-hour itinerary – a playful mix of *Mona Lisa* obvious and up-to-the-minute unexpected.

Arriving by the stunning main entrance, pick up colour-coded floor plans at the lower-ground-floor **information desk** 1 beneath IM Pei's glass pyramid, ride the escalator up to the Sully Wing and swap passport for multimedia guide (there are limited descriptions in the galleries) at the wing entrance.

The Louvre is as much about spectacular architecture as masterly art. To appreciate this zip up and down Sully's Escalier Henri II to admire **Venus de Milo** 2, then up parallel Escalier Henri IV to the palatial displays in **Cour Khorsabad** 3. Cross room 1 to find the escalator up to the 1st floor and staircase-as-art **L'Esprit d'Escalier** 4. Next traverse 25 consecutive galleries (thank you, floor plan!) to flip conventional contemplation on its head with Cy Twombly's **The Ceiling** 5, and the hypnotic **Winged Victory of Samothrace sculpture** 6 – just two rooms away – which brazenly insists on being admired from all angles. End with the impossibly famous **The Raft of Medusa** 7, **Mona Lisa** 8 and **Virgin & Child** 9.

TOP TIPS

➡ **Floor Plans** Don't even consider entering the Louvre's maze of galleries without a *Plan/Information Louvre* brochure, free from the information desk in the Hall Napoléon

➡ **Crowd dodgers** The Denon Wing is always packed; visit on late nights Wednesday or Friday or trade Denon in for the notably quieter Richelieu Wing

➡ **2nd floor** Not for first-timers: save its more specialist works for subsequent visits

Mission Mona Lisa

If you just want to venerate the Louvre's most famous lady, use the Porte des Lions entrance (closed Tuesday and Friday), from where it's a five-minute walk. Go up one flight of stairs and through rooms 26, 14 and 13 to the Grande Galerie and adjoining room 6.

L'Esprit d'Escalier
Escalier Lefuel, Richelieu
Discover the 'Spirit of the Staircase' through François Morellet's contemporary stained glass, which casts new light on old stone. DETOUR» Napoleon III's gorgeous gilt apartments.

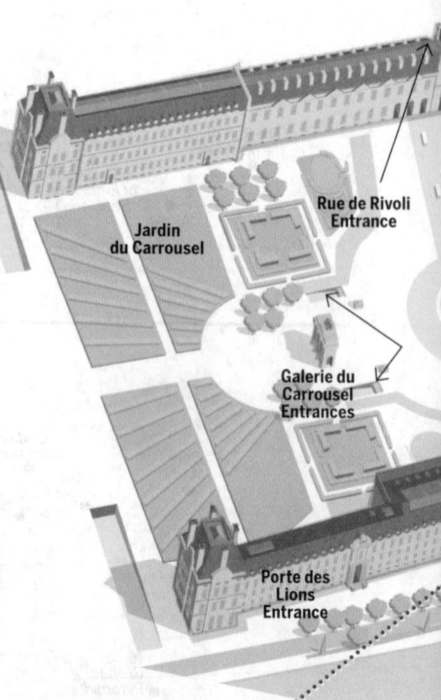

The Raft of the Medusa
Room 77, 1st Floor, Denon
Decipher the politics behind French romanticism in Théodore Géricault's *Raft of the Medusa*.

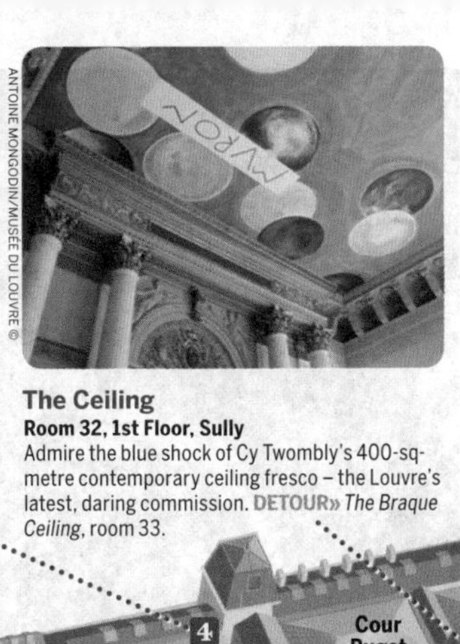

ANTOINE MONGODIN/MUSÉE DU LOUVRE ©

Cour Khorsabad

Ground Floor, Richelieu

Time travel with a pair of winged human-headed bulls to view some of the world's oldest Mesopotamian art. **DETOUR»** Night-lit statues in Cour Puget.

WITOLD SKRYPCZAK/GETTY ©

Venus de Milo

Room 16, Ground Floor, Sully

No one knows who sculpted this seductively realistic goddess from Greek antiquity. Naked to the hips, she is a Hellenistic masterpiece.

The Ceiling

Room 32, 1st Floor, Sully

Admire the blue shock of Cy Twombly's 400-sq-metre contemporary ceiling fresco – the Louvre's latest, daring commission. **DETOUR»** *The Braque Ceiling*, room 33.

Virgin & Child

Room 5, Grande Galerie, 1st Floor, Denon

In the spirit of artistic devotion save the Louvre's most famous gallery for last: a feast of Virgin-and-child paintings by Raphael, Domenico Ghirlandaio, Giovanni Bellini and Francesco Botticini.

Mona Lisa

Room 6, 1st Floor, Denon

No smile is as enigmatic or bewitching as hers. Da Vinci's diminutive *La Joconde* hangs opposite the largest painting in the Louvre – sumptuous, fellow Italian Renaissance artwork *The Wedding at Cana.*

TERRY SMITH IMAGES/ALAMY ©

Winged Victory of Samothrace

Escalier Daru, 1st Floor, Sully

Draw breath at the aggressive dynamism of this headless, handless Hellenistic goddess. **DETOUR»** The razzle-dazzle of the Apollo Gallery's crown jewels.

GIANNI DAGLI ORTI / THE ART ARCHIVE / ALAMY ©

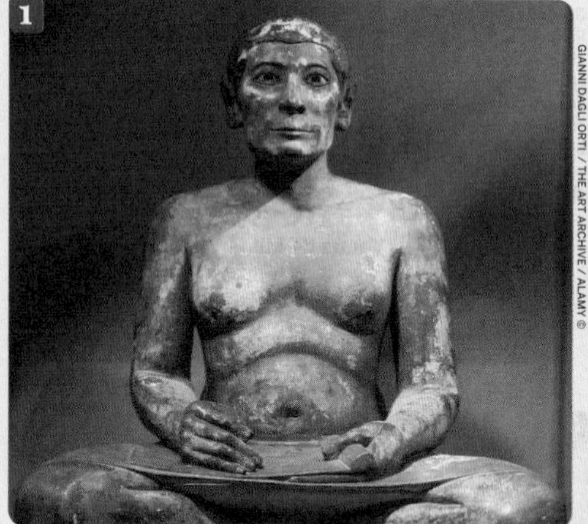

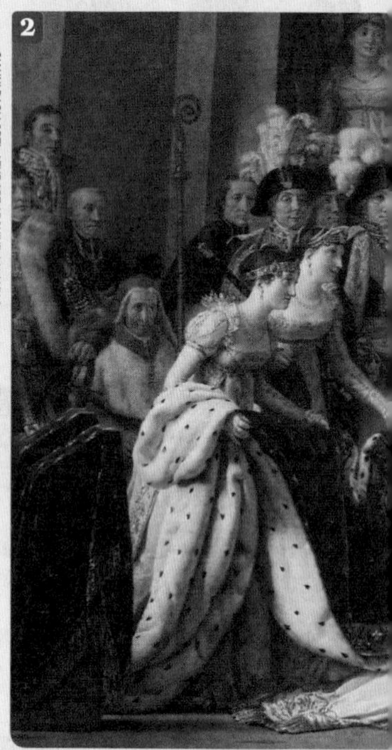

1. Seated Scribe
A painted limestone statue with crystal inlaid eyes.

2. The Coronation of Empereur Napoleon I
A magnificent painting depicting the coronation of Napoleon, by Jean-Louis David.

3. The Dying Slave
Michelangelo's marble statue from the Renaissance.

4. Mona Lisa
Visitors to the Louvre line up to see the world's most famous painting: Leonardo da Vinci's *La Joconde* (better known as *Mona Lisa*).

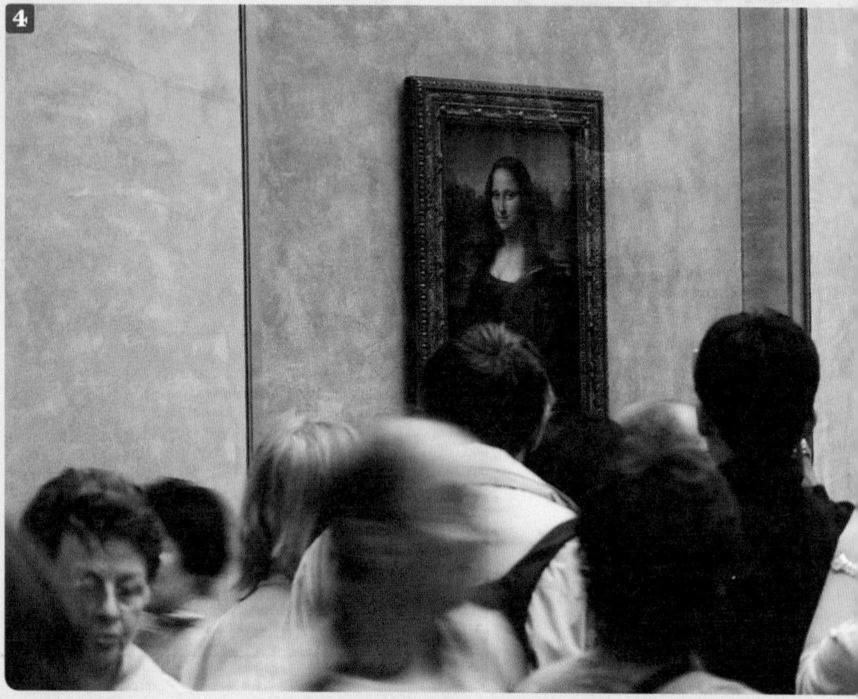

EXOTICA.IM 10 / ALAMY ©

GLENN BEANLAND / GETTY IMAGES ©

ADAM WOOLFITT / CORBIS ©

THE PYRAMID: INSIDE & OUT

A 21m-high glass pyramid designed by Chinese-born American architect IM Pei bedecks the main entrance to the Louvre. Beneath Pei's **Grande Pyramide** (Map p388; place du Louvre) is the **Hall Napoléon**, a split-level public area comprising a temporary exhibition hall, bookshop, souvenir store, cafe and auditoriums for lectures and films. To revel in another Pei pyramid, head towards the **Carrousel du Louvre** (Map p388; ☎01 43 16 47 10; www.carrouseldulouvre.com; 99 rue de Rivoli; ⏲8am-11pm, shops 10am-8pm daily; Ⓜ Palais Royal–Musée du Louvre), a shopping mall that loops underground from the Grande Pyramide to the Arc de Triomphe du Carrousel (p114) – its centrepiece is Pei's **Pyramide Inversée** (inverted glass pyramid).

Avoid queues outside the Grande Pyramide: use the Porte des Lions entrance (⏲closed Tuesday and Friday) or the Carrousel du Louvre entrance at 99 rue de Rivoli. Buy tickets in advance – by telephone (☎08 92 68 46 94, 01 41 57 32 28), online, or from machines in the Carrousel du Louvre.

Interior gallery of the Denon Wing

Northern European & French Painting

The 2nd floor of the Richelieu Wing holds Flemish and Dutch paintings spearheaded by works by Peter Paul Rubens and Pieter Bruegel the Elder.

An amble through 17th-century Flanders and the 15th- to 16th-century Netherlands (don't miss *Gabrielle d'Etrées and Her Sister* off Room 7, 2nd floor, Richelieu Wing) brings visitors into the Sully Wing where works by 18th- and 19th-century French painters excite. Look out for Ingres' *The Turkish Bath* (off Room 60, 2nd floor, Sully), Géricault's *The Raft of the Medusa* (Room 77, 1st floor, Denon), Jean-Louis David's monumental *The Coronation of Empereur Napoleon I* (Room 75, 1st floor, Denon) and works by Delacoix, Corot and Fragonard.

Trails & Tours

Self-guided thematic trails (1½ hours to three hours) range from Louvre masterpieces to the art of eating. There's also several trails for kids (hunt lions, the history of horses). Download trail brochures in advance from the website. Alternatively, rent a **Nintendo 3DS multimedia guide** (adult/child €5/3) at ticket desks or machines in the Hall Napoléon. More formal, English-language **guided tours** (☎reservations 01 40 20 51 77; ⏲11am & 2pm Wed-Mon except 1st Sun of month) depart from the Hall Napoléon. Reserve a spot up to 14 days in advance or sign up on arrival at the museum.

TOP SIGHTS
CENTRE POMPIDOU

The Centre Pompidou has amazed and delighted visitors ever since it opened in 1977, not just for its outstanding collection of modern art but also for its radical architectural statement. The dynamic and vibrant arts centre delights and enthrals with its irresistible cocktail of galleries and exhibitions, hands-on workshops, dance performances, free wi-fi hotspot, bookshop, design boutique, cinemas and other entertainment venues.

Musée National d'Art Moderne

France's national collection of modern art – almost 75,000 works in all – fills the bright and airy, well-lit galleries of the National Museum of Modern Art covering two complete floors of the Pompidou. All the major movements and artists of modern art (from 1905 to 1960) are well represented on the 5th floor, including Fauvist Matisse (don't miss his cut-outs *Deux danseurs*; 1937–38), cubists Braque and Picasso, and surrealists Max Ernst, Dalí, Miró and Man Ray.

One floor down on the 4th, works created from 1960 to the present take centre stage. Highlights include *Ten Lizes* (1963) by pop art-wizard Andy Warhol and Yves Klein's monochromes (including a 1960 marine-blue monochrome that gave rise to the term 'Klein blue').

Every genre – sculpture, photography, painting, design, installation art and so on – gets a look in, and the museum also has an **Espace des Collections Nouveaux Médias et Film** (New Media & Film Centre; ⏲11am-8.30pm Wed-Mon) where visitors can discover 40 years of image and sound experimentation and art.

DON'T MISS

- The 245-piece Matisse Collection, Musée National d'Art Moderne
- The 6th Floor and its Sweeping Panorama of Paris
- Kandinsky's *Auf Weis II*

PRACTICALITIES

- Map p392
- ☎01 44 78 12 33
- www.centrepompidou.fr
- place Georges Pompidou, 1er
- museum, exhibitions & panorama €13 or €11, under 18yr & 1st Sun of month free
- ⏲11am-9pm Wed-Mon
- Ⓜ Rambuteau

LUNCH OPTIONS

Georges (Map p392; ☎01 44 78 47 99; www.centrepompidou.fr; place Georges Pompidou, 6th fl, Centre Pompidou; starters €20, mains €40; ⊙lunch & dinner to 1am Wed-Mon; ⓂRambuteau) on the 6th floor of the Pompidou is the chic design lunch option. The inexpensive mezzanine cafe on the 1st floor is unmemorable: walk instead to Café La Fusée (p125) or Café Beaubourg (p125) for an affordable lunch or well-deserved, postmuseum aperitif.

The full monty Pompidou experience is as much about hanging out in the busy streets and squares around it, packed with souvenir shops and people, as absorbing the centre's inside contents. West of the Centre Pompidou, fun-packed place Georges Pompidou and its nearby pedestrian streets attract bags of buskers, musicians, jugglers and mime artists. Don't miss place Igor Stravinsky with its fanciful mechanical fountains of skeletons, hearts, treble clefs and a big pair of ruby-red lips by Jean Tinguely and Niki de St-Phalle.

Blockbuster temporary exhibitions, generally arranged around the work of a single artist in galleries on the 6th floor, complete the modern-art museum's prestigious and exciting repertoire.

The Musée National d'Art Moderne is one of the major holders of work by Moscow-born artist **Vassily Kandinsky**, with around 700 pieces. The museum's collection charts his journey from impressionist-style works to the abstract paintings, such as *Auf Weiss II* (On White II; 1923), for which he's best known.

Architecture & Views

Former French President Georges Pompidou wanted an ultracontemporary artistic hub and he got it: competition-winning architects Renzo Piano and Richard Rogers designed the building inside out, with utilitarian features like plumbing, pipes, air vents and electrical cables forming part of the external facade. The building was completed in 1977.

Viewed from a distance (such as from Sacré-Cœur), the Centre Pompidou's primary-coloured, boxlike form amid a sea of muted grey Parisian rooftops makes it look like a child's Meccano set abandoned on someone's elegant living-room rug. Although the Centre Pompidou is just six storeys high, the city's low-rise cityscape means stupendous views extend from its roof (reached by external escalators enclosed in tubes). Rooftop admission is included in museum and exhibition admission – or buy a **panorama ticket** (admission €3; ⊙11am-11pm Wed-Mon) just for the roof.

Children's Gallery

Interactive art exhibitions fill the fabulous children's gallery on the 1st floor. There are also regular workshops for kids aged six to 10 years (in French only; check the website for costs and registration details), and a great website, www.junior.centrepompidou.fr (in English and French), which is loaded with inspirational activities to fire kids' creativity.

Tours & Guides

Guided tours are only in French (the information desk in the central hall on the ground floor has details), but the gap is easily filled by the excellent **multimedia guide** (adult/under 13yr €5/3), which explains 62 works of art in the Musée National d'Art Moderne in detail on a 1½-hour trail. There is also a shorter 45-minute tour; another covering the unique architecture of the Centre Pompidou; and one created with kids in mind.

TOP SIGHTS
ÉGLISE ST-EUSTACHE

Just north of the gardens snuggling up to the city's old marketplace, now the soulless Forum des Halles, is one of the most beautiful churches in Paris. Majestic, architecturally magnificent and musically outstanding, St-Eustache has made souls soar for centuries.

Richelieu and Molière were baptised here (Molière also wed here), Louis XIV celebrated his first Holy Communion in the church, and Voltaire is buried here. Mozart chose St-Eustache for the funeral mass of his mother, and in 1855 Berlioz's *Te Deum* premiered here.

Art & Architecture

Built between 1532 and 1637, the church is primarily Gothic, although a neoclassical facade was added on the western side in the mid-18th century. Inside, many of the stained glass and paintings were given by guilds and merchants from the nearby Les Halles. Highlights include several works by Rubens in the side chapels, the colourful bas-relief of Parisian market porters (1969) by British sculptor Raymond Mason, and the exquisite altarpiece – bronze with white gold leaf (1990) – completed by 31-year-old American artist Keith Haring weeks before his death. Outside the church is a gigantic sculpture of a head and hand entitled *L'Écoute* (Listen; 1986) by Henri de Miller.

DON'T MISS

- ➡ Free Sunday-Afternoon Organ Recitals
- ➡ Altarpiece by Keith Haring
- ➡ Paintings by Rubens

PRACTICALITIES

- ➡ Map p392
- ➡ www.st-eustache.org
- ➡ 2 impasse St-Eustache, 1er
- ➡ admission free
- ➡ ⌚9.30am-7pm Mon-Fri, 10am-7pm Sat, 9am-7pm Sun
- ➡ Ⓜ Les Halles

The Organ

France's largest organ, above the church's western entrance and dating from 1854, has 101 stops and 8000 pipes. Organ recitals at 5.30pm on Sunday are a must for music lovers, as is June's Festival des 36 Heures de St-Eustache – 36 hours of nonstop music embracing a symphony of genres, world music, choral and jazz included.

SIGHTS

History and culture meet head on along the banks of the Seine in the 1er arrondissement, home to some of the most important sights for visitors to Paris, including the world-renowned Louvre and Centre Pompidou. It was in this same neighbourhood that Louis VI created *halles* (markets) in 1137 for merchants who converged on the city centre to sell their wares and for over 800 years they were, in the words of Émile Zola, the 'belly of Paris'. The wholesalers were moved lox, stock and cabbage out to the suburbs in 1971.

MUSÉE DU LOUVRE — ART MUSEUM

See p103.

LES ARTS DÉCORATIFS — ART MUSEUM

Map p388 (www.lesartsdecoratifs.fr; 107 rue de Rivoli, 1er; adult/18-25yr/under 18yr €9.50/8/free; 11am-6pm Tue-Sun; M Palais Royal–Musée du Louvre) A trio of privately administered museums collectively known as the Decorative Arts sit in the Rohan Wing of the vast Palais du Louvre. Admission includes entry to all three here as well as the Musée Nissim de Camondo in the 8e. Temporary exhibitions, open until 9pm on Thursday, command an additional fee.

The **Musée des Arts Décoratifs** (Applied Arts Museum) displays furniture, jewellery and such objets d'art as ceramics and glassware from the Middle Ages and the Renaissance through the art nouveau and art deco periods to modern times.

The much smaller **Musée de la Publicité** (Advertising Museum) has some 100,000 posters in its collection dating as far back as the 13th century, and innumerable promotional materials touting everything from 19th-century elixirs and early radio advertisements to Air France as well as electronic publicity. Only certain items are exhibited at any one time; most of the rest of the space is given over to special exhibitions.

Haute couture (high fashion) creations by the likes of Chanel and Jean-Paul Gaultier can be ogled in the **Musée de la Mode et du Textile** (Museum of Fashion & Textiles), home to some 16,000 costumes from the 16th century to present day. Most of the outfits are warehoused, however, and are only displayed during regularly scheduled themed exhibitions.

ART IN THE MAKING: 59 RUE DE RIVOLI

In such a classical part of Paris crammed with elegant historic architecture, **59 Rivoli** (Map p392; http://59rivoli-eng.org; 59 rue de Rivoli, 1er; 1-8pm Tue-Sun; M Louvre-Rivoli) is quite the bohemian breath of fresh air. Take time out to watch artists at work in the 30 *ateliers* (studios) strung on six floors of the long-abandoned bank building, now a legalised squat where some of Paris' most creative talent works (but doesn't live). The ground-floor gallery hosts a new exhibition every fortnight and free gigs, concerts and shows pack the place out most weekends. Look for the sculpted façade festooned with catchy drapes, banners and unconventional recycled piping above the shopfronts.

ÉGLISE ST-GERMAIN L'AUXERROIS — CHURCH

Map p392 (www.saintgermainauxerrois.cef.fr; 2 place du Louvre, 1er; 9am-7pm Mon-Sat, to 8pm Sun; M Louvre Rivoli or Pont Neuf) Built between the 13th and 16th centuries in a mixture of Gothic and Renaissance styles and with similar dimensions and ground plans to those of Notre Dame, this once royal parish church stands on a site at the eastern end of the Louvre that has been used for Christian worship since about AD 500.

After being mutilated in the 18th century by clergy intent on 'modernisation', and damaged during the Revolution, the church was restored by the Gothic Revivalist architect Eugène Viollet-le-Duc in the mid-19th century. Peek inside at its fine Renaissance stained glass.

ARC DE TRIOMPHE DU CARROUSEL — LANDMARK

Map p388 (place du Carrousel, 1er; M Palais Royal–Musée du Louvre) This triumphal arch, erected by Napoleon to celebrate his battlefield successes of 1805, sits with aplomb in the **Jardin du Carrousel**, the gardens immediately next to the Louvre. The arch was once crowned by the ancient Greek sculpture called *The Horses of St Mark's*, 'borrowed' from the portico of St Mark's Basilica in Venice by Napoleon but returned after his defeat at Waterloo in 1815.

TOP SIGHTS
JARDIN DES TUILERIES

Laid out by André Le Nôtre (garden architect at Versailles) in 1664, this 28-hectare expanse of manicured green is much loved today by city joggers and Sunday-afternoon strollers. A funfair sets up here in midsummer. Look out for Louise Bourgeois' *The Welcoming Hands* (1996) facing place de la Concorde.

Set in an 19th-century orangery built to shelter the garden's orange trees in winter, the **Orangerie Museum** (www.musee-orangerie.fr; adult/18-25yr/under 18yr €7.50/5/free, after 5pm €5, 1st Sun of month free; ⌚9am-6pm Wed-Mon; Ⓜ Concorde) exhibits important Impressionist works, including a series of Monet's *Decorations des Nymphéas* (Waterlilies) in two huge oval rooms purpose-built in 1927 on the artist's instructions. Works by Cézanne, Matisse, Picasso, Renoir, Sisley, Soutine and Utrillo complete the gallery's outstanding playlist. The wonderfully airy **gallery** (Map p388; ☎01 47 03 12 50; www.jeudepaume.org; 1 place de la Concorde, 8e; adult/18-25yr/under 18yr €7.50/5/free; ⌚noon-9pm Tue, noon-7pm Wed-Fri, 10am-7pm Sat & Sun; Ⓜ Concorde) in the erstwhile ***jeu de paume*** (real, or royal, tennis court) is all that remains of the **Palais des Tuileries** after it burnt down during the 1871 Revolution.

DON'T MISS

➡ Monet's *Waterlilies*

PRACTICALITIES

➡ Map p388

➡ ⌚7am-7.30pm, 9pm or 11pm

➡ Ⓜ Tuileries or Concorde

The quadriga (the two-wheeled chariot drawn by four horses) that replaced it was added in 1828 and celebrates the return of the Bourbons to the French throne after Napoleon's downfall. The sides of the arch are adorned with depictions of Napoleonic victories and eight pink-marble columns, atop each of which stands a soldier of the emperor's Grande Armée.

PLACE VENDÔME CITY SQUARE

Map p388 (Ⓜ Tuileries or Opéra) Octagonal place Vendôme and the arcaded and colonnaded buildings around it were constructed between 1687 and 1721. In March 1796 Napoleon married Josephine, Viscountess Beauharnais, in the building at No 3. Today the buildings surrounding the square house the posh Hôtel Ritz Paris and some of the city's most fashionable boutiques.

The 43.5m-tall **Colonne Vendôme** (Vendôme Column) in the centre of the square consists of a stone core wrapped in a 160m-long bronze spiral made from hundreds of Austrian and Russian cannons captured by Napoleon at the Battle of Austerlitz in 1805. The statue on top depicts Napoleon in classical Roman dress.

JARDIN DU PALAIS ROYAL GARDEN

Map p388 (2 place Colette, 1er; ⌚7.30am-10pm Apr & May, 7am-11pm Jun-Aug, 7am-9.30pm Sep, 7.30am-8.30pm Oct-Mar; Ⓜ Palais Royal–Musée du Louvre) This elegant urban space, 21 hectares large, is fronted by the neoclassical **Palais Royal** (Royal Palace; closed to the public), constructed in 1624 by Cardinal Richelieu but mostly dating to the late 18th century. Louis XIV hung out here in the 1640s and today it is the governmental **Conseil d'État** (State Council).

Jardin du Palais Royal is a perfect spot to sit, contemplate, picnic between boxed hedges and shop in the trio of arcades that frame the garden so beautifully: **Galerie de Valois** (east), where Charlotte Corday, Jean-Paul Marat's assassin once worked in a shop, is the most upmarket with designer boutiques like Stella McCartney, Pierre Hardy and Didier Ludot (p126) and coat-of-arms engraver Guillaumot, at work at Nos 151 to 154 since 1785. Across the garden, in **Galerie de Montpensier** (west), the Revolution broke out on a warm mid-July day just three years after the galleries opened in the Café du Foy. The third arcade, tiny **Galerie Beaujolais**, is crossed by **Passage du**

START **METRO LOUVRE RIVOLI**

END **METRO LE PELETIER**

DISTANCE **3KM**

DURATION **TWO HOURS**

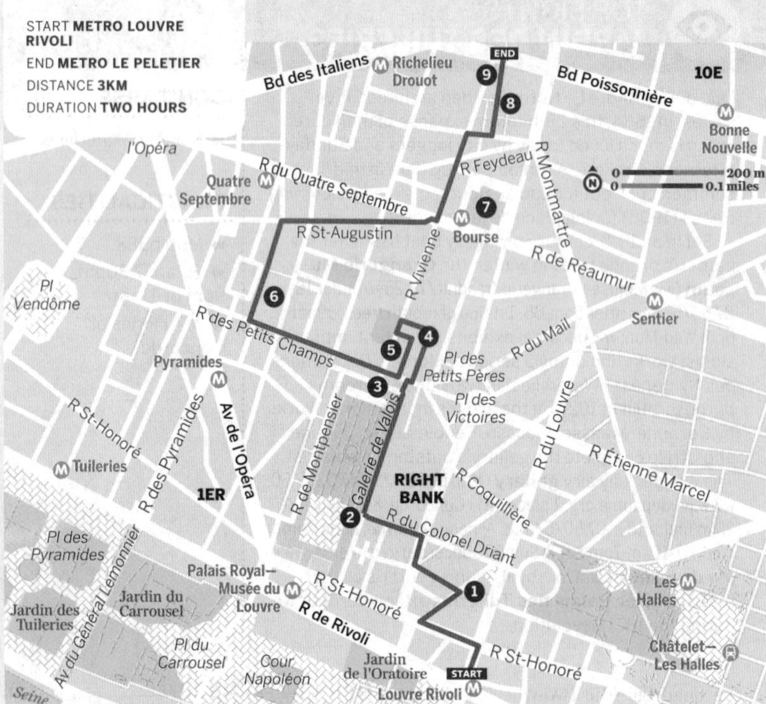

Neighbourhood Walk

Stepping Foot into 19th-century Paris

➡ Step into the Right Bank's lushly decorated *passages couverts* (covered arcades) – this was where early-19th-century Parisians gathered to stroll, shop, dine and go to the theatre. This walking tour is perfect for a rainy day; avoid Sundays.

From the metro, cross rue de Rivoli, walk north along rue du Louvre, turn left onto rue St-Honoré then right onto rue Jean-Jacques Rousseau. At No 19 enter **1 Galerie Véro Dodat** (1823), fitted with skylights, ceiling murals, Corinthian columns and gas globe lamps (now electric). Bijou art galleries, jewellers, a music shop and furniture restorer fill its quaint shopfronts.

The gallery's western exit leads to rue du Bouloi and rue Croix des Petits Champs. Head north to the corner of rue du Colonel Driant, turn left and walk to rue de Valois. At No 5 is an entrance to **2 Jardin du Palais Royal** and its arcades. Cut through **3 Passage du Perron** to rue du Beaujolais and beyond (north) to rue des Petits Champs. Turn right and duck into **4 Galerie Vivienne** at No 4. Decorated in 1826 with bas-reliefs of snakes (signifying prudence), scales (justice), anchors (hope), lute (harmony) and cockerel (vigilance), this is Paris' poshest *passage* with a lovely wine shop, flower boutique and old-fashioned bookshop much loved by Colette.

Exiting at 6 rue Vivienne, turn left and explore **5 Galerie Colbert** at No 2. Built in 1826 and now part of Paris University, the *passage* served as a car workshop-garage as recently as the 1980s. Follow the passage to its exit at 6 rue des Petits Champs and enter tatty **6 Passage Choiseul** (1824); Paul Verlaine (1844–96) drank absinthe here and Céline (1894–1961) grew up in his mother's lace shop at No 62.

Leave at 23 rue St-Augustin, stroll east to rue du Quatre Septembre – the building across the square is the **7 Bourse de Commerce**. Turn left up rue Vivienne, then right along rue St-Marc to **8 Passage des Panoramas**. Lunch at **9 L'Arbre à Cannelle**, **Racines** or **Passage 53**.

Perron, a passageway above which writer Colette (1873–1954) lived out the last dozen years of her life.

The far southern end of the square is polka-dotted with the black-and-white striped columns of various heights by **sculptor Daniel Buren**. It was started in 1986, interrupted by irate Parisians and finished – following the intervention of the Ministry of Culture and Communication – in 1995. The story (invented by Buren?) goes that if you toss a coin and it lands on one of the columns, your wish will come true.

In between the two rises a somewhat imposing wooden building, a temporary construction put up to house part of the neighbouring national theatre (France's oldest), the **Comédie Française**, while its main colonnaded building dating to 1860 is renovated.

CENTRE POMPIDOU — ART MUSEUM

See p111.

FORUM DES HALLES — SHOPPING MALL

Map p392 (www.forumdeshalles.com; 1 rue Pierre Lescot, 1er; ⏱shops 10am-8pm Mon-Sat; Ⓜ Les Halles or RER Châtelet–Les Halles) Don't get too excited. Tragically, the Forum des Halles is no longer a market, rather an unspeakably ugly, four-level, underground shopping centre constructed in 1970s glass-and-chrome style after Paris' main wholesale food market dating to the early 12th century was moved to the southern suburb of Rungis, near Orly.

The upside is, dramatic change (for the better) is afoot. The dodgy park and dated arbours topping the underground shopping mall have been demolished, and cranes, diggers and an army of builders are busy at work creating **La Canopée** – a thoroughly contemporary, glass-topped, curvilinear building by architects Patrick Berger and Jacques Anziutti, inspired by the natural shade canopy of a rainforest. Spilling out from the translucent, leaflike rooftop will be state-of-the-art gardens by landscape designer David Mangin with *pétanque* courts (a variant on the game of bowls) and chess tables, a central patio and pedestrian walkways. Final completion will be 2016.

The mall itself will receive a relatively light renovation in stages; hence business should continue more or less as usual, with minimal disruption to the city's largest metro/RER hub. Follow the project at www.parisleshalles.fr or pop into the information centre on **place Jean du Bellay**, a pretty square pierced by the **Fontaine des Innocents** (1549). The multitiered Renaissance fountain is named after the Cimetière des Innocents, a cemetery formerly on this site from which two million skeletons were disinterred after the Revolution and transferred to the Catacombes. The square buzzes in summer with street musicians, fire-eaters and other street performers.

ÉGLISE ST-EUSTACHE — CHURCH

See p113.

MUSÉE EN HERBE — ART MUSEUM

Map p392 (☎01 40 67 00 37; www.musee-en-herbe.com; 21 rue Herold, 1er; admission €6; ⏱10am-8pm Fri-Wed, to 9pm Thu; Ⓜ Les Halles) One of the city's great backstreet secrets, this children's museum is a surprise gem for art lovers of every age, not just kids. Its permanent exhibition changes every March and focuses on the work of one artist through a series of interactive displays.

Captions are in English as well as French, children get a *jeu de piste* (activity sheet) to guide and entertain, and additional workshops and guided visits for kids and adults – think hands-on art workshops, afternoon tea, early evening aperitif and so on (€6 to €10, reserve in advance) – add to the playful experience.

FREE BOURSE DE COMMERCE — MONUMENT

Map p392 (2 rue de Viarmes, 1er; ⏱9am-6pm Mon-Fri; Ⓜ Les Halles) At one time the city's grain market, the circular Trade Exchange was capped with a copper dome in 1811. The murals running along internal walls below the galleries were painted by five different artists in 1889 and restored in 1998. They represent French trade and industry through the ages.

TOUR JEAN SANS PEUR — TOWER

Map p392 (www.tourjeansanspeur.com; 20 rue Étienne Marcel, 1er; adult/7-18yr €5/3; ⏱1.30-6pm Wed-Sun Apr-early Nov, 1.30-6pm Wed, Sat & Sun early Nov-Mar; Ⓜ Étienne Marcel) This Gothic, 29m-high tower called Tower of John the Fearless was built by the Duke of Bourgogne so he could take refuge from his enemies at the top. Part of a splendid mansion in the early 15th century, it is one of the very few examples of feudal military architecture extant in Paris. Climb 140 steps up the spiral staircase to the top turret.

TOUR ST-JACQUES TOWER

Map p392 (square de la Tour St-Jacques, 1er; MChâtelet) Just north of place du Châtelet, the Flamboyant Gothic, 52m-high St James Tower is all that remains of the Église St-Jacques la Boucherie, built by the powerful butchers guild in 1523 as a starting point for pilgrims setting out for the shrine of St James at Santiago de Compostela in Spain.

The church was demolished by the Revolutionary Directory in 1797, but the sand-coloured bell tower, perfectly clean, was spared so it could be used to drop globules of molten lead in the manufacture of shot.

EATING

TOP CHOICE BEEF CLUB STEAK €€

Map p392 (☎09 54 37 13 65; 58 rue Jean-Jacques Rousseau, 1er; mains €20-45; ⊙dinner Tue-Sat; MLes Halles) No steak house is more chic or hipper than this. Packed out ever since it threw its first T-bone on the grill in spring 2012, this beefy address is all about steak, prepared to sweet perfection by legendary Paris butcher Yves-Marie Le Bourdonnec. The vibe is hip New York and the downstairs cellar bar, the Ballroom du Beef Club, shakes a mean cocktail (€12 to €15) courtesy of the cool guys from the Experimental Cocktail Club. An address not to be missed – if you are lucky enough to score a table that is!

LOCAL KNOWLEDGE

CHEAP EAT

It's as cheap as chips, a mug of sweet lemon tea gets you change from €2, and punters can eat in or take away. In the heart of Paris' Japantown, **Ace Gourmet Bento** (Map p388; 18 rue Thérèse, 1er; ⊙noon-midnight Mon-Sat; MPalais Royal-Musée du Louvre) is a bijou Japanese-Korean canteen-bistro with bright white walls, flowery pop-art deco, and an unbeatable-value €8.10 lunch deal. Pick your meat or fish main with rice or noodles, choose five veggie salads and side dishes, and plop yourself and fuchsia-pink tray down at a table. Proof of the pudding of just how low-cost this address is – the fresh fruit salad is thrown in for free.

TOP CHOICE FRENCHIE BISTRO €€

(☎01 40 39 96 19; www.frenchie-restaurant.com; 5-6 rue du Nil, 2e; menus €34, €38 & €45; ⊙dinner Mon-Fri; MSentier) Tucked down an alley you wouldn't venture down otherwise, this bijou bistro with wooden tables and old stone walls is iconic. Frenchie is always packed and for good reason: excellent-value dishes are modern, market-driven (the menu changes daily with a choice of two dishes by course) and prepared with just the right dose of unpretentious creative flair by French chef Gregory Marchand.

The only hiccup is snagging a table: reserve for one of two sittings (7pm or 9.30pm) two months in advance or arrive at 7pm and pray for a cancellation or – failing that – share tapas-style small plates with friends across the street at Frenchie Bar à Vin. No reservations – write your name on the sheet of paper strung outside, loiter in the alley and wait for your name to be called.

KUNITORAYA JAPANESE €

Map p388 (www.kunitoraya.com; 39 rue Ste-Anne, 1er; mains €12-14; ⊙11.30am-10pm; MPyramides) Some of the best-value *udon* (handmade Japanese noodles) is what this buzzing address in Paris' eat-rich Japantown is all about. Grab a stool at the kitchen bar and watch the hip young chefs strut their stuff over steaming bowls of soup, *grands bols de riz* (big bowls of rice) laced with battered prawns, sweet duck or beef, and other meal-in-one dishes. In summer go for one of the cold noodle dishes served on bamboo.

Whatever the season, arrive well before by 1pm (or 8pm for dinner) or risk leaving disappointed (and hungry). No credit cards and no advance reservations.

TOP CHOICE CLAUS BREAKFAST, BRUNCH €

Map p392 (☎01 42 33 55 10; www.clausparis.com; 14 rue Jean-Jacques Rousseau, 1er; breakfast €13-18, lunch €19; ⊙7.30am-6pm Mon-Fri, 9.30am-5pm Sat & Sun; MÉtienne Marcel) Dubbed the 'haute-couture breakfast specialist' in Parisian foodie circles, this inspired *épicerie du petit-dej* (breakfast grocery shop) has everything you could possibly desire for the ultimate gourmet breakfast and brunch – organic mueslis and cereals, fresh juices, jams, honey and so on.

Breakfast or brunch on site, shop at Claus to create your own or ask for a luxury breakfast hamper to be delivered to your

A HIDDEN KITCHEN

So successful were the twice-weekly clandestine dinners they hosted in an apartment near the Louvre that American duo Braden and Laura shut their Hidden Kitchen supper club and opened **Verjus** (Map p388; 01 42 97 54 40; www.verjusparis.com; 52 rue de Richelieu, 1er; 4-/6-course tasting menu €55/70, with wine pairings €85/110; dinner Mon-Fri; M Bourse or Palais Royal–Musée du Louvre) a hidden but hyped restaurant you need to know about to find. Cuisine is contemporary and international – think brown butter monkfish with brussel sprouts, apple and Tabasco broth or hangar steak with hazelnuts and horseradish. An English-language menu plays to Paris' many anglophones in love with this address, and wine pairings are impeccable.

Reservations are essential Thursday and Friday, but walk-ins Monday to Wednesday often end up with a table. And for diners who don't strike gold or simply yearn for something less, there's Braden and Laura's **Verjus Bar à Vin** (Map p388; 47 rue Montpensier, 1er; 6-11pm Mon-Fri; M Bourse or Palais Royal–Musée du Louvre). The pocket-sized wine bar, with old cream-stone walls in the restaurant cellar, cooks up what Parisian foodies rightfully claim to be the best fried buttermilk chicken (€10) in the city. The crispy Basque pork belly slices and string-thin fries come a close second. No reservations – arrive early to snag one of 10 bar stools.

door. Its lunchtime salads, soups and tarts are equally tasty.

SPRING — MODERN FRENCH €€

Map p388 (01 45 96 05 72; www.springparis.fr; 6 rue Bailleul, 1er; lunch/dinner menu €44/76; lunch & dinner Wed-Fri, dinner Tue & Sat; M Palais Royal–Musée du Louvre) One of the Right Bank's 'talk-of-the-town' addresses, with an American in the kitchen and stunning food. It has no printed menu, meaning hungry gourmets put their appetites in the hands of the chef and allow multilingual waiting staff to reveal what's cooking as each course is served. Advance reservations essential.

At lunchtime, nip to the **Spring Épicerie** (Map p388; 52 rue de l'Arbre Sec, 1er; noon-8pm Tue-Sat) a tiny wine shop which serves steaming bowls of market-inspired, 'hungry worker-style' *bouillon du poule* (chicken soup; €12) loaded with veg, a poached farm egg, herbs and so on. Eat at a bar stool or on the trot.

KAÏ — JAPANESE €€€

Map p388 (01 40 15 10 99; 18 rue du Louvre, 1er; lunch/dinner menu €28 & €42/69; lunch Tue-Sat, dinner Tue-Sun; M Louvre Rivoli) This exquisite Japanese restaurant is where we want to go when we die and have been deemed worthy of paradise. The decor – bamboo ceiling, blond-wood flooring – is an exercise in restraint, and the food is out of this world, with its own style of sushi and excellent grilled dishes. Try the aubergine with miso.

LE SAUT DU LOUP — TRADITIONAL FRENCH €€

Map p388 (01 42 25 49 55; 107 rue de Rivoli, 1er; lunch/dinner menu €19/22; lunch & dinner; M Louvre Rivoli) Given its location inside the Decorative Arts Museum, its interior design is naturally chic and impeccable. But it is the sweeping summer terrace with crunchy gravel underfoot and elegant tables overlooking the pea-green lawns of Jardin du Carrousel that is the real reason to eat here.

Post-Louvre visit, afternoon tea or early-evening aperitif here is an equally desirable and cinematic Paris moment.

L'ARDOISE — BISTRO €€

Map p388 (01 42 96 28 18; www.lardoise-paris.com; 28 rue du Mont Thabor, 1er; menu €35; lunch Tue-Sat, dinner Tue-Sun; M Concorde or Tuileries) This is a lovely little bistro with no menu as such (*ardoise* means 'blackboard', which is all there is), but who cares? The food – fricassee of corn-fed chicken with morels, pork cheeks in ginger, hare in black pepper, prepared dextrously by chef Pierre Jay (ex-Tour d'Argent) – is superb. The menu changes every three weeks and the three-course *prix fixe* (set menu) offers good value.

L'Ardoise is bound to attract a fair number of tourists due to its location, but generally they too are on a culinary quest.

LE SOUFFLÉ — TRADITIONAL FRENCH €€

Map p388 (01 42 60 27 19; www.lesouffle.fr; 36 rue du Mont Thabor, 1er; lunch/dinner menu €25/35; lunch & dinner Mon-Sat; M Concorde or Tuileries) The faintly vintage, aqua-blue

LOCAL KNOWLEDGE

PICNICKING IN PALATIAL SPLENDOUR

There is no lovelier spot around the Louvre to picnic in palatial splendour than Jardin du Palais Royal (p115), the courtyard gardens of Palais Royal with benches overlooking box-hedged flowerbeds, crunchy gravel paths and Daniel Buren's distinctive zebra-striped columns at one end. The real secret though is the filled baguette sandwiches (€3.25 to €4.50) sold at Paris' oldest bakery, a two-minute walk away beneath the arches on the western side of the gardens. **Boulangerie Pâtisserie du Grand Richelieu** (Map p388; 51 rue de Richelieu, 1er; Mon-Sat; M Palais Royal–Musée du Louvre) has been in the biz since 1810, bakes 16-odd different types of *pain* (bread) and is something of a city legend. To speak to the man himself, ask for *boulanger* Claude Esnault.

façade of this concept kitchen is reassuringly befitting of the timeless French classic it serves inside – the soufflé. The light fluffy dish served in white ramekins comes in dozens of different flavours, both savoury and sweet; *andouillette* (pig intestine sausage) is the top choice for fearless gourmets.

If you're egged out by dessert or simply crave something a bit different, go for the *soufflé glacé Grand Marnier* (frozen soufflé doused in Grand Marnier). Sweet!

RACINES — WINE BAR €€

Map p388 (01 40 13 06 41; 8 Passage des Panoramas, 2e; mains €15-30; lunch & dinner Mon-Fri; M Grands Boulevards or Bourse) Snug inside a former 19th-century *marchand de vin* (wine merchant's; look up to admire the lovely old gold lettering above the door), Racines (meaning 'Roots') is an address that shouts Paris at every turn. Shelves of wine bottles curtain the windows, the old patterned floor smacks of feasting and merriment, and the menu chalked on the *ardoise* (blackboard) is a straightforward choice of three starters, three mains and a trio of desserts, deeply rooted in the best local produce.

An impressive choice of organic and natural *vins* makes the wine list stand out.

PASSAGE 53 — MODERN FRENCH €€€

Map p388 (01 42 33 04 35; www.passage53.com; 53 Passage des Panoramas, 2e; lunch/dinner menu €60/110; lunch & dinner Tue-Sat; M Grands Boulevards or Bourse) No address inside Passage des Panoramas contrasts more dramatically with the outside hustle and bustle than this elegant restaurant at No 53. An oasis of calm and tranquillity (with window blinds pulled firmly down when closed), this gastronomic address is an ode to only the best French produce – worked to perfection in a series of tasting courses by Japanese chef Shinichi Sato. Advance reservations recommended.

YAM'TCHA — FUSION €€€

Map p392 (01 40 26 08 07; www.yamtcha.com; 4 rue Sauval, 1er; lunch/dinner menus from €50/85; lunch Wed-Sun, dinner Wed-Sat; M Louvre Rivoli) Adeline Grattard's ingeniously fused French and Chinese flavours recently earned the female chef a Michelin star. Pair dishes on the frequently changing menu with wine or exotic teas. Book well ahead.

DROUANT — MODERN FRENCH €€€

Map p388 (01 42 65 15 16; www.drouant.com; 16-18 place Gaillon, 2e; lunch/dinner menu €44/42 & €54; lunch & dinner; M Quatre Septembre) A mecca for literary groupies, this is where the Prix Goncourt (p327), France's equivalent of the Booker or Pulitzer, is awarded each year. Packed out with business suits at lunchtime, it's one of those timeless Parisian addresses with a classical interior, great-value *plat du jour* (€18) and superb tapas-style dishes prepared by Alsatian chef Antoine Westerman.

RESTAURANT DU PALAIS ROYAL — INTERNATIONAL €€€

Map p388 (01 40 20 00 27; www.restaurantdupalaisroyal.com; 110 Galerie de Valois, 1er; mains €38-42; lunch & dinner Mon-Sat; M Palais Royal–Musée du Louvre) The terrace of this Parisian classic overlooking the Palais Royal is one of the capital's most coveted in fine weather. In colder months the traditional, redder-than-red dining room is a cosy and stylish backdrop to international dishes with an Italian spin by chef Bruno Hees – think exquisite meat and fish dishes paired with creative risottos.

LE GRAND VÉFOUR TRADITIONAL FRENCH €€€

Map p388 (☎01 42 96 56 27; www.grand-vefour.com; 17 rue de Beaujolais, 1er; lunch/dinner menu €96/282; ⏱lunch Mon-Fri, dinner Mon-Thu; Ⓜ Pyramides) This 18th-century jewel on the northern edge of the Jardin du Palais Royal has been a dining favourite of the Parisian elite since 1784; just look at who gets their names ascribed to each table – from Napoleon to Victor Hugo and Colette (who lived next door). The food is tip-top; expect a voyage of discovery in one of the most beautiful restaurants in the world.

LE GRAND COLBERT TRADITIONAL FRENCH €€

Map p388 (☎01 42 86 87 88; www.legrandcolbert.fr; 2-4 rue Vivienne, 2e; lunch menus €25.50 & €32.50; ⏱noon-1am; Ⓜ Pyramides) This former workers' *cafétéria* transformed into a fin de siècle showcase is more relaxed than many similarly restored restaurants and is a convenient spot for lunch after visiting the neighbouring covered shopping arcades – the daily *formule ardoise* (blackboard fixed menu; €16) chalked on the board is good value – or cruising the streets at night (last orders: midnight).

Don't expect gastronomic miracles, but portions are big and service is friendly. Sunday ushers in a pricier €41 *menu*.

BIOBOA ORGANIC €€

Map p388 (☎01 40 28 02 83; www.bioboa.fr; 93 rue Montmartre, 2e; 2-/3-course lunch menu €21/26, mains €16-24; ⏱9am-midnight Mon-Sat; Ⓜ Sentier or Bourse) Potted olive trees salute the entrance to this organic food cafe, a lovely space with retro mirrors, violet walls and funky collection of lampshades mixing a dozen and one fabrics, textures and materials. Order an apple and kiwi juice, kick back in an armchair and revel in a menu that mixes organic farm meats with a generous dose of tasty vegetarian dishes.

Don't miss the restaurant's adjoining, small but select *épicerie* (grocery store).

LA MAUVAISE RÉPUTATION MODERN FRENCH €€

Map p388 (☎01 42 36 92 44; www.lamauvaisereputation.fr; 28 rue Léopold-Bellan, 2e; lunch menus €17-21, dinner menus €35; ⏱lunch Tue-Fri & Sun, dinner Tue-Sat; Ⓜ Sentier) The name alone – Bad Reputation (yep, also a Georges Brassens album) – immediately makes you want to poke your nose in and see what's happening behind that bright orange canopy and oyster-grey façade just footsteps from busy rue Montorgueil.

Great bistro cooking and warm engaging service in a catchy designer space with coloured spots on the wall and fresh flowers on each table is the answer.

RACINES (2) MODERN FRENCH €€

Map p392 (☎01 4 60 77 34; 39 rue de l'Arbre Sec, 1er; mains €28; ⏱lunch & dinner Mon-Fri; Ⓜ Louvre Rivoli) R2 is a cousin of Racines in Passage des Panoramas, but that is about the extent of the family resemblance. No 2 is a thoroughly modern, urban bistro with a

LOCAL KNOWLEDGE

RUE D'ARGOUT

It's a slip of a street from the 13th century, but it's one of those short, stumble-upon strips where Paris' young bright things like to be, where you just know you'll walk down that same street tomorrow, or next week, or next month perhaps, and another trendsetter will have popped up.

Take **Blend** (Map p392; www.blendhamburger.com; 44 rue d'Argout, 2e; burgers €10, lunch menus €15 & €17; ⏱lunch & dinner Mon-Sat; Ⓜ Sentier), a gourmet burger bar the size of a pocket handkerchief that has been the talk of the town since its 2012 opening. Easy to spot by the hungry crowd lingering outside waiting for a table, the sharp, smart, black-and-wood space cooks up bijou-sized burgers with homemade buns and meat from celebrity butcher Yves-Marie Le Bourdonnec of Beef Club (p118).

Across the street and a few doors down, bagels are stuffed with different sweet and savoury fillings, and hot dogs served New York–style at **Adèle's Family** (Map p392; www.adelesfamily.com; 67 rue d'Argout, 2e; ⏱11.45am-7pm Tue-Fri, 11.30am-6pm Sat & Sun ; 📶; Ⓜ Sentier); while next-door neighbour **Fée Nature** (Map p392; 67 rue d'Argout, 2e; ⏱11am-6pm Mon-Sat; Ⓜ Sentier) thinks green with its inventive, wholly *'bio et sain'* (organic & healthy) menu. Orange blossom tapioca anyone? If the line's too long further up the street, you know where to go.

contemporary Philippe Starck interior and an open stainless-steel kitchen where you can watch the hip, young black-outfitted chefs, tattoos et al, at work.

What's cooking – just two or three choices for each course – is chalked on the board and the Louvre, handily so, is just around the corner.

AUX LYONNAIS LYONNAIS €€

Map p388 (☎01 42 96 65 04; www.auxlyonnais.com; 32 rue St-Marc, 2e; lunch menu €30, mains €20-27; ⊙lunch & dinner Tue-Fri, dinner Sat; Ⓜ Richelieu-Drouot) This is where top French chef Alain Ducasse (who has three Michelin stars at his restaurant over at the Plaza Athénée) and his followers 'slum' it. The venue is an art nouveau masterpiece that feels more real than movie set and the food is perfectly restructured Lyonnais classics.

L'ARBRE À CANNELLE BISTRO €

Map p388 (☎01 45 08 55 87; www.arbre-a-cannelle.fr; 57 Passage des Panoramas, 2e; mains €13.50-15.90; ⊙lunch Mon & Tue, lunch & dinner Wed-Sat; Ⓜ Grands Boulevards or Bourse) Tucked inside one of the Right Bank's most vibrant early-19th-century *passages couverts* (covered arcades), the 'Cinnamon Tree' is as much about ogling original 19th-century decor – check that ceiling, man! – as feasting on good-value bistro fare. More delicate appetites will appreciate the tasty selection of salads, savoury tarts and quiches. Predictably, the place gets packed at lunchtime.

THE CITY'S MOST FAMOUS HOT CHOCOLATE

Clink china with lunching ladies, their posturing poodles and half the students from Tokyo University at **Angelina** (Map p388; 226 rue de Rivoli, 1er; ⊙daily; Ⓜ Tuileries), a grand dame of a tearoom dating to 1903. Breakfast, lunch and weekend brunch are all served here, against a fresco backdrop of belle époque Nice, but it is the superthick, decadently sickening 'African' hot chocolate (€7.20), served with a pot of whipped cream and carafe of water, that prompts the constant queue for a table at Angelina. Buy it bottled to take home from Angelina's small boutique.

AU PIED DE COCHON BRASSERIE €€

Map p392 (☎01 40 13 77 00; www.pieddecochon.com; 6 rue Coquillère, 1er; lunch menu €18.50, mains €18.60-24.35; ⊙24hr; Ⓜ Les Halles) This venerable establishment, which once satisfied the appetites of both market porters and theatre-goers with its famous onion soup and *pieds de cochon* (grilled pig's trotters), has become more uniformly upmarket and touristy since Les Halles was moved to the suburbs.

But it still opens round the clock seven days a week as it has since the end of WWII, and its pig's trotters, tails, ears and snouts are definitely worth writing a postcard home about. Children's *menu* €7.90.

DJAKARTA BALI INDONESIAN €€

Map p392 (☎01 45 08 83 11; www.djakarta-bali.com; 9 rue Vauvilliers, 1er; menus €25-55; ⊙dinner Tue-Sun; Ⓜ Louvre Rivoli) OK, it might look like Hollywood's idea of an Indonesian restaurant with all those Balinese handicrafts adorning the walls, but this is the real thing, run by the progeny of an Indonesian diplomat exiled when President Sukarno was overthrown in 1967.

If you think you can handle it, order one of four *rijstafels* (Dutch for 'rice table') – a seemingly endless feast of seven to 10 courses. Those with nut allergies beware: peanuts appear in many dishes.

LE VÉRO DODAT FRENCH €

Map p388 (☎01 45 08 92 06; 1st fl, 19 Galerie Véro Dodat, 2 rue du Bouloi, 1er; menu €17.50; ⊙lunch & dinner to 10.30pm Mon-Sat; Ⓜ Louvre Rivoli) This friendly little place in the heart of the Véro Dodat *passage couvert* has seating downstairs and up. Workers from the nearby Bourse de Commerce fill it at lunchtime.

JOE ALLEN AMERICAN €€

Map p392 (www.joeallenparis.com; 30 rue Pierre Lescot, 1er; lunch/dinner menu €14/18.50 & €23.50; ⊙noon-1am; 🚸; Ⓜ Étienne Marcel) A Parisian institution since 1972, Joe Allen brings a touch of New York to the city with its Californian wines, excellent weekend brunches and vibrant atmosphere. Food is simple but finely prepared – the ribs and hamburgers are both grand.

BAAN BORAN THAI €

Map p388 (www.baan-boran.com; 43 rue de Montpensier, 1er; lunch menu €14.80, mains €11.60-21; ⊙lunch & dinner Mon-Fri, dinner Sat; Ⓜ Palais Royal–Musée du Louvre) A handy stop

LOCAL KNOWLEDGE

RUE MONTMARTRE

No street is so well clad with appealing places to sip *café* or cocktails as this. Start at rue Montmartre's southern end with heritage-listed, hole-in-the-wall **Christ Inn's Bistrot** (Map p392; ☎01 42 36 07 56; 15 rue Montmartre, 1er; ⏰Tue-Sat; Ⓜ Les Halles), a historic gem with its railway-carriage-style slatted wooden seats and belle époque tiles featuring market scenes of Les Halles and an *oh très bobo* (hip), late-20s crowd. Equally 'vintage' is **Le Tambour** (Map p392; ☎01 42 33 06 90; 41 rue Montmartre; ⏰8am-6am; Ⓜ Étienne Marcel or Sentier), a mecca for Parisian night owls with its long hours (food until 3.30am or 4am) and hip mix of recycled street furniture and old metro maps. The Crazy Heart, aka **Le Cœur Fou** (Map p392; ☎01 42 33 91 33; 55 rue Montmartre; ⏰5pm-2am; Ⓜ Étienne Marcel), a few doors up, is a tiny gallery-bar with candles nestled in whitewashed walls and an *oh très bobo*, late-20s crowd.

en route to or from the Louvre, this provincial Thai joint – one of a trio behind the Palais Royal – is authentic and friendly to vegetarians.

CAFÉ MARLY — CAFE €€

Map p388 (☎01 46 26 06 60; www.maisonthierrycostes.com/cafe-marly; 93 rue de Rivoli, 1er; mains €18-39; ⏰8am-2am; Ⓜ Palais Royal–Musée du Louvre) This chic venue facing the Louvre's inner courtyard serves contemporary French fare throughout the day under the palace colonnades. Views of the glass pyramid are priceless.

KHATAG — TIBETAN €

Map p392 (http://restaurantkhatag.free.fr; 68 rue Quincampoix, 3e; lunch menu €7.50-11, dinner menu €13-22; ⏰lunch & dinner Tue-Sun; Ⓜ Rambuteau) This oasis of calm in frenetic Les Halles serves what many reckon to be the city's best Tibetan food.

SAVEURS VÉGÉT'HALLES — VEGAN €

Map p392 (☎01 40 41 93 95; www.saveursvegethalles.fr/; 41 rue des Bourdonnais, 1er; salads €11.90; ⏰lunch & dinner Mon-Sat; ✍; Ⓜ Châtelet) This vegan eatery offers quite a few mock-meat dishes like *poulet végétal aux champignons* ('chicken' with mushrooms). No alcohol.

LINA'S BEAUTIFUL SANDWICH — SANDWICHES, SALADS €

Map p392 (www.linasparis.com; 50 rue Étienne Marcel, 2e; sandwiches €4.50-7; ⏰8.30am-6pm Mon-Fri, 9am-6.30pm Sat; 📶; Ⓜ Sentier or Bourse) For made-to-measure sandwiches built from five different bread types and countless fillings and dressings, there is no better address than this large, bright, contemporary 1er space with bags of comfy seating. Free wi-fi is the icing on the cake.

COJEAN — SANDWICHES, SALADS €

Map p388 (www.cojean.fr; 3 place du Louvre, 1er; sandwiches €6-7; ⏰10am-4pm Mon-Fri, 11am-6pm Sat; 📶; Ⓜ Palais Royal–Musée du Louvre) Across the street from the Louvre, this stylish sandwich and salad bar promises a quick lunch for less than €10 beneath the splendour of an elegant moulded period ceiling.

TA SUSHI — JAPANESE €

Map p392 (4 rue Étienne Marcel, 2e; menu €11-16.90; ⏰lunch & dinner Mon-Sat; Ⓜ Étienne Marcel) This is arguably the pick of the crop of affordable sushi bars that have sprouted in Paris in recent years.

LA BAGUE DE KENZA — PATISSERIE

Map p392 (www.labaguedekenza.com; 136 rue St-Honoré, 1er; Ⓜ Louvre Rivoli) Astonishing, exquisite and seductively sweet Algerian cakes and pastries is what this speciality patisserie with tearoom and restaurant up top does best.

DRINKING & NIGHTLIFE

TOP CHOICE EXPERIMENTAL COCKTAIL CLUB — COCKTAIL BAR

Map p392 (www.experimentalcocktailclub.com; 37 rue St-Saveur, 2e; ⏰daily; Ⓜ Réaumur-Sebastopol) Called ECC by trendies, this fabulous speakeasy with grey façade and old-beamed ceiling is effortlessly hip. Oozing spirit and soul, the cocktail bar – with retro-chic decor by American interior designer Cuoco Black, and sister bars in London and New York – is a sophisticated flashback to those *années folles* (crazy years) of prohibition New York.

JAZZ DUO

Rue des Lombards, 2e, is the street to swing by for live jazz.

Le Baiser Salé (Map p392; www.lebaisersale.com; 58 rue des Lombards, 2e; daily; Châtelet) Known for its Afro and Latin jazz, and jazz fusion concerts, the Salty Kiss combines big names and unknown artists. The place has a relaxed vibe, with sets starting at 7.30pm and 10pm.

Sunset & Sunside (Map p392; www.sunset-sunside.com; 60 rue des Lombards, 1er; daily; Châtelet) Two venues in one at this trendy, well-respected club: electric jazz, fusion and the odd salsa session downstairs; acoustics and concerts upstairs.

Cocktails (€12 to €15) are individual and fabulous, and DJs set the space partying until dawn at weekends. The same guys are behind the equally hip Ballroom cocktail bar in the cellar of the New Yorker-style Beef Club (p118).

JEFREY'S — COCKTAIL BAR

Map p392 (www.jefreys.fr; 14 rue St-Saveur, 2e; Tue-Sat; Réaumur-Sebastopol) Oh how dandy this trendy drawing room with wooden façade, leather Chesterfields and old-fashioned gramophone is! Gentlemen's club in soul, yes, but creative cocktails are shaken for both him and her, and never more so than during happy hour (7pm to 10.30pm Tuesday and Thurday) when cocktails (€11 to €13) dip to €9.

Favourites include I Wanna be This Drink (rum, strawberry juice, fresh raspberries and balsamic vinegar caramel) and the Grand Marnier–based Cucumber Cooler. Well-aged whisky and other spirits are another reason to drink chez Jefrey.

KONG — BAR

Map p392 (www.kong.fr; 1 rue du Pont Neuf, 1er; daily; Pont Neuf) Late nights at this Philippe Starck–designed riot of iridescent champagne-coloured vinyl booths, Japanese cartoon cut-outs and garden gnome stools see Paris' glam young set guzzling Dom Pérignon, nibbling on tapas-style platters (mains €20 to €40) and shaking their designer-clad booty on the tables.

If you can, try to snag a table *à l'étage* (upstairs) in the part-glass-roofed terrace-gallery, where light floods across the giant geisha swooning horizontal across the ceiling, and stunning river views (particularly at sunset) make you swoon. Smokers will appreciate the *fumoir* (a tiny heated room with no windows or ceiling) accessible from here.

LE FUMOIR — COCKTAIL BAR

Map p392 (www.lefumoir.com; 6 rue de l'Amiral de Coligny, 1er; daily; Louvre Rivoli) This colonial-style bar-restaurant is a fine spot to sip top-notch gin from quality glassware while nibbling on olives from the vintage mahogany bar, or discover new cocktails with friends during happy hour (6pm to 8pm). A buoyant, corporate crowd packs out the place weekday evenings after work, while the restaurant revs into gear with late-morning breakfasts during the week and Sunday brunch.

The best seats in the house are in the 'library' and on the pavement terrace.

HARRY'S NEW YORK BAR — COCKTAIL BAR

Map p388 (www.harrysbar.fr; 5 rue Daunou, 2e; daily; Opéra) One of the most popular American-style bars in the prewar years, Harry's once welcomed writers like F Scott Fitzgerald and Ernest Hemingway, who no doubt sampled the bar's unique cocktail and creation: the Bloody Mary. The Cuban mahogany interior dates from the mid-19th century and was brought over from a Manhattan bar in 1911.

There's a basement piano bar called Ivories where Gershwin supposedly composed *An American in Paris* and, for the peckish, old-school hot dogs and generous club sandwiches to snack on. The advertisement for Harry's that occasionally appears in the papers still reads 'Tell the Taxi Driver Sank Roo Doe Noo' and is copyrighted.

Ô CHATEAU — WINE BAR

Map p392 (www.o-chateau.com; 68 rue Jean-Jacques Rousseau, 1er; 4pm-midnight, Tue-Sat; Les Halles or Étienne Marcel) Wine aficionados can thank this young, fun, cosmopolitan *bar à vin* for bringing affordable tasting on tap to Paris. Sit at the long trendy bar and savour your pick of 40-odd *grands vins* served by the glass (500-odd by the bottle!). Or sign up in advance for a guided cellar tasting in English over lunch (€75), dinner (€100) or with six *grands crus* (wines of the highest grade) and cheese (€120).

DEPUR BAR

Map p392 (www.depur.fr; 4bis rue St-Saveur, 2e; daily; ; Étienne Marcel or Sentier) It's glitzy and chic, a definite after-dark dress-up. But what really gives this hybrid bar-restaurant wow-factor is its courtyard terrace – covered in winter, open and star-topped in summer. Cocktails are shaken from 5pm.

CAFÉ BEAUBOURG CAFE

Map p392 (100 rue St-Martin, 3e; daily; Les Halles) This upbeat minimalist cafe across from the Centre Pompidou has been drawing a well-heeled crowd on its terrace for two dozen years now.

CAFÉ LA FUSÉE BAR

Map p392 (168 rue St-Martin, 3e; daily; Rambuteau or Étienne Marcel) A short walk from the Pompidou, the Rocket is a lively, laid-back hang-out with red-and-white striped awnings strung with fairy lights outside, and paint-peeling, tobacco-coloured walls evoking 101 great nights out inside. Its wine selection by the glass (€2.70 to €5.50) is notably good.

MKP OPÉRA COCKTAIL BAR

Map p388 (www.mkpbar.com; 4 rue Daunou, 2e; Mon-Sat; Quatre Septembre) Big, black and glitzy, this glamorous after-work hang-out lures a buoyant crowd with its lavish cocktails, festive spirit and *planchas* (tasting platters of cheese, meats and foie gras). Around midnight it morphs into a club.

LE REX CLUB CLUB

(www.rexclub.com; 5 bd Poissonnière, 2e; Wed-Sat; Bonne Nouvelle) Attached to the art deco Grand Rex cinema, this is Paris' premier house and techno venue where some of the world's hottest DJs strut their stuff on a 70-speaker, multidiffusion sound system.

SOCIAL CLUB CLUB

Map p388 (www.parissocialclub.com; 142 rue Montmartre, 2e; Wed-Sun; Grands Boulevards) These subterranean rooms showcasing electro, hip hop, funk and live acts are a magnet for clubbers who take their music seriously. Across the street at No 146 is the cafe where French socialist Jean Jaurès was assassinated in 1914.

LA CHAMPMESLÉ BAR

Map p388 (www.lachampmesle.com; 4 rue Chabanais, 2e; daily; Pyramides) The *grande dame* of Parisian dyke bars, around since 1979, is a cosy, relaxed spot that attracts an older crowd (about 75% are lesbians, the rest mostly gay men). Expect cabaret nights, tarot-card reading, fortune-telling sessions and art exhibitions.

LE TROISÈME LIEU BAR

Map p392 (62 rue Quincampoix, 4e; Tue-Sun; Rambuteau) Billing itself as *la cantine des ginettes armées* (canteen of armed gals), this kooky place for chic young lesbians is part bar, part club, part restaurant. There's a large, colourful bar and big wooden tables at street level, with good-value meals available. The vaulted cellar below leaves space for dancing to DJs (house, electro) and rock/alternative music concerts.

ENTERTAINMENT

COMÉDIE FRANÇAISE THEATRE

Map p388 (www.comedie-francaise.fr; place Colette, 1er; Palais Royal–Musée du Louvre) Founded in 1680 under Louis XIV, the 'French Comedy' theatre bases its repertoire around the works of classic French playwrights. The theatre has its roots in an earlier company directed by Molière at the Palais Royal – the French playwright and actor was seized by a convulsion on stage during the fourth performance of the

PARIS' FILM ARCHIVE

Cinemas showing films set in Paris are the centrepiece of the city's film archive, the **Forum des Images** (Map p392; www.forumdesimages.net; 1 Grande Galerie, Porte St-Eustache, Forum des Halles, 1er; 12.30-11.30pm Tue-Fri, from 2pm Sat & Sun; Les Halles). Created in 1988 to establish 'an audiovisual memory bank of Paris', and recently renovated in dramatic shades of pink, grey and black, the five-screen centre has a new library and research centre with newsreels, documentaries and advertising. Check its program online including thematic series and frequent festivals and events.

Imaginary Invalid in 1673 and died later at his home on nearby rue de Richelieu.

Admire an oversized replica of Molière's director chair outside the Comédie Française on place Colette.

OPÉRA COMIQUE — OPERA

Map p388 (www.opera-comique.com; 1 place Boïeldieu, 2e; Ⓜ Richelieu Drouot) This century-old hall has premiered many important French operas and continues to host classic and less-known works.

THÉÂTRE DU CHÂTELET — CLASSICAL

Map p392 (www.chatelet-theatre.com; 1 place du Châtelet, 2e; Ⓜ Châtelet) This venue hosts concerts as well as operas, musical performances, theatre, ballet and popular Sunday-morning concerts.

THÉÂTRE DE LA VILLE — DANCE

Map p392 (www.theatredelaville-paris.com; 2 place du Châtelet, 2e; Ⓜ Châtelet) It hosts theatre and music too but Théâtre de la Ville is best known for its contemporary dance productions.

SHOPPING

There's no denying it or escaping it, so why not embrace it; the 1e and 2e *arrondissements* are mostly about fashion. Indeed the Sentier district is something of a garment heaven, while rue Étienne Marcel, place des Victoires and rue du Jour flaunt prominent labels and shoe shops. Nearby rue Montmartre and rue Tiquetonne are the streets to shop for streetwear and avant-garde designs; the easternmost part of the 1e around Palais Royal, for fancy period and conservative label fashion.

TOP CHOICE DIDIER LUDOT — FASHION

Map p388 (www.didierludot.fr; 19-20 & 23-24 Galerie de Montpensier, 1er; Ⓜ Palais Royal–Musée du Louvre) In the rag trade since 1975, collector Didier Ludot sells the city's finest couture creations of yesteryear in his exclusive twinset of boutiques. Didier also hosts exhibitions and has published a book portraying the evolution of the little black dress, brilliantly brought to life in his boutique that sells just that, **La Petite Robe Noire** (Map p388; 125 Galerie de Valois, 1er; Ⓜ Palais Royal–Musée du Louvre).

E DEHILLERIN — HOMEWARES

Map p392 (www.dehillerin.com; 18-20 rue Coquillière, 1er; ⊙9am-12.30pm & 2-6pm Mon & Wed-Fri, 8am-6pm Tue & Sat; Ⓜ Les Halles) Founded in 1820, this extraordinary two-level store – think old-fashioned warehouse rather than shiny chic boutique – carries an incredible selection of professional-quality *matériel de cuisine* (kitchenware). Poultry scissors, turbot poacher, old-fashioned copper pot or Eiffel Tower–shaped cake tin – it's all here.

COLETTE — CONCEPT STORE

Map p388 (www.colette.fr; 213 rue St-Honoré, 1er; Ⓜ Tuileries) Uber-hip is an understatement. Ogle at designer fashion on the 1st floor, and streetwear, limited-edition sneakers, art books, music, gadgets and other hi-tech, inventive and/or plain unusual items on the ground floor. End with a drink in the basement 'water bar' and pick up free design magazines and flyers for some of the city's hippest happenings by the door upon leaving.

PASSAGE DES PANORAMAS — SHOPPING ARCADE

Map p388 (10 rue St-Marc, 2e; Ⓜ Bourse) Built in 1800, this is the oldest covered arcade in Paris and the first to be lit by gas (1817). It's a bit faded around the edges now, but retains a real 19th-century charm with several outstanding eateries, a theatre from where spectators would come out to shop during the interval, and autograph dealer Arnaud Magistry (at No 60).

ROOM SERVICE — FASHION

Map p392 (www.roomservice.fr; 52 rue d'Argout, 2e; Ⓜ Les Halles) *'Atelier Vintage'* (vintage workshop) is the thrust of this chic boutique which reinvents vintage pieces as new. Scarves, headpieces, sequins, bangles and beads casually strung up to be admired...the place oozes the femininity and refinement of an old-fashioned Parisian boudoir.

2WS — FASHION

Map p392 (www.2ws.fr; 68 rue Jean-Jacques Rousseau, 1er; Ⓜ Étienne Marcel) As much about street art as wear, this fashion boutique with rough concrete floor and industrial fittings is achingly hip. DJs spin tunes Saturday afternoons, and tank tops, reverse sweatshirts and jumpsuits are the backbone of its lifestyle range for men, women and kids.

GALIGNANI
BOOKS

Map p388 (http://galignani.com; 224 rue de Rivoli, 1er; MConcorde) Proudly claiming to be the 'first English bookshop established on the continent', this ode to literature stocks French and English books and is the best spot in Paris for picking up just-published titles.

ANTOINE
FASHION

Map p388 (10 av de l'Opéra, 1er; ⊙10.30am-3pm & 4-6.30pm Mon-Sat; MPyramides or Palais Royal–Musée du Louvre) Antoine has been the Parisian master of bespoke canes, umbrellas, fans and gloves since 1745.

JAMIN PUECH
FASHION

Map p388 (www.jamin-puech.com; 26 rue Cambon, 1er; MConcorde) Among Paris' most creative handbag designers, Jamin Puech is known for its bold mix of colours, fabrics, leathers and textures – lots of beads, pompoms, shells, feathers and so on. If you're all about label spotting, you'll be impressed to learn its Cocotte handbag starred in *Sex in the City 2*.

COMPTOIR DE LA GASTRONOMIE
FOOD, DRINK

Map p392 (www.comptoir-gastronomie.com; 34 rue Montmartre, 1er; ⊙6am-8pm Mon, 9am-8pm Tue-Sat; MLes Halles) This elegant *épicerie fine* (specialist grocer) stocks a scrumptious array of gourmet goods to take away; it adjoins a striking art nouveau dining room dating to 1894.

LIBRAIRIE GOURMANDE
BOOKS

Map p388 (www.librairie-gourmande.fr; 92 rue Montmartre, 1er; ⊙11am-7pm Mon-Sat; MSentier) The city's leading bookshop dedicated to things culinary and gourmet.

WH SMITH
BOOKS

Map p388 (www.whsmith.fr; 248 rue de Rivoli, 1er; ⊙9am-7pm Mon-Sat, 12.30-7pm Sun; MConcorde) This branch of the British-owned chain is supposedly Paris' largest English-language bookshop.

ALLSAINTS SPITALFIELDS
FASHION

Map p392 (www.allsaints.com; 49 rue Étienne Marcel, 2e; MSentier) The industrial design of this British fashion house is eye-catching. Hundreds of vintage sewing machines fill its windows and garments inside are hung on old bits of hand-operated machinery.

LOCAL KNOWLEDGE

BACKSTAGE AT THE FLICKS

A trip to the 1932 art-deco cinematic icon **Le Grand Rex** (www.legrandrex.com; 1 bd Poissonnière, 2e; tour adult/child €9.80/8; ⊙tours 10am-7pm Wed-Sun; MBonne Nouvelle) is like no other trip to the flicks. Screenings aside, the cinema runs 50-minute behind-the-scenes tours (English soundtracks available) during which visitors – tracked by a sensor slung around their neck – are whisked right up (via a lift) behind the giant screen, tour a soundstage and get to have fun in a recording studio. Whizz-bang special effects along the way will stun adults and kids alike.

AESOP
COSMETICS

Map p388 (www.aesop.com; 256 rue St-Honoré, 1er; MPalais Royal–Musée du Louvre) Browsing this Australian boutique is as much about admiring smart design as swooning over the lavender stems, camomile buds, roses, parsley seeds and other plants (or parts) that go into this sophisticated range of hair, skin and body-care products.

KABUKI FEMME
FASHION

Map p392 (www.barbarabui.com; 25 rue Étienne Marcel, 2e; MÉtienne Marcel) Opened some 20 years ago, this is the shop that brought Barbara Bui to world attention. Her own eponymous store is next door and you'll find Kabuki for men two doors down. Judicious selections from other brands too, including Prada, Balenciaga, Stella McCartney, Yves Saint Laurent and Dior.

KILIWATCH
FASHION

Map p392 (http://espacekiliwatch.fr; 64 rue Tiquetonne; ⊙2-7.15pm Mon, 11am-7.45pm Tue-Sat; MÉtienne Marcel) A Parisian institution, Kiliwatch gets jam-packed with hip guys and gals rummaging through racks of new and used streetwear. Startling vintage range of hats and boots plus art/photography books, eyewear and the latest sneakers.

MARITHÉ & FRANÇOIS GIRBAUD
FASHION

Map p392 (www.girbaud.com; 38 rue Étienne Marcel, 2e; MÉtienne Marcel) This globetrotting designer couple call themselves 'jeanologists', having devoted themselves to more than 30 years of denim. They have four other boutiques in Paris.

BUKIYA FASHION

Map p388 (12 rue Thérèse, 1er; Ⓜ Pyramides) Stylish in its simplicity, this minimalist white space sells Japanese *tenugi* (headscarves) and ecofriendly *furosiki* (square wrapping cloths). Don't miss the socks with toes and the kimonos downstairs.

LAVINIA FOOD, DRINK

Map p388 (www.lavinia.com; 3 bd de la Madeleine, 8e; Ⓜ Madeleine) Among the largest and most exclusive drinks shops is this bastion of booze with a top collection of *eaux-de-vie* (fruit brandies).

LEGRAND FILLES & FILS FOOD, DRINK

Map p388 (www.caves-legrand.com; 1 rue de la Banque, 2e; Ⓜ Pyramides) This shop, tucked inside Galerie Vivienne since 1880, sells fine wine and all the accoutrements: corkscrews, tasting glasses, decanters etc. It also has a fancy wine bar, *école du vin* (wine school) and *éspace dégustation* with several tastings a month; check its website for details.

BOÎTES À MUSIQUE ANNA JOLIET GIFTS, SOUVENIRS

Map p388 (www.boitesamusique-paris.com; Passage du Perron, 1er; Ⓜ Pyramides) This wonderful shop at the northern end of the Jardin du Palais Royal specialises in music boxes, new and old, from Switzerland.

Montmartre & Northern Paris

MONTMARTRE & PIGALLE | CLICHY | GARE DU NORD & CANAL ST-MARTIN

Neighbourhood Top Five

❶ Hike up the steps to the **Basilique du Sacré-Cœur** (p131) for panoramic views from the outside and a glittering mosaic within.

❷ Catch a performance at the **Parc de la Villette** (p133), the city's largest cultural playground.

❸ Step back into 19th-century opulence at the elegant **Musée Jaquemart Andre** (p135).

❹ Discover the tombs of French royalty at the **Basilique de St-Denis** (p138).

❺ Treat the kids to a day at the **Cité des Sciences** (p136).

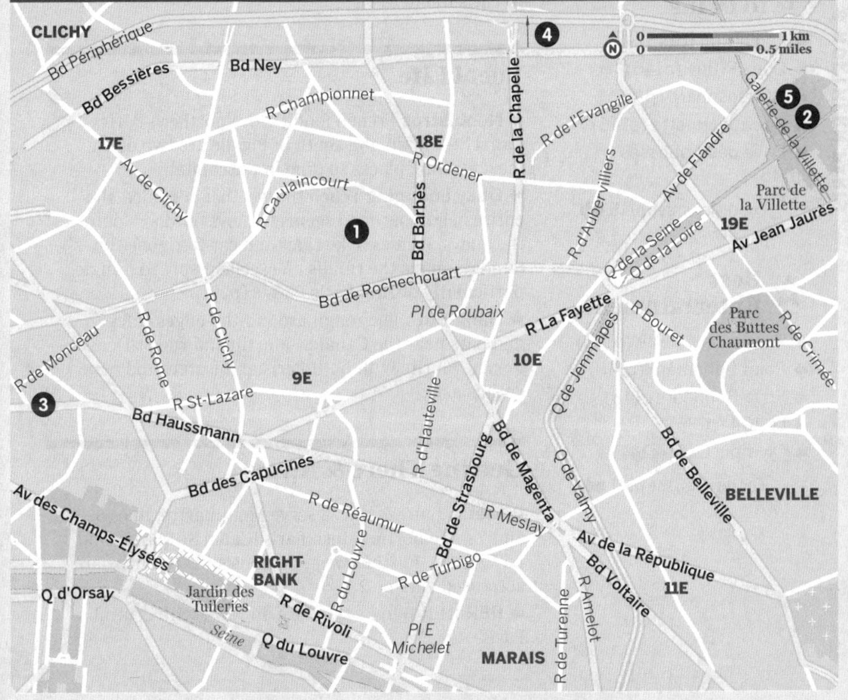

For more detail of this area, see Map p394, p398 and p400 ➡

Lonely Planet's Top Tip

Although gritty, the neighbourhoods in the north and northeast of Paris are fairly safe as far as big cities go. If there's one place you need to stay on your guard, it's at the foot of the hill that leads up to Sacré-Cœur. It's not unusual for pickpockets and con artists to work the crowds here.

Best Places to Eat

- Chez Michel (p142)
- Vivant (p142)
- Cul de Poule (p139)
- Le Verre Volé (p143)
- Le Miroir (p139)

For reviews, see p139

Best Places to Drink

- La Fourmi (p145)
- Chez Prune (p146)
- L'Atmosphère (p146)
- Chez Jeannette (p146)
- Cave des Abbesses (p145)

For reviews, see p145

Best Entertainment

- Parc de la Villette (p133)
- Point Éphemère (p148)
- Rosa Bonheur (p148)
- Le 104 (p136)
- Olympic Café (p147)

For reviews, see p147

Explore: Montmartre & Northern Paris

One of the wellsprings of Parisian myth, Montmartre has always stood apart. Bohemians, revolutionaries, artists, can-can girls and headless martyrs have all played a role in its story, and while it may belong to Paris today, vestiges of the original village – ivy-clad buildings, steep, narrow streets – remain. Crowned by the white domes of Sacré-Cœur, dragged back to earth by red-light Pigalle, it has forever encompassed contrast and conflict.

An ideal place to base yourself, Montmartre is fairly self-contained – it has plenty in the way of sights, cuisine, shopping and entertainment. Most visitors here spend half a day or more exploring the side streets that tumble down from the summit in all directions, searching valiantly for that one perfect vista looking out over the city.

And while packed with crowds, there's still plenty of local life to enjoy – whether in the sizzling culinary hot spot south of Pigalle or the rarely visited streets on the backside of the Butte (as the hill is known).

Some excellent museums are located to the west, beyond place de Clichy, but for a taste of a more modern-day *bobo* (bourgeois bohemian) lifestyle, you'll need to head further east to the Canal St-Martin. The quays here have undergone an urban renaissance in the past decade, making it one of the most vibrant neighbourhoods in Paris today.

Local Life

- **Neobistros** French foodies love northern Paris: Canal St-Martin and south of Pigalle are two of the most exciting places to dine in the capital.
- **Quay Lounging** When the weather gets nice, the entire neighbourhood seems to move outdoors onto the quays. Picnics, bike rides and car-free zones on Sundays make the canals an excellent spot to mingle, particularly during Paris Plages (p28).
- **Hang-outs** The rough-around-the-edges cafes and bars near the Canal St-Martin and rue St-Denis are a favourite with both Parisian hipsters and wine enthusiasts.

Getting There & Away

- **Metro** Lines 2 and 12 serve Montmartre; lines 5 and 7 serve northeastern Paris (Canal St-Martin and La Villette). Further west, the museums in Clichy are acccessed via line 2.
- **RER** RER B links the Gare du Nord with central Paris.

TOP SIGHTS
BASILIQUE DU SACRÉ-CŒUR

Although some may poke fun at Sacré-Cœur's unsubtle design, the view from its parvis (courtyard) is one of those perfect Paris postcards. More than just a basilica, Sacré-Cœur is a veritable experience, from the musicians performing on the steps and the groups of friends picnicking on the hillside park. We can't deny that it's touristy, but beneath it all, Sacré-Cœur's heart still shines gold.

DON'T MISS

- The Views from the Parvis
- The Apse Mosaic *Christ in Majesty*
- The Dome

PRACTICALITIES

- Map p394
- www.sacre-coeur-montmartre.com
- place du Parvis du Sacré Cœur
- Basilica dome admission €5, cash only
- ⏲6am-10.30pm, dome 9am-7pm Apr-Sep, to 5.30pm Oct-Mar
- Ⓜ Anvers

The Basilica

The tranquil basilica may appear to be a place of peacefulness and worship today, but in truth Sacré-Cœur's foundations were laid amid bloodshed and controversy. Its construction began in 1876, in the wake of France's humiliating defeat to Prussia and the chaotic Paris Commune, when workers overthrew the reactionary government and took over the city. The resulting battle for control was essentially a civil war, ending with mass executions, exiles and rampant destruction.

In this context, the construction of an enormous basilica to expiate the city's sins seemed like a gesture of peace and forgiveness – indeed, the 7 million French francs needed to construct the church came solely from the contributions of local Catholics. Unfortunately, the Montmartre location was no coincidence: the conservative old guard desperately wanted to assert their power in what was then a hotbed of revolution. The battle between the two camps – Catholic versus secular, royalists versus republican – raged on, and it wasn't until 1919 that Sacré-Cœur was finally consecrated, even then standing in utter contrast to the bohemian lifestyle that surrounded it.

A PLACE OF PILGRIMAGE

In a sense, atonement here has never stopped: a prayer 'cycle' that began in 1835 before the basilica's completion still continues around the clock, with perpetual adoration of the Blessed Sacrament continually on display above the high altar. The basilica's travertine stone exudes calcite, ensuring it remains white despite weathering and pollution.

In 1944, 13 Allied bombs were dropped on Montmartre, falling just next to Sacré-Coeur. Although the stained glass windows all shattered from the force of the explosions, miraculously no one died and the basilica sustained no other damage.

While criticism of its design and white travertine stone has continued throughout the decades (one poet called it a giant baby's bottle for angels), the interior is enlivened by the glittering apse mosaic *Christ in Majesty*, designed by Luc-Olivier Merson in 1922 and one of the largest in the world.

The Dome

Outside, some 234 spiralling steps lead you to the basilica's dome, which affords one of Paris' most spectacular panoramas; they say you can see for 30km on a clear day. In the tower above and weighing in at 19 tonnes, the bell, known as La Savoyarde, is the largest in France. The chapel-lined crypt, visited in conjunction with the dome, is huge but not very interesting.

You can avoid some of the climb up to the basilica with the short but useful **funicular railway** (one metro ticket; ⏲6am-midnight) or the **tourist train** (€6; ⏲10am-midnight Apr-Sep, 10am-6pm Oct-Mar), which leaves from place Blanche.

ATLANTIDE PHOTOTRAVEL/ CORBIS©

TOP SIGHTS
PARC DE LA VILLETTE

The largest park in Paris, Parc de la Villette is a cultural centre, kids' playground and landscaped urban space all rolled into one. The French love of geometric forms defines the layout – the colossal mirror-like sphere of the Géode cinema, an undulating strip of corrugated steel stretching for hundreds of metres, the bright-red cubical pavilions known as folies – but it's the intersection of two canals, the Ourcq and the St-Denis, that brings the most natural and popular element: water. Although it's a fair hike from central Paris, consider the trip here for one of the many events or if you have children.

Events throughout the year are staged in the wonderful old Grande Halle (formerly a slaughterhouse - the Parisian cattle market was located here from 1867 to 1974), Le Zénith, the Cabaret Sauvage (p148) and the Cité de la Musique (p149). The new **Paris Philharmonic hall** (Map p400; Parc de la Villette, 19e; MPorte de Pantin) is due to be completed here in 2015.

DON'T MISS

- Evening Performances
- The Themed Gardens
- The Cité des Sciences (p136)

PRACTICALITIES

- Map p400
- www.villette.com
- MPorte de la Villette or Porte de Pantin

For Children

When the weather's pleasant, children (and adults) will enjoy exploring the numerous themed gardens, the best of which double as playgrounds. These include the Jardin du Dragon (Dragon Garden), with an enormous dragon slide between the Géode and the nearest bridge, the Jardin des Dunes (Dunes Garden) and Jardin des Miroirs (Mirror Garden).

However, for the young ones, the star attraction is the Cité des Sciences (p136) and its attached cinemas. Here, kids from ages two and up can explore a variety of interactive exhibits: the brilliant Cité des Enfants is probably the most popular section, with a construction site, TV studio, robots and water-based physics experiments all designed for children.

An information centre is at the park's southern edge; pick up a map here so you can get your bearings.

SIGHTS

Montmartre & Pigalle

BASILIQUE DU SACRÉ-CŒUR BASILICA

See p131.

PLACE DU TERTRE CITY SQUARE

Map p394 (MAbbesses) It would be difficult to miss the place du Tertre, one of the most touristy spots in all of Paris. Although today it's filled with visitors, buskers and portrait artists, it was originally the main square of the village of Montmartre before it was incorporated into the city proper.

One of the more popular claims of Montmartre mythology is staked to La Mère Catherine at No 6: in 1814, so it's said, Cossack soldiers first introduced the term *bistro* (Russian for 'quickly') into the French lexicon. Another big moment came on Christmas Eve, 1898, when Louis Renault's first car was driven up the Butte to the place du Tertre, igniting the start of the French auto industry.

ÉGLISE ST-PIERRE DE MONTMARTRE CHURCH

Map p394 (MAbbesses) This church, all that remains of the former Benedictine Abbey of Montmartre, dates back to the 12th century and is one of the oldest in Paris, though it has been much restored. Built atop a Roman temple to Mars, it was witness to the founding of the Jesuits in 1534, who met in the crypt under the guidance of Ignatius of Loyola.

There are some who say that the name Montmartre is derived from 'Mons Martis' (Latin for Mount of Mars); others prefer the Christian 'Mont Martyr' (Mount of the Martyr), a reference to the 3rd-century St Denis. According to legend, St Denis walked across Montmartre and on to the site of what is today's Basilique de St-Denis after having been beheaded by Roman priests.

MUSÉE DE MONTMARTRE HISTORY MUSEUM

Map p394 (www.museedemontmartre.fr; 12 rue Cortot, 18e; adult/18-25yr/10-17yr €8/6/4; 10am-6pm; MLamarck–Caulaincourt) The Montmartre Museum displays paintings, lithographs and documents mostly relating to the area's rebellious and bohemian past. It's located in one of the oldest houses in Montmartre, a 17th-century manor home where over a dozen artists, including Renoir and Utrillo, once resided. There's an excellent bookshop here that sells small bottles of the wine produced from grapes grown in the Clos Montmartre.

Although it is undergoing significant renovations, the museum should remain open.

MUSÉE DE LA HALLE ST-PIERRE ART MUSEUM

Map p394 (www.hallesaintpierre.org; 2 rue Ronsard, 18e; adult/senior & under 26yr €8/6.50; 10am-6pm daily, noon-6pm Mon-Fri Aug; MAnvers) Founded in 1986, this museum and gallery is in the lovely old, covered St Peter's Market. It focuses on the primitive and Art Brut schools; there is no permanent collection but the museum stages three temporary exhibitions a year. There's a lovely cafe on-site.

DALÍ ESPACE MONTMARTRE ART MUSEUM

Map p394 (www.daliparis.com; 11 rue Poulbot; adult/senior/8-25yr €11/7/6; 10am-6pm, to 8pm Jul & Aug; MAbbesses) More than 300 works by Salvador Dalí (1904–89), the flamboyant Catalan surrealist printmaker, painter, sculptor and self-promoter, are on display at this surrealist-style basement museum located just west of place du Tertre. The collection includes Dalí's strange sculptures (most in reproduction), lithographs, many of his illustrations and furniture, including the famous Mae West lips sofa.

FREE **MUSÉE DE LA VIE ROMANTIQUE** MUSEUM

Map p394 (www.vie-romantique.paris.fr; 16 rue Chaptal, 9e; permanent collections free; 10am-6pm Tue-Sun; MBlanche or St-Georges) This small museum is dedicated to two artists active during the Romantic era: the writer George Sand and the painter Ary Scheffer. Located at the end of an atmospheric cobbled lane, which, incidentally, would make a perfect film location, the villa housing the museum originally belonged to Scheffer. The museum was the setting for popular salons of the day, attended by such notable figures as Delacroix, Liszt and Chopin (Sand's lover).

The ground floor is devoted to Sand and is full of paintings, objets d'art and personal effects, while the 1st floor displays a selection of Scheffer's portraits.

CIMETIÈRE DE MONTMARTRE — CEMETERY

Map p394 (admission free; 8am-5.30pm Mon-Fri, from 8.30am Sat, from 9am Sun; MPlace de Clichy) Established in 1798, this 11-hectare cemetery is perhaps the most celebrated necropolis in Paris after Père Lachaise. It contains the graves of writers Émile Zola (whose ashes are now in the Panthéon), Alexandre Dumas (fils) and Stendhal, composers Jacques Offenbach and Hector Berlioz, artist Edgar Degas, film director François Truffaut and dancer Vaslav Nijinsky, among others.

The entrance closest to the Butte de Montmartre is at the end of av Rachel, just off bd de Clichy, or down the stairs from 10 rue Caulaincourt. Maps showing the location of the tombs are available free from the **conservation office** (20 av Rachel) at the cemetery's entrance.

MUSÉE DE L'ÉROTISME — ART MUSEUM

Map p394 (www.musee-erotisme.com; 72 bd de Clichy, 18e; adult/student €10/6; 10am-2am; MBlanche) The Museum of Erotic Art attempts to raise around 2000 titillating statuary, stimulating sexual aids and fetishist items to a loftier plane, with antique and modern erotic art from four continents spread out across several floors. Some of the exhibits are, well, breathtaking, to say the least. Open late.

Clichy

MUSÉE NISSIM DE CAMONDO — HISTORIC RESIDENCE

Map p401 (www.lesartsdecoratifs.fr; 63 rue de Monceau, 8e; adult/18-25yr/under 18yr €7.50/5.50/free; 10am-5.30pm Wed-Sun; MMonceau or Villiers) The Nissim de Camondo Museum, housed in a sumptuous mansion modelled on the Petit Trianon at Versailles, displays 18th-century furniture, wood panelling, tapestries, porcelain and other objets d'art collected by Count Moïse de Camondo, a Sephardic Jewish banker who moved from Constantinople to Paris in the late 19th century.

He bequeathed the mansion and his collection to the state on the proviso that it would be turned into a museum named in memory of his son Nissim (1892–1917), a pilot killed in action during WWI. It is part of Les Arts Décoratifs, the trio of museums in the Louvre's Rohan Wing.

TOP SIGHTS MUSÉE JACQUEMART-ANDRÉ

If you belonged to the cream of Parisian society in the late 19th century, chances are you would have been invited to one of the dazzling soirées held at this mansion. The home of art collectors Nélie Jacquemart and Édouard André, this opulent residence was designed in the then-fashionable eclectic style, which combined elements from different eras – seen here in the presence of Greek and Roman antiquities, Egyptian artefacts, period furnishings and portraits by Dutch masters.

A wander through the 16 rooms offers an absorbing glimpse of the lifestyle and tastes of Parisian high society: from the library, hung with canvases by Rembrandt and Van Dyck, to the marvelous Jardin d'Hiver – a glass-paned garden room backed by a magnificent double-helix staircase. Upstairs is more art – an impressive collection of Italian Renaissance works by Botticelli, Donatello and Titian, among others.

The mansion's architect, Henri Parent, was nearly hired to work on the even more prestigious Paris opera house, Palais Garnier (p92) – he was beat out only by the then-unknown Charles Garnier.

After the tour, stop in at the **salon de thé** (☎11.45am to 5.30pm), which serves pastries as extravagant as the decor.

DON'T MISS...

- The Library
- The Jardin d'Hiver
- The Italian Art Collection

PRACTICALITIES

- Map p401
- ☎01 45 62 11 59
- www.musee-jacquemart-andre.com
- 158 bd Haussmann
- adult/7-17yr €11/9.50
- 10am-6pm, to 9.30pm Mon & Sat during temporary exhibits
- MMiromesnil

FREE MUSÉE CERNUSCHI ART MUSEUM

Map p401 (www.cernuschi.paris.fr; 7 av Vélasquez, 8e; permanent collections free; ⌚10am-6pm Tue-Sun; Ⓜ Villiers) The Cernuschi Museum is comprised of an excellent and rare collection of ancient Chinese art (funerary statues, bronzes, ceramics), much of which predates the Tang dynasty (618–907), in addition to diverse pieces from Japan. Milan banker and philanthropist Henri Cernuschi (1821–96), who settled in Paris before the unification of Italy, assembled the collection during a world tour from 1871–73.

Gare du Nord & Canal St-Martin

PARC DE LA VILLETTE PARK

See p133.

CITÉ DES SCIENCES SCIENCE MUSEUM

Map p400 (☎01 40 05 12 12; www.cite-sciences.fr; Parc de la Villette; adult/under 26yr €8/6; ⌚10am-6pm Tue-Sat, to 7pm Sun; Ⓜ Porte de la Villette) This is the city's top museum for kids, with three floors of hands-on exhibits for children aged two and up, plus two special-effects cinemas, a planetarium and a retired submarine. The only drawback is that each exhibit has a separate admission fee (though some combined tickets do exist), so you'll have to do some pretrip research in order to figure out what's most appropriate.

Make sure to reserve tickets in advance via the website if you plan on coming on a weekend or during school holidays. Packing a picnic is also a good idea.

FREE LE 104 GALLERY

Map p398 (www.104.fr; 104 rue d'Aubervilliers or 5 rue Curial, 19e; admission free; ⌚noon-7pm Tue-Fri, 11am-7pm Sat & Sun; Ⓜ Stalingrad or Crimée) A former funeral parlour turned city-funded art space, Le 104 has provided a much-needed jolt of vitality to an otherwise neglected neighbourhood. Spread out over a massive 39,000 sq metres, the complex is a hive of activity: a random wander through the public areas will turn up breakdancers, wacky art installations and rehearsing actors.

Check the schedule for events to make the most of it: there's circus, theatre, music, monthly balls and even magic shows. Some things are free; others require admission. Also on-site are a pizza truck, a cafe and a restaurant-bar.

CANAL ST-MARTIN PARK

Map p398 (Ⓜ République, Jaurès, Jacques Bonsergent) The tranquil, 4.5km-long Canal St-Martin was inaugurated in 1825 to provide a shipping link between the Seine and the northeastern Parisian suburbs. Emerging from below ground near place République, its shaded towpaths take you past locks, metal bridges and ordinary Parisian neighbourhoods. It's a great place for a romantic stroll or cycle.

Note that many neighbourhood shops and bistros here are closed on Sundays and Mondays.

CANAL CRUISES

Everyone takes the river boats down the Seine, but if you're up for something slightly different, why not try a canal cruise? Two companies run 2½-hour trips along the Canal St-Martin, chugging back and forth between central Paris and Parc de la Villette. Boats go at a leisurely pace, passing through four locks and an underground section (livened up somewhat by an art installation).

Canauxrama (Map p398; ☎01 42 39 15 00; www.canauxrama.com; adult/student & senior/4-12yr €16/12/8.50) Departures are at 9.45am and 2.30pm from the Port de l'Arsenal at the Bastille and Parc de la Villette. There are also evening cruises on Fridays and Saturdays in July and August.

Paris Canal Croisières (Map p422; ☎01 42 40 96 97; www.pariscanal.com; adult/senior & 12-25yr/4-11yr €19/16/12; ⌚mid-Mar–mid-Nov) Cruises depart from near the Musée d'Orsay (quai Anatole France) at 9.30am and from Parc de la Villette at 2.30pm.

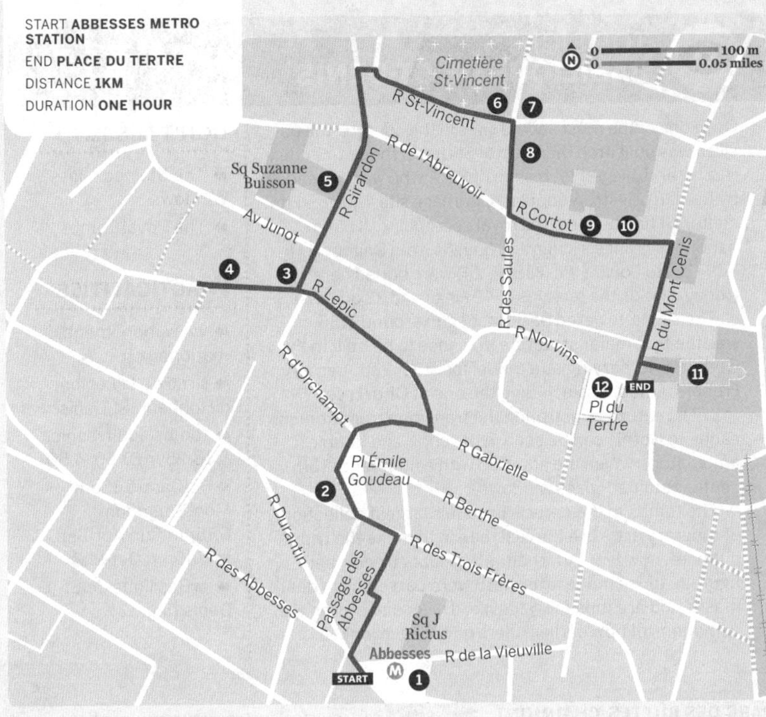

Neighbourhood Walk

Montmartre Tour

Begin the walk at ❶ **place des Abbesses**, where Hector Guimard's iconic art nouveau metro entrance (1900) still stands. Deep underground, beneath a maze of gypsum mines, is one of Paris' deepest metro stations.

Exit the square, heading up the passage des Abbesses to place Émile Goudeau. At No 11bis you'll find the ❷ **Bateau Lavoir**, where Max Jacob, Amedeo Modigliani and Pablo Picasso – who painted his seminal *Les Demoiselles d'Avignon* (1907) here – once lived in great poverty. Originally at No 13, the Bateau Lavoir burned down in 1970 and was rebuilt in 1978.

Continue the climb up rue Lepic to Montmartre's two surviving windmills: the ❸ **Moulin Radet** (now a restaurant), and, 100m west, the ❹ **Moulin Blute-Fin**. In the 19th century, they were turned into the open-air dance hall Le Moulin de la Galette, immortalised by Renoir in his 1876 tableau *Le Bal du Moulin de la Galette* (displayed at the Musée d'Orsay). Just north of the windmills is Sq Suzanne Buisson, which holds a ❺ **statue of St-Denis**, the 3rd-century martyr and patron saint of France who was beheaded by Roman priests.

After passing by the ❻ **Cimetière St-Vincent**, where local painter Maurice Utrillo is buried, you'll come upon the celebrated cabaret ❼ **Au Lapin Agile**, which features a mural of a rabbit jumping out of a cooking pot by caricaturist André Gill. Just opposite is the ❽ **Clos Montmartre**, a small vineyard dating from 1933.

Up the hill is Montmartre's oldest building, a manor house built in the 17th century. Once a home to painters Renoir, Utrillo and Raoul Dufy, it's now the ❾ **Musée de Montmartre**. Continue on past composer ❿ **Eric Satie's former residence** (No 6;) and then turn right onto rue du Mont Cenis; you'll soon come across the historic ⓫ **Église St-Pierre de Montmartre**. End the tour at the busy ⓬ **place du Tertre**, once the main square of the village.

TOP SIGHTS
BASILIQUE DE ST-DENIS

Once one of the most sacred sites in the country, the basilica was built atop the tomb of St Denis, the 3rd-century martyr and alleged 1st bishop of Paris who was beheaded by Roman priests. A popular pilgrimage site, by the sixth century it had become the royal necropolis: all but a handful of France's kings and queens from Dagobert I (r 629–39) to Louis XVIII (r 1814–24) were buried here (today it holds the remains of 42 kings and 32 queens).

The single-towered basilica, begun around 1136, was the first major structure in France to be built in the Gothic style, serving as a model for other 12th-century French cathedrals, including the one at **Chartres** (p277). Features illustrating the transition from Romanesque to Gothic can be seen in the choir and double ambulatory, which are adorned with a number of 12th-century stained-glass windows.

The tombs in the crypt – Europe's largest collection of funerary art – are the real reason to make the trip out here, however. Adorned with *gisants* (recumbent figures), those made after 1285 were carved from death masks and are thus fairly lifelike; earlier sculptures are depictions of how earlier rulers might have looked.

DON'T MISS...

- The Stained-Glass Windows
- The Royal Tombs

PRACTICALITIES

- www.monuments-nationaux.fr
- 1 rue de la Légion d'Honneur, St Denis
- tombs adult/senior & 18-25yr €7.50/4.50
- 10am-6.15pm Mon-Sat, noon-6.15pm Sun Apr-Sep, to 5.15pm Oct-Mar
- M Basilique de St-Denis (line 13)

PARC DES BUTTES-CHAUMONT PARK

Map p400 (rue Manin & rue Botzaris, 19e; 7.30am-11pm May-Sep, to 9pm Oct-Apr; M Buttes-Chaumont or Botzaris) This quirky park is one of the city's largest green spaces; its landscaped slopes hide grottoes, waterfalls, a lake and even an island topped with a temple to Sybil. Once a gypsum quarry and rubbish dump, it was given its present form by Baron Haussmann in time for the opening of the 1867 Exposition Universelle.

It's a favourite with Parisians, who come here to practise tai chi, take the kids to a puppet show or simply to relax with a bottle of wine and a picnic dinner. The tracks of an abandoned 19th-century railway line (La Petite Ceinture, which once circled Paris) also run through the park.

CITÉ DE LA MUSIQUE MUSIC MUSEUM

Map p400 (www.cite-musique.fr; 221 av Jean Jaurès, 19e; noon-6pm Tue-Sat, 10am-6pm Sun; M Porte de Pantin) The Cité de la Musique, on the southern edge of Parc de la Villette, is a striking, triangular-shaped concert hall whose mission is to introduce music from around the world to Parisians. The **Musée de la Musique** (Music Museum; Map p400; adult/under 26yr €8/free) inside displays some 900 rare musical instruments; you can hear many of them being played on the audioguide.

Next door is the new Paris Philharmonic hall (estimated opening 2015) as well as the prestigious Conservatoire National Supérieur de Musique et de Danse, a top school for classical musicians and dancers.

MUSÉE DE L'ÉVANTAIL MUSEUM

Map p398 (www.annehoguet.fr; 2 bd de Strasbourg, 10e; adult €6; 2-6pm Mon-Wed; M Strasbourg-St-Denis) Around 900 handheld fans are on display here, dating as far back as the mid-18th century. The small museum is housed in what was once a well-known fan manufactory, and its original showroom, dating from 1893, is sublime. It closes during August.

PORTE ST-DENIS & PORTE ST-MARTIN LANDMARK

Map p398 (cnr rue du Faubourg St-Denis & bd St-Denis, 10e; M Strasbourg St-Denis) These two triumphal arches were both built in the late 17th century to commemorate victories by Louis XIV's armies. At the time of their construction, they replaced gates in the Paris city walls.

EATING

Not much changes in the staid western Paris culinary scene, but once you cross over that invisible border somewhere in the middle of the 9e *arrondissement*, it's a different world. Every year sees a flurry of new openings in the neighbourhoods south of Pigalle or along the Canal St-Martin, and the young chefs at work here boast some of the most exciting dining venues in Paris today.

Montmartre & Pigalle

LE MIROIR — BISTRO €€

Map p394 (☎01 46 06 50 73; 94 rue des Martyrs, 18e; lunch menus €18 & dinner €25-40; ⏲lunch Tue-Sun, dinner Tue-Sat; Ⓜ Abbesses) This unassuming modern bistro is smack in the middle of the Montmartre tourist trail, yet it remains a local favourite. There are lots of delightful pâtés and rillettes to start off with – guinea hen with dates, duck with mushrooms, haddock and lemon – followed by well-prepared standards like stuffed veal shoulder.

The lunch special includes a glass of wine, coffee and dessert; the Sunday brunch also gets the thumbs up. If you feel like imbibing afterwards, pop into its wine shop across the street.

LE PANTRUCHE — BISTRO €€

Map p394 (☎01 48 78 55 60; www.lepantruche.com; 3 rue Victor Masse, 9e; menus lunch/dinner €17/32; ⏲Mon-Fri; Ⓜ Pigalle) Named after a nearby 19th-century theatre, classy Pantruche has been making waves in the already crowded dining hot spot of South Pigalle. No surprise, then, that it hits all the right notes: seasonal bistro fare, reasonable prices and an intimate setting. The menu runs from classics (steak with béarnaise sauce) to more daring creations (scallops served in a parmesan broth with cauliflower mousseline). It's wise to reserve well in advance.

TOP CHOICE CUL DE POULE — MODERN FRENCH €€

Map p394 (☎01 53 16 13 07; 53 rue des Martyrs, 9e; 2-/3-course lunch menus €15/18, dinner €23/28; ⏲closed Sun lunch; Ⓜ Pigalle) With plastic orange cafeteria seats outside looking less than inviting, you probably wouldn't wander into the Cul de Poule by accident. But the light-hearted spirit (yes, there is a mounted chicken's derrière on the wall) is deceiving; this is one of the best and most affordable kitchens in Pigalle, with excellent neobistro fare that emphasises quality ingredients from the French countryside.

LE GARDE TEMPS — MODERN FRENCH €€

Map p394 (☎09 81 48 50 55; 19bis rue Pierre Fontaine, 9e; 2-/3-course menus €22/31; ⏲lunch & dinner Mon-Fri; Ⓜ Pigalle) The chalkboard menus at this contemporary bistro are framed and hung on the walls, and thankfully the promise of gastronomic art does not disappoint. Old bistro standards have been swept away in favour of more imaginative creations (fondant of red cabbage topped with quail confit) and – here's where the Garde Temps scores big points – the dinner prices aren't much more than that ho-hum cafe down the street.

LE CAFÉ QUI PARLE — MODERN FRENCH €€

Map p394 (☎01 46 06 06 88; 24 rue Caulaincourt, 18e; lunch 2-/3-course menus €12.50/17, mains €17-25; ⏲8.30am-11pm Mon-Sat, lunch Sun;

WORTH A DETOUR

MUSÉE D'ART ET D'HISTOIRE

To the southwest of the Basilica de St-Denis is the **Museum of Art and History** (www.musee-saint-denis.fr; 22bis rue Gabriel Péri, St-Denis; adult/student & senior €5/3; ⏲10am-5.30pm Mon, Wed & Fri, to 8pm Thu, 2-6.30pm Sat & Sun; Ⓜ St-Denis Porte de Paris), housed in a restored Carmelite convent founded in 1625 and later presided over by Louise de France, the youngest daughter of Louis XV. Displays include reconstructions of the Carmelites' cells, an 18th-century apothecary and, in the archaeology section, items found during excavations around the basilica.

There's a section on modern art, with a collection of work by a local son, the surrealist artist Paul Éluard (1895–1952), as well as an important collection of politically charged posters, cartoons, lithographs and paintings from the 1871 Paris Commune.

(📶; Ⓜ Lamarck–Caulaincourt or Blanche) The Café qui Parle is a fine example of where modern-day eateries are headed in Paris. It offers inventive, reasonably priced dishes prepared by owner-chef Damian Moeuf amid comfortable surroundings. Regulars love the art on the walls and ancient safes down below (the building was once a bank), but not as much as the brunch, served from 10am on Saturdays and Sundays.

LE PETIT TRIANON CAFE €

Map p394 (☎01 44 92 78 08; www.trianoncafe.fr; 80 boulevard Rochechouart, 18e; lunch menu €13.20, mains €6.50-17.90; ⏰10am-2pm; Ⓜ Anvers) With its large windows and a few carefully chosen antiques, this recently revived belle époque cafe at the foot of Montmartre feels about as timeless as the Butte itself. Dating back to 1894 and attached to the century-old Le Trianon theatre, it's no stretch to imagine artists like Toulouse-Lautrec and crowds of show-goers once filling the place in the evening.

Well-prepared standards (steak tartare, grilled swordfish) are served throughout the day; you can also just stop in for a drink.

LA MASCOTTE SEAFOOD, CAFE €€

Map p394 (☎01 46 06 28 15; www.la-mascotte-montmartre.com; 52 rue des Abbesses, 18e; lunch/dinner menus €25/41; ⏰7am-midnight; Ⓜ Abbesses) Founded in 1889, this unassuming bar is about as authentic as it gets in Montmartre. It specialises in quality seafood – oysters, lobster, scallops – and regional dishes (Auvergne sausage), but you can also pull up a seat at the bar for a simple glass of wine and a plate of charcuterie.

LE COQ RICO POULTRY €€€

Map p394 (☎01 42 59 82 89; www.lecoqrico.com; 98 rue Lepic, 18e; mains €20-38, whole roast chicken €95; ⏰7am-8.30pm Wed-Mon; Ⓜ Abbesses) The first haute cuisine restaurant to open in Montmartre in years, Le Coq Rico specialises in poultry – and not just any poultry, but red-ribbon birds that have been raised in five-star chicken coops.

A selection of eggs, gizzards, bouillons, foie gras ravioli and other delicacies whet the appetite before the arrival of the pièce de résistance: an entire just-roasted chicken or guineafowl, which can be split up to four ways.

ARNAUD DELMONTEL BOULANGERIE €

Map p394 (39 rue des Martyrs, 9e; ⏰7am-8.30pm Wed-Mon; Ⓜ Pigalle) One of several Montmartre bakeries to win Paris' 'best baguette' prize in the past decade, Delmontel specialises in gorgeous pastries, cakes and a variety of artisanal breads.

LE GRENIER À PAIN BOULANGERIE €

Map p394 (38 rue des Abbesses, 18e; ⏰7.30am-8pm Thu-Mon; Ⓜ Abbesses) The Grenier is another Montmartre bakery that won Paris' 'best baguette' prize (2010), though you'd be forgiven for thinking that their real specialty lies in the savoury *fougasses* (flatbread) and mini breads that come with a range of alluring toppings (fig and goat cheese, bacon and olives).

CRÊPERIE PEN-TY CRÊPES €

Map p394 (☎01 48 74 18 49; 65 rue de Douai, 9e; galettes €3-9.80, crêpes €3.90-8.80; ⏰lunch & dinner to 11pm Mon-Sat; Ⓜ Place de Clichy) Hailed as the best *crêperie* in northern Paris, Pen-Ty is worth the detour – but be sure to book ahead. Need to brush up on Breton Cuisine 101? A *galette* is a savoury crêpe made from buckwheat flour; a regular crêpe is sweet and made from white flour.

LE COQUELICOT BOULANGERIE €

Map p394 (24 rue des Abbesses, 9e; omelettes €6.50, quiche with salad €4.20; ⏰8.30am-5pm; Ⓜ Abbesses) Although nothing to blog about, the Coquelicot bakery is nonetheless a good spot for an easy meal, offering omelettes, quiches, sandwiches and yummy pastries. The outdoor tables occupy a prime location alongside rue des Abbesses. It also serves breakfast.

L'ÉTÉ EN PENTE DOUCE BISTRO €

Map p394 (☎01 42 64 02 67; 23 rue Muller, 18e; mains €9.70-17, dinner menu €20; ⏰noon-midnight daily; Ⓜ Anvers) Parisian terraces don't get much better than this: a secret square wedged in between two flights of steep staircases on the backside of Montmartre, in a neighbourhood that's very much the real thing. Quiches, giant salads and classic dishes like Niçois-style stuffed veggies make up the menu.

MICHELANGELO SICILIAN €€

Map p394 (☎01 42 23 10 77; 3 rue André-Barsacq, 18e; menu €30; ⏰dinner Tue-Sat; Ⓜ Anvers or Abbesses) A one-man show, chef Michelangelo does it all – the shopping, the chopping, the table waiting, the cooking, the sitting down with guests for a glass of wine while the pasta is boiling…it's the equivalent of being invited over to a Sicilian's house for dinner. Michelangelo chooses the menu (three courses, cash only), so you'll have to be somewhat adventurous. Bookings essential.

LE CHÉRI BIBI TRADITIONAL FRENCH **€€**

Map p394 (☎01 42 54 88 96; 15 rue André del Sarte, 18e; menus €23 & €26; ⊙dinner Mon-Sat; Ⓜ Anvers) Taking its name from the series of detective novels by Gaston Leroux (1868–1927), this odd little place can be found on a little-visited side of the Butte de Montmartre. There's no sign outside, so just look for the thick black drapes in the shopfront window and enter what feels like the 1950s, with its postwar decor and excellent 'family' cooking.

LE RELAIS GASCON REGIONAL CUISINE **€**

Map p394 (☎01 42 58 58 22; www.lerelaisgascon.fr; 6 rue des Abbesses, 18e; mains €12-15.50, menu €25.50; ⊙10am-2am daily; Ⓜ Abbesses) Situated just a short stroll from the place des Abbesses, the Relais Gascon has a relaxed atmosphere and authentic regional cuisine at very reasonable prices. The giant salads and *confit de canard* will satisfy big eaters, while the traditional *cassoulet* and *tartiflette* are equally delicious.

Another **branch** (Map p394; ☎01 42 52 11 11; 13 rue Joseph de Maistre) is just down the street. Credit cards not accepted at the main restaurant.

ROSE BAKERY VEGETARIAN **€€**

Map p394 (☎01 42 82 12 80; 46 rue des Martyrs, 18e; mains €14.50-17.50; ⊙9am-6.30pm Tue-Sat; 🌶; Ⓜ St-Georges) The original branch of the always hip Rose Bakery. Another branch (p163) is in the Marais.

L'ÉPICERIE ITALIAN **€**

Map p394 (51 rue des Martyrs, 9e; dishes €9.50-15; ⊙noon-10pm; Ⓜ Pigalle) A buzzy Italian caterer, L'Épicerie serves all sorts of delicacies from 'the Boot', including risottos (artichokes, peppers and olives), plates of pasta, and stuffed veggies and cannelloni. Meal times are less formal than elsewhere and you can even order out for an improv picnic.

AU GRAIN DE FOLIE VEGETARIAN **€**

Map p394 (☎01 42 58 15 57; 24 rue de la Vieuville, 18e; salads €12, menus €13 & €18; ⊙lunch 1-2.30pm Tue-Sun, dinner to 10.30pm Tue-Sat; Ⓜ Abbesses) This hole-in-the-wall macrobiotic and organic eatery is run by a woman from Cambridge and has been in business for over 25 years. It has excellent vegetarian pâté, and vegan quiche.

LE MONO AFRICAN **€**

Map p394 (☎01 46 06 99 20; 40 rue Véron, 18e; mains €11-15; ⊙dinner to 1am Thu-Tue; Ⓜ Abbesses or Blanche) Le Mono, run by a cheery Togolese family, offers West African specialities, including *lélé* (flat, steamed cakes of white beans and prawns), *azidessi* (beef or chicken with peanut sauce), *gbekui* (goulash with spinach, onions, beef, fish and prawns) and *djenkoumé* (grilled chicken with semolina noodles). The rum-based punches are an excellent prelude.

HÔTEL AMOUR BISTRO **€**

Map p394 (☎01 48 78 31 80; www.hotelamourparis.fr; 8 rue Navarin, 9e; mains €13-25; ⊙8am-midnight; 📶; Ⓜ St-Georges or Pigalle) Attached to the arty hotel of the same name, this buzzing hot spot is a cross between an American diner and a hip French bistro. The food is definitely not gourmet (croque monsieur, bacon cheeseburger), but it is served nonstop until midnight, making this a great after-hours stop. There is also fantastic garden seating – if you can get it.

CHEZ TOINETTE TRADITIONAL FRENCH **€€**

Map p394 (☎01 42 54 44 36; 20 rue Germain Pilon; mains €16-25; ⊙dinner Mon-Sat; Ⓜ Abbesses) The atmosphere of this convivial restaurant is rivalled only by its fine cuisine. In the heart of one of the capital's most touristy neighbourhoods, Chez Toinette has kept alive the tradition of old Montmartre with its simplicity and culinary expertise.

LE REFUGE DES FONDUS SAVOIE **€€**

Map p394 (☎01 42 55 22 65; 17 rue des Trois Frères, 18e; menu €21; ⊙dinner to 2am daily; Ⓜ Abbesses or Anvers) This odd place has been a Montmartre favourite for nigh on four decades. The single *menu* provides an aperitif, hors d'oeuvre, red wine and a good quantity of either *fondue savoyarde* (cheese fondue) or *fondue bourguignonne* (meat fondue). The last sitting is at midnight.

CHEZ PLUMEAU TRADITIONAL FRENCH **€€**

Map p394 (☎01 46 06 26 29; 4 place du Calvaire, 18e; mains €12.50-22; ⊙noon-11pm Thu-Tue Apr-Sep, lunch & dinner Thu-Mon Oct-Mar; Ⓜ Abbesses) Chez Plumeau caters to those who have just had their portraits done on place du Tertre. But for a tourist haunt it's not too bad (it even has veggie options), and the back terrace is great on a warm spring or summer afternoon.

Clichy

BISTRO DES DAMES BISTRO €€

Map p401 (01 45 22 13 42; 18 rue des Dames, 17e; mains €12-20; lunch & dinner; Place de Clichy) This charming little bistro will appeal to lovers of simple, authentic cuisine, with hearty salads, tortillas and glorious charcuterie platters of *pâté de campagne* and paper-thin Serrano ham. The dining room, which looks out onto the street, is lovely, but in the summer it's the cool and tranquillity of the small back garden that pulls in the punters.

CHARLOT, ROI DES COQUILLAGES SEAFOOD €€

Map p401 (01 53 20 48 00; www.charlot-paris.com; 12 place de Clichy; mains €15.50-35.90, lunch menus €22.10 & €29.50; Place de Clichy) 'Charlot, the King of Shellfish' is an art deco palace that is one of the best places in town for no-nonsense seafood. The platters and oysters are why everyone is here, but don't ignore the wonderful fish soup and mains, such as grilled sardines, *sole meunière* and bouillabaisse.

LA MAFFIOSA DI TERMOLI PIZZERIA €

Map p401 (01 55 30 01 83; 19 rue des Dames; pizzas & pasta €9.30-10.40; closed Sun lunch; Place de Clichy) This place has more than 40 pizzas that are too good to ignore, as well as decent garlic bread with or without Parma ham.

AU BON COIN CAFE €

Map p401 (01 58 60 28 72; 52 rue Lemercier, 17e; mains €9.60-15.50; lunch Mon-Fri, dinner to midnight Tue-Fri; La Fourche) If you're looking for solid cafe food and a quintessential Parisian eating experience, look no further than Au Bon Coin. It's up the street from place de Clichy in a rarely visited neighbourhood.

MARCHÉ BATIGNOLLES-CLICHY MARKET €

Map p401 (Bd des Batignolles, 8e & 17e; 9am-2pm Sat; Place de Clichy) Near place de Clichy, this market is excellent for *produits biologiques* (organic produce).

Gare du Nord & Canal St-Martin

CHEZ MICHEL BRETON, SEAFOOD €€

Map p398 (01 44 53 06 20; 10 rue Belzunce, 10e; menu €50; lunch Tue-Fri, dinner Mon-Fri; Gare du Nord) If all you know about Breton cuisine is crêpes and cider, a visit to Chez Michel is in order. The only option is to order the four-course menu, which features excellent seafood (scallop tartare, hake with Breton white beans) as well as specialities like *keuz breizh* (Breton cheeses) and *kouign* (butter cake).

If you can't book a table, don't despair – it also prepares four-course picnic baskets (€52 for two people) if you order ahead. Two doors down is little brother **Chez Casimir** (Map p398; 6 rue Belzunce, 10e; menus €24-32; lunch & dinner Mon-Fri, 10am-7pm Sat & Sun), with decent bistro fare.

L'OFFICE MODERN FRENCH €€

Map p398 (01 47 70 67 31; 3 rue Richer; lunch menus €19-24, dinner menus €27-33; Mon-Fri; Poissonière or Bonne Nouvelle) Straddling the east–west Paris divide, L'Office is off the beaten track but unusual enough to merit a detour for those serious about their food. The market-inspired menu is mercifully short – as in there are only two choices for lunch – but outstanding. Don't judge this one by the menu; the simple chalkboard descriptions ('beef/polenta') belie the rich and complex flavours emerging from the kitchen.

VIVANT MODERN FRENCH €€€

Map p398 (01 42 46 43 55; www.morethanorganic.com; 43 rue des Petites Écuries, 10e; mains €21-28; Mon-Fri; Bonne Nouvelle) Pierre Jancou, the mind behind natural-wine bars like Racines (p120) and La Crèmerie, has moved on to his latest adventure set in a century-old exotic bird shop, where simple but elegant dishes – creamy burratta, crispy duck leg with mashed potatoes, foie gras and roasted onion, an Italian cheese plate – are created to showcase the carefully sourced ingredients.

The Swiss-born Jancou is a natural-wine activist, so make sure you treat yourself to at least a glass: it's an essential part of the meal here.

TOP CHOICE **LE VERRE VOLÉ** WINE BAR €

Map p398 (☎01 48 03 17 34; 67 rue de Lancry, 10e; mains €13-16; ⏰lunch & dinner; Ⓜ Jacques Bonsergent) The tiny 'Stolen Glass' – a wine shop with a few tables – is just about the most perfect wine-bar-cum-restaurant in Paris, with excellent wines and expert advice. Unpretentious and hearty *plats du jour* (dishes of the day) are excellent. Reserve well in advance for meals, or stop by just for a tasting.

PINK FLAMINGO PIZZERIA €

Map p398 (☎01 42 02 31 70; www.pinkflamingopizza.com; 67 rue Bichat, 10e; pizzas €10.50-16; ⏰lunch Tue-Sun, dinner daily; Ⓜ Jacques Bonsergent) Not another pizza place? *Mais non, chérie!* Once the weather warms up, the Flamingo unveils its secret weapon – pink helium balloons that the delivery guy uses to locate you and your perfect canal-side picnic spot (GPS not needed).

Order a Poulidor (duck, apple and *chèvre*) or a Basquiat (gorgonzola, figs and cured ham), pop into Le Verre Volé across the canal for the perfect bottle of vino and you're set.

ALBION WINE BAR €€

Map p398 (☎01 42 46 02 44; 80 rue du Faubourg Poissonnière, 10e; mains €17-21; ⏰lunch Tue-Fri, dinner Tue-Sat; Ⓜ Poissonnière) Albion is the ancient Greek name for England and it's no coincidence that it's a mere five-minute jaunt from the Gare du Nord and, what's more, run by two affable English speakers. But don't read into the name too much: this sleek new place is still very Paris, with bottles of wine lining one wall, waiting to be paired with the modern cuisine.

DU PAIN ET DES IDÉES BOULANGERIE €

Map p398 (34 rue Yves Toudic, 10e; ⏰7am-8pm Mon-Fri; Ⓜ Jacques Bonsergent) Fabulous traditional bakery with naturally leavened bread, orange-blossom brioche and *escargots* (similar to cinnamon rolls) in four decadent flavours – pistachio and chocolate anyone? The bakery itself dates back to 1889.

PHILOU BISTRO €€

Map p398 (☎01 42 38 00 13; 12 av Richerand, 10e; 2-/3-course menus €25/30; ⏰lunch & dinner Mon-Fri; Ⓜ Jacques Bonsergent) The walls at this swanky new bistro are nearly 100% chalkboard, with the day's temptations writ large. The brainchild of seasoned chef Philippe Damas – the man who founded Le Square Trousseau (p189) – Philou steers away from the latest trends, preferring instead succulent French comfort food prepared with top-of-the-line ingredients.

BOB'S JUICE BAR VEGETARIAN €

Map p398 (☎09 50 06 36 18; www.bobsjuicebar.com; 15 rue Lucien Sampaix, 10e; juice €4-6.50, sandwiches €6.50; ⏰7.30am-3pm Mon-Fri; 📶; Ⓜ République) In need of some vitamin C? Sweet potato soup? This tiny outpost (and do note that it is tiny) with bags of rice flour and flaxseed lining the walls serves delicious smoothies, freshly squeezed organic juices, vegan breakfasts, hummus sandwiches...in short, all those things you might have trouble finding elsewhere in Paris.

JARDIN DES VOLUPTÉS ORGANIC €

Map p398 (☎01 48 24 38 68; 10 rue de l'Échiquier, 10e; mains €11.90, 2-/3-course menus €13.90/20; ⏰11am-4pm Mon-Sat, 10am-3pm Sun; Ⓜ Strasbourg-St-Denis) A cosy teahouse attached to a bona fide qigong (ch'i kung) centre, this health-oriented place would have no trouble fitting in in California. What's surprising is how popular it is with Cartesian-esque Parisians, attracted by both the quality of the organic ingredients and the original cooking.

Kids might shy away from the quinoa vegetable stir-fry, but other dishes (meatless chilli, salmon-and-leek gratin, dairy-free lemon meringue pie) can do no wrong. Sunday brunch is by reservation only.

KRISHNA BHAVAN INDIAN, VEGETARIAN €

Map p398 (☎01 42 05 78 43; 24 rue Cail, 10e; thaali €10-12, menu €15; ⏰lunch & dinner; Ⓜ La Chapelle) This is about as authentic an Indian vegetarian canteen as you'll find in Paris. If in doubt as to what to order, ask for a *thaali*, a circular steel tray with samosas, dosas and other wrapped goodies. Wash it all down with a yoghurt-based lassi, which comes in five flavours, including mango and rose.

BISTROT DES FAUBOURGS BISTRO €€

Map p398 (☎01 46 07 09 49; 55 rue des Vinaigriers, 10e; mains €14-19, lunch menu €14; ⏰lunch & dinner Mon-Fri; Ⓜ Jacques Bonsergent) A tiny 1920s-style bistro with chequerboard floor, red banquettes and an oak-and-tin bar, this local fave fills up in the blink of an eye, so book a table or show up early. The fabulous starters – langoustine raviolis, oxtail pâté – are followed by the types of traditional French dishes that you're likely to dream about once you're back home.

LA ROTONDE BRASSERIE, BAR €€

Map p398 (☎01 80 48 33 40; www.larotonde.com; 6-8 place de la Bataille de Stalingrad, 19e; lunch menu €19, mains €15-23, bar food from €3.50; ⏰8am-2am; 📶; Ⓜ Stalingrad) Overlooking the Bassin de la Villette, this striking 18th-century edifice went from customs station to police barracks to salt warehouse before its most recent conversion in late 2011 to hip new brasserie. The light-filled circular atrium is the show stealer, but the casual bar-cafe with quay-side lounge chairs and inexpensive meals is what draws in the crowds.

LE GRENIER À PAIN BOULANGERIE €

Map p398 (91 rue Faubourg Poissonnière, 9e; ⏰8am-8pm Thu-Tue, to 1.30pm Sun; Ⓜ Poissonnière) Michel Galloyer founded this string of artisan bakeries, which also includes an award-winning branch (p140) in Montmartre.

JAMBO AFRICAN €€

Map p398 (☎01 42 45 46 55; 23 rue Ste-Marthe, 10e; 3-course menu €28; ⏰dinner daily; 📶; Ⓜ Belleville) This charming restaurant, decorated with shields and masks from different parts of Africa, was opened by a former aid worker and his Rwandan wife. The cuisine is inspired by Central African cuisine; many of the ingredients are imported direct from Kigali, the Rwandan capital.

LA CANTINE DE QUENTIN TRADITIONAL FRENCH €

Map p398 (☎01 42 02 40 32; 52 rue Bichat, 10e; lunch menu €16; ⏰lunch Tue-Sun, shop 10am-7.30pm; Ⓜ Jacques Bonsergent or Gare de l'Est) A bewitching combination of gourmet food shop and lunchtime bistro, La Cantine de Quentin stocks quality products from the countryside (cassoulet, charcuterie, wine, tapenade, vinegar, mushrooms), many of which find their way into the back-room kitchen. There's plenty of temptation and you won't leave empty handed.

LE RÉVEIL DU XE BISTRO €

Map p398 (☎01 42 41 77 59; 35 rue du Château d'Eau, 10e; mains €9.30-13.80; ⏰lunch Mon-Sat, dinner Mon-Fri; Ⓜ Château d'Eau) This corner bistro is slightly out of the way, but if you're in search of a locals' place you won't regret the trip. Plates of charcuterie (saucisson, rillettes, pâté) and Auvergne cheeses (cantal, St-Nectaire, bleu) supplement French standards, and there are even mixed salads for those hoping for a glimpse of the colour green.

MARCHÉ ST-QUENTIN FOOD MARKET €

Map p398 (85bis bd de Magenta, 10e; ⏰8am-8pm Tue-Sat, 8am-1.30pm Sun; Ⓜ Gare de l'Est) This iron-and-glass covered market, built in 1866, has the usual range of French specialities and produce, as well as afforable lunches at a range of stalls (including African and Lebanese).

LA SARDINE CAFE, BAR €

Map p398 (www.barlasardine.com; 32 place Ste-Marthe, 10e; tapas €3-6, lunch menu €12; ⏰9am-2am Apr-Sep, closed Mon Oct-Mar; 📶; Ⓜ Belleville) Out in the western flanks of Belleville, it's easy to miss the rue Ste-Marthe, filled with colourful restaurants and bars exerting a dilapidated, funky charm. At the top is this convivial cafe-wine bar, a bit of Marseille in Paris, with an enormous terrace on sheltered place Ste-Marthe. It's brilliant for warm afternoons, casual meals and to sample a few organic wines.

LE CAMBODGE CAMBODIAN €

Map p398 (☎01 44 84 37 70; www.lecambodge.fr; 10 av Richerand, 10e; dishes €9.50-13; ⏰lunch & dinner Mon-Sat; Ⓜ Goncourt) Hidden in a peaceful street between the gargantuan Hôpital St-Louis and Canal St-Martin, this favourite establishment among students serves enormous spring rolls and the ever-popular *pique-nique Angkorien* (rice vermicelli and sautéed beef, which you wrap up yourself in lettuce leaves). The food tastes homemade (if not especially authentic) and the vegetarian options are especially good.

ZUZU'S PETALS ORGANIC €

Map p398 (☎09 51 79 00 31; http://zuzuspetals.fr; 8 rue Marie et Louise, 10e; mains €8-15, lunch menus €10.50-12.80; ⏰lunch Mon-Tue & Thu-Fri, dinner Fri & Sat; Ⓜ Goncourt) Named after a phrase in the 1946 classic *It's a Wonderful Life*, this organic deli serves soups, sandwiches, vegetable gratins, smoothies and other health-conscious (and delicious) dishes.

MADAME SHAWN THAI €€

Map p398 (☎01 42 38 07 37; www.mmeshawn.com; 56 rue de Lancry, 10e; mains €12.50-18.50 (add €1 to prices for dinner); ⏰lunch & dinner; Ⓜ Jacques Bonsergent) The Mme started out in a humble French cafe that was deftly transformed into a sophisticated Thai restaurant. The heat may be turned down a few degrees, but you can still taste the flavours of Chiang Mai in the *tôm yam* soup, invigorating green curries and…chocolate *nem* (a small spring roll) for dessert?

LA MARINE BAR, CAFE €€

Map p398 (☎01 42 39 69 81; 55bis quai de Valmy, 10e; lunch menu €15; mains €13-22; ⏰7.30am-2am Mon-Fri, from 9am Sat & Sun; 📶; Ⓜ République) This large, airy hang-out overlooking Canal St-Martin has been multi-tasking as a cafe, restaurant and bar for years now, and offfers a good cross-section of the neighbourhood population.

DISHNY INDIAN €

Map p398 (☎01 40 05 18 36; 212 rue du Faubourg St-Denis, 10e; mains €6-11, menus lunch €7-16/dinner €9 & €16; ⏰lunch & dinner to midnight; Ⓜ La Chapelle or Gare du Nord) Probably the most famous Indian restaurant situated along rue Cail – Paris' Little India – the Dishny offers an array of inexpensive choices, many from the south.

TERMINUS NORD BRASSERIE €€

Map p398 (☎01 42 85 05 15; 23 rue de Dunkerque, 10e; mains €18.50-31.50, menus €23.50 & €31.50; ⏰7.30am-midnight daily; Ⓜ Gare du Nord) Directly across from the Gare du Nord, the 'North Terminus' brasserie has a copper bar, waiters in white uniforms, brass fixtures and mirrored walls that look as they did when it opened in 1925. Breakfast is available from 7.30am to 10.30am.

LE CHANSONNIER BRASSERIE €€

Map p398 (☎01 42 09 40 58; www.lechansonnier.com; 14 rue Eugène Varlin; starters €8.20, mains €17, menus €11.60 (lunch only) & €24; ⏰lunch & dinner Mon-Fri, dinner only Sat & Sun; Ⓜ Château Landon or Louis Blanc) The 'Singer' (named after the 19th-century Lyonnais socialist singer-songwriter Pierre Dupont) could be a film set, with its curved zinc bar and art nouveau mouldings. The food is very substantial with mains that range from *noix St-Jacques provençal* (scallops in herbed tomato sauce) and bouillabaisse to *daube de sanglier* (boar stew).

DRINKING & NIGHTLIFE

Crowded around the hillside of Montmartre you'll find an eclectic selection of places to drink. This area offers an unusual medley of tourist-trap bars at Sacré-Cœur, picturesque Parisian spots around Abbesses, anything-goes venues (from hostess bars to Irish pubs) at Pigalle and cool African outposts at Château Rouge. In contrast, Canal St-Martin offers a trendy bohemian atmosphere and wonderful summer nights (and days) in casual canal-side hang-outs.

Montmartre & Pigalle

TOP CHOICE LA FOURMI BAR, CAFE

Map p394 (74 rue des Martyrs, 18e; ⏰8am-1am Mon-Thu, to 3am Fri & Sat, 10am-1am Sun; Ⓜ Pigalle) A Pigalle institution, La Fourmi hits the mark with its high ceilings, long zinc bar and unpretentious vibe. Get up to speed on live music and club nights or sit down for a reasonably priced meal and drinks.

LE PROGRÈS BAR, CAFE

Map p394 (7 rue des Trois Frères, 18e; ⏰9am-2am; Ⓜ Abbesses) A real live *café du quartier* perched in the heart of Abbesses, the 'Progress' occupies a corner site with huge windows and simple seating and attracts a relaxed mix of local artists, shop staff, writers and hangers-on. It's great for convivial evenings, but it's also a good place to come for inexpensive meals and cups of coffee.

CAVE DES ABBESSES WINE BAR

Map p394 (43 rue des Abbesses, 18e; cheese and charcuterie €7-13; ⏰5-9.30pm Tue-Fri, noon-9.30pm Sat & Sun; Ⓜ Pigalle) Pass through the door at the back of the Cave des Abbesses wine shop and you'll discover, no, not a storage room or a portal to another dimension, but instead a quirky little bar. It feels like one of those places only regulars know about, but don't be intimidated; sit down, order a plate of cheese and a glass of Corbières, and you'll blend right in.

KOOKA BOORA CAFE

Map p394 (53 ave Trudaine, 9e; 8.45am-7pm; ; Pigalle) If you can't stomach another cup of carelessly brewed Parisian coffee, take note, Kooka Boora was probably opened just for you. The pros behind the counter can serve up the sacred bean in all of its myriad forms, along with freshly squeezed juices and baked nibbles for breakfast and lunch.

LE SANCERRE BAR, CAFE

Map p394 (35 rue des Abbesses, 18e; 7am-2am; ; Abbesses) Le Sancerre is a popular, rather brash bistro-cum-bar that's often crowded to capacity in the evening, especially on Saturdays. Scruffy yet attractive with its classic bistro decor and hip local mood, it has a prized terrace that gets the late morning sun.

AU P'TIT DOUAI BAR, CAFE

Map p394 (92 rue Blanche, 9e; 8am-2am Sat, 11am-8pm Sun; ; Blanche) This colourful neighbourhood cafe is just down the street from the Moulin Rouge, but it might as well be light years away. Trade in the mayhem for some tranquillity over coffee, wines by the glass or traditional French fare at mealtimes.

AU RENDEZ-VOUS DES AMIS BAR, CAFE

Map p394 (23 rue Gabrielle, 18e; 8am-2am; Abbesses) If you need to ease your way up or down the steps of Montmartre, look no further than this kick-back cafe-bar, which serves inexpensive espresso and pitchers of beer. Sandwiches and snacks are prepared in Hell's Kitchen.

WORTH A DETOUR

CHEZ LOUISETTE

Here since 1967, **Chez Louisette** (Marché aux Puces de St-Ouen; noon-5pm Sat-Mon; Porte de Clignancourt) is popular with tourists visiting Paris' largest flea market, the Marché aux Puces de St-Ouen. The food is as abysmal as the service; the real reason people come here is to hear old-time *chanteuses* and *chanteurs* belt out numbers by Piaf and other classic French singers.

Clichy

LE WEPLER CAFE

Map p401 (14 place de Clichy; 8am-1am; Place de Clichy) This large cafe-brasserie founded in 1892 is celebrated for its oysters. Great people-watching and friendly service.

Gare du Nord & Canal St-Martin

CHEZ PRUNE BAR, CAFE

Map p398 (71 quai de Valmy, 10e; 8am-2am Mon-Sat, 10am-2am Sun; République) This Soho-boho cafe put Canal St-Martin on the map a decade ago and its good vibes and rough-around-the-edges look show no sign of fading in the near future. Excellent news for longtime fans of Chez Prune.

CHEZ JEANETTE BAR, CAFE

Map p398 (www.chezjeannette.com; 47 rue du Faubourg Saint-Denis, 10e; 11am-11.30pm; Château d'Eau) Cracked tile floors and original 1950s decor have turned Chez Jeanette into one of the 10e's most popular hot spots. It's Macbooks by day, pints by night and reasonably priced meals around the clock. What more could you possibly want?

TOP CHOICE **L'ATMOSPHÈRE** BAR, CAFE

Map p398 (49 rue Lucien Sampaix, 10e; 9.30am-1.45am Mon-Sat, till midnight Sun; Jacques Bonsergent or Gare de l'Est) A nod to the 1938 Canal St-Martin flick *Hôtel du Nord*, this timber-and-tile cafe along the canal has an arty, spirited ambience (or, should we say, atmosphere), well-priced drinks and good food.

SWINGING LONDRESS BAR, CAFE

Map p398 (97 rue du Faubourg St-Denis, 10e; 7am-2am daily; ; Gare de l'Est) The latest addition to the St-Denis drinking scene, Swinging Londress is a funky ode to 1960s design, with tripped-out wallpaper that will have you seeing things before the night is through. Cheap drinks, decent grub and a sense of humour make this place a winner.

BREAD AND WINE BY THE GARE DU NORD

Yes, restaurant owners and chefs go out to eat, too. Charles Compagnon, owner of L'Office (p142), filled us in on his staff's top dining picks in Paris' burgeoning culinary hot spot, the 10e arrondissement.

Le Grenier à Pain (p140) They bake the bread we serve at L'Office. We really like *le pain de trois*, which is a kind of country bread that's made with three different types of flour. We also recommend their *gâteau basque* (a small round pastry filled with sweet almond paste).

Vivant (p142) This is a great restaurant. The quality of the products is simply outstanding and the atmosphere is really *charmant*. It's located in an old *oisellerie* (a place where exotic birds were raised and sold); the original faience tiling is still on the walls.

Albion (p143) We really like this restaurant because of the quality of the cooking and the diverse wine selection.

LE JEMMAPES — BAR

Map p398 (82 quai de Jemmapes, 10e; ⌚4pm-2am daily; Ⓜ Jacques Bonsergent or Goncourt) This canal-side bar has several Belgian beers on tap. If you'd like to take your drinking closer to the canal, it also has no-frills plastic cups for when the party spills outside in nicer weather.

CAFÉ CHÉRI(E) — BAR, CAFE

Map p398 (44 bd de la Villette, 19e; ⌚noon-1am; Ⓜ Belleville) An imaginative, colourful bar with its signature red lighting, infamous mojitos and caiparinhas and commitment to quality tunes, Chéri(e) is everyone's darling in this part of town. There's a gritty art-chic crowd and electro DJs Thursday to Saturday.

HÔTEL DU NORD — BAR, CAFE

Map p398 (www.hoteldunord.org; 102 quai de Jemmapes, 10e; ⌚9am-2.30am; 📶; Ⓜ Jacques Bonsergent) The setting for the eponymous 1938 French film (p148) starring Louis Jouvet and Arletty, the interior of this vintage cafe feels as if it was stuck in a time warp with its zinc counter, red velvet curtains and old piano. Come for the atmosphere and nostaliga. Skip the food.

DELAVILLE CAFÉ — BAR, CAFE

Map p398 (34 bd de Bonne Nouvelle, 10e; ⌚11am-2.30am; 📶; Ⓜ Bonne Nouvelle) This grand erstwhile brothel has an alluring mix of restored history and industrial chic. Between the high-ceilinged restaurant, one of the best terraces on the grands boulevards and the bar-lounge areas, you're sure to find your niche somewhere at Delaville Café. A great spot to unwind.

☆ ENTERTAINMENT

☆ Montmartre & Pigalle

MOULIN ROUGE — CABARET

Map p394 (☎01 53 09 82 82; www.moulinrouge.fr; 82 bd de Clichy, 18e; Ⓜ Blanche) Immortalised in the posters of Toulouse-Lautrec and later on screen by Baz Luhrmann, the Moulin Rouge twinkles beneath a 1925 replica of its original red windmill. Yes, it's rife with bus-tour crowds, but from the opening bars of music to the last high kick it's a whirl of fantastical costumes, sets, choreography and champagne. Bookings are advised.

OLYMPIC CAFÉ — LIVE MUSIC

Map p394 (☎01 42 52 29 93; www.rueleon.net; 20 rue Léon, 18e; ⌚11am-2am Tue-Sat; Ⓜ Château Rouge) This community bar in the Goutte d'Or neighbourhood is the best place in Paris to catch live African music along with jazz and reggae groups. The monthly program also includes events at the **Lavoir Moderne Parisien** (Map p394; ☎01 42 52 09 14; 35 rue Léon), another springboard for young talent down the road. There's African specialities for lunch and dinner.

LA MACHINE DU MOULIN ROUGE — CLUB

Map p394 (www.lamachinedumoulinrouge.com; 90 bd de Clichy, 18e; ⌚10pm-5am Thu-Sat; Ⓜ Blanche) Part of the original Moulin Rouge (well, the boiler room anyway), this club packs 'em in on weekends with a dance floor, concert hall, champagne bar and outdoor terrace.

LA CIGALE ROCK, JAZZ

Map p394 (☎01 49 25 81 75; www.lacigale.fr; 120 bd de Rochechouart; admission €25-60; MAnvers or Pigalle) Now classed as a historical monument, this music hall dates from 1887 but was redecorated 100 years later by Philippe Starck. Among the many artists who have performed here recently are Rufus Wainwright, Ryan Adams, Richard Hawley, Tindersticks, Lambchop, Julia Stone and Ibrahim Maalouf.

LE DIVAN DU MONDE LIVE MUSIC

Map p394 (www.divandumonde.com; 75 rue des Martyrs, 18e; ⊙Fri & Sat, sometimes open for events Mon-Fri; MPigalle) Take some cinematographic events, Gypsy gatherings, *nouvelles chansons françaises* (new French songs). Add in soul/funk fiestas, air-guitar face-offs and rock parties of the Arctic Monkeys/Killers/Libertines persuasion and stir with an Amy Winehouse swizzle stick. You may now be getting some idea of the inventive, open-minded approach at this excellent cross-cultural venue in Pigalle.

BUS PALLADIUM CLUB

Map p394 (www.lebuspalladium.com; 6 rue Pierre Fontaine, 9e; ⊙11pm-5am Tue, Fri, Sat; MBlanche) Once the place to be back in the 1960s, the Bus is now back in business 50 years later, with funky DJs and a mixed bag of performances by indie and pop groups.

AU LAPIN AGILE CABARET

Map p394 (☎01 46 06 85 87; www.au-lapin-agile.com; 22 rue des Saules, 18e; adult €24, student except Sat €17; ⊙9pm-1am Tue-Sun; MLamarck–Caulaincourt) This rustic cabaret venue was favoured by artists and intellectuals in the early 20th century and traditional *chansons* are still performed here. The four-hour show starts at 9.30pm and includes singing and poetry. Some love it, others feel it's a bit of a trap.

It's named after *Le Lapin à Gill,* a mural of a rabbit jumping out of a cooking pot by caricaturist André Gill, which can still be seen on the western exterior wall.

☆ Gare du Nord & Canal St-Martin

POINT ÉPHÉMÈRE LIVE MUSIC

Map p398 (www.pointephemere.org; 200 quai de Valmy, 10e; ⊙noon-2am Mon-Sat, noon-10pm Sun; 📶; MLouis Blanc) This arts and music venue by the Canal St-Martin attracts an underground crowd from noon till past midnight, for drinks, meals, concerts, dance nights and even art exhibitions. At the time of writing gourmet-hamburger food truck Le Camion qui Fume was setting up shop here on Sundays.

ROSA BONHEUR DANCE HALL

Map p400 (www.rosabonheur.fr; Parc des Buttes Chaumont, 19e; ⊙noon-midnight Wed-Sun; MBotzaris) This self-styled *guinguette* (old-fashioned dance hall) morphs from outdoor cafe by day into a jam-packed dance floor by night. Its setting inside the Parc des Buttes Chaumont is surely the most bucolic getaway in the action-packed capital, and even if the tapas won't set your world on fire, good vibes are virtually guaranteed. If the park is closed, you'll need to enter at 7 rue Botzaris.

CABARET SAUVAGE WORLD MUSIC

Map p400 (www.cabaretsauvage.com; 221 av Jean Jaurès, 19e; MPorte de la Villette) This very cool space in the Parc de la Villette (it

HÔTEL DU NORD

If you want a glimpse of life along the canal before it became cool, the movie to watch is Marcel Carné's *Hôtel du Nord* (1938). The story revolves around the residents of the hotel – including a canal worker, prostitute, drifting criminal and lovesick girl – and is hardly short on drama; it begins with a botched double suicide and ends with a murder. The highlight, though, is the dialogue, delivered with an old-fashioned Parisian accent that, let's face it, is a lot more fun than the French you hear today. One of the most unforgettable lines in all French cinema belongs to Arletty's character (the prostitute). Accused of being a 'suffocating atmosphere' in a lovers' spat, she responds, '*Atmosphère? Atmosphère?! Est-ce que j'ai une gueule d'atmosphère?!*' (Atmosphere? Atmosphere?! Do I look like an atmosphere?!) Today the movie is referenced in the names of a local hotel, restaurant and cafe.

looks like a gigantic yurt) is host to African, reggae and raï concerts as well as DJ nights that last till dawn. There are also occasional hip-hop and indie acts that pass through.

CITÉ DE LA MUSIQUE WORLD MUSIC

Map p400 (www.citedelamusique.fr; 221 av Jean Jaurès, 19e; box office noon-6pm Tue-Sat, 10am-6pm Sun, to 8pm on day of performance; Porte de Pantin) Every imaginable type of music and dance, from classical to North African to Japanese, is hosted at this venue's 1200-seat main auditorium. Smaller concerts are in the smaller Amphithéâtre du Musée de la Musique.

LE 104 THEATRE

Map p398 (www.le104.fr; 104 rue d'Aubervilliers or 5 rue Curial, 19e; noon-7pm Tue-Fri, 11am-7pm Sat & Sun; ; Stalingrad or Crimée) Circus, theatre, music, monthly balls and even magic shows are held at this former funeral parlour turned city-funded art space (p136). Some shows are free; others require admission.

ALHAMBRA LIVE MUSIC

Map p398 (www.alhambra-paris.com; 21 rue Yves Toudic, 10e; République or Jacques Bonsergent) The Subways and Clap Your Hands Say Yeah are among the artists who have recently played at this 1930s cinema-theatre, which now serves as a music hall for pop, rock and soul concerts.

NEW MORNING JAZZ, BLUES

Map p398 (www.newmorning.com; 7-9 rue des Petites Écuries, 10e; Château d'Eau) New Morning is a highly regarded auditorium with excellent acoustics that hosts big-name jazz concerts as well as a variety of blues, rock, funk, salsa, Afro-Cuban and Brazilian music.

LE REGARD DU CYGNE DANCE

(www.leregarducygne.com; 210 rue de Belleville, 20e; Place des Fêtes) Le Regard du Cygne prides itself on being an independent, alternative performance space. Situated in the creative 20e, this is where many of Paris' young and daring talents in movement, music and theatre congregate to perform. If you're in the mood for some innovative and experimental modern dance, performance or participation, this is the place to come.

WORTH A DETOUR

MARCHÉ AUX PUCES DE ST-OUEN

A vast flea market, the **Marché aux Puces de St-Ouen** (www.marcheauxpuces-saintouen.com; rue des Rosiers, av Michelet, rue Voltaire, rue Paul Bert & rue Jean-Henri Fabre; 9am-6pm Sat, 10am-6pm Sun, 11am-5pm Mon; Porte de Clignancourt) was founded in the late 19th century. It's said to be Europe's largest market, and has more than 2500 stalls grouped into a dozen *marchés* (market areas), each with its own speciality (eg Paul Bert for 17th-century furniture, Malik for clothing, Biron for Asian art). There are miles upon miles of 'freelance' stalls; come prepared to spend some time.

SHOPPING

Montmartre & Pigalle

LA CITADELLE FASHION, ACCESSORIES

Map p394 (1 rue des Trois Frères, 18e; 11am-8pm Mon-Sat, to 7pm Sun; Abbesses) This designer discount shop hidden away in Montmartre has some real finds from new French, Italian and Japanese designers. Look out for such labels as Les Chemins Blancs and Yoshi Kondo.

ANTOINE ET LILI FASHION, HOMEWARES

Map p394 (90 rue des Martyrs, 18e; 11am-8pm Mon-Sat, 1-7pm Sun; Abbesses) Fashion from the Canal St-Martin label (p150).

ETS LION FOOD, DRINK

Map p394 (7 rue des Abbesses, 18e; 10.30am-8pm Tue-Sat, 11am-7pm Sun; Abbesses) An essential pitstop on the foodie trail, this gourmet and gardening shop sells homemade jams, packaged *riz au lait* (rice pudding), multicoloured Eiffel Tower pasta and olive oils.

TATI DEPARTMENT STORE

Map p394 (4 bd de Rochechouart, 18e; 10am-7pm Mon-Fri, 9.30am-7pm Sat; Barbès Rochechouart) This bargain-filled, rough and tumble, frill-free department store is every fashionable Parisian's guilty secret. It could be yours too.

THE FIVE BASIC CHEESE TYPES

The choices on offer at a *fromagerie* (cheese shop) can be spectacularly overwhelming, but vendors will always allow you to sample what's on offer before you buy, and they are usually very generous with their guidance and pairing advice. The following list divides French cheeses into five main groups – as they are usually divided in a shop – and recommends several types in each family to try. You'll be putting a cheese plate together in no time.

Fromage à pâte demi-dure 'Semi-hard cheese' means uncooked, pressed cheese. Among the finest are Tomme de Savoie, made from either raw or pasteurised cow's milk; Cantal, a cow's milk cheese from Auvergne that tastes something like Cheddar; St-Nectaire, a pressed cheese that has a strong, complex taste; and Ossau-Iraty, a ewe's milk cheese made in the French Basque Country.

Fromage à pâte dure 'Hard cheese' is always cooked and then pressed. Among the most popular are: Beaufort, a grainy cow's milk cheese with a slightly fruity taste from Rhône-Alpes; Comté, a cheese made with raw cow's milk in Franche-Comté; Emmental, a cow's milk cheese made all over France; and Mimolette, an Edam-like dark-orange cheese from Lille that can be aged for up to 36 months.

Fromage à pâte molle 'Soft cheese' is moulded or rind-washed. The ever popular Camembert, a classic moulded cheese from Normandy that for many is synonymous with 'French cheese', and Brie de Meaux are both made from raw cow's milk; Munster from Alsace, mild Chaource and strong-smelling Langres from Champagne, and the odorous Époisses de Bourgogne are rind-washed, fine-textured cheeses.

Fromage à pâte persillée 'Marbled' or 'blue cheese' is so called because the veins often resemble *persille* (parsley). Roquefort is a ewe's milk veined cheese that is to many the king of French cheeses. Fourme d'Ambert is a mild cow's milk cheese from Rhône-Alpes. Bleu du Haut Jura (also called Bleu de Gex) is a mild, blue-veined mountain cheese.

Fromage de chèvre 'Goat's milk cheese' is usually creamy and both sweet and slightly salty when fresh, but hardens and gets much saltier as the cheese matures. Among the best varieties are: Ste-Maure de Touraine, a creamy, mild cheese from the Loire region; Crottin de Chavignol, a classic though saltier variety from Burgundy; Cabécou de Rocamadour from Midi-Pyrenées, often served warm with salad or marinated in oil and rosemary; and Saint Marcellin, a soft white cheese from Lyon.

Clichy

FROMAGERIE ALLÉOSSE FOOD, DRINK

Map p401 (www.alleosse.com; 13 rue Poncelet, 17e; ⌚9am-1pm & 4-7pm Tue-Thu, 9am-6pm Fri & Sat; Ⓜ Ternes) Although there are cheese shops throughout the city, this one is actually worth a trip across town. Cheeses are sold as they should be, grouped into five main categories: *fromage de chèvre* (goat's milk cheese), *fromage à pâte persillée* (veined or blue cheese), *fromage à pâte molle* (soft cheese), *fromage à pâte demi-dure* (semihard cheese) and *fromage à pâte dure* (hard cheese).

Gare du Nord & Canal St-Martin

ANTOINE ET LILI FASHION, HOMEWARES

Map p398 (95 quai de Valmy, 10e; ⌚11am-7pm Sun & Mon, 10.30am-7.30pm Tue-Fri, 10am-8pm Sat; Ⓜ République or Gare de l'Est) All the colours of the rainbow and all the patterns in the world congregate in this wonderful Parisian institution with designer clothing for women (pink store) and children (green store), and hip home decorations (yellow store).

BAZAR ÉTHIC FASHION, HOMEWARES

Map p398 (25 rue Beaurepaire, 10e; 11am-7.30pm Mon-Sat, 2.30-7pm Sun; République or Jacques Bonsergent) An excellent shop for a browse, Bazar Éthic specialises in chic fair-trade and ecofriendly products. It carries a range of clothing (organic cotton jeans, children's wear) and home-design handicrafts, such as lacquered bamboo bowls.

LIZA KORN FASHION

Map p398 (19 rue Beaurepaire, 10e; 11.30am-7.30pm Mon-Sat; Jacques Bonsergent) From rock 'n' roll fashion to a new children's line, this designer's tiny boutique is a portal into a rich and playful imagination.

MAJE FASHION, ACCESSORIES

Map p398 (6 rue de Marseille, 10e; 11am-8pm Mon-Sat, 1.30-7.30pm Sun; Jacques Bonsergent) A Parisian prêt-à-porter brand featured regularly on the pages of *Elle, Glamour* and *Marie Claire,* Maje doesn't come cheaply – that is, unless you know about this outlet store, which sells most items at a 30% discount.

SPORTS & ACTIVITIES

HAMMAM MEDINA SPA

Map p400 (01 42 02 31 05; www.hammam-medina.com; 43-45 rue Petit, 19e; 11am-10pm Mon-Fri, 10am-9pm Sat, 9am-7pm Sun; Laumière) The rhythmic release of eucalyptus-scented steam into this *hammam* (Turkish steambath) will set mind and body at ease in minutes. Also included is an excruciating (but effective) exfoliation rubdown. The almond-oil massage and mint tea are extra, but an indulgent way to end any session. Saturdays are mixed (men and women), otherwise it's women only.

STADE DE FRANCE STADIUM STADIUM

(www.stadefrance.com; rue Francis de Pressensé, St-Denis la Plaine; St-Denis-Porte de Paris or La Plaine Stade de France) This 80,000-seat stadium was built for the 1998 football World Cup, which France won by miraculously defeating Brazil 3-0 in the finals. Today it hosts football and rugby matches, major gymnastic events and big-ticket music concerts.

Le Marais & Ménilmontant

Neighbourhood Top Five

❶ Pay your respects to the rich, famous and infamous at **Cimetière du Père Lachaise** (p154).

❷ Take an elegant walk through the history of Paris, from prehistory to modern times, at the city's atmospheric **Musée Carnavalet** (p156), secreted in a pair of richly furnished 16th- and 17th-century mansions.

❸ No square exalts Paris-hungry souls more than **place des Vosges** (p157), a triumph of symmetry and understated *bon goût.*

❹ Learn about German-occupied Paris and Holocaust horrors at the **Mémorial de la Shoah** (p160).

❺ Enjoy Paris for free with an art exhibition and twirl on ice at Paris' neo-Renaissance **Hôtel de Ville** (p157).

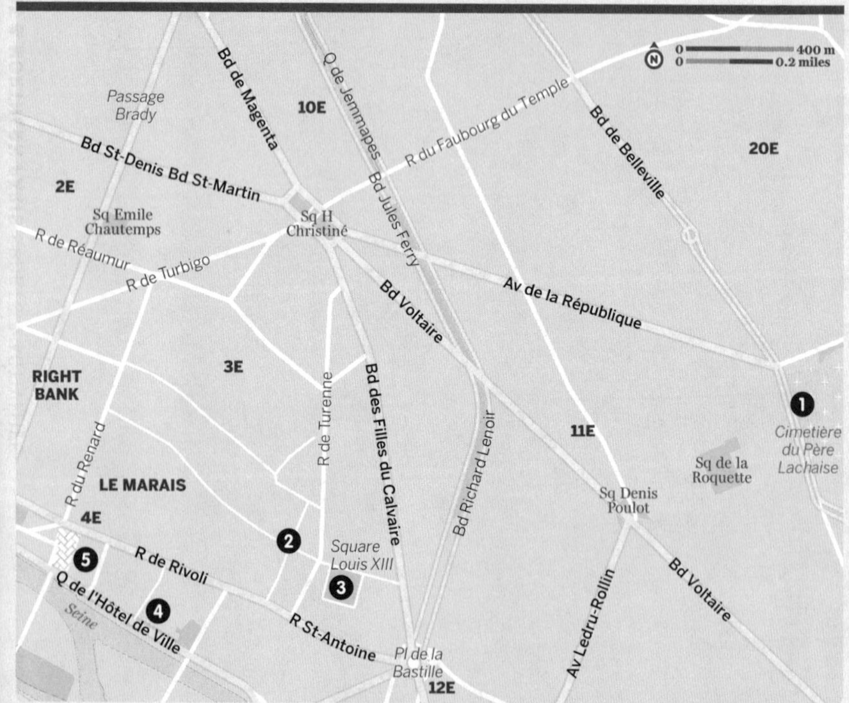

For more detail of this area, see Map p402 and p404 ➡

Explore Le Marais & Ménilmontant

Sublime place des Vosges is a perfect starting point, geographically and historically. The cafe terraces of place de la Bastille are not far away, or meander west along rue de Rivoli or rue du Roi de Sicile – a parallel twinset with a liberal sprinkling of shops, cafes and bars. Essential stop for history buffs is the Mémorial de la Shoah (with some of the city's best coffee at La Caféthèque, a two-minute walk away). Bearing north towards the Haut Marais, hipster strips laden with appealing drinking and dining options include rue Vieille du Temple (which takes you near the Musée Picasso), rue du Bourg Tibourg, and rue Rosiers in the heart of the historic Jewish quarter known as Pletzl. From the Haut Marais, trendy rue Oberkampf and rue Jean-Pierre Timbaud delve east into the solidly working-class Ménilmontant and, further on, Belleville.

Local Life

➡ **Hang-outs** Lap up the local vibe over *un café* or *apéro* on the pavement terrace of a neighbourhood cafe like Café Crème (p161), Le Progrès (p171), Café Charlot (p168) or Aux Deux Amis (p168).

➡ **Gay Life** The Marais is the epicentre of gay and lesbian Paris (p68). Favourite addresses include Open Café (p172) and Scream Club (p172).

➡ **Belleville** Savour the vibrant, multicultural make-up of this unpretentious and working-class 'village' on rue de Belleville and at bd de Belleville's busy market.

➡ **Rue de Ménilmontant** Watch for new bar, club and restaurant openings as the traditional working-class *quartier* of Ménilmontant morphs into a trendsetter.

Getting There & Away

➡ **Metro** Stops for the lower Marais include Chemin Vert, Hôtel de Ville and St-Paul (line 1), Rambuteau (line 11), or Filles du Calvaire and St-Sébastien–Froissart (line 8). For the Haut Marais, get off at Temple (line 3); for Ménilmontant, hop off at Belleville (lines 2 and 11), Couronnes or Ménilmontant (line 2), or Oberkampf (line 5).

➡ **Bus** Take bus 29 from rue des Francs Bourgeois to Bastille and Gare de Lyon; and bus 76 from rue de Rivoli to the 20e and Porte de Bagnolet.

➡ **Bicycle** Handy Vélib' stations next to metro stations: 7 place de l'Hôtel de Ville, 49 rue Rambuteau and place Pasdeloup (next to Filles du Calvaire). In Ménilmontant try 81bis rue Jean-Pierre Timbaud or 137 bd Ménilmontant.

Lonely Planet's Top Tip

The lower Marais has long been fashionable, but the real buzz today is in Haut Marais (upper or northern Marais; NoMa), a very cool neighbourhood with market-square twinset Marché du Temple and Marche aux Enfants Rouges (p168) at its heart and bags of addresses showcasing rising design talent, vintage fashion, hip art and cool dines. Watch for new openings on rue de Bretagne, rue Dupetit Thouars, rue Charles François Dupuis and rue Charlot among others.

Best Places to Eat

➡ Au Passage (p161)
➡ Chatomat (p162)
➡ Le Chateaubriand (p161)
➡ Le Petit Marché (p162)
➡ Nanashi (p162)

For reviews, see p161 

Best Places to Drink

➡ La Chaise au Plafond (p172)
➡ La Mangerie (p169)
➡ Cinéma Café Merci (p168)
➡ Le Barav (p168)
➡ Andy Walhoo (p169)

For reviews, see p168

Best Weekend Brunch

➡ Derrière (p161)
➡ Candelaria (p162)
➡ La Bellevilloise (p174)
➡ Le Dôme du Marais (p165)
➡ Soya Cantine BIO (p163)

For reviews, see p161 

RYAN GREEN / GETTY IMAGES ©

TOP SIGHTS

CIMETIÈRE DU PÈRE LACHAISE

The world's most visited cemetery opened its one-way doors in 1804. Its 44 hectares entomb some 70,000 ornate, often ostentatious tombs, rendering a stroll here akin to exploring a verdant sculpture garden. Indeed Père Lachaise was intended as a park for Parisians – local neighbourhood graveyards were full and this was a ground-breaking project for Parisians to be buried outside the quartier in which they'd lived and died.

Jesuit Roots

Cimitière du Père Lachaise is named after Louis XIV's confessor, a Jesuit father known as Le Père La Chaise, who was resident on the estate where the cemetery is now located. The Jesuits bought the land in the 17th century but sold it a century later and in 1803 the land fell into city hands. Père Lachaise was built at the same time as cemeteries in Montmartre and Montparnasse. but Parisians, wary of entombing their dead so far from home, proved reluctant to purchase grave space here. It was only in 1817, after the remains of immortal 12th-century lovers Abélard and Héloïse were disinterred and reburied here beneath a neo-Gothic tombstone, that the cemetery really took off.

Famous Occupants

The only criteria to become a permanent resident of Cimitière du Père Lachaise was Paris residency; nationality did not matter, hence the cosmopolitan population of the city's most extravagant cemetery.

DON'T MISS

- Oscar Wilde
- Jim Morrison
- Monsieur Noir
- Édith Piaf
- Mur des Fédérés

PRACTICALITIES

- ☎01 43 70 70 33
- www.pere-lachaise.com
- 16 rue du Repos & bd de Ménilmontant, 20e
- admission free
- ⏲8am-6pm Mon-Fri, to 8.30am Sat, to 9am Sun
- Ⓜ Père Lachaise or Philippe Auguste

The 800,000 or so buried here include: the composer Chopin; the playwright Molière; the poet Apollinaire; writers Balzac, Proust, Gertrude Stein and Colette; the actors Simone Signoret, Sarah Bernhardt and Yves Montand; the painters Pissarro, Seurat, Modigliani and Delacroix; the *chanteuse* Édith Piaf alongside her two-year-old daughter; and the dancer Isadora Duncan.

Oscar Wilde

One of the most visited graves is that of Oscar Wilde (1854–1900), interred in division 89 in 1900. As camp as a row of tents and as fresh as tomorrow, the flamboyant Irish playwright and humorist proclaimed on his deathbed in what is now L'Hôtel (p295): 'My wallpaper and I are fighting a duel to the death – one of us has *got* to go.' Wilde was sentenced to two years in prison in 1895 for gross indecency stemming from his homosexual relationship with Lord Alfred 'Bosie' Douglas (1870–1945).

Jim Morrison

The cemetery's other big hitter is 1960s rock star Jim Morrison (1943–71), who died in a flat in the Marais at 17-19 rue Beautreillis, 4e, in 1971 and is now buried in division 6 of the Cimitière du Père Lachaise. His tomb is something of a grave concern for the cemetery these days – a security guard had to be posted near the grave of the rock singer not long ago after fans began taking drugs and having sex on his tomb.

Monsieur Noir

A few years back, up in division 92, a protest by women saw the removal of a metal fence placed around the grave of one Victor Noir, pseudonym of the journalist Yvan Salman (1848–70), who was shot and killed by Pierre Bonaparte, great-nephew of Napoleon, at the age of just 22. According to legend, a woman who strokes the amply filled crotch of Monsieur Noir's prostrate bronze effigy will enjoy a better sex life or even become pregnant. Apparently some would-be lovers and mothers were rubbing a bit too enthusiastically and the larger-than-life-size package was being worn down.

Mur des Fédérés

On 27 May 1871, the last of the Communard insurgents, cornered by government forces, fought a hopeless, all-night battle among the tombstones. In the morning, the 147 survivors were lined up against the **Mur des Fédérés** (Wall of the Federalists), shot and buried where they fell in a mass grave.

A PERFECT CITY STROLL

For fans of Paris' exceptional art and architecture, this vast cemetery – the city's largest – is not a bad starting point. It's one of central Paris' biggest green spaces, laced with 5300 trees and magnificent 19th-century sculptures by artists such as David d'Angers, Hector Guimard, Visconti and Chapu. Many graves are crumbling, overgrown and in need of a good clean, but such is the nature of the cemetery's faded-grandeur charm. Consider the walking tour detailed in the photographic book *Meet Me At Pèere Lachaise* by Anna Erikssön and Masson Bendewald, or start with architect Étienne-Hippolyte Godde's neoclassical chapel and portal at the main entrance and get beautifully lost.

The cemetery has five entrances, two of which are on bd de Ménilmontant. Maps indicating the location of noteworthy graves are available for free from the Conservation Office (16 rue du Repos) in the southwestern corner of the cemetery. Organised tours (in French) also depart from here.

TOP SIGHTS
MUSÉE CARNAVALET

A poetic ode to Parisian *histoire*, this unusual history museum secreted in a pair of remarkable *hôtels particuliers* is one of the city's quiet surprises. Its maze of period rooms chart the city's history from prehistory to modern times through a 600,000-piece fest of art, artefacts and historic objects. A half day can easily be spent savouring the permanent collection (free) and temporary exhibitions (admission fee).

Hôtel Carnavalet

This sublime Renaissance-style mansion was home to letter-writer Madame de Sévigné between 1677 and 1696. Some of her belongings are displayed on the 1st floor beside portraits of prominent literary figures like Molière and Jean de la Fontaine, and other artworks and objects evocative of Paris in the 17th and 18th centuries. Rooms on the ground floor focus mainly on the 16th century, with a colourful collection of vintage street and shop signs. Don't miss the *chat noir* (black cat) from Montmartre and various tools depicting shop trades.

Hôtel Le Peletier

A covered gallery on the 1st floor links Hôtel Carnavalet with 17th-century Hôtel Le Peletier de St-Fargeau. The lovely ground-floor orangery showcases the museum's archaeological collection from prehistory and the Gallo-Roman period. Some of the nation's most important documents, paintings and other objects from the French Revolution (rooms 100 to 113) are on the 2nd floor. First-floor highlights include Fouquet's art nouveau jewellery shop from rue Royale and Marcel Proust's cork-tiled bedroom from his apartment on bd Haussmann (room 147), where he wrote most of the 7350-page literary cycle *À la Recherche du Temps Perdu* (Remembrance of Things Past).

DON'T MISS

- ➡ Marcel Proust's Bedroom
- ➡ Fouquet's Art Nouveau Shop
- ➡ Paul Signac's *Le Pont des Arts* (1928)

PRACTICALITIES

- ➡ Map p404
- ➡ www.carnavalet.paris.fr
- ➡ 23 rue de Sévigné, 3e
- ➡ ⌚10am-6pm Tue-Sun
- ➡ Ⓜ St-Paul, Chemin Vert or Rambuteau

SIGHTS

The Marais (meaning 'marsh' or 'swamp' in French) was exactly what its name implies right up until the 13th century, when it was converted to farmland. In the early 17th century Henri IV built place Royale (today's place des Vosges), turning the area into Paris' most fashionable residential address. When the aristocracy moved out of Paris to Versailles and Faubourg St-Germain, the Marais and its townhouses passed into the hands of ordinary Parisians. The 110-hectare area was given a major facelift in the late 1960s and early '70s, and today it is one of the city's most coveted addresses.

FREE PLACE DES VOSGES — CITY SQUARE

Map p404 (place des Vosges, 4e; MSt-Paul or Bastille) Inaugurated in 1612 as place Royale and thus the oldest square in Paris, place des Vosges is a strikingly elegant ensemble of 36 symmetrical houses with ground-floor arcades, steep slate roofs and large dormer windows arranged around a large and leafy square with four symmetrical fountains and an 1829 copy of a mounted statue of Louis XIII, originally placed here in 1639.

Only the earliest houses were built of brick; to save time, the rest were given timber frames and faced with plaster, which was later painted to resemble brick. The square received its present name in 1800 to honour the Vosges *département* (administrative division) for being the first in France to pay its taxes.

Between 1832 and 1848 writer Victor Hugo lived in an apartment on the 3rd floor of the square's Hôtel de Rohan-Guéménée, moving to the mansion a year after the publication of *Notre Dame de Paris* (The Hunchback of Notre Dame) and completing *Ruy Blas* while living here. The **Maison de Victor Hugo** (Map p404; www.musee-hugo.paris.fr; admission free; 10am-6pm Tue-Sun; MSt-Paul or Bastille) is now a small museum devoted to the life and times of the celebrated novelist and poet, with an impressive collection of his personal drawings and portraits. Temporary exhibitions command an admission fee.

HÔTEL DE SULLY — MANSION

Map p404 (62 rue St-Antoine, 4e; MSt-Paul or Bastille) In the southwestern corner of place des Vosges is the back entrance to this aristocratic mansion, built in 1625 and home to the headquarters of the Centre des Monuments Nationaux, responsible for many of France's historical monuments. From the square, duck beneath the arch and be instantly wooed by two beautifully decorated late-Renaissance courtyards, both festooned with allegorical reliefs of the seasons and the elements.

In the northern courtyard look to the southern side for spring (flowers and a bird in hand) and summer (wheat sheaves); in the southern courtyard turn to the northern side for autumn (grapes) and winter, with a symbol representing both the end of the year and the end of life. In the second courtyard are symbols for the elements: on the western side 'air' on the left and 'fire' on the right and on the eastern side 'earth' on the left and 'water' on the right.

> **LOCAL KNOWLEDGE**
>
> **SECRET CITY VIEWS**
>
> A few blocks east of bd de Belleville, the lovely but little-known **Parc de Belleville** (Map p402; MCouronnes) ensnares a hill almost 200m above sea level amid 4.5 hectares of greenery. Climb to the top for some of the best views of the city.

FREE HÔTEL DE VILLE — CITY HALL

Map p404 (www.paris.fr; place de l'Hôtel de Ville, 3e; MHôtel de Ville) Paris' beautiful neo-Renaissance town hall was gutted during the Paris Commune of 1871 and rebuilt in luxurious neo-Renaissance style between 1874 and 1882. The ornate facade is decorated with 108 statues of illustrious Parisians and outstanding temporary exhibitions held inside in the **Salle St-Jean** (Map p404; 5 rue Lobau) generally have a Parisian theme and are free.

From December to early March, an **ice-skating rink** (Patinoire de l'Hôtel de Ville; Map p404; admission free, skate rental €5; noon-10pm Mon-Fri, 9am-10pm Sat & Sun, Dec-Mar; MHôtel de Ville) sets up outside this beautiful building, creating something of a picture-book experience.

FREE MUSÉE COGNACQ-JAY — ART MUSEUM

Map p404 (www.cognacq-jay.paris.fr; 8 rue Elzévir, 3e; admission free; 10am-6pm Tue-Sun; MSt-Paul or Chemin Vert) This museum in Hôtel de

THE NEW-LOOK PICASSO MUSEUM

One of Paris' most beloved art collections re-opens its doors in 2013 after massive renovations. Housed in the stunning, mid-17th-century Hôtel Salé, the **Musée Picasso** (Map p404; ☎01 42 71 25 21; www.musee-picasso.fr; 5 rue de Thorigny; Ⓜ St-Paul or Chemin Vert) woos art lovers with more than 3500 drawings, engravings, paintings, ceramic works and sculptures by the *grand maître* (great master) Pablo Picasso (1881–1973). The extraordinary collection was donated to the French government by the artist's heirs in lieu of paying inheritance tax.

Donon brings together oil paintings, pastels, sculpture, objets d'art, jewellery, porcelain and furniture from the 18th century assembled by Ernest Cognacq (1839–1928), founder of La Samaritaine department store, and his wife Louise Jay.

Although Cognacq appreciated little of his collection, boasting to all who would listen that he had never visited the Louvre and was only acquiring collections for the status, the artwork and objets d'art give a pretty good idea of upper-class tastes during the Age of Enlightenment. Temporary exhibitions command an admission fee.

MUSÉE DE L'HISTOIRE DE FRANCE — HISTORY MUSEUM

Map p404 (60 rue des Francs Bourgeois, 3e; adult/student/under 18yr €3/2.30/free; ⏲10am-5.30pm Mon & Wed-Fri, 2-5.30pm Sat & Sun; Ⓜ Rambuteau or St-Paul) Paris' French History museum, inside the early 18th-century Hôtel de Rohan-Soubise, contains antique furniture, 18th-century paintings and documents – everything from medieval incunabula and letters written by Joan of Arc to the wills of Louis XIV and Napoleon. The ceiling and walls of the interior are extravagantly painted and gilded in the rococo style.

Look out for the Cabinet des Singes, a room filled with frescoes of playful, cheeky monkeys painted by Christophe Huet between 1749 and 1752. France's **National Archives** (Map p404; ☎01 40 27 60 96; www.archivesnationales.culture.gouv.fr; 60 rue des Francs Bourgeois; Ⓜ Rambuteau or St-Paul) are housed in the Soubise wing of the same building.

MUSÉE DES ARTS ET MÉTIERS — MUSEUM

Map p402 (www.arts-et-metiers.net; 60 rue de Réaumur, 3e; adult/student/child €6.50/4.50/free; ⏲10am-6pm Tue, Wed & Fri-Sun, to 9.30pm Thu; Ⓜ Arts et Métiers) The Arts & Crafts Museum, dating to 1794 and the oldest museum of science and technology in Europe, is a must for anyone with an interest in how things tick or work. Housed inside the sublime 18th-century priory of St-Martin des Champs, some 3000 instruments, machines and working models from the 18th to 20th centuries are displayed according to theme (from Construction and Energy to Transportation) across three floors.

Taking pride of place in the choir of the attached church of St-Martin des Champs is Foucault's original pendulum, which he introduced to the world at the Universal Exhibition in Paris 1855, and Louis Blériot's monoplane from 1909. Guided tours are in French only but the excellent English-language audioguide (€5) more than compensates.

MUSÉE DE LA CHASSE ET DE LA NATURE — MUSEUM

Map p404 (www.chassenature.org; 62 rue des Archives, 3e; adult/18-25yr/under 18yr €6/4.50/free; ⏲11am-6pm Tue-Sun; Ⓜ Rambuteau or Hôtel de Ville) The Hunting & Nature Museum may sound like an oxymoron to the politically correct, but in France, where hunting is a very big deal, to show your love for nature is to go out and shoot something – or so it would seem. The delightful Hôtel Guénégaud (1651) is positively crammed with weapons, paintings, sculpture and objets d'art related to hu nting and, of course, lots and lots of trophies – horns, antlers, heads.

MUSÉE DE LA POUPÉE — DOLL MUSEUM

Map p404 (www.museedelapoupeeparis.com; impasse Berthaud; adult/3-12yr €8/4, under 12yr free Sun, everyone free 2nd Fri of month; ⏲10am-6pm Tue-Sat; Ⓜ Rambuteau) Frightening to some – all those beady little eyes and silent screams – the Doll Museum is more appropriate for adults than for children. There are around 500 of the lifeless creatures here, dating back to 1800, all arranged in scenes representing Paris through the centuries.

There are temporary exhibitions (think Barbie and Sindy and 'France's best plush animals'), as well as workshops, storytelling sessions and a 'hospital' for antique dolls.

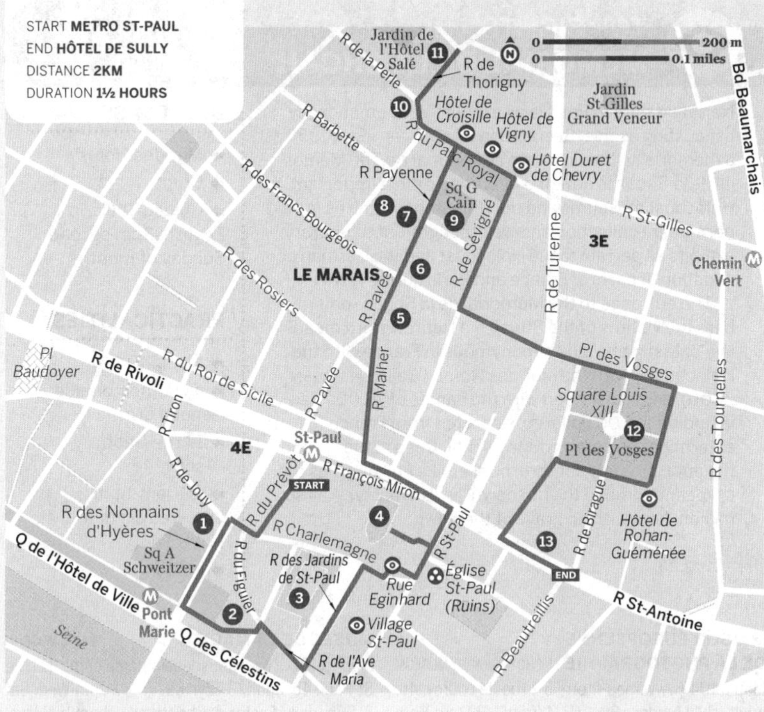

Neighbourhood Walk

Medieval Marais Meanderings

While Henri IV was busy having place Royale (place des Vosges) built, aristocrats were commissioning gold-brick *hôtels particuliers* – beautiful Renaissance structures that lend the Marais an architectural harmony unknown elsewhere in Paris.

From rue François Miron, walk south on rue du Prévôt to rue Charlemagne. To the right at 7 rue de Jouy stands the **1 Hôtel d'Aumont**, built around 1650. Continue south along rue des Nonnains d'Hyères and turn left onto rue de l'Hôtel de Ville. At 1 rue du Figuier is **2 Hôtel de Sens**, the oldest Marais mansion with geometric gardens and a neo-Gothic turret. Begun around 1475, it was built as digs for the powerful archbishops of Sens and later rented out. It was restored in mock Gothic style in 1911.

Continue southeast along rue de l'Ave Maria, then northeast along rue des Jardins de St-Paul. To the left, the two truncated towers are all that remain of Philippe-Auguste's **3 enceinte**, a fortified wall (1190) once guarded by 39 towers. Cross rue Charlemagne, duck into rue Eginhard and follow it to rue St-Paul and **4 Église St-Paul St-Louis** (1641). At the end of rue St-Paul, turn left, then walk north up rue Malher and rue Pavée, the first cobbled road in Paris. At No 24 is the late Renaissance **5 Hôtel Lamoignon**, built for the legitimised daughter of Henri II.

North along rue Payenne is the back of the **6 Musée Carnavalet**; the Revolutionary-era 'Temple of Reason' **7 Chapelle de l'Humanité** at No 5; and the rear of the **8 Musée Cognacq-Jay**. From grassy **9 Sq George Cain** opposite 11 rue Payenne, walk northwest to more spectacular 17th-century *hôtels particuliers:* **10 Hôtel de Libéral Bruant** at 1 rue de la Perle, and **11 Hôtel Salé** crammed with Picassos at 5 rue de Thorigny.

Retrace your steps to rue du Parc Royal, walk south down rue de Sévigné and then follow rue des Francs Bourgeois eastwards to end with sublime **12 place des Vosges** and **13 Hôtel de Sully**.

TOP SIGHTS
MÉMORIAL DE LA SHOAH

No single sight in Paris is as exhaustive or emotionally exhausting as this. Secreted in what began life in 1956 as a memorial to the unknown Jewish martyr, the Mémorial de la Shoah is now one of Europe's most important Holocaust museums and documentation centres. A vast permanent collection and well-thought-out temporary exhibits all pertain to the Holocaust and the German occupation of parts of France and Paris during WWII.

The entrance to the Mémorial de la Shoah remembers the victims of the Shoah – a Hebrew word meaning 'catastrophe' and synonymous in France with the Holocaust – with the Mur des Noms (Wall of Names; 2006), a wall inscribed with the names of 76,000 Jews, including 11,000 children, deported from France to Nazi extermination camps during WWII. Deep in the crypt of the appropriately sombre, bunker-like building, lies the crypt and tomb to the unknown Jewish martyr – all six million Jews with no grave of their own.

DON'T MISS

- ➡ Mur des Noms
- ➡ Crypt
- ➡ Guided Tours in English, 3pm second Sunday of month

PRACTICALITIES

- ➡ Map p404
- ➡ www.memorialdelashoah.org
- ➡ 17 rue Geoffroy l'Asnier, 4e
- ➡ ⏲10am-6pm Sun-Wed & Fri, to 10pm Thu
- ➡ Ⓜ St-Paul

MAISON EUROPÉENNE DE LA PHOTOGRAPHIE — PHOTOGRAPHY MUSEUM

Map p404 (www.mep-fr.org; 5-7 rue de Fourcy, 4e; adult/child/under 8yr €7/4/free; ⏲11am-8pm Wed-Sun; Ⓜ St-Paul or Pont Marie) The European House of Photography, housed in the overly renovated Hôtel Hénault de Cantorbe (dating – believe it or not – from the early 18th century), has cutting-edge temporary exhibits (usually retrospectives on single photographers), as well as an enormous permanent collection on the history of photography and its connections with France.

There are frequent showings of short films and documentaries on weekend afternoons. The Japanese garden at the entrance is a delight.

FREE MUSÉE ÉDITH PIAF — MUSEUM

Map p402 (☎01 43 55 52 72; 5 rue Crespin du Gast, 11e; admission free; ⏲by appointment 1-6pm Mon-Wed, 10am-noon Thu; Ⓜ Ménilmontant) This private museum in Ménilmontant, some 1.5km from the birthplace of the iconic singer Édith Piaf and closer to her final resting place in Cimetière du Père Lachaise, follows the life and career of the 'urchin sparrow' through memorabilia, recordings, personal objects, letters and other documentation. Admission by advance reservation; book a week in advance.

MUSÉE DE LA MAGIE — MAGIC MUSEUM

Map p404 (www.museedelamagie.com; 11 rue St-Paul, 4e; adult/3-12yr €9/7; ⏲2-7pm Wed, Sat & Sun, daily Easter & Christmas school holidays; Ⓜ St-Paul) The ancient arts of magic, optical illusion and sleight of hand are explored in this Magic Museum, in the 16th-century *caves* (cellars) of the Marquis de Sade's former home. Admission includes a magic show and a combination ticket covering admission to the adjoining Musée des Automates – a collection of antique wind-up toys – is available (€12/9).

MUSÉE D'ART ET D'HISTOIRE DU JUDAÏSME — MUSEUM

Map p404 (www.mahj.org; 71 rue du Temple; adult/under 26yr €6.80/free; ⏲11am-6pm Mon-Fri, 10am-6pm Sun; Ⓜ Rambuteau) To delve into the historic heart of the Marais' long-established Jewish community visit this facinating museum, housed in the sumptuous Hôtel de St-Aignan dating from 1650. The museum traces the evolution of Jewish communities from the Middle Ages to the present, with particular emphasis on French Jewish history and the history of Jewish communities in other parts of Europe and North Africa. Highlights include documents relating to the Dreyfus Affair; and works by Chagall, Modigliani and

Soutine. A creative array of music, writing and history workshops for children, adults and families complement the excellent exhibitions; see the website for details.

The area in which the musuem sits is known as Pletzl (from the Yiddish for 'little square'). This colourful Jewish quarter starts in rue des Rosiers and continues along rue Ste-Croix de la Bretonnerie to rue du Temple. Don't miss the **Art Nouveau synagogue** (Map p404; 10 rue Pavée) designed in 1913 by Hector Guilard, also responsible for the city's famous metro entrances.

MARCHÉ DU TEMPLE — MARKET

Map p402 (btwn rue Perrée & rue Dupetit Thouars, 3e; MTemple) Easily the most exciting project in this constantly changing and evolving *quartier*, this old covered market has art nouveau ironwork to die for. Also known as the Carreau du Temple, the market started life in 1809 as a set of four wooden pavilions where silks, lace, leather and other materials were sold. In 1863 they were replaced by a glass-and-iron structure, now the focus of a mammoth reconstruction and restoration project that will see the covered market transformed by the end of 2013 into a vibrant, state-of-the-art cultural and sports centre for the local community. The pavement terrace of **Café Crème** (Map p402; 4 rue Dupetit Thouars, 3e; MTemple) is the perfect spot for savouring this exciting architectural project.

EATING

Packed with restaurants and bistros of every imaginable type, the Marais is one of Paris' premier dining neighbourhoods. Book ahead for weekends.

TOP CHOICE LE DAUPHIN — BISTRO €€

Map p402 (01 55 28 78 88; 131 av Parmentier, 11e; 2-/3-course lunch menu €23/27; lunch & dinner Tue-Fri, dinner Sat; MGoncourt) Advance reservations are essential at this buzzing wine bar. Run by the same team as Le Chateaubriand a few doors down, the stark white space with marble floor, marble bar, marble ceiling and marble walls (and the odd mirror) is a temple to taste. Lunch is a choice of two starters and two mains (one fish, one meat), presented like a work of art on (predictably) white china.

But the pièce de résistance is evening dining when foodies pick and choose their way through an exquisite succession of *petites assiettes comme tapas* (small tapas-style dishes).

TOP CHOICE AU PASSAGE — BISTRO €

Map p402 (01 43 55 07 52; www.facebook.com/aupassage; 1bis passage de St-Sébastien, 11e; 2-/3-course lunch menu €13.50/19.50, dinner €20-35; lunch & dinner Mon-Fri, dinner Sat; MSt-Sébastien-Froissart) Have faith in talented Australian chef James Henry at this raved-about *petit bar de quartier* (neighbourhood bar) with vegetable crates piled scruffily in the window and a fridge filling one corner of the old-fashioned dining room.

The lunch menu – a good-value, uncomplicated choice of two starters and two mains – is chalked on the blackboard, while dinner sees waiting staff in jeans twirl in and out of the pocket-sized kitchen with tapas-style starters to share, followed by a feisty shoulder of lamb, side of beef or other meaty cut for the entire table. Advance reservations essential.

LE CHATEAUBRIAND — MODERN FRENCH €€€

Map p402 (01 43 57 45 95; www.lechateaubriand.fr; 129 av Parmentier, 11e; mains €27-46; lunch & dinner Tue-Sat; MGoncourt) The quintessential *neobistro*, Le Chateaubriand is a simple but elegantly tiled art deco dining room with some of the most imaginative cuisine in town. Chef Iñaki Aizpitarte – a name that could only be Basque – is well travelled and his dishes show that global exposure again and again in their odd combinations (watermelon and mackerel, milk-fed veal with langoustines and truffles).

Dinner is a five-course tasting menu with no choices. Divine. Advance reservations essential.

DERRIÈRE — MODERN FRENCH €€

Map p402 (01 44 61 91 95; www.derriere-resto.com; 69 rue des Gravilliers, 3e; lunch menu €25, mains €17-24; lunch & dinner Mon-Fri & Sun, dinner Sat; MArts et Métiers) Play table ping pong between courses, sit on the bed glass of champers in hand, lounge between book cases, or entertain a dinner party of 12 – such is the nature of this apartment restaurant with courtyard seating in summer. Its vibe might be chilled in a trendy 'shoes off' kind of way, but Derrière (literally, 'Behind') is deadly serious in the kitchen.

LOCAL KNOWLEDGE

EAT STREETS

Rue Oberkampf, 11e, & rue de Ménilmontant, 11e & 20e Mainstream Marais bistros and bags of hip hang-outs, the streets buzz with diners and denizens of the night, every night.

Rue Jean-Pierre Timbaud, 11e This increasingly happening street is perfect for casual cafe-bar dining and snacking over drinks.

Rue des Rosiers, 4e Jewish restaurants (some Ashkenazic, some Sephardic, not all kosher) serving specialities from Central Europe, North Africa and Israel. Many are closed Friday evenings, Saturdays and Jewish holidays.

Rue Au Maire, 3e Small Chinese noodle shops and restaurants run riot here, perfect for those craving authentic Chinese food without the trek to the larger Chinatown in the 13e.

Rue de Belleville, 20e Dine on Chinese, Southeast Asian or Middle Eastern on this busy road and the streets around it.

Bd de Belleville, 11e & 20e Several couscous restaurants dot this busy thoroughfare.

Classic French bistro dishes and more inventive creations are excellent, as is its Sunday brunch. Advance reservations for dinner essential.

LE PETIT MARCHÉ — BISTRO €€

Map p404 (☎01 42 72 06 67; 9 rue de Béarn, 3e; mains €17-20; Ⓜ Chemin Vert) A faintly fusion-cuisine is what makes this cosy bistro with old cream beams, candles on the tables and mirrors on the walls stand out. Raw tuna wrapped in sesame seeds, ginger-spiced prawns, and monkfish medallions with figs give a creative Asian kick to a menu that otherwise reassures with old French bistro favourites around for centuries.

Lunch menus are excellent value, but evening dining – à la carte only – is a pricier affair. Best of all, this address is just footsteps from Paris' utterly gorgeous place des Vosges.

CHATOMAT — MODERN FRENCH €€

Map p402 (☎01 47 97 25 77; 6 rue Victor Letalle, 20e; mains €15-20; ⊙dinner Wed-Sun; Ⓜ Ménilmontant, Couronnes or Père Lachaise) No dinner address is worth the trek to lesser known Ménilmontant more than this contemporary bistro with signature plain white walls, pinch of post-industrial flavour and bags of foodie buzz. Fronted with flare by Brazilian Antonio and manned with much creativity in the kitchen by Alice and Victor, the old shop-turned-restaurant cooks up just three starters, three mains and three desserts each night – and none disappoint. Book at least a few days in advance.

NANASHI — FUSION €

Map p402 (☎09 60 00 25 59; www.nanashi.fr; 57 rue Charlot, 3e; bento €14-16; ⊙noon-midnight Mon-Fri, to 6pm Sat & Sun; Ⓜ Filles du Calvaire) A fabulous lunch and after-dark address wedged between boutiques in the Haut Marais, this hip industrial space with large street-facing windows and concrete floor is uber-cool, ultra-healthy and great value. Pick from creative salads, soups and bento boxes chalked on the board, and whatever you do, don't miss out on the amazing and astonishing, freshly squeezed fruit and veg cocktails. Weekend brunch €17.

CANDELARIA — TAQUERIA

Map p402 (www.candelariaparis.com; 52 rue Saintonge; tacos €3, quesadillas & tostadas €3.50; ⊙noon-midnight Thu-Sat, to 11pm Sun-Wed; ❄; Ⓜ Filles du Calvaire) You definitely need to know about this cool, two-room taqueria to find it. Wedged between boutiques in the Haut Marais, Candelaria is pure, unadulterated hipness in that nonchalant manner Paris does so well. Lunch and weekend brunch is served at the bar at the front, or wait for the secret back room to open to indulge in authentic tacos, quesadillas and tostadas around a candlelit shared table. The party can get raucous at times, and occasional DJ sets, tastings, post-gallery drinks and other happenings only amplify the cool factor to sky high. The Bloody Marys and other more creative cocktails shaken at weekend brunches (noon to 4pm) are addictive. No surprise that Carina Soto

Velasquez, the Colombian woman behind Candelaria, once worked at the Experimental Cocktail Club. Check its Facebook page or Twitter feed for events.

404 NORTH AFRICAN €€

Map p402 (☎01 42 74 57 81; www.404-resto.com; 69 rue des Gravilliers, 11e; lunch menu €17, mains €17-26; ⊙lunch & dinner daily; MArts et Métiers) Plump on one of the Marais' trendiest dining 'n' drinking streets, this Maghreb (North African) caravanserai is as comfortable as you get in Paris – and it's fabulous! Marvel at the Thousand and One Nights decor – a real feast for the eyes with all those antiques and curios – and gorge on excellent couscous dishes (€16 to €26), *tajines* (€16 to €21), grills (€15 to €26) and fish *pastilla* (Moroccan pie).

Hot date tip: weekend *brunch berbère* (Berber brunch, €21).

CHEZ JANOU PROVENÇAL €€

Map p404 (☎01 42 72 28 41; www.chezjanou.com; 2 rue Roger Verlomme, 3e; mains €15-20; ⊙lunch & dinner; MChemin Vert) Push your way in, order a kir or one of 80 different pastis from the jam-packed bar while you wait for a table, and revel in the buzz of this busy spot. Cuisine is Provençal (or as close as you get to Provençal in Paris) with all the southern classics like *brandade de morue* (salt cod purée with potatoes), ratatouille, and lavender-scented *crème brulée* well covered.

Not recommended for the claustrophobic (unless it's summer and you succeed in nabbing a seat on the terrace). Advance reservations essential.

CANTINE MERCI CAFE €

Map p404 (www.merci-merci.com; 111 bd Beaumarchais, 3e; mains €12-18; ⊙lunch Mon-Sat; MSt-Sébastien–Froissart) This basement canteen might well share the shop floor with nifty bathroom gadgets and designer kitchen gear, but its gastronomic thrust is as inspired as the hip concept store (p174) in which it squats. Lunch is what girlfriends come here for (by the droves), to feast on healthy and zesty salads, soups and savoury tarts, all oozing bags of vegetable creativity.

ROSE BAKERY CAFE €

Map p402 (☎01 49 96 54 01; 30 rue Debelleyme, 3e; mains €7-18; ⊙9am-6.30pm Tue-Sun; MFilles du Calvaire or St-Sébastien–Froissart) Savoury tarts, salads, risotto, great breakfasts, feisty organic fruit juices and lots of different teas at this hip, English-style daytime eating address with gold-stone walls and an open kitchen.

SOYA CANTINE BIO VEGETARIAN €€

Map p402 (☎01 48 06 33 02; www.soya75.fr; 20 rue de la Pierre Levée, 11e; mains €15-20, 2-/3-course lunch menu €16/19; ⊙lunch & dinner Tue-Sat, lunch Sun; MGoncourt) A real favourite for its hip location in an old industrial *atelier* (think bare cement, metal columns and big windows), Soya is a full-on vegetarian eatery in what was once a staunchly working-class district. Dishes, many tofu-based, are 95% organic and the weekend brunch buffet (€23.50) is a deliciously lazed, languid and organic affair. A glass floor floods the basement area with light.

L'ALLER-RETOUR BISTRO

Map p402 (5 rue Charles-François Dupuis, 3e; mains €10-20; ⊙lunch & dinner Tue-Fri, dinner Sat; MTemple) One of a cluster of trendy boutique addresses in the Haut Marais, this bistro is overtly retro in its interior design and a complete carnivore in the kitchen – a *bar à viande* (meat bar) is how it describes itself. Grilled meat and fine wine is its Holy Grail, with staggering success, and its €10.90 lunch deal, including a glass of *vin*, is a steal.

Know how to say *bleu* (blue), *saignant* (rare), *à point* (medium) and *bien cuit* (well done) before stepping foot in here.

BISTROT DE L'OULETTE REGIONAL CUISINE €€€

Map p404 (☎01 42 71 43 33; www.l-oulette.com; 38 rue des Tournelles, 20e; 2-/3- course lunch menu €13/18, dinner menus €26 & €33; ⊙lunch & dinner Mon-Fri, dinner Sat; MBastille or Chemin Vert) A younger cousin of the chic **L'Oulette** (Map p411; ☎01 40 02 02 12; www.l-oulette.com; 15 place Lachambeaudie; starters €16-32, mains €26-41, 2-/3-course menus €38/42, with wine €44/48; ⊙lunch & dinner to 10.15pm Mon-Fri; Cour St-Émilion) in Bercy, this bistro bustles by day and night with a mix of locals and tourists who are here for the capable south-western provincial cooking. Duck features heavily – try the *foie gras de canard* (fattened duck livers) or the *magret de canard* (fillet of duck breast).

Wines include almost a dozen from the southwest.

LE VILLARET FRENCH €€€

Map p402 (☎01 43 57 89 76; 13 rue Ternaux, 11e; mains €20-40; ⏰lunch Mon-Fri, dinner Mon-Sat; Ⓜ Parmentier) Twinned boxed bay leaf trees herald the entrance to this discreet neighbourhood bistro that gets packed out with a wealthy suited clientele at lunchtime. Indeed diners are said to cross Paris to sample Le Villaret's rich specialities such as *velouté de cèpes* (mushroom soup) and *jarret de veau à la poudre foie gras* (veal shank sprinkled with foie gras).

QUI PLUME LA LUNE FUSION, GASTRONOMIC €€€

Map p404 (☎01 48 07 45 48; 50 rue Amelot, 3e; lunch menu €35, dinner menus €45-82; ⏰lunch & dinner Tue-Sat; Ⓜ St-Sébastien–Froissart) The attention to detail at this gastronomic restaurant named after a film is extraordinary. From the driftwood sculptures and miniature vase strung with a ribbon by the door to the exquisite culinary creations with Japanese overtones, Who Plucked the Moon invites a generous intimacy. Old stone walls add a certain romance.

LE REPAIRE DE CARTOUCHE MODERN FRENCH €€€

Map p404 (☎01 47 00 25 86; 8 bd des Filles du Calvaire & 99 rue Amelot, 3e; mains €25-30; ⏰lunch & dinner Tue-Sat; Ⓜ St-Sébastien–Froissart) With entrances at the front and back, 'Cartouche's Den' – a reference to the 18th-century Parisian 'Robin Hood' Louis-Dominique Cartouche – looks to the past and future. It's an old-fashioned place that takes a very modern, innovative approach to French food under the direction of Norman chef Rodolphe Paquin.

As its name implies and the rifle on the wall underscores, it focuses on meat and game, though there are some excellent fish and shellfish dishes on the menu.

LE GRAND APPÉTIT VEGAN €

Map p404 (☎01 40 27 04 95; 9 rue de la Cerisaie, 4e; mains €11.50-13; ⏰noon-3pm & 7-9pm Mon-Thu, 11am-2.15pm Fri; Ⓜ Bastille) No eggs, no sugar, no dairy products, no meat and no preprepared products is the culinary mantra of this *végétalien* (vegan) lunch address, with an excellent organic and macrobiotic shop next door selling vegan food products. Pick from a *petite* or *grande* veggie plate, a miso soup, or an inventive *bol garni* (bowl) of rice, organic cereals, seaweed and vegetables.

The sushi-style *norimaki* (seaweed-wrapped rice rolls with veg and tofu) are delicious.

L'AS DU FELAFEL JEWISH €

Map p404 (34 rue des Rosiers, 4e; takeaway dishes €5-8; ⏰noon-midnight Sun-Thu, to 5pm Fri; Ⓜ St-Paul) The lunchtime queue stretching halfway down the street from this place says it all! This Parisian favourite, 100% worth the inevitable wait, is *the* address for kosher, perfectly deep-fried chickpea balls and turkey or lamb shwarma sandwiches. Do as every Parisian does and takeaway.

LE HANGAR BISTRO €€

Map p404 (☎01 42 74 55 44; 12 impasse Berthaud, 3e; mains €15-22; ⏰Tue-Sat; Ⓜ Rambuteau) Unusual for big mouths like us, we almost balk at revealing details of this perfect little restaurant tucked away down an alley. It serves all the bistro favourites – *entrecôte* (beef steak), rillettes, steak tartare – in relaxing, very quiet surrounds. The terrace is a delight in fine weather and the service both professional and personal.

LE BARATIN BISTRO €€€

Map p402 (☎01 43 49 39 70; 3 rue Jouye-Rouve, 20e; mains €20-30, lunch menu €18; ⏰lunch & dinner Tue-Fri, dinner Sat; Ⓜ Pyrénées or Belleville) *Baratin* (chatter) rhymes with *bar à vin* (wine bar) in French and this animated venue just steps from the lively Belleville *quartier* does both awfully well. In addition it offers some of the best (and very affordable) French food in the 20e on its ever-changing blackboard. The selection of wine (some organic) by the glass or carafe is excellent. Reservations essential.

CHEZ MARIANNE JEWISH €

Map p404 (2 rue des Hospitalières St-Gervais, 4e; mains €18.50-24; ⏰noon-midnight; Ⓜ St-Paul) Absolutely heaving at lunchtime, Chez Marianne translates as elbow-to-elbow eating beneath age-old beams on copious portions of falafel, hummus, purées of aubergine and chickpeas, and 25-odd other *zakouski* (hors d'œuvres; €12/14/16 for plate of 4/5/6). Fare is Sephardic rather than Ashkenazi (the norm at most Pletzl eateries), not Beth Din kosher, and a hole-in-the-wall window sells falafel in pita (€6) to munch on the move.

BREAKFAST IN AMERICA AMERICAN €

Map p404 (www.breakfast-in-america.com; 4 rue Malher, 4e; burgers €8.50-11.50, lunch menu student/adult €7.95/9.95; 8.30am-11pm; St-Paul) No reservations meaning pretty much you'll have to queue, especially on weekends, to get into this busy American-style diner with red banquettes, Formica surfaces, chicken wings and bottomless mugs of coffee. BIA (p213) is also in the Latin Quarter.

CHEZ NÉNESSE — BISTRO €

Map p404 (01 42 78 46 49; 17 rue Saintonge, 3e; mains €15-18; lunch & dinner Mon-Fri; Filles du Calvaire) Old-world bistro is the atmosphere at this tiny spot with lace curtains and a quality kitchen that only cooks classic French dishes eaten for oodles of centuries. Its *salade de canard au vinaigre d'hydromel* (duck salad in honey vinegar) and sweet *medallions de veau au miel* (veal medallions pan fried in honey) are not to be scoffed at.

L'ENOTECA — ITALIAN €€

Map p404 (01 42 78 91 44; www.enoteca.fr; 25 rue Charles V, 4e; menu €31, with wine €46; lunch & dinner; Sully-Morland or Pont Marie) The 'Vinotheque', a trattoria across the street from the historic Village St-Paul, serves *haute cuisine à l'italienne* and an excellent list of Italian wines by the glass to accompany it. It's no secret that this is one of the few Italian wine bars in Paris to take its *vino* seriously (there are 400 labels in the cellar), so book ahead.

Pasta dishes (€17 to €23) are excellent, as is the generous *tavola antipasti* (antipasto buffet table) served at lunch.

AMBASSADE D'AUVERGNE — TRADITIONAL FRENCH €€

Map p402 (01 42 72 31 22; www.ambassade-auvergne.com; 22 rue du Grenier St-Lazare; lunch menu €20, mains €16-20, ; lunch & dinner; Rambuteau) For truly hungry carnivores with a fetish for only the best products, the Auvergne embassy – an easy walk from the Centre Pompidou – is the place to head. Traditional cuisine from the Auvergne has been the restaurant's mantra for more than a century and dishes like *salade tiède de lentilles vertes du Puy* (warm green Puy lentil salad) and *saucisse de Parlan à l'aligot* (feisty pork sausage) will make you want to trip it straight to this tasty rural region in central France.

GEORGET (ROBERT ET LOUISE) — TRADITIONAL FRENCH €

Map p404 (01 42 78 55 89; 64 rue Vieille du Temple, 4e; lunch menu €12, plat du jour €16; lunch & dinner Wed-Sun, dinner Mon & Tue; St-Sébastien–Froissart) This 'country inn' with red gingham curtains offers simple and inexpensive French food, including *côte de bœuf* (side of beef 2/3 people, €42/63), cooked on an open fire. Arrive early to snag the farmhouse table next to the fireplace – the makings of a real jolly Rabelaisian evening.

HISTORIC INTERIORS

Depending where you eat, Parisian dining can be as much about feasting on a vintage interior as food.

Bofinger (Map p404; 01 42 72 87 82; www.bofingerparis.com; 5-7 rue de la Bastille, 4e; mains €20-38; lunch & dinner; Bastille) Scoff *choucroute* (sauerkraut with assorted meats), seafood dishes and other quintessential brasserie fare between art nouveau brass, glass and mirrors in Paris' oldest brasserie dating to 1864. Ask for a table downstairs beneath the *coupole* (stained-glass dome).

Le Dôme du Marais (Map p404; 01 42 74 54 17; www.ledomedumarais.fr; 53bis rue des Francs Bourgeois, 4e; 2-/3-course menu €26/32; lunch & dinner Tue-Sat; Rambuteau) Classic French dishes in a sublime, pre-Revolution building and former auction room with a glassed-in courtyard and knock-out, octagonal-shaped dining room. Brunch (€33) is help yourself to as much as you can eat.

Chez Jenny (Map p402; 01 44 54 39 00; www.chezjenny.com; 39 bd du Temple, 3e; mains €19-30; noon-midnight Sun-Thu, to 1am Fri & Sat; République) Feast on huge Alsatian *choucroute garnie* (sauerkraut with smoked or salted pork, frankfurters and potatoes), *baeckeoffe* (Alsatian meat and veg stew) and stunning marquetry of Alsatian scenes by Charles Spindler on the 1st floor at this cavernous brasserie c 1932.

CRÊPES, PANCAKES & TARTINES

The Marais ensnares some tip-top crêpe and pancake addresses – the perfect cheap lunch, sweet treat between meals or late-night munch.

Breizh Café (Map p404; www.breizhcafe.com; 109 rue Vieille du Temple, 3e; crêpes & galettes €3.80-11.80; ⊙lunch & dinner Wed-Sun; MSt-Sébastien–Froissart) Everything at the Breton Café (*breizh* is 'Breton' in Breton) is 100% authentic, be it the Cancale oysters, the 20 types of cider, or the organic-flour crêpes cooked to perfection.

Marche ou Crêpe (Map p402; 88 rue Oberkampf, 11e; crêpes & galettes €3-10; ⊙6pm-midnight Tue-Thu, 6pm-2am Fri & Sat, 5pm-midnight Sun; MParmentier) This little crêperie just south of the rue Jean-Pierre Timbaud bars and clubs has the added advantage of staying open late.

Bob's Kitchen (Map p402; 74 rue des Gravilliers, 11e; pancakes €5-8.50; ⊙8am-3pm Mon-Fri, 10am-4pm Sat & Sun; MArts et Métiers) If it's pancakes US-style you're after without a spot of cow's milk in sight, Bob's your man (although you might be hard pushed to even get in this tiny space, let alone snag a pew). Expect sweet and savoury pancakes, milk- and gluten-free, alongside one of the most creative vegetarian lunch menus in town that changes daily and flits all over the globe.

Cuisine de Bar (Map p402; 38 rue Debelleyme, 3e; tartines €10-15; MFilles du Calvaire) Paris' most famous bread-maker, Poilâne, cooks up savoury and sweet *tartines* (open sandwiches) in the Marais too. There is another branch (p236) in St-Germain.

LE CLOWN BAR — TRADITIONAL FRENCH €€

Map p402 (☎01 43 55 87 35; 114 rue Amelot, 11e; plat du jour €10.50; ⊙lunch & dinner Mon-Sat; P; MFilles du Calvaire) A wonderful wine-bar-cum-bistro next to the **Cirque d'Hiver** (1852), the Clown Bar is quite similar to a museum with its painted ceilings, mosaics on the wall, lovely zinc bar and circus memorabilia that touches on one of our favourite themes (especially cinematically) of all time: the evil clown. Don't be scared: the food is simple and unpretentious traditional French.

Parmentier de boudin à la normande (black pudding Parmentier with apple) is its most popular dish.

AUX VINS DES PYRÉNÉES — TRADITIONAL FRENCH €€

Map p404 (☎01 42 72 64 94; 25 rue Beautreillis, 4e; mains €15-20; ⊙lunch & dinner Sun-Fri, dinner Sat; MSt-Paul or Bastille) Tucked in a former wine warehouse, this is a lovely place to enjoy an unpretentious French meal with much exemplary wine. The fish, meat and game dishes are all good, but the foie gras and *pavé de rumsteak* (thick rump steak) are both worth a special mention – as is the wine list that features both celebrated and little-known estate wines.

Local *bobos* (bohemian bourgeois) love the old-world charm.

POZZETTO — ICE CREAM, CAFE €

Map p404 (www.pozzetto.biz; 39 rue du Roi de Sicile, 4e; ⊙11.30am-9pm Mon-Thu, to 11.30pm Fri-Sun; MSt-Paul) Urban myth says this gelato maker opened when a group of friends from northern Italy couldn't find their favourite ice cream in Paris so they imported the ingredients to create it from scratch. Twelve flavours – spatula'd, not scooped – include *gianduia torinese* (hazelnut chocolate from Turin) and *zabaione*, made from egg yolks, sugar and sweet Marsala wine, along with the more usual peach, pistachio and poire William. Great Italian coffee, too.

CAFFÉ BOBOLI — ITALIAN €€

Map p404 (www.caffeboboli.com; 13 rue du Roi de Sicile, 4e; pasta €13-14.50, mains €14.60-17; ⊙dinner Mon, lunch & dinner Tue-Sat; MSt-Paul) Affordable Italian fare in the heart of the Marais is what this small bright restaurant run by two young Florentines is about. Original paintings and photographs strung on the walls change every few months.

LE TRUMILOU — BISTRO €€

Map p404 (☎01 42 77 63 98; www.letrumilou.com; 84 quai de l'Hôtel de Ville, 4e; menus €16.50 & €19.50; MHôtel de Ville) This no-frills bistro is located just round the corner from the Hôtel de Ville and faces the posh Île de St-Louis square. Relax and unwind in a Parisian institution that's been in situ for over a century. If you're looking for an authentic menu from the early 20th century and prices (well, almost) to match, you won't do better than this. Specialities of the house include *canard aux pruneaux* (duck with prunes) and *ris de veau grand-mère* (veal sweetbreads in mushroom cream sauce).

LE PETIT DAKAR SENEGALESE €€

Map p404 (☎01 44 59 34 74; www.lepetitdakar.com; 6 rue Elzévir, 3e; mains €15-22, menu €15 (lunch only); ⏲lunch & dinner Tue-Sat, dinner Sun; Ⓜ St-Paul) Many consider this to be the most authentic Senegalese restaurant in Paris, and its *tiéboudienne* (rice, fish and vegetables, €18) – served Fridays and Saturdays – is definitely worth a return trip. It also runs cooking courses should you have the urge to cook the same back home.

LE POROKHANE AFRICAN, SENEGALESE €

Map p402 (☎01 40 21 86 74; http://www.restaurantporokhane.com; 3 rue Moret, 11e; ⏲dinner; Ⓜ Ménilmontant or Parmentier) A large dining room in hues of ochre and terracotta, this is a popular meeting place for Senegalese artists. The clientele apparently has *un peu tendance show-biz* (a bit of a show-biz bent), and live *kora* (a traditional string instrument) music is not unusual on weekends. Great address for dining after midnight.

TAI YIEN CHINESE €

Map p402 (☎01 42 41 44 16; 5 rue de Belleville, 11e; mains €8-15; ⏲lunch & dinner; Ⓜ Belleville) Packed to the rafters at lunchtime, this wholly authentic Hong Kong–style 'steam restaurant' is an experience – there is no better address for a rice or noodle fix, especially late in the evening. It's hard to imagine better *char siu* (barbecued pork) outside Chinatown.

DONG HUONG VIETNAMESE €

Map p402 (☎01 43 57 42 81; 14 rue Louis Bonnet, 11e; dishes €7-12; ⏲lunch & dinner Wed-Mon; Ⓜ Belleville) Despite a name that sounds like a Spanish Lothario, this no-frills Vietnamese noodle-shop-cum-restaurant serves great bowls of *pho* (noodles) to rooms full of appreciative regulars. The fact that the regulars are all Asian (and mainly Vietnamese) and the food comes out so fast is a testament to its authenticity and freshness.

REUAN THAI THAI €€

Map p402 (☎01 43 55 15 82; 36 rue de l'Orillon; mains €10-20; ⏲lunch & dinner; Ⓜ Belleville) This fragrant place offers some of the most authentic Thai food in Paris and has all your favourite Thai dishes. Half a dozen or so are vegetarian.

L'AVE MARIA FUSION €€

Map p402 (☎01 47 00 61 73; 1 rue Jacquard, 11e; mains €15-17; ⏲7pm-2am; Ⓜ Parmentier) This colourful canteen fuses the flavours of the southern hemisphere with hearty, hybrid and harmonious food. The music really livens up from midnight.

PIZZA PICK

Pink Flamingo (Map p404; ☎01 42 71 28 20; www.pinkflamingopizza.com; 105 rue Vieille du Temple, 3e; pizza €10.50-16; ⏲noon-3pm & 7-11.30pm; Ⓜ St-Sébastien–Froissart) The capital's most inventive, dare we say romantic, pizza joint on the Canal St-Martin (p136) has spawned a balloon base in the Marais too. Yes!

Al Taglio (Map p402; 2bis rue Neuve Popincourt, 11e; pizza €15-35 per kg; ⏲noon-11pm Sun-Thu, to midnight Fri & Sat; Ⓜ St-Sébastien–Froissart) Pizza *au poids* (by weight) is the trademark of this thoroughly contemporary pizza space with a trio of shared high tables with bar stools and a couple of regular tables spilling out onto a side alley. Its **second branch** (Map p404; 27 rue de Saintonge, 3e; pizza €15-35 per kg; ⏲noon-11pm Sun-Thu, to midnight Fri & Sat; Ⓜ Filles-du-Calvaire) in the 3e gets more crowded.

La Briciola (Map p402; ☎01 42 77 34 10; 64 rue Charlot, 3e; pizzas €10-20; ⏲lunch & dinner Mon-Sat; Ⓜ Oberkampf) Excellent pizzas, salads and wine at this friendly hole-in-the-wall Italian eatery in the northern Marais.

Grazie (Map p404; ☎01 42 78 11 96; www.graziegrazie.fr; 91 bd Beaumarchais, 3e; pizzas €10-20; ⏲lunch & dinner; Ⓜ Filles du Calvaire) Pizza chic is what this oh-so *bobo* Italian pizzeria and cocktail bar is all about. The place is designed like a New York loft and beautiful people are a constant. Not the best place for the most authentic in town, but the best for posing over a pizza slice or mozzarella ball.

MARCHÉ AUX ENFANTS ROUGES INTERNATIONAL

Map p402 (39 rue de Bretagne, 3e; ⏲8.30am-1pm & 4-7.30pm Tue-Fri, 4-8pm Sat, 8.30am-2pm Sun; Ⓜ Filles du Calvaire) Built in 1615, Paris' oldest covered market is secreted behind an inconspicuous green metal gate – and for good reason. A glorious maze of 20-odd food stalls selling ready-to-eat dishes from around the globe, it is a great place to come for a meander and munch with locals. Grab a Japanese bento box, Caribbean platter or a more traditional French crêpe, and consume at communal tables. End with a coffee across the street at **Café Charlot** (Map p402; www.cafecharlotparis.com; 38 rue de Bretagne, 3e; ⏲7-2am daily; Ⓜ Filles du Calvaire), a great neighbourhood cafe in a former bakery with retro white tiles and the perfect pavement terrace to lap up authentic Haut Marais vibe.

DRINKING & NIGHTLIFE

A lively mix of gay-friendly (and gay-only) cafe society and bourgeois arty spots, with an interesting sprinkling of eclectic bars and relatively raucous pubs, the Marais is a spot par excellence when it comes to a night out. Rue Oberkampf is the essential hub of the Ménilmontant bar crawl, springing from a few cafes to being the epicentre of a vibrant, rapidly expanding bar scene. But as Oberkampf commercialises, the arty/edgy crowd is moving steadily outwards, through cosmopolitan Belleville and towards La Villette.

AUX DEUX AMIS CAFE, BAR

Map p402 (☎01 58 30 38 13; 45 rue Oberkampf, 11e; ⏲8am-2am Tue-Sat; Ⓜ Oberkampf) From the well-worn, tiled floor to the day's menu scrawled in marker on the vintage mirror behind the bar and the *tarif des consommations* (drinks price list) stuck on a tatty sheet in the window, Aux Deux Amis is the quintessential Parisian neighbourhood bar if ever there was one. The place – steps from the noisy fruit, veg and cheese stalls of the Tuesday and Friday morning market, **Marché Popincourt** (Map p402; bd Richard Lenoir; Ⓜ Oberkampf) – is perfect for a coffee any time from dawn to dark, and it serves a great choice of tapas-style nibbles and wine in the evening. But to get the full flavour of Aux Deux Amis, you have to come after the market on Friday when the house speciality – *tartare de cheval* (finely cut horsemeat seasoned with a secret mix of herbs and seasonings) – is cooked up (or rather not cooked) as a *plat du jour* (dish of the day) at lunchtime and as tapas in the evening. Bon appétit!

CINÉMA CAFÉ MERCI CAFE

Map p404 (www.merci-merci.com; 111 bd Beaumarchais, 3e; ⏲Mon-Sat; Ⓜ St-Sébastien–Froissart) A suitably stark, retro interior dresses this small cafe run by concept store Merci (p174) and dedicated to the 7th art (aka cinema). B&W snaps of Vivien Leigh, Katherine Hepburn and other movie stars grace the walls; seating is a hip mix of banquet, low coffee table etc; and its retro *citronnade maison* – extra tart and tongue-tickling homemade lemonade is out of this world.

If books, not flicks, is your zeitgeist head next door to Merci's equally trendy **Used Book Café Merci** (Map p404; www.merci-merci.com; 11 bd Beaumarchais, 3e; ⏲10am-6pm Mon-Sat; Ⓜ St-Sébasten–Froissart).

PANIC ROOM BAR

Map p404 (www.panicroomparis.com; 101 rue Amelot, 11e; ⏲Mon-Sat; Ⓜ St-Sébastien–Froissart) This brazenly wild bar just east of the Haut Marais is not quite as terrifying or forbidding as its name suggests. A wildly flavoured cocktail – such as gin shaken with strawberries and basil, or a cognac-based creation mixing cucumber, coriander and ginger – is the thing to sip here, especially during happy hour (6.30pm to 8.30pm). Check its website for DJ sets, gigs and happenings.

LE BARAV WINE BAR

Map p402 (☎01 48 04 57 59; www.lebarav.fr; 6 rue Charles-François Dupuis, 3e; ⏲Tue-Sat; Ⓜ Temple) This hipster *bar à vin*, sitting smartly on one of the trendiest streets in the Haut Marais, oozes atmosphere – and one of the city's loveliest pavement terraces. Its extensive wine list is complemented by tasty food (lunch *plat du jour* €10.50), seating is at vintage bistro tables or on bar stools, and its wine shop a few doors down hosts great *dégustations à thème* (themed wine tastings; reserve in advance).

LA MANGERIE TAPAS BAR

Map p404 (☎01 42 77 49 35; http://la-mangerie.com; 7 rue de Jarente, 4e; tapas €5-11; ⏲Mon-Sat; ⓂSt-Paul) A heaving 'after work' drinks venue if ever there was one, La Mangerie cooks up a colourful choice of Spanish-inspired tapas – grab a pencil, paper and tick the boxes to order – and good choice of wine by the glass. But it's the buoyant vibe and buzzing atmosphere, orchestrated to perfection by charismatic owner and front-of-house, Serge, that are the real reasons to come here.

Reserve in advance to ensure a street-level pew; tables in the cellar are less appealing. Love the bicycle strung on the wall!

ZÉRO ZÉRO BAR

Map p404 (www.radiozerozero.com; 89 rue Amelot, 11e; ⏲Mon-Sat; ⓂSt-Sébastien–Froissart) A heaving Saturday-night address on rue Amelot, Zéro Zéro screams Berlin with its banquet seating and tag-covered walls (and ceiling and windows and bar...). Electro and house is the sound and the house cocktail, a potent rum-and-ginger concoction, ensures a wild party spirit.

LA BELLE HORTENSE WINE BAR

Map p404 (www.cafeine.com; 31 rue Vieille du Temple, 4e; ⏲daily; ⓂHôtel de Ville or St-Paul) Another creative venue from Xavier Denamur (p172), this literary wine bar named after a Jacques Roubaud novel fuses shelf after shelf of good books to read with an equally good wine list and enriching weekly agenda of book readings, signings and art events. A zinc bar and original 19th-century ceiling set the mood perfectly.

LA PERLA MEXICAN, BAR

Map p404 (www.cafepacifico-laperla.com; 26 rue François Miron, 4e; ⏲Thu-Wed; ⓂSt-Paul or Hôtel de Ville) The tables at this saloon-style Mexican joint with centrepiece-bar were clearly an afterthought. Grab a bar stool, knock back one of 60-odd tequila types neat or with salt and lemon, and graze on some of the best guacamole (€7.50), nachos (from €6.50), quesadillas (€11.50) and enchiladas (€9) in town. Happy hour 5pm to 8pm Monday to Friday shakes a mean €5 cocktail.

But the real queen of the drinks card is the Margherita – seven types (€9.50 to €12) any way you like it: frozen, shaken, smoky or in a six-glass pitcher (€50).

ANDY WALHOO BAR

Map p402 (69 rue des Gravilliers, 3e; ⏲Tue-Sat; ⓂArts et Métiers) Casablanca meets pop-artist Andy Warhol in this cool, multicoloured cocktail lounge hidden away just north of the Centre Pompidou. Its clever name means 'I have nothing' in Arabic and is a major misnomer: its acid-yellow colour, sweet cocktails, pushy staff and loud house music may be too much for some palates. Happy hour, 5pm to 8pm, ushers in a great-value €5 *cocktail du jour* and the courtyard behind is paradise for smokers and partiers.

LE NOUVEAU CASINO CLUB

Map p402 (www.nouveaucasino.net; 109 rue Oberkampf, 11e; ⏲Tue-Sun; ⓂParmentier) This club-concert annexe of Café Charbon (p169) has made a name for itself amid the bars of Oberkampf with its live music concerts (usually Tuesday, Thursday and Friday) and lively club nights on weekends. Electro, pop, deep house, rock – the program is eclectic, underground and always up to the minute. Check the website for up-to-date listings.

LE PICK-CLOPS BAR, CAFE

Map p404 (16 rue Vieille du Temple, 4e; ⏲Mon-Sun; 📶; ⓂHôtel de Ville or St-Paul) This buzzy bar-cafe – all shades of yellow and lit by neon – has Formica tables, ancient bar stools and plenty of mirrors. Attracting a friendly flow of locals and passers-by, it's a great place for morning or afternoon coffee, or that last drink alone or with friends. Great rum punch served with copious amounts of peanuts.

LA CARAVANE BAR

Map p402 (35 rue de la Fontaine au Roi, 11e; ⏲daily; 📶; ⓂGoncourt) This funky, animated bar is a little jewel tucked away between République and Oberkampf; look for the tiny campervan above the pavement. The bar is surrounded by colourful kitsch furnishings, and the people around it and behind it are amiable and relaxed.

CAFÉ CHARBON BAR, CAFE

Map p402 (www.lecafecharbon.com; 109 rue Oberkampf, 11e; ⏲daily; 📶; ⓂParmentier) With its post-industrial belle époque ambience, the Charbon was the first of the hip cafes and bars to catch on in Ménilmontant. It's always crowded and worth heading to for the distressed decor with high ceilings, chandeliers and perched DJ booth. Food (mains €12.50 to €15) and evening tapas (€6) are both good.

LIZARD LOUNGE PUB

Map p404 (18 rue du Bourg Tibourg, 4e; daily; Hôtel de Ville or St-Paul) A quality outpost of Anglo-Saxon attitude in the heart of the Marais, this relaxed pub has beer on tap, cocktails, and grub along the lines of club sandwiches and burgers. Its Sunday brunch is a real hit, as is its cellar space with stone walls where DJs spin tunes on weekends. Happy hour from 8pm to 10pm sees 1.5L pitchers of beer cost a bargain €12.

AU P'TIT GARAGE BAR

Map p402 (63 rue Jean-Pierre Timbaud, 11e; daily; Parmentier) Just about the last 'neighbourhood' bar in the *quartier*, the 'Little Garage' attracts local custom (think grease monkeys and others with cleaner hands) with its rock 'n' roll, laid-back staff and rough-and-ready decor. It's still our favourite venue on rue JPT.

LA PERLE BAR

Map p404 (78 rue Vieille du Temple, 3e; daily; St-Paul or Chemin Vert) Notorious for being the bar next door where shamed fashion designer John Galliano hung out (and, indeed, was arrested in February 2011), this party bar is where *bobos* (bohemian bourgeois) come to slum it over *un rouge* (glass of red wine) in the Marais until the DJ arrives to liven things up. Unique trademarks: the (for real) distressed look of the place and the model locomotive over the bar.

L'ALIMENTATION GÉNÉRALE BAR

Map p402 (64 rue Jean-Pierre Timbaud, 11e; Wed-Sun; Parmentier) A rue JPT stalwart, the 'Grocery Store' is a massive space, with crazy retro decor and some outrageous toilets. Music is a very big deal here. DJs rock the joint on weekends.

LES ÉTAGES BAR

Map p404 (35 rue Vieille du Temple, 4e; daily; ; Hôtel de Ville or St-Paul) Students and expats find the 'Storeys' (all three floors) with its faded sage-green façade a viable alternative to the standard Marais fare, and happily appropriate the upgraded lounge rooms upstairs. Happy hour is 5pm to 9pm.

POP IN BAR

Map p404 (http://popin.fr; 105 rue Amelot, 4e; daily; St-Sébastien–Froissart) All skinny jeans and cultivated pop-rock nonchalance, the Pop In somehow got itself on the in-crowd map but maintains a relaxed regulars' vibe. It's popular with expats and Parisian students starting out the evening, and the drinks are reasonably priced. Whisper sweet nothings as you leave; it's had a lot of problems with noise-sensitive neighbours.

CAFÉ BAROC BAR, CAFE

Map p404 (37 rue du Roi de Sicile, 4e; Tue-Sun; St-Paul) The old cinema seats here are ideal for sipping flavoured beer (a big deal here). Normally a chilled, almost classy little place, things get hyper when bar staff play fabulously camp 1980s tunes.

LITTLE CAFÉ BAR, CAFE

Map p404 (62 rue du Roi de Sicile, 4e; daily; St-Paul) What you see is what you get at this unpretentious yet fashionable corner cafe where street-smart locals linger between boutiques to chat 'n relax over great coffee, good wine and tasty food. Sunday brunch (€21) packs out the place, both inside and outside on the pavement. Electronic music predominates after dark.

AU CHAT NOIR CAFE

Map p402 (76 rue Jean-Pierre Timbaud, 11e; daily; ; Parmentier or Couronnes) This attractive corner cafe with high ceilings and a long, wooden bar is a happening but relaxed drinking space. It's also a great cafe in which to hang out or read emails during the day. Downstairs is more animated, with occasional live concerts.

CAFÉ DES PHARES CAFE

Map p404 (7 place de la Bastille, 4e; daily; Bastille) There is no better spot to bask in the morning sun and watch Parisian traffic twirl around the July Column (p183) than the Beacons Café, the city's original *bistrot philo* (philosophers' bistro) where pensive Parisians meet on Sunday morning to debate the meaning of life and all that. Posy Paris at its best!

L'AUTRE CAFÉ CAFE

Map p402 (www.lautrecafe.com; 62 rue Jean-Pierre Timbaud, 11e; daily; ; Parmentier) A young mixed crowd of locals, artists, filmmakers and party-goers remains faithful to this literary cafe with its 8m-long zinc-topped bar, spacious seating areas, relaxed

TOP TIPS FOR TEA & COFFEE

For die-hard connoisseurs craving a genuine cup of tea or espresso shot, there are surprisingly few addresses in Paris. For authentic Italian, Pozzetto (p166) is the pick. Other recommendations:

Le Loir dans La Théière (Map p404; 3 rue des Rosiers, 4e; daily; M St-Paul) Cutesy name (Dormouse in the Teapot) notwithstanding, this is a wonderful old space filled with retro toys, comfy couches and scenes from *Through the Looking Glass* on the walls. Its dozen different types of tea poured in the company of tip-top savoury tarts and crumble-type desserts ensure a constant queue on the street outside. Breakfast (€12) and brunch (€19.50) too.

Mariage Frères (Map p404; www.mariagefreres.com; 30, 32 & 35 rue du Bourg Tibourg, 4e; daily; M Hôtel de Ville)) Founded in 1854, this is Paris' first and arguably finest tearoom with a shop where you can also choose from more than 500 varieties of tea sourced from some 35 countries.

La Caféthèque (Map p404; www.lacafeotheque.com; 52 rue de l'Hôtel de Ville, 4e; daily; ; M St-Paul or Hôtel de Ville) From the industrial grinder by the door to the elaborate tasting notes in the menu, this coffee house is serious. Grab a pew (next to the piano perhaps or, if you're lucky, in the corner leather armchair), pick your bean (Guatemala, Panama, Brazil, Honduras, Peru etc) and get it served just the way you like it (espresso, ristretto, latte etc). The *café du jour* (coffee of the day) keeps well-travelled tastebuds on their toes and, in keeping with French cafe tradition, a coffee at the bar (€1.80) is cheaper than sitting at a table (€3).

Merce and the Muse (Map p402; http://merceandthemuse.com; 1bis rue Charles-François Dupuis, 3e; Tue-Sun; ; M Temple) The smell of freshly ground beans fills this small 100% retro New York coffee shop, run with passion by a New Yorker gal called Merce (pronounced 'Merci') and a bunch of English-speaking pals. Jasmine tea, lavender milk, home-made cakes and a tasty brunch (€9 to €20) lend to the faded charm.

environment, reasonable prices and exhibition openings.

It's a great place to open your laptop and indulge in a little work or surf, browse the newspapers and art magazines, or hang with mates in the small lounge upstairs. Sunday brunch, noon to 5pm, is a hip date.

LE PROGRÈS CAFE

Map p402 (1 rue de Bretagne, 3e; Mon-Sat; M St-Sébastien–Froissart or Filles du Calvaire) This sunlit, art deco-tiled corner cafe is a sociable spot to chat with locals over strong coffee, inexpensive bistro fare and pitchers of wine.

CAFÉ SUÉDOIS CAFE

Map p404 (11 rue Payenne, 3e; Tue-Sun; ; M Chemin Vert) Housed in the beautiful 16th-century Hôtel de Marle, this gorgeous cafe in the Swedish Cultural Institute lures Parisians like bees to a honey pot with its delicious soups, sandwiches and cakes eaten inside or – best up – outside in the tranquil paved courtyard.

CAFÉ MARTINI BAR

Map p404 (www.cafemartini.fr; 9 rue du Pas de la Mule, 4e; daily; M Chemin Vert) Skip the pair of cafe-bars on place des Vosges and nip around the corner instead to this cosy den with wood-panelled entrance, beamed ceiling and buzzing after-work crowd – the saggy sofa is the hot spot! Spoil yourself with smoothies and *chocolat chaud à l'ancienne* by day, copious cheese and cold meat platters (€6) at dusk, and €5 cocktails during happy hour from 5pm to 9pm.

L'APPAREMMENT CAFÉ CAFE

Map p404 (18 rue des Coutures St-Gervais, 3e; daily; M St-Sébastien–Froissart) This tasteful haven, tucked behind the Musée Picasso, is just like home with its wood panelling, leather sofas, scattered parlour games to play and dog-eared books to read. Come for Sunday brunch.

LA TARTINE WINE BAR

Map p404 (24 rue de Rivoli & 17 rue du Roi de Sicile, 11e; daily; M St-Paul) A wine bar where little

TASTEFUL TOILETTES

Clustered on one of the most happening streets in the Marais is a trio of hybrid, uber-cool drinking-dining spots created by the hugely charismatic, vocal and politically active entrepreneur Xavier Denamur. All three are quintessentially Parisian with their down-to-earth pavement terraces, staunchly local crowd and – completely atypically – hmm, designer *toilettes* (toilets).

Le Petit Fer à Cheval (Map p404; 30 rue Vieille du Temple, 4e; ⌚daily; Ⓜ Hôtel de Ville or St-Paul) A Marais institution, The Little Horseshoe is a pocket-sized cafe-bar with an original horseshoe-shaped zinc bar from 1903 leaving little room for much else. But nobody seems to mind at this genial place, overflowing with regulars from dawn to dark. Great *apéro* spot and great WC – the stainless-steel toilets stall are straight out of a Flash Gordon film (inspired, in fact, by the interior of the *Nautilus* submarine in Jules Verne's *20,000 Leagues under the Sea*).

L'Étoile Manquante (Map p404; 34 rue Vieille du Temple, 4e; ⌚daily; Ⓜ Hôtel de Ville or St-Paul) A fabulous pavement terrace, this time spilling out onto rue Ste-Croix de la Bretonnerie, The Missing Star is a trendy, gay-friendly bar with a retro interior topped by star-lit vaults. But it's the TV cameras in the loos and the electric toy train that chugs between the girls' and the boys' that create the real buzz.

La Chaise au Plafond (Map p404; 10 rue du Trésor, 4e; ⌚daily; Ⓜ Hôtel de Ville or St-Paul) Bohemian Marais at its best: The Chair on the Ceiling is a peaceful, warm place, with wooden tables outside on a terrace giving onto tranquil, boutique-encrusted rue du Trésor (p177) – a real oasis from the frenzy of the Marais. Its wine list is fine, and its food menu is an ode to local producers – vegetables, eggs for its all-day brunch (€21), apples for a juice not to be missed and so on, all arrive fresh from an organic farm 30km outside Paris. And *les toilettes*, a sharp mix of shiny stainless steel and sculpted bronze.

has changed since the days of gas lighting (some of the fixtures are still in place), this place offers 15 selected reds, whites and rosés by the *pot* (46cL). There's not much to eat except lots of *tartines* (open-faced sandwiches).

PURE MALT — PUB

Map p404 (4 rue Caron, 4e; ⌚daily; Ⓜ St-Paul) A little Scottish pub-bar just south of lovely place du Marché Ste-Catherine, this is an address for the discerning whisky connoisseur – more than 150 types of whisky, mainly single malts, as well as beer of course and a TV screen to watch sport.

OPEN CAFÉ — CAFE, GAY

Map p404 (www.opencafe.fr; 17 rue des Archives, 4e; ⌚daily; Ⓜ Hôtel de Ville) A gay venue for all types at all hours, this spacious bar-cafe with twinkling disco balls strung from the starry ceiling has bags of appeal – not least, a big buzzing pavement terrace, a kitchen serving breakfast (€8.50) and all-day *tartines* (€7), and four-hour happy hour kicking in daily at 6pm.

LE COX — BAR, GAY

Map p404 (www.coxbar.fr; 15 rue des Archives, 4e; ⌚daily; Ⓜ Hôtel de Ville) This small gay bar with decor that changes every quarter is *the* meeting place for an interesting (and interested) cruisy crowd throughout the evening from dusk on. OK, we don't like the in-your-face name either, but what's a boy to do? Happy hour runs 6pm to 9pm daily.

SCREAM CLUB — CLUB, GAY

Map p402 (www.scream-paris.com; 18 rue Faubourg du Temple, 11e; ⌚daily; Ⓜ Belleville or Goncourt) What started out as a summer party is now a permanent fixture on the city's gay scene (marketed as Paris' biggest gay party). The Saturday-night *soirée gay* brings clubbers together on two dance floors – one dedicated to pop, the other to sets by an international DJ – and a ooh la la! *espace cruising*.

LE QUETZAL — BAR, GAY

Map p404 (10 rue de la Verrerie, 4e; ⌚daily; Ⓜ Hôtel de Ville) This perennial favourite gay bar – one of the first in the Marais – is opposite rue des Mauvais Garçons (Bad Boys' Street), a road named after the brigands who congregated here in 1540. It's always busy, with house and dance music playing at night, and cruisy at all hours; plate-glass windows allow you to check out the talent before it arrives.

3W KAFÉ BAR, GAY

Map p404 (8 rue des Écouffes, 4e; ⏲Tue-Sat; Ⓜ St-Paul) The name of this flagship cocktail bar-pub on a street with several lesbian bars means 'Women with Women' so it can't be any clearer. It's relaxed and there's no ban on men (but they must be accompanied by a girl). On weekends there's dancing downstairs with a DJ and themed evenings take place regularly.

LES JACASSES BAR, GAY

Map p404 (5 rue des Écouffes, 4e; ⏲Wed-Sun; Ⓜ St-Paul) Girls looking for something a bit more authentic in the Marais should cross over rue des Écouffes to the 3W's sister bar, which looks like it's been transplanted from Normandy. Softer music, more hard-core evenings.

LE DUPLEX BAR, GAY

Map p402 (www.duplex-bar.com; 25 rue Michel le Comte, 3e; ⏲daily; Ⓜ Rambuteau) Attracting a crowd that is *ni fashion ni folle* (neither into fashion nor queeny), the (very) long-established Duplex is comatose during the week but fills up on weekends with 'boys next door' from out of town. Hosts interesting exhibitions too, agenda online.

LE TANGO CLUB, GAY

Map p402 (www.boite-a-frissons.fr; 13 rue au Maire, 3e; ⏲Fri-Sun; Ⓜ Arts et Métiers) Billing itself as a *boîte à frissons* (club of thrills), Le Tango hosts a mixed and cosmopolitan, gay and lesbian crowd in a historic 1930s dancehall. Its atmosphere and style is retro and festive, with waltzing, salsa and tango getting going from the moment it opens. From about 12.30am onwards DJs play. Sunday's gay tea dance is legendary.

★ ENTERTAINMENT

THÉÂTRE LE POINT VIRGULE COMEDY

Map p404 (www.lepointvirgule.com; 7 rue Ste-Croix de la Bretonnerie, 4e; Ⓜ Hôtel de Ville) This tiny and convivial comedy spot in the Marais has been going strong for well over five decades. It offers cafe-theatre at its best – stand-up comics, performance artists, musical acts. The quality is variable, but it's great fun and the place has a reputation for discovering new talent.

LA FAVELA CHIC WORLD MUSIC

Map p402 (www.favelachic.com; 18 rue du Faubourg du Temple, 11e; ⏲Tue-Sat; Ⓜ République) It starts as a chic, convivial restaurant (open for lunch and dinner to 11pm) and gives way to caipirinha- and mojito-fuelled bumping, grinding, flirting and dancing (mostly on the long tables). The music is traditionally bossa nova, samba, *baile* (dance), funk and Brazilian pop, and it can get very crowded and hot.

LA JAVA WORLD MUSIC

Map p402 (www.la-java.fr; 105 rue du Faubourg du Temple, 11e; Ⓜ Goncourt) Built in 1922, this is the dance hall where Édith Piaf got her first break, and it now reverberates to the sound of live salsa, rock and world music. Live concerts usually take place during the week at 8pm or 9pm. Afterwards a festive crowd gets dancing to electro, house, disco and Latino DJs.

LE BATACLAN ROCK, POP

Map p402 (www.bataclan.fr; 50 bd Voltaire, 11e; Ⓜ Oberkampf or St-Ambroise) Built in 1864 and Maurice Chevalier's debut venue in 1910, this excellent little concert hall – a symphony of lively red, yellow and green hues – draws big-ticket French (and some international) rock and pop legends. Le Bataclan also masquerades as a theatre and dance hall.

LA MAROQUINERIE ROCK, POP

(http://lamaroquinerie.fr; 23 rue Boyer, 20e; ⏲daily; Ⓜ Ménilmontant) This tiny but trendy venue in Ménilmontant entices a staunchly local, in-the-know set with real cutting-edge gigs – many bands kick off their European tour here. The al fresco courtyard and restaurant renders La Maroquinerie impossible to resist; to see for yourself head east along rue Ménilmontant and take the second right after place de Ménilmontant.

SATELLIT CAFÉ WORLD MUSIC

Map p402 (www.satellit-cafe.com; 44 rue de la Folie Méricourt, 11e; ⏲Tue-Sat; Ⓜ Oberkampf or St-Ambroise) A great venue for world music and not as painfully trendy as some others in Paris, come to listen to everything from blues and flamenco to African and Bollywood.

LE VIEUX BELLEVILLE LIVE MUSIC

Map p402 (www.le-vieux-belleville.com; 12 rue des Envierges, 20e; Ⓜ Pyrénées) This old-fashioned bistro at the top of Parc de Belleville is an atmospheric venue for performances of *chansons* featuring accordions and an organ grinder three times a week. It's a lively favourite with locals, though, so booking ahead is advised. The 'Old Belleville' serves classic bistro food (open for lunch Monday to Friday, dinner Tuesday to Saturday).

LA BELLEVILLOISE CULTURAL CENTRE

(☎01 46 36 07 07; www.labellevilloise.com; 19-21 rue Boyer, 20e; ⊙Wed-Sun; Ⓜ Ménilmontant) Gigs, concerts, theatrical performances, exhibitions, readings, dance classes and workshops… Vibrant, alternative and dynamic, the arts centre and club La Bellevilloise is where it all happens after dark in Ménilmontant. The morning after Saturday night, return for a jazz brunch – Sunday brunch (adult/child €29/13) accompanied by live jazz – in its trendy cafe-restaurant. You'll find it particularly gorgeous in summer with its sunlit tables and 100-year-old olive trees. Advance reservations recommended; head east along rue Ménilmontant and take the second right after place de Ménilmontant.

SHOPPING

The Marais boasts excellent speciality stores and an ever-expanding fashion presence. Hip young designers have colonised the upper reaches of the 3e towards rue Charlot as well as rue de Turenne. Meanwhile, rue des Francs Bourgeois and, towards the other side of rue de Rivoli, rue François Mirron in the 4e have well-established boutique shopping for clothing, hats, home furnishings and stationery. Place des Vosges is lined with very high-end art and antique galleries with some amazing sculpture for sale.

TOP CHOICE **MERCI** CONCEPT STORE

Map p404 (www.merci-merci.com; 111 bd Beaumarchais, 3e; Ⓜ St-Sébastien–Froissart) The landmark Fiat Cinquecento in the courtyard marks the entrance to this unique multistorey concept store whose rallying cry is one-stop shopping. Fashion, accessories, linens, lamps and various other nifty designs for the home (a kitchen brush made from recycled egg shells and coffee grounds anyone?).

And a trio of inspired eating-drinking spaces (p163) complete Paris' hippest shopping experience. All proceeds go to a children's charity in Madagascar.

TOP CHOICE **LIEU COMMUN** CONCEPT STORE

Map p402 (www.lieucommun.fr; 5 rue des Filles du Calvaire, 3e; Ⓜ Filles du Calvaire) Music, fashion, jeans, household items, furniture and gadgets are the essential pillars of this alternative design space on one of the Marais' most interesting shopping streets.

GRAND BONTON KIDS

Map p404 (www.bonton.fr; 5 bd des Filles du Calvaire, 3e; Ⓜ Filles du Calvaire) Chic and stylish, this concept store designed squarely with kids in mind stocks vintage-inspired fashion, furnishings and knick-knacks for babies, toddlers and children. Don't leave without donning an old-fashioned, floppy sunhat or pair of oversized sunglasses and getting your photo snapped in its retro photo booth.

BY SOPHIE KIDS

Map p402 (www.bysophie.fr; 50 rue Jean-Pierre Timbaud, 11e; ⊙11am-7pm Tue-Fri; Ⓜ Parmentier) Stylish parents keen to don their kids in chic, retro fashion should make a beeline for this vintage-style boutique with clothes and accessories for babies, toddlers and young children. Sophie also hosts hip knitting workshops.

ANDREA CREWS FASHION

Map p402 (www.andreacrews.com; 25 rue Vaucouleurs, 11e; Ⓜ Belleville) Using everything from discarded clothing to electrical fittings and household bric-a-brac, this collective sews, recycles and reinvents to create the most extraordinary pieces not everyone would wear.

LIBRAIRIE DE L'HÔTEL DE SULLY BOOKS

Map p404 (www.editions.monuments-nationaux.fr; 62 rue St-Antoine, 4e; ⊙10am-7pm; Ⓜ St-Paul) This bookshop is located inside an early 17th-century aristocratic mansion housing the Centre des Monuments Nationaux (the body responsible for many of France's historical monuments). It's the best address in

LOCAL KNOWLEDGE

MARAIS À LA MODE

It's certainly no surprise that New Yorker Kasia Dietz, when she moved to Europe, intuitively plumped for a part of Paris that subsequently morphed into the city's trendiest neighbourhood: Le Marais. This handbag designer more often than not dreams up new creations over *un café* or three in one of her favourite local hang-outs.

Perfect Saturday

Wandering around **Village St-Paul** (p177), a hidden enclave with tiny boutiques, galleries, cafes and restaurants. Sometimes there is a farmers market or fair. Lunch at **La Petite Maison dans La Cour** (Map p404; 9 rue St-Paul, 4e; ⌚lunch Wed-Sun; Ⓜ St-Paul), a tiny place with tasty home-cooking and gorgeous summer terrace.

Best Vintage

I pass **Violette et Léonie** (p175) almost every day and usually end up popping in to try something on. The window seems to change daily and it stocks a real mix of fashions and labels, everything from H&M to Chanel.

Forget the buzz! Hypeless Dines

Le Petit Marché (p162), nicely understated, is the best address around place des Vosges. Then there's **L'Aller-Retour** (p163), which is quite meat-heavy. Rather than ordering wine by the glass they simply bring the bottle to your table and you pay for what you drink (really unusual for Paris). It's on my favourite street in the Marais.

Evening Apéro

Café Crème (p161) is a quintessential Parisian bistro, a really local, unpretentious place with good burgers and a great terrace – perfect for an easy *apéro* (predinner drink). **Café Charbon** (p169) is more 'the scene', very hip, an address I love. Then there is **La Perle** (p170), a lively spot on any given night, where locals mix with expats.

the city for Paris-related titles – historical texts, biographies, picture books, atlases, you name it…

TRÉSOR FASHION

Map p404 (5 rue du Trésor, 4e; Ⓜ Hotel de Ville or St-Paul) Tucked at the end of pedestrian rue du Trésor, this bohemian boutique by Brigitte Masson injects a fresh, individual take on women's fashion. From its catchy salmon-orange façade strung with old-fashioned fairy lights to its overtly retro ambience inside, this address is Paris-perfect for picking up something a little different. There's also a great range of spectacular accessories.

VIOLETTE ET LÉONIE FASHION

Map p404 (www.violetteleonie.com; 1 rue de Saintonge, 3e; Ⓜ Filles du Calvaire) So chic and of such high quality that it really doesn't seem like secondhand, Violette et Léonie is a first-class *depôt-vente* boutique specialising in vintage. It stocks new items daily, with the option of shopping *sur place* (there's also an address at 27 rue de Poitou in the 3e) or you can take advantage of bargains online.

PAULINE PIN ACCESSORIES

Map p402 (www.paulinepin.com; 51 rue Charlot, 3e; Ⓜ Filles du Calvaire) Invest in a super-soft, and stylish handbag made by designer Clarisse at her flagship store and workshop. She now has a handful of boutiques in France and beyond.

MY E-CASE ACCESSORIES

Map p404 (http://myecase.com; 3 rue de Birague & 27 rue des Écouffes, 4e; Ⓜ Chemin Vert or St-Paul) Studded in sparkling diamante, shaped like an old tape cassette, covered in 'sugar' like a donut, or encrusted with miniature cupcakes…from wild and wacky, to Cath Kidston flowers and plain grey, this boutique sells protective coverings for smartphones in every imaginable design. Gloves with touch-screen tips too: a must for tech fiends.

I LOVE MY BLENDER BOOKS

Map p404 (www.ilovemyblender.fr; 36 rue du Temple, 3e; ⌚10am-7pm Tue-Sat, to 5pm Sun; Ⓜ Rambuteau) Shoppers who are particularly fond of their blenders should not get too excited. As far removed from kitchenware as you can imagine, this bookshop is stocked almost exclusively with books written in English, whatever the provenance. They're available here in their original editions and in French translation.

ROUGIER & PLÉ SUPPLIES, ARTS

Map p402 (www.rougier-ple.fr; 13 bd des Filles du Calvaire, 3e; ⏲11am-7pm Tue-Sat, 2.30-7pm Sun & Mon; MFilles du Calvaire) The city's oldest *beaux arts* (fine arts), in business since 1854, sells paper, pens, arts and crafts materials – everything imaginable in fact for *le plaisir de crée* (the pleasure of creation).

CHOCOLATERIE JOSÉPHINE VANNIER CHOCOLATE

Map p404 (www.chocolats-vannier.com; 4 rue du Pas de la Mule, 3e; ⏲11am-7pm Tue-Sat, 2.30-7pm Sun & Mon; MChemin Vert) Miniature piano keyboards, violins, smiley-face boxes or a pair of jogging shoes...you name it, *chocolatier* Joséphine Vannier can create it out of chocolate.

TOP CHOICE MAISON GEORGES LARNICOL CHOCOLATE

Map p404 (www.chocolaterielarnicol.fr; 9 rue du Roi de Sicile & 14 rue Rivoli, 4e; ⏲9.30am-10pm; MChemin Vert) Coco-ginger bites, buttery caramels and chocolate objects d'art (a pair of red stilettos perhaps, an alarm clock or football?) are among the sweet treats displayed so enticingly at this master chocolate maker and pastry chef from Brittany.

But it is his syrupy, chewy *kouignettes,* traditional Breton butter cakes unusually made in mini dimensions and 16 different flavours (€2.50 per 100g), that are the real reason to come here. Oh, and the glass jars of *caramel au beurre salé* (butter caramel) that come complete with a small spoon...

POPELINI CAKES

Map p402 (29 rue Debelleyme, 3e; ⏲11am-7pm Tue-Sat, 10am-3pm Sun; MSt-Sébastien–Frossart) Forget cupcakes and *macarons*! The hottest thing to buy at this bijou, bright pink cube of a shop is bite-sized *choux* (éclairs), flavoured a dozen and more different ways: jasmine, pistachio and cherry jam, strawberry and lychee, Grand Marnier, Baileys, the list is endless. The *chou du jour* (éclair of the day, €2.80) promises to thrill.

FLEUX DESIGN, HOMEWARES

Map p404 (www.fleux.com; 39 & 52 rue Sainte Croix de la Bretonnerie, 4e; ⏲11am-7.30pm Mon-Fri, 10.30am-8pm Sat, 2-7.30pm Sun; MHôtel de Ville) Innovative designs by European designers fill this big white space. Think products for the home that range from kitsch to clever to plain crazy.

BHV DEPARTMENT STORE

Map p404 (www.bhv.fr; 14 rue du Temple, 4e; MHôtel de Ville) BHV (bay-ash-vay) is a fairly straightforward, if faintly flashy, department store where you can buy everything from guidebooks on Paris to every imaginable type of hammer, power tool, nail, plug and hinge.

RED WHEELBARROW BOOKSTORE BOOKS

Map p404 (www.theredwheelbarrow.com; 22 rue St-Paul, 4e; MSt-Paul) It's always a pleasure to visit this English-language bookshop of the old school with a fine selection of literature and 'serious reading', and helpful, well-read staff.

TUMBLEWEED TOYS, FASHION

Map p404 (www.tumbleweedparis.com; 19 rue de Turenne, 4e; ⏲11am-7pm; MSt-Paul or Chemin Vert) This little shop specialises in leather slippers for kids and *l'artisanat d'art ludique* (crafts of the playing art): think handmade wooden toys and exquisitely made brain teasers and puzzles for adults, such as Japanese 'spin' and 'secret' boxes that defy entry.

FRAGONARD COSMETICS

Map p404 (www.fragonard.com; 51 rue des Francs Bourgeois, 4e; ⏲10.30am-7.30pm Mon-Sat, noon-7pm Sun; MSt-Paul) This Parisian perfume maker has alluring natural scents in elegant bottles as well as candles, essential oils and soaps. In addition to the splendid smells, there's a small, expensive and very tasteful selection of clothing, hand-stitched linen tablecloths and napkins.

L'ARTISAN PARFUMEUR PERFUME

Map p404 (www.artisanparfumeur.com; 32 rue du Bourg Tibourg, 4e; MSt-Paul) This artisan has been making exquisite original scents and candles for decades. Products are expensive but of very high quality and attractively packaged, or try your hand at creating your own scent during a three-hour workshop (€170).

LE STUDIO DES PARFUMS PERFUME

Map p404 (☎01 40 29 90 84; www.artisanparfumeur.com; 23 rue du Bourg Tibourg, 4e; MSt-Paul) Learn how a perfume maker's organ with more than 150 different scents works and create your own fragrance (€95/175 for one/three hours) at this charming perfume studio. Little girls will love the scent workshops for children (€30 for 45 minutes).

LOSCO ACCESSORIES

Map p404 (www.losco.fr; 20 rue de Sévigné, 4e; 2-7pm Sun-Tue, 11am-1pm & 2-7pm Wed-Sat; MSt-Paul) This artisan *ceinturier* epitomises the main draw of shopping in Paris – stumbling upon tiny boutique-workshops selling 101 quality variations of one single item, in this case *ceintures* (belts). Pick leather, length and buckle to suit just you.

K JACQUES ACCESSORIES

Map p404 (www.kjacques.fr; 6 rue Pavée, 4e; MSt-Paul) Traditional strappy sandals, supposedly inspired by a simple leather pair brought by writer Colette from Greece to show her cobbler, is the speciality of this shoemaker from St-Tropez. Celebrity clients include Picasso, Brigitte Bardot and the Baba Cool Generation.

GREEN IN THE CITY FASHION

Map p404 (www.greeninthecity.fr; 9 rue Malher, 4e; MSt-Paul) Great name for a shop and great products: 'Green and sexy' is the strapline of this tasteful boutique specialising in organic designs by Leaf, Racine, Reine Mère, Camilla Norrback and other environmentally conscious fashion designers who work with organic wool and cotton, nonviolent silk, vegetal dyes and so forth.

MADE IN USED FASHION

Map p404 (www.madeinused.com; 36 rue de Poitou, 3e; MFilles du Calvaire) 'Genetic vintage' is the strapline of Vic Caserta's stylish boutique in the Haut Marais where vintage clothes and materials get a new lease of life.

ABOU D'ABI BAZAR FASHION

Map p404 (www.aboudabibazar.com; 125 rue Vieille du Temple, 4e; 2-7.15pm Mon, 10.30am-7.15pm Tue-Sat, 2-7pm Sun; MChemin Vert) This fashionable boutique is a treasure trove of smart and affordable ready-to-wear pieces from sought-after designers such as Paul & Joe and Isabel Marant.

L'ÉCLAIREUR FASHION

Map p404 (www.leclaireur.com; 40 rue de Sévigné, 4e; MSt-Paul) Part art space, part lounge and part deconstructionist fashion statement, this shop for women is known for having the next big thing first. The nearby **menswear store** (Map p404; www.leclaireur.com; 12 rue Malher, 4e; MSt-Paul) on rue Malher fills an equally stunning, old warehouse-turned-art space.

LOCAL KNOWLEDGE

SECRET SHOPPING

Some of the Marais' sweetest boutique shopping is secreted down peaceful alleyways and courtyards, free of cars, as they were centuries ago. Take **Rue du Trésor** (p172), a pedestrian dead-end passage off rue du Vieille du Temple, encrusted with an exclusive handful of hip boutiques and cafe terraces abuzz with Parisians at lunchtime and after work. Favourites are **Trésor** (p175) and **La Chaise au Plafond** (p172).

Monday to Friday its cobbled alleys are mostly mouse quiet, but come the weekend savvy trendsetters mingle at **Village St-Paul** (Map p404; rue St-Paul, des rue Jardins St-Paul & rue Charlemagne, 4e; MSt-Paul), a designer set of five vintage courtyards, refashioned in the 1970s from the 14th-century walled gardens of King Charles V. Meander away Saturday afternoon with a courtyard-to-courtyard stroll, paved in old stone, pierced with ancient fountains and riddled with tiny artisan boutiques, galleries, antique shops and the odd old-fashioned tearoom.

L'HABILLEUR FASHION, ACCESSORIES

Map p404 (44 rue de Poitou, 4e; MSt-Sébastien–Froissart) For 15 years this shop has been known for its discount designer wear – offering 50% to 70% off original prices. It generally stocks last season's collections including such lines as Paul & Joe, Giorgio Brato and Belle Rose.

LA BOUTIQUE EXTRAORDINAIRE FASHION

Map p402 (67 rue Charlot, 3e; 11am-8pm Tue-Sat, 3-7pm Sun; MFilles du Calvaire) Mohair, silk and other natural, organic and ethical materials are hand-knitted into exquisite garments, almost too precious to wear, at this unusual and captivating Haut Marais boutique.

FINGER IN THE NOSE KIDS

Map p402 (www.fingerinthenose.com; 60 rue Saintonge, 3e; MFilles du Calvaire) What a

TAKE NOTE

Contrary to elsewhere in the city, most shops in the Marais only open at 11am and close at 7pm or a little later. Many are open Sunday afternoon, too, typically from 2pm to 7pm.

great image of tough kids kitted out in cool clobber, finger up nose, does this friendly bijou boutique evoke! Fashions are street-hip and refreshingly unisex, meaning lots of neutral and darker tones, no 'Hello Kitty' pink (alleluia!).

ISABEL MARANT FASHION

Map p402 (www.isabelmarant.fr; 47 rue Saintonge, 3e; Ⓜ Filles du Calvaire) The historic setting – an old *atelier de rémoulage* (remoulding workshop) complete with faded gold lettering above the shopfront – makes the shopping experience at this Haut Marais boutique filled with Isabel Marant (p315) designs all the more pleasurable.

SHINE FASHION

Map p404 (15 rue de Poitou, 3e; Ⓜ Filles du Calvaire) A limited but discerning collection of designer stuff in the trendsetting 3e: women's clothing, excellent shoes and handbags with plenty of Marc Jacobs, See by Chloé and K by Karl Lagerfeld, as well as jewellery by Bijoux de Sophie.

FIESTA GALERIE DESIGN, HOMEWARES

Map p404 (www.fiesta-galerie.fr; 24 rue du Pont Louis-Philippe, 4e; noon-7pm Wed-Sat, 2-7pm Sun; Ⓜ Pont Marie) The red neon 'Open' sign strung on the door immediately sets the tone for this stylish and eye-catching gallery specialising in vintage objects for the home – lamps, furniture, cushions and so on – from the 1940s to 1970s. Great website too.

SIC AMOR FASHION, ACCESSORIES

Map p404 (www.french-jewellery.fr; 20 rue du Pont Louis-Philippe, 4e; Ⓜ Pont Marie) Bright and colourful contemporary jewellery by local designers from a shop located opposite the headquarters of the all-but-moribund Partie Communiste Française is what this address is all about.

For bold, frilly, gorgeous, oftentimes out of-this-world hats and scarves walk south along the same street to its sister boutique **Mi Amor** (Map p404; 10 rue du Pont Louis-Philippe, 4e; Ⓜ Pont Marie).

UN CHIEN DANS LE MARAIS FASHION, ACCESSORIES

Map p404 (www.unchiendanslemarais.com; 35bis rue du Roi de Sicile, 4e; Ⓜ St-Paul) Only in Paris: this pocket-sized boutique has to be seen to be believed: ballerina tutus, fur coats, woolly jumpers, black tailed coats, hoodies, frilly blouses and sweaters with 101 different logos – all for your dog.

SURFACE TO AIR FASHION, ACCESSORIES

Map p404 (www.surfacetoair.com; 108 rue Vieille du Temple, 3e; 11.30am-7.30pm Mon-Sat, noon-6pm Sun; Ⓜ St-Sébastien–Froissart or Filles du Calvaire) This shop has very edgy clothing as well as arty books and accessories. With an exceedingly up-to-date collection of daring local and international designs, the space also welcomes regular installations and collaborative events with artists.

JULIEN CAVISTE WINE

Map p402 (50 rue Charlot, 3e; Ⓜ Filles du Calvaire) This independent wine shop focuses on small, independent producers and organic wines. The enthusiastic merchant Julien will locate and explain (and wax lyrical about) the wine for you, whatever your budget.

LE REPAIRE DE BACCHUS FOOD, DRINK

Map p402 (40 rue de Bretagne, 3e; Ⓜ Arts et Métiers) 'The Den of Bacchus' stocks a good selection of New World wines and an excellent supply of French vintages, Cognac, Armagnac and whiskies.

VERT D'ABSINTHE DRINK

Map p404 (www.vertdabsinthe.com; 11 rue d'Ormesson, 4e; Ⓜ St-Paul) Fans of the *fée verte* (green fairy), as absinthe was known during the belle époque, will think they've died and gone to heaven here. You can buy not only bottles of the best-quality hooch here but all the paraphernalia as well: glasses, water jugs and tiny slotted spoons for the all-important sugar cube.

BOUTIQUE OBUT GAMES, HOBBIES

Map p402 (www.labouleobut.com; 60 av de la République, 11e; Ⓜ Parmentier) This is the Parisian mecca for fans of *pétanque* or the similar (though more formal) game of boules, a form of bowls played with heavy steel balls wherever a bit of flat and shady ground can be found. It will kit you out with all the equipment necessary to get a game going and even has team uniforms.

LA MAISON DE L'ASTRONOMIE — GAMES, HOBBIES

Map p404 (www.maison-astronomie.com; 33-35 rue de Rivoli, 11e; Ⓜ Hôtel de Ville) Astronomical books, sky maps, star globes, gyroscopes, stellascopes, spacesuit pyjamas or your very own miniature space shuttle: if star-gazing is your passion, this large shop is for you babe. Telescopes, some running into tens of thousands of euros, cram the 1st floor.

ATELIER D'AUTREFOIS — GIFTS, SOUVENIRS

Map p404 (61 bd Beaumarchais, 11e; ⏲10am-6pm; Ⓜ Chemin Vert) This treasure chest of a shop stocks exquisite music boxes – both new and antique – and will repair any that are ailing. It's a shop that will attract both collectors and souvenir hunters.

CSAO BOUTIQUE & GALLERY — GIFTS, SOUVENIRS

Map p404 (www.csao.fr; 9 & 9bis rue Elzévir, 4e; ⏲11am-7pm Tue-Fri, 11am-7.30pm Sat, noon-7pm Sun; Ⓜ St-Paul or Chemin Vert) This wonderful shop and gallery, owned and operated by the charitable Compagnie du Sénégal et de l'Afrique de l'Ouest (CSAO; Senegal and West Africa Company), distributes the work of African craftspeople and artists. Many of the colourful fabrics and weavings are exquisite. Included are items handmade from recycled handbags, aluminium cans and tomato-paste tins.

PUZZLE MICHÈLE WILSON — GAMES, HOBBIES

Map p402 (www.puzzles-et-jeux.com; 39 rue de la Folie Méricourt, 11e; Ⓜ St-Ambroise) *Puzzleurs* and *puzzleuses* will love the selection of hand-cut wooden jigsaw puzzles available in this shop. Ranging in size (and degree of difficulty) from 80 to 5000 pieces, the puzzles depict for the most part major works of art; everyone from Millet and Bosch to the impressionists is represented.

The ones of medieval stained glass and 18th-century fans are particularly fine. There are two other outlets in Paris.

MÉLODIES GRAPHIQUES — GIFTS

Map p404 (10 rue du Pont Louis-Philippe, 4e; Ⓜ Pont Marie) Here you'll find all sorts of

SOLE DESIGN

The real joy of mooching around the Marais is stumbling across tiny *ateliers* (workshops) and boutiques to watch just-established or rising designers at work. Break with lunch à la mode at Nanashi (p162).

Moon Young Hee (Map p402; 62 rue Charlot, 3e; Ⓜ Filles du Calvaire) Watch fanciful 'origami' creations being cut by hand in the studio of designer Moon Young Hee. Ancient beams, exposed stone walls and huge street-facing windows form the perfect stage.

Valentine Gauthier (Map p402; www.valentinegauthier.com; 58 rue Charlot, 3e; Ⓜ Filles du Calvaire) Indulge your inner-cowgirl with leather jackets, mules, cowboy boots and other romantic, at times Wild West–inspired, designs by one of Paris' most talented new designers.

Yukiko (Map p404; www.yukiko.fr; 97 rue Vieille du Temple, 3e; Ⓜ St-Paul) This elegant, drawing room-style boudoir – an orgy of soft creams, gold and pastels – provides the perfect backdrop for the vintage-chic designs for women by Tokyo-born, Paris-based Yukiko.

Anne Elisabeth (Map p404; www.anne-elisabeth.com; 8 rue Malher, 4e; ⏲11am-7pm Mon-Sat, 2-7pm Sun; Ⓜ St-Paul) Every creation of Anne Elisabeth is named after a river, town, character in a novel or simply something that happens to inspire this well-travelled Parisian designer of the moment. Bold colours, printed housecoats and wide trousers are among her signature 'arty-couture' garments inspired by 1950s and 1960s fashion. Find a second **boutique** (Map p402; Ⓜ République) at 3 rue de la Corderie, 3e.

Kate Mack (Map p402; www.kate-mack.com; 15 rue Oberkampf, 11e; Ⓜ Oberkampf) A hardcore address for getting to the core of Parisian trend, this studio-boutique is a real delight. Ogle at silver-skinned mannequins modelling overtly feminine but funky *femme fatale* designs.

items made from exquisite Florentine *papier à cuve* (paper hand-decorated with marbled designs). There are several other fine stationery shops along the same street.

LES MOTS À LA BOUCHE BOOKS

Map p404 (www.motsbouche.com; 6 rue Ste-Croix de la Bretonnerie, 4e; ⏲11am-11pm Mon-Sat, 1-9pm Sun; Ⓜ Hôtel de Ville) 'On the Tip of the Tongue' is Paris' premier gay and lesbian bookshop with some English-language books too. If you're feeling naughty, go downstairs.

SPORTS & ACTIVITIES

LES BAINS DU MARAIS SPA

Map p404 (☎01 44 61 02 02; www.lesbainsdumarais.com; 31-33 rue des Blancs Manteaux, 4e; Ⓜ Rambuteau or Hôtel de Ville) Luxury personified, this *hammam* (Turkish steambath) combines the classical with the modern – mint tea and Levantine decor with as many pampering treatments as you'd care to name. The *hammam* is reserved for men and for women on certain days; 'mixed days', when bathing suits are obligatory, are Wednesday evening and all day Saturday and Sunday.

NOMADES INLINE SKATING

Map p404 (www.nomadeshop.com; 37 bd Bourdon, 4e; half-/full day Mon-Fri €5/8, Sat & Sun €6/9, weekend/week €15/30; Ⓜ Bastille) Paris' 'Harrods for roller-heads' rents and sells equipment and accessories, including wheels, helmets (€2), elbow and knee guards (€1).

FREE ROLLERS & COQUILLAGES INLINE SKATING

Map p404 (www.rollers-coquillages.org; 37 bd Bourdon, 4e; ⏲2.30-5.30pm Sun, arrive 2pm) Suitable for all levels of ability, Rollers & Coquillages sets off on 21km-or-so routes from Nomades, where you can buy or rent inline skates and protective equipment.

Bastille & Eastern Paris

Neighbourhood Top Five

❶ Take in a performance at the **Opéra Bastille** (p192), one of the late President François Mitterrand's most enduring projects.

❷ Pay your respects to timeless cinema at the **Cinémathèque Française** (p192).

❸ Go rails to trails on the elevated **Promenade Plantée** (p183).

❹ Explore the picture-perfect **Château de Vincennes** (p187), the only medieval castle in Paris.

❺ Kick back at an outdoor concert while the kids cut loose at the **Parc Floral** (p187).

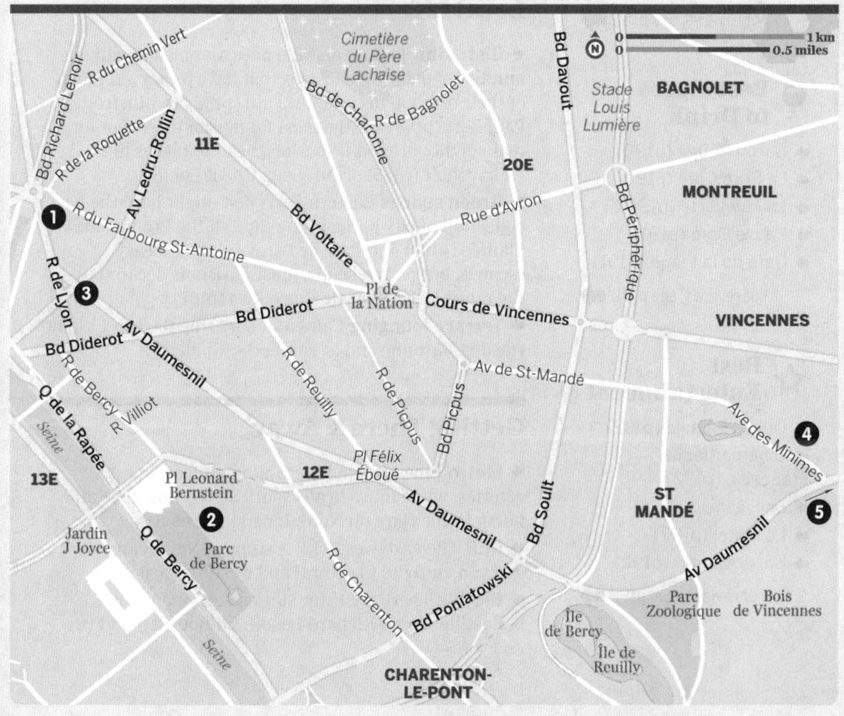

For more detail of this area, see Map p408 and p411 ➡

Lonely Planet's Top Tip

While the area immediately surrounding the Bastille has spawned a clutch of faceless bars and restaurant chains, walking a little bit further north on rue de Charonne or east to Ledru-Rollin and Faidherbe-Chaligny will bring you to a much more interesting neighbourhood, filled with exciting restaurants, modest cafes and all the quirky, unusual shops that make a city great.

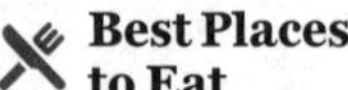

Best Places to Eat

- Septime (p184)
- Le Siffleur de Ballons (p184)
- Eat Intuition (p185)
- La Gazzetta (p185)
- Bistrot Paul Bert (p185)

For reviews, see p184

Best Places to Drink

- Baron Rouge (p190)
- Le Pure Café (p190)
- La Fée Verte (p190)
- Pause Café (p191)
- Café de la Plage (p191)

For reviews, see p190

Best Entertainment

- Opera Bastille (p192)
- Cinémathèque Française (p192)
- La Flèche d'Or (p192)
- Le Motel (p192)
- Barrio Latino (p192)

For reviews, see p192

Explore: Bastille & Eastern Paris

The Bastille is not known for its sights, but it is nonetheless a fascinating area to explore on foot. Still authentically residential in most areas, a wander along the streets northeast of the place de la Bastille – particularly around the metro stops Charonne and Faidherbe-Chaligny – will give you a taste of everyday life in one of Paris' most dynamic neighbourhoods. For a more voyeuristic glimpse of city life, ascend to the elevated park, the Promenade Plantée, which offers fabulous views looking down on the streets around you, and even the occasional peek through an apartment window.

Bastille's main attraction is not aimless *flâneurie* (strolling the city streets) – this former working-class district doesn't exactly have the same visual knockout factor as central Paris. No, Bastille is best for dipping your toes into a vibrant restaurant scene dominated by young, creative chefs; its scores of popular, inexpensive bars and cafes; and the profusion of evening entertainment, from avant-garde opera to indie rock.

A trip to the Bois de Vincennes, the city's largest park, never disappoints. From castles to outdoor concerts, bike excursions and football matches to picnics, it's one of the most-loved spots in the capital to unwind.

Local Life

- **Bistro life** The 11e and 12e have an unusually high number of old-school bistros that have preserved much of their original decor. Chez Paul (p186) and Bistrot Paul Bert (p185) are the most famous of these, but for real neighbourhood favourites, head to places like L'Ébauchoir (p188) or Au Vieux Chêne (p188).
- **Green spaces** Eastern Paris just might have the best collection of city parks in the capital: the Promenade Plantée (p183) and Parc de Bercy (p183) are easy escapes, but on weekends, most Parisians decamp to the much larger Bois de Vincennes (p187).
- **Terrace lounging** Cafes and bars rule the roost along rue de Charonne and at Faidherbe-Chaligny.

Getting There & Away

- **Metro** Lines 1, 8 and 9 are all major east–west arteries, while line 5 heads south across the Seine and north to the Gare du Nord. Line 14 serves Bercy.
- **RER** The east–west RER A stops at Nation and Gare de Lyon en route to central and western Paris.
- **Bicycle** There are three stations around the place de la Bastille: on bd Richard Lenoir, bd Bourdon and rue de Lyon.

SIGHTS

PLACE DE LA BASTILLE CITY SQUARE

Map p408 (MBastille) The Bastille, a 14th-century fortress built to protect the city gates, is the most famous monument in Paris that no longer exists. Transformed into a dreaded state prison under Cardinal Richelieu, it was demolished shortly after a mob stormed it on 14 July 1789 and freed a total of just seven prisoners.

The *place* still resonates with the French as a symbol of revolutionary change, but first impressions of today's busy traffic circle can be a bit underwhelming. The most obvious monument is the lone bronze Colonne de Juillet (July Column) topped with the gilded Spirit of Liberty, but you'll notice that the column has little to do with the famous storming of the prison; it instead commemorates the victims of the later revolutions of 1830 and 1848.

If you're keen to find the Bastille's onetime foundations, look for a triple row of paving stones which traces the building's outline on the ground between bd Henri IV and rue St-Antoine. The foundations are also marked below ground in the Bastille metro station, on the platform of line 5.

CINÉMATHÈQUE FRANÇAISE FILM MUSEUM

Map p411 (www.cinemathequefrancaise.com; 51 rue de Bercy, 12e; exhibits adult/18-25yr/under 18yr €6/5/3; noon-7pm Mon & Wed-Sat, to 8pm Sun; MBercy) A little-known gem near the Parc de Bercy, the Cinémathèque Française was originally created in 1936 by film archivist Henri Langlois. On site are two museums, one devoted to temporary exhibits (usually taking a behind-the-scenes look at a particular film) and the other devoted to the history of cinema, with props (including some from Méliès' classic, *A Trip to the Moon*, featured in *Hugo*), early equipment and short clips of a few classics.

Also here is a vast film library for researchers and a theatre which screens up to 10 films daily.

PROMENADE PLANTÉE PARK

Map p408 (8am-9.30pm May-Aug, to 5.30pm Sep-Apr; MBastille or Gare de Lyon) The most innovative green space in the city, the elevated Promenade Plantée was built atop the old Vincennes Railway, in operation from 1859 to 1969. Three stories above ground level, it provides all the usual park amenities – benches, rose trellises, corridors of bamboo – but its real attraction is the unique aerial vantage point on city life and the surrounding architecture.

The viaduct drops back to street level at the Jardin de Reuilly (1.5km), but it's possible to follow the line all the way to the Bois de Vincennes at the city's edge. This latter section, known as the Coulée Verte (3km), can also be done on a bike or inline skates. Access to the elevated section is via staircase; there is usually at least one per city block. Beneath the park at street level is the **Viaduc des Arts** (Map p408; Gare de Lyon or Daumesnil), which runs along av Daumesnil.

OPÉRA BASTILLE OPERA HOUSE

Map p408 (www.operadeparis.fr; 2-6 place de la Bastille, 12e; guided tours adult/10-25yr/under 10yr €12/10/6; MBastille) In 1984, the former railway station on place de la Bastille was demolished to make way for the new opera house, the Opéra Bastille. One of former President Mitterand's pet projects, the 3400-seat venue was built with the intention of stripping opera of its elitist airs – hence the notable inauguration date of 13 July 1989, the eve of the 200th anniversary of the storming of the Bastille.

There are 1¼-hour **guided tours** of the building, which depart at wildly different times depending on the date – you'll need to check in at the **box office** (01 40 01 19 70; 130 rue de Lyon, 12e; 2.30-6.30pm Mon-Sat). Tickets go on sale 10 minutes before tours begin.

MAISON ROUGE GALLERY

Map p408 (www.lamaisonrouge.org; 10 bd de la Bastille; adult/13-18yr €7/5; 11am-7pm Wed-Sun, to 9pm Thu; MQuai de la Rapée) Subtitled 'Fondation Antoine de Galbert' after the man who endowed it, this cutting-edge gallery shows contemporary artists and seldom-seen works from private collections. The hip, health-conscience Rose Bakery (p163) has a branch here. Note that everything closes between exhibits.

PARC DE BERCY PARK

Map p411 (rue Paul Belmondo; 8am-sunset Mon-Fri, from 9am Sat & Sun; MCour St-Émilion or Bercy) Built atop the site of a former wine depot, this large, well-landscaped park is a great place to break for a picnic and let the kids run free. Bercy reached its height as the 'world's wine cellar' in the 19th century: it was right on the Seine, close to Paris yet

ELEPHANTS IN PARIS

After the Bastille fortress was torn down, there was quite naturally a debate as to what should replace it. A fountain? A monument to the Revolution? Finally, in 1808, Napoleon Bonaparte provided the solution: a gigantic 24m-high bronze elephant with a viewing platform on the top. *Mais, bien sûr*! Always one for larger-than-life projects, Napoleon's intent was for the elephant to serve as an architectural counterpoint to another massive monument he had proposed just two year earlier: the Arc de Triomphe. Designs were drawn up and in 1813 a full-scale plaster-and-wood model was actually installed at the *place* (featured in Victor Hugo's *Les Misérables*). Unfortunately, after Napoleon lost the Battle of Waterloo in 1815, funds dried up and permanent construction came to a halt. The plaster model fell into disrepair and was torn down in 1846, but you have to wonder: would Bastille today be more memorable if the project had actually gone through?

outside the city walls, meaning that shipping was convenient and commerce tax-free.

Vestiges of its former incarnation are spread across the park and the Cour St-Émilion, where the warehouses were located. In some spots you'll see the old railroad tracks; in others you'll find grape vines.

MUSÉE DU FUMEUR MUSEUM
Map p408 (www.museedufumeur.net; 7 rue Pache, 11e; adult/senior & student €5/3; ⏲12.30-7pm Tue-Sat; Ⓜ Voltaire) The Smoker's Museum traces the history of one of humankind's greatest vices: the smoking of tobacco. Hardcore butt-fiends will feel vindicated, though the museum takes an impartial stance, providing (as it states on entry) 'a vantage point for the observation of changing behaviours'. Done up as an old tobacco warehouse, it has a wonderful collection of portraits.

CITÉ NATIONALE DE L'HISTOIRE DE L'IMMIGRATION MUSEUM
(www.histoire-immigration.fr; 293 av Daumesnil, 12e; adult €3-5; ⏲10am-5.30pm Tue-Fri, to 7pm Sat & Sun; Ⓜ Porte Dorée) This heavyweight museum documents the hot-potato topic of immigration through a series of informative historical displays that cover groups as diverse as the Vietnamese, Portuguese, Jews and Russians. The multimedia permanent collection called Repères (Landmarks) and the gallery of personal items donated by members of the public are emotive and informative. It's housed in the lavish 1931 Palais de la Porte Dorée.

AQUARIUM TROPICAL AQUARIUM
(www.aquarium-portedoree.fr; 293 av Daumesnil, 12e; adult/child €6.50/5; ⏲10am-5.30pm Tue-Fri, to 7pm Sat & Sun; Ⓜ Porte Dorée) Although this aquarium is a bit dated, the inexpensive admission makes it a popular choice with many a Parisian family. It's located in the basement of the Palais de la Porte Dorée, beneath the immigration museum.

EATING

Bastille dining tends to swing between a highly lauded group of up-and-coming chefs, who run the hip new neobistros that have reinspired Parisian cooking, and the die-hard traditionalists, who rarely venture beyond the much-loved standards of French cuisine. Thankfully, there's plenty of room for everybody.

TOP CHOICE SEPTIME MODERN FRENCH €€€
Map p408 (☎01 43 67 38 29; 80 rue de Charonne, 11e; lunch/5-course menus €26/55; ⏲lunch Tue-Fri, dinner Mon-Fri; Ⓜ Charonne) Reading the menu at Septime won't get you far, as it looks mostly like an obscure shopping list (hanger steak/chicory/roots, chicken's egg/foie gras/*lardo*). And that's if you even get a menu – if you order the excellent five-course meal (available for both lunch and dinner), you won't even know what's being served until it arrives.

But rest assured, the alchemists in the kitchen here, run by Bertrand Grébaut, are capable of producing some truly beautiful creations, and the blue-smocked waitstaff go out of their way to ensure that the culinary surprises are all pleasant ones. Reserve in advance.

TOP CHOICE LE SIFFLEUR DE BALLONS WINE BAR €
Map p408 (www.lesiffleurdeballons.com; 34 rue de Citeaux, 12e; lunch menu €14, mains €7-15;

⏰10.30am-3pm & 5.30-10pm Tue-Sat; Ⓜ Faidherbe Chaligny) With Tom Waits on the stereo and a few cactuses atop the register, this contemporary wine bar clearly has a dash of California in its soul. The wines, though, are all French – and all natural – and paired with a quality selection of simple but delicious offerings: tartines, soups, lentil salad with truffle oil, cheeses and Iberian charcuterie plates.

Look out for the weekly tastings with winemakers. No reservations, so don't waltz in too late.

EAT INTUITION MODERN FRENCH **€€**

Map p408 (☎01 43 46 12 94; http://eatintuition.com; 53 rue de Charenton, 12e; lunch/dinner menus €28/37; ⏰lunch Thu & Fri, dinner Tue-Sat; 👶; Ⓜ Bastille or Ledru-Rollin) Rarely do you see the words sophisticated and Bastille in the same sentence, but Venezuelan chef Isabella Losada De Armas has managed to break through a couple of stereotypes at this wonderful off-the-radar restaurant. A refreshing change from the same old same, expect haute cuisine with a distinctly personal style, a welcome that's warmer than usual and a wine list that's particularly notable – it only features wine from vineyards run by women.

LA GAZZETTA MODERN FRENCH **€€€**

Map p408 (☎01 43 47 47 05; www.lagazzetta.fr; 29 rue de Cotte, 12e; lunch menus €17, 5-/7-course dinner menus €42/56; lunch Tue-Sat, dinner to 11pm Mon-Sat; ⏰lunch Tue-Sat, dinner to 11pm Mon-Sat; Ⓜ Ledru-Rollin) This fabulous neo-brasserie has gained a substantial following under the tutelage of Swedish chef Petter Nilsson, who is as comfortable producing daring creations (milk-fed lamb confit and ice bleu d'Auvergne cheese) as he is more subtle ones (gnocchi with roasted almonds and lemon). Nilsson's penchant for unusual flavour combinations is quite a polariser, so sample the lunch menu before splashing out for a five-course dinner.

CAFFÈ DEI CIOPPI SICILIAN **€€**

Map p408 (☎01 43 46 10 14; 159 rue du Faubourg Saint-Antoine, 11e; mains €16-20; ⏰Tue-Fri; Ⓜ Ledru-Rollin) Sheltered inside the narrow Passage St-Bernard is this tiny neighbourhood Sicilian, where the open kitchen takes up about as much space as the tables. Federica and Fabrizio do it all: expect simple but flavour-filled dishes like artichoke risotto or linguine with squid. Bookings essential, even for the seating that spills out into the hidden alleyway in warm weather.

RINO MODERN FRENCH **€€€**

Map p408 (☎01 48 06 95 85; 46 rue Trousseau, 11e; 2-/3-course lunch menus €20/25, 2-/3-course dinner menus €38/55; ⏰Tue-Fri; Ⓜ Bastille) For contemporary market-driven cuisine, Giovanni Passerini's buzzy bistro remains one of the most respected addresses in eastern Paris. His Italian roots come through in both the menu and the wine list, though he mastered his technique under some of Paris' top chefs (Alain Passard, Petter Nilsson) – it's a superb combination. Portions are small, however.

BOULANGERIE BAZIN BOULANGERIE **€**

Map p408 (85bis rue de Charenton, 12e; ⏰7.30am-8pm Fri-Tue; Ⓜ Ledru-Rollin) Dating from 1906, this belle époque bakery run by Jacques Bazin has an extraordinary array of award-winning breads, brioches and pastries.

WALY FAY AFRICAN **€€**

Map p408 (☎01 40 24 17 79; 6 rue Godefroy Cavaignac, 11e; mains €13-19; ⏰dinner Mon-Sat; Ⓜ Charonne) This easygoing 'loungin' restaurant' attracts a rather hip crowd for African food with a West Indian twist. Dishes to sample include Senegal's national dish, *tiéboudienne* (rice, fish and vegetables), and the beef *n'dole* with wild greens; you might also consider the copious *mafé* (beef simmered in peanut sauce) served with rice and *aloko* (fried plantain bananas). The ginger ice cream goes down a treat.

BISTROT PAUL BERT BISTRO **€€**

Map p408 (☎01 43 72 24 01; 18 rue Paul Bert, 11e; 3-course lunch/dinner menus €18/36; ⏰lunch & dinner Tue-Sat; Ⓜ Faidherbe-Chaligny) When food writers make lists of the best Paris bistros, one of the names that almost always pops up is Paul Bert. The timeless decor and perfectly executed classic dishes guarantee that you'll need to reserve well in advance, even if the service isn't always up to snuff. Favourites here include the *steak-frites* and the *Paris-Brest* (a cream-filled pastry).

L'ÉCAILLER DU BISTROT SEAFOOD **€€€**

Map p408 (☎01 43 72 76 77; 22 rue Paul Bert, 11e; mains €24-40, seafood platter €36; ⏰lunch & dinner Tue-Sat; Ⓜ Faidherbe-Chaligny) Oyster lovers should make a beeline for Bistrot Paul Bert's famous seafood annex, which serves up a dozen varieties of fresh bivalves, freshly shucked and accompanied by a little lemon juice. Other delights are platters of seafood, a half-dozen *oursins* (sea urchins), minute-cooked tuna steak with sesame oil and the très extravagant lobster *menu.*

CHEZ PAUL BISTRO €€

Map p408 (☎01 47 00 34 57; www.chezpaul.com; 13 rue de Charonne, 11e; mains €16-28; ⊙lunch & dinner; MLedru-Rollin) As far as cinematic French bistros are concerned, Chez Paul gives nearby Paul Bert a run for its money. This is Paris as your grandmother would have known it: checquered red-and-white napkins, faded photographs on the walls, old red banquettes and traditional French dishes handwritten on a yellowing menu. Stick with the simplest of dishes and make sure you've booked ahead. Open to 12.30am daily.

MARCHÉ D'ALIGRE MARKET €

Map p408 (http://marchedaligre.free.fr; rue d'Aligre, 12e; ⊙8am-1pm & 4-7.30pm Tue-Sat, 8am-2pm Sun; MLedru-Rollin) All the staples of French cuisine can be found in this chaotic market street: cheese, coffee, chocolate, wine, charcuterie and even Tunisian pastries. It's a fantastic place to put together a DIY lunch, have a shot of espresso or simply soak up the atmosphere. In the centre of place d'Aligre is the covered **Beauvau Market**, where the offerings are a bit more gourmet.

Other places to look out for here include **Pink Flamingo** (23 rue de l'Aligre) and the Moisan bakery.

MOISAN BOULANGERIE €

Map p408 (5 place d'Aligre, 12e; ⊙7am-8pm Tue-Sun; MLedru-Rollin) One of the oldest organic bakeries in Paris, located just around the corner from the animated Marché d'Aligre. Lunchtime offers include bruschetta and pizzas fresh out of the oven.

MAMA SHELTER PIZZERIA €

(☎01 43 48 48 48; www.mamashelter.com; 109 rue de Bagnolet, 20e; pizzas €8-12; ⊙noon-1.30am Mon-Sat; 📶; MAlexandre Dumas, Gambetta, 🚌76) If you're headed to a concert at La Flèche d'Or (p192), kick off the evening with pizzas and beer on the rooftop terrace at Mama Shelter, just across the street. The pizzeria itself is on the ground floor and features a wood-fired oven and a superb selection of pies, including the mysterious chocolate pizza. Great hours.

ÉTOILE ROUGE BISTRO €€

Map p408 (☎01 53 17 02 44; www.letoilerouge.fr; 75 rue Crozatier, 12e; mains €10-19; ⊙closed Sun night & Mon; MLedru-Rollin) It's not clear where they're going with the retro-Bolshevik motif, but all that really matters is that this is a first-class bistro with enticing French classics (pheasant with foie gras and figs) and an excellent selection of natural wines. It's a two-minute stroll from the Marché d'Aligre.

MAMIE TEVENNEC CRÊPERIE €

Map p408 (☎01 44 93 92 42; 41 rue Faidherbe, 11e; lunch menus €10, crêpes from €8; ⊙Tue-Sat; MCharonne) Georges Brassens on the stereo and old-fashioned decor make this neighbourhood crêperie a fave with everyone, from indulgent grandparents at lunch to star-crossed twenty-somethings at dinner. For that quirky extra touch, it also serves excellent Corsican charcuterie and substantial salads. Everyone goes gaga for the salted-butter-caramel dessert crêpe.

40/60 PIZZERIA €

Map p408 (44 rue Trousseau, 11e; pizza slices from €7; ⊙Tue-Sat; MLedru-Rollin) You'd be hard-pressed to find a hipper pizzeria than 40/60, which features black-and-white Qbert-style floor tiles (imported from Spain) and Genovese pizza baked on large trays and cut by the rectangle. The pricing system is a bit complex if you're not a math whiz, but hey, the thick-crust gourmet pizza is worth the mental workout. Also does takeaway.

MANSOURIA NORTH AFRICAN €€

Map p408 (☎01 43 71 00 16; www.mansouria.fr; 11 rue Faidherbe, 11e; mains €18-26, menus €28 & €36; ⊙lunch Tue-Sat, dinner Mon-Sat; MFaidherbe-Chaligny) This particularly attractive Moroccan restaurant serves excellent milk-fed steamed lamb, and what some say is the best *kascsou* (couscous) and *touagin* (tajine) in town. The signature dish is the *mourouzia*, lamb simmered in a complex combination of some 27 spices and served with a sauce of honey, raisins and almonds. There are different options available for the three-course *menus.*

MARCHÉ BASTILLE MARKET €

Map p408 (bd Richard Lenoir, 11e; ⊙7am-2.30pm Thu & Sun; MBastille or Richard Lenoir) If you only get to one open-air market in Paris, this one – stretching between the Bastille

BOIS DE VINCENNES

Paris is flanked by two large parks, the Bois de Boulogne in the west and the Bois de Vincennes in the east. Originally royal hunting grounds, the Bois de Vincennes was annexed by the army following the Revolution and then donated to the city in 1860 by Napoleon III. A fabulous place to escape the endless stretches of Parisian concrete, the Bois de Vincennes also contains a handful of notable sights. Metro lines 1 (St-Mandé, Château de Vincennes) and 8 (Porte Dorée, Porte de Charenton) will get you to the eastern edges of the park.

Château de Vincennes (www.chateau-vincennes.fr; av de Paris, Vincennes; adult/18-25yr/under 18yr €8.50/5.50/free; ⌚10am-6.15pm Apr-Sep, to 5.15pm Oct-Mar; Ⓜ Château de Vincennes) Originally a meagre 12th-century hunting lodge, the castle here was expanded several times throughout the centuries until it reached its present size under Louis XIV. Notable features include the beautiful 52m-high keep (1370) and the royal chapel (1552), both of which are open to visitors. Note that the chapel is only open between 11am and noon, and 3pm and 4pm.

Parc Floral de Paris (Esplanade du Chateau de Vincennes; adult/7-18yr/under 7yr €5/2/free; ⌚9.30am-9pm May-Aug, shorter hr rest of year; Ⓜ Château de Vincennes) This magnificent botanical park is one of the highlights of the Bois de Vincennes. Natural landscaping and a magnificent collection of plants will keep amateur gardeners happy, while Paris' largest play area (giant climbing webs and slides, jungle gyms, sand-boxes, etc) will absolutely thrill families. Open-air concerts are staged throughout summer, making it a first-rate picnic destination.

Lac Daumesnil (Ⓜ Porte Dorée) The largest lake in the Bois de Vincennes, this is a popular destination for walks and rowboat excursions in warmer months. A Buddhist temple is located nearby.

Vincennes (Ⓜ Château de Vincennes or RER A Vincennes) Often overlooked, a stop in Vincennes itself will give you a feel for a typical well-heeled French town. Shopping is the main activity, with dozens of stores lining the main street, rue de Midi, where you can also pick up plenty of gourmet picnic supplies.

Parc Zoologique de Paris (Ⓜ Porte Dorée) This zoo, home to some 600 animals, has been undergoing major renovations since 2008 and is expected to reopen in spring 2014.

and Richard Lenoir metro stations – is among the very best.

SARDEGNA A TAVOLA — SARDINIAN €€€

Map p408 (☎01 44 75 03 28; 1 rue de Cotte, 12e; mains €16-38; ⌚lunch Tue-Sat, dinner to 11pm Mon-Sat; Ⓜ Ledru-Rollin) Sardegna a Tavola claims it will introduce you to the flavours, colours and fragrances of the Mediterranean, and you barely have to walk though the door for the last two. But stick around for the flavours and you won't be disappointed. Sardinian specialities include spaghetti with *bottarga* (cured mullet roe), cooked with garlic, parsley and red-pepper flakes.

CAFÉ CARTOUCHE — BISTRO €€

Map p411 (☎01 40 19 09 95; 4 rue de Bercy, 12e; mains €17-22, 2-/3-course lunch menus €15/18; ⌚lunch Mon-Fri, dinner Mon-Sat; Ⓜ Cour St-Émilion) The only authentic eats within walking distance of Bercy Village, this regular's spot is always bustling, particularly at lunch, when securing a table may well be mission impossible. Bistro fare changes daily and is prepared in the best French carnivore tradition: think blood sausage, steak with Roquefort sauce or roast chicken with wild mushrooms.

EL GALPON DE UNICO — ARGENTINE €€

Map p408 (☎01 43 67 68 08; www.resto-unico.com; 15 rue Paul Bert, 11e; lunch menu €17, mains €23-35; ⌚lunch & dinner; Ⓜ Faidherbe-Chaligny) This very trendy, very orange Argentine *parillada* (steakhouse) took over an old butcher's shop and put a retro 1970s spin on it. Unico is all about meat – especially the barbecued *entrecôte* (rib steak) with chunky *frites*. To order, study the diagram of the steer and choose your territory.

L'ENCRIER

BISTRO €

Map p408 (☎01 44 68 08 16; 55 rue Traversière, 12e; mains €16, 2-/3-course menus lunch €12.50/14.50, dinner €19.80/24.80; ⌚lunch Mon-Fri, dinner to 11pm Mon-Sat; ⓂLedru-Rollin or Gare de Lyon) Always heaving but especially at lunch, the 'Inkwell' attracts punters with a decent variety of dishes, ranging from steak with Roquefort sauce or delicate pig's cheeks with spices to simple veggie lasagne. Ideally located just off the Viaduc des Arts, the assortment of set *menus*, open kitchen and large picture window make this place a winner.

PARIS HANOI

VIETNAMESE €

Map p408 (74 rue de Charonne, 11e; mains €9-11; ⌚lunch & dinner; ⓂCharonne) This upbeat, very yellow restaurant is an excellent place to come for *pho* (soup noodles with beef) and other classic Vietnamese dishes. There's no reservations and the place is a veritable legend, so be prepared to join the queue.

BAR À SOUPES

SOUP €

Map p408 (33 rue de Charonne, 11e; soups from €5.30, lunch menu €9.95; ⌚Mon-Sat; ⓂLedru-Rollin) With 36 varieties of soup served per week (six daily), chances are you'll always find something here to please your palate. A few of Mme Bley's stalwarts include pumpkin-chestnut borscht, creamed red lentils and coconut milk, and the vodka-laced Bloody Mary.

LE SOUK

NORTH AFRICAN €€

Map p408 (☎01 49 29 05 08; 1 rue Keller, 11e; menus €19.50 & €26; ⌚lunch Sat & Sun, dinner Tue-Sat; ⓂLedru-Rollin) You'll enjoy this place almost as much for the decor as the food – from the clay pots overflowing with spices on the outside to the exuberant Moroccan interior. Exuberant furnishings aside, what about the food? As authentic as the decoration – notably the duck *tajine*, the pigeon pastilla and vegetarian couscous. Portions are surprisingly generous for Paris.

LES AMIS DE MESSINA

SICILIAN €€

Map p408 (☎01 43 67 96 01; www.lesamisdesmessina.com; 204 rue du Faubourg St-Antoine, 12e; pasta €12-17, mains €18-25; ⌚lunch Mon-Fri, dinner to 11.30pm Mon-Sat; ⓂFaidherbe-Chaligny) Chef Ignazio Messina works the open kitchen here, preparing gorgeous pasta dishes alongside the fresh *pisci* (fish) and *carni* (meat), not to mention all the other decadent Sicilian specialties. Start off with the two-person platter of house antipasti.

AU VIEUX CHÊNE

BISTRO €€

Map p408 (☎01 43 71 67 69; 7 rue du Dahomey, 11e; starters €10-16, mains €21-24, lunch menus €15, 2-/ 3-course dinner menus €28/33; ⌚lunch & dinner Mon-Fri; ⓂFaidherbe-Chaligny) Along a quiet side street in a neighbourhood full of traditional woodworking studios, this retro bistro offers an excellent seasonal menu, with specialities like rabbit stuffed with foie gras, and some well-chosen wines. Three of the cast-iron columns holding the place up are registered monuments.

L'ÉBAUCHOIR

BISTRO €€

Map p408 (☎01 43 42 49 31; www.lebauchoir.com; 45 rue de Cîteaux, 12e; mains €19-24, lunch menus €13-25; ⌚lunch Tue-Sat, dinner to 11pm Mon-Sat; ⓂFaidherbe-Chaligny) This one-time workers' eatery has been upgraded to a convivial gourmet bistro, where regulars drop in for personal creations from chef Thomas Dufour, like lentils with Beaufort cheese or veal liver with honey and ginger.

LES PASSAGES DE LA BASTILLE

The area east of the Bastille was originally outside city limits and under the control of the nearby Abbey de Saint-Antoine (now the St-Antoine Hospital). In 1471 King Louis XI granted the abbey an unusual privilege: craftsmen living on the abbey's land were granted exemption from city taxes and, more importantly, from the the stringent guild regulations that stifled innovation of any sort. Cabinetmakers, gilders, varnishers and others flooded into the area, and the result was a flurry of creativity that resulted in the introduction of prized new furniture styles over the centuries, such as Louis XIV, Louis XV and Louis XVI. The imaginatively named passages and courtyards once inhabited by artisans still exist – you'll find plenty if you look closely while walking down rue du Faubourg St-Antoine – but the sounds of hammer and saw have since been replaced by the secluded live-work spaces of architects and graphic designers, as well as a quite a few ever-popular restaurants.

JACQUES MÉLAC WINE BAR €

Map p408 (☎01 43 70 59 27; 42 rue Léon Frot, 11e; mains €16-20, lunch menus €14.50; ⊙lunch & dinner Mon-Sat; MCharonne) Fringed with its very own venerable grape vine (Château Charonne), this quintessential neighbourhood wine bar has been defending French culinary traditions since 1938.

LE SQUARE TROUSSEAU BISTRO €€

Map p408 (☎01 43 43 06 00; 1 rue Antoine Vollon, 12e; mains €18-24; ⊙8am-2am; MLedru-Rollin) This vintage bistro (c 1900) with etched glass, zinc bar and polished wood panelling has become a Parisian landmark of sorts – you won't catch Mathieu Kassovitz here anymore, but a meal, or even a simple coffee and croissant on the terrace, will delight no matter whom you're seated next to.

LE TIFFIN INDIAN €

Map p408 (☎01 48 07 32 28; www.letiffin.fr; 42 rue de Charonne, 11e; mains €6-8, menus €9-13; ⊙lunch Mon-Sat, dinner Tue-Sat; MLedru-Rollin) This hip new Indian makes a killer kati roll, which is essentially a chapati-curry sandwich. Not filling enough? Order one of the more substantial dishes (tandoori chicken, vegetarian curry) and rice on the side, and kick back to the indie-rock soundtrack. No surprises there – it was opened up by the team behind Le Motel (p192).

LE MOUTON NOIR BISTRO €€

Map p408 (☎01 48 07 05 45; www.lemoutonnoir.fr; 65 rue de Charonne, 11e; mains €18, 3-course menus €29; ⊙dinner Tue-Sat; MCharonne) This tiny dinner place with a mere two-dozen covers is something of a neighbourhood secret. The focus is supposed to be on its 'hippygroove' cuisine (apparently French fusion; strangely, the term never took off), but the menu is surprisingly conservative: what they really do well here is source quality ingredients and prepare dishes to perfection.

CHALET SAVOYARD FONDUE €€

Map p408 (☎01 48 05 13 13; www.chalet-savoyard.fr; 58 rue de Charonne, 11e; mains €12-18, menus €28; ⊙lunch & dinner; MLedru-Rollin) Fondue restaurants are a fairly rare breed in Paris, which probably accounts for the incredible popularity of the hearty, rib-stickin' cuisine at this spacious place. Fill up on alpine specialities like *tartiflette* (melted reblochon cheese and bacon baked with potatoes), 14 different types of cheese fondues (served with bread and potatoes) or raclette (another type of melted cheese that's served over – surprise! – potatoes).

LES DOMAINES QUI MONTENT WINE BAR €€

Map p408 (136 bd Voltaire, 11e; menus €15; ⊙lunch Mon-Sat; MVoltaire) Les Domaines Qui Montent has been around since before the *cave à manger* trend began, and although it's not quite as trendy as most newcomers, it is very much the real thing. Above all a wine shop, it offers simple 2-course menus at lunch which you can pair with any of their available bottles.

À LA RENAISSANCE CAFE €€

Map p408 (☎01 43 79 83 09; 87 rue de la Roquette, 11e; mains €13-22, lunch/dinner menus €22/30; ⊙lunch & dinner; MVoltaire) This popular local's cafe is certainly out of the way, but if you're looking for an authentic meal in a neighbourhood setting, it's definitely a good bet – it's always full up at meal times. Along with wine and plates of cheese, it serves mackerel *rillettes,* steak tartare and that all-time favourite, *œufs à la coq aux tartines* (soft-boiled eggs with toast).

SWANN ET VINCENT ITALIAN €€

Map p408 (☎01 43 43 49 40; www.swann-vincent.fr; 7 rue St-Nicolas, 12e; mains €13-19, lunch menus €17.50; ⊙lunch & dinner; MLedru-Rollin) Paris meets Italy in this elegant, old-fashioned restaurant. Unpretentious staff will help you select from the huge blackboard, whose offerings include temptations such as saffron risotto with speck and veal cutlets drizzled with lemon. Go easy on the olive-and-herb bread – you need to leave room for the tiramisu.

AGUA LIMÓN SPANISH €

Map p408 (☎01 43 44 92 24; www.restaurant-agualimon.com; 12 rue Théophile Roussel; tapas €5-13, 2-/3-course lunch menus €11.50/16; ⊙lunch & dinner Tue-Sat; 📶; MLedru-Rollin) Head to this lemon-coloured tapas place for a shot of Mediterranean sunlight. The menu includes standards such as Catalan-style octopus, goat cheese in olive oil and *patatas bravas* (fried potatoes with spicy tomato sauce). There's a decent selection of Spanish wines and sangria.

À LA BANANE IVOIRIENNE AFRICAN €

Map p408 (☎01 43 70 49 90; 10 rue de la Forge Royale, 11e; mains €10-15, menus €28.50; ⊙dinner Tue-Sat; MLedru-Rollin) West African specialities (including a generous vegetarian platter) are served in a relaxed and friendly setting, with lots of West African gewgaws on display. It's been an African institution in Paris for over 20 years and is said to serve the best Ivorian food in the capital. It's open until midnight and there's live African music in the cellar restaurant starting at 10pm on Fridays.

LES GALOPINS FRENCH €€

Map p408 (☎01 47 00 45 35; 24 rue des Taillandiers, 11e; lunch menus €13, 2-/3-course dinner menus €15/21; ⊙lunch Mon-Fri, dinner Mon-Sat; Ⓜ Bastille) The meals at this cute neighbourhood bistro are straightforward and in the best tradition of French cuisine, with such offerings as *raviolis de pétoncles* (queen-scallop raviolis), *médaillons de lotte au gingembre* (monkfish medallions with ginger) and *côte de veau aux pleurotes* (veal chop with oyster mushrooms).

CHEZ RAMULAUD FRENCH €€

Map p408 (☎01 43 72 23 29; 269 rue du Faubourg St-Antoine, 11e; lunch menus €14-16, dinner menus €29; ⊙lunch Mon-Fri, dinner Mon-Sat; Ⓜ Faidherbe-Chaligny) With its peaceful, retro atmosphere, this old-school brasserie is reminiscent of an established provincial restaurant. The blackboard offerings are both comforting and substantial: daily soups, terrines, coddled eggs with seasonal mushrooms and other French classics.

CAFÉ DE L'INDUSTRIE CAFE €

Map p408 (☎01 47 00 13 53; 16 & 17 rue St-Sabin, 11e; mains €7-14.50, lunch menus €10.50; ⊙9.15am-2am; Ⓜ Bastille) This popular cafe-restaurant with neocolonial decor has two locations, with **Café de l'Industrie Annexe** (Map p408) directly opposite. It's a pleasant space and a preferable alternative to one of the crowded cafes or bars just off the place de la Bastille. You'll find the food is competitively priced but not always up to scratch; to avoid disappointment stick with the simple entrées or just graze off the fabulous dessert table.

LE TRAIN BLEU BRASSERIE €€€

Map p408 (☎01 43 43 09 06; www.le-train-bleu.com; 1st fl, Gare de Lyon, 26 place Louis Armand, 12e; starters €18-28, mains €30-45, menus lunch €56, dinner €68 & €98; ⊙7.30am-11pm Mon-Sat, 9am-11pm Sun; 📶; Ⓜ Gare de Lyon) In all probability you've never – ever – seen a railway station restaurant as sumptuous as this heritage-listed belle époque showpiece. This is a top-end spot to dine on such fare as foie gras with a confiture of red onions, grapes and hazelnuts, Charolles beef steak tartare and chips, and the house-made *baba au rhum*.

Sunday brunch is from 11.30am to 2.30pm, which leaves just enough time to board that train to the sunny south.

DRINKING & NIGHTLIFE

Place de la Bastille has become increasingly crass over the years, but it invariably draws a crowd, particularly to heaving rue de Lappe. The options become much more appealing as you head further east.

TOP CHOICE LE BARON ROUGE WINE BAR

Map p408 (1 rue Théophile Roussel, 12e; ⊙10am-2pm & 5-10pm Mon-Fri, 10am-10pm Sat, 10am-4pm Sun; Ⓜ Ledru-Rollin) Just about the ultimate Parisian wine-bar experience, this place has a dozen barrels of the stuff stacked up against the bottle-lined walls. As unpretentious as you'll find, it's a local meeting place where everyone is welcome and is especially busy on Sundays after the Marché d'Aligre (p186) wraps up. All the usual suspects – cheese, charcuterie and oysters – will keep your belly full.

For a small deposit, you can even fill up one-litre bottles straight from the wine barrel for under €5.

LE PURE CAFÉ CAFE

Map p408 (14 rue Jean Macé, 11e; ⊙daily; Ⓜ Charonne) A classic Parisian haunt, this rustic, cherry-red corner cafe was featured in the art-house film *Before Sunset* but it's still a refreshingly unpretentious spot for a drink or well-crafted fare like veal with chestnut purée.

LA FÉE VERTE BAR

Map p408 (108 rue de la Roquette, 11e; dishes €10-16; ⊙daily; 📶; Ⓜ Voltaire) You guessed it, the 'Green Fairy' specialises in absinthe (served traditionally with spoons and sugar cubes), but this fabulously old-fashioned neighbourhood cafe and bar also serves terrific food, including Green Fairy cheeseburgers.

PAUSE CAFÉ BAR

Map p408 (41 rue de Charonne, 11e; dishes from €12.50; ⌚daily; Ⓜ Ledru-Rollin) With an established pedigree that dates back to the 1990s, this happening cafe does it all: drinks, meals, coffee and brunch. Well situated away from the fray of Bastille, its generous terrace, covered in winter, fills up with fashionable locals and the almost famous. French film buffs may recognize it from the Gen-X hit *Chacun cherche son chat* (When the Cat's Away, 1996).

CAFÉ DE LA PLAGE BAR

Map p408 (59 rue de Charonne, 11e; ⌚Tue-Sat; Ⓜ Ledru-Rollin) A collection of flip-flop keychains dangle over the bar, setting the party atmosphere for this divey favourite that fills up to bursting on weekends. There's live music most nights in the basement, cheap drinks and a young, international crowd.

MOJITO LAB COCKTAIL BAR

Map p408 (www.mojitolab.com; 28 rue Keller, 11e; ⌚daily; 📶; Ⓜ Bastille) A good deal classier than pretty much any bar in the Bastille area, the Lab is a study in mojito mixology – some 20 different versions, from the Mojito flambé to the magical MojiPotter – are available for connoisseurs. Ninety-minute mixing classes are also held here, beginning at 6pm (except Wednesday).

LES FUNAMBULES BAR

Map p408 (12 rue Faidherbe, 11e; ⌚daily; 📶; Ⓜ Faidherbe-Chaligny) Like so many small cafes in Paris, Les Funambules turns into a fashionable bar as evening approaches. While the original architecture provides character (check out the frescoes), nowadays the terrace is crammed with beautiful people on warm summer evenings.

The rest of the year customers take shelter inside under the bird cages and stunning coffered ceiling with chandelier, and enjoy a cocktail at the bar or a snack of tapas in the back room.

TROLL CAFÉ BAR

Map p408 (27 rue de Cotte, 12e; ⌚daily; Ⓜ Ledru-Rollin) This fun-loving music and beer bar just up from the Marché d'Aligre takes Brittany as its theme (at least the eponymous Troll, 90 years old if a day, is supposedly from there) but mixes in something of a northern France angle by selling Ch'ti beer.

LE BISTROT DU PEINTRE BAR, BISTRO

Map p408 (116 av Ledru-Rollin, 11e; meals from €11; ⌚daily; 📶 👪; Ⓜ Bastille) This lovely belle époque bistro and wine bar could just as easily count as a restaurant rather than a drinking place; after all, the food is great. But it's the 1902 art nouveau bar, elegant terrace and spot-on service that has put it on the apéritif A-list of local artists, *bobos* and local celebs.

LE CHINA COCKTAIL BAR

Map p408 (www.lechina.eu; 50 rue de Charenton, 12e; ⌚daily; Ⓜ Ledru-Rollin or Bastille) Although China is present in name only, this is nonetheless a delightfully plush place to meet for drinks, with deep leather couches, 1930s Shanghai decor and live shows in the basement.

RUE DE LAPPE

Although at night it's one of the rowdiest bar-hopping streets in Paris, rue de Lappe is actually quite peaceful during the day and worth a quick wander. Like most streets in the area, it dates back to the 17th century and was originally home to cabinetmakers, who first moved into the area to escape the taxes and restrictions imposed by guilds operating within city limits. In the centuries that followed, the street was gradually taken over by metalworkers, who equipped the city with its zinc bars, copper piping and the like. At the same time, immigrants from the central French region of Auvergne also moved in, opening up *cafés-charbons*, places where you could go for a drink and buy coal at the same time. In this way the street eventually became a popular drinking strip, and its accordion-driven dance halls, which hosted *bals-musettes*, were to become famous throughout Paris. The dance hall Le Balajo (p192) dates back to 1936 and still hosts a *bal-musette* on Monday afternoons. You can also find a few Auvergne specialty shops here, such as the one at No 6, as well as a beautiful old bistro, Les Sans-Culottes, at No 27.

LA LIBERTÉ BAR

Map p408 (196 rue de Faubourg St-Antoine, 11e; daily; ; Faidherbe-Chaligny) A delightfully messy local institution infused with the spirit of the '68 revolution, the 'Liberty' does simple meals and wine by day, and is a heaving mix of regulars and drop-ins, raspy-voiced arguments and glasses going clink by night. It's the kind of place where *bobos,* artists and old rockers find their common point: a passionate love of drink and talk.

TAPE BAR BAR

Map p408 (21 rue de la Roquette, 11e; daily; Bastille) Graffiti tags are scrawled on every possible surface inside the Tape Bar, marking this as the only underground hangout within a minute's walk of the Bastille. Cheap drinks and decent music.

BARRIO LATINO CLUBBING

Map p408 (46-48 rue du Faubourg St-Antoine, 11e; daily; Bastille) Still squeezing the salsa theme for all that it's worth, this enormous over-the-top bar-restaurant with serious dancing is spread over three highly impressive floors. It attracts Latinos, Latino wannabes, Latino wannahaves and a gay crowd. Don't arrive too late; the queue to get in can be formidably long.

LE BALAJO CLUBBING

Map p408 (www.balajo.fr; 9 rue de Lappe, 11e; daily; Bastille) A mainstay of Parisian nightlife since 1936, this ancient ballroom is devoted to salsa classes and Latino music during the week, with an R&B slant on weekends. At times, depending on your sensitivies, it can be somewhat tacky, but it scores a mention for its historical value and its old-fashioned *musette* (accordion music) gigs on Monday afternoons.

LA SCÈNE BASTILLE CLUBBING

Map p408 (www.scenebastille.com; 2bis rue des Taillandiers, 11e; Thu-Sun; Bastille or Ledru-Rollin) The 'Bastille Scene' puts on a mixed bag of concerts but focuses on electro, funk and hip hop.

SANZ SANS CLUBBING

Map p408 (01 44 75 78 78; 49 rue du Faubourg St-Antoine; 9am-2am Mon, 9am-5am Tue-Sat, 6pm-5am Sun; Bastille) A little cheesy, a little sleazy, this lively bar clad in red velvet and zebra stripes continues to hold out as a busy drinking venue on the Bastille beat. DJs spin everything from electronic to funk and soul, and the crowd is similarly unpredictable.

★ ENTERTAINMENT

OPÉRA BASTILLE OPERA, BALLET

Map p408 (08 92 89 90 90; www.operadeparis.fr; 2-6 place de la Bastille, 12e; Bastille) This 3400-seat venue is the city's main opera hall; it also occasionally stages ballet and classical concerts. Tickets for performance always go on sale online two weeks before they're available by telephone or at the box office (p183). Standing-only tickets (*places débouts*) are available for €5, going on sale 90 minutes before performances begin.

If you want to try your luck, last-minute seats sometimes go on sale 45 minutes before the curtain goes up to people aged under 28 or over 60.

CINÉMATHÈQUE FRANÇAISE CINEMA

Map p411 (www.cinemathequefrancaise.com; 51 rue Bercy, 12e; daily; Bercy) This national institution is a temple to the 'seventh art' and always screens its foreign offerings in their original versions. Up to 10 movies a day are shown, usually retrospectives (Spielberg, Altman, Eastwood) mixed in with related but more obscure films. Tickets €6.50.

LA FLÈCHE D'OR LIVE MUSIC

(www.flechedor.fr; 102bis rue de Bagnolet, 20e; daily; Alexandre Dumas or Gambetta) Just over 1km northeast of place de la Nation and housed in a former railway station on the outer edge of central Paris, this music venue attracts a young alternative crowd with both indie rock concerts and house/electro DJ nights. The 'Golden Arrow' – that was the train to Calais in the 1930s – has a solid reputation for promoting young talent.

LE MOTEL CLUB

Map p408 (8 passage Josset, 11e; Tue-Sun; Ledru-Rollin) This hole-in-the wall venue in the hot-to-the-boiling-point 11e has become the go-to indie bar around Bastille. It's particularly well loved for its comfy sofas, inexpensive but quality drinks (Belgian beers on tap) and excellent music. Live bands and DJs throughout the week.

LES DISQUAIRES DANCE

Map p408 (www.lesdisquaires.com; 6 rue des Taillandiers, 11e; daily; ; Ledru-Rollin or Bastille) This oh-so-Bastille club and music venue spins a variety of beats (Latin, funk, soul) and also hosts the occasional live concert. This being France, there's usually some decent food (cheese and charcuterie) to be had alongside the drinks.

LA CHAPELLE DES LOMBARDS CLUB

Map p408 (19 rue de Lappe, 11e; Tue-Sun; Bastille) This perennially popular Bastille dance club has happening Latino DJs and reggae, funk and Afro jazz concerts – in a word, a bit of everything. Concerts usually take place at 8.30pm on Friday and Saturday.

PALAIS OMNISPORTS DE PARIS-BERCY CONCERTS

Map p411 (www.bercy.fr; 8 bd de Bercy, 12e; Bercy) This indoor sports arena, whose sloping exterior is covered with a lawn, hosts the largest concerts and events to come through Paris (Cirque du Soleil, Lenny Kravitz) as well as various sporting competitions and matches.

SHOPPING

BERCY VILLAGE HOME, GARDEN

Map p411 (www.bercyvillage.com; cour St-Émilion, 12e; daily; Cour St-Émilion) Set in the former Bercy wine warehouses is this popular commercial centre, with cafes, a large cinema, and a string of stores catering to the needs of Parisian families. A good spot for a browse, you'll find home design, clever kitchen supplies and quality toy stores among other options.

VIADUC DES ARTS ARTS, CRAFTS

Map p408 (www.viaducdesarts.fr; av Daumesnil, 12e; vary; Bastille or Gare de Lyon) Beneath the red-brick arches of the Promenade Plantée (p183) is the Viaduc des Arts, where traditional artisans and contemporary designers carry out antique renovations and create new items using traditional methods. Artisans include furniture and tapestry restorers, interior designers, cabinet makers, violin- and flute-makers, embroiderers and jewellers.

ISABEL MARANT FASHION, ACCESSORIES

Map p408 (www.isabelmarant.tm.fr; 16 rue de Charonne, 11e; Mon-Sat; Bastille) Great cardigans and trousers, interesting accessories, ethnic influences and beautiful fabrics: just a few reasons why Isabel Marant has become the darling of Paris fashion. Bohemian and stylish, these are clothes that people actually look good in.

FERMOB HOME, GARDEN

Map p408 (www.fermob.com; 81-83 av Ledru-Rollin, 12e; Mon-Sat; Ledru Rollin) If you want to create the 'Jardin du Luxembourg look' in your own backyard or garden, head for Fermob. It makes French park-style benches and folding chairs in a range of yummy colours – from carrot and lemon to fuchsia and aubergine.

CHEMINS DE BRETAGNE FOOD, DRINK

Map p408 (15 rue de Prague, 12e; 10am-1.30pm & 2.30-7pm Tue-Sat; Ledru Rollin) Can't live without buttery *kouign amann* (a kind of Breton cake)? Sights set on *cidre* (cider)? This is the place for all things Breton – from fish products and cakes to organic herbal teas and sea salt.

PREMIÈRE PRESSION PROVENCE FOOD, DRINK

Map p408 (www.ppprovence.com; 3 rue Antoine Vollon, 12e; 11am-2.30pm & 3.30-7pm Tue-Fri, 11am-7pm Sat, 11am-2pm Sun & Mon; Ledru-Rollin) By and large France does not make a lot of olive oil – a mere 0.02% of world production – but what it does press is lighter, more fruity and easier to digest than the olive oils of Spain, Italy or Greece. Come here for the finest Appellation d'Origine Contrôlée (AOC)-rated cold-pressed *huile d'olive* (olive oil) from Provence.

ALBUM BOOKS, COMICS

Map p411 (www.album.fr; 46 cour St-Émilion, 12e; daily; Cour St-Émilion) Album specialises in *bandes dessinées* (graphic novels), which have an enormous following in France, with everything from Tintin and Babar to erotic comics and the latest Japanese manga.

MARCHÉ AUX PUCES D'ALIGRE FLEA MARKET

Map p408 (place d'Aligre; 8am-1pm Tue-Sun; Ledru-Rollin) Smaller but more central than Paris' other flea markets, rummage through boxes of clothes and accessories worn decades ago, as well as assorted bric-a-brac.

The Islands

Neighbourhood Top Five

❶ Revel in the crowning glory of medieval Gothic architecture and its brilliantly bestial rooftop walk: **Cathédrale de Notre Dame de Paris** (p196).

❷ Read richly coloured biblical tales, exquisitely told with a stained-glass grace and beauty impossible to find elsewhere at **Sainte Chapelle** (p202).

❸ Learn how Marie Antoinette and thousands of others lived out their final days before being beheaded at the **Conciergerie** (p201).

❹ Skip across **Pont Neuf** (p201) and imagine it Christo-wrapped.

❺ Savour the sweetness of a famous Parisian **Berthillon** (p202) ice cream.

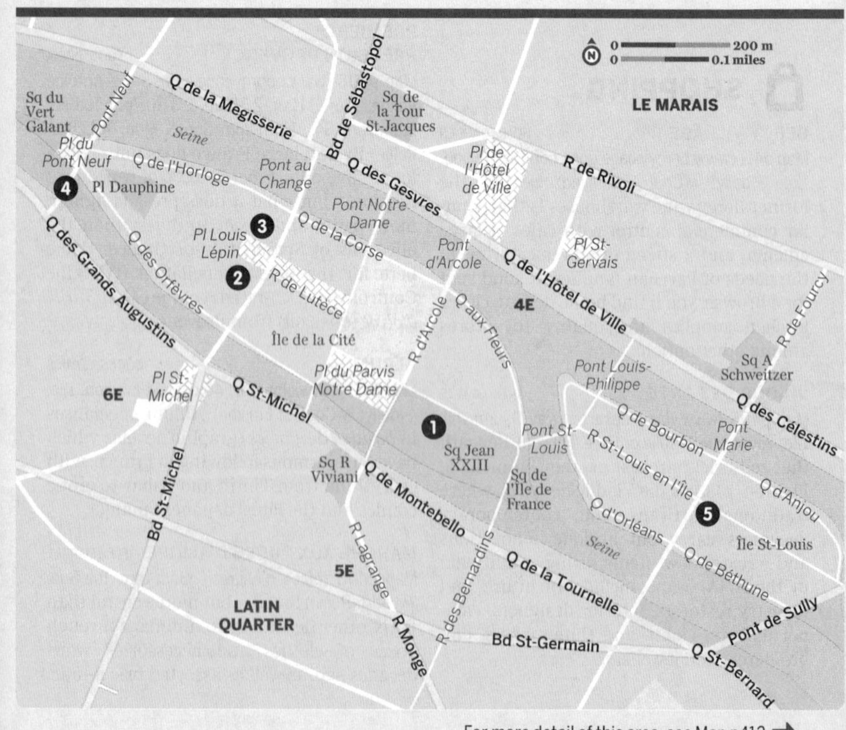

For more detail of this area, see Map p412 ➡

Explore the Islands

Paris' island duo could not be more different – or so enchanting to meander on foot. Start the day on Île de la Cité where the Conciergerie, Sainte Chapelle and Pont Neuf offer historical drama and intrigue. Indulge in a light lunch and glass of wine at Taverne Henri IV, then stroll east, cutting through the flower and bird markets to Cathédrale de Notre Dame. Scale the cathedral towers, tour the interior and then relax in the pretty gardens behind the flying-buttress-festooned edifice.

Or squirrel away the finer details of Notre Dame for day two and splurge the afternoon instead on exploring the quaint car-free lanes and bijou portfolio of street plaques celebrating famous past residents on neighbouring Île St-Louis – the islet with ample eating and boutique-shopping opportunities. End the day in the area around Pont St-Louis and Pont Louis-Philippe, one of the city's most romantic spots.

Local Life

- **Opera at the Cathedral** The occasional sound-and-images 'operas' staged at Cathédrale de Notre Dame de Paris (p196) cast the cathedral in a very different, impossibly romantic, light.
- **Art Exhibitions** Viewing one of the cutting-edge, contemporary art exhibitions hosted by the Conciergerie (p201) is the most exciting way to experience Europe's largest surviving medieval hall.
- **Markets** Île de la Cité's daily flower market, Marché aux Fleurs (p203), has brightened up place Louis Lépin since 1808 and on Sundays it becomes a bird market.
- **Free Entertainment** Pont au Double (linking Notre Dame with the Left Bank) and Pont St-Louis (linking the two islands) buzz with buskers, musicians and other street entertainment in summer.

Getting There & Away

- **Metro** The closest stations are Cité (line 4) and Pont Marie (line 7).
- **Bus** Bus 47 links Île de la Cité with the Marais and Gare de l'Est; bus 21 with Opéra and Gare St-Lazare. On Île St Louis it's bus 67 to Jardin des Plantes and Place d'Italie, and bus 87 through the Latin Quarter to École Militaire and Champ de Mars.
- **Bicycle** Île de la Cité has a trio of handy Vélib' stations: one at place Louis Lépine by the Cité metro station; others at 1 quai aux Fleurs and 5 rue d'Arcole, both by Cathédrale de Notre Dame.

Lonely Planet's Top Tip

Queues to see the sunlight stream through spectacular stained-glass at **Sainte Chapelle** (p202) are staggeringly long. To dodge the line and sail through with little or no waiting, first visit the **Conciergerie** (p201) and buy a combination ticket covering admission to both the old prison and the chapel. With this *billet jumelé* firmly in hand, you skip the painfully long ticket queue at Sainte Chapelle and enter via the line for museum pass holders and combination tickets.

Best Places to Eat

- Berthillon (p202)
- Café St-Régis (p201)
- Le Tastevin (p202)
- Mon Vieil Ami (p202)

For reviews, see p202

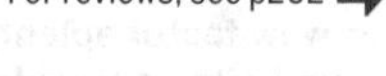

Best Places to Drink

- Café St-Régis (p201)
- Taverne IV (p203)
- La Charlotte de l'Île (p203)

For reviews, see p203

Best Places to Romance

- Hidden corners, stairwells and rooftop of Tours de Notre Dame (p197)
- Pont St-Louis & Louis-Philippe
- Pont Neuf (p201)
- Square du Vert Galant

For reviews, see p201 

OCEAN / CORBIS ©

TOP SIGHTS
CATHÉDRALE DE NOTRE DAME DE PARIS

Notre Dame, the most visited unticketed site in Paris with upwards of 14 million people crossing its threshold a year, is not just a masterpiece of French Gothic architecture but was also the focus of Catholic Paris for seven centuries. Its stained-glass lit interior has wow factor aplenty, but it is the sky-high meander around its gargoyle-guarded rooftop that most visitors swoon over.

Architecture

Built on a site occupied by earlier churches and, a millennium before that, a Gallo-Roman temple, Notre Dame was begun in 1163 and largely completed by the early 14th century. The cathedral was badly damaged during the Revolution, prompting architect Eugène Emmanuel Viollet-le-Duc to oversee extensive renovations between 1845 and 1864. Enter the magnificent forest of ornate **flying buttresses** that encircle the cathedral chancel and support its walls and roof.

Notre Dame is known for its sublime balance, though if you look closely you'll see all sorts of minor asymmetrical elements introduced to avoid monotony, in accordance with standard Gothic practice. These include the slightly different shapes of each of the three main **portals**, whose statues were once brightly coloured to make them more effective as a *Biblia pauperum* – a 'Bible of the poor' to help the illiterate faithful understand Old Testament stories, the Passion of the Christ and the lives of the saints.

Learn more on a **guided tour** (☎01 42 34 56 10; free) in English.

DON'T MISS

- ➡ Flying Buttresses
- ➡ Rose Windows
- ➡ Treasury
- ➡ Towers

PRACTICALITIES

- ➡ Map p412
- ➡ www.cathedraledeparis.com
- ➡ 6 place du Parvis Notre Dame, 4e
- ➡ admission free
- ➡ ⏲7.45am-7pm
- ➡ Ⓜ Cité

Rose Windows

Entering the cathedral, its grand dimensions are immediately evident: the interior alone is 130m long, 48m wide and 35m high and can accommodate more than 6000 worshippers.

The most spectacular interior features are three rose windows. The most renowned is the 10m-wide window over the western façade above the 7800-pipe organ, and the window on the northern side of the transept (virtually unchanged since the 13th century).

Treasury

In the southeastern transept, the **trésor** (Treasury; adult/student/child €4/2/1; ⌚9.30am-6pm Mon-Fri, 9.30am-6.30pm Sat, 1.30-6.30pm Sun) contains artwork, liturgical objects and first-class relics. Among these is the **Ste-Couronne** (Holy Crown), purportedly the wreath of thorns placed on Jesus' head before he was crucified. It is exhibited between 3pm and 4pm on the first Friday of each month, 3pm to 4pm every Friday during Lent, and 10am to 5pm on Good Friday.

The Mays

Walk past the **choir**, with its carved wooden stalls and statues representing the Passion of the Christ, to admire the cathedral's wonderful collection of paintings in its nave side chapels. From 1449 onwards, city goldsmiths offered to the cathedral each year on 1 May a tree strung with devotional ribbons and banners to honour the Virgin Mary to whom Notre Dame (Our Lady) is dedicated. Fifty years later the goldsmiths' annual gift, known as a **May**, had become a tabernacle decorated with scenes from the Old Testament, and, from 1630, a large canvas – 3m tall – commemorating one of the Acts of the Apostles accompanied by a poem or literary explanation. By the early 18th century when the brotherhood of goldsmiths was dissolved, the cathedral had received 76 such monumental paintings – just 13 of which can be admired today.

Towers

A constant queue marks the entrance to the **Tours de Notre Dame** (Notre Dame Towers; rue du Cloître Notre Dame, 4e; adult/18-25yr/under 18yr €8.50/5.50/free; ⌚10am-6.30pm daily Apr-Jun & Sep, 10am-6.30pm Mon-Fri, 10am-11pm Sat & Sun Jul & Aug, 10.30am-5.30pm daily Oct-Mar). Climb the 422 spiralling steps to the top of the western façade of the **north tower** (Map p412) where you'll find yourself face-to-face with the cathedral's most frightening of its fantastic gargoyles, 13-tonne bell **Emmanuel** in the **South**

THE HEART OF PARIS

Notre Dame really is the heart of the city, so much so that distances from Paris to every part of metropolitan France are measured from **place du Parvis Notre Dame**, the square in front of it across which Charlemagne (AD 742–814), emperor of the Franks, rides his **steed** (Map p412). A bronze star across the street from the cathedral's main entrance marks the exact location of **Point Zéro des Routes de France** (Map p412).

Music has been a sacred part of Notre Dame's soul since birth and there's no better day to revel in the cathedral's rousing musical heritage than on Sunday at a Gregorian or polyphonic Mass (10am and 6.30pm respectively) or a free organ recital (4.30pm). October to June, the cathedral stages evening sound-and-image 'operas' (admission free) and a wonderful repertoire of evening concerts; buy tickets (€18) at the welcome desk inside the main entrance reception and find the program online at www.musique-sacree-notredamedeparis.fr.

TIMELINE

1160 Maurice de Sully becomes bishop of Paris. Mission: to grace growing Paris with a lofty new cathedral.

1182–90 The **choir with double ambulatory** 1 is finished and work starts on the nave and side chapels.

1200–50 The **west facade** 2, with rose window, three portals and two soaring towers, goes up. Everyone is stunned.

1345 Some 180 years after the foundation stone was laid, the Cathédrale de Notre Dame is complete. It is dedicated to *notre dame* (our lady), the Virgin Mary.

1789 Revolutionaries smash the original **Gallery of Kings** 3, pillage the cathedral and melt all its bells except the great bell Emmanuel. The cathedral becomes a Temple of Reason then a warehouse.

1831 Victor Hugo's novel *The Hunchback of Notre Dame* inspires new interest in the half-ruined Gothic cathedral.

1845–50 Architect Viollet-le-Duc undertakes its restoration. Twenty-eight new kings are sculpted for the west facade. The heavily decorated **portals** 4 and **spire** 5 are reconstructed. The neo-Gothic **treasury** 6 is built.

1860 The area in front of Notre Dame is cleared to create the *parvis*, an alfresco classroom where Parisians can learn a catechism illustrated on sculpted stone portals.

1935 A rooster bearing part of the relics of the Crown of Thorns, St Denis and St Geneviève is put on top of the cathedral spire to protect those who pray inside.

1991 The architectural masterpiece of Notre Dame and its Seine-side riverbanks become a Unesco World Heritage Site.

2013 Notre Dame celebrates 850 years since construction began with a bevy of new bells and restoration works.

Virgin & Child
Spot all 37 artworks representing the Virgin Mary. Pilgrims have revered the pearly-cream sculpture of her in the sanctuary since the 14th century. Light a devotional candle and write some words to the *Livre de Vie* (Book of Life).

North Rose Window
See prophets, judges, kings and priests venerate Mary in vivid blue and violet glass, one of three beautiful rose blooms (1225–70), each almost 10m in diameter.

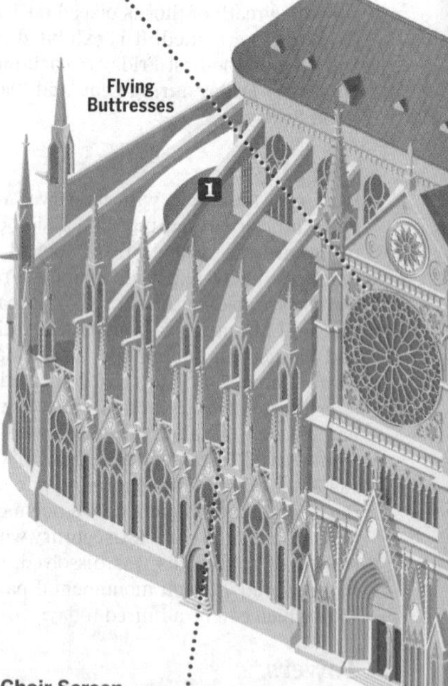

Choir Screen
No part of the cathedral weaves biblical tales more evocatively than these ornate wooden panels, carved in the 14th century after the Black Death killed half the country's population. The faintly gaudy colours were restored in the 1960s.

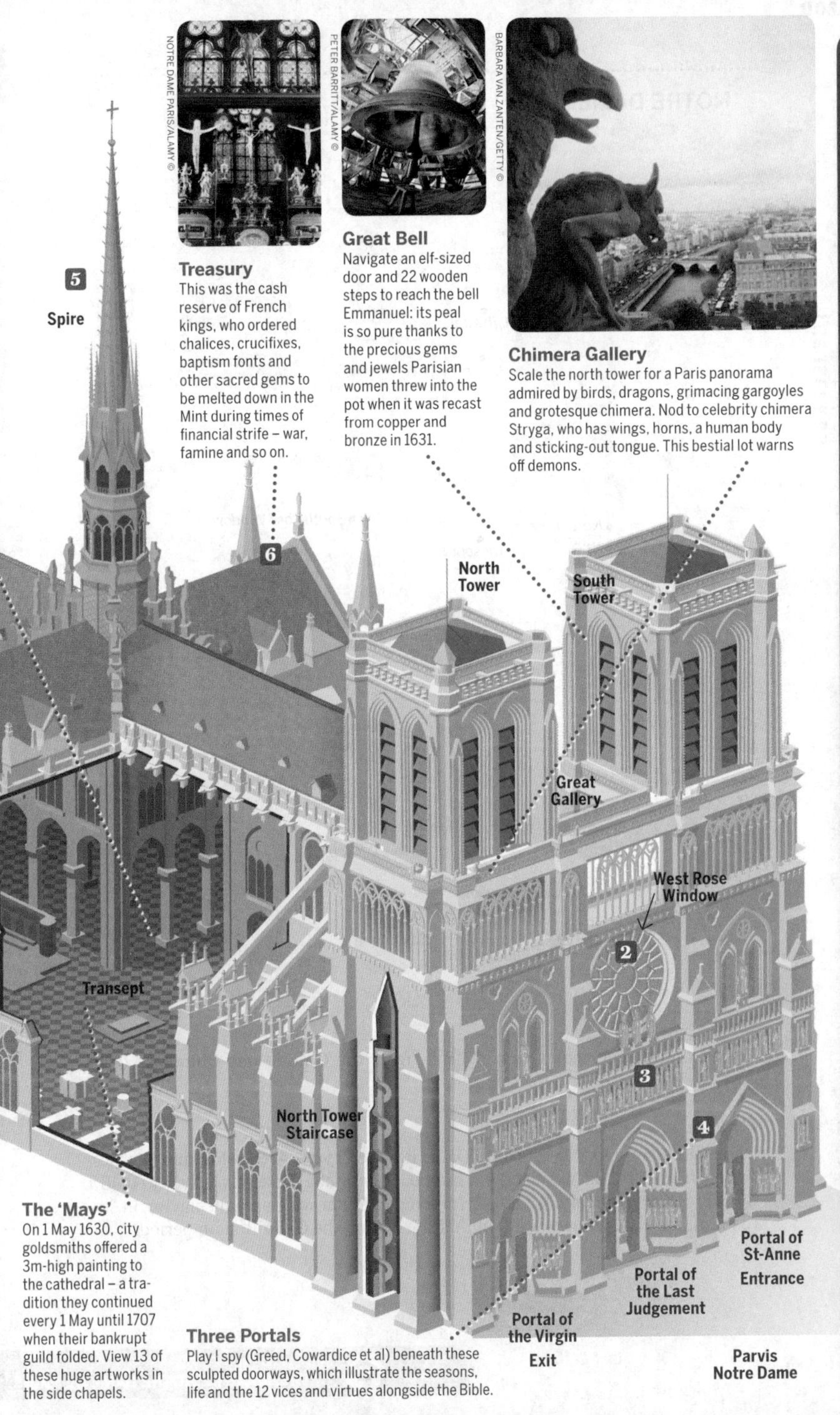

Treasury
This was the cash reserve of French kings, who ordered chalices, crucifixes, baptism fonts and other sacred gems to be melted down in the Mint during times of financial strife – war, famine and so on.

Great Bell
Navigate an elf-sized door and 22 wooden steps to reach the bell Emmanuel: its peal is so pure thanks to the precious gems and jewels Parisian women threw into the pot when it was recast from copper and bronze in 1631.

Chimera Gallery
Scale the north tower for a Paris panorama admired by birds, dragons, grimacing gargoyles and grotesque chimera. Nod to celebrity chimera Stryga, who has wings, horns, a human body and sticking-out tongue. This bestial lot warns off demons.

The 'Mays'
On 1 May 1630, city goldsmiths offered a 3m-high painting to the cathedral – a tradition they continued every 1 May until 1707 when their bankrupt guild folded. View 13 of these huge artworks in the side chapels.

Three Portals
Play I spy (Greed, Cowardice et al) beneath these sculpted doorways, which illustrate the seasons, life and the 12 vices and virtues alongside the Bible.

NOTRE DAME

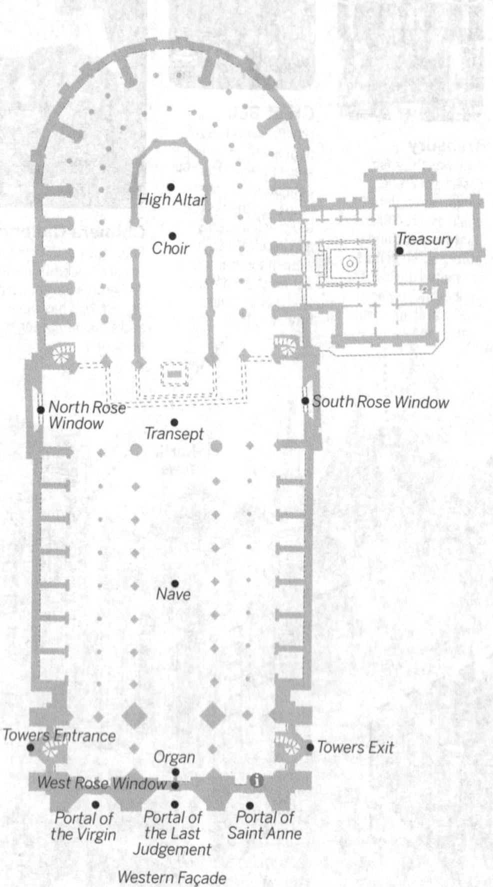

Tower, and a spectacular view of Paris from the **Galerie des Chimères** (Gargoyles Gallery).

Crypt

Under the square in front of Notre Dame lies the **Crypte Archéologique** (Archaeological Crypt; Map p412; www.paris.fr; 1 place du Parvis Notre Dame; adult/student/14-18yr €4/3/2; ⏲10am-6pm daily; Ⓜ Cité) a 117m-long and 28m-wide area displaying in situ the remains of structures built on this site during the Gallo-Roman period.

SIGHTS

Île de la Cité was the site of the first settlement in Paris (c 3rd century BC) and later the centre of Roman Lutetia. The island remained the hub of royal and ecclesiastical power, even after the city spread to both banks of the Seine in the Middle Ages. Smaller Île St-Louis was actually two uninhabited islets called Île Notre Dame (Our Lady Isle) and Île aux Vaches (Cows Island) in the early 17th century – until a building contractor and two financiers worked out a deal with Louis XIII to create one island and build two stone bridges to the mainland.

CATHÉDRALE DE NOTRE DAME DE PARIS — CATHEDRAL

See p196.

CONCIERGERIE — MONUMENT

Map p412 (www.monuments-nationaux.fr; 2 bd du Palais, Île de la Cité, 1er; adult/under 18yr €8.50/free, 1st Sun of month Nov-Mar free; ⌚9.30am-6pm; MCité) The Conciergerie was built as a royal palace in the 14th century, but later lost favour with the kings of France and became a prison and torture chamber. During the Reign of Terror (1793–94) it was used to incarcerate alleged enemies of the Revolution before they were brought before the Revolutionary Tribunal, next door in the Palais de Justice.

Among the almost 2800 prisoners held in the dungeons here (in various 'classes' of cells, no less) before being sent in tumbrils to the guillotine were Queen Marie Antoinette (see a reproduction of her cell) and, as the Revolution began to turn on its own, the radicals Danton, Robespierre and, finally, the judges of the Tribunal themselves. The 14th-century **Salle des Gens d'Armes** (Cavalrymen's Hall), a fine example of Rayonnant Gothic style, is Europe's largest surviving medieval hall in Europe.

A joint ticket with Sainte Chapelle costs €12.50.

PONT NEUF — BRIDGE

Map p412 (MPont Neuf) Paris' oldest bridge has linked the western end of Île de la Cité with both river banks since 1607 when the king inaugurated it by crossing the bridge on a white stallion. The occasion is commemorated by an equestrian **statue of Henri IV** (Map p412), known to his subjects as the Vert Galant ('jolly rogue' or 'dirty old man', perspective depending).

View the bridge's seven arches, decorated with humorous and grotesque figures of barbers, dentists, pickpockets, loiterers etc, from a spot along the river or a boat. Pont Neuf and nearby place Dauphine were used for public exhibitions in the 18th century. In the last century the bridge became an objet d'art in 1963, when School of Paris artist Nonda built, exhibited and lived in a huge Trojan horse of steel and wood on the bridge; in 1984 when Japanese designer Kenzo covered it with flowers; and in 1985 when Bulgarian-born 'environmental sculptor' Christo famously wrapped the bridge in beige fabric.

MÉMORIAL DES MARTYRS DE LA DÉPORTATION — MONUMENT

Map p412 (Square de l'Île de France, 4e; ⌚10am-noon & 2-7pm Apr-Sep, to 5pm Oct-Mar; St-Michel–Notre Dame) The Memorial to the Victims of the Deportation, erected in 1962, remembers the 160,000 residents of France (including 76,000 Jews, of whom 11,000 were children) deported to and murdered in Nazi concentration camps during WWII. A single barred 'window' separates the bleak, rough concrete courtyard from the waters of the Seine. Inside lies the **Tomb of the Unknown Deportee**.

LOCAL KNOWLEDGE

CAFÉ ST-REGIS

Hip and historical with a dose of retro vintage thrown in for good measure, **Le Saint Regis** (Map p412; http://cafesaintregisparis.com; 6 rue du Jean de Bellay, 4e; ⌚daily; wi-fi; MPont Marie) – as those in the know call this cafe – is a deliciously Parisian hang-out any time of day. From boiled eggs with *bio* bread for breakfast to a midmorning pancake, brasserie lunch or early-evening oyster platter, Café St-Regis hits the spot. Its pick-and-mix breakfast menu (€6 to €12) features eggs cooked in every conceivable manner; crepes (€6.50 to €9.50) are an all-day mainstay, and its weekend brunch (€18 or €23) jostles with happy hour (7pm to 9pm daily) for best crowd-packed moment. Free wi-fi, magazines and newspapers to read, and a lovely white ceramic-tiled interior complete the appealing ensemble.

EATING

Île St-Louis is a nice if pricey place to eat, but forget Île de la Cité – recommended eating spots are almost nonexistent.

TOP CHOICE BERTHILLON — ICE CREAM €

Map p412 (31 rue St-Louis en l'Île, 4e; ⏲10am-8pm Wed-Sun; Ⓜ Pont Marie) Berthillon is to ice cream what Château Lafite Rothschild is to wine and Valhrona is to chocolate. And with nigh on 70 flavours to choose from, you'll be spoiled for choice.

While the fruit-flavoured sorbets (cassis, blackberry etc) produced by this celebrated *glacier* (ice-cream maker) are renowned, the chocolate, coffee, *marrons glacés* (candied chestnuts), Agenaise (Armagnac and prunes), *noisette* (hazelnut) and *nougat au miel* (honey nougat) are richer. Eat in or grab a cone with one/two/three/four small scoops (€2.30/3.60/4.90/6.20) to takeaway.

LE TASTEVIN — TRADITIONAL FRENCH €€€

Map p412 (☎01 43 54 17 31; www.letastevin-paris.com; 46 rue St-Louis en l'Île, 4e; starters €16-24.50, mains €23-31, menus €28-67; ⏲lunch Wed-Sun, dinner to 11pm Tue-Sun; Ⓜ Pont Marie) With its old-fashioned lace curtains, wood panelling and beamed ceiling, this lovely old-style address in a 17th-century building smacks of charm. Its excellent cuisine is equally traditional: think *escargots* (snails), foie gras, sole, or *ris de veau* (calf sweetbreads) with morels and tagliatelli.

MON VIEIL AMI — TRADITIONAL FRENCH €€€

Map p412 (☎01 40 46 01 35; www.mon-vieil-ami.com; 69 rue St-Louis en l'Île, 4e; plat du jour €13, menu €41; ⏲lunch & dinner Wed-Sun; Ⓜ Pont Marie) Alsatian chef Antoine Westermann is the creative talent behind this sleek black neobistro where guests are treated like old friends (hence the name) and vegetables get royal treatment. The lunchtime *plat du jour* (dish of the day) is especially good value and a perfect reflection of the season.

For dinner try artichokes and potatoes cooked with lemon confit and pan-fried skate-fish. Unusually for Paris, Mon Veil Ami opens for dinner at 6.30pm – handy for those seeking an early dine.

LES FOUS DE L'ÎLE — BRASSERIE €€

Map p412 (www.lesfousdelile.com; 33 rue des Deux Ponts, 4e; lunch 2-/3-course menu €18/24, dinner €22/27; ⏲10am-2am; Ⓜ Pont Marie) This

TOP SIGHTS SAINTE CHAPELLE

Try to save Sainte Chapelle for a sunny day when Paris' oldest, finest stained glass is at its dazzling best. Enshrined within the **Palais de Justice** (Law Courts), this Holy Chapel is Paris' most exquisite Gothic monument. Peek at its exterior from across the street, by the law courts' gilded 18th-century gate facing rue de Lutèce.

Sainte Chapelle was built in just six years (compared with nearly 200 years for Notre Dame) and was consecrated in 1248. The chapel was conceived by Louis IX to house his personal collection of holy relics, including the famous Holy Crown (now in Notre Dame) – acquired by the French king in 1239 from the emperors of Constantinople for an amount easily exceeding the amount it cost to build the chapel!

The bijou chapel is decorated with statues, foliage-decorated capitals, angels and so on. But it is the 1113 scenes depicted in its 15 floor-to-ceiling stained-glass windows – 15.5m high in the nave, 13.5m in the apse – that stun. From the bookshop in the former ground-floor chapel reserved for palace staff, head up the staircase to the upper chapel where only the king and his close friends were allowed. Grab a storyboard in English to 'read' the 15-window biblical story.

DON'T MISS

- Stained Glass

PRACTICALITIES

- Map p412
- 4 bd du Palais, 1er
- adult/under 18yr €8.50/free
- ⏲9.30am-5pm Nov-Feb, to 6pm Mar-Oct
- Ⓜ Cité

typical brasserie is a somewhat genteel address with a lovely open kitchen and unusual cockerel theme (we don't know either) throughout. Hearty fare like 'real' (its claim, not ours) *cassoulet* (traditional Languedoc stew with beans and meat) and lighter Spanish-inspired tapas dishes are served continuously from noon to 11pm.

DRINKING & NIGHTLIFE

Drinking venues on the islands are scarce. They do exist but use them as a starting point as very few places stay open after the bewitching hour of midnight.

TAVERNE HENRI IV WINE BAR

Map p412 (13 place du Pont Neuf, 1er; ⌚Mon-Fri; ⓂPont Neuf) One of the very few places to drink on Île de la Cité, this is a serious wine bar dating back to 1885. A tasty choice of inexpensive *tartines* (open sandwiches), *charcuterie* (cold cooked meats) and cheese platters complement its extensive wine list, making it a lovely riverside place to drink.s.

Predictably, it lures a fair few legal types from the nearby Palais de Justice.

LA CHARLOTTE DE L'ISLE TEA ROOM

Map p412 (www.lacharlottedelisle.fr; 24 rue St-Louis en l'Île, 4e; ⌚11am-7pm Wed-Sun; ⓂPont Marie) This tiny place is a particularly lovely *salon de thé* (tearoom) with a quaint fairytale theme, old-fashioned glass sweet jars on the shelf and a fine collection of tea to taste in situ or buy to sip at home. Hot chocolate, chocolate sculptures, cakes and pastries are other sweet reasons to come here.

LE FLORE EN L'ÎLE CAFE

Map p412 (www.lefloreenlile.com; 42 quai d'Orléans, 4e; ⌚8am-1am; ⓂPont Marie) A tourist crowd piles into this excellent people-watching spot with prime views of the buskers on Pont St-Louis.

SHOPPING

Île de St-Louis is a shopper's delight for crafty boutiques and tiny charm-rich specialist stores, Île de la Cité for souvenirs and tourist kitsch.

MARCHÉ AUX FLEURS MARKET

Map p412 (place Louis Lépin, 4e; ⌚8am-7.30pm Mon-Sat; ⓂCité) Blooms have been sold at this flower market since 1808, making it the oldest market of any kind in Paris. On Sunday, between 9am and 7pm, it transforms into a twittering bird market, **Marché aux Oiseaux** (Map p412; ⌚9am-7pm).

IL CAMPIELLO CRAFTS

Map p412 (www.ilcampiello.com; 88 rue St-Louis en l'Île, 4e; ⌚11am-7pm; ⓂPont Marie) Venetian carnival masks – intricately crafted from papier mâché, ceramics and leather – are the speciality of this exquisite shop, which also sells jewellery made from Murano glass beads. It was established by a native of Venice, to which the Île St-Louis bears more than a passing resemblance.

LA PETITE SCIERIE FOOD

Map p412 (www.lapetitescierie.fr; 60 rue St-Louis en l'Île, 4e; ⌚11am-7pm Thu-Mon; ⓂPont Marie) The Little Sawmill sells every permutation of duck edibles with the emphasis on foie gras.

LIBRAIRIE ULYSSE BOOKS

Map p412 (www.ulysse.fr; 26 rue St-Louis en l'Île, 4e; ⌚2-8pm Tue-Fri; ⓂPont Marie) You can barely move in between this shop's antiquarian and new travel guides, *National Geographic* back editions and maps. Opened in 1971 by the intrepid Catherine Domaine, this was the world's first travel bookshop. Hours vary, but ring the bell and Catherine will open up if she's around.

CLAIR DE RÊVE TOYS

Map p412 (www.clairdereve.com; 35 rue St-Louis en l'Île, 4e; ⓂPont Marie) This shop is all about wind-up toys, music boxes and puppets – mostly marionettes, which sway and bob suspended from the ceiling.

PREMIÈRE PRESSION PROVENCE OLIVE OIL

Map p412 (51 rue St-Louis en l'Île, 4e; 👪; ⓂPont Marie) Its name evokes the first pressing of olives to make olive oil in the south of France and that is precisely what this gourmet boutique sells – be it as oil or in any number of spreads and sauces (pesto, tapenade etc). The gigantic mill stone in the window makes the small shopfront impossible to miss.

Latin Quarter

Neighbourhood Top Five

❶ Allow as much time to savour the exterior as the newly renovated museum inside the **Institute of the Arab World** (p210), a visionary example of 1980s architecture (and don't miss the view from the roof!).

❷ Time travel back to the Middle Ages at the **Musée National du Moyen Âge** (p206).

❸ Pay homage to France's greatest thinkers buried beneath the neoclassical **Panthéon** (p208).

❹ Curl up with a volume of poetry in the magical bookshop **Shakepeare & Company** (p216).

❺ Stroll around Paris' sprawling botanical gardens, the **Jardin des Plantes** (p207).

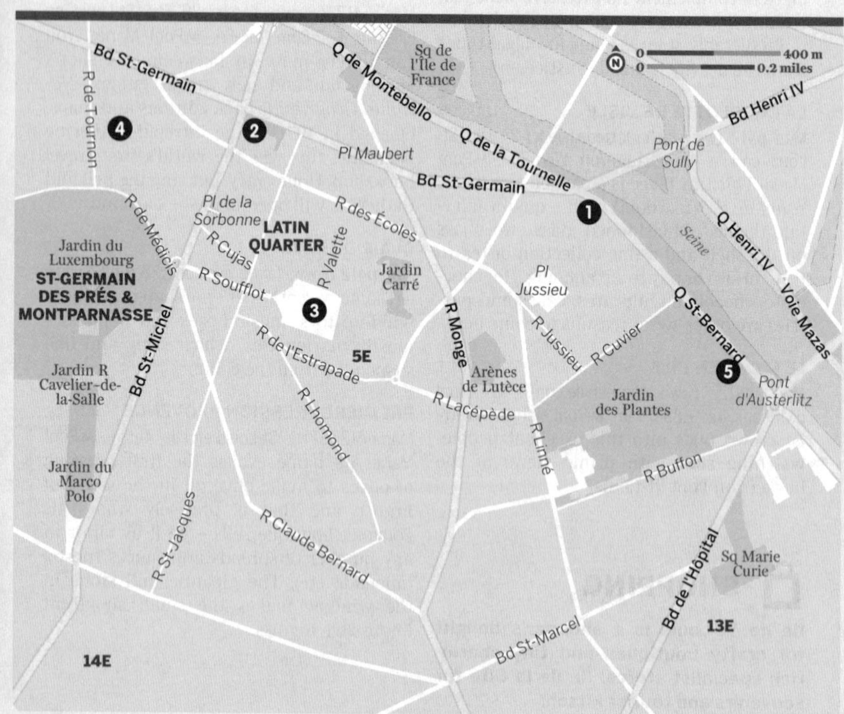

For more detail of this area, see Map p414 and p416 ➡

Explore Latin Quarter

Paris' botanical gardens, the Jardin des Plantes, are a serene spot to start the day, before checking out the Institut du Monde Arabe and sipping a sweet mint tea in the courtyard of the Mosquée de Paris.

There's no better strip to see, smell and taste the *Quartier Latin* (Latin Quarter) than the thriving market street rue Mouffetard, so it's worth coinciding a flit from food stall to fabulous food shop here with lunch at one of the many restaurants utilising its produce (but skip it on Mondays when the market stalls are shut).

Descend to the Panthéon's crypt to visit France's great thinkers, then spend the afternoon in the Musée National du Moyen Âge for the ultimate history lesson.

Excellent bistros are constantly popping up in this neighbourhood. Medieval cellars (many used as Revolutionary prisons) provide an atmospheric setting for live jazz and jam sessions, or join the area's students at the *quartier's* lively pubs.

Local Life

➡ **Sporting Life** Join the locals playing *boules* and *pétanque* (a variant on the game of bowls) in the 2nd-century Roman amphitheatre Arènes de Lutèce (p208).

➡ **Student Life** Clink drinks during extended Latin Quarter happy hours (p214) and there will almost certainly be a student or academic affiliated with the Sorbonne sitting next to you.

➡ **Cinematic Life** Catch an all-night movie marathon followed by breakfast at the art deco Le Champo (p216).

Getting There & Away

➡ **Metro** The most central stations to jump off at are St-Michel by the Seine; Cluny–La Sorbonne or Maubert-Mutualité on bd St-Germain; and Censier Daubenton or Gare d'Austerlitz by the Jardin des Plantes.

➡ **Bus** Convenient bus stops include the Panthéon for the 89 to Jardin des Plantes and 13e (Bibliothèque National de France François Mitterrand); bd St-Michel for the 38 to Centre Pompidou, Gare de l'Est & Gare du Nord; and rue Gay Lussac for the 27 to Île de la Cité, Opéra & Gare St-Lazare.

➡ **Bicycle** Handy Vélib' stations include 42 rue St-Severin, 5e, just off bd St-Michel; 40 rue Boulangers, 5e, near Cardinal Lemoine metro station; and 27 rue Lacépède, 5e, near Place Monge.

➡ **Boat** The hop-on, hop-off Batobus docks opposite Notre Dame on quai de Montebello, and at the Jardin des Plantes on quai St-Bernard.

Lonely Planet's Top Tip

First-time visitors often think the maze of tiny streets between the Seine and bd St-Germain in the 5e comprise the Latin Quarter. And while it's worth a look – find Paris' narrowest street, the 1.8m-wide rue du Chat qui Pêche ('street of the fishing cat') – this neighbourhood, named for the international language spoken here by students until the French Revolution, has so much more: there are great pubs, cafes, wine bars and squares throughout the *arrondissement*.

Best Places to Eat

➡ L'AOC (p209)

➡ L'Agrume (p210)

➡ La Tour d'Argent (p210)

➡ Le Coupe-Chou (p210)

➡ Bistrot Les Papilles (p211)

➡ Boulangerie Bruno Solques (p211)

For reviews, see p209

Best Places to Drink

➡ Café de la Nouvelle Mairie (p214)

➡ Le Verre à Pied (p214)

➡ Le Pub St-Hilaire (p214)

For reviews, see p214

Best Jazz Clubs

➡ Café Universel (p215)

➡ Le Caveau des Oubliettes (p216)

➡ Le Petit Journal St-Michel (p216)

For reviews, see p215

TOP SIGHTS

MUSÉE NATIONAL DU MOYEN ÂGE

CRAIG PERSHOUSE / GETTY IMAGES ©

Medieval history comes to life at France's Musée National du Moyen Âge. This National Museum of the Middle Ages is often referred to as the Musée de Cluny (or just Cluny), due to the fact that it's partly – and atmospherically – housed in the 15th-century Hôtel de Cluny, Paris' finest civil medieval building. Spectacular displays include illuminated manuscripts, weapons, suits of armour, furnishings and objets d'art made of gold, ivory and enamel.

Long before construction began on the Hôtel de Cluny, the **Gallo-Romans** built *thermes* (baths) here around AD 200. The Musée National du Moyen Âge now occupies not only the Hôtel de Cluny but the *frigidarium* (cooling room), which holds remains of the **baths**. Look for the display of the fragment of mosaic, *Love Riding a Dolphin*.

Initially the residential quarters of the Cluny Abbots, the **Hôtel de Cluny** was later occupied by Alexandre du Sommerard, who moved here in 1833 with his collection of medieval and Renaissance objects. Bought by the state after his death, the museum opened a decade later, retaining the Hôtel de Cluny's original layout and features.

The museum's circular Room 13 on the 1st floor displays *La Dame à la Licorne* (The Lady with the Unicorn), a sublime series of late-15th-century **tapestries** from the southern Netherlands. Five are devoted to the senses; the sixth is the enigmatic *À Mon Seul Désir* (To My Sole Desire), a reflection on vanity.

Small **gardens** to the museum's northeast, including the Jardin Céleste (Heavenly Garden) and the Jardin d'Amour (Garden of Love), are planted with flowers, herbs and shrubs that appear in masterpieces hanging throughout the museum. To the west, the **Forêt de la Licorne** (Map p414, Unicorn Forest) is based on the illustrations in the tapestries.

DON'T MISS

- The Gallo-Roman Baths
- The Hôtel de Cluny
- The Tapestries
- The Gardens

PRACTICALITIES

- Map p414
- www.musee-moyenage.fr
- 6 place Paul Painlevé
- adult/18-25yr/under 18yr €8.50/6.50/free
- 9.15am-5.45pm Wed-Mon
- M Cluny–La Sorbonne

SIGHTS

JARDIN DES PLANTES BOTANIC GARDEN

Map p416 (www.jardindesplantes.net; 57 rue Cuvier, 5e; admission free to adult/child €6/4, depending on section; ⏲most sections 7.30am-7.45pm Apr-Oct, 8.30am-5.30pm Oct-Mar; MGare d'Austerlitz, Censier Daubenton or Jussieu) Founded in 1626 as a medicinal herb garden for Louis XIII, Paris' 24-hectare botanical gardens are a serious institute rather than a leisure destination, but fascinating all the same, and idyllic to stroll or jog around.

Sections include a winter garden, tropical greenhouses and an alpine garden with 2000 mountainous plants, as well as the gardens of the École de Botanique, used by students of the School of Botany and green-fingered Parisians studying up on horticultural techniques. It also encompasses a zoo, the Ménagerie du Jardin des Plantes, and the Musée National d'Histoire Naturelle, three separate centres comprising France's natural-history museum. A two-day pass covering access to all areas of the Jardin des Plantes costs €25/20 per adult/child.

MÉNAGERIE DU JARDIN DES PLANTES ZOO

Map p416 (www.mnhn.fr; 57 rue Cuvier & 3 quai St-Bernard, 5e; adult/child €9/7; ⏲9am-5pm; MGare d'Austerlitz, Censier Daubenton or Jussieu) Like the Jardin des Plantes in which it's located, this 1000-animal zoo is more than a tourist attraction, also doubling as a research centre for the reproduction of rare and endangered species. During the Prussian siege of 1870, the animals of the day were themselves endangered, when almost all were eaten by starving Parisians. No vegetarians back then!

MUSÉE NATIONAL D'HISTOIRE NATURELLE HISTORY MUSEUM

Map p416 (www.mnhn.fr; 57 rue Cuvier, 5e; Galerie d'Anatomie Comparée et de Paléontologie adult/child €7/5, Grande Galerie de l'Évolution adult/child €7/5; ⏲Galerie d'Anatomie Comparée et de Paléontologie 10am-5pm Wed-Mon, Grande Galerie de l'Évolution 10am-6pm Wed-Mon; MCensier Daubenton or Gare d'Austerlitz) France's National Museum of Natural History within the Jardin des Plantes incorporates the **Galerie de Minéralogie et de Géologie** (Mineralogy & Geology Gallery; Map p416; 36 rue Geoffroy St-Hilaire; adult/child €8/6; ⏲10am-6pm Wed-Mon) (closed for renovation at the time of writing); the **Galerie d'Anatomie Comparée et de Paléontologie** (Map p416; 2 rue Buffon; adult/child €7/free; ⏲10am-5pm or 6pm Wed-Mon), covering anatomy and fossils; and the topical **Grande Galerie de l'Évolution** (Great Gallery of Evolution; Map p416; 36 rue Geoffroy St-Hilaire; adult/child €7/free; ⏲10am-6pm Wed-Mon), highlighting humanity's effect on the planet's ecosystems.

The National Museum of Natural History was created in 1793 and became a site of significant scientific research in the 19th century. Of its three museums, the Grande Galerie de l'Évolution is a particular winner if you're travelling with kids: life-sized elephants, tigers and rhinos play safari and imaginative exhibits on evolution and global warming fill 6000 sq metres. Rare specimens of endangered and extinct species dominate the Salle des Espèces Menacées et des Espèces Disparues (Hall of Threatened and Extinct Species) on level 2, while down on level 1 the Salle de Découverte (Room of Discovery) houses interactive exhibits for children.

FREE **MUSÉE DE LA SCULPTURE EN PLEIN AIR** SCULPTURE MUSEUM

Map p414 (quai St-Bernard, 5e; admission free; ⏲24hr; MGare d'Austerlitz) Along quai St-Bernard, this open-air sculpture museum (also known as the Jardin Tino Rossi) has over 50 late-20th-century unfenced sculptures, and makes a great picnic spot. A salad beneath a César or a baguette with creamy brie beside a Brancusi is a pretty classy way to see the Seine up close, short of actually getting on it by joining a cruise.

LOVE LOCKS

Stretching from the Latin Quarter's quai de la Tournelle, 5e, to the southern tip of the Île de la Cité, the **Pont de l'Archevêché** footbridge is one of many Parisian bridges covered in padlocks (to the chagrin of city authorities, whose attempts to eradicate them have proved temporary at best). Inscribed with initials and sometimes adorned with ribbons, the locks are attached by couples who then throw the key into the Seine as a symbol of eternal love. Pont de l'Archevêché has so many that it's often dubbed 'the love bridge'.

TOP SIGHTS PANTHÉON

The Panthéon is a superb example of 18th-century **neoclassicism**. The domed landmark was commissioned by Louis XV around 1750 as an abbey but due to financial and structural problems it wasn't completed until 1789 – not a good year for church openings in Paris. Two years later the Constituent Assembly turned it into a secular mausoleum.

Louis XV originally dedicated the church to Ste Geneviève in thanksgiving for his recovery from an illness. It reverted to its religious duties twice more after the Revolution but has played a secular role ever since 1885, and now is the resting place of some of France's greatest thinkers.

Beneath the dome is **Foucault's pendulum**, which he used to demonstrate the earth's rotation on its axis.

Narrow stairs lead from behind the pendulum down to the labyrinthine **crypt**. Among its 80 or so permanent residents are Voltaire, Jean-Jacques Rousseau, Louis Braille, Émile Zola and Jean Moulin. The first woman to be interred in the Panthéon was the two-time Nobel Prize–winner Marie Curie (1867–1934), reburied here (along with her husband, Pierre) in 1995.

DON'T MISS

- The Architecture
- Foucault's Pendulum
- The Crypt

PRACTICALITIES

- Map p416
- www.monum.fr
- place du Panthéon
- adult/under 18yr €8.50/free
- ⌚10am-6.30pm Apr-Sep, to 6pm Oct-Mar
- Ⓜ Maubert-Mutualité, Cardinal Lemoine or RER Luxembourg

MOSQUÉE DE PARIS — MOSQUE

Map p416 (☎01 45 35 97 33; www.la-mosquee.com; 2bis place du Puits de l'Ermite, 5e; adult/child €3/2; ⌚mosque 9am-noon & 2-6pm Sat-Thu, souk 11am-7pm daily; ⓂCensier Daubenton or Place Monge) Paris' central mosque with its striking 26m-high minaret was built in 1926 in an ornate art deco Moorish style. The complex includes a wonderful North African–style *salon de thé* (tearoom) and restaurant and a *hammam* (traditional Turkish-style bathhouse), as well as a vibrant Moroccan-style *souk* (market). Visitors must be modestly dressed.

SORBONNE — UNIVERSITY

Map p414 (12 rue de la Sorbonne, 5e; ⓂCluny–La Sorbonne or RER Luxembourg) The crème de la crème of academia flock to this distinguished university, one of the world's most famous. Founded in 1253 by Robert de Sorbon, confessor to Louis IX, as a college for 16 impoverished theology students, the Sorbonne soon grew into a powerful body with its own government and laws.

Today, 'La Sorbonne' embraces most of the 13 autonomous universities – 35,500-odd students in all – created when the University of Paris was reorganised after the student protests of 1968. Until 2015, when an ambitious, 10-year modernisation program costing €45 million reaches completion, parts of the complex will be under renovation.

Place de la Sorbonne links bd St-Michel and the **Chapelle de la Sorbonne** (Map p414), the university's distinctive domed church, built between 1635 and 1642. The remains of Cardinal Richelieu (1585–1642) lie in a tomb with an effigy of a cardinal's hat suspended above.

MUSÉE NATIONAL DU MOYEN ÂGE — HISTORY MUSEUM

See p206.

FREE ARÈNES DE LUTÈCE — ROMAN RUINS

Map p416 (www.arenesdelutece.com; 49 rue Monge, 5e; ⌚9am-9.30pm Apr-Oct, 8am-5.30pm Nov-Mar; ⓂPlace Monge) The 2nd-century Roman amphitheatre Lutetia Arena once sat 10,000 people for gladiatorial combats and other events. Found by accident in 1869 when rue Monge was under construction, it's now used by locals playing football and, especially, boules and *pétanque* (p218).

ÉGLISE ST ÉTIENNE DU MONT CHURCH

Map p416 (www.saintetiennedumont.fr; 1 place Ste-Geneviève, 5e; ⊙8am-noon & 2-7pm Tue-Sat, 9am-noon & 2.30-7pm Sun; Ⓜ Cardinal Lemoine) This is one for the history buffs. The Church of Mount St Stephen, built between 1492 and 1655, contains Paris' only surviving rood screen (1535), separating the chancel from the nave; the other rood screens were removed during the late Renaissance because they prevented the faithful in the nave from seeing the priest celebrate Mass. In the nave's southeastern corner, the tomb of Ste Geneviève lies in a chapel.

Ste Geneviève, patroness of Paris, was born at Nanterre in AD 422 and turned away Attila the Hun from Paris in AD 451. A highly decorated reliquary near her tomb contains all that is left of her earthly remains – a finger bone.

MUSÉE DE L'ASSISTANCE PUBLIQUE-HÔPITAUX DE PARIS HOSPITAL MUSEUM

(www.aphp.fr/musee; 47 quai de la Tournelle, 5e; adult/13-18yr €4/2; ⊙10am-6pm Tue-Sun Sep-Jul; Ⓜ Maubert-Mutualité) A museum devoted to the history of Parisian hospitals since the Middle Ages may not sound like a crowd-pleaser, but some of the paintings, sculptures, drawings and medical instruments are very evocative of their times. You'll be appreciative of medicinal improvements.

EATING

From chandelier-lit palaces loaded with history to cheap-eat student haunts, the 5e *arrondissement* has something to suit every budget and culinary taste. Rue Mouffetard is famed for its food market and food shops, while its side streets, especially pedestrian rue du Pot au Fer, cook up some fine budget dining. The maze of narrow streets between rue St-Jacques, bd St-Germain and bd St-Michel tend to be overly touristy.

TOP CHOICE **L'AOC** REGIONAL CUISINE **€€**

Map p414 (☎01 43 54 22 52; www.restoaoc.com; 14 rue des Fossés St-Bernard, 5e; 2-/3-course lunch menus €21/29, mains €18-32; ⊙lunch & dinner Tue-Sat; Ⓜ Cardinal Lemoine) *'Bistrot carnivore'* is the strapline of this ingenious restaurant concocted around France's most respected culinary products. The concept here is Appellation d'Origine Contrôlée (AOC), meaning everything has been reared or made according to strict guidelines designed to protect a product unique to a particular village, town or area. The result? Only the best!

Rare is the chance to taste *porc noir de Bigorre,* a type of black pig bred in the Pyrénées.

LATIN QUARTER LITERARY ADDRESSES

Like its Left Bank neighbours, the Latin Quarter is steeped in literary history.

James Joyce's flat (Map p416; Ⓜ Cardinal Lemoine) Peer down the passageway at 71 rue du Cardinal Lemoine, 5e: Irish writer James Joyce (1882–1941) lived in the courtyard flat at the back marked 'E' when he arrived in Paris in 1921; he finished editing *Ulysses* here.

Ernest Hemingway's apartment (Map p416; Ⓜ Cardinal Lemoine) At 74 rue du Cardinal Lemoine, 5e, is the apartment where Ernest Hemingway (1899–1961) lived with his first wife Hadley from January 1922 until August 1923. Just below was Bal au Printemps, a popular *bal musette* (dancing club) that served as the model for the one where Jake Barnes meets Brett Ashley in Hemingway's *The Sun Also Rises*.

Paul Verlaine's garret (Map p416; Ⓜ Cardinal Lemoine) Hemingway lived on rue du Cardinal Lemoine but wrote in a top-floor garret of a hotel round the corner at 39 rue Descartes, 5e, the very hotel where the poet Paul Verlaine (1844–96) died. Ignore the incorrect plaque.

Place de la Contrescarpe Rue Descartes runs south into place de la Contrescarpe, 5e (Ⓜ Place Monge), now a well-scrubbed square with four Judas trees and a fountain, but once a 'cesspool' (said Hemingway), especially Café des Amateurs at 2-4 place de la Contrescarpe, now Café Delmas (p214).

George Orwell's boarding house (Map p416; Ⓜ Place Monge) In 1928 George Orwell (1903–50) stayed in a cheap boarding house above 6 rue du Pot de Fer, 5e, while working as a dishwasher. Read about it and the street, which he called 'rue du Coq d'Or' (Street of the Golden Rooster), in *Down and Out in Paris and London* (1933).

TOP SIGHTS
INSTITUTE OF THE ARAB WORLD

The Institute of the Arab World, set up by France and 20 Arab countries to promote cultural contacts between the Arab world and the West, is housed in a building designed by Jean Nouvel, and opened in 1987. Its new-look museum, showcasing Arab art, artisanship and science, was unveiled in 2012.

Inspired by traditional latticed-wood windows, the **building** blends modern and traditional Arab and Western elements, with thousands of *mushrabiyah* (or *mouche-arabies*, photo-electrically sensitive apertures built into the glass walls that allow you to see out without being seen).

The overhauled **museum** paints a global vision of the Arab world through 9th- to 19th-century art and artisanship, instruments from astronomy and other fields of scientific endeavour in which Arab technology once led the world, as well as contemporary Arab art.

From the top (9th) floor **observation terrace**, incredible views stretch across the Seine as far as Basilica du Sacré-Cœur. In addition to a panoramic restaurant here, the building also contains a cafe and a cafeteria, as well as a cinema and library.

DON'T MISS

- The Architecture
- The Museum
- The Observation Terrace

PRACTICALITIES

- Institut du Monde Arabe
- Map p414
- www.imarabe.org
- 1 place Mohammed V
- adult/under 26yr €8/free
- 10am-6pm Tue-Fri, to 7pm Sat & Sun
- M Jussieu

L'AGRUME NEOBISTRO €€

Map p416 (01 43 31 86 48; 15 rue des Fossés St-Marcel, 5e; 2-/3-course lunch menus €19/24, mains €26-39; lunch & dinner Tue-Sat; M Censier Daubenton) Snagging a table at L'Agrume – meaning 'Citrus Fruit' – is tough; reserve several days ahead. The reward is watching chefs work with seasonal products in the open kitchen while you dine – at a table, bar stool or *comptoir* (counter) – at this pocket-sized contemporary bistro on a little-known street on the Latin Quarter's southern fringe.

Lunching is magnificent value and a real gourmet experience. Evening dining is an exquisite, no-choice *dégustation* (tasting) melody of five courses, different every day.

LA TOUR D'ARGENT GASTRONOMIC €€€

Map p414 (01 43 54 23 31; www.latourdargent.com; 15 quai de la Tournelle, 5e; lunch menu €65, dinner menus €170-190; lunch & dinner Tue-Sat; M Cardinal Lemoine or Pont Marie) The venerable 'Silver Tower' is famous for its *caneton* (duckling), rooftop garden with glimmering Notre Dame views and a fabulous history harking back to 1582 – from Henry III's inauguration of the first fork in France to inspiration for the winsome animated film *Ratatouille*. Its wine cellar is one of Paris' best; dining is dressy and exceedingly fine.

Reserve eight to 10 days ahead for lunch, three weeks ahead for dinner – and don't miss its chocolate and coconut sphere with banana and lime sorbet for dessert. Buy fine food and accessories in its **boutique** (Map p414) directly across the street.

LE COUPE-CHOU TRADITIONAL FRENCH €€

Map p414 (01 46 33 68 69; www.lecoupechou.com; 9 & 11 rue de Lanneau, 5e; 2-/3-course lunch menus €26.50/32, mains €17.50-25; Mon-Sat; M Maubert-Mutualité) This maze of candle-lit rooms inside a vine-clad 17th-century townhouse is overwhelmingly romantic. Ceilings are beamed, furnishings are antique, and background classical music mingles with the intimate chatter of diners. As in the days when Marlene Dietrich et al dined here, advance reservations are essential.

Timeless French dishes include Burgundy snails, steak tartare and bœuf bourguignon, finished off with fabulous cheeses sourced from *fromagerie* (cheese shop) Quatrehomme and a silken crème brûlée.

Le Coupe-Chou, incidentally, has nothing to do with cabbage *(chou);* rather it's named after the barber's razor once wielded with a deft hand in one of its seven rooms.

BISTROT LES PAPILLES — BISTRO €€

Map p416 (01 43 25 20 79; www.lespapillesparis.com; 30 rue Gay Lussac, 5e; lunch/dinner menus €22/31; 10.30am-midnight Mon-Sat; M Raspail or RER Luxembourg) This hybrid bistro, wine cellar and *épicerie* (specialist grocer) with a sunflower-yellow façade offers a fabulous dining experience: the place is always packed. Dining is at simply dressed tables wedged beneath bottle-lined walls, and fare is market-driven: each weekday cooks up a different *marmite du marché* (market casserole). But what really sets it apart is its exceptional wine list.

It only seats around 15 people; reserve a few days in advance to guarantee a table. After your meal, stock your own *cave* (wine cellar) at Les Papilles' *cave à vin*.

BOULANGERIE BRUNO SOLQUES — BOULANGERIE, PATISSERIE €

Map p416 (243 rue St-Jacques, 5e; 6.30am-8pm Mon-Fri; ; M Place Monge or RER Luxembourg) Inventive *pâtissier* Bruno Solques crafts oddly shaped flat tarts with mashed fruit, fruit-filled brioches and subtly spiced gingerbread. This small, bare-boards shop is also filled with wonderfully rustic breads. It's on the pricey side, but worth it – kids from the school across the way can't get enough.

LES PIPOS — WINE BAR €€

Map p414 (01 43 54 11 40; www.les-pipos.com; 2 rue de l'École Polytechnique, 5e; mains €13.50-25; 8am-2am Mon-Sat; M Maubert-Mutualité) A feast for the eyes and the senses, this *bar à vins* is above all worth a visit for its food. Its *charcuteries de terroir* (regional cold meats and sausages) is mouth-watering, as is its cheese board, which includes all the gourmet names (bleu d'Auvergne, St-Félicien, St-Marcellin etc). No credit cards.

CHEZ NICOS — CRÊPERIE €

Map p416 (44 rue Mouffetard, 5e; crêpes €3.50-6; 10am-2am; ; M Place Monge) The signboard outside crêpe artist Nicos' unassuming little shop chalks up dozens of fillings but ask by name for his masterpiece, 'La Crêpe du Chef', stuffed with aubergines, feta, mozzarella, lettuce, tomatoes and onions. There's a handful of tables inside; otherwise get it wrapped up in foil and head to a nearby park.

LE PETIT PONTOISE — BISTRO €€

Map p414 (01 43 29 25 20; 9 rue de Pontoise, 5e; mains €19.50-28; lunch & dinner daily; M Maubert-Mutualité) Sit down at a wooden table behind the lace curtains hiding you from the world and indulge in fantastic old-fashioned classics like *rognons de veau à l'ancienne* (calf kidneys), *boudin campagnard* (black pudding) and sweet apple purée or roast quail with dates. Dishes – like the decor – might seem simple, but you'll leave pledging to return.

LA MOSQUÉE DE PARIS — NORTH AFRICAN €€

Map p416 (01 43 31 38 20; www.la-mosquee.com; 39 rue Geoffroy St-Hilaire, 5e; mains €12-21; restaurant lunch & dinner daily, tearoom 9am-11.30pm daily; M Censier Daubenton or Place Monge) Dig into one of nine types of couscous, or choose a heaping *tajine* or meaty grill at this richly decorated, authentic-as-it-gets North African restaurant tucked within the walls of the city's stunning art deco Moorish mosque, or sip a sweet peppermint tea and nibble on a *pâtisserie orientale* between trees and chirping birds in the courtyard of the tearoom.

Feeling decadent? Book in for a *formule orientale* (€58), which includes a body scrub, 10-minute massage and a lounge in the *hammam* (Turkish bath) as well as lunch, mint tea and sweet pastry.

MOISSONNIER — LYONNAIS €€€

Map p414 (01 43 29 87 65; 28 rue des Fossés St-Bernard, 5e; 4-/6-course dinner menus €75/115, mains €35-49; lunch & dinner Tue-Sat; M Cardinal Lemoine) It's Lyon, not Paris, that French gourmets venerate as the French food capital. Take one bite of an *andouillette* (sausage made from pig intestine), *tablier de sapeur* (breaded, fried stomach), traditional *quenelles* (dumplings) or *boudin noir aux pommes* (black pudding with apples) and you'll realise why. A perfect reflection of unforgettable regional cuisines.

LE JARDIN DES PÂTES — ORGANIC, PASTA €

Map p416 (01 43 31 50 71; 4 rue Lacépède, 5e; pasta €10-16.50; lunch & dinner daily; ; M Place Monge) A crisp white-and-green façade handily placed next to a Vélib' station flags the Pasta Garden, a simple, smart 100% *bio* (organic) place where pasta comes in every guise imaginable – barley, buckwheat, rye, wheat, rice, chestnut and so on. Try the *pâtes de chataignes* (chestnut pasta) with duck breast, nutmeg, crème fraiche and mushrooms.

LA PARISIENNE BOULANGERIE, PATISSERIE €

Map p416 (28 rue Monge, 5e; ⏲7am-8.30pm Mon-Fri; Ⓜ Cardinal Lemoine) Look for the vivid, violet-coloured façade framing tiled murals of historic French scenes of the wheat-harvesting and bread-baking process (or just the queue out the door) to find this award-winning *boulangerie*. Pick up '*un tradi*' (a 70cm-long artisan *baguette tradition* distinguished by pointy tips and coarse hand-crafted surface) or sugary-sweet, pastel-shaded *macarons* costing just €10.80 per dozen.

ANAHUACALLI MEXICAN €€

Map p414 (☎01 43 26 10 20; www.anahuacalli.fr; 30 rue des Bernardins, 5e; mains €16-22; ⏲lunch Sun, dinner daily; Ⓜ Maubert-Mutualité) Mexican food is riding a wave of popularity in Paris and this upmarket restaurant – behind a discreet rosemary-coloured façade, with a sparingly decorated interior lined with mirrors and statuettes – offers some of the best. Authentic enchiladas, tamales and tacos are all elegantly presented; fish aficionados should try the salmon with papaya salsa.

LE POT DE TERRE TRADITIONAL FRENCH €

Map p416 (☎01 43 31 15 51; www.lepotdeterre.com; 22 rue du Pot de Fer, 5e; lunch/dinner menus from €9/17.50; ⏲lunch & dinner daily; 👪; Ⓜ Place Monge) This place was built in 1539, and legend has it that d'Artagnan and the musketeers slaked their thirst here between sword duels. The great-value fare – *tartatouille* (puff pastry–encased ratatouille), *magret de canard aux framboises* (duck breast in raspberry sauce) and old-fashioned desserts like chocolate mousse make it worth hunting down on this restaurant-clad street.

LE POT O'LAIT CRÊPERIE €

Map p416 (www.lepotolait.com; 41 rue Censier, 5e; lunch menus €12, crêpes €2.80-11.50; ⏲lunch & dinner Tue-Sat; 👪; Ⓜ Censier Daubenton) It might not have the lace-and-china atmosphere of a traditional Breton crêperie, but this bright, contemporary crêperie is the business when it comes to *galettes* (savoury buckwheat crêpes) like *andouille* (Breton sausage), onions and creamy mustard sauce, and sweet crêpes (pistachio ice cream, zesty orange, hot chocolate and whipped cream, or strawberry ice cream, cherries, almonds and whipped cream).

Salads are spectacular; kids will love the ice-cream sundaes.

LE PRÉ VERRE BISTRO €€

Map p414 (☎01 43 54 59 47; www.lepreverre.com; 25 rue Thénard, 5e; 2-/3-course lunch menus €13.50/29.50, mains €18.50; ⏲lunch & dinner Tue-Sat; 👪; Ⓜ Maubert-Mutualité) Busy and buzzing, the Delacourcelle brothers' jovial bistro plunges diners into the heart of a Parisian's Paris. At lunchtime join the flock and go for the *formule dejeuner* (lunch menu), which might be curried chickpea soup, guinea-fowl thigh spiced with ginger on a bed of red and green cabbage, a glass of wine and loads of ultracrusty, ultrachewy baguette (the best).

Desserts mix Asian spices with traditional French equally well, thanks to chef Philippe's extended sojourns in China, Malaysia, Japan and India. Marc is the man behind the interesting wine list, which features France's small independent *vignerons* (wine producers).

TEA CADDY TEAROOM €€

Map p414 (☎01 43 54 15 56; www.the-tea-caddy.com; 14 rue St-Julien le Pauvre, 5e; brunch/lunch menus €29/30, dinner mains €11-18; ⏲11am-7pm Sat-Wed, to 11pm Thu & Fri; Ⓜ St-Michel) Arguably the most English of the 'English' tearooms in Paris, this institution, founded in 1928, is a fine place to break for lunch or a nice genteel tea with a Devon scone, double cream and jam (€5.95) after a tour of nearby Notre Dame, Ste-Chapelle or the Conciergerie.

LE COMPTOIR DU PANTHÉON CAFE, BRASSERIE €€

Map p416 (☎01 43 54 75 56; 5 rue Soufflot, 5e; salads €10-15, mains €12-26; ⏲cafe 7am-2am Mon-Sat, to 11pm Sun, brasserie 11am-11pm Mon-Sat, to 7pm Sun; Ⓜ Cardinal Lemoine or RER Luxembourg) Enormous, creative meal-sized salads are the reason to pick this as a dining spot. Magnificently placed across from the domed Panthéon on the shady side of the street, its pavement terrace is big, busy and oh so Parisian – turn your head away from Voltaire's burial place and the Eiffel Tower pops into view.

Service is superspeedy and food is handily served all day.

MACHU PICCHU SOUTH AMERICAN €

Map p416 (☎01 43 26 13 13; 9 rue Royer-Collard, 5e; 3-course lunch menu €10.50, mains €8.50-15; ⏰lunch & dinner Mon-Sat; Ⓜ Cluny–La Sorbonne or RER Luxembourg) Students adore this place, named after the lost city of the Incas in Peru. But doesn't Peruvian food mean guinea-pig fricassee? No. This hidey-hole, going strong since the 1980s, serves excellent meat and seafood dishes as well as a bargain-basement lunch *menu* and *plats du jour* (dishes of the day). No credit cards.

LE PUITS DE LÉGUMES VEGETARIAN €

Map p414 (☎01 43 25 50 95; www.lepuitsdelegumes.com; 18 rue du Cardinal Lemoine, 5e; mains €9.50-16; ⏰lunch & dinner Mon-Sat; Ⓜ Cardinal Lemoine) Homemade tarts, quiches and rice dishes loaded with fresh seasonal vegetables are the draw of the 'Vegetable Well', a vegetarian (plus fish) student favourite. From the tiny kitchen out back a comforting waft of homemade cooking pervades the simple dining room, filled with a handful of condiment-laden tables. Specials are chalked on the board outside.

KOOTCHI AFGHAN €

Map p414 (☎01 44 07 20 56; 40 rue du Cardinal Lemoine, 5e; lunch menus €9-15.50, mains €11-14.50; ⏰lunch & dinner Mon-Sat; Ⓜ Cardinal Lemoine) Behind a sky-blue façade, carpets, traditional instruments and other jumble lend this Afghan restaurant a Central Asian caravanserai air. The welcome is warm and the food is warming. Specialities include *qhaboli palawo* (veal stew with nuts and spices); *dogh,* a drink similar to salted Indian lassi; and traditional *halwa* (sweet cake) perfumed with rose and cardamom.

Vegetarians keen to spice up their culinary life should go for the *borani palawo* (spicy vegetable stew) as a main course.

LA SALLE À MANGER TRADITIONAL FRENCH €

Map p416 (☎01 55 43 91 99; 138 rue Mouffetard, 5e; mains €11.50-15; ⏰8am-4pm Mon-Fri, to 7pm Sat & Sun; Ⓜ Censier Daubenton) With a sunny pavement terrace beneath trees enviably placed at the foot of foodie street rue Mouffetard, the 'Dining Room' is prime real estate. Its 360-degree outlook – market stalls, fountain, church and garden with playground for tots – couldn't be prettier, and its salads, *tartines* (open-faced sandwiches), tarts and pastries ensure packed tables at breakfast, lunch and weekend brunch.

AUX CÉRISES DE LUTÈCE TEAROOM €

Map p416 (86 rue Monge, 5e; mains €9.50-13; ⏰10am-7pm daily; 👪; Ⓜ Place Monge) Heaped with colourful teapots, jugs and jumble, this cosy eating space is the type of place that would wear flowery wellies. As much cafe and tearoom as lunchtime restaurant, it serves breakfast all day alongside salads, quiches and *tartines.* Market mornings see the trio of pavement tables hotly contested.

TASHI DELEK TIBETAN €

Map p416 (☎01 43 26 55 55; 4 rue des Fossés St-Jacques, 5e; menus from €12, mains €7-13.50; ⏰lunch & dinner Mon-Sat; Ⓜ Cardinal Lemoine or RER Luxembourg) Cheap, tasty Tibetan fare spans from *tsampa* (vegetable and barley soup) to delicious *daril seu* (meatballs with garlic, ginger and rice) or *tselmok* (cheese and vegetable ravioli). Wash it down with traditional or salted-butter tea. Don't forget to say *tashi delek* upon entering – it means *bonjour* in Tibetan.

LE FOYER DU VIETNAM VIETNAMESE €

Map p416 (☎01 45 35 32 54; 80 rue Monge, 5e; mains €6.50-10; ⏰lunch & dinner Mon-Sat; 👪; Ⓜ Place Monge) The Vietnam Club, with its self-proclaimed *ambiance familiale* (family atmosphere), might be nothing more than a long room with peeling walls and tables covered in oilcloths and plastic flowers, but everyone flocks here to feast on its hearty house specialities, 'Saigon' or 'Hanoi' soup (noodles, soya beans and pork flavoured with lemon grass, coriander and chives) included.

Dishes come in medium or large portions and the price to quality ratio is astonishing.

BREAKFAST IN AMERICA AMERICAN €

Map p414 (www.breakfast-in-america.com; 17 rue des Écoles, 5e; menus €8-16; ⏰8.30am-11pm daily; 👪; Ⓜ Cardinal Lemoine or Jussieu) States-style breakfasts – including blueberry pancakes drowning in maple syrup – are just the start at this authentic diner (known as BIA to its devoted US of A clientele), which also serves up towering burgers, wraps, omelettes, cheesecake, bagels, chilli con carne and classic milkshakes throughout the day, all in American-size portions.

LE BUISSON ARDENT BISTRO €€

Map p416 (☎01 43 54 93 02; www.lebuissonardent.fr; 25 rue Jussieu, 5e; lunch/dinner menus from €17/20; ⏰lunch daily, dinner Mon-Sat; Ⓜ Jussieu) Classy fare at this rose-toned bistro includes roasted quail, pan-fried veal kidneys, and scorpion fish.

LE BABA BOURGEOIS MODERN FRENCH €€

Map p414 (☎01 44 07 46 75; http://lebababourgeois.com; 5 quai de la Tournelle, 5e; 2-/3-course lunch menus €17/20, 2-/3-course dinner menus €25/36; ⏰11am-11.30pm Tue-Sat, to 5pm Sun; Ⓜ Cardinal Lemoine or Pont Marie) In a former architect's studio with a 1970s Italian designer interior, 'le BB' opens to a superb Seine-side pavement terrace facing Notre Dame. The menu – *tartes salées* (savoury tarts) and salads – makes for a simple stylish bite any time; Sunday ushers in a splendid all-day buffet brunch, *à volonté* (all you can eat, €27).

DRINKING & NIGHTLIFE

Rive Gauche romantics, well-heeled cafe society types and students by the gallon drink in the 5e *arrondissement*, where old-but-good recipes, nostalgic formulas and a deluge of early-evening happy hours ensure a quintessential Parisian soirée. It's not ground-breaking, but it's all good fun.

CAFÉ DE LA NOUVELLE MAIRIE WINE BAR

Map p416 (19 rue des Fossés-Saint-Jacques, 5e; ⏰9am-8pm Mon-Fri; Ⓜ Cardinal-Lemoine) Shhhh...just around the corner from the Panthéon but hidden away on a small, fountained square, the narrow wine bar Café de la Nouvelle is a neighbourhood secret, serving blackboard-chalked wines by the glass as well as bottles. Accompanying tapas-style food is simple and delicious.

LE VERRE À PIED CAFE

Map p416 (http://leverreapied.fr; 118bis rue Mouffetard, 5e; ⏰9am-9pm Tue-Sat, 9.30am-4pm Sun; Ⓜ Censier Daubenton) This *café-tabac* is a pearl of a place where little has changed since 1870. Its nicotine-hued mirrored wall, moulded cornices and original bar make it part of a dying breed, but the place oozes the charm, glamour and romance of an old Paris everyone loves, including stall holders from the rue Mouffetard market who yo-yo in and out.

Contemporary photography and art adorns one wall. Lunch is a busy, lively affair, and live music quickens the pulse a couple of evenings a week.

LE PUB ST-HILAIRE PUB

Map p414 (www.pubsainthilaire.com; 2 rue Valette, 5e; ⏰3pm-2am Mon-Thu, 3pm-4am Fri, 4pm-4am Sat, 4pm-midnight Sun; Ⓜ Maubert-Mutualité) The term 'buzzing' fails to do justice to the pulsating vibe inside this student-loved pub. Generous happy hours last several hours and the place is kept packed with a trio of pool tables, board games, music on two floors, hearty bar food and various gimmicks to rev up the party crowd (a metre of cocktails, 'be your own barman' etc). Expect wild times.

CURIO PARLOR COCKTAIL CLUB COCKTAIL BAR

Map p414 (www.curioparlor.com; 16 rue des Bernardins, 5e; ⏰7pm-2am Mon-Thu, to 4am Fri-Sun; Ⓜ Maubert-Mutualité) Run by the same switched-on, chilled-out team as the Experimental Cocktail Club (p123) et al, this hybrid bar-club looks to the interwar *années folles* (crazy years) of 1920s Paris, London and New York for inspiration. Its racing-green façade with a simple brass plaque on the door is the height of discretion.

Go to its Facebook page to find out which party is happening when.

L'ACADÉMIE DE LA BIÈRE PUB

Map p416 (www.academie-biere.com; 88bis bd de Port Royal, 5e; ⏰10am-2am Sun-Thu, to 3am Fri & Sat; Ⓜ Vavin or RER Pont Royal) Serious students of Belgian beer should head to this 'beer academy' to try its 12 beers on tap or choose from over 300 bottled varieties, including Trappist (Monk-made) beers like prized Westmalle, abbey beers including Grimbergen and Leffe, fruit beers and Cantillon gueuze (double-fermented Lambic beer made in Brussels).

In true Belgian tradition, it also serves *moules* (mussels), delivered and cleaned each morning, cooked in creative ways including with mustard, curry, roquefort or gueuze, and served continuously.

CAFÉ DELMAS CAFE

Map p416 (www.cafedelmasparis.com; 2 place de la Contrescarpe, 5e; ⏰8am-2am Sun-Thu, to 4am Fri & Sat; Ⓜ Place Monge) Enviably situated on tree-studded place de la Contrescarpe, the Delmas is a hot spot for chilling over *un café* or cappuccino or all-day breakfast. Cosy up beneath overhead heaters outside to soak up the street atmosphere or snuggle up between books in the library-style interior – awash with students from the nearby universities.

If you're looking for the bathrooms, note that Jacqueline is for women, Jacques for men.

LE CROCODILE BAR

Map p416 (6 rue Royer-Collard, 5e; ⌚6pm-2am Mon-Sat; Ⓜ Odén or RER Luxembourg) This green-shuttered bar has been dispensing cocktails (more than 200 on the list) since 1966. The '70s were 'epic' in this bar, and the dream kicks on well into the new millennium. Arrive late for a truly eclectic crowd, including lots of students, and an atmosphere that can go from quiet tippling to raucous revelry. Hours can vary.

LE PIANO VACHE BAR, LIVE MUSIC

Map p414 (www.lepianovache.com; 8 rue Laplace, 5e; ⌚noon-2am Mon-Fri, 6pm-2am Sat; Ⓜ Maubert-Mutualité) Down the hill from the Panthéon, this bar is covered in old posters above old couches and is drenched in 1970s and '80s rock ambience. Effortlessly underground and a real student fave, bands and DJs play mainly rock, plus some goth, reggae and pop.

LE VIEUX CHÊNE BAR

Map p416 (69 rue Mouffetard, 5e; ⌚9am-2am Sun-Thu, to 5am Fri & Sat; Ⓜ Place Monge) This rue Mouffetard institution is reckoned to be Paris' oldest bar. Indeed, a revolutionary circle met here in 1848 and it was a popular *bal musette* (dancing club) in the late 19th and early 20th centuries. These days it's a student favourite, especially during happy 'hour' (4pm to 9pm Tuesday to Sunday, and from 4pm until closing on Monday).

Resident DJs mix it up on Friday and Saturday nights.

CAVE LA BOURGOGNE CAFE, BAR

Map p416 (144 rue Mouffetard, 5e; ⌚7am-2am Mon-Sat, to 11pm Sun; Ⓜ Censier Daubenton) A prime spot for lapping up rue Mouffetard's 'saunter-all-day' spirit, this neighbourhood hang-out sits on square St-Médard, one of the Latin Quarter's loveliest squares – picture a flower-bedecked fountain, centuries-old church and market stalls spilling across one side. Inside, old ladies and their pet dogs meet for coffee around dark wood tables alongside a local wine-sipping set. In summer everything spills outside.

LE VIOLON DINGUE PUB

Map p414 (46 rue de la Montagne Ste-Geneviève, 5e; ⌚7pm-5am Tue-Sat, 8pm-4am Sun; Ⓜ Maubert-Mutualité) A loud, lively bar adopted by revolving generations of students, The Crazy Violin attracts lots of young English-speakers with big-screen sports shown upstairs and the flirty 'Dingue Lounge' downstairs. The name 'Crazy Violin' is a pun on the expression *le violon d'Ingres,* meaning 'hobby' in French because the celebrated painter Jean-Auguste-Dominique Ingres played fiddle in his spare time.

LE PANTALON BAR

Map p416 (7 rue Royer-Collard, 5e; ⌚5.30pm-2am; Ⓜ Cluny–La Sorbonne or RER Luxembourg) Ripped vinyl seats, coloured-glass light fittings and old stickers plastered on the walls make this rockin' little bar a favourite hang-out of Parisian musicians.

LE MAUZAC WINE BAR

Map p416 (www.lemauzac.net; 7 rue de l'Abbé de l'Epée, 5e; ⌚11.30am-midnight Mon-Sat; Ⓜ Place Monge or RER Luxembourg) Fronted by a leafy garden terrace, this wine bar has street lamps and stone floors indoors, giving it the atmosphere of a Parisian street – although the wine bottles lining the walls are a greater indication of its raison d'être. Some 60 varieties of red, white and rosé wines are available by the glass; food includes Landes foie gras and Breton oysters.

☆ ENTERTAINMENT

TOP CHOICE CAFÉ UNIVERSEL LIVE MUSIC

Map p416 (☎01 43 25 74 20; http://cafeuniversel.com; 267 rue St-Jacques, 5e; admission free; ⌚from 9pm Tue-Sat; 📶; Ⓜ Censier Daubenton or RER Port Royal) Café Universel hosts a brilliant array of live concerts with everything from bebop and Latin sounds to vocal jazz sessions. Plenty of freedom is given to young producers and artists, and its convivial relaxed atmosphere attracts a mix of students and jazz lovers. *La Confiture des Mardis* (Tuesday jam sessions) are particularly lively, with vocal jams until just after midnight.

Its complete monthly agenda is posted online. Concerts are free but bring money to tip artists when they pass the hat around.

LE CHAMPO CINEMA

Map p414 (www.lechampo.com; 51 rue des Écoles, 5e; MSt-Michel or Cluny–La Sorbonne) This is one of the most popular of the many Latin Quarter cinemas, featuring classics and retrospectives looking at the films of such actors and directors as Alfred Hitchcock, Jacques Tati, Alain Resnais, Frank Capra, Tim Burton and Woody Allen. One of the two *salles* (cinemas) has wheelchair access.

A couple of times a month Le Champo screens films all night for night owls, kicking off at midnight (three films plus breakfast €15).

LE CAVEAU DES OUBLIETTES LIVE MUSIC

Map p414 (01 46 34 24 09; www.caveaudesoubliettes.fr; 52 rue Galande, 5e; 5pm-4am daily; MSt-Michel) From the 16th-century ground-floor pub, descend to the 12th-century dungeon for cutting-edge jazz, blues and funk concerts and jam sessions (from 10pm).

LE PETIT JOURNAL ST-MICHEL LIVE MUSIC

Map p416 (01 43 26 28 59; www.petitjournalsaintmichel.com; 71 bd St-Michel, 5e; admission incl 1 drink €17-20, with dinner €46-50; Mon-Sat; MCluny–La Sorbonne or RER Luxembourg) Classic jazz concerts kick off at 9.15pm in the atmospheric downstairs cellar of this sophisticated jazz venue across from the Jardin du Luxembourg. Everything ranging from Dixieland and vocals to big band and swing sets patrons' toes tapping. Dinner is served at 8pm.

CAVEAU DE LA HUCHETTE LIVE MUSIC

Map p414 (01 43 26 65 05; www.caveaudelahuchette.fr; 5 rue de la Huchette, 5e; admission Sun-Thu €12, Fri & Sat €14, under 25yr €10; 9.30pm-2.30am Sun-Wed, to 4am Thu-Sat; MSt-Michel) Housed in a medieval *caveau* (cellar) used as a courtroom and torture chamber during the Revolution, this club is where virtually all the jazz greats have played since the end of WWII. It attracts its fair share of tourists, but the atmosphere can be more electric than at the more serious jazz clubs. Sessions start at 10pm.

L'EPÉE DE BOIS CINEMA

Map p416 (www.cinema-epee-de-bois.fr; 100 rue Mouffetard, 5e; MCensier Daubenton) Even locals find it easy to miss the small doorway leading to rue Mouffetard's little cinema, which screens art-house flicks such as Julie Delpy–directed films.

MÉTAMORPHOSIS MAGIC SHOWS

Map p414 (01 43 54 08 08; www.metamorphosis-spectacle.fr; 3 quai de Montebello, 5e; Tue-Sun; MMaubert-Mutualité) Old-fashioned magic shows in a magical setting – aboard a boat moored on the stunning Seine opposite Notre Dame. From Tuesday to Saturday nights you can catch dinner at 7.30pm (adult/child *menus* including show €60/32), or a show only at 9.30pm (adult/child €30/16). Shows are in French only, but the illusionary tricks transcend language barriers. Sundays are especially geared towards kids.

Sunday brunch from 12.30pm (adult/child including show €38/32) is followed by shows at 3pm (all ages €16).

SHOPPING

The Latin Quarter is a shopper's paradise and bookworms in particular will love this part of the Left Bank, which is home to some wonderful bookshops. Other student-frequented shops include camping stores, comic shops, old-school music shops where collectors browse for hours, and cheap, colourful homewares stores, interspersed by the occasional *droguerie-quincaillerie* (hardware store) – easily spotted by the jumble of laundry baskets, buckets etc piled on the pavement in front.

TOP CHOICE **SHAKESPEARE & COMPANY** BOOKS

Map p414 (www.shakespeareandcompany.com; 37 rue de la Bûcherie, 5e; 10am-11pm Mon-Fri, from 11am Sat & Sun; MSt-Michel) A kind of spell descends as you enter this enchanting bookshop, where nooks and crannies overflow with new and secondhand English-language books. Fabled for nurturing writers, at night its couches turn into beds where writers stay in exchange for stacking shelves. Readings by emerging to illustrious authors take place at 7pm most Mondays; it also hosts workshops and literary festivals.

The bookshop is the stuff of legends. The original shop (12 rue l'Odéon, 6e; closed by the Nazis in 1941 – see p233) was run by Sylvia Beach and became the meeting point for Hemingway's 'Lost Generation'. American-born George Whitman opened the present incarnation in 1951, attracting a Beat poet

LOCAL KNOWLEDGE

FOOD SHOPPING ALONG RUE MOUFFETARD

The narrow, sloping cobblestone street rue Mouffetard is one of Paris' earliest, beginning its life as a Roman road to Rome via Lyon. It acquired its current name in the 18th century, when the then-nearby River Bievre (now piped underground) became the communal waste disposal for local tanners and wood-pulpers. The resulting odours gave rise to the name Moffettes (French for 'skunk'), which was transmuted over the years to Mouffetard.

Today the aromas on 'La Mouffe', as it's nicknamed by locals, are infinitely more enticing. Grocers, butchers, fishmongers and other food purveyors set their goods out on street stalls during the **Marché Mouffetard** (Map p416; ⌚8am-7.30pm Tue-Sat, to noon Sun; Ⓜ Censier Daubenton).

You won't even have to worry about the aromas if you're taking home the scrumptious cheeses from *fromagerie* **Androuet** (Map p416; http://androuet.com; 134 rue Mouffetard; ⌚9.30am-1pm & 4-7.30pm Tue-Thu, to 7.30pm Fri & Sat, to 1.30pm Sun; Ⓜ Censier Daubenton) – all of its cheeses can be vacuum packed for free. (Be sure to look up to see the beautiful murals on the building's façade, and look out for others along this street.)

Stuffed olives and capsicums and marinated aubergine are among the picnic goodies at gourmet Italian deli **Delizius** (Map p416; 134 rue Mouffetard; ⌚9.30am-8pm Tue-Fri, 9am-8pm Sat, 9am-2pm Sun; Ⓜ Censier Daubenton), which also sells ready-to-eat hot meals and fresh and dried pasta.

Light, luscious *macarons* in flavours like jasmine, raspberry and blackcurrant, and a mouthwatering range of chocolates by three *maîtres chocolatiers* (master chocolate-makers) – Fabrice Gillotte, Jacques Bellanger and Patrice Chapoare – are laid out like jewels at **Chocolats Mococha** (Map p416; www.chocolatsmococha.com; 89 rue Mouffetard; Ⓜ Censier Daubenton).

The charming *épicerie fine* (specialist grocer) **Le 4** (Map p416; www.le4epiceriefine.com; 4 rue Mouffetard; ⌚11am-8pm; Ⓜ Place Monge or Cardinal Lemoine) stocks a hand-picked range of foie gras, sweets, oils, vinegars, tea and champagne – as well as eclectic homewares such as bottles, vases and scented candles, and accessories like offbeat key rings and bags.

clientele, and scores of authors have since passed through its doors. In 2006 Whitman was awarded the Officier des Arts et Lettres by the French Minister of Culture, recognising 'significant contribution to the enrichment of the French cultural inheritance'. Whitman died in 2011, aged 98; he is buried in Division 73 of Cimetière du Père Lachaise. Today his daughter, Sylvia Beach Whitman, maintains Shakespeare & Company's serendipitous magic.

MAGIE — GAMES, HOBBIES

Map p414 (☎01 43 54 13 63; www.mayette.com; 8 rue des Carmes, 5e; ⌚1-8pm Mon-Sat; Ⓜ Maubert-Mutualité) One of a kind, this 1808-established magic shop is said to be the world's oldest. Since 1991 it's been in the hands of world-famous magic pro Dominique Duvivier. Professional and hobbyist magicians flock here to discuss king sandwiches, reverse assemblies, false cuts and other card tricks with Duvivier and his daughter, Alexandra.

Should you want to learn the tricks of the trade, Duvivier has magic courses up his sleeve.

CROCODISC — MUSIC

Map p414 (www.crocodisc.com; 40 & 42 rue des Écoles, 5e; ⌚11am-7pm Tue-Sat; Ⓜ Maubert-Mutualité) Music might be more accessible than ever before thanks to iPods, tablets and smartphones but for many it will never replace rummaging through racks for treasures. New and secondhand CDs and vinyl discs at No 40 rue des Écoles span world music, rap, reggae, salsa, soul and disco, while No 42 has pop, rock, punk, new wave, electro and soundtracks.

Its nearby sister shop **Crocojazz** (Map p414; 64 rue de la Montagne-Ste-Geneviève, 5e; ⌚11am-7pm Tue-Sat; Ⓜ Maubert-Mutualité) specialises in jazz, blues, gospel and timeless crooners, with books and DVDs as well as recordings.

FROMAGERIE LAURENT DUBOIS FOOD, DRINK

Map p414 (www.fromageslaurentdubois.fr; 47ter bd St-Germain, 5e; ⏲8.30am-7.30pm Tue-Sat, to 1pm Sun; ⓂMaubert-Mutualité) One of the best *fromageries* in Paris, this cheese-lover's nirvana is filled with to-die-for delicacies such as St-Félicien with Périgord truffles. Rare, limited-production cheeses include blue Termignon and Tarentaise goat's cheese. All are appropriately cellared in warm, humid or cold environments. There's also a 15e branch (p264).

ABBEY BOOKSHOP BOOKS

Map p414 (☎01 46 33 16 24; rue de la Parcheminerie, 5e; ⏲10am-7pm Mon-Sat; ⓂSt-Michel or Cluny–La Sorbonne) In a heritage-listed townhouse, this welcoming Canadian-run bookshop serves free coffee (sweetened with maple syrup) to sip while you browse tens of thousands of new and used books, and organises literary events and countryside hikes.

ALBUM COMICS

Map p414 (www.album.fr; 67 bd St-Germain, 5e; ⏲10am-8pm Mon-Sat, noon-7pm Sun; ⓂCluny–La Sorbonne) Album specialises in *bandes dessinées* (comics), which have an enormous following in France, with everything from Tintin and Babar to erotic comics and the latest Japanese manga. Serious comic collectors – and anyone excited by Harry Potter wands, Star Wars, Superman and other superhero figurines and t-shirts (you know who you are!) – shouldn't miss it.

LIBRAIRIE EYROLLES BOOKS

Map p414 (☎01 44 41 11 72; www.eyrolles.com; 61 bd St-Germain, 5e; ⏲9.30am-7.30pm Mon-Fri, to 8pm Sat; ⓂMaubert-Mutualité) Art, design, architecture, dictionaries and kids' books are the mainstay of this large bookshop with titles in English and stacks of browsing space.

For maps, guides and travel lit hop two doors over to its **Librairie de Voyage** (Map p414; ☎01 46 34 82 75; 63 bd St-Germain; ⏲10.30am-7.30pm Mon, 9.30am-7.30pm Tue-Fri, 9.30am-8pm Sat; ⓂMaubert Mutualité).

AU VIEUX CAMPEUR OUTDOOR EQUIPMENT

Map p414 (www.auvieuxcampeur.fr; 48 rue des Écoles, 5e; ⏲11am-8pm Mon-Wed & Fri-Sat, to 9pm Thu; ⓂMaubert-Mutualité or Cluny–La Sorbonne) This sporting-gear chain runs 29 shops in the Latin Quarter, each selling equipment for a specific outdoor activity. This is the flagship shop (specialising in mountaineering); you can find walking gear at **2–4 rue Thénard** (Map p414); camping gear and a fabulous range of accessories (torches, knives, flasks, folding buckets, pack showers) at **6 rue Thénard** (Map p414); and Paris' most complete range of maps and guides at **2 rue de Latran** (Map p414).

Clothing for *le froid urbain* (urban cold) is stocked at 50 rue des Écoles and 3 rue de Latran.

LA BOUTIQUE DU CRÉATEUR DE JEUX GAMES, HOBBIES

Map p414 (www.laboutiqueducreateurdejeux.fr; 40 rue St-Jacques, 5e; ⏲11.30am-7pm Tue-Sat; ⓂCluny–La Sorbonne) This shop sells brand-new board and card games created in the last couple of years in France; several are bilingual (French and English). Its *jeux de mesure* are made-to-measure, limited editions often focusing on a social issue such as alcohol abuse, immigrant equality etc.

MOUFFETARD FOLIE'S HOMEWARES

Map p416 (51 rue Mouffetard, 5e; ⏲11am-8.30pm; ⓂCensier Daubenton) From rue Mouffetard, step down into the basement housing this colourful homewares shop crammed with cute, kitsch, inexpensive new items such as battery-powered flying Fresian-cow mobiles and gumdrop-coloured lamps.

MARCHÉ MAUBERT MARKET

Map p414 (place Maubert, 5e; ⏲7am-2.30pm Tue, Thu & Sat; ⓂMaubert-Mutualité) The Left Bank's bohemian soul lives on at this colourful street market. Expect regular market fare: fresh food and veggies.

MARCHÉ MONGE MARKET

Map p416 (place Monge, 5e; ⏲7am-2pm Wed, Fri & Sun; ⓂPlace Monge) The open-air Marché Monge is laden with wonderful cheeses, baked goods and a host of other temptations.

SPORTS & ACTIVITIES

HAMMAM DE LA MOSQUÉE DE PARIS SPA

Map p416 (☎01 43 31 38 20; www.la-mosquee.com; 39 rue Geoffroy St-Hilaire, 5e; admission €15; ⏲men 2-9pm Tue, 10am-9pm Sun, women 10am-9pm Mon, Wed, Thu & Sat, 2-9pm Fri; ⓂCensier

Daubenton or Place Monge) Massages at this atmospheric *hammam* cost €1 a minute and come in 10-, 20- or 30-minute packages. Should you fancy an exfoliating body scrub and mint tea, get the 10-/30-minute massage *formule* (€38/58). There are also lunch deals at La Mosquée de Paris (p211). Bring a swimsuit but hire a towel/dressing gown (€4/5). No kids under 12.

BOWLING MOUFFETARD BOWLING

Map p416 (☎01 43 31 09 35; www.bowling-mouffetard.abcsalles.com; 13 rue Gracieuse & 73 rue Mouffetard, 5e; games €4.90, shoes €2; ⏰3pm-2am Mon-Fri, 10am-2am Sat & Sun; Ⓜ Place Monge) Intimate, friendly alley with eight lanes and two entrances.

PISCINE PONTOISE SWIMMING

Map p414 (☎01 55 42 77 88; http://piscine.equipement.paris.fr; 19 rue de Pontoise, 5e; adult/concession €4.50/2.70; ⏰vary; Ⓜ Maubert-Mutualité) A beautiful art deco–style indoor pool in the heart of the Latin Quarter; a €10.50 evening ticket (from 8pm) covers entry to the pool, gym and sauna. It has shorter hours during term time – check up-to-date opening times online.

WILL SALTER / GETTY IMAGES ©

SYLVAIN SONNET / HEMIS / CORBIS ©

STEFANO BROZZI / GRAND TOUR / CORBIS ©

SONNET SYLVAIN / HEMIS / CORBIS ©

1. Jardin des Tuileries (p115)
A couple strolling in part of the 28-hectare gardens, laid out by André Le Nôtre in 1664.

2. Bois de Boulogne (p86)
The 845-hectare park with 400,000 trees was inspired by London's Hyde Park.

3. Parc des Buttes-Chaumont (p138)
The temple to Sybil sits atop an island in this Parisian park.

4. Jardin du Luxembourg (p228)
Home to Palais du Luxembourg, the gardens blend French and English styles.

St-Germain & Les Invalides

ST-GERMAIN | LES INVALIDES

Neighbourhood Top Five

❶ Revel in a wealth of world-famous impressionist masterpieces and art nouveau architecture in resplendently renovated surrounds at the glorious **Musée d'Orsay** (p224).

❷ Indulge in an exquisitely Parisian moment in the sculpture-filled gardens of the **Musée Rodin** (p230).

❸ Feast your eyes on the fantastical food displays at **La Grande Épicerie de Paris** (p245).

❹ Sip a *café crème* on the terrace of famous literary cafe **Les Deux Magots** (p242).

❺ Visit Napoleon's tomb in the monumental **Hôtel des Invalides** (p231) complex.

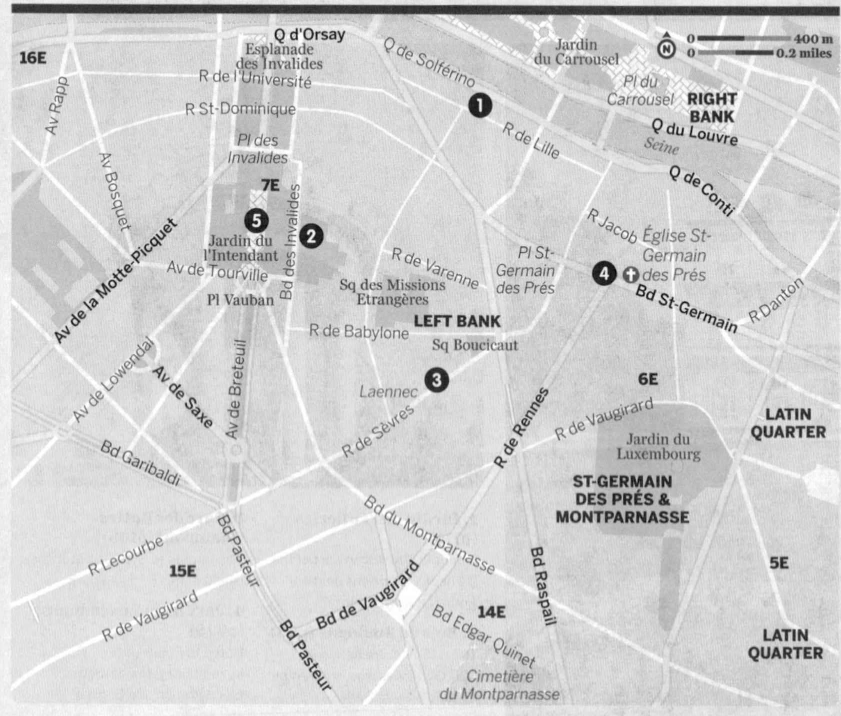

For more detail of this area, see Map p418 and p422

Explore St-Germain & Les Invalides

Despite gentrification since its early 20th century bohemian days, there remains a startling cinematic quality to this soulful part of the Left Bank where artists, writers, actors and musicians cross paths and *la vie germanopratine* (St-Germain life) is belle.

Allow plenty of time to stroll the neighbourhood side streets and stop at its fabled literary cafes, its *prêt-à-porter* stores and vast white spaces showcasing interior design. In between, view Delecroix's works at the Église St-Sulpice and his former studio, the Musée National Eugène Delacroix, and soak up the serenity of the masterpiece-filled sculpture garden of the Musée Rodin.

Entry to the Musée d'Orsay is less expensive in the late-afternoon, so it's an ideal time to check out its breathtaking collections, before dining at the area's stylish restaurants and swizzling cocktails at its bars.

Local Life

➡ **Park Life** To see Parisians at a play, its most popular park, the beautiful Jardin du Luxembourg, is a must-stroll, particularly at weekends.

➡ **Market Life** Street markets where locals stock up on mouthwatering produce include Marché Raspail and rue Cler.

➡ **Fashion Finds** Scour the designer cast-off racks at St-Germain's secondhand boutiques (p245).

Getting There & Away

➡ **Metro** This area is well served by metro and RER. Get off at metro stations St-Germain des Prés, Mabillon or Odéon for its busy bd St-Germain heart.

➡ **Bus** Buses stop on bd St-Germain for the 86 to Odéon, Pont Sully (Île St-Louis) and Bastille; on rue de Rennes for the 96 to place Châtelet, Hôtel de Ville, St-Paul (Marais), rue Oberkampf and rue de Ménilmontant; and on Quai d'Orsay for the 63 to Gare d'Austerlitz and Gare de Lyon, and the 83 to Grand Palais, Rond Point des Champs-Élysées and rue du Faubourg St-Honoré. The 73 links the Musée d'Orsay with place de la Concorde, av des Champs-Élysées and La Défense.

➡ **Bicycle** Handy Vélib' stations include 141 bd St-Germain, 6e; opposite 2 bd Raspail, 6e; and 62 rue de Lille, 7e.

➡ **Boat** Batobus boats dock by quai Malaquais for St-Germain des Prés and quai de Solférino for the Musée d'Orsay. Paris Canal uses the pier at quai Anatole France for canal boats to Bassin de la Villette (19-21 quai de la Loire).

Lonely Planet's Top Tip

Particularly around the Seine, in an increasingly common ruse scammers pretend to 'find' a gold ring (by subtly dropping it on the ground) then offer it to you as a diversionary tactic to surreptitiously reach into your pockets or bags to get money. Don't fall for it!

Best Places to Eat

➡ Bouillon Racine (p235)
➡ Huîterie Regis (p236)
➡ Ze Kitchen Galerie (p235)
➡ L'Arpège (p240)
➡ Cuisine de Bar (p236)

For reviews, see p235 

Best Places to Drink

➡ Les Deux Magots (p242)
➡ Au Sauvignon (p242)
➡ Brasserie O'Neil (p243)
➡ Café Thoumieux (p244)
➡ La Mezzanine (p243)

For reviews, see p242

Best Churches

➡ Église St-Germain des Prés (p234)
➡ Église St-Sulpice (p232)
➡ Chapelle Notre Dame de la Medaille Miraculeuse (p232)

For reviews, see p232 

TOP SIGHTS
MUSÉE D'ORSAY

BERTRAND GARDEL / HEMIS / CORBIS ©

The home of France's national collection from the impressionist, postimpressionist and art nouveau movements is, appropriately, the glorious former Gare d'Orsay railway station, itself an art nouveau showpiece designed by competition-winning architect Victor Laloux. Transforming the languishing building into the country's premier showcase for art from the period 1848 to 1914 was the grand project of President Valéry Giscard d'Estaing, who signed off on it in 1977. The museum opened its doors in 1986, with a roll call of instantly recognisable works from French and international masters.

Far from resting on its laurels, the Musée d'Orsay is fresh from a renovation program known as the 'Nouvel d'Orsay' that incorporates a re-energised layout and increased exhibition space. Rather than being lost in a sea of white, prized paintings now gleam from richly coloured walls that create a much more intimate, stately home-like atmosphere, with high-tech illumination literally casting the masterpieces in a new light.

For a thorough introduction to the museum, 90-minute 'Masterpieces of the Musée d'Orsay' guided tours (€6) in English generally run at least once a day from Tuesday to Saturday – check the website for seasonal departure times. Kids under 13 aren't permitted on tours.

Under new rules, photography of all kinds (including from mobile phones) is now forbidden in the Musée d'Orsay to avoid crowd bottlenecks. If you want something more tangible than memories to take with you, there's an excellent book and gift shop.

DON'T MISS

- The Building
- Painting Collections
- Decorative Arts Collections
- Sculptures
- Graphic Arts Collections

PRACTICALITIES

- Map p422
- www.musee-orsay.fr
- 62 rue de Lille, 7e
- adult/under 25yr/under 18yr €9/6.50/free
- 9.30am-6pm Tue, Wed & Fri-Sun, to 9.45pm Thu
- M Assemblée Nationale or RER Musée d'Orsay

The Building

Even on its completion, just in time for the 1900 Exposition Universelle, painter Edouard Detaille declared that the new station looked like a Palais des Beaux Arts. But by 1939 the increasing electrification of the rail network meant the Gare d'Orsay's platforms were too short for mainline trains, and within a few years all rail services ceased.

The station was used as a mailing centre during WWII, and in 1962 Orson Welles filmed Kafka's *The Trial* in the building. It was saved from being demolished and replaced with a hotel complex by a Historical Monument listing in 1973, before the government set about establishing the palatial museum.

Painting Collections

Top of every visitor's must-see list is the world's largest collection of impressionist and postimpressionist art. Just some of its highlights include Manet's *On The Beach* and *Woman With Fans*; Monet's gardens at Giverny and *Rue Montorgueil, Paris, Festival of June 30, 1878*; Cézanne's card players, *Green Apples* and *Blue Vase*; Renoir's *Ball at the Moulin de la Galette* and *Young Girls at the Piano*; Degas' ballerinas; Toulouse-Lautrec's cabaret dancers; Pissarro's *The Harvest*; Sisley's *View of the Canal St-Martin*; and Van Gogh's self-portraits, *Bedroom in Arles* and *Starry Night over the Rhône*. One of the museum's newest acquisitions is James Tissot's 1868 painting *The Circle of the Rue Royale*, classified as a national treasure.

Decorative Arts Collections

Household items such as candlesticks, desks, chairs, bookcases, vases, pot-plant holders, free-standing screens, wall mirrors, water pitchers, plates, goblets, bowls – and even soup terrines – become works of art in the hands of their creators from the era, incorporating exquisite design elements and motifs.

Sculptures

The cavernous former station is a magnificent setting for sculptures, including works by Degas, Gaugin, Claudel, Renoir and Rodin.

Graphic Arts Collections

Drawings, pastels and sketches from major artists are another of the d'Orsay's lesser-known highlights. Look for Georges Seurat's *The Black Bow* (c 1882) which uses crayon on paper to define forms by contrasting between black and white, and Paul Gaugin's poignant self-portrait (c 1902-1903), drawn near the end of his life.

MONEY SAVING TIPS

Save money by purchasing a combined ticket with the Musée de l'Orangerie, costing €14 to visit both within four days. Musée d'Orsay admission drops to €6.50 for entry after 4.30pm (after 6pm on Thursday).

The museum is busiest on Tuesdays and Sundays, followed by Thursdays and Saturdays. Save time queuing by pre-purchasing tickets online; head directly to Entrance C.

DINING TIPS

Designed like a fantasy underwater world, **Café Campana** (Map p422; dishes €9-18; ⏲10am-5pm Tue, Wed & Fri-Sun, to 9pm Thu), adjacent to the impressionist gallery, serves dishes such as PPP (penne rigate, Parma ham and parmesan shavings – plus pesto). Don't miss the view through the former station's giant glass clockface. Time has scarcely changed the museum's – and originally the station's – chandeliered **Restaurant Musée d'Orsay** (Map p422; ☎01 45 49 47 03; lunch/dinner menus €16.50/55; ⏲lunch Tue-Sun, dinner Thu, afternoon tea 2.45-5.45pm Tue-Sun).

1. La Clownesse Cha-U-Kao
Henri de Toulouse-Lautrec's painting of a cabaret dancer.

2. Danseuses Bleues
Edgar Degas' ballerinas.

3.Portrait de l'artiste
Vincent Van Gogh's self-portrait from 1889, one of several of Van Gogh's self-portraits in the museum.

4. Bal du Moulin de la Galette
Auguste Renoir's *Ball at the Moulin de la Galette* is a highlight of the collection.

THE GALLERY COLLECTION / CORBIS ©

MASTERPICS / ALAMY ©

PETER BARRITT / ALAMY ©

TOP SIGHTS
JARDIN DU LUXEMBOURG

This inner-city oasis of formal terraces, chestnut groves and lush lawns has a special place in the hearts of Parisians. Napoleon dedicated the 23 gracefully laid-out hectares of the Luxembourg Gardens to the children of Paris, and many residents spent their childhood watching puppet shows, and riding the carousel or ponies. All those activities are still here today, as well as modern play equipment, tennis and other sporting venues.

The Jardin du Luxembourg's history stretches further back than Napoleon. The gardens are a backdrop to the Palais du Luxembourg, built in the 1620s for Marie de Médici, Henri IV's consort, to assuage her longing for the Pitti Palace in Florence. The Palais is now home to the French Senate, which, in addition to parliamentary activities, is charged with promoting the palace and its gardens.

Numerous overhauls over the centuries have given the Jardin du Luxembourg a blend of both traditional French- and English-style gardens – studded with over 100 sculptures, including statues of Stendhal, Chopin, Baudelaire, and Delacroix – that is unique in Paris.

Grand Bassin

All ages love the octagonal **Grand Bassin** (Map p418), a serene ornamental pond where adults can lounge and kids can prod 1920s **toy sailboats** (per 30/60 minutes €2/3.20; ⏲Apr-Oct) with long sticks. Nearby, littlies can take **pony rides** (€2.50; ⏲Apr-Oct) or romp around the **playgrounds** (Map p418) – the green half is for kids aged seven to 12 years, the blue half for under-sevens.

DON'T MISS

- Grand Bassin
- Puppet Shows
- Orchards
- Palais du Luxembourg
- Musée du Luxembourg

PRACTICALITIES

- Map p418
- numerous entrances
- ⏲between 7.30am and 8.15am to between 5pm and 10pm; seasonal entry times are posted at entrance gates
- Ⓜ St-Sulpice, Rennes or Notre-Dames des Champs, or RER Luxembourg

Puppet Shows

You don't have to be a kid or speak French to be delighted by marionette shows, which have entertained audiences in France since the Middle Ages. The lively puppets perform in the little **Théâtre du Luxembourg** (Map p418; http://guignolduluxembourg.monsite-orange.fr; tickets €4.70; usually 3.15pm Wed, 11am & 3.15pm Sat & Sun, daily during school holidays). Show times can vary; check the program online and arrive half an hour early.

Orchards

Dozens of apple varieties grow in the **orchards** (Map p418). Bees have produced honey in the nearby apiary, the **Rucher du Luxembourg** (Map p418), since the 19th century. The annual Fête du Miel (Honey Festival), in late September, offers two days of tasting and buying the sweet harvest in the ornate **Pavillon Davioud** (Map p418; 55bis rue d'Assas).

Palais du Luxembourg

Since 1958 the **Palais du Luxembourg** (Map p418; rue de Vaugirard) has housed the **Sénat** (Upper House of French Parliament; Map p418; 01 44 54 19 49; www.senat.fr; rue de Vaugirard; adult/18-25yr €8/6). It's occasionally visitable by guided tour.

East of the palace is the Italianate **Fontaine des Médici** (Map p418), an ornate fountain built in 1630. During Baron Haussmann's 19th-century reshaping of the roads, it was moved 30m and the pond and dramatic statues of the giant bronze Polyphemus discovering the white-marble lovers Acis and Galatea were added.

Musée du Luxembourg

Prestigious temporary art exhibitions, such as 'Cézanne et Paris', take place in the **Musée du Luxembourg** (Map p418; www.museeduluxembourg.fr; 19 rue de Vaugirard, 6e; adult/child generally €13.50/9; 10am-8pm Sun-Thu, to 10pm Fri & Sat). It was the first French museum to be opened to the public, in 1750, before relocating here in 1886; following closures, it's mounted exhibitions regularly here since 1979.

Around the back of the museum, lemon and orange trees, palms, grenadiers and oleanders shelter from the cold in the palace's **Orangery** (Map p418). Nearby, the heavily guarded **Hôtel du Petit Luxembourg** was where Marie de Médici lived while Palais du Luxembourg was being built. The president of the Senate has called it home since 1825.

PICNICKING

Kiosks and cafes are dotted throughout the park, including places selling fairy (candy) floss. If you're planning on picnicking, forget bringing a blanket – the elegantly manicured lawns are off-limits apart from a small wedge on the southern boundary. Instead, do as Parisians do, and corral one of the iconic green metal chairs (designed in 1923) and find your own favourite part of the park.

The Jardin du Luxembourg plays a pivotal role in Victor Hugo's *Les Misérables*: the novel's lovers Marius and Cosette meet here for the first time.

DINING

For delicious dining and decadent-and-then-some hot chocolate, the salon de thé **Angelina** (Map p418; www.angelina-paris.fr; rue de Vaugirard; snacks €14-25 , mains €23-35; 10am-7.30pm Sun-Thu, to 11.30pm Fri & Sat), whose flagship establishment is beneath the rue de Rivoli's cloisters, has made its long-awaited Left Bank debut with a cafe/restaurant/tearoom adjacent to the Musée du Luxembourg.

TOP SIGHTS

MUSÉE RODIN

Sculptor, painter, sketcher, engraver and collector Auguste Rodin donated his entire collection to the French state in 1908 on the proviso they dedicate his former workshop and showroom, the Hôtel Biron (1730), to displaying his works. The collection, including works by artists Van Gogh and Renoir, is now installed not only in the mansion itself, but in its rose-covered garden. The museum also features fifteen sculptures by Camille Claudel, Rodin's muse and protégé.

The Thinker

The first large-scale cast of Rodin's famous sculpture *The Thinker* (Le Penseur), made in 1902, resides in the garden – the perfect place to contemplate this heroic naked figure conceived by Rodin to represent intellect and poetry (it was originally titled *The Poet*).

The Gates of Hell

The Gates of Hell (La Porte de l'Enfer) was commissioned in 1880 as the entrance for a never-built museum, and Rodin worked on his sculptural masterwork up until his death in 1917. Standing 6m high by 4m wide, its 180 figures comprise an intricate scene from Dante's *Inferno*.

The Kiss

The marble monument to love, *The Kiss* (Le Baiser), was originally part of *The Gates of Hell*. The sculpture's entwined lovers caused controversy on its completion due to Rodin's then-radical approach of depicting women as equal partners in ardour.

DON'T MISS

- Camille Claudel Sculptures
- Collections
- The Thinker
- The Gates of Hell
- The Kiss

PRACTICALITIES

- Map p422
- www.musee-rodin.fr
- 79 rue de Varenne, 7e
- permanent exhibition adult/under 25yr €7/5, garden €1/free
- 10am-5.45pm Tue-Sun
- (wheelchair access)
- M Varenne

TOP SIGHTS

HÔTEL DES INVALIDES

The Hôtel des Invalides was built in the 1670s by Louis XIV to provide housing for 4000 *invalides* (disabled war veterans). On 14 July 1789, a mob forced its way into the building and seized 32,000 rifles before heading on to storm the prison at Bastille and start the French Revolution. At the southern end of the esplanade, laid out between 1704 and 1720, is the final resting place of Napoleon. The Hôtel des Invalides now houses the Musée des Plans-Reliefs, a museum full of scale models of towns, fortresses and châteaux across France.

North of the main courtyard is the **Musée de l'Armée** (Army Museum; Map p422; www.invalides.org; 129 rue de Grenelle, 7e; adult/child €9/free; ⌚10am-6pm Mon & Wed-Sat, to 9pm Tue) – the nation's largest collection on French military history. Sobering wartime footage screens at this army museum, which also has weaponry, flag and medal displays as well as a multimedia area dedicated to Charles de Gaulle.

South of the main courtyard is the **Église du Dôme**, which, with its sparkling golden dome (1677–1735), is one of the finest religious edifices erected under Louis XIV, and was the inspiration for the United States Capitol building. The very extravagant **Tombeau de Napoléon 1er** (Napoleon's Tomb), in the centre of the Église du Dôme, comprises six coffins fitting into one another like a Russian doll.

Also south of the main courtyard is the **Église St-Louis des Invalides**, once used by soldiers.

Within the Hôtel des Invalides, the esoteric **Musée des Plans-Reliefs** is full of scale models of towns, fortresses and châteaux across France.

DON'T MISS

- Musée de l'Armée
- Église du Dôme
- Tombeau de Napoléon 1er
- Église St-Louis des Invalides
- Musée des Plans-Reliefs

PRACTICALITIES

- Map p422
- www.invalides.org
- 129 rue de Grenelle, 7e
- adult/child under 18yr €9/free
- ⌚10am-6pm Mon & Wed-Sat, 10am-9pm Tue, 10am-6.30pm Sun Apr-Sep, to 5pm Oct-Mar, closed 1st Mon of month
- Ⓜ Invalides

SIGHTS

St-Germain

MUSÉE NATIONAL EUGÈNE DELACROIX — RESIDENCE MUSEUM

Map p418 (www.musee-delacroix.fr; 6 rue de Furstemberg, 6e; adult/under 18yr €5/free; 9.30am-5pm Wed-Mon; M Mabillon or St-Germain des Prés) The Eugène Delacroix Museum, in a courtyard off a magnolia-shaded square, was the romantic artist's home and studio at the time of his death in 1863, and contains a collection of his oil paintings, watercolours, pastels and drawings, including many of his more intimate works, such as *An Unmade Bed* (1828) and his paintings of Morocco.

If you want to see Delacroix's major works, pay a visit to the Musée du Louvre or the Musée d'Orsay, or check out his frescoes at Église St-Sulpice.

ÉGLISE ST-SULPICE — CHURCH

Map p418 (www.paroisse-saint-sulpice-paris.org; place St-Sulpice, 6e; 7.30am-7.30pm; M St-Sulpice) In 1646 work started on the twin-towered Church of St Sulpicius and took six architects 150 years to finish. What draws most people to the church is not its striking Italianate façade with two rows of superimposed columns, Counter-Reformation-influenced neoclassical decor or even the frescoes by Delecroix, but its setting for a murderous scene in Dan Brown's *The Da Vinci Code*.

Inside, the church is lined with 21 side chapels. The frescoes in the Chapelle des Sts-Anges (Chapel of the Holy Angels), first to the right as you enter the chapel, depict Jacob wrestling with the angel (to the left) and Michael the Archangel doing battle with Satan (to the right) and were painted by Eugène Delacroix between 1855 and 1861. The monumental, 20m-tall organ loft dates back to 1781. You can hear the organ in its full glory during 10.30am Mass on Sunday or the occasional Sunday-afternoon organ concert.

CHAPELLE NOTRE DAME DE LA MEDAILLE MIRACULEUSE — CHURCH

Map p418 (01 49 54 78 88; www.chapellenotredamedelamedaillemiraculeuse.com; 140 rue du Bac, 6e; 7.45am-1pm & 2.30-7pm Mon & Wed-Sat, 7.45am-7pm Sun; M Rue du Bac or Vaneau) Tucked away at the end of a courtyard across from Le Bon Marché department store, this extraordinary chapel is where, in 1830, the Virgin Mary spoke to 24-year-old Catherine Labouré. In a series of three miraculous apparitions that took place here, the young novice seminary sister was told to have a medal made that would protect and grace those who wore it.

The first Miraculous Medals were made in 1832 – the same year a cholera epidemic plagued Paris – and their popularity spread rapidly as wearers of the medal found themselves miraculously cured or protected from the deadly disease. Devout Roman Catholics around the world still wear the medal today.

Catherine Labouré (1806–76), the eighth child of a Burgundy farmer, was beatified in 1933 and her body moved to a reliquary beneath the altar of Our Lady of the Globe (to the right as you face the main altar) inside the Chapel of Our Lady of the Miraculous Medal.

JARDIN DU LUXEMBOURG — PARK

See p228.

MUSÉE ERNEST HÉBERT — RESIDENCE MUSEUM

Map p418 (www.rmn.fr/Musee-Hebert; 85 rue du Cherche Midi, 6e; 12.30-6pm Mon & Wed-Fri, 2-6pm Sat & Sun; M St-Placide) Portrait painter Ernest Hébert (1817–1908) created likenesses of society people of the Second Empire and the belle époque and was therefore not short of a coin or two. The artist's wonderful 18th-century townhouse and its baubles – not his saccharine, almost cloying portraits – is the drawcard here. The museum was closed for renovations at the time of research.

FREE MUSÉE ATELIER ZADKINE — RESIDENCE MUSEUM

Map p418 (www.zadkine.paris.fr; 100bis rue d'Assas, 6e; free; 10am-6pm Tue-Sun; M Vavin) Russian cubist sculptor Ossip Zadkine (1890–1967) arrived in Paris in 1908 and lived and worked in this cottage for almost 40 years. Zadkine produced an enormous catalogue of sculptures made from clay, stone, bronze and wood. The museum covers his life and work; one room displays figures he sculpted in contrasting woods including walnut, pear, ebony, acacia, elm and oak.

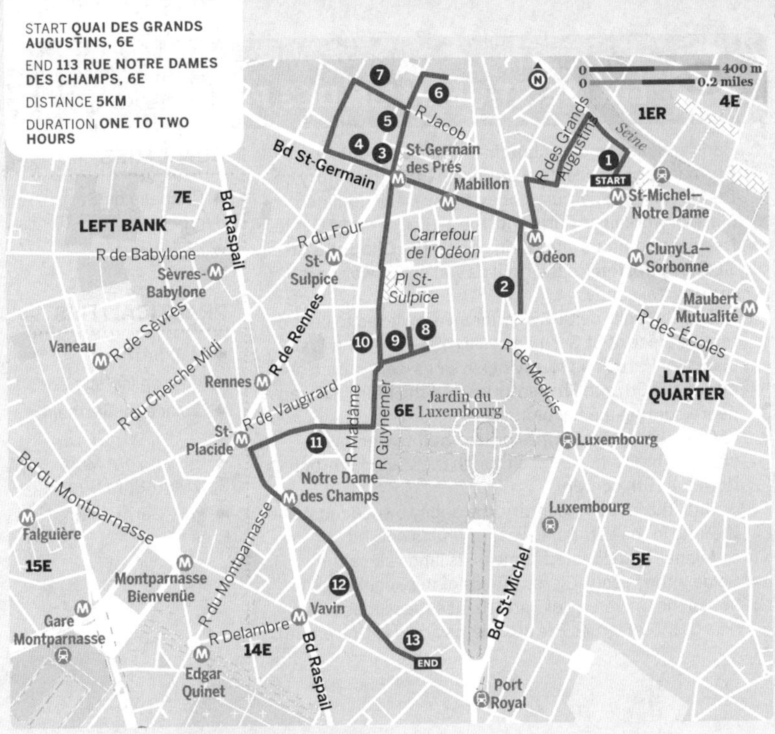

Neighbourhood Walk

Left Bank Literary Loop

To retrace the footsteps of Left Bank literary luminaries, begin by following the Seine west past the *bouquinistes* (secondhand booksellers) that Ernest Hemingway loved. The 'Beat Hotel', now the **1 Relais Hôtel du Vieux Paris**, is where Allen Ginsberg, Jack Kerouac, William S Burroughs and others holed up in the 1950s.

At **2 12 rue de l'Odéon** stood the original Shakespeare & Company bookshop where owner Sylvia Beach lent books to Hemingway, and edited, retyped and published *Ulysses* for James Joyce in 1922. It was closed during the occupation when Beach refused to sell her last copy of Joyce's *Finnegan's Wake* to a Nazi officer.

Bd St-Germain's **3 Les Deux Magots** and **4 Café de Flore** were favourite cafes of post-war Left Bank intellectuals Jean-Paul Sartre and Simone de Beauvoir.

At **5 36 rue Bonaparte** Henry Miller stayed in a 5th-floor mansard room in 1930, which he later wrote about in *Letters to Emil* (1989).

The **6 L'Hôtel**, the former Hôtel d'Alsace, is where Oscar Wilde died in 1900.

Hemingway spent his first night in Paris in Room 14 of the **7 Hôtel d'Angleterre** in 1921.

In 1925 William Faulkner stayed several months at what's now the posh **8 Hôtel Luxembourg Parc**, and Hemingway's last years in Paris were at **9 6 rue Férou**. F Scott and Zelda Fitzgerald lived at **10 58 rue de Vaugirard** in 1928, near **11** 27 rue de Fleurus where Gertrude Stein lived and entertained artists and writers including Matisse, Picasso, Braque, Gauguin, Fitzgerald, Hemingway and Ezra Pound.

Pound lived at **12 70bis rue Notre Dame des Champs** in a flat filled with Japanese paintings and packing crates, while Hemingway's first apartment in this area was above a sawmill at **13 113 rue Notre Dames des Champs**.

TOP SIGHTS
ÉGLISE ST-GERMAIN DES PRÉS

Paris' oldest standing church, the Romanesque St Germanus of the Fields, was built in the 11th century on the site of a 6th-century abbey and was the dominant place of worship in Paris until the arrival of Notre Dame. Despite numerous alterations since, the **Chapelle de St-Symphorien** (to the right as you enter) was part of the original abbey.

The Chapelle de St-Symphorien is believed to be the resting place of St Germanus (AD 496–576), the first bishop of Paris. The Merovingian kings were buried here during the 6th and 7th centuries, but their tombs disappeared during the Revolution.

Over the western entrance, the **bell tower** has changed little since 990, although the spire dates only from the 19th century.

Until the late 17th century, the abbey owned most of the land in the Left Bank west of what's now bd St-Michel, and donated some of its lands along the Seine – the Préaux Clercs (Fields of the Scholars) – to house the University of Paris (hence the names of the nearby streets, rues Pré aux Clercs and de l'Université).

DON'T MISS

- Chapelle de St-Symphorien
- Bell Tower

PRACTICALITIES

- Map p418
- www.eglise-sgp.org
- 3 place St-Germain des Prés, 6e
- 8am-7pm Mon-Sat, 9am-8pm Sun
- St-Germain des Prés

FONDATION DUBUFFET ART MUSEUM

Map p422 (www.dubuffetfondation.com; 137 rue de Sèvres, 6e; adult/under 10yr €6/free; 2-6pm Mon-Fri Sep-Jul; Duroc) Situated in a lovely 19th-century *hôtel particulier* (private mansion) at the end of a courtyard, the foundation houses the collection of Jean Dubuffet (1901–85), chief of the Art Brut school (a term he coined to describe all works of artistic expression not officially recognised). Much of his work is incredibly modern and expressive.

MUSÉE DE LA MONNAIE DE PARIS MINT MUSEUM

Map p418 (01 40 46 55 35; www.monnaiedeparis.fr; 11 quai de Conti, 6e; Pont Neuf) Closed for renovations at the time of writing, the Parisian Mint Museum traces the history of French coinage from antiquity onwards, with displays that help to bring to life this otherwise niche subject. It's housed in the 18th-century royal mint, the Hôtel de la Monnaie, which is still used by the Ministry of Finance to produce commemorative medals and coins.

The overhaul of this sumptuous neoclassical building with one of the longest façades on the Seine is slated to incorporate triple Michelin starred chef Guy Savoy's new cafe and restaurant.

INSTITUT DE FRANCE HISTORIC BUILDING

Map p418 (www.institut-de-france.fr; 23 quai de Conti, 6e; Mabillon or Pont Neuf) The French Institute, created in 1795, brought together five of France's academies of arts and sciences. The most famous of these is the **Académie Française** (Map p418; French Academy), founded in 1635 by Cardinal Richelieu. Its 40 members, known as the Immortels, have the Herculean (some say impossible) task of safeguarding the purity of the French language.

The domed building housing the institute, across the Seine from the Louvre's eastern end, is a masterpiece of French neoclassical architecture.

BIBLIOTHÈQUE MAZARINE LIBRARY

Map p418 (01 44 41 44 06; www.bibliotheque-mazarine.fr; 23 quai de Conti, 6e; 2-day admission pass free, annual membership/10-visit carnet to borrow books €15/7.50; 10am-6pm Mon-Fri; Mabillon or Pont Neuf) Within the Institut de France, the Mazarine Library is France's oldest public library, founded in 1643. You can visit the bust-lined, late-17th-century reading room or consult the library's collection of 500,000 volumes, using a two-day pass obtained by leaving your ID at the office to the left of the entrance; bring two photos for annual membership or the 10-visit *carnet* (book of tickets).

Les Invalides

MUSÉE MAILLOL-FONDATION DINA VIERNY SCULPTURE MUSEUM

Map p422 (www.museemaillol.com; 61 rue de Grenelle, 7e; adult/11-25yr €11/9; ⌚10.30am-7pm Sat-Thu, to 9.30pm Fri; Ⓜ Rue du Bac) This splendid little museum focuses on the work of sculptor Aristide Maillol (1861–1944) and also includes works by Matisse, Gauguin, Kandinsky, Cézanne and Picasso. All are from the private collection of Odessa-born Dina Vierny (b 1915–2009), Maillol's principal model for 10 years from the age of 15. The museum is located in the stunning 18th-century Hôtel Bouchardon.

MUSÉE RODIN MUSEUM, GARDEN

See p230.

HÔTEL DES INVALIDES MONUMENT, MUSUEM

See p231.

ASSEMBLÉE NATIONALE PARLIAMENT

Map p422 (www.assemblee-nationale.fr; 33 quai d'Orsay & 126 rue de l'Université, 7e; Ⓜ Assemblée Nationale or Invalides) The lower house of the French parliament, known as the National Assembly, meets in the 18th-century Palais Bourbon, which fronts the Seine. Tours are available through local deputies, making citizens and residents the only ones eligible. Next door is the Second Empire-style **Ministère des Affaires Étrangères** (Ministry of Foreign Affairs; 37 quai d'Orsay, 7e), built between 1845 and 1855.

MUSÉE D'ORSAY ART MUSEUM

See p224.

MUSÉE DES ÉGOUTS DE PARIS SEWERS

Map p422 (place de la Résistance, 7e; adult/child €4.20/3.40; ⌚11am-5pm Sat-Wed May-Sep, 11am-4pm Sat-Wed Oct-Dec & Feb-Apr; Ⓜ Alma Marceau or RER Pont de l'Alma) Raw sewage flows beneath your feet as you walk through 480m of odoriferous tunnels in this working sewer museum. Exhibitions cover the development of Paris' waste-water disposal system, including its resident rats (an estimated one sewer rat for every Parisian above ground). Enter via a rectangular maintenance hole topped with a kiosk across the street from 93 quai d'Orsay, 7e.

The sewers keep regular hours except – God forbid – when rain threatens to flood the tunnels. Toy rats are sold at its gift shop.

EATING

The picnicking turf of the Jardin de Luxembourg is complemented by some fabulous places to pick up picnic ingredients. But even if it's not picnic weather, the neighbourhood's streets are lined with places to dine as lightly or lavishly as your heart desires – from quintessential Parisian bistros to chic designer restaurants. Rue St-André des Arts and its continuation, rue du Buci, are good hunting grounds, as is the area between Église St-Sulpice and Église St-Germain des Prés.

St-Germain

TOP CHOICE **BOUILLON RACINE** BRASSERIE €€

Map p418 (☎01 44 32 15 60; www.bouillonracine.com; 3 rue Racine, 6e; ⌚noon-11pm; Ⓜ Cluny-La Sorbonne) Inconspicuously situated in a quiet street, this heritage-listed 1906 art nouveau 'soup kitchen', with mirrored walls, floral motifs and ceramic tiling, was built in 1906 to feed market workers. Despite the magnificent interior, the food – inspired by age-old recipes – is by no means an afterthought.

Superbly executed dishes include stuffed, spit-roasted suckling pig, pork shank in Rodenbach red beer, and scallops and shrimps with lobster coulis. Finish off your foray in gastronomic history with an old-fashioned sherbet.

ZE KITCHEN GALERIE GASTRONOMIC €€€

Map p418 (☎01 44 32 00 32; www.zekitchengalerie.fr; 4 rue des Grands Augustins, 6e; lunch/dinner menus €26.50/65; ⌚lunch & dinner Mon-Fri, dinner Sat; Ⓜ St-Michel) William Ledeuil's passion for Southeast Asian travel shows in the feisty dishes he creates in his

Michelin-starred glass-box kitchen. Hosting three to five art exhibitions a year, the restaurant/gallery's menu is a vibrant feast of broths loaded with Thai herbs and coconut milk, meat and fish cooked à *la plancha* and inventive desserts like white chocolate and wasabi ice cream.

HUÎTERIE REGIS OYSTER BAR €€

Map p418 (☎01 44 41 10 07; 3 rue de Montfaucon, 6e; dozen oysters, glass wine & coffee from €26; ⏱11am-midnight Tue-Sun; Ⓜ Mabillon) Hip, trendy, tiny and white, this is *the* spot for slurping oysters on crisp winter days. They come only by the dozen, along with fresh bread and butter, but wash them down with a glass of chilled Muscadet and *voilà,* one perfect lunch. Only two tables loiter on the pavement outside; otherwise it's all inside.

CUISINE DE BAR SANDWICH BAR €

Map p418 (8 rue du Cherche Midi, 6e; dishes €7.50-13; ⏱8.30am-7pm Tue-Sat; 📶; Ⓜ Sèvres-Babylone) As next-door neighbour to one of Paris' most famous bakers, this is not any old sandwich bar. Rather, it is an ultrachic spot to lunch between designer boutiques on open sandwiches cut from celebrated Poilâne (p239) bread and fabulously topped with gourmet goodies such as foie gras, smoked duck, gooey St-Marcellin cheese and Bayonne ham.

BRASSERIE LIPP BRASSERIE €€

Map p418 (☎01 45 48 53 91; 151 bd St-Germain, 6e; mains €17-24; ⏱11.45am-12.45am; Ⓜ St-Germain des Prés) Waiters in black waistcoats, bow ties and long white aprons serve brasserie favourites like *choucroute garnie* and *jarret de porc aux lentilles* (pork knuckle with lentils) at this celebrated wood-panelled establishment. Opened by Léonard Lipp in 1880, it achieved immortality when Hemingway sang its praises in *A Moveable Feast.* Arrive hungry: salads aren't allowed as meals.

LA BOTTEGA DI PASTAVINO ITALIAN €

Map p418 (18 rue de Buci, 6e; dishes €4-5.50; ⏱9am-8.15pm Mon-Sat; Ⓜ St-Germain des Prés) Crammed with imported Italian groceries – marinated capsicums, artichokes and olives, dozens of varieties of dried and fresh pasta, white truffle cream and bottles of Italian *vino* – this Aladdin's Cave–style deli also dishes up freshly cooked pasta, salads, and piping-hot, authentic panini for lunch on the run.

LA JACOBINE TEAROOM €€

Map p418 (☎01 46 34 15 95; www.lajacobine.com; 59-61 rue St-André des Arts, 6e; mains €16-21; ⏱5-11.30pm Mon, noon-11.30pm Tue-Sun; Ⓜ Odéon) Old-world tearoom/busy lunch spot La Jacobine is packed to the rafters by noon for its homemade tarts, giant-sized salads and crêpes. Its lovely location inside Cour du Commerce St-André, a glass-covered passageway built in 1735 to link two Jeu de Paume (old-style tennis) courts, makes it all the more romantic.

POLIDOR TRADITIONAL FRENCH €€

Map p418 (☎01 43 26 95 34; www.polidor.com; 41 rue Monsieur le Prince, 6e; menus from €22; ⏱lunch & dinner; Ⓜ Odéon) A meal at this quintessentially Parisian *crèmerie-restaurant*

PARIS' OLDEST RESTAURANT & CAFE

St-Germain claims both the city's oldest restaurant and its oldest cafe.

À la Petite Chaise (Map p418; ☎01 42 22 13 35; www.alapetitechaise.fr; 36 rue de Grenelle; lunch/dinner menus from €27/33; ⏱lunch & dinner Mon-Sat; Ⓜ Sèvres-Babylone) hides behind an iron gate that's been here since it opened in 1680, when wine merchant Georges Rameau served food to the public to go with his wares. Classical decor and cuisine to match (onion soup, foie gras, duck, lamb and unexpected delights like truffled asparagus) make it worth a visit above and beyond its history.

Hot on the heels of À la Petite Chaise's opening, **Le Procope** (Map p418; www.procope.com; 13 rue de l'Ancienne Comédie; 2-/3-course menus from €20.90/27.90; ⏱11.30am-midnight; 👪; Ⓜ Odéon) welcomed its first patrons in 1686, and was frequented by Voltaire, Molière and Balzac et al. Its chandeliered interior also has an entrance onto the glass-roofed passageway Cour du Commerce St-André (c 1735). Along with house specialties like coq au vin, calf's head casserole in veal stock, and calf kidneys with violet mustard, it serves its own sorbets and ice creams, which it's been making here since 1686 too.

FAUBOURG ST-GERMAIN

In the 18th century, Faubourg St-Germain – a formal world of exquisite ironwork, gold leaf and conventional manners west of St-Germain des Prés – was Paris' most fashionable neighbourhood. French nobility moved across the river from the more crowded, polluted Marais and built magnificent *hôtels particuliers* (private mansions), particularly around rue de Lille, rue de Grenelle and rue de Varenne. Balzac captures its aristocratic way of life in his novel *La Duchesse de Langeais*.

After the Revolution, many of these mansions were turned into national institutions, and there's now an overdose of embassies and government ministries; **Hôtel Matignon** (Map p422; 57 rue de Varenne, 7e) has been the official residence of the French prime minister since the start of the Fifth Republic (1958). Rodin worked and exhibited in the palatial Hôtel Biron (c 1730), now the Musée Rodin, and it was to the stylish pad at No 53 that Edith Wharton moved in 1910 to write *Le Temps de l'Innocence* (The Age of Innocence).

But the area's finest example of timeless extravagance is **5bis rue Verneuil** (Map p418) – the house where Parisian singer, sexpot and provocateur Serge Gainsbourg lived from 1969 until his death in 1991. Neighbours have long since given up scrubbing off the reappearing graffiti and messages from fans.

is like a trip to Victor Hugo's Paris: the restaurant and its decor date from 1845. *Menus* of tasty, family-style French cuisine ensure a never-ending stream of diners eager to sample *bœuf bourguignon*, *blanquette de veau à l'ancienne* (veal in white sauce) and Polidor's famous *tarte Tatin*. Expect to wait.

ROGER LA GRENOUILLE — TRADITIONAL FRENCH €€

Map p418 (☎01 56 24 24 34; 26-28 rue des Grands Augustins, 6e; lunch/dinner menus from €19/24; ⏰lunch Tue-Sat, dinner Mon-Sat; Ⓜ St-Michel) Nine varieties of frogs' legs are served at the time-worn institution Roger the Frog. À la Provençale is with tomato, Orientale sees the pin-sized legs spiced with pine kernels and fresh mint, while Indienne has a splash of curry. If you're squeamish about devouring Roger and his mates, dishes like roast pheasant with dried figs are also on the menu.

Frog sculptures and statues scatter throughout the restaurant, along with B&W pictures of 1920s Paris on the whitewashed walls and an array of old lamps illuminating the low sepia-coloured ceiling.

LE PARC AUX CERFS — MODERN FRENCH €€

Map p418 (☎01 43 54 87 83; 50 rue Vavin, 6e; 2-/3-course menus €19.50/26; ⏰lunch & dinner; Ⓜ Notre Dame de Champs) Evening reservations are essential at this small, stylish restaurant known for its creative dishes: two-cabbage salad, *tartare de saumon* (raw chopped salmon) with pink peppercorns and grapefruit, goat's cheese and almonds and so on. Elegant air and friendly service aside, *the pièce de résistance* has to be its delightful patio garden out back.

The name Parc aux Cerfs was given to the clearings used as French aristocracy hunting fields prior to the French Revolution.

GROM — ICE CREAM €

Map p418 (www.grom.fr; 81 rue de Seine, 6e; ice cream from €3.50; ⏰1pm-10.30pm Mon-Wed, 1pm-midnight Thu-Sat, noon-10.30pm Sun; 👪; Ⓜ Mabillon) Flavours change monthly at France's only outlet of prestigious Turin gelato-maker Grom. All include sustainably sourced, high-grade ingredients like Syrian pistachio nuts and Venezuelan chocolate chips.

PIZZA CHIC — PIZZA €€

Map p418 (☎01 45 48 30 38; www.pizzachic.fr; 13 rue Mézières, 6e; pizza €19-22; ⏰lunch & dinner; 👪; Ⓜ St-Sulpice) The antithesis of fast-food chains-that-shall-not-be-mentioned, Pizza Chic's cast iron walls and crisp white tablecloths set the scene for rarefied pizzas like artichoke with parmesan aged for two years, accompanied by a lush wine list. *Apertivi* and *antipasti* choices are many; desserts include a rich panna cotta and even richer tiramisù.

CASA BINI — ITALIAN €€

Map p418 (☎01 46 34 05 60; www.casabini.fr; 36 rue Gregoire de Tours, 6e; 2-/3-course lunch menus €23/27, mains €16-34; ⏰lunch & dinner;

; Odéon) At this highly recommended Italian restaurant, homemade pasta is cooked to al dente perfection and children are treated like gods. Dishes span squid and creamed courgette soup, *tagliolini* studded with white summer truffles or a classic veal *saltimbocca* (veal escalope flavoured with ham, thyme and sage).

KGB FUSION €€

Map p418 (01 46 33 00 85; http://zekitchen-galerie.fr; 25 rue des Grands Augustins, 6e; 2-/3-course lunch menus €27/34, mains €27-32; lunch & dinner Tue-Sat; St-Michel) Overtly art gallery in feel, KGB ('Kitchen Galerie Bis', in reference to **Ze Kitchen Galerie**) draws a hip crowd for its casual platters of Asian-influenced *hors d'œvres*, creative pastas like *orecchiette* studded with octopus, squid and crab, and mains spanning roast pigeon with ginger and cranberry condiment, suckling lamb and grilled seabass with lemongrass and mandarin dressing.

LE PETIT ZINC BRASSERIE €€

Map p418 (01 42 86 61 00; www.petit-zinc.com; 11 rue St-Benoît, 6e; 2-/3-course menus €21/28.50, seafood platters from €24; noon-midnight; St-Germain des Prés) Not a 'little bar' as its name would suggest, but a large, wonderful brasserie serving mountains of fresh seafood, traditional French cuisine and regional specialities from the south-west in art nouveau splendour. That said, the term 'brasserie' is used loosely here; you'll feel more like you're in a starred restaurant, so book a table in advance and dress accordingly.

CHEZ ALLARD BISTRO €€

Map p418 (01 43 26 48 23; 41 rue St-André des Arts, 6e; lunch menus €27.90, mains €21-40; lunch & dinner; St-Michel) Staff couldn't be kinder or more professional at this Left Bank favourite, even during its enormously busy lunchtime. The food is superb: try a dozen snails, some *cuisses de grenouilles* (frogs' legs) or *un poulet de Bresse* (France's most fêted chicken, from Burgundy) for two. Reservations are essential. Enter from 1 rue de l'Éperon.

COSI SANDWICH BAR €

Map p418 (54 rue de Seine, 6e; sandwich menus €10-15; noon-11pm; ; Odéon) An institution in the 6e for a quick, cheap eat in its upstairs dining room or to take to a park, Cosi might just be Paris' most imaginative sandwich maker, with sandwich names like Stonker, Tom Dooley and Naked Willi chalked on the blackboard. Classical music plays in the background and homemade foccacia bread is still warm from the oven.

GIRAUDET LYONNAIS €

Map p418 (www.giraudet.fr; 5 rue Princesse, 6e; menus €10.50-13.60; 10.30am-4pm Mon-Fri, to 7pm Sat; Mabillon) Newly arrived from Lyon, where its name is synonymous with contemporary takes on Lyonnais staples, this sleek spot specialises in soups and *quenelles* (feather-light flour, egg and cream dumplings). There's also a take-away **Giraudet Boutique** (Map p418; 16 rue Mabillon, 6e; 2.30-7pm Mon, 10am-2pm & 2-7.30pm Tue-Fri, 10am-7.30pm Sat; Mabillon) around the corner.

LA RÔTISSERIE D'EN FACE MODERN FRENCH €€

Map p418 (01 43 26 40 98; www.jacques-cagna.com; 2 rue Christine, 6e; lunch menus €23-37, dinner mains €20-38; lunch Mon-Fri, dinner Mon-Sat; St-Michel or Odéon) Situated *en face* (opposite) Jacques Cagna's eponymous (and, until 2012, Michelin-starred) restaurant on rue des Grands Augustins, his less expensive alternative is, in fact, better. Dine between mustard-coloured walls on superb fish (eg deep-fried plaice with seaweed tartare) and meat (wild boar in red wine stew) accompanied by six-grain bread baked on the premises.

LE CHERCHE MIDI ITALIAN €€

Map p418 (01 45 48 27 44; www.lecherchemidi.fr; 22 rue du Cherche Midi, 6e; mains €16; lunch & dinner; Sèvres- Babylone) This popular restaurant with red awning and classic interior buzzes all the more at weekends when Saturday shoppers and Sunday strollers make a beeline for its small sunlit pavement terrace. Cuisine is classic and elegant. Get here by 12.30pm and 8pm respectively to be sure of getting a table.

LE CHRISTINE MODERN FRENCH €€

Map p418 (01 40 51 71 64; www.restaurantlechristine.com; 1 rue Christine, 6e; lunch/dinner menus from €22/35; lunch & dinner Mon-Fri; St-Michel or Odéon) Behind its pumpkin-coloured façade with a giant fork stuck over the door, wood-beamed ceilings and stone walls hung with contemporary artwork set a suitably Left Bank scene for dining on pared-down French classics.

POILÂNE BOULANGERIE €

Map p418 (www.poilane.fr; 8 rue du Cherche Midi, 6e; ⌚7.15am-8.15pm Mon-Sat; Ⓜ Sèvres-Babylone) Pierre Poilâne opened his *boulangerie* upon arriving from Normandy in 1932. Today his granddaughter runs the company, which still turns out wood-fired, rounded sourdough loaves made with stone-milled flour and Guérande sea salt.

GÉRARD MULOT PATISSERIE €

Map p418 (www.gerard-mulot.com; 76 rue de Seine, 6e; ⌚6.45am-8pm; Ⓜ Odéon or Mabillon) Fruit tarts (peach, lemon, apple), *tarte normande* (apple cake) and *clafoutis* (cherry flan) are among this celebrated patisserie's specialties.

LE COMPTOIR DU RELAIS BISTRO €€€

Map p418 (☎01 44 27 07 97; 9 Carrefour de l'Odéon, 6e; dinner menus €55, mains €12-45; ⌚lunch & dinner; Ⓜ Odéon) Simply known as Le Comptoir (the Counter) among the in crowd, this gourmet bistro has provoked a real stir ever since it opened. The culinary handiwork of top chef Yves Camdeborde, it cooks up seasonal bistro dishes with a seriously creative and gourmet twist like fancy asparagus and foie gras salad.

Bagging a table at lunchtime is just about doable providing you're here at 12.30pm sharp, but forget evening dining – more gastronomic than at lunch – unless you've reserved your table *weeks* in advance.

LES ÉDITEURS CAFE €€

Map p418 (☎01 43 26 67 76; 4 Carrefour de l'Odéon, 6e; 2-/3-course menus €19.50/24.50; ⌚8am-2am; Ⓜ Odéon) A hybrid cafe, restaurant, library (there are more than 5000 books on hand), bar and *salon de thé*, Les Éditeurs' floor-to-ceiling windows make it a great place to watch *la vie germanopratin* (yes, there is a descriptor for St-Germain des Prés) goings-on. Breakfasts and weekend brunch are big here.

Outside, a statue of **Georges Danton** (Map p418), a leader of the Revolution and later one of its guillotined victims, stands head intact.

LADURÉE PATISSERIE €

Map p418 (21 rue Bonaparte, 7e; ⌚8.30am-7.30pm Mon-Fri, 8.30am-8.30pm Sat, 10am-7.30pm Sun; Ⓜ St-Germain des Prés) Queues stretch around the block from the St-Germain branch of famous patisserie Ladurée for its pricey but picture-perfect delicacies, including its magnificent rainbow of *macarons*, and *le baiser Ladurée* (layered almond cake with strawberries and cream). There's another branch on the Champs Élysées (p95).

LE SALON D'HÉLÈNE GASTRONOMIC €€€

Map p418 (☎01 42 22 00 11; www.helenedarroze.com; 4 rue d'Assas, 6e; lunch/dinner menus from €28/85; ⌚lunch & dinner Tue-Sat; Ⓜ Sèvres-Babylone) Female star chefs are a rarity in Paris, but Hélène Darroze is a stellar exception. These premises house both her elegant Michelin-starred restaurant upstairs and this relaxed downstairs salon renowned for its multicourse tasting *menus*, where dishes reflect Darroze's native southwestern France, such as wood-grilled foie gras.

L'ATELIER DE JOËL ROBUCHON FUSION, GASTRONOMIC €€€

Map p418 (☎01 42 22 56 52; www.restaurants-joel-robuchon.com; 5 rue de Montalembert, 7e; mains €32-67; ⌚lunch & dinner; Ⓜ Rue du Bac) Celebrity chef Joël Robuchon takes diners on a mind-blowing culinary tour of the finer things in French gastronomy, lobster, sardines, foie gras and milk-fed lamb included. Dining is stool-style around a communal U-shaped black lacquer bar in a Japanese-accented dining room with bamboo in glass vases.

CHEZ HANAFOUSA JAPANESE €€

Map p418 (☎01 43 26 50 29; www.hanafousa.com; 4 passage de la Petite Boucherie, 6e; lunch/dinner menus from €13.50/33; ⌚lunch Wed-Sun, dinner daily; Ⓜ St-Germain des Prés) Sit around a steely-topped U-shaped 'hot table' and watch fish, meat, spices, vegetables and herbs chopped, sliced, ground and flamed *teppanyaki*-style before your eyes, and end the show with a flaming vanilla ice-cream fritter or wasabi ice-cream.

FISH LA BOISSONNERIE BISTRO €€

Map p418 (☎01 43 54 34 69; 69 rue de Seine, 6e; lunch menus €26, mains €12.50-19.50; ⌚lunch & dinner Tue-Sun; Ⓜ Mabillon) This former fish shop, with its wonderful old mosaic on the front façade, rustic communal seating and bonhomie, is almost as much a wine bar as a restaurant. Dishes like pork tenderloin with fennel risotto are complemented by outstanding wines.

LE MÂCHON D'HENRI BISTRO €€

Map p418 (☎01 43 29 08 70; 8 rue Guisarde, 6e; menus €35; ⊙lunch & dinner; Ⓜ St-Sulpice or Mabillon) Feisty French staples at this tiny, jam-packed bistro might include Lyonnais *boudin noir aux pommes* (black pudding with apples), Jura *saucisse de Morteau* (a type of sausage) and lentils or tripe cooked Caen-style.

AU PIED DE FOUET BISTRO €

Map p418 (☎01 43 54 87 83; www.aupieddefouet.com; 50 rue St-Benoît, 6e; mains €9-12.50; ⊙Mon-Sat; Ⓜ St-Germain des Prés) Wholly classic bistro dishes such as *entrecôte* (steak), *confit de canard* (duck cooked slowly in its own fat) and *foie de volailles sauté* (pan-fried chicken livers) at this busy bistro are astonishingly good value. Round off your meal with a *tarte Tatin*, wine-soaked prunes or bowl of *fromage blanc* (a cross between yoghurt, sour cream and cream cheese).

Les Invalides

L'ARPÈGE GASTRONOMIC €€€

Map p422 (☎01 47 05 09 06; www.alain-passard.com; 84 rue de Varenne, 7e; menus from €120; ⊙lunch & dinner Mon-Fri; Ⓜ Varenne) Triple Michelin-starred chef Alain Passard specialises in vegetables and inspired desserts like his signature tomatoes stuffed with a veritable orchard of a dozen dried and fresh fruits and served with aniseed ice cream. Book at least two weeks ahead.

LA GRANDE ÉPICERIE LE COMPTOIR PICNIC CAFETERIA €

Map p422 (www.lagrandeepicerie.fr; 26 rue de Sèvres, 6e; dishes €8.50-13.50; ⊙8.30am-8pm Mon-Sat; 🚸; Ⓜ Sèvres-Babylone) Hover around the bar in the food hall of Le Bon Marché department store over a wok-cooked hot dish, design your own sandwich (bread type and fillings), salad or 11-piece sushi plate. You'll pay marginally less to take the same away; alternatively put together your own gourmet picnic from the food hall.

LES COCOTTES CONTEMPORARY €€

Map p422 (www.leviolondingres.com; 135 rue Ste-Dominique, 7e; 2-/3-course lunch menus €9/15, mains €14-28; ⊙lunch & dinner Mon-Sat; Ⓜ École Militaire or RER Port de l'Alma) Christian Constant's chic concept space is devoted to *cocottes* (casseroles), with a buoyant crowd feasting on inventive seasonal creations cooked to perfection in little black enamel, oven-to-table *cocottes* (casserole dishes). Seating is on bar stools around high tables and it doesn't take reservations: get here at noon sharp or by 7.15pm.

If the queue's out the door, nip a couple of doors down for a drink at Café Constant (p241).

LE SQUARE REGIONAL CUISINE €€

Map p422 (☎01 45 51 09 03; www.restaurant-lesquare.com; 31 rue St-Dominique, 7e; lunch/dinner menus from €19.50/26; ⊙lunch & dinner Mon-Sat; Ⓜ Solférino) The terrace tables along rue Casimir-Périer are the best seats in the house for views of the neighbouring twin-spired Basilique Ste Clotilde, which resembles a mini-Notre Dame. Inside, wood panelled decor and autumnal hued banquettes make an elegant spot to dine on classical dishes with a southwestern accent such as beef with béarnaise sauce and potato gratin.

To drink in the views, the bar opens from 8am to 11pm.

CHEZ LUCIE CARIBBEAN €€

Map p422 (☎01 45 55 08 74; 15 rue Augereau, 7e; lunch/dinner menus from €16/25; ⊙lunch & dinner; Ⓜ École Militaire) The often-staid 7e is the last place you'd expect to find this riotous little Caribbean restaurant. Colourful, closely packed tables, comedic staff, spicy creole *gambas* (prawns) and smoked chicken – and feisty rum punch! – give it a Calypso party atmosphere. Book ahead.

BESNIER BOULANGERIE €

Map p422 (40 rue de Bourgogne, 7e; ⊙7am-8pm Mon-Fri Sep-Jul; Ⓜ Varenne) You can watch baguettes being made through the viewing window of this award-winning *boulangerie/patisserie*.

TANTE MARGUERITE REGIONAL CUISINE €€€

Map p422 (☎01 45 51 79 42; www.bernard-loiseau.com; 5 rue de Bourgogne, 7e; lunch/dinner menus €38/52; ⊙lunch & dinner Mon-Fri; Ⓜ Assemblée Nationale) Opened by one of France's most decorated chefs, the late Bernard Loiseau, and helmed by chef Pedro Gomes, this elegant wood-panelled restaurant celebrates the rich flavours of Burgundy. Immortal Loiseau recipes include snail ragout.

LOCAL KNOWLEDGE

PATRICIA WELLS' CULINARY SHOPPING SECRETS

Cookery teacher and author of *The Food Lover's Guide to Paris*, American Patricia Wells (www.patriciawells.com) has lived, cooked and shopped in Paris since 1980, and is considered to have truly captured the soul of French cuisine.

What is it that makes Paris so wonderful for culinary shopping? The tradition, the quality, the quantity, the atmosphere and physical beauty!

Where do you buy your weekly groceries? All over: the Sunday organic market at Rennes (Marché Raspail) – I love the dried fruits and nuts; Poilâne for bread; Quatrehomme for cheese; and Poissonnerie du Bac for fish.

What about for an extraspecial gourmet meal? I shop regularly at Le Bon Marché's La Grande Épicerie de Paris because it is right down the street from me. But for special meals I always order things in advance and go from shop to shop – La Maison du Chocolat and Pierre Hermé for chocolate and cakes, and La Dernière Goutte for wine. That is the fun of Paris, and of France.

Your top food shopping tip? If you live in Paris, become a *client fidèle* so they reach in the back and give you the best stuff. If you only go once in a while, just smile and be friendly.

A perfect culinary souvenir from Paris? Fragonard, the perfume maker, has a great shop on bd St-Germain. They have a changing selection of *great* things for the home, such as fabulous vases with an Eiffel Tower theme, lovely embroidered napkins with a fish or vegetable theme, great little spoons with a cake or pastry theme. Nothing is very expensive and the offerings change every few months, so you have to pounce when you find something you love. The gift wrapping in gorgeous Fragonard bags is worth it alone!

Interviewed by Nicola Williams

CAFÉ DE L'ALMA — CAFE €€

Map p422 (www.cafe-de-l-alma.com; 5 av Rapp, 7e; mains €7-40; ⌚breakfast, lunch & dinner; MAlma-Marceau or RER Pont de l'Alma) At this table-fronted cafe, the bistro-style fare is as stylish as the contemporary charcoal-, rose- and violet-hued decor.

CAFÉ CONSTANT — NEOBISTRO €€

Map p422 (www.cafeconstant.com; 139 rue Ste-Dominique, 7e; 2-/3-course menus €16/23; ⌚lunch & dinner Tue-Sun; MÉcole Militaire or RER Port de l'Alma) Take a former Michelin-star chef and a dead-simple corner cafe and what do you get? This jam-packed address with original mosaic floor, wooden tables and huge queues every meal time. The pride and joy of Christian and Catherine Constant, it doesn't take reservations but you can enjoy a drink at the bar (or on the pavement outside) while you wait.

Cuisine is creative bistro, mixing old-fashioned grandma staples like *purée de mon enfance* (mashed potato from my childhood) with Sunday treats like foie-gras-stuffed quail and herb-roasted chicken. Les Cocottes (p240), a couple of doors down on the same street, is another Constant hit.

BRASSERIE THOUMIEUX — TRADITIONAL FRENCH €€

Map p422 (☎01 47 05 49 75; www.thoumieux.com; 79 rue St-Dominique; mains €20-23; ⌚noon-midnight; MLa Tour Maubourg) An old-school institution, Thoumieux was founded in 1923, and has been worshipped by generations of diners ever since for its menu of duck thighs, veal and snails and its smooth-as-silk service.

BELLOTA BELLOTA — SPANISH €€

Map p422 (☎01 53 59 96 96; www.bellota-bellota.com; 18 rue Jean Nicot, 7e; mains €21-39; ⌚lunch & dinner to 11pm Tue-Sat; MLa Tour Maubourg) Huge Iberian hams hang in the window and piggy legs dangle from the ceiling of this fabulously tiled Spanish-style bar/cafe. It's a perfect spot for lunch before or after the Musée d'Orsay, an aperitif at the end of the day or to pick up caviar, smoked salmon and cold meats to take away.

MAMIE GÂTEAUX — TEAROOM €

Map p422 (www.mamie-gateaux.com; 66-70 rue du Cherche Midi, 6e; lunch €10-15; ⌚11.30am-6pm Tue-Sat; MSt-Placide or Sèvres-Babylone) Screened by lace curtains and filled with *brocante* (secondhand) furniture, this retro tearoom positively heaves at lunchtime, as the electrifying buzz of shoppers tucking into homemade quiches, savoury cakes, tarts and salads testifies. The ratatouille-and-mozzarella tart is a treat.

BOULANGERIE-PÂTISSERIE STÉPHANE SECCO BOULANGERIE €

Map p422 (20 rue Jean Nicot, 7e; 8am-8.30pm Tue-Sat; MLa Tour-Maubourg) Don't miss Stéphane Secco's signature *Paris-Brest* (wheel-shaped choux pastry with butter cream and almonds, which was created in 1891 to commemorate the bicycle race between Paris and Brest in Brittany), delicate *madeleines* (traditional lemon-flavoured shell-shaped cakes) and zero-fat cheesecake (yes, really).

LA PÂTISSERIE DES RÊVES PATISSERIE €

Map p422 (www.lapatisseriedesreves.com; 93 rue du Bac, 7e; 10am-8.30pm Tue-Sat, 8.30am-2pm Sun; MRue du Bac) The most extraordinary cakes, far too beautiful to eat, are showcased beneath glass domes at this Patisserie of Dreams of big-name *pâtissier* Philippe Conticini. Each month cooks up a different fruit tart – banana in January, almond in March, purple figs and quince in November and so on.

CAFÉ DE L'ESPLANADE FUSION €€€

Map p422 (01 47 05 38 80; 52 rue Fabert, 7e; starters €15-20, mains €20-44; lunch & dinner; MLa Tour Maubourg) An address to impress (so dress to impress), the hobnobbing Café de l'Esplanade is the only cafe-restaurant on the magnificent Esplanade des Invalides. No *menus* – just à la carte.

RUE CLER MARKET €

Map p422 (rue Cler, 7e; 8am-7pm Tue-Sat, 8am-noon Sun; MÉcole Militaire) Pick up fresh bread, sandwich fillings, pastries and wine for a picnic along the lively market street rue Cler, which buzzes with local shoppers, especially on weekends.

MARCHÉ RASPAIL MARKET €

Map p422 (bd Raspail, btwn rue de Rennes & rue du Cherche Midi, 6e; regular market 7am-2.30pm Tue & Fri, organic market 9am-3pm Sun; MRennes) A traditional open-air market on Tuesday and Friday, Marché Raspail is especially popular on Sundays when it's filled with organic produce.

POISSONNERIE DU BAC SEAFOOD €

Map p422 (69 rue du Bac, 7e; 9am-1pm & 4-7.30pm Tue-Sat, 9.30am-1pm Sun; MRue du Bac) Self-caterers shouldn't miss this superb aquamarine- and cobalt-tiled fishmonger. Even if you don't have access to a kitchen in Paris, the fish, scallops, prawns, crabs and other crustaceans laid out on beds of crushed ice constitute a visual feast.

DRINKING & NIGHTLIFE

St-Germain's Carrefour de l'Odéon has a cluster of lively bars and cafes. Rue de Buci, rue St-André des Arts and rue de l'Odéon enjoy a fair slice of night action with their arty cafes and busy pubs, while place St-Germain des Prés buzzes with the pavement terraces of fabled literary cafes. Students pile into the bars and pubs on atmospheric 'rue de la soif' (street of thirst), aka rue Princesse. An indisputable day rather than night venue, government ministries and embassies outweigh drinking venues hands-down in Les Invalides.

St-Germain

TOP CHOICE LES DEUX MAGOTS CAFE

Map p418 (www.lesdeuxmagots.fr; 170 bd St-Germain, 6e; 7.30am-1am; MSt-Germain des Prés) If ever there were a cafe that summed up St-Germain des Prés' early-20th-century literary scene, it's this former hang-out of anyone who was anyone. You will spend *beaucoup* to sip a coffee in a wicker chair on the terrace shaded by dark-green awnings and geraniums spilling from window boxes, but it's an undeniable piece of Parisian history.

If you're feeling decadent, order its famous hot chocolate, served in porcelain jugs. The name refers to the two *magots* (grotesque figurines) of Chinese dignitaries at the entrance.

TOP CHOICE AU SAUVIGNON WINE BAR

Map p418 (80 rue des Saintes Pères, 7e; 8.30am-10pm; MSèvres-Babylone) There's no more authentic *bar à vin* than this. Grab a table in the evening sun or head to the quintessential bistro interior, with an original zinc bar, tightly packed tables and hand-painted ceiling celebrating French viticultural tradition. Order a plate of *casse-croûtes au pain Poilâne* – toast with ham, pâté, terrine, smoked salmon, foie gras and so on.

BRASSERIE O'NEIL MICROBREWERY

Map p418 (www.oneilbar.fr; 20 rue des Canettes, 6e; ⏲noon-2am; Ⓜ St-Sulpice or Mabillon) Paris' first microbrewery was opened by a French restaurateur and French brewer over two decades ago, and still brews four fabulous beers (blond, amber, bitter brown and citrusy white) on the premises. Soak them up with thin-crusted *flammekueches* (Alsatian pizzas) – in a nod to the brasserie's name, there's an Irish version with cheddar and bacon.

CAFÉ DE FLORE CAFE

Map p418 (www.cafedeflore.fr; 172 bd St-Germain, 6e; ⏲7am-1.30am; St-Germain des Prés) The red upholstered benches, mirrors and marble walls at this art deco landmark haven't changed much since the days when Jean-Paul Sartre and Simone de Beauvoir essentially set up office here, writing in its warmth during the Nazi occupation. It also hosts a monthly English-language philo-café session (p34).

LES ETAGES ST-GERMAIN BAR

Map p418 (5 rue de Buci, 6e; ⏲noon-2am; Ⓜ Odéon) Busy and bustling on shop-lined rue de Buci, this shabby-chic terrace bar with retro stools makes a fabulous people-watching pit stop between boutiques. Grab a coffee or summer-time strawberry mojito in the sun, or plump for happy hour (3pm to 8pm) when the price of cocktails plummets.

LE PRÉ BAR

Map p418 (www.cafelepreparis.com; 4-6 rue du Four; ⏲24-hr; Ⓜ Mabillon) Mauve-and-orange wicker chairs line the terrace of this hip drinking spot, while inside the chrome-and-laminex bar resembles a 1950s Airstream trailer.

CUBANA CAFÉ COCKTAIL BAR

Map p418 (www.cubanacafe.com; 47 rue Vavin, 6e; ⏲10.30am-4am; Ⓜ Vavin) A post-work crowd sinks into leather armchairs beneath oil paintings of daily life in Cuba for a huge range of Cuban cocktails made with Havana rum and regular live Cuban music (check the program online).

CAFÉ LA PALETTE CAFE

Map p418 (www.cafelapaletteparis.com; 43 rue de Seine, 6e; ⏲6.30am-2am Mon-Sat; Ⓜ Mabillon) In the heart of gallery land, this *fin-de-siècle* cafe and erstwhile stomping ground of Paul Cézanne and Georges Braque attracts a grown-up set of fashion people and local art dealers. Its summer terrace is beautiful.

PRESCRIPTION COCKTAIL CLUB COCKTAIL BAR

Map p418 (www.prescriptioncocktailclub.com; 23 rue Mazarine, 6e; ⏲7pm-1am Mon-Thu, 7pm-4am Fri & Sat; Ⓜ Odéon) With bowler and flat-top hats as lampshades and a 1930s speakeasy New York air to the place, this club – one in a trio run by the same successful team as Curio Parlor and Experimental – is very Parisian-cool. Getting past the doorperson can be tough but, once in, it's friendliness and old-fashioned cocktails all round. Watch its Facebook page for events such as Mad Hatters pyjama parties.

LE ZÉRO DE CONDUITE BAR

Map p418 (☎01 46 34 26 35; www.zerodeconduite.fr; 14 rue Jacob, 6e; ⏲8.30pm-1.30am Mon-Thu, 6pm-2am Fri & Sat, 9pm-1am Sun; Ⓜ Odéon) In the house where Richard Wagner lived briefly in the 1840s, Le Zéro De Conduite goes all out to rekindle your infancy, serving cocktails in *biberons* (baby bottles) and throwing *concours de grimaces* (face-pulling competitions), with cards, dice and board games. Book ahead for a table.

L'URGENCE BAR BAR

Map p418 (www.urgencebar.com; 45 rue Monsieur-le-Prince, 6e; ⏲9pm-4am Tue-Sat; Ⓜ Odéon or RER Luxembourg) At this medical-themed 'emergency room' just south of the École de Médecine, the future doctors of France imbibe luridly coloured liquor from babies' bottles and test tubes, loosen their stethoscopes and point to the 'X-ray art' – making comments like '*Mais non!* Clarisse, that's so not the tibia!'

LA MEZZANINE COCKTAIL BAR

Map p418 (www.alcazar.fr; 62 rue Mazarine, 6e; ⏲7pm-2am; Ⓜ Odéon) Overlooking the sleek restaurant Alcazar, this hip white-and-glass mezzanine bar is narcissistic but alluring, with fancy cocktails, *nouvelle cuisine* dinners and a fashionable supper-club clientele. Wednesday to Saturday, DJs 'pass records' in the corner – this place is famous for its excellent trip-hop/house/lounge music compilations.

LE 10 PUB

Map p418 (10 rue de l'Odéon, 6e; ⌚6pm-2am; Ⓜ Odéon) A local institution, the cellar pub 'Le Dix' is plastered with posters and is a student favourite, not least for its cheap sangria. An eclectic selection emerges from the jukebox – everything from jazz and the Doors to traditional French *chansons* (à la Édith Piaf). It's the ideal spot for plotting the next revolution or conquering a lonely heart.

KILÀLI TEAROOM

Map p418 (3-5 rue des Quatre Vents, 6e; ⌚noon-10pm Tue-Sat, 1-9pm Sun; Ⓜ Odéon) Style personified, this Japanese tearoom-cum-art gallery is a peaceful oasis amid the bustling shops. Finesse, nobility and other elevated qualities describe the different varieties of green teas served in pottery teapots with matching *yunomi* (goblets).

LE WAGG CLUB

Map p418 (www.wagg.fr; 62 rue Mazarine, 6e; ⌚Fri-Sun; Ⓜ Odéon) Although it's not as hip as many Right Bank party spots, this slick, contemporary club (associated with the popular Fabric in London) isn't as hard to get into, either. The dance floor starts filling up in the wee hours; check the website for parties and events including Sunday salsa class followed by *une soirée 100% cubaine.*

Les Invalides

TOP CHOICE **ALAIN MILLIART** JUICE BAR

Map p422 (☎01 45 55 63 86; www.alain-milliat.com; 159 rue de Grenelle, 7e; ⌚10am-10pm Tue-Sat; Ⓜ La Tour Maubourg) Alain Milliart's fruit juices, bottled in the south of France, were until recently reserved for ultra-exclusive hotels and restaurants. But the opening of his Parisian juice bar/bistro means you can pop in to buy one of 33 varieties of juices and nectars, or sip them in-house. Milliart's jams and compotes are equally lush.

Stunning flavours include rosé grape or green tomato juice and white peach nectar. There's also a short but stellar, regularly changing blackboard menu (*menus* €22 to €36) influenced by the markets and seasons; be sure to book ahead for dinner.

CAFÉ THOUMIEUX CAFE

Map p422 (www.thoumieux.fr; 4 rue de la Comète, 7e; ⌚noon-midnight; Ⓜ La Tour-Maubourg) The trendy tapas annexe of Brasserie Thoumieux is always full of well-heeled young Parisians enjoying the Iberian ambience. Tapas and San Miguel beer set the scene, but perfumed vodka is the house speciality, with no fewer than 40 different types (including chocolate, fig, watermelon and mint tea) to choose from.

☆ ENTERTAINMENT

LE LUCERNAIRE CULTURAL CENTRE

Map p418 (☎01 42 22 26 50, reservations 01 45 44 57 34; www.lucernaire.fr; 53 rue Notre Dame des Champs, 6e; ⌚restaurant & bar 10am-10pm Mon-Fri, from 3pm Sat & Sun; Ⓜ Notre Dame des Champs) Sunday-evening concerts are a permanent fixture on the impressive repertoire of this dynamic Centre National d'Art et d'Essai (National Arts Centre). Be it classical guitar, baroque, French *chansons* or oriental music, these weekly concerts starting at 6.30pm are a real treat. Art and photography exhibitions, cinema, theatre, lectures, debates and guided walks round off the packed cultural agenda.

LA PAGODE CINEMA CINEMA

Map p422 (☎01 45 55 48 48; www.etoile-cinema.com; 57bis rue de Babylone, 7e; ⌚vary; Ⓜ St-François Xavier) This 19th-century Japanese pagoda was converted into a cinema in the 1930s and remains the most atmospheric spot in Paris to catch arthouse and classic films. Don't miss a moment or two in its bamboo-enshrined garden.

A classified historical monument, the pagoda was shipped to France, piece by piece, in 1895 by Monsieur Morin (the then proprietor of Le Bon Marché), who had it rebuilt in his garden on rue de Babylone as a present for his wife. The wife wasn't too impressed – she left him a year later. But Parisian *cinéphiles* who flock here to revel in its eclectic program clearly approve.

SHOPPING

The northern wedge of the 6e between Église St-Germain des Prés and the Seine is a dream to roam around with its

bijou art galleries, antique shops, stylish vintage clothes, and fashion boutiques (PennyBlack, Vanessa Bruno, Joseph, Isabel Marant et al), while St-Germain des Prés' natural style continues along the western half of bd St-Germain and rue du Bac – two streets with a striking collection of contemporary furniture, kitchen and design shops.

CIRE TRUDON HOME, GARDEN

Map p418 (www.ciretrudon.com; 78 rue de Seine, 6e; ⌚10-7pm Mon-Sat, closed Mon Aug; Ⓜ Odéon) Claude Trudon began selling candles here in 1643, and the company – which officially supplied Versailles and Napoleon with light – is now the world's oldest candle-maker (look for the plaque to the left of the shop's awning). A rainbow of candles and candlesticks fill the shelves inside.

LE BON MARCHÉ DEPARTMENT STORE

Map p422 (www.bonmarche.fr; 24 rue de Sèvres, 7e; ⌚10am-8pm Mon-Wed & Fri, to 9pm Thu & Sat; Ⓜ Sèvres-Babylone) Built by Gustave Eiffel as Paris' first department store in 1852, Le Bon Marché translates as 'good market' but also means 'bargain', which it isn't. But it is the epitome of style, with a superb concentration of men's and women's fashions, beautiful homewares, stationery and a good range of books and toys as well as chic dining options.

The icing on the cake is its glorious food hall, La Grande Épicerie de Paris.

LA GRANDE ÉPICERIE DE PARIS FOOD, DRINK

Map p422 (www.lagrandeepicerie.fr; 36 rue de Sèvres, 7e; ⌚8.30am-9pm Mon-Sat; Ⓜ Sèvres-Babylone) Among other edibles, Le Bon Marché's magnificent food hall sells vodka-flavoured lollipops with detoxified ants inside and fist-sized Himalayan salt crystals to grate over food. Its fantastical displays of chocolates, pastries, biscuits, cheeses, fresh fruit and vegetables and deli goods are a sight to behold.

LA CHAUMIÈRE À LA MUSIQUE MUSIC

Map p418 (www.chaumiereonline.com; 5 rue de Vaugirard, 6e; ⌚11am-7.30pm Mon-Fri, to 8pm Sat, 2-8pm Sun; Ⓜ Odéon) Behind its teal-blue façade, La Chaumière à la Musique buys, sells and exchanges thousands of rare classical music recordings. It also stocks books on composers as well as sheet music, and is a point of contact for tapping into Paris' contemporary classical music scene.

AU PLAT D'ÉTAIN GAMES, HOBBIES

Map p418 (16 rue Guisarde, 6e; ⌚11am-12.30pm & 2-7pm Tue & Thu-Sat; Ⓜ Odéon) Nail-sized tin *(étain)* and lead soldiers, snipers, cavaliers, military drummers and musicians (great for chessboard pieces) cram this fascinating boutique. In business since 1775, the shop itself is practically a collectable.

LA MAISON DE POUPÉE ANTIQUES

Map p418 (☎06 09 65 58 68; 40 rue de Vaugirard, 6e; ⌚2.30-7pm Mon-Sat, by appt Sun; Ⓜ Odéon or RER Luxembourg) Opposite the residence

SECONDHAND CHIC

When St-Germain's well-heeled residents spring-clean their wardrobes, they take their designer and vintage cast-offs to *dépôt-vente* (secondhand) boutiques, where savvy locals snap up serious bargains. Try your luck at the following addresses:

Chercheminippes (Map p422; www.chercheminippes.com; 102, 109-111 & 124 rue du Cherche Midi, 6e; ⌚11am-7pm Mon-Sat; Vaneau) Five beautifully presented boutiques on one street selling secondhand pieces by current designers. Each specialises in a different genre (haute couture, kids, menswear etc) and perfectly ordered by size and designer. There are even changing rooms.

Le Dépôt-Vente de Buci (Map p418; 4 rue Bourbon le Château; ⌚9.30am-6pm Tue-Sat; Ⓜ Mabillon) Fronted by a black wooden façade, this stylish 'boutique of curiosities' stocks hand-me-downs mainly from the 1960s on consignment, returning anything that hasn't sold after three months.

Ragtime (Map p418; 23 rue de l'Échaude; ⌚2.30-7.30pm Mon-Sat; Ⓜ Mabillon) Madame Auguet's boutique sells vêtements anciens (vintage clothes) from 1870 to 1970.

L'Embellie (Map p422; 2 rue du Regard; ⌚1pm-7.30pm Mon, 11am-7.30pm Tue-Sat; Ⓜ Sèvres-Babylone) Superb selection of vintage fashion.

of the French Senate's president, this delightful little shop sells its namesake dolls houses as well as *poupées anciennes* (antique dolls).

CARINE GILSON FASHION

Map p418 (www.carinegilson.com; 18 rue de Grenelle, 7e; ⊙10.30am-6.30pm Mon-Sat; MSt-Sulpice) Silks and lace sourced in Lyon and Calais are turned into seductive lingerie in beautifully muted tones by Belgian-born designer Carine Gilson, who trained at the prestigious Antwerp Academy (alma mater of Dries Van Noten, among others).

FRÉDÉRIC MALLE PERFUME

Map p418 (www.fredericmalle.com; 37 rue de Grenelle, 7e; ⊙noon-7pm Mon, 11am-7pm Tue-Sat; MRue du Bac) Taking the approach of an 'editor', Malle works with his perfume 'authors' to produce unique fragrance 'editions' (all are refrigerated until sold). These apartment-styled premises were his first Paris shop; there are now a couple of others plus one in New York.

THEATR'HALL FASHION

Map p418 (www.theatrhall.com; 3 Carrefour de l'Odéon, 6e; ⊙11am-7.30pm Mon-Sat; MOdéon) Should you have an upcoming masquerade ball, this wonderful old space selling theatrical garb – shirts in medieval, Revolution and belle époque styles, capes, top hats and Venetian masks – is the place to come to look the part.

HERMÈS CONCEPT STORE

Map p418 (www.hermes.com; 17 rue de Sèvres, 6e; ⊙10.30am-7pm Mon-Sat; MSèvres-Babylone) A stunning art deco swimming pool now houses luxury label Hermès' first-ever concept store. Retaining its original mosaic tiles and iron balustrades and adding enormous timber pod-like 'huts', the vast, tiered space showcases new directions in home furnishings including fabrics and wallpaper, as well as classic lines including its signature scarves.

DEYROLLE ANTIQUES, HOMEWARES

Map p418 (www.deyrolle.com; 46 rue du Bac, 7e; ⊙10am-7pm Tue-Sat; MRue du Bac) Overrun with creatures including lions, tigers, zebras and storks, taxidermist Deyrolle opened in 1831. In addition to stuffed animals (for rent and sale), this fascinating place stocks minerals, shells, corals and crustaceans, stand-mounted ostrich eggs and pedagogical storyboards. There are also rare and unusual seeds (including many old types of tomato), gardening tools and accessories.

ALEXANDRA SOJFER ACCESSORIES

Map p418 (www.alexandrasojfer.fr; 218 bd St-Germain, 7e; ⊙9.30am-6.30pm Tue-Sat; MSt-Germain des Prés) Become Parisian chic with a frivolous, frilly, fantastical or frightfully fashionable *parapluie* (umbrella), parasol or walking cane, handcrafted by Alexandra Sojfer at this *parapluie*-packed St-Germain boutique, in the trade since 1834.

ART & ANTIQUE STREETS

Art and antique dealers congregate within the **Carré Rive Gauche** (www.carrerivegauche.com; MRue du Bac or Solférino). Bounded by quai Voltaire and rues de l'Université, des St-Pères and du Bac, this 'Left Bank square' is home to more than 120 specialised merchants. Antiques fairs are usually held in spring, while exhibitions take place during the year.

To the east, exploring the art galleries on rue Mazarine, rue Jacques Callot, rue des Beaux Arts and rue de Seine is a real feast for the designer soul. Among the edgier galleries here are the courtyard **Galerie Loft** (Map p418; www.galerieloft.com; 3bis rue des Beaux Arts; ⊙10.30am-6.30pm Tue-Sat; MSt-Germain des Prés), featuring all forms of art including digital video and performance photography; **Galerie Onega** (Map p418; www.galerie-onega.com; 60 rue Mazarine; ⊙11am-7pm Tue-Sat; MSt-Germain des Prés), showcasing street art and graffiti; and **La Galerie Moderne** (Map p418; www.lagaleriemoderne.com; 52 rue Mazarine; ⊙10am-7pm Mon-Sat; MSt-Germain des Prés) with original designer furniture and lights from the 1950s, '60s and '70s. Antique shops in this area include the pocket handkerchief–size **Hapart** (Map p418; 72 rue Mazarine; ⊙2-7pm Tue-Sun; MOdéon), which recalls lost childhood with its romantic selection of old and antique toys.

LE BAIN ROSE HOME, GARDEN

Map p418 (www.le-bain-rose.fr; 11 rue d'Assas, 6e; ⏰10am-7pm Mon-Sat; Ⓜ Rennes) The antique and retro mirrors, perfume spritzers, soap dishes, mirrors (hand-held and on stands) and even basins and tapware at this long-established shop can transform your bathroom into a belle époque sanctum.

QUATREHOMME FOOD, DRINK

Map p422 (62 rue de Sèvres, 6e; ⏰8.45am-1pm & 4-7.45pm Tue-Thu, 8.45am-7.45pm Fri & Sat; Ⓜ Vanneau) Buy the best of every French cheese you can find, many with an original take (eg Epoisses boxed in chestnut leaves, Mont d'Or flavoured with black truffles, spiced honey and Roquefort bread etc), at this king of *fromageries*. The smell alone as you enter is heavenly.

A LA RECHERCHE DE JANE ACCESSORIES

Map p418 (http://alarecherchedejane.wordpress.com; 41 rue Dauphine, 6e; ⏰11.30am-7.30pm Tue-Sat, 12.30-7pm Sun; Ⓜ St-Germain des Prés) This *chapelier* (milliner) has literally thousands of handcrafted hats on hand for both men and women, and can also make them to order. Hours can vary.

JB GUANTI ACCESSORIES

Map p418 (www.jbguanti.fr; 59 rue de Rennes, 6e; ⏰10am-7pm Mon-Sat; Ⓜ St-Sulpice or Mabillon) For the ultimate finishing touch, the men's and women's gloves at this boutique, which specialises solely in gloves, are the epitome of both style and comfort, whether unlined, silk lined, cashmere lined, lambskin lined or trimmed with rabbit fur.

Buying for someone else? To get their glove size, measure the length in centimetres of their middle finger from the top to where it joins their hand – the number of centimetres equals the size (eg 5cm is a size 5).

GALERIE FRANÇOIS RÉNIER ACCESSORIES

Map p418 (☎01 45 49 26 88; www.unjourunsac.com; 27 bd Raspail; ⏰10am-7pm Tue-Sat; Ⓜ Sèvres-Babylone) *Un jour un sac* (a bag a day) is the philosophy of handbag designer François Rénier, who creates bags from paper, fabric or leather and leaves his customer to pick which handles to attach. Buy a couple to mix 'n' match at home.

LIN ET CIE ACCESSORIES

Map p418 (www.linetcie.com; 16 rue Bréa, 6e; ⏰1-7pm Mon, 11am-7pm Tue-Sat; Ⓜ Notre Dame des Champs) Simplicity is the charm of the organic jewellery created for mother and baby at this unusual boutique. Its tiny silver, precious stone or porcelain motifs, delicately strung on nylon and tied with knots, can also be ordered online.

CAVE ST-SULPICE FOOD, DRINK

Map p418 (www.cavesaintsulpice.com; 3 rue St-Sulpice, 6e; ⏰11am-8.15pm Mon-Sat, 10am-1pm Sun; Ⓜ Odéon) Champagne is the specialty of this lovely little boutique. Spend as little or as much as you fancy, on a half-bottle, bottle or magnum, choose pink, white or designer.

LA DERNIÈRE GOUTTE FOOD, DRINK

Map p418 (www.laderniergoutte.net; 6 rue du Bourbon le Château, 6e; ⏰10am-1.30pm & 3.30-8.30pm; Ⓜ Mabillon) 'The Last Drop' is the brainchild of Cuban-American sommelier Juan Sánchez, whose tiny wine shop is packed with exciting French *vins de propriétaires* (estate-bottled wines) made by small independent producers. Check the website for the shop's program of talks and tastings.

PÂTISSERIE SADAHARU AOKI FOOD, DRINK

Map p418 (www.sadaharuaoki.com; 35 rue de Vaugirard, 6e; ⏰11am-7pm Tue-Sat, 10am-6pm Sun; Ⓜ Rennes or St-Sulpice) 'Exquisite' fails to describe the creations of one of Paris' top pastry chefs, Tokyo-born Sadaharu Aoki. His gourmet works include boxes of 72 different flavoured macaroons and green-tea chocolate.

PIERRE HERMÉ FOOD, DRINK

Map p418 (www.pierreherme.com; 72 rue Bonaparte, 6e; ⏰10am-7pm Sun-Fri, to 8pm Sat; Ⓜ Odéon or RER Luxembourg) It's the size of a chocolate box but once in, your tastebuds will go wild. Pierre Hermé is one of Paris' top chocolatiers and this boutique is a veritable feast of perfectly presented petits fours, cakes, chocolate, nougats, *macarons* and jam.

ROUGE ET NOIR GAMES, HOBBIES

Map p418 (www.rouge-et-noir.fr; 26 rue Vavin, 6e; ⏰11am-7pm Tue-Sat; Ⓜ Vavin) Trivial Pursuit Paris, Rubik's cubes, juggling balls, backgammon, chess, tarot and playing cards... This small family-run boutique specialising in traditional and not-so-traditional games offers bags of fun.

FLAMANT HOME INTERIORS HOMEWARES

Map p418 (www.flamant.com; 8 place de Furstenberg, 6e; ⌚10.30am-7pm Mon-Sat; Ⓜ Mabillon) Silverware, curtains, cutlery, tableware, linen and other quality home furnishings: this maze of a store with two entrances (you can also enter via 8 rue de l'Abbaye) is the place where moneyed Parisians shop for the home.

BONTON BAZAR KIDS

Map p422 (www.bonton.fr; 122 rue du Bac, 7e; ⌚10am-7pm Mon-Sat; Ⓜ Sèvres-Babylone) This ode to childhood sells a mix of toys, kids' chopsticks (handy for families dining out a lot in Paris), kitchen and bathroom wares (including polka-dotted cutlery and black rubber ducks with fishing rods), bedroom decorations, pedal-powered metal cars and so on.

Quaint, retro fashion of the same timeless ilk for babies and kids respectively is the focus of nearby boutiques including **Bébé Bonton** (Map p422; 82 rue de Grenelle; Rue du Bac) and **Grenelle Bonton** (Map p422; 82 rue de Grenelle; Rue du Bac). Its 800 sq metre concept store Grand Bonton (p174) is on the Right Bank.

LA CLEF DES MARQUES FASHION

Map p418 (www.laclefdesmarques.com; 122-126 bd Raspail, 6e; ⌚12.30-7pm Tue-Sat; Ⓜ Vavin) This designer outlet specialises in *grandes marques* (big names) at knock-down prices for men, women and kids, with labels like Emilio Pucci, Ralph Lauren, Calvin Klein, Le Petit Bateau, Diesel and stacks of sportswear. Bargains also span handbags, jewellery, perfume and shoes. For secondhand designer wear, see p245.

PLASTIQUES HOMEWARES

Map p418 (www.plastiques-paris.fr; 103 rue de Rennes, 6e; ⌚10.15am-7pm Mon-Sat; Ⓜ Rennes) Lollypop-coloured tableware (trays, serving bowls, dinner settings etc) and cookware (whisks, mixing bowls and much more) fill this original, inexpensive boutique.

MAX MAROQUINERIE BAGAGERIE ET ACCESSOIRES ACCESSORIES

Map p418 (45 rue Dauphine, 6e; ⌚noon-7pm Mon-Sat; Ⓜ Odéon) Among the wares of this handbag boutique are small-run, limited-edition Frederic T totes at extremely reasonable prices.

GÉRARD DURAND ACCESSORIES

Map p422 (www.accessoires-mode.com; 75-77 rue du Bac, 7e; ⌚9am-7pm Mon-Sat; Ⓜ Rue du Bac) Brightly coloured, boldly printed *collants* and *bas* (tights and stockings) are the specialty of this boutique, which also stocks equally vibrant socks, scarves and gloves.

SONIA RYKIEL FASHION

Map p418 (www.soniarykiel.com; 175 bd St-Germain, 6e; ⌚10.30am-7pm Mon-Sat; Ⓜ St-Germain des Prés) In the heady days of May 1968 amid Paris' student uprisings, Sonia Rykiel opened her inaugural Left Bank boutique here, and went on to revolutionise garments with inverted seams, 'no hems' and 'no lining'. Her diffusion labels (including children's wear) are housed in separate boutiques nearby, with other outlets around Paris.

CINÉ REFLET BOOKS

Map p418 (14 rue Monsieur-le-Prince, 6e; ⌚1-8pm Mon-Tue & Thu-Sat, to 9.15pm Wed; Ⓜ Odéon) An old projector takes pride of place at this cinema-dedicated bookshop.

LA MAISON DU CHOCOLAT FOOD, DRINK

Map p418 (www.lamaisonduchocolat.com; 19 rue de Sèvres, 6e; ⌚10am-7.30pm Mon-Sat, to 1pm Sun; Ⓜ Sèvres-Babylone) Pralines, ganaches and fruit chocolates are the hallmark of this exquisite chocolatier. Other treats include *macarons* inspired by its signature chocolates, such as Rigoletto (chocolate and salted caramel) and Salvador (chocolate and raspberry), as well as sinful éclairs.

FRAGONARD BOUTIQUE PERFUME

Map p418 (☎01 42 84 12 12; 196 bd St-Germain; ⌚11am-9pm Mon-Sat, 2-7.30pm Sun; Ⓜ Rue du Bac or St-Germain des Prés) The bd St-Germain boutique of perfumer maker Fragonard (which runs Paris' perfume museum (p94) stocks a heady range of souvenirs – from scarves to cookbooks – evoking the sights, scents and flavours of France.

SAN FRANCISCO BOOK COMPANY BOOKS

Map p418 (www.sanfranciscobooksparis.com; 17 rue Monsieur le Prince, 6e; ⌚11am-9pm Mon-Sat, 2-7.30pm Sun; Ⓜ Odéon) Art, architecture, literary criticism, politics and science are among the non-fiction titles at this haven of a little secondhand English-language bookshop. You could easily lose hours browsing its shelves brimming with classic and contemporary novels.

CENTRALE DU FUSIL D'OCCASION

ANTIQUES

Map p422 (69 rue de Grenelle, 7e; ⏲10am-12.30pm & 2.30-6.30pm Tue-Sun; Ⓜ Rue du Bac) If antique pistols and rifles fire your interest, this musty gunsmith is one not to miss.

TEA & TATTERED PAGES

BOOKS

Map p422 (www.teaandtatteredpages.com; 24 rue Mayet, 6e; ⏲11am-7pm Mon-Sat, noon-6pm Sun; Ⓜ Duroc) More than 15,000 volumes cram two floors at this secondhand English-language bookshop. The tearoom has a clutch of tables and doesn't serve food, but is still a cosy spot for a cuppa.

TASCHEN

BOOKS

Map p418 (www.taschen.com; 2 rue du Buci, 6e; ⏲11am-8pm Mon-Thu, to midnight Fri & Sat; Ⓜ Odéon) Illustrated books on art, design, architecture, fashion and urban culture fill this striking Philippe Starck–designed split-level shop and its pavement bargain bins.

Montparnasse & Southern Paris

MONTPARNASSE & 15E | PLACE D'ITALIE & CHINATOWN

Neighbourhood Top Five

❶ Ignore the '70s smoked-glass exterior of **Tour Montparnasse** (p252) – or give thanks that the outcry over its construction prompted a crackdown on similarly soulless skyscrapers – and zip to the top for one of the finest panoramas of Paris.

❷ Prowl the spine-prickling skull-and bone-packed tunnels of Paris' creepy ossuary, **Les Catacombes** (p253).

❸ Visit Jean-Paul Sartre, Simone de Beauvoir and Serge Gainsbourg at **Cimetière du Montparnasse** (p255).

❹ Savour belle époque Paris at the lovely museum and garden of the **Musée Bourdelle** (p252).

❺ Catch superb exhibitions at France's national library, the book-shaped **Bibliothèque Nationale de France** (p254).

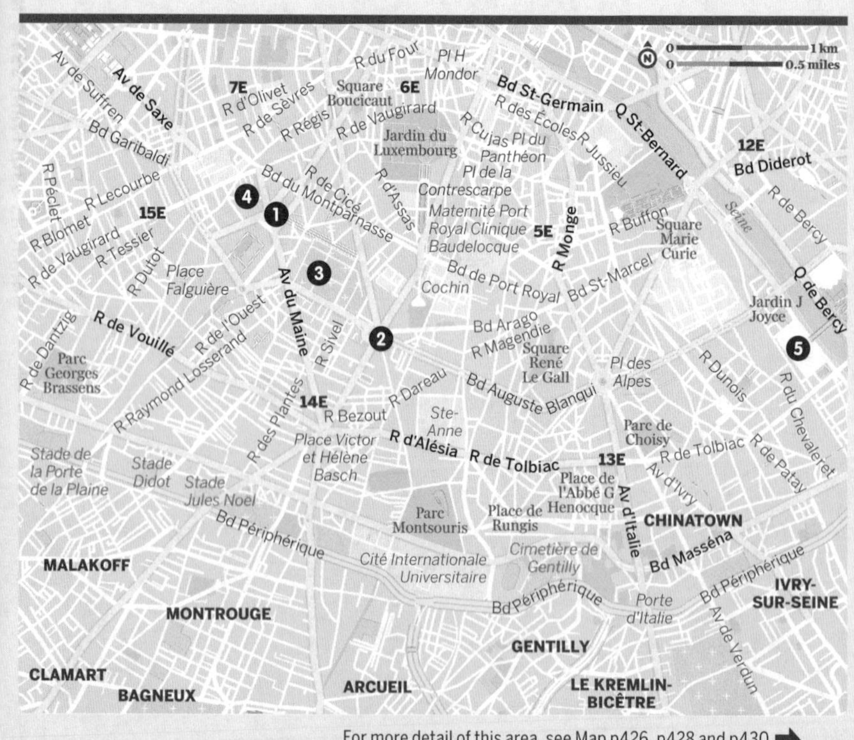

For more detail of this area, see Map p426, p428 and p430 ➡

Explore Montparnasse & Southern Paris

Tour Montparnasse is an unavoidable sight, but its observation deck is an unrivalled spot to get to grips with the lay of the land. At its feet are the cafes, brasseries and backstreets where some of the early 20th century's most seminal artists and writers hung out – albeit now swathed by urban grit. The area's tree-filled cemetery is a peaceful spot to escape – and to visit famous graves.

After exploring the area's museums, drift west into the gentrified 15e where, for more great views, you can board a balloon 'flight' in the Parc André-Citroën, one of the capital's most innovative open spaces.

To Montparnasse's east, the ever regenerating 13e is home to the country's national library and state-of-the-art national museum of sport. Also in the 13e is Paris' largest Chinatown. Wherever you end up for dinner in this sprawling southern sector of Paris, head back to the river to dance until dawn on the floating bars and nightclubs moored on the Seine's quays.

Local Life

➡ **Village Life** Join locals singing revolutionary songs from the time of the Paris Commune in the trendy restaurants and bars of the Butte aux Cailles *quartier*.

➡ **Breton Life** Take a crêperie crawl through Montparnasse's 'Little Brittany' (p259).

➡ **Fashion Finds** Browse for bargain designer seconds, samples and last season's stock on the 14e's rue d'Alésia (p263).

Getting There & Away

➡ **Metro** Montparnasse Bienvenüe is the transport hub for Montparnasse and 15e. Bibliothèque and Place d'Italie are the main stops in Place d'Italie and Chinatown.

➡ **Bus** From Gare Montparnasse, bus 91 goes to Gare d'Austerlitz, Gare de Lyon and Bastille; bus 92 to Charles de Gaulle-Étoile; bus 94 to Sèvres-Babylone. Pick up bus 82 on bd du Montparnasse for Invalides and the Eiffel Tower; bus 95 on rue de Rennes for St-Germain des Prés, Louvre, Opéra and Montmartre. Bus 62 from the Bibliothèque Nationale de France crosses the 13e to rue d'Alésia and rue de la Convention. At place d'Italie, take bus 67 to Mosquée de Paris, Jardin des Plantes, Île de St-Louis, Hôtel de Ville and Pigalle, and bus 83 to Jardin de Luxembourg and Les Invalides.

➡ **Bicycle** Handy Vélib' stations include 5-7 rue d'Odessa, 14e; 13 bd Edgar Quinet, 14e; and 2 av René Coty, 14e; and two facing Place d'Italie, 13e.

Lonely Planet's Top Tip

The metro is tailor-made for crosstown trips, but to whizz around Paris' perimeter, hop on the new T3 tram. The first section of the tramline opened in 2006, skimming the city's southern quarters from the Pont du Garigliano, 15e, to Porte d'Ivry, 13e. Its ambitious extension, inaugurated in late 2012, stretches from Porte d'Ivry to Porte de la Chapelle, 18e, encircling some two-thirds of the city. Passengers use standard t+ tickets (see p340). For updates on Paris' tramways, see www.tramway.paris.fr.

Best Places to Eat

➡ La Cabane à Huîtres (p256)

➡ Jadis (p256)

➡ Pho 14 (p259)

➡ L'Avant Goût (p259)

➡ Chez Paul (p259)

For reviews, see p256 ➡

Best Places to Drink

➡ Le Select (p261)

➡ Tandem (p261)

➡ Auto Passion Café (p261)

For reviews, see p261 ➡

Best Floating Nightclubs

➡ Le Batofar (p262)

➡ Peniche El Alamein (p262)

➡ La Dame de Canton (p262)

For reviews, see p261 

SIGHTS

Montparnasse & 15e

GARE MONTPARNASSE TRAIN STATION

Map p428 (place Raoul Dautry, 14e; Ⓜ Montparnasse Bienvenüe) Several unusual attractions sit on the rooftop of this sprawling train station. The **Jardin de l'Atlantique** (Map p428; place des Cinq Martyr du Lycée Buffon), whose 3.5 hectares of green park terraces carpet the roof of the station, offers greenery and tranquillity in the heart of a very busy district. The garden's futuristic **Observatoire Météorologique** 'sculpture' measures precipitation, temperature and wind speed.

Next to the garden the small **Musée Jean Moulin** (Map p428; www.ml-leclerc-moulin.paris.fr; 23 allée de la 2e DB; admission free; ⏲10am-6pm Tue-Sun) is devoted to the WWII German occupation of Paris, with its focus on the Resistance and its leader, Jean Moulin (1899–1943). The attached **Mémorial du Maréchal Leclerc de Hauteclocque et de la Libération de Paris** shows a panoramic film on the eponymous general (1902–47), who led the Free French units during the war and helped to liberate the city in 1944.

To get here, walk up the metal staircase next to platform 1 inside the station.

TOUR MONTPARNASSE PANORAMIC TOWER

Map p428 (www.tourmontparnasse56.com; rue de l'Arrivée, 15e; adult/under 20yr/7-15yr €7/4/3; ⏲9.30am-11.30pm Apr-Sep, to 10.30pm Sun-Thu, to 11pm Fri & Sat Oct-Mar; Ⓜ Montparnasse Bienvenüe) The 210m-high Montparnasse Tower, built in 1973 with steel and smoked glass and housing offices for 5000 workers, affords spectacular views over the city. (Bonus: its observation floor and terrace are about the only spots in Paris you can't see this startlingly ugly, oversized lipstick tube, which in low-rise Paris sticks out like a sore thumb.)

Europe's fastest lift whisks visitors up in 38 seconds to the indoor observatory on the 56th floor, with an exhibition centre, video clips, multimedia terminals and Paris' highest restaurant, Le Ciel de Paris (p258). Finish with a hike up the stairs to the open-air terrace on the 59th floor.

FONDATION CARTIER POUR L'ART CONTEMPORAIN CONTEMPORARY ART

Map p428 (www.fondation.cartier.com; 261 bd Raspail, 14e; adult/11-26yr €9.50/6.50; ⏲11am-10pm Tue, to 8pm Mon & Wed-Sun; Ⓜ Raspail) This stunning glass-and-steel building, designed by Jean Nouvel, is a work of art in itself. It hosts temporary exhibits on contemporary art (from the 1980s to today) in a wide variety of media – from painting and photography to video and fashion, as well as performance art.

FREE **MUSÉE BOURDELLE** SCULPTURE MUSEUM

Map p428 (www.bourdelle.paris.fr; 18 rue Antoine Bourdelle, 15e; ⏲10am-6pm Tue-Sun; Ⓜ Falguière) The Bourdelle Museum contains monumental bronzes in the house and workshop where sculptor Antoine Bourdelle (1861–1929), a pupil of Rodin, lived and worked. The three sculpture gardens are particularly lovely and impart a flavour of belle époque and post-WWI Montparnasse. The museum usually has a temporary exhibition (which generally has an admission charge) going on alongside its permanent collection.

LES MONTPARNOS

Peer long and hard (and long and hard again) around the unfortunate 1960s Gare Montparnasse complex and glimmers of the area's bohemian past occasionally emerge: after WWI writers, poets and artists of the avant-garde abandoned Montmartre on the Right Bank and crossed the Seine, shifting the centre of Paris' artistic ferment to the area around bd du Montparnasse. Known as les Montparnos, artists Chagall, Modigliani, Léger, Soutine, Miró, Matisse, Kandinsky and Picasso, composer Stravinsky, and writers Hemingway, Ezra Pound and Cocteau were among those who hung out here, talking endlessly in the cafes and restaurants for which the *quartier* became famous. It remained a creative hub until the mid-1930s.

Historic brasseries that recall les Montparnos' legacy include Le Select (p261), La Coupole (p257), with muraled columns painted by artists including Chagall, Le Dôme (p256), where Gertrude Stein is said to have encouraged Matisse to open his artist academy, and the hedged La Closerie des Lilas (p257).

TOP SIGHTS
LES CATACOMBES

Paris' most gruesome and macabre sight is its series of underground tunnels lined with skulls and bones exhumed from the city's overflowing cemeteries. In 1785 it was decided to solve the hygienic and aesthetic problems posed by the cemeteries by exhuming the bones and storing them in the tunnels of three disused quarries.

The Catacombes is one such ossuary, created in 1810. The route through the Catacombes begins at a small, dark-green belle époque building in the centre of a grassy area of av Colonel Henri Roi-Tanguy, adjacent to Place Denfert Rochereau. After descending 20m (130 steps) from street level, you follow 2km of subterranean passages with a mind-boggling amount of bones and skulls of millions of Parisians neatly packed along every wall. During WWII these tunnels were used as a headquarters by the Resistance; thrill-seeking cataphiles are often caught (and fined) roaming the tunnels at night.

Renting an audioguide greatly enhances the experience. In the tunnels the temperature is a cool 14° Celsius – bring a jacket, even in summer. The exit is back up 83 steps on rue Remy Dumoncel (MMouton-Duvernet), 700m southwest of av Colonel Henri Roi-Tanguy.

DON'T MISS

- Tunnels

PRACTICALITIES

- Map p428
- www.catacombes.paris.fr
- 1 av Colonel Henri Roi-Tanguy, 14e
- adult/under 26yr/under 13yr €8/4/free
- 10am-5pm Tue-Sun
- MDenfert Rochereau

MUSÉE DE LA POSTE — POSTAL MUSEUM

Map p428 (www.ladressemuseedelaposte.fr; 34 bd de Vaugirard, 15e; adult/under 26yr €5/free; 10am-6pm Mon-Sat; MMontparnasse Bienvenüe or Pasteur) Not only posties and philatelists but anyone who enjoys travel, exploration and communication will enjoy this contemporary postal museum. Billed as 'L'Adresse' (the Address), the museum offers a fascinating overview of the history of the French postal service, with exhibits spanning several floors. Imaginative temporary exhibitions might be anything from artist-designed letter boxes to wartime postal services or postcards.

Before leaving, don't miss the shop selling every imaginable French stamp, from *Harry Potter* designs to romantic red heart-shaped stamps, as well as stamps from overseas French territories including New Caledonia and French Polynesia.

MUSÉE DU MONTPARNASSE — MUSEUM

Map p428 (www.museedumontparnasse.net; 21 av du Maine, 15e; adult/12-18yr €6/5; 12.30-7pm Tue-Sun; MMontparnasse Bienvenüe) Housed in the studio of Russian cubist artist Marie Vassilieff (1884–1957) down a delightfully leafy alleyway off av du Maine, Montparnasse Museum doesn't have a permanent collection; rather it recalls the great role Montparnasse played during various artistic periods of the 20th century, offered through temporary exhibitions.

MUSÉE PASTEUR — RESIDENCE MUSEUM

Map p428 (Institut Pasteur; www.pasteur.fr; 25 rue du Docteur Roux, 15e; adult/student €7/3; 2pm, 3pm & 4pm Mon-Fri Sep-Jul; MPasteur) Housed in the apartment where the famous chemist and bacteriologist spent the last seven years of his life (1888–95), a tour of this museum takes you through Pasteur's private rooms, with odds and ends including gifts presented to him by heads of state and drawings he did as a young man.

After Pasteur's death, the French government wanted to entomb his remains in the Panthéon, but his family, acting in accordance with his wishes, obtained permission to have him buried at his institute. The great savant lies in the basement crypt.

Tours lasting 45 minutes to one hour are in French; printed English guides are available. Note that you need to show a passport or ID card to gain entrance.

PARC ANDRÉ-CITROËN PARK

(quai André-Citroën, 15e; MBalard) In 1915 automotive entrepreneur André Citroën built a vast car manufacturing plant here in the 15e. After it closed in the 1970s, the vacated site was eventually turned into this forward-looking 14-hectare urban park. Its central lawn is flanked by greenhouses, dancing fountains, an elevated reflecting pool, and smaller gardens themed around movement and the (six) senses.

LE BALLON AIR DE PARIS SCENIC BALLOON

Map p430 (01 44 26 20 00; www.ballondeparis.com; Parc André Citroën, 2 rue de la Montagne de la Fage, 15e; admission adult/child Mon-Fri €10/9, Sat & Sun €12/10; 9am-30min prior to park closure; MBalard or Lourmel) Drift up and up but not away – this helium-filled balloon remains tethered to the ground as it elevates you 150m into the air for spectacular panoramas over Paris. The balloon also plays an active environmental role, changing colour depending on the air quality and pollution levels. Make sure you confirm ahead as the balloon doesn't ascend in windy conditions.

Place d'Italie & Chinatown

BIBLIOTHÈQUE NATIONALE DE FRANCE NATIONAL LIBRARY

Map p426 (01 53 79 40 41; www.bnf.fr; 11 quai François Mauriac, 13e; temporary exhibitions adult/18-26yr from €7/5; 10am-7pm Tue-Sat, 1-7pm Sun; MBibliothèque) The four glass towers of the €2 billion National Library of France – conceived as a 'wonder of the modern world' and opened in 1995 – were one of President Mitterand's most ambitious and costliest *grands projets*. It's well worth visiting for its excellent temporary exhibitions (entrance E), which revolve around 'the word' – from storytelling to bookbinding and French heroes.

The national library contains around 12 million tomes stored on some 420km of shelves and can hold 2000 readers and 2000 researchers.

No expense was spared to carry out the library's grand design, which many claimed defied logic. While books and historical documents are shelved in the sunny, 23-storey and 79m-high towers (shaped like half-open books), patrons sit in artificially lit basement halls built around a 'forest courtyard' of 140 50-year-old pines, trucked in from the countryside. The towers have since been fitted with a complex (and expensive) shutter system but the basement is prone to flooding from the Seine.

MUSÉE NATIONAL DU SPORT SPORT MUSEUM

Map p426 (www.museedusport.fr; 93 av du France, 13e; adult/18-26yr €4/2, 1st Sun of month free; 10am-6pm Tue-Fri, 2-6pm Sat & Sun; MBibliothèque) A recent addition to the increasingly happening 13e, Paris' National Museum of Sport covers just that: football, tennis, polo, the Tour de France...you name it, there is sporting paraphernalia to match in this modern space with bags of kid appeal.

Check out skis used by triple gold medallist and 1968 French skiing legend Jean-Claude Killy; see the prototype motorcycle with three wheels used by Jean Naud to bike from Paris to Timbuktu in 1986; or sign the kids up for one-hour 'how to be a sports commentator' or Olympic Games *ateliers* (workshops, €5) in French.

LES FRIGOS GALLERY

Map p426 (www.les-frigos.com; 19 rue des Frigos, 13e; vary; MBibliothèque) The name of this gallery translates as 'The Refrigerators', which is what this 1920s industrial building plastered from head to foot in graffiti used to be – a storage depot for refrigerated railway wagons. Inside it's become a little bit different: some 200 artists use what is now an established artists' squat (artists pay rent to the city, which now owns the place) as gallery and studio space.

Les Frigos' many galleries have no fixed opening hours: hedge your bets and hope you bump into someone willing to show you around, or look out for one of the fabulous open days and other events Les Frigos hosts (click 'Agenda' on its website).

GALERIE ITINERRANCE GALLERY

Map p426 (http://itinerrance.fr; 7bis, rue René Goscinny, 13e; 2-7pm Wed-Sat; MBibliothèque) A sign of the 13e's creative renaissance, this very funky gallery showcases graffiti and street art. Artists and events vary – check the program online.

DOCKS EN SEINE CULTURAL CENTRE

Map p426 (Cité de la Mode et du Design; www.paris-docks-en-seine.fr; 36 quai d'Austerlitz,

TOP SIGHTS
CIMETIÈRE DU MONTPARNASSE

Opened in 1824, Montparnasse Cemetery, Paris' second-largest after Père Lachaise, sprawls over 19 hectares. Although it doesn't have the sheer scale of celebrities laid to rest here as its better-known counterpart, there are still numerous famous graves (free maps are available from the conservation office).

Some of the illustrious 'residents' at Cimetière du Montparnasse include poet Charles Baudelaire, writer Guy de Maupassant, playwright Samuel Beckett, photographer Man Ray, industrialist André Citroën, Captain Alfred Dreyfus of the infamous affair, actress Jean Seberg, and philosopher Jean-Paul Sartre and his partner, writer Simone de Beauvoir.

Like Père Lachaise too, Cimetière du Montparnasse has its time-honoured tomb traditions. One of the most popular is fans leaving metro tickets atop the grave of crooner Serge Gainsbourg (in division 1, just off av Transversale) in reference to his 1958 song '*Le Poinçonneur des Lilas*' (The Ticket Puncher of Lilas), which depicts work-a-day monotony through the eyes of a metro ticket-puncher. Gainsbourg enacted the soul-destroying job (since eclipsed by machines) on film when recording the song in the Porte des Lilas station.

DON'T MISS

- ➡ Charles Baudelaire's Grave
- ➡ Jean-Paul Sartre & Simone de Beauvoir's Graves
- ➡ Serge Gainsbourg's Grave

PRACTICALITIES

- ➡ Map p428
- ➡ www.paris.fr
- ➡ bd Edgar Quinet & rue Froidevaux, 14e
- ➡ ⌚8am-6pm Mon-Fri, 8.30am-6pm Sat, 9am-6pm Sun
- ➡ Ⓜ Edgar Quinet or Raspail

13e; Ⓜ Gare d'Austerlitz) Framed by a lurid-lime wave-like glass façade, a transformed Seine-side warehouse, the Docks en Seine houses the French Fashion Institute – the Institut Français de la Mode (hence the docks' alternative name, Cité de la Mode et du Design), with a growing program of fashion and design exhibitions and events throughout the year.

One of Paris' most exciting projects, the docks occupy a 20,000 sq metre riverside warehouse built in 1907 (the first industrial complex in Paris to use reinforced concrete), where goods were delivered by barge. It was transformed post-millennium into a state-of-the-art cultural centre with a sun deck and waterside promenades across which concerts and other al fresco festivities spill in summer. Its hottest new drawcard is the 2012-opened 'creative space' **Wanderlust** (Map p426; 32 Quai d'Austerlitz, 13e; ⌚noon-6am, Wed-Sun; Ⓜ Gare d'Austerlitz), with the city's largest terrace – a whopping 1600 sq metres – as well as an open-air cinema, bar, club, restaurant, markets and more.

For the best view of the water-facing façade, cross the Seine over Pont Charles de Gaulle.

MANUFACTURE DES GOBELINS — FACTORY, GALLERY

Map p426 (☎01 44 08 52 00; www.mobiliernational.culture.gouv.fr; 42 av des Gobelins, 13e; gallery adult/7-25yr €8/6, tour & gallery €10/7.50; ⌚gallery 12.30-6.30pm Tue-Sun, guided tours 2-4.30pm Tue-Thu; Ⓜ Les Gobelins) The Gobelins Factory has been weaving *haute lisse* (high relief) tapestries on specialised looms since the 18th century along with Beauvais-style *basse lisse* (low relief) ones and Savonnerie rugs. Superb examples are showcased in its gallery. Factory visits (1½ hours), by guided tour, take you through the *ateliers* (workshops) and exhibits of the thousands of carpets and tapestries woven here.

Buy tickets in advance at Fnac (p63)or turn up well ahead of time for same-day tour tickets.

PARC MONTSOURIS — PARK

Map p426 (av Reille, 14e; ⌚sunrise to sunset; Ⓜ Porte d'Orléans or RER Cité-Universitaire) The name of this sprawling lakeside park – planted with horse-chestnut, yew, cedar, weeping beech and buttonwood trees – derives from *moque souris* (mice mockery) because the area was once over-run

RENAISSANCE OF THE 13E

Serious change is afoot in the 13e *arrondissement* (city district), centred on a once nondescript area south of the Latin Quarter that spirals out from the big busy traffic hub Place d'Italie. The area's renaissance was heralded in the 1990s by the controversial Bibliothèque Nationale de France and by the arrival of the high-speed Météor metro line, followed, among other additions, by the MK2 entertainment complex, the floating Piscine Joséphine Baker swimming pool on the Seine, and Paris' most recent bridge, the Passerelle Simone de Beauvoir (2006), providing a cycle and pedestrian link to the Right Bank. And it's not slated to stop until 2020, when the ZAC Paris Rive Gauche redevelopment project ends.

Pivotal to this 130-hectare redevelopment zone is a university that will ultimately host 30,000 students. Other institutions to have moved in include Institut Français de la Mode (French Fashion Institute) in the stylised former warehouse, the Docks en Seine and its buzzing new 'creative space', Wanderlust.

The area's mainline train station, the Gare d'Austerlitz, is getting a €600 million makeover from celebrated architect Jean Nouvel. Not only will the station itself be overhauled (including €200 million alone on the grand hall's glass roof, beneath which hot air balloons were manufactured during the 1870 siege of Paris), but shops, cafes and green spaces will fill the surrounding streets. The renovation is also due to wrap up in 2020. Track updates on the area at www.parisrivegauche.com.

with rodents. Today it's a delightful spot for a picnic, and has endearing playground areas such as a concrete 'road system' where littlies can trundle matchbox cars (BYO cars).

The park adjoins the groundbreaking 1920s-built Cité Universitaire (student halls of residence); you're free to wander around the campus.

EATING

Since the 1920s, bd du Montparnasse has been one of the city's premier avenues for enjoying Parisian cafe life, with legendary brasseries and cafes. The down-to-earth 15e cooks up fabulous bistro fare – key streets are rues de la Convention, de Vaugirard, St-Charles, du Commerce and south of bd de Grenelle. For Asian food, try Chinatown's avs de Choisy and d'Ivry and rue Baudricourt. The villagey Butte aux Cailles is buzzing with interesting addresses.

Montparnasse & 15e

TOP CHOICE LA CABANE À HUÎTRES — SEAFOOD €

Map p428 (☎01 45 49 47 27; 4 rue Antoine Bourdelle, 14e; dozen oysters €14.50, menu €19.50; ⊙lunch & dinner Wed-Sat; MMontparnasse Bienvenüe) Wonderfully rustic, this wooden-styled *cabane* (cabin) with just nine tables is the pride and joy of fifth-generation oyster farmer Françis Dubourg, who splits his week between the capital and his oyster farm in Arcachon on the Atlantic Coast. The fixed menu includes a dozen oysters, foie gras, *magret de canard fumé* (smoked duck breast) or smoked salmon and scrumptious desserts.

JADIS — NEOBISTRO €€€

Map p430 (☎01 45 57 73 20; www.bistrot-jadis.com; 202 rue de la Croix Nivert, 15e; lunch/dinner menus from €29/36; ⊙lunch & dinner Mon-Fri; MBoucicaut) This upmarket neobistro on the corner of a very unassuming street in the 15e is one of Paris' most raved about (ie reserve in advance). Traditional French dishes pack a modern punch thanks to the daring of rising star chef Guillaume Delage, who braises pork cheeks in beer and uses black rice instead of white.

The lunch *menu* is extraordinarily good value and the chocolate soufflé – order it at the start of your meal – is divine.

LE DÔME — BRASSERIE €€€

Map p428 (☎01 43 35 25 81; 108 bd du Montparnasse, 14e; mains €37-49, seafood platter €54; ⊙lunch & dinner; MVavin) A 1930s art deco extravaganza, Le Dôme is a monumental place for a dining experience of the formal white-tablecloth and bow-tied waiter variety. It's one of the swishest places around for shellfish platters piled high with fresh oysters, king prawns, crab claws and so on, followed by traditional creamy home-made *millefeuille* for dessert, wheeled in on a trolley and cut in front of you.

The brasserie is awash with history: so the stories go, it was here that Gertrude Stein allegedly convinced Henri Matisse to open his artists' academy – only for Matisse to later add his voice to the 'Testimony against Gertrude Stein' pamphlet, published in 1935, condemning Stein's interpretation of how cubism emerged and her own influence in its emergence in her 1933 *Autobiography of Alice B Toklas*.

LA CLOSERIE DES LILAS — BRASSERIE €€

Map p428 (☎01 40 51 34 50; www.closeriedeslilas.fr; 171 bd du Montparnasse, 6e; restaurant mains €23-49, brasserie mains €23-27; ⊙restaurant lunch & dinner daily, brasserie noon-1am daily, piano bar 11am-1am daily; MVavin or RER Port Royal) As anyone who has read Hemingway knows, what is now the American Bar at the 'Lilac Enclosure' is where Papa did a lot of writing (including much of *The Sun Also Rises*), drinking and oyster slurping; brass plaques tell you exactly where he and luminaries such as Picasso, Apollinaire, Man Ray, Jean-Paul Sartre and Samuel Beckett stood, sat or fell.

La Closerie des Lilas is split into a late-night piano bar, chic restaurant and more lovable (and cheaper) brasserie with a hedged-in pavement terrace.

LA COUPOLE — BRASSERIE €€€

Map p428 (☎01 43 20 14 20; www.lacoupoleparis.com; 102 bd du Montparnasse, 14e; lunch menus €28-33.50, mains €19.50-37; ⊙8am-1am Sun-Thu, to 1.30am Fri & Sat; ♿; MVavin) The reason for visiting this enormous, 450-seat brasserie, designed by the Solvet brothers and opened in 1927, is more history than gastronomy. Its famous mural-covered columns (painted by such artists as Brancusi and Chagall), dark wood panelling and soft lighting have hardly changed an iota since the days of Sartre, Soutine, Man Ray, the dancer Josephine Baker and other regulars.

You can book for lunch, but you'll have to queue for dinner; though there's always breakfast. It's a great option if you're travelling *en famille*: kids are given pencils and game-filled notebooks, and can choose waffles, fruit cocktails and more from their own menu.

LA CAGOUILLE — SEAFOOD €€

Map p428 (☎01 43 22 09 01; www.la-cagouille.fr; 10 place Constantin Brancusi, 14e; lunch/dinner menus €26/42; ⊙lunch & dinner daily; MGaîté) Chef Gérard Allemandou, one of the best seafood chefs (and cookery book writers) in Paris, gets glowing reviews for his fish and shellfish dishes at this cafe-restaurant. Given the quality of the produce, the three-course *menus* are outstanding value.

L'OS À MOËLLE — MODERN FRENCH €€

Map p430 (☎01 45 57 27 27; 3 rue Vasco de Gama, 15e; lunch/dinner menus from €17/35; ⊙lunch Tue-Fri, dinner Tue-Sat; MLourmel) Marrow-bone chef Thierry Faucher's affordable *menus* embrace delicacies like scallops with coriander, sea bass in cumin butter or half a quail with endives and chestnuts, and his chocolate *quenelle* (dumpling) with saffron cream is award-winning. Should you fail to snag a table, try his neighbouring wine bar, **La Cave de L'Os à Moëlle**.

SAWADEE — THAI €€

Map p430 (☎01 45 77 68 90; http://restaurant-thai-sawadee.com; 53 av Émile Zola, 15e; menus €23-35; ⊙lunch & dinner Mon-Sat; MCharles Michels) For 20 years this well-known restaurant has been bidding *sawadee* (welcome) to Thai-food lovers. The decor is rather impersonal, but the sophisticated cuisine more than makes up for it. Classics include prawn or chicken soup flavoured with lemongrass, spicy beef salad (a real treat), and satay sticks (chicken, beef, lamb and pork) with peanut sauce.

LE CRISTAL DE SEL — NEOBISTRO €€

Map p430 (☎01 42 50 35 29; www.lecristaldesel.fr; 13 rue Mademoiselle, 15e; 2-/3-course lunch menu €15/18, mains €21-23; ⊙lunch & dinner to 10pm Tue-Sat; MCommerce) The raved-about stage of young rising chef Karl Lopez, this modern bistro has a distinct kitchen feel with its small brightly lit white walls and white-painted beams. The only decorative feature is a candle-lit crystal of rose-tinted salt on each table – a sure sign that food is what the Salt Crystal is all about.

Lopez's langoustine ravioli is luscious, and his *tarte à la bergamote fraîche meringuée* (lemon meringue pie) has to be the zestiest in Paris.

KIM ANH — VIETNAMESE €€

Map p430 (☎01 45 79 40 96; www.kimanh-restaurant.com; 49 av Émile Zola, 15e; menu €35; ⊙lunch

Tue-Sat, dinner Tue-Sun; MCharles Michels) The antithesis of the typically Parisian canteen-style Vietnamese restaurant, Kim Anh greets diners with tapestries, white tablecloths, fresh flowers and extraordinarily fresh, flavoursome and elaborately presented food. The *émincé de bœuf à la citronnelle* (beef with lemongrass) is a skillful combination of flavours, but the true sensation is the caramelised langoustine.

L'ENTREPÔT MODERN FRENCH **€€**

Map p428 (01 45 40 07 50; www.lentrepot.fr; 7-9 rue Francis de Préssensé, 14e; lunch/Sunday brunch menus €15/26, mains €15-22; lunch Mon-Sat, brunch Sun, dinner daily; MPernety or Plaisance) Industrial in mood and open-minded in spirit (people of all ages come here), this dynamic cultural centre happens to be a fantastic place to eat, too. Service is fast, friendly and French – start with goat's cheese marinated in nut oil, or half a dozen snails followed by ravioli in chestnut cream or chicken and chunky hand-cut fries.

The real show stealer, live band line-up aside, is its leafy back garden with dozens of tables beneath trees. Reserve tables al fresco in advance, especially for Sunday brunch.

LE SÉVÉRO BISTRO **€€€**

Map p428 (01 45 40 40 91; 8 rue des Plantes, 14e; mains €30-50; lunch & dinner Mon-Fri; MMouton Duvernet) Meat is the mainstay of this cosy neighbourhood bistro (it's run by ex-butcher William Bernet), served with sensational fries and washed down with any number of excellent wines, which are chalked on an entire wall.

LE CIEL DE PARIS TRADITIONAL FRENCH **€€€**

Map p428 (01 40 64 77 64; www.cieldeparis.com; level 56, Tour Montparnasse, 33 av du Maine, 14e; mains €24-59; restaurant 8.30am-11pm; MMontparnasse Bienvenüe) Views don't get much better than 'the sky of Paris', the Tour Montparnasse's 56th-floor restaurant, renovated in 2012 and accessed by private lift. Starters include Burgundy snails and pigs' trotters; seafood is a speciality, as is the Aveyron lamb cooked for 12 hours. No need to rush straight off – the bar stays open until 1am.

MARCHÉ EDGAR QUINET MARKET **€**

Map p428 (bd Edgar Quinet, 14e; 7am-2pm Wed & Sat; MEdgar Quinet or Montparnasse Bienvenüe) Opposite Tour Montparnasse, this open-air street market buzzes with neighbourhood shoppers. There's always a great range of cheeses, as well as stalls sizzling up snacks to eat on the run, from crêpes to spicy falafels.

MARCHÉ BRANCUSI MARKET **€**

Map p428 (place Constantin Brancusi, 14e; 9am-3pm Sat; MGaîté) Overdose on organic produce at this weekly open-air market.

MARCHÉ GRENELLE MARKET **€**

Map p430 (bd de Grenelle, btwn rue de Lourmel & rue du Commerce, 15e; 7am-2.30pm Wed & Sun; MLa Motte-Picquet-Grenelle) Arranged below an elevated railway and surrounded by stately Haussmann boulevards and art nouveau apartment blocks, this outdoor street market attracts a well-heeled clientele.

MARCHÉ ST-CHARLES MARKET **€**

Map p430 (rue St-Charles, btwn rue de Javel & rond-point St-Charles, 15e; 7am-2.30pm Tue & Fri; MCharles Michels or Javel-André Citroën) This street market may appear somewhat far-flung off in the western 15e, but shoppers will go any distance for its quality produce, including organic goods.

POILÂNE BOULANGERIE **€**

Map p430 (www.poilane.fr; 49 bd de Grenelle, 15e; 7.15am-8.15pm Mon-Sat; MDupleix) Pick up handcrafted sourdough bread from this branch of one of Paris' most famous bakeries (p239), as well as its delicious *Punitions* (crispy butter biscuits).

Place d'Italie & Chinatown

L'AUBERGE DU 15 GASTRONOMIC **€€**

Map p426 (01 47 07 07 45; www.laubergedu15.com; 15 Rue de la Santé, 13e; lunch menus €26, mains €28-50; lunch & dinner Tue-Sat; MSt-Jacques or RER Port Royal) Rising chef Nicolas Castelet and his *pâtissier* brother Florent run this charming 'inn', with rough-hewn stone walls, chocolate-toned decor and classic dishes that evoke a country retreat. Choose dining companions who share your culinary tastes – most mains must be ordered by a minimum of two people, and the €68 *dégustation* menu must be ordered by the entire table. This place is definitely one to watch.

PHO 14 VIETNAMESE €

Map p426 (129 avenue de Choisy, 13e; ⌚9am-11pm; Ⓜ Tolbiac) Factor in a wait at this small, simple Vietnamese restaurant (also known as Pho Banh Cuon 14) – it doesn't take bookings and is wildly popular with in-the-know locals for its authentic and astonishingly cheap *pho* (noodles). The steaming Vietnamese broth is richly flavoured with cinnamon and incorporates noodles and traditional beef; the chicken *pho* is likewise divine.

ENTOTO ETHIOPIAN €€

Map p426 (☎01 45 87 08 51; www.restaurant-entoto.com; 145 rue Léon-Maurice Nordmann, 13e; dinner menus €22-28; ⌚dinner daily; Ⓜ Glacière) Tear off a piece of *injera* (spongy Ethiopian flatbread) and scoop up delectable vegetable and spicy meat accompaniments at France's first Ethiopian restaurant, which opened in 1983 and is filled with redolent photos of the country's people and landscapes. A potent pot of Ethiopian coffee is the traditional way to finish the meal – prepare to be wired all night.

L'OURCINE FRENCH BASQUE €€

Map p426 (☎01 47 07 13 65; 92 rue Broca, 13e; lunch/dinner menus €26/34; ⌚lunch & dinner Tue-Sat; Ⓜ Les Gobelins) A perfect example of a neobistro, this intimate place may be casual (no dress code) and affordable, but it takes its food seriously. The focus of the superb menu is on the flavours of the French Basque Country, including succulent pan-fried baby squid with fiery Espelette peppers.

CHEZ PAUL TRADITIONAL FRENCH €€

Map p426 (☎01 45 89 22 11; 22 rue de la Butte aux Cailles, 13e; mains €16-22; ⌚lunch & dinner; Ⓜ Corvisart or Place d'Italie) Paul's pad is a classic in Butte aux Cailles. Soak up the relaxed, chatty feel and indulge in Frencher-than-French dishes cooked to perfection. Despite its name *gras double* (double fat) is not fatty; rather, it's pork belly pan-fried with garlic and parsley, as the friendly note on the menu explains.

L'AVANT GOÛT NEOBISTRO €€

Map p426 (☎01 53 80 24 00; www.lavantgout.com; 26 rue Bobillot, 13e; starters/mains

'LITTLE BRITTANY'

Trains leave from Gare Montparnasse for the windswept region of Brittany, a couple of hours' away, but you don't even have to leave the capital to take a mini-tour: due to the Breton population congregating here, rue du Montparnasse, 14e, is lined with over a dozen authentic Breton crêperies, many of which are named for the region's locales, such as St-Malo, Quimper, Pont Aven and Bigoudene.

Unlike the rolled-up crêpes sold on street corners, Breton crêpes are folded envelope-style at the edges, served flat on a plate and eaten using cutlery – and are best washed down with bowls of Breton cider. Savoury *galettes* use *blé noir* – (buckwheat flour; *sarrasin* in Breton), while both *galettes* and sweet crêpes made from white flour use salted Breton butter. Traditional toppings include *andouille* (Breton sausage), and *caramel au beurre salé* (salty caramel sauce; *salidou* in Breton).

Rue Montparnasse's top two crêperies:

Crêperie Josselin (Map p428; ☎01 43 20 93 50; 67 rue du Montparnasse, 14e; savoury crêpes €6-9, sweet crêpes €4-7; ⌚lunch & dinner Tue-Fri, noon-11pm Sat & Sun; 👪; Ⓜ Edgar Quinet) Filled with dark timber furniture, painted plates and screened by lace curtains, Josselin (named for the eastern Breton village crowned by a 14th-century castle), locals crowd around the open kitchen waiting for a table. Delicious *galettes* include Roquefort with walnuts.

Crêperie Plougastel (Map p428; ☎01 01 42 79 90 63; 47 rue du Montparnasse, 14e; 2-/-3/-course menus €14.80/16.80; ⌚11am-midnight daily; 👪; Ⓜ Edgar Quinet) Named for the Breton commune near Brest, Plougastel's decor might be spartan, but its *galettes* and crêpes are anything but, with generous toppings including St-Jacques scallops.

One block west of rue du Montparnasse, rue Odessa, 14e, also has a handful of Breton crêperies.

€10/16.50, menu lunch/dinner €14/31; lunch & dinner Tue-Sat; M Place d'Italie) A prototype of the Parisian neobistro, The Foretaste has chef Christophe Beaufront serving some of the most inventive modern cuisine around. Tables count little more than a dozen and the place gets noisy. But the food is different and divine – don't miss his signature dish, *pot au feu au cochon aux épices* (spicy pork stew).

Advance reservations are vital but, should you miss out, you can get takeaway dishes from its nearby wine shop, **L'Avant-Goût Coté Cellier** (Map p426; 01 53 81 14 06; www.lavantgout.com; 37 rue Bobillot; noon-8pm Tue-Fri, 10.30am-1.30pm & 3.30-8.30pm Sat; M Place d'Italie).

LA TROPICALE — ICE CREAM €

Map p426 (www.latropicaleglacier.com; 180 bd Vincent Auriol, 13e; ice cream from €2.50, lunch menus €8-12; noon-7pm Mon-Sat, closed mid-late Aug; ; M Place d'Italie) All-natural flavours like lycee, guava, mango and papaya, honey and pine nut as well as a pina-colada-like coconut, rum and pineapple transport you to the tropics at this mint-coloured *glacier-salon de thé*. It also serves seasonally changing lunchtime quiches, flans and a *plat du jour* (dish of the day).

CHEZ NATHALIE — FUSION €€

Map p426 (01 45 80 20 42; www.cheznathalie.fr; 41 rue Vandrezanne, 13e; starters €10-15, mains €17-23; lunch & dinner; M Corvisart or Place d'Italie) On a quiet street with summertime tables, this pocket-sized restaurant is a lovely spot to dine *tête à tête*. Transparent Kartell chairs and deep-purple table tops complement the stylised menu, which fuses traditional French with world food such as sesame-encrusted tuna, beef bourguignon with caramelised carrots, and squid pan-fried with Espelette peppers.

LES CAILLOUX — ITALIAN €€

Map p426 (01 45 80 15 08; 58 rue des Cinq Diamants, 13e; pasta/mains €16/20; lunch & dinner Tue-Sat; M Corvisart or Place d'Italie) The pavement terrace of this pricey, chic hang-out in the heart of Butte aux Cailles is the spot to sit and be seen. In keeping with the cool crowd that gathers here, decor is minimalist: understated chocolate façade, shabby-chic wooden floor and simple tables lit by low-hanging lamps. Although almost secondary to the hip scene, the Italian food is delicious.

LA CHINE MASSÉNA — CHINESE €€

Map p426 (01 45 83 98 88; 18 av de Choisy, 13e; lunch/dinner menus from €11/16; lunch & dinner Mon-Sat; M Porte de Choisy) This enormous restaurant specialising in Cantonese and Chiu Chow cuisine is a real favourite in Chinatown. The dim sum is especially good and waiters still go around the dining area with trolleys calling out their wares.

LE TEMPS DES CÉRISES — TRADITIONAL FRENCH €

Map p426 (01 45 89 69 48; www.cooperativetempsdescerises.eu; 18-20 rue de la Butte aux Cailles, 13e; mains €11-19.50; lunch Mon-Fri, dinner Mon-Sat; M Corvisart or Place d'Italie) Run by a workers' cooperative for over three decades, The Time of Cherries (ie 'days of wine and roses') is an easygoing restaurant (provided you switch off your phone, lest there be hell to pay) serving faithfully solid fare in a quintessentially Parisian atmosphere. Buy their *coton-bio* T-shirt upon departure.

CHEZ GLADINES — FRENCH BASQUE €

Map p426 (01 45 80 70 10; 30 rue des Cinq Diamants, 13e; mains €8.50-12.80; lunch daily, dinner Mon-Sat; ; M Corvisart) Colossal 'meal-in-a-metal-bowl' salads are the prime draw of this down-to-earth Basque bistro with red-and-checked tablecloths in Buttes aux Cailles. It buzzes with students and spendthrift diners, and is always a hoot. Traditional Basque specialities include *pipérade* (eggs scrambled with tomato and peppers) and *poulet basque* (chicken cooked with tomatoes, onions, peppers and white wine). Arrive early to grab a seat.

HAO HAO — CHINESE €

Map p426 (28 rue de Choisy, 13e; 9am-2am; M Porte de Choisy) Opening to a snug dining room clattering with diners until late in the night, Hao Hao's open kitchen cooks up cheap, filling and delicious Chinese dishes such as Sichuan chicken.

LE PETIT MARGUERY — TRADITIONAL FRENCH €€

Map p426 (01 43 31 58 59; http://petitmarguery.com; 9 bd de Port Royal, 13e; lunch menus €23-26, dinner menus €30-35; lunch & dinner Tue-Sun; M Les Gobelins) This traditional restaurant isn't the kind of place you'd rearrange your itinerary around but if you're in the area, it's a perfect choice for hearty dishes like pan-fried cod with braised chicory and lemon butter, and Grand Marnier soufflée. It's popular with locals though, so book ahead to avoid a lengthy wait.

DRINKING & NIGHTLIFE

The comings and goings of the Gare Montparnasse train station and a dynamic cultural centre keep things lively. Southwest of Place d'Italie, the area around the Butte aux Cailles molehill has some good options. It's a pretty area that's popular with students and local residents; places here tend to have die-hard regulars.

Montparnasse & 15e

AUTO PASSION CAFÉ — CAFE

(www.autopassioncafe.fr; 197 bd Brune, 14e; ⏲10am-2am; 🚸; Ⓜ Porte d'Orléans) Rev heads will be in heaven at this cafe run by three motoring enthusiasts. Filled with racing memorabilia, including engines, petrol pumps and some very cool cars, even its menu *('la kart')* reflects the race track: starters are listed under 'grid', mains 'pit stop' and desserts 'finishing line', or go for the three-course 'grand prix' (€28).

Many of its excellent cocktails have auto themes too, such as *injecteur* (vodka, guava, strawberries, passionfruit and grenadine); nonalcoholic options include *autostoppeuse* (orange juice, pineapple, banana and strawberries).

LE SELECT — CAFE

Map p428 (99 bd du Montparnasse, 6e; ⏲7am-2.30am; Ⓜ Vavin) Dating from 1923, this Montparnasse institution was the first of the area's grand cafes to stay open late into the night, and it still draws everyone from beer-swigging students to whisky-swilling politicians. *Tartines* made with Poilâne bread are a speciality.

LE ROSEBUD — COCKTAIL BAR

Map p428 (11bis rue Delambre, 14e; ⏲7pm-2am; Ⓜ Edgar Quinet or Vavin) Like the sleigh of that name in *Citizen Kane,* Rosebud harkens to the past. In this case it's to Montparnasse's early 20th-century heyday (the decor has scarcely changed since Sartre drank here). Enjoy a Champagne cocktail amid the quiet elegance of polished wood and aged leather.

LA CAVE DE L'OS À MOËLLE — WINE BAR

Map p430 (rue Vasco de Gama, 15e; ⏲noon-10.30pm Tue-Sun; Ⓜ Lourmel) Warming the cockles with a *vin chaud* (mulled wine) and *pain d'épice* (honey spiced bread) around a wine-barrel-turned-table on the pavement outside this cosy wine bar is a winter treat.

LE REDLIGHT — CLUBBING

Map p428 (www.leredlight.com; 34 rue du Départ, 14e; ⏲midnight to 6am Sat & Sun; Ⓜ Montparnasse Bienvenüe) Beneath Tour Montparnasse, this huge, laser-lit venue, fittingly called *l'enfer* (hell) in a previous life, is up there among Paris' busiest house, techno and electro clubs. Its podiums get packed out with a young, dance-mad crowd well past dawn. Hours often vary depending on the *soirée* – see its website for flyers.

LA RUCHE — CAFE

Map p428 (73 bd du Montparnasse, 14e; ⏲6am-2am; Ⓜ Montparnasse Bienvenüe) Even when other cafes in the Montparnasse area are quiet, this cherry-red, split-level cafe hung with funky light fittings buzzes with a young, fun crowd.

FÉLICIE — CAFE, BAR

Map p428 (www.felicie.info; 174 ave du Maine, 14e; ⏲7am-2am; Ⓜ Lourmel) Be it breakfast, lunch, pre- or post-dinner drinks, this unpretentious neighbourhood brasserie-bar with a big heated pavement terrace is a quintessentially Parisian spot to Zen any time of day. Throw in Sunday brunch, 'express' lunch deals built around bistro classics like steak tartare and a laid-back late-night vibe, and chances are you'll be back.

Place d'Italie & Chinatown

TANDEM — WINE BAR

Map p426 (10 rue de la Butte aux Cailles, 13e; ⏲noon-2.30pm & 7.30-11pm Tue-Sat; Ⓜ Corvisart or Place d'Italie) If wine's your love, make a beeline for this overwhelmingly old-fashioned *bar à vins* crammed with regulars. Two brothers with a fierce oenological passion home in on 'boutique' *(vins de proprietés)* and organic wines as well as those produced by new *vignerons* (wine makers). A traditional bistro menu com plements the wine list.

FROG & BRITISH LIBRARY — MICROBREWERY, PUB

Map p426 (www.frogpubs.com; 114 av de France, 13e; ⏲7.30am-2am Mon-Fri, noon-2am Sat & Sun; 📶; Ⓜ Bibliothèque) A hybrid English pub-French brasserie, this spacious drinking venue around the corner from the

Bibliothèque Nationale is propped up by expats and French students who flock here between library visits for food (apple pie and custard, potato wedges, weekend brunches) with a pint.

The pick of the drinks list is its half-dozen beers brewed on the premises with inspired names like 'Dark de Triomphe', 'In-seine' and 'Parislytic'.

LA DAME DE CANTON CLUBBING

Map p426 (www.damedecanton.com; opposite 11 quai François Mauriac, 13e; ⏲7pm-2am Tue-Thu, to dawn Fri & Sat; Ⓜ Quai de la Gare or Bibliothèque) This floating *boîte* (club) aboard a three-masted Chinese junk with a couple of world voyages under its belt bobs beneath the Bibliothèque Nationale de France. Concerts range from pop and indie to electro, hip-hop, reggae and rock; afterwards DJs keep the young crowd moving. There's also a popular restaurant and bar.

LE BATOFAR CLUBBING

Map p426 (www.batofar.org; opp 11 quai François Mauriac, 13e; ⏲9pm-midnight Mon & Tue, to 4am or later Wed-Sun; Ⓜ Quai de la Gare or Bibliothèque) This incongruous, much-loved, red-metal tugboat has a rooftop bar that's terrific in summer, and a respected restaurant, while the club underneath provides memorable underwater acoustics between its metal walls and portholes. Le Batofar is known for its edgy, experimental music policy and live performances, mostly electro-oriented but also incorporating hip-hop, new wave, rock, punk or jazz. Hours can vary.

LE DJOON CLUBBING

Map p426 (www.djoon.fr; 22-24 bd Vincent Auriol, 13e; ⏲7.30pm-1am Thu, 11.30pm-5am Fri & Sat, 6pm-midnight Sun; Ⓜ Quai de la Gare) In an area increasingly known for its cutting-edge venues, this urbanite, New York–inspired loft club and restaurant has carved out a name for itself as a super-stylish weekend venue for soul, funk, deep house, garage and disco, courtesy of visiting DJs. Thursday and Sunday evenings are tamer but still DJ-fed dance. Look for the striking glass-and-steel façade.

PENICHE EL ALAMEIN LIVE MUSIC

Map p426 (http://elalamein.free.fr; opposite 11 quai François Mauriac, 13e; ⏲hours vary; Ⓜ Quai de la Gare or Bibliothèque) Strung with terra-cotta pots of flowers, this deep-purple boat is a lovely spot on the Seine to sip away summer evenings. Sit amid tulips and enjoy live bands; flyers are stuck on the lamp post at the front. Less hectic than Paris' other floating clubs moored here, hence the older crowd, its sound spans jazz, world and Piaf-style *chansons*.

LE MERLE MOQUEUR BAR

Map p426 (11 rue de la Butte aux Cailles, 13e; ⏲5pm-2am; Ⓜ Corvisart) Friendly and convivial, the tiny, retro Mocking Magpie serves a huge selection of rum punches (over 20 at last count) and unearths great '80s tracks from the musical vaults.

LA TAVERNE DE LA BUTTE PUB

Map p426 (13 rue de la Butte aux Cailles, 13e; ⏲5pm-2am; Ⓜ Corvisart) A pint of Guinness is the choice drink at this Irish-ish pub. Staff generously replenish bar snacks, but the TV can be a bit of an atmosphere killer depending on what's on.

LA FOLIE EN TÊTE BAR

Map p426 (http://lafolieentete.blogspot.com; 33 rue de la Butte aux Cailles, 13e; ⏲5pm-2am Mon-Sat, 6pm-midnight Sun; Ⓜ Corvisart) Guitars and brass instruments strung on the walls attest to this jammed little bar's musical roots. Although it no longer hosts the profusion of acts it did in decades past, it still hosts occasional live *chansons*, world music, jazz and rock; check the line-up online (click on '*prochain événement*'). Already-cheap, drinks are even cheaper during happy hour (6pm to 8pm).

SPUTNIK BAR

Map p426 (www.sputnik.fr; 14 rue de la Butte aux Cailles, 13e; ⏲2pm-2am Mon-Sat, 4pm-midnight Sun; 📶; Ⓜ Corvisart or Place d'Italie) This large bar with a wi-fi zone and a dozen machines to surf is far more than an internet cafe. With its buzzing pavement terrace on one of Paris' funkiest streets and art exhibitions, Sputnik is a hip student haven, particularly between 6pm and 8pm during happy hour and brunch from 11am to 4pm on Saturday and Sunday.

☆ ENTERTAINMENT

L'ENTREPÔT CULTURAL CENTRE

Map p428 (☎01 45 40 07 50; www.lentrepot.fr; 7-9 rue Francis de Préssensé, 14e; Ⓜ Pernety or Plaisance) Everything from film screenings to jazz and world music concerts, poetry slams, photography, painting and sculpture exhibitions, art installations and much more take place at this dynamic cultural space near Gare Montparnasse.

DANCING LA COUPOLE DANCING

Map p428 (☎01 43 27 56 00; www.lacoupole-paris.com; 102 bd du Montparnasse, 14e; ⏰hours vary; Ⓜ Vavin) Roaring 1920s-style tea dances are held above the historic brasserie of the same name from 2.30pm to 7pm on Sundays; check the website or posters outside for details of salsa and Latino, tango, foxtrot and other styles.

LE PETIT JOURNAL MONTPARNASSE JAZZ, BLUES

Map p428 (☎01 43 21 56 70; http://petitjournalmontparnasse.com; 13 rue du Commandant René Mouchotte, 14e; admission incl 1 drink €25, with dinner €70; ⏰Mon-Sat; Ⓜ Gaîté) Like its sister club Le Petit Journal St-Michel (p216), this jazz and blues club near Gare Montparnasse serves meals (at 8.15pm), followed by a fabulous range of jazz and blues concerts (starting at 10pm).

MK2 BIBLIOTHÈQUE CINEMA, PHOTOGRAPHY

Map p426 (www.mk2.com; 128-162 av de France, 13e; Ⓜ Bibliothèque) This branch of the ever-growing chain next to the Bibliothèque Nationale is the most ambitious yet, with 14 screens showing a variety of blockbusters and studio films, a trendy cafe, brasserie, restaurant, late-night bar, and shops specialising in DVDs, books and comics and graphic novels.

Inside the complex, **Studio Harcourt** (Map p426; www.studio-harcourt.eu), the mythical 1934-founded Parisian photography studio famed for its black-and-white portraits of film stars, has installed a hi-tech photo booth for glamour portraits at a fraction of the price of its studio sittings. The booth, which premiered at the Cannes Film Festival, uses continuous light rather than flash to snap glamorous black-and-white shots (four for €10).

SHOPPING

The concrete-block shopping mall opposite Gare Montparnasse includes a branch of department store Galeries Lafayette. In-the-know Parisians head to the southern 14e to shop for discount designer wear, while the neighbouring 15e is privy to a clutch of specialist addresses. In the 13e you'll find Asian grocery stores and supermarkets.

TOP CHOICE **ADAM MONTPARNASSE** ART SUPPLIES

Map p428 (www.adamparis.com; 11 bd Edgar Quinet, 14e; ⏰9.30am-12.30pm & 1.30-7pm Mon, 9.30am-7pm Tue-Sat; Ⓜ Edgar Quinet) If Paris' glorious art galleries have awoken your inner artist, pick up paint brushes, charcoals, pastels, sketchpads, watercolours, oils, acrylics, canvases and all manner of art supplies at this historic shop. Picasso,

DISCOUNT DESIGNER OUTLETS

For previous seasons' collections, surpluses, prototypes and seconds by name-brand designers, save up to 70% off men's, women's and kids' fashions at the discounted outlet stores along rue d'Alésia, 14e, particularly between av de Maine to rue Raymond-Losserand. Exiting the Alésia metro station, walk west along rue d'Alésia to uncover its line-up of outlets, including the following:

Cacharel (Map p428; 114 rue d'Alésia, 14e; ⏰10am-7pm Mon-Sat; Ⓜ Alésia) Cut-price men's, women's and children's wear from French label.

SR Store (Map p428; 64 & 110-112 rue d'Alésia, 14e; ⏰10.45am-6.45pm Mon-Fri, to 7pm Sat; Ⓜ Alésia) Two shops stocking Sonia Rykiel designs. No 64 has lower-priced, more casual clothes, while No 110-112 has Sonia Rykiel's classic lines.

Dorotennis (Map p428; 74 rue d'Alésia, 14e; ⏰2-7.30pm Mon, 10.30am-7.30pm Tue-Sat; Ⓜ Alésia) Sleek, stylish women's sportswear.

Naf Naf Stock (Map p428; 143 rue d'Alésia, 14e; ⏰11am-7pm Mon-Fri, 10am-7pm Sat; Ⓜ Alésia) Fun, flirty female fashions.

For slashed prices on *grandes marques* (big names) under one roof, head to the 15e's **Mistigriff** (Map p430; www.mistigriff.fr; 83-85 rue St-Charles, 15e; Ⓜ Charles Michels)

Brancusi and Giacometti were among Édouard Adam's clients.

Another seminal client was Yves Klein, with whom Adam developed the ultramarine 'Klein blue' – the VLB25 'Klein Blue' varnish is sold exclusively here.

FROMAGERIE LAURENT DUBOIS FOOD

Map p430 (www.fromageslaurentdubois.fr; 2 rue de Lourmel, 15e; ⏲9am-1pm & 4-7.45pm Tue-Fri, 8.30am-7.45pm Sat, 9am-1pm Sun; Ⓜ Dupleix) The finest French cheeses are tantalisingly displayed at this branch of fêted Fromagerie Laurent Dubois. It also has a Latin Quarter premises (p218).

TANG FRÈRES FOOD, DRINK

Map p426 (48 av d'Ivry, 13e; ⏲9am-7.30pm Tue-Sun; Ⓜ Porte d'Ivry) You'd be forgiven for thinking you'd been transported to another continent upon entering this enormous Asian supermarket. Spices, sauces, freezers full of frozen dumplings, and kitchen utensils are imported from Asia along with beverages including Chinese beer. If your appetite's fired up, ready-to-eat snacks are sold opposite the entrance.

PIERRE HERMÉ FOOD

Map p428 (www.pierreherme.com; 185 rue Vaugirard, 15e; ⏲10am-7pm Tue-Sat; Ⓜ Pasteur) Petits fours, cakes, chocolate, nougats, jam and, of course, *macarons* from maestro Pierre Hermé. There is also a branch (p247) in St-Germain.

MARCHÉ AUX PUCES DE LA PORTE DE VANVES FLEA MARKET

(http://pucesdevanves.typepad.com; av Georges Lafenestre & av Marc Sangnier, 14e; ⏲from 7am Sat & Sun; Ⓜ Porte de Vanves) The Porte de Vanves flea market is the smallest and one of the friendliest of the lot. Av Georges Lafenestre has lots of 'curios' that don't quite qualify as antiques. Av Marc Sangnier is lined with stalls of new clothes, shoes, handbags and household items for sale.

L'ARBRE À BEURRE FOOD, COSMETICS

Map p430 (www.codina.net; 24 rue Violet, 15e; ⏲9.30am-6.30pm Tue-Sat; Ⓜ Av Émile Zola) Organic oils (pumpkin-seed, avocado, daisy, carrot, cashew and cherry) are made at this sky-blue Codina atelier. Be it your hair or health you need to boost, Codina has something to suit.

LE PETIT BAZAR KIDS

Map p430 (☎01 76 90 73 17; www.lepetitbazar.com; 128 av Émile Zola, 15e; ⏲1.15-6.15pm Mon, 10am-6.30pm Tue-Fri, 10am-7pm Sat; Ⓜ Av Émile Zola) A real *quartier* boutique with a distinctly 'green' philosophy, this emporium for tots has it all: imaginative games and toys, clothes, bedroom furnishings and accessories, stuff for school and babycare products – all organic, recycled or made by local artisans. Help yourself to a herbal tea or juice and slice of homemade cake (fill in your own bill and pay at the counter).

There's a clutch of music workshops for toddlers (aged one to five).

SPORTS & ACTIVITIES

PISCINE JOSÉPHINE BAKER SWIMMING

Map p426 (☎01 56 61 96 50; www.paris.fr; quai François Mauriac, 13e; pool adult/child €3/1.70, sauna €10/5; ⏲1-9pm Mon, Wed & Fri, 1pm-11pm Tue & Thu, noon-8pm Sat, 10am-8pm Sun; Ⓜ Bibliothèque or Quai de la Gare) Floating on the Seine, this striking swimming pool is style indeed (named after the sensual 1920s American singer, what else could it be?). More of a spot to be seen than thrash laps, the two 25m-×-10m pools lure Parisians like bees to a honey pot in summer when the roof slides back.

FREE **PARI ROLLER** INLINE SKATING

Map p428 (www.pari-roller.com; to/from place Raoul Dautry, 14e; admission free; ⏲10pm-1am Fri, arrive 9.30pm; Ⓜ Montparnasse Bienvenüe) The world's largest inline mass skate, Pari Roller regularly attracts over 10,000 bladers. Dubbed 'Friday Night Fever', this fast-paced skate covers a different 30km-odd route each week. Most incorporate cobblestones and downhill stretches, and are geared for experienced bladers only (for your safety and everyone else's). It takes place year-round except when wet weather makes conditions treacherous.

Like its gentler counterpart, the Marais-based Rollers & Coquillages (p180), it's accompanied by yellow-jersey-clad volunteer marshals, along with police (some on inline skates), and ambulances. Wear bright clothes to make yourself visible to drivers and other skaters.

FOREST HILL AQUABOULEVARD SWIMMING

Map p430 (☎01 40 60 10 00; www.aquaboulevard.fr; 4-6 rue Louis Armand, 15e; adult/child 3-11yr €22/15, high season €28/18; ⏰9am-11pm Mon-Thu, 9am-midnight Fri, 8am-midnight Sat, 8am-11pm Sun; Ⓜ Balard) Just outside the *Périphérique* (ring road), this huge tropical 'beach' and aquatic park is well worth a visit, particularly if you're travelling with kids over three years (under threes aren't allowed), with water slides, waterfalls and wave pools. To keep fit without getting wet, you can also play tennis, squash, golf, use the gym and take dance classes. Last admission is 9pm.

PISCINE KELLER SWIMMING

Map p430 (☎01 45 71 81 00; http://piscine.equipement.paris.fr; 14 rue de l'Ingénieur Keller, 15e; adult/child €3/1.70; ⏰noon-10pm Mon & Fri, 7am-8.30am & noon-10pm Tue & Thu, 7am-8pm Wed, 9am-9pm Sat, 9am-7pm Sun; Ⓜ Charles Michels) This revamped 1960s indoor pool with state-of-the-art glass roof that slides back on warm days is a splash with Parisians. It has slightly different hours during school holidays.

PISCINE DE LA BUTTE AUX CAILLES SWIMMING

Map p426 (☎01 45 89 60 05; http://piscine.equipement.paris.fr; 5 place Paul Verlaine, 13e; adult/child €3/1.70; ⏰7am-8.30am, 11.30am-1.30pm & 4.30-9pm Tue, 7am-7pm Wed, 7am-8.30am & 11.30am-6.30pm Thu & Fri, 7am-8.30am & 10am-6.30pm Sat, 8am-6pm Sun; Ⓜ Place d'Italie) This stunning pool, built in 1924, takes advantage of the lovely warm water issuing from a nearby artesian well. Come summer, its two outdoor pools buzz with swimmers frolicking in the sun. Open extended hours during school holidays.

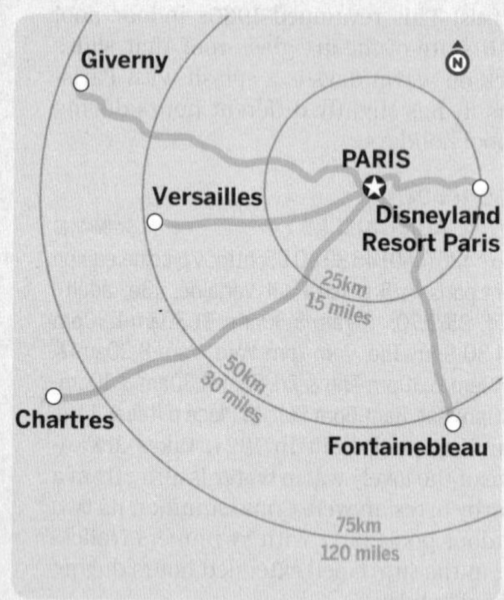

Day Trips from Paris

TOP SIGHTS
VERSAILLES

Louis XIV transformed his father's hunting lodge into the monumental Château de Versailles in the mid-17th century, and it remains France's most famous, grandest palace. Situated in the prosperous, leafy and bourgeois suburb of Versailles (population 84,225), the baroque château was the kingdom's political capital and the seat of the royal court from 1682 up until the fateful events of 1789 when Revolutionaries massacred the palace guard and dragged Louis XVI and Marie Antoinette back to Paris, where they were ingloriously guillotined.

Intended to house his court of 6000 people, Louis XIV hired four talented men to take on the gargantuan task: architect Louis Le Vau; Jules Hardouin-Mansart, who took over from Le Vau in the mid-1670s; painter and interior designer Charles Le Brun; and landscape designer André Le Nôtre, under whom entire hills were flattened, marshes drained and forests moved to create the seemingly endless gardens, ponds and fountains for which Versailles is so well known. It has been on Unesco's World Heritage list since 1979.

Sprawling over 900 hectares, the estate is divided into four main sections: the 580m-long palace; the gardens, canals and pools to the west of the palace; two smaller palaces known as the Grand Trianon and the Petit Trianon to the northwest; and the Hameau de la Reine (Queen's Hamlet) north of the Petit Trianon.

The basic palace ticket and more elaborate Passport both include an English-language audioguide and allow visitors to freely visit the King's and Queen's State Apartments, the chapel and various galleries. The Passport additionally gets you into the Grand and Petit Trianons and, in high season,

DON'T MISS

- Château de Versailles
- The Gardens
- Marie Antoinette's Estate
- The Trianon Palaces

PRACTICALITIES

- 01 30 83 78 00
- www.chateauversailles.fr
- admission Passport (estate-wide access) €18, with musical events €25, palace €15
- 8am-6pm Tue-Sat, 9am-6pm Sun Apr-Oct, 8.30am-5.30pm Tue-Sat, 9am-5.30pm Sun Nov-Mar

A DAY IN COURT

Visiting Versailles – even just the State Apartments – may seem overwhelming at first, but think of it as a house where people ate, drank, worked, slept and conspired and you'll be on the right path.

Some two decades into his long reign, Louis XIV began turning his father's hunting lodge into a palace large enough to house his entire court (to keep closer tabs on the 6000-strong army of courtiers). Sparing no expense, the Sun King employed the greatest artists and craftspeople of the day and by 1682 he'd created the most extravagant dormitory in history.

The royal schedule was as accurate and predictable as a Swiss watch. By following this itinerary of rooms you can recreate the king's day, starting with the **King's Bedchamber** 1 and the **Queen's Bedchamber** 2, where the royal couple was roused at about the same time. The royal procession then leads through the **Hall of Mirrors** 3 to the **Royal Chapel** 4 for morning Mass and returns to the **Council Chamber** 5 for late-morning meetings with ministers. After lunch the king might ride or hunt or visit the **King's Library** 6. Later he could join courtesans for an 'apartment evening' starting from the **Hercules Drawing Room** 7 or play billiards in the **Diana Drawing Room** 8 before supping at 10pm.

VERSAILLES BY NUMBERS

- **Rooms** 700 (11 hectares of roof)
- **Windows** 2153
- **Staircases** 67
- **Gardens and parks** 800 hectares
- **Trees** 200,000
- **Fountains** 50 (with 620 nozzles)
- **Paintings** 6300 (measuring 11km laid end to end)
- **Statues and sculptures** 2100
- **Objets d'art and furnishings** 5000
- **Visitors** 5.3 million per year

Queen's Bedchamber
Chambre de la Reine
The queen's life was on constant public display and even the births of her children were watched by crowds of spectators in her own bedchamber. DETOUR » The Guardroom, with a dozen armed men at the ready.

Lunch Break

Diner-style food at Sister's Café, crêpes at Le Phare St-Louis or picnic in the park.

Guardroom

South Wing

King's Library
Bibliothèque du Roi
The last resident, bibliophile Louis XVI, loved geography and his copy of *The Travels of James Cook* (in English, which he read fluently) is still on the shelf here.

Savvy Sightseeing

Avoid Versailles on Monday (closed), Tuesday (Paris' museums close, so visitors flock here) and Sunday, the busiest day. Also, book tickets online so you don't have to queue.

JOHN ELK III/GETTY ©

Hall of Mirrors

Galerie des Glaces

The solid-silver candelabra and furnishings in this extravagant hall, devoted to Louis XIV's successes in war, were melted down in 1689 to pay for yet another conflict. **DETOUR»** The antithetical Peace Drawing Room, adjacent.

DENNIS JOHNSON/GETTY ©

King's Bedchamber

Chambre du Roi

The king's daily life was anything but private and even his *lever* (rising) at 8am and *coucher* (retiring) at 11.30pm would be witnessed by up to 150 sycophantic courtiers.

MIKE BOOTH/ALAMY ©

Council Chamber

Cabinet du Conseil

This chamber, with carved medallions evoking the king's work, is where the monarch met his various ministers (state, finance, religion etc) depending on the days of the week.

DANITA DELIMONT/ALAMY ©

Diana Drawing Room

Salon de Diane

With walls and ceiling covered in frescos devoted to the mythical huntress, this room contained a large billiard table reserved for Louis XIV, a keen player.

Royal Chapel

Chapelle Royale

This two-storey chapel (with gallery for the royals and important courtiers, and the ground floor for the B-list) was dedicated to St Louis, patron of French monarchs. **DETOUR»** The sumptuous Royal Opera.

RADIUS IMAGES/ALAMY ©

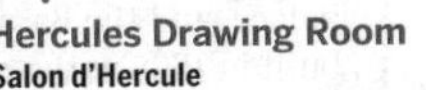

Hercules Drawing Room

Salon d'Hercule

This salon, with its stunning ceiling fresco of the strong man, gave way to the State Apartments, which were open to courtiers three nights a week. **DETOUR»** Apollo Drawing Room, used for formal audiences and as a throne room.

PLANNING FOR VERSAILLES

By noon queues for tickets and entering the château spiral out of control: arrive early and avoid Tuesday and Sunday, the busiest days. Save time by pre-purchasing tickets on the château's website or at **Fnac** (www.fnac.com) and go to Entrance A.

The estate is so vast that the only way to see it all is to hire a four-person electric car (☎01 39 66 97 66; per hr €30); hop aboard the shuttle train (www.train-versailles.com; adult/11-18yr €6.70/5); or rent a bike (☎01 39 66 97 66; per hr €6.50) or boat (☎01 39 66 97 66; per hr €15).

DINING AT VERSAILLES

Eateries within the estate include two branches of tearoom **Angelina** (www.angelina-versailles.fr; mains €10-24; ⏲10am-6pm Tue-Sat Apr-Oct, to 5pm Tue-Sat Nov-Mar), one inside the palace, and one by the Petit Trianon. Both are decadent settings for enjoying hot chocolate (p122). In the Louis XIV–created town of Versailles, rue de Satory is lined with restaurants serving food from around the world.

the Hameau de la Reine and the daytime musical fountain displays.

Château de Versailles

Few alterations have been made to the château since its construction, apart from most of the interior furnishings disappearing during the Revolution and many of the rooms being rebuilt by Louis-Philippe (r 1830–48), who opened part of the château to the public in 1837. The current €400 million restoration program is the most ambitious yet and until it's completed in 2020 part of the palace is likely to be clad in scaffolding when you visit.

To access areas that are otherwise off limits and to learn more about Versailles' history, take a 90-minute **guided tour** (☎01 30 83 77 88; tours €16; ⏲English-language tours 9.30am & 2pm Tue-Sun) of the Private Apartments of Louis XV and Louis XVI and the Opera House or Royal Chapel. Tour tickets include access to the most famous parts of the palace, such as the Hall of Mirrors and the King's and Queen's State Apartments; prebook online.

Note that prams (pushchairs), even folded, aren't allowed inside the palace; they must be left at Entrance A.

Hall of Mirrors

The palace's opulence peaks in its shimmering Galerie des Glaces (Hall of Mirrors). This 75m-long ballroom has 17 sparkling mirrors on one side and an equal number of windows on the other.

The King's & Queen's State Apartments

Luxurious, ostentatious appointments – frescoes, marble, gilt and woodcarvings, with themes and symbols drawn from Greek and Roman mythology – adorn every moulding, cornice, ceiling and door in the palace's Grands Appartements du Roi et de la Reine (King's and Queen's State Apartments).

The Gardens

Don't miss a stroll through the château's magnificent **gardens** (admission free except during musical events; ⏲8am-8.30pm Apr-Oct, 8am-6pm Tue-Sat Nov-Mar). The best view over the rectangular pools is from the Hall of Mirrors. Pathways include the Royal Walk's verdant 'green carpet', with smaller paths leading to leafy groves.

The gardens' largest fountains are the 17th-century Bassin de Neptune (Neptune's Fountain), a dazzling mirage of 99 fountains 300m north of the palace, and the Bassin d'Apollon (Apollo's Fountain), built in 1668 at the eastern end of the Grand Canal.

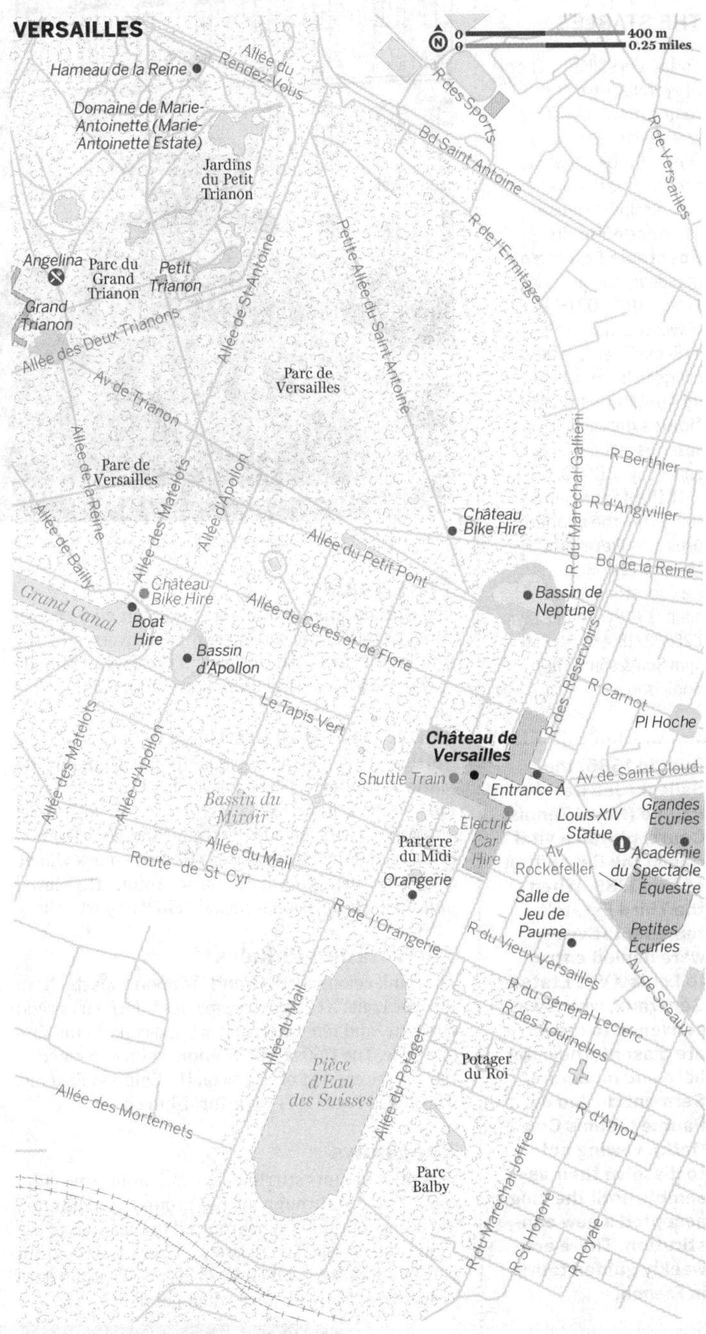
VERSAILLES
0 400 m
0 0.25 miles
Hameau de la Reine
Allée du Rendez-Vous
Domaine de Marie-Antoinette (Marie-Antoinette Estate)
Jardins du Petit Trianon
R des Sports
Bd Saint Antoine
R de Versailles
R de l'Ermitage
Angelina
Parc du Grand Trianon
Petit Trianon
Grand Trianon
Allée des Deux Trianons
Allée de St-Antoine
Petite Allée du Saint Antoine
Parc de Versailles
Av de Trianon
Allée de la Reine
Parc de Versailles
Allée des Matelots
Allée d'Apollon
R du Maréchal Gallieni
R Berthier
R d'Angiviller
Château Bike Hire
Allée de Bailly
Allée du Petit Pont
Bd de la Reine
Château Bike Hire
Grand Canal
Boat Hire
Allée de Céres et de Flore
Bassin de Neptune
Bassin d'Apollon
R des Reservoirs
R Carnot
Le Tapis Vert
Pl Hoche
Château de Versailles
Allée des Matelots
Allée d'Apollon
Shuttle Train
Entrance A
Av de Saint Cloud
Bassin du Miroir
Grandes Écuries
Louis XIV Statue
Electric Car Hire
Allée du Mail
Parterre du Midi
Av Rockefeller
Académie du Spectacle Équestre
Route de St Cyr
Orangerie
Salle de Jeu de Paume
R de l'Orangerie
Petites Écuries
R du Vieux Versailles
Av de Sceaux
R du Général Leclerc
R des Tournelles
Allée du Mail
Allée du Potager
Pièce d'Eau des Suisses
Potager du Roi
Allée des Mortemets
R d'Anjou
Parc Balby
R du Maréchal Joffre
R St Honoré
R Royale

THE STABLES

Today Versailles' school of architecture and restoration workshops fill the Petites Écuries (Little Stables), while the Grandes Écuries (Big Stables) house the **Académie du Spectacle Équestre** (Academy of Equestrian Arts; ☎01 39 02 07 14; www.acadequestre.fr; 1 av Rockefeller, Grandes Écuries). In addition to its 45-minute **Les Matinales** (morning training sessions; adult/13-18yr/under 13yr €12/10/6.50; ⏲11.15am Sat & Sun & some Thu) the academy presents **Reprises Musicales** (Musical Equestrian Shows; adult/13-18yr/under 13yr €25/22/16; ⏲6pm Sat, 3pm Sun & some Thu); book ahead.

Built in 1686, the Salle du Jeu de Paume (Royal Tennis Court) played a vital role in the Revolution of May 1789. When the Third Estate's representatives were denied entry to Louis XVI's États-Généraux, which was convened to moderate dissent, they met here and made the Serment du Jeu de Paume (Tennis Court Oath), vowing not to dissolve their assembly until the king accepted a new constitution. There are weekly guided tours in French.

Fountain in the gardens of Versailles

The Canals

The Grand Canal, 1.6km long and 62m wide, is oriented to reflect the setting sun. It's traversed by the 1km-long Petit Canal, forming a cross-shaped body of water with a perimeter of more than 5.5km.

Marie Antoinette's Estate

Northwest of the main palace is the **Domaine de Marie Antoinette** (Marie Antoinette's Estate; admission €10; ⏲noon-6.30pm Tue-Sat Apr-Oct, to 5.30pm Tue-Sat Nov-Mar). Tickets include the Grand and Petit Trianon palaces, and the **Hameau de la Reine** (a mock village completed in 1784, where Marie Antoinette played milkmaid); admission is included in Passport tickets.

The Trianon Palaces

The pink-colonnaded **Grand Trianon** was built in 1687 for Louis XIV as an escape from the court's rigid etiquette, and renovated under Napoleon I in the Empire style. The 1760s **Petit Trianon** was redecorated in 1867 by the consort of Napoleon III, Empress Eugénie, who added Louis XVI–style furnishings.

The Shows

Versailles mounts stirring day- and night-time *spectacles* (shows) throughout the grounds in summer, including fountains synchronised to the tones of baroque and classical composers, . Check the program and buy **tickets** (☎01 30 83 78 89; www.chateauversaillesspectacles.fr) in advance when possible.

TOP SIGHTS
DISNEYLAND RESORT PARIS

It took almost €4.6 billion to turn fields east of Paris into Europe's first Disney theme park. What started as Euro-Disney in 1992 sees families pouring in to share magical moments with Mickey and co. The resort comprises the Disneyland Park theme park, the film-oriented Walt Disney Studios Park, and hotel-, shop- and restaurant-filled Disney Village. And the kids can't get enough.

One-day admission includes unlimited access to attractions in *either* Disneyland Park or Walt Disney Studios Park. The latter includes entry to Disneyland Park three hours before it closes. Multiday passes and packages are available.

Picnics aren't allowed but there are ample restaurants. Most have meal coupons for adults/children (€28/15). The resort's seven American-styled hotels are linked by free shuttle bus to the parks. Rates vary hugely.

Devote a good hour on its website planning your day and buy tickets in advance where possible to avoid queues.

Disneyland Park

Disneyland Park (10am-8pm Mon-Fri, 9am-8pm Sat & Sun Sep-May, 9am-11pm Jun-Aug, hours can vary) has five themed 'lands': 1900s-styled **Main Street USA**; **Frontierland**, home to the Big Thunder Mountain ride; **Adventureland**, which evokes exotic lands (think *Pirates of the Caribbean*); **Fantasyland**, crowned by Sleeping Beauty's castle; and **Discoveryland**, with massive-queue rides such as Space Mountain: Mission 2.

Walt Disney Studios Park

Walt Disney Studios Park (9am-7pm late Jun-early Sep, 10am-7pm Mon-Fri & 9am-7pm Sat & Sun early Sep-late Jun) has behind-the-scenes tours showcasing film, animation and TV production, larger-than-life characters and wild rides like the Twilight Zone Tower of Terror.

DON'T MISS

- Disneyland Park
- Walt Disney Studios Park

PRACTICALITIES

- hotel booking 01 60 30 60 30, restaurant reservations 01 60 30 40 50
- www.disneylandparis.com
- one-day admission adult/3-11yr €59/53
- RER A4 to Marne-la-Vallée/Chessy from central Paris (€7)

Fontainebleau

Explore

Fresh air fills your lungs on arriving in the smart town of Fontainebleau (population 21,800), which is enveloped by the 20,000-hectare Forêt de Fontainebleau, one of France's loveliest woods.

The town grew up around its magnificent château, which has a list of former tenants and visitors that reads like a who's who of French royalty. Although it's less crowded and pressured than Versailles, exploring it can still take the best part of a day.

Rich in game and walking, cycling, rock-climbing and horse-riding opportunities, the surrounding forest is as big a playground today as it was in the 16th century, so it's worth prolonging your stay if you can. Fontainebleau also has a cosmopolitan drinking and dining scene, thanks to the town's lifeblood, the international graduate business school Insead.

The Best...

- **Sight** Château de Fontainebleau (p276)
- **Place to Eat** Dardonville (p275)
- **Place to Drink** Le Ferrare (p276)

SLEEPING IN FONTAINEBLEAU

- **Hôtel de Londres** (01 64 22 20 21; www.hoteldelondres.com; 1 place Général de Gaulle; d €100-180;) Classy, cosy and beautifully kept, the mostly air-conditioned 16-room Hotel London is furnished in warm reds and royal blues. The priciest rooms (eg room 5) have balconies with dreamy château views.
- **La Guérinière** (06 13 50 50 37; balestier.gerard@wanadoo.fr; 10 rue de Montebello; d incl breakfast €70; @) This charming B&B provides some of the best-value accommodation around. Owner Monsieur Balestier speaks English and has five generously proportioned rooms, each dressed in white linens and period wooden furniture. Breakfast includes homemade jam.

Top Tip

Train tickets to Fontainebleau Avon are sold at Gare de Lyon's SNCF Transilien counter/Billet Ile-de-France machines, *not* SNCF mainline counters/machines. On returning, tickets include travel to any Paris metro station.

Getting There & Away

Travel time The trip takes 35 to 60 minutes by train.

Train Up to 40 daily SNCF Transilien (www.transilien.com) trains link Paris' Gare de Lyon with Fontainebleau Avon station (€8.40).

Bus Line A links the train station with the château (€1.90), 2km southwest, every 10 minutes from 5.30am to 10.30pm (9.30pm Saturday, 11.30pm Sunday).

Taxi Book a taxi in Fontainebleau on 06 21 76 68 10.

Need to Know

- **Location** 69km southeast of Paris
- **Tourist Office** (01 60 74 99 99; www.fontainebleau-tourisme.com; 4 rue Royale; 10am-6pm Mon-Sat, 10am-12.30pm & 3-5pm Sun May-Oct, 10am-6pm Mon-Sat, 10am-1pm Sun Nov-Apr) Fontainebleau's poorly signposted tourist office sells loads of walking and rock-climbing guides and maps covering the Forêt de Fontainebleau. It also rents bikes (€5/15/19 per hour/half-day/24 hours; reserve in advance).

SIGHTS

Contact the tourist office for details of Fontainebleau's Musée National des Prisons (National Museum of Prisons), Musée Motocycliste de la Gendarmerie (Police Motorcycle Museum), and Centre Sportif d'Equitation Militaire (Sporting & Military Horseriding Centre), all visitable on monthly guided tours.

EATING & DRINKING

There are lovely cafe terraces on place Napoléon Bonaparte and some appealing

Fontainebleau

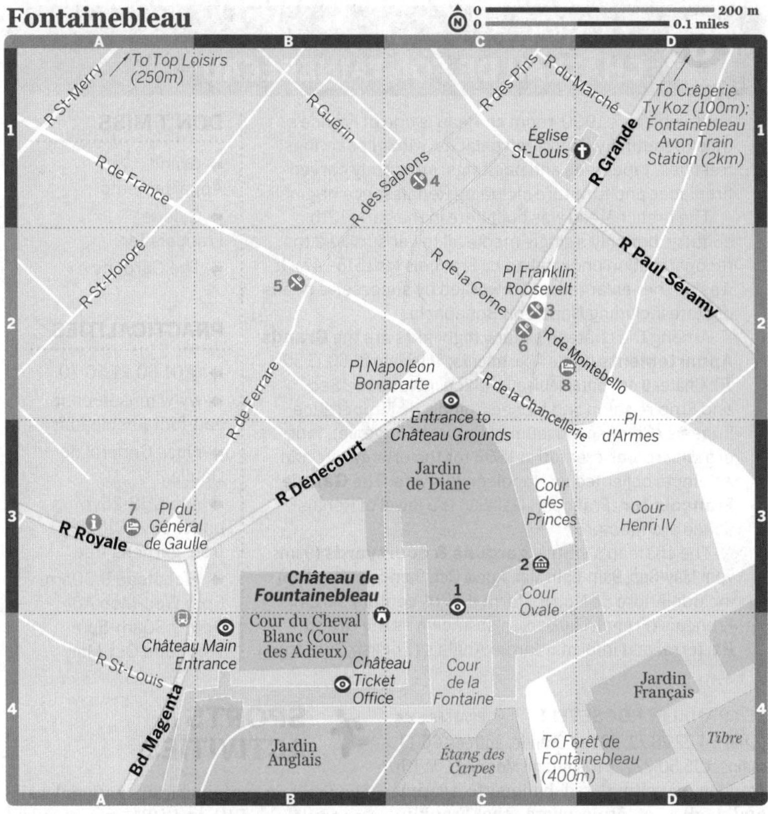

drinking options on rue de la Corne. Rue de Montebello tours the world with Indian, Lebanese and other international cuisines. For fabulous *fromageries* (cheese shops), head to rue des Sablons and rue Grande.

TOP CHOICE **DARDONVILLE** PATISSERIE, BOULANGERIE €
(24 rue des Sablons; ⏱7am-1.30pm & 3.15-7.30pm Tue-Sat, 7am-1.30pm Sun) Melt-in-your-mouth *macarons* in flavours like poppy seed and gingerbread cost just €4.50 per dozen (per *dozen!*) at this exceptional patisserie/*boulangerie*. Queues also form out the door for its amazing breads and savoury *petits fours* like tiny pastry-wrapped sausages and teensy coin-size quiches that are perfect picnic fare.

CÔTÉ SUD REGIONAL CUISINE €€
(☎01 64 22 00 33; 1 rue Montebello; lunch menu €14.50, mains €16.50-22; ⏱lunch & dinner daily) Dishes at this welcoming bistro have a southern accent, such as *daube de sanglier* (wild boar stew) and *salade landoise* (an enormous salad of fresh and cooked vegetables, goose liver and preserved gizzards). Bring your appetite.

Fontainebleau

Top Sights

Sights

Eating

Sleeping

TOP SIGHTS
CHÂTEAU DE FONTAINEBLEAU

Fontainbleau's 1900-room château is one of France's most beautifully decorated palaces, with gilt carvings, frescoes, tapestries and paintings, intricately carved fireplaces and furniture including Renaissance originals.

The first château was built here in the early 12th century, but only a single medieval tower survived the reconstruction undertaken by François I (r 1515–47). It was further enlarged and reworked by successive heads of state including Napoleon Bonaparte.

Among the château's many highlights are the **Grands Appartements** (State Apartments; ☎tel info 01 60 71 50 70; Château de Fontainebleau), which include the Second Empire salon and Musée Chinois de l'Impératice Eugénie (Chinese Museum of Empress Eugénie), four drawing rooms created in 1863 for the oriental art and artefacts collected by Napoleon III's wife. The **Galerie François 1er** (François I Gallery) is a jewel of Renaissance architecture.

The château's stately **gardens & courtyards** (9am-7pm May-Sep, 9am-6pm Mar, Apr & Oct, 9am-5pm Nov-Feb) include André Le Nôtre's formal, 17th-century Jardin Français (French Garden), also known as the Grand Parterre, and informal Jardin Anglais (English Garden).

DON'T MISS

- Grands Appartements
- Galerie François 1er
- The Gardens

PRACTICALITIES

- ☎01 60 71 50 70
- www.musee-chateau-fontainebleau.fr
- place Général de Gaulle
- adult/18-25yr/under 18yr €10/8/free; gardens free
- ⏲château 9.30am-6pm Wed-Mon Apr-Sep, 9.30am-5pm Wed-Mon Oct-Mar

LE FRANKLIN ROOSEVELT BRASSERIE €€
(☎01 64 22 28 73; 20 rue Grande; entrées €6-13, mains €15.50-22; ⏲10am-1am Mon-Sat) With wooden panelling, red banquette seating and oodles of atmosphere, the Franklin keeps locals well-fed: the *salades composées* (salads with meat or fish) are healthy and huge.

LE FERRARE BRASSERIE €
(☎01 60 72 37 04; 23 rue de France; 2-/3-course menus €11.50-13; ⏲7.30am-4pm Mon, to 10.30pm Tue-Thu, to 1am Fri & Sat) Locals pile into this quintessential bar/brasserie, which has a blackboard full of Auvergne specialities and bargain-priced *plats du jour* (daily specials).

CRÊPERIE TY KOZ CRÊPERIE €
(☎01 64 22 00 55; 18 rue de la Cloche; crêpes & galettes €3-10.80; ⏲lunch & dinner Tue-Sun) Tucked in a courtyard, this Breton hidey-hole whips up sweet crêpes and savoury galettes in regular (*simple*) or double-thickness (*pourleth*). Wash them down with traditional Val de Rance cider.

SPORTS & ACTIVITIES

The Forêt de Fontainebleau's national walking trails, the GR1 and GR11, are excellent for jogging, walking, cycling and horse riding, and for climbers the forest is a veritable paradise. Rock-climbing enthusiasts have long come to its sandstone ridges, cliffs and overhangs to hone their skills before setting off for the Alps. There are different grades marked by colours, with white representing easy climbs (suitable for children) and black representing climbs up and over death-defying boulders. The website **Bleau** (http://bleau.info) has stacks of information on climbing in the forest.

To give it a go, contact **Top Loisirs** (☎01 60 74 08 50; www.toploisirs.fr; 16 rue Sylvain Collinet) about equipment hire and instruction. Two gorges worth visiting are the **Gorges d'Apremont**, 7km northwest near Barbizon, and the **Gorges de Franchard**, a few kilometres south of Gorges d'Apremont.

Chartres

Explore

Step off the train in Chartres (population 45,600) and the two very different spires – one Gothic, the other Romanesque – of its glorious 13th-century cathedral beckon. Follow them to check out the cathedral's brilliant blue stained glass windows and its collection of relics – including the Sainte Voile (Holy Veil) said to have been worn by the Virgin Mary when she gave birth to Jesus – which have lured pilgrims since the Middle Ages.

After visiting the town's museums, don't miss a stroll around Chartres' carefully preserved old town. Adjacent to the cathedral, staircases called *tertres* and steep streets lined with half-timbered medieval houses lead downhill to the narrow western channel of the Eure River, romantically spanned by footbridges.

The Best...

➡ **Sight** Cathédrale Notre Dame (p277)

➡ **Place to Eat** Le Saint-Hilaire (p279)

➡ **Place to Drink** La Chocolaterie (p280)

Top Tip

Allow one-and-a-half to two hours to walk the signposted *circuit touristique* taking in Chartres' key sights. Free town maps from the tourist office also mark the route.

Getting There & Away

Travel time 55 to 70 minutes by train

Train Frequent SNCF trains link Paris' Gare Montparnasse (€14.50) with Chartres, some of which stop at Versailles-Chantiers (€12, 45 to 60 minutes).

Taxi For a local taxi ring ☎02 37 36 00 00.

Need to Know

➡ **Location** 91km southwest of Paris

➡ **Tourist Office** (☎02 37 18 26 26; www.chartres-tourisme.com; place de la Cathédrale; ⏲9am-7pm Mon-Sat, 9.30am-5.30pm Sun Apr-Sep, 9am-6pm Mon-Sat, 9.30am-5pm Sun Oct-Mar) Rents 1½-hour English-language

TOP SIGHTS
CATHÉDRALE NOTRE DAME

France's best-preserved medieval cathedral was built in the Gothic style in the 13th century to replace a Romanesque cathedral devastated by fire in 1194.

Covering 2.6 sq km, the cathedral's 172 stained glass windows are mostly 13th-century originals. Over the west entrance the most important, dating from 1150, are renowned for their dazzling colour, called 'Chartres blue'.

The 105m-high **Clocher Vieux** (Old Bell Tower) is the tallest Romanesque steeple still standing. A visit to the 112m-high **Clocher Neuf** (adult/18-25yr/under 18yr €7/4.50/free; ⏲9.30am-12.30pm & 2-6pm Mon-Sat, 2-6pm Sun May-Aug, 9.30am-12.30pm & 2-5pm Mon-Sat, 2-5pm Sun Sep-Apr) justifies the spiralling 350-step climb.

In Chartres since 876, the **Sainte Voile** (Holy Veil) is displayed at the end of the cathedral's north aisle.

Tours in French of the cathedral's 110m-long **crypt** (guided tour adult/7-18yr €2.70/2.10; ⏲tours 11am Mon-Sat & 2.15pm, 3.15pm, 4.30pm & 5.15pm daily late Jun-late Sep, 11am Mon-Sat & 2.15pm, 3.15pm & 4.30pm daily Apr-late Jun & late Sep-Oct, 11am Mon-Sat & 4.15pm Nov-Mar) run year-round. There are seasonal English-language **tours** (☎02 37 28 15 58; millerchartres@aol.com; tour €10; ⏲noon & 2.45pm Mon-Sat Apr-Oct).

DON'T MISS

➡ Stained Glass Windows

➡ Clocher Neuf

➡ Sainte Voile

➡ Crypt

PRACTICALITIES

➡ www.diocese-chartres.com

➡ place de la Cathédrale

➡ ⏲8.30am-7.30pm, to 10pm Tue, Fri & Sun Jun-Aug

Chartres

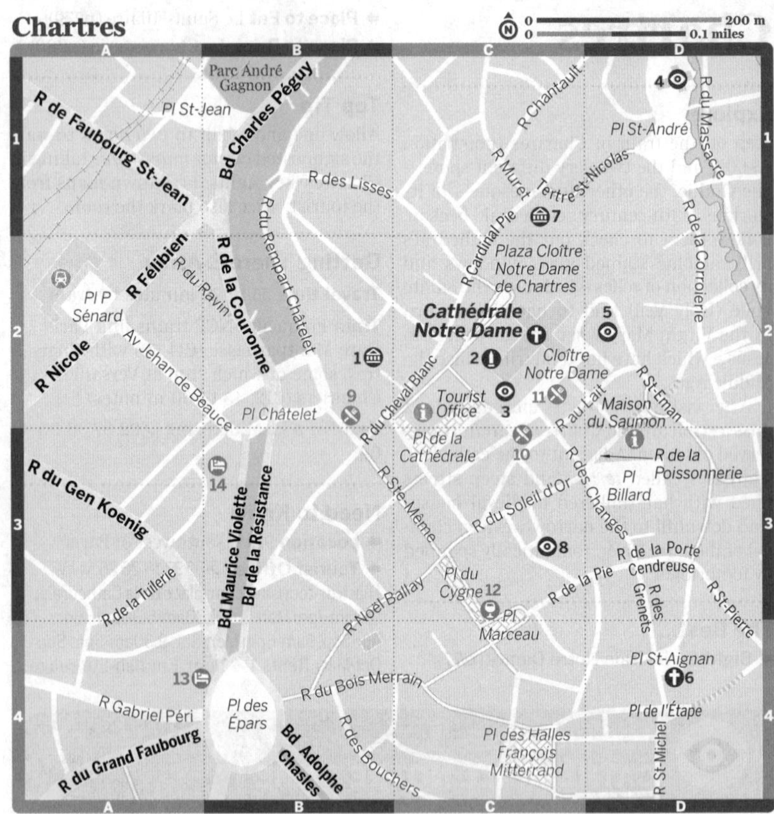

Chartres

Top Sights
- Cathédrale Notre Dame C2

Sights
1. Centre International du Vitrail B2
2. Clocher Neuf C2
3. Clocher Vieux C2
4. Collégiale St-André D1
5. Crypt D2
6. Église St-Aignan D4
7. Musée des Beaux-Arts C1
8. Old Town C3

Eating
9. La Passacaille B2
10. Le Bistro de la Cathédrale C3
11. Le Serpente C2

Drinking & Nightlife
12. La Chocolaterie C3

Sports & Activities
- La Crypte .... (see 5)

Sleeping
13. Best Western Le Grand Monarque A4
14. Hôtel du Bœuf Couronné B3

audioguide tours (€5.50/8.50 for one/two) of the medieval city as well as binoculars (€2), fabulous for seeing details of the cathedral close up. There's a branch with an exhibition on Chartres' history in the 16th-century **Maison du Saumon** (8-10 rue de la Poissonnerie; 10am-1pm & 2-6pm Mon-Sat Apr-Oct, 10am-noon & 1-6pm Mon-Sat Nov-Mar).

SIGHTS

CENTRE INTERNATIONAL DU VITRAIL MUSEUM

(www.centre-vitrail.org; 5 rue du Cardinal Pie; adult/16-18yr/under 15yr €4/3/free; ⏲9.30am-12.30pm & 1.30-6pm Mon-Fri, 10am-12.30pm & 2.30-6pm Sat, 2.30-6pm Sun) After visiting Chartres' cathedral, view more stained glass close up by nipping into its International Stained-Glass Centre, housed in a half-timbered former granary.

MUSÉE DES BEAUX-ARTS MUSEUM

(29 Cloître Notre Dame; adult/under 18yr €3.20/free; ⏲2-6pm Wed, Sat & Sun May-Oct, 2-5pm Wed, Sat & Sun Nov-Mar) Chartres' fine-arts museum, accessed via the gate next to the cathedral's north portal, is in the former Palais Épiscopal (Bishop's Palace), built in the 17th and 18th centuries. Its collections include 16th-century enamels of the Apostles made for François I, paintings from the 16th to 19th centuries and polychromatic wooden sculptures from the Middle Ages.

OLD TOWN HISTORIC QUARTER

Chartres' old town is northeast and east of the cathedral. Highlights include the 12th-century **Collégiale St-André** (place St-André), a Romanesque church that's now an exhibition centre; **rue de la Tannerie** and its extension **rue de la Foulerie**, lined with flower gardens, mill races and the restored remnants of riverside trades: wash houses, tanneries and the like; and **rue des Écuyers**, with many structures dating from around the 16th century.

Flying buttresses hold up the 12th- and 13th-century **Église St-Pierre** (place St-Pierre), which was once part of a Benedictine monastery founded in the 7th century. Its location outside the city walls meant it was vulnerable to attack, and the fortress-like, pre-Romanesque bell tower, which dates from around 1000, was once used as a refuge by monks. The fine, brightly coloured clerestory windows in Église St-Pierre's nave, choir and apse date from the early 14th century.

Église St-Aignan (place St-Aignan) is interesting for its wooden barrel-vault roof (1625), arcaded nave and painted interior of faded blue and gold floral motifs (c 1870). The stained glass and the Renaissance Chapelle de St-Michel date from the 16th and 17th centuries.

SLEEPING IN CHARTRES

➡ **Best Western Le Grand Monarque** (☎02 37 18 15 15; www.bw-grand-monarque.com; 22 place des Épars; d/tr from €132/195; ❄@📶) With its teal-blue shutters gracing its 1779 façade, lovely stained-glass ceiling and treasure trove of period furnishings, old B&W photos and knick-knacks, the refurbished Grand Monarch (with air-con in some rooms) is a historical gem and very central. Its restaurant has a Michelin star; check the website for its program of three-hour cooking lessons (€55).

➡ **Hôtel du Bœuf Couronné** (☎02 37 18 06 06; www.leboeufcouronne.com; 15 place Châtelet; s €65-85, d €75-109; @📶) The red-curtained entrance lends a theatrical air to this recently renovated Logis guesthouse in the centre of everything. Its summertime terrace restaurant cooks up cathedral-view dining and the Dickens music bar is right next door.

LE PETIT CHART' TRAIN TOURIST TRAIN

(www.promotrain.fr/gbcircuit.htm; adult/child €6/3; ⏲10.30am-7pm Apr-Oct) Chartres' electric tourist train covers the main sights in 35 minutes; it departs from in front of the tourist office.

EATING & DRINKING

TOP CHOICE **LE SAINT-HILAIRE** REGIONAL CUISINE €€

(☎02 37 30 97 57; www.restaurant-saint-hilaire.fr; 11 rue du Pont Saint-Hilaire; 2-/3-course menus from €27/42; ⏲lunch & dinner Tue-Sat) Local products are ingeniously used in to-die-for dishes like stuffed mushrooms with lentils, snails in puff pastry with leek fondue, a seasonal lobster menu, and aromatic cheese platters at this pistachio-painted, wood-beamed charmer.

LE SERPENTE BRASSERIE, TEAROOM €

(☎02 37 21 68 81; www.leserpente.com; 2 Cloître Notre Dame; mains €16-18.50; ⏲11am-11pm) Its location opposite the cathedral ensures this traditional brasserie and *salon de thé* – one of the oldest in Chartres – is always full. Specialities span pigs trotters and veal kidneys to fresh fish and meal-sized salads.

LA PASSACAILLE ITALIAN €

(☎02 37 21 52 10; www.lapassacaille.fr; 30 rue Ste-Même; 2-/3-course menus €15/18, pizzas €7.50-11.50, pasta €9; lunch & dinner Thu-Tue;) This welcoming spot has particularly good pizzas (try the Montagnarde with tomato, mozzarella, nutty-flavoured Reblochon cheese, potatoes, red onions, cured ham and crème fraîche). Homemade pasta with toppings including *pistou* (pesto) made on the premises.

LE BISTRO DE LA CATHÉDRALE BISTRO, BAR €€

(☎02 37 36 59 60; 1 Cloître Notre Dame; menus €22-24; lunch & dinner Thu-Tue) In the shadow of the cathedral, this stylish wine bar is ideally situated for a long lazy lunch of pâté, duck breast and the like over a glass or three of wine. Service is friendly and efficient.

LA CHOCOLATERIE TEAROOM, PATISSERIE

(14 place du Cygne; 8am-7.30pm Tue-Sat, 10am-7.30pm Sun & Mon) Soak up local life overlooking the open-air **flower market** (place du Cygne; 8am-1pm Tue, Thu & Sat). This tearoom/patisserie's hot chocolate and *macarons* (flavoured with orange, apricot, peanut, pineapple and so on) are sublime, as are its sweet homemade crêpes and miniature madeleine sponge cakes (dishes from €3.35).

Giverny

Explore

The village's two main draws, the impressionist museum the Musée des Impressionismes Giverny and Monet's former home, the Maison de Claude Monet, are only open from April to October (as are most places to eat, drink and sleep). Alas, outside these times, there's no reason to visit Giverny (population 525). If you are here during these months, the Maison de Claude Monet's gardens are magnificent, so factor in plenty of time to enjoy them. From early to late spring, daffodils, tulips, wisteria and irises appear, followed by poppies and lilies. By June, nasturtiums, roses and sweet peas are in blossom. Around September, there are dahlias, sunflowers and hollyhocks.

TOP SIGHTS MAISON DE CLAUDE MONET

The prized drawcard of tiny Giverny is the home and flower-filled garden of the seminal impressionist painter and his family from 1883 to 1926. Here Monet painted some of his most famous series, including *Décorations des Nymphéas* (Waterlilies).

Unfortunately, Monet's hectare of land has become two distinct areas, cut by the Chemin du Roy, a small railway line that has been converted into the D5 road.

The northern area of the property is **Clos Normand**, where Monet's famous pastel-pink-and-green house and the Atelier des Nymphéas (Water Lilies Studio) stand. These days the studio is the entrance hall, adorned with precise reproductions of his works. Outside are the symmetrically laid-out gardens.

From the Clos Normand's far corner a foot tunnel leads under the D5 to the **Jardin d'Eau** (Water Garden). Having bought this land in 1895 after his reputation (and bank account) had swelled, Monet dug a pool, planted water lilies and built the famous Japanese bridge, since rebuilt. Draped with purple wisteria, the bridge blends into the asymmetrical foreground and background, creating the intimate atmosphere for which the 'Painter of Light' was famous.

DON'T MISS

- Clos Normand
- Jardin d'Eau

PRACTICALITIES

- ☎02 32 51 28 21
- www.fondation-monet.com
- 84 rue Claude Monet
- adult/7-12yr/under 7yr €9/5/free
- 9.30am-6pm daily Apr-Oct

The Best...

➡ **Sight** Maison de Claude Monet (p280)

➡ **Place to Paint** Musée des Impressionismes Giverny (p281)

➡ **Place to Eat** Auberge du Vieux Moulin (p281)

Top Tip

Be aware that the village has no public toilets, ATMs or bureaux de change.

Getting There & Away

Travel time 45 minutes by train to Vernon, then 20 minutes by bus (or by taxi or bike).

Train From Paris' Gare St-Lazare SNCF, trains run to Vernon (€13.30, 1¼ hours).

Bus Seasonal shuttle buses (€4 return, from April to October) link Vernon's station with Giverny.

Taxi A taxi from Vernon's station to Giverny costs about €15 one way. Call ☎02 32 51 10 24.

Bike Hire a bike from Bar-Restaurant du Chemin de Fer (€12 per day), opposite Vernon's station, or at Cyclo News (7 cours du Marché aux Chevaux; €12.20 per day; ⏲8:30am to 7.30pm Tuesday-Saturday).

Need to Know

➡ **Location** 74km northwest of Paris

➡ **Tourist Office** (☎02 32 51 39 60; www.cape-tourisme.fr; 36 rue Carnot; ⏲9am-12.30pm & 2-6pm Tue-Sat, 10am-noon Sun May-Sep, 9am-12.30pm & 2-5.30pm Tue-Sat Oct-Apr) The closest tourist office – and the transport springboard for Giverny – is in Vernon, 7km northwest. The website www.vernon-visite.org is also packed with information.

SIGHTS

MUSÉE DES IMPRESSIONNISMES GIVERNY — ART MUSEUM

(☎02 32 51 94 65; www.mdig.fr; 99 rue Claude Monet; adult/child €6.50/3; ⏲10am-5.30pm daily Apr-Oct) About 100m northwest of the Maison de Claude Monet is the Giverny Museum of Impressionisms. Set up in partnership with the Musée d'Orsay, among others, the pluralised name reinforces its coverage of all aspects of impressionism and related movements.

Until 2009 the museum was known as the Musée d'Art Américain (American Art Museum), which focused on a fine collection of works by American impressionist painters who flocked to France in the late 19th and early 20th centuries; the new museum covers impressionists and their works both home-grown and abroad, while still exhibiting American works.

Reserve ahead for two-hour **art workshops** offering an introduction to watercolour, drawing, sketching or pastels (high season only). Lectures, readings, concerts and documentaries also take place regularly – check the program on the website.

SLEEPING IN GIVERNY

➡ **Le Clos Fleuri** (☎02 32 21 36 51; www.giverny-leclosfleuri.fr; 5, rue de la Dîme; s/d €90/95; ⏲Apr-Oct; 📶) Big rooms with king-size beds and exposed wood beams overlook the hedged gardens of this delightful B&B within strolling distance of the Maison de Claude Monet and Musée des Impressionismes Giverny. Each of its three rooms is named after a different flower; green-thumbed host Danielle speaks fluent English.

EATING & DRINKING

AUBERGE DU VIEUX MOULIN — TRADITIONAL FRENCH €€

(☎02 32 51 46 15; www.vieuxmoulingiverny.com; 21 rue de la Falaise; salads €12, lunch menus €15-18, dinner menus €24-35; ⏲lunch daily, dinner Fri & Sat Apr-Oct, lunch Fri-Sun Nov-Mar) The Old Mill Inn, a couple of hundred metres east of the Maison de Claude Monet, is an excellent place for lunch and has a lovely terrace.

LA MUSARDIÈRE — BRASSERIE €€

(☎02 32 21 03 18; www.lamusardiere.fr; 123 rue Claude Monet; d €83-97; ⏲hotel Feb–mid-Dec, restaurant daily Apr-Oct; 🅿📶) Dining at the crêperie-oriented restaurant of this 1880-established hotel is a pleasure. It's set amid a lovely garden less than 100m northeast of the Maison de Claude Monet.

Sleeping

Paris has a huge choice of accommodation, from hostels to deluxe hotels, some of which rank among the finest in the world. Yet although the city has more than 150,000 beds in over 1500 establishments, you'll still need to book well ahead during the warmer months (April to October) and all public and school holidays.

Hotels

Hotels in Paris are inspected by government authorities and classified from no-star to five stars. The majority are two- and three-star hotels, which are generally excellent value. All hotels must display their rates, including TVA (*taxe sur la valeur ajoutée*; valued-added tax).

Rooms tend to be small by international standards – a family of four will probably need two connecting rooms, though it's possible to make do with triples, quads or suites in some places.

Cheaper hotels may not have lifts and/or air conditioning. Some don't accept credit cards.

Breakfast is rarely included in hotel rates; heading to a cafe is often better value.

Hostels

Paris is awash with hostels, and standards are improving. Rates often include breakfast.

More institutional hostels have daytime lock-outs and curfews; some have a maximum three-night stay. Places with upper age limits tend not to enforce them except at the busiest of times. Official *auberges de jeunesse* (youth hostels) require guests to have Hostelling International (HI) cards or their equivalent.

B&Bs & Homestays

Bed-and-breakfast (B&B) accommodation (*chambres d'hôte* in French) is increasingly popular. The city of Paris has inaugurated a scheme, Paris Quality Hosts (Hôtes Qualité Paris), to foster B&Bs – not just to offer accommodation, but also to ease the isolation of Parisians, half of whom live alone. There's often a minimum stay of three or four nights.

Apartments

Families or those wanting to self-cater should consider renting a short-stay apartment. Paris has some excellent apartment hotels, such as the international chain **Apart'hotels Citadines** (www.citadines.com/apart_hotels).

For an even more authentic experience, apartment rental agencies offer furnished residential apartments for stays of a few days to several months. Apartments often include wi-fi and washing machines, and can be superb value. Beware of direct-rental scams.

Websites

- Lonely Planet (www.lonelyplanet.com/hotels) Reviews of Lonely Planet's top choices.
- Paris Hotel Service (www.parishotelservice.com) Specialises in boutique hotels.
- Paris Hotel (www.hotels-paris.fr) Well-organised hotel booking site.
- Paris Quality Hosts (www.hqp.fr) B&B accommodation in the city.
- Guest Apartment Services (www.guestapartment.com) Romantic apartment rentals on and around Paris' islands.
- Room Sélection (www.room-selection.com) Select apartment rentals centred on the Marais.
- Paris Attitude (www.parisattitude.com) Thousands of apartment rentals, professional service, reasonable fees.

Lonely Planet's Top Choices

Hôtel Crayon (p286) Artist line- drawings, retro furnishings and coloured-glass shower doors.

Le Pradey (p286) This newcomer is the last word in luxury hotel design.

Mama Shelter (p292) Philippe Starck-designed hipster haven with a cool in-house pizzeria.

L'Hôtel (p295) The stuff of romance, Parisian myths and urban legends.

L'Apostrophe (p295) Cutting-edge design invoking wild interpretations of the written word.

Le Citizen Hotel (p289) Modern and tech-savvy, with a warm minimalist design.

Best by Budget

€

Hôtel Tiquetonne (p286)

Hôtel Monte Carlo (p285)

Hôtel Eldorado (p289)

Hôtel du Nord – Le Pari Vélo (p289)

Cosmos Hôtel (p290)

Hôtel St-André des Arts (p295)

€€

Hôtel St-Louis en l'Île (p293)

Hôtel Amour (p287)

Hôtel Perreyve (p295)

Hôtel Jeanne d'Arc (p290)

Hôtel Minerve (p294)

Le Citizen Hotel (p289)

€€€

Hidden Hotel (p285)

Hôtel du Jeu de Paume (p293)

Hôtel Les Jardins du Marais (p290)

Relais Christine (p296)

Hôtel des Académies et des Art (p296)

Best Design Hotels

W Paris - Opéra (p285)

Hôtel Joyce (p285)

BLC Design Hotel (p293)

Five Hotel (p293)

Le Bellechasse (p295)

Hôtel de la Paix (p297)

Best Boutique Hotels

Hôtel Caron de Beaumarchais (p291)

Hôtel du Petit Moulin (p291)

Hôtel Sezz (p285)

Hôtel Particulier Montmartre (p288)

La Maison (p297)

Select Hôtel (p293)

Best B&Bs

Gentle Gourmet (p285)

Au Sourire de Montmartre (p288)

A Room in Paris (p289)

Manoir de Beauregard (p289)

Hôtel du Haut Marais (p290)

Best Historic Hotels

Hôtel Langlois (p285)

Hôtel Chopin (p286)

Le Pavillon de la Reine (p290)

Hôtel St-Merry (p287)

Hôtel Favart (p287)

Hôtel d'Angleterre (p295)

NEED TO KNOW

Price Ranges

In this book, the following price ranges apply for a double room with en suite bathroom in high season (breakfast not included).

€	less than €110
€€	€110 to €200
€€€	over €200

Taxe de Séjour

The city of Paris levies a *taxe de séjour* (tourist tax) of between €0.20 (campgrounds, 'NN' or unclassified hotels) and €1.50 (four-star hotels) per person per night on all forms of accommodation.

Internet Access

Most hotels and hostels in Paris have some form of internet access available. Increasingly, wi-fi (pronounced wee-fee in French) is free of charge. Some establishments have a computer terminal in the reception area for guest use and may charge guests an access fee. You may find that in many hotels, especially older ones, the higher the floor, the less reliable the wi-fi connection.

Smoking

Smoking is now officially banned in all Paris hotels, so don't be afraid to complain if you get a smoky room.

Where To Stay

Neighbourhood	For	Against
Eiffel Tower & Western Paris	Close to Paris' iconic tower and museums. Upmarket area with quiet residential streets.	Short on budget and midrange accommodation options. Limited nightlife.
Champs-Élysées & Grands Boulevards	Luxury hotels, famous boutiques and department stores, gastronomic restaurants, great nightlife.	Some areas extremely pricey. Nightlife hot spots can be noisy.
Louvre & Les Halles	Epicentral location, excellent transport links, major museums, shopping galore.	Not many bargains. Ongoing Forum des Halles construction work may be noisy and inconvenient.
Montmartre & Northern Paris	Village atmosphere and some lively multicultural areas. Many places have views across Paris.	Hilly streets, less central than some areas, and some parts very touristy. Red light district around Pigalle, although well-lit and safe, won't appeal to some travellers.
Le Marais & Ménilmontant	Buzzing nightlife, hip shopping, great range of eating options in all price ranges. Excellent museums. Lively gay and lesbian scene. Busier on Sundays than most areas. Very central.	Can be seriously noisy in areas where bars and clubs are especially concentrated.
Bastille & Eastern Paris	Few tourists, allowing you to see the 'real' Paris up close. Excellent markets, loads of nightlife options.	Some areas slightly out of the way.
The Islands	As geographically central as it gets. Almost all accommodation situated on the peaceful, romantic Île St-Louis.	No metro station on the Île St-Louis. Limited self-catering options, zero nightlife.
Latin Quarter	Energetic student area, stacks of eating and drinking options, late-opening bookshops.	Popularity with students and visiting academics makes rooms hardest to find during conferences and seminars from March to June and in October.
St-Germain & Les Invalides	Stylish, central location, superb shopping, sophisticated dining, proximity to the Jardin du Luxembourg.	Budget accommodation is seriously short changed.
Montparnasse & Southern Paris	Good value, few tourists, excellent links to both airports.	Some areas slightly out of the way.

Eiffel Tower & Western Paris

HÔTEL SEZZ BOUTIQUE HOTEL €€€

Map p382 (01 56 75 26 26; www.hotelsezz.com; 6 av Frémiet, 16e; d €353, ste €428-910; Passy) Punning on the number of the posh *arrondissement* – 16 (*seize* in French) – in which it finds itself, this boutique bonanza is heavy on design (think Christophe Pillet), technology and Zen spirit. The 27 rooms, more than half of which are suites, are spacious and done up in reds and blacks, and feature lots of glass.

There's a *hammam* (Turkish steambath), Jacuzzi and massage room, and the bar specialises in Champagne. Each guest has their own personal assistant during their stay.

MON HÔTEL BOUTIQUE HOTEL €€€

Map p382 (01 45 02 76 76; www.monhotel.fr; 1-5 rue d'Argentine, 16e; d €299-428; Argentine) The Mac of the Paris hotel world, Mon Hôtel is a sleek boutique property located just behind the Arc de Triomphe. The vision here is contemporary design, and the 37 rooms feature unusual touches like alcantara (a kind of synthetic suede) walls and, of course, cool ring-shaped iPod docks.

Added luxuries like Compagnie de Provence bath products and a massage and sauna room make this one of the nicer choices near the Champs-Élysées.

GENTLE GOURMET B&B €€

Map p382 (01 45 00 46 55; www.gentlegourmetbandb.com; 21 rue Duret, 16e; s €135-155, d €160-200; Argentine) A vegan bed and breakfast, the Gentle Gourmet is definitely a unique concept in Paris. In addition to getting a comfortable room in an apartment building, there are loads of other extras, including vegan dinners (reservations essential) and tours of the kitchen gardens of France. There are only a few beds available, however, so you'll need to book ahead.

Champs-Élysées & Grands Boulevards

HIDDEN HOTEL BOUTIQUE HOTEL €€€

Map p384 (01 40 55 03 57; www.hidden-hotel.com; 28 rue de l'Arc de Triomphe, 17e; s & d from €376; Charles de Gaulle-Étoile) The Hidden is one of the Champs-Élysées' best secrets: an ecofriendly boutique hotel, it's serene, stylish, reasonably spacious, and it even sports green credentials. The earth-coloured tones are the result of natural pigments (there's no paint), and all rooms feature handmade wooden furniture, stone basins for sinks, and linen curtains surrounding Coco-Mat beds. The Emotion rooms are among the most popular.

W PARIS - OPÉRA DESIGN HOTEL €€€

Map p386 (01 77 48 94 94; www.wparisopera.fr; 4 rue Meyerbeer, 9e; d €340-500; Chausée d'Antin-La Fayette) Melding 1870s Haussmann style with modern design, this sleek new hotel boasts the plushest rooms on the Grands Boulevards. Don't sell yourself short with a Cozy or Wonderful room: what you want is a Spectacular room – or maybe even a Wow suite – with superlative-inducing views of the Palais Garnier next door.

HÔTEL JOYCE DESIGN HOTEL €€€

Map p386 (01 55 07 00 01; www.hotel-joyce.com; 29 rue La Bruyère, 9e; €259-294; St-Georges) This design hotel is located in a lovely residential area in between Montmartre and l'Opéra. It's got all the modern design touches (iPod docks, a sky-lit breakfast room fitted out with old Range Rover seats) and even makes some ecofriendly claims – it relies on 50% renewable energy and uses organic products when available. Rates drop significantly outside of high season.

HÔTEL LANOGLOIS HISTORIC HOTEL €€

Map p386 (01 48 74 78 24; www.hotel-langlois.com; 63 rue St-Lazare, 9e; s €110-120, d €140-150; Trinité) If you're looking for a bit of belle époque Paris, the Langlois won't let you down. Built in 1870, this 27-room hotel has kept its charm, from the tiny caged elevator to sandstone fireplaces (sadly decommissioned) in many rooms as well as original bathroom fixtures and tiles. Room 64 has wonderful views of Montmartre's rooftops.

HÔTEL MONTE CARLO HOTEL €

Map p386 (01 47 70 36 75; www.hotelmontecarlo.fr; 44 rue du Faubourg Montmartre, 9e; s €45-120, d €59-147, tr €119-179; Le Peletier) A unique budget hotel, the Monte Carlo is a steal, with colourful, personalised rooms and a great neighbourhood location. The owners go the extra mile and even provide a partly organic breakfast. The cheaper rooms come without bathroom or shower, but overall it outclasses many of the other choices in its price range. Rates vary with the season.

HÔTEL AMARANTE BEAU MANOIR HOTEL €€€
Map p386 (01 53 42 28 28; www.amarantebeaumanoir.com; 6 rue de l'Arcade, 8e; s & d €216-255; ; Madeleine) Among the cosier hotels in the 8e, the Amarante has traditional-style rooms, with exposed rafters, wooden furniture and oak panelling, and it has a prime location just around the corner from place Madeleine. There's a small fitness room downstairs. Wi-fi access here costs an additional €22 per day.

HÔTEL CHOPIN HISTORIC HOTEL €
Map p386 (01 47 70 58 10; www.hotelchopin.fr; 46 passage Jouffroy, 9e; s €72-88, d €98-114, tr €136; ; Grands Boulevards) Dating to 1846, the 36-room Chopin is down one of Paris' most delightful 19th-century arcades. The rooms don't have much in the way of personality, but the belle époque location is fabulous.

Louvre & Les Halles

HÔTEL TIQUETONNE HOTEL €
Map p392 (01 42 36 94 58; www.hoteltiquetonne; 6 rue Tiquetonne, 2e; d with shower €65, with shared shower €45 ; ; Etienne Marcel) Heart-warmingly good value, this 45-room address in the heart of party land has been in the hotel biz since the 1900s and is much-loved by a loyal clientele of all ages. Rooms straddle seven floors, are spick and span, and sport an inoffensive mix of vintage decor – roughly 1930s to the 1980s with brand new bathrooms and parquet flooring in recently renovated rooms.

Ask for a room in the rooftops with a view of Basilique du Sacré-Cœur (rooms 701, 702 or 703) or Eiffel Tower (rooms 704 and 705)! Shared shower *jeton* (tokens) are €5; ask at reception.

TOP CHOICE **HÔTEL CRAYON** BOUTIQUE HOTEL €€
Map p392 (01 42 36 54 19; www.hotelcrayon.com; 25 rue du Bouloi, 1er; s €129-249, d €149-299; ; Les Halles or Sentier) Line drawings by French artist Julie Gauthron bedeck walls and doors at this creative boutique hotel – a work of art. The pencil *(le crayon)* is the theme, with rooms sporting a different shade of each floor's chosen colour – we love the coloured-glass shower doors and the books on the bedside table that guests can swap and take home.

Beautiful pieces of 1950s and 1960s furniture add a dash of retro, and doodling on the walls is a unique perk for guests sleeping in the dazzling white-and-silver suite. Pick which fragrance you'd like your room perfumed with, help yourself to coffee or grab a drink from the fridge, and make yourself at home. *Quel bonheur!*

LE PRADEY DESIGN HOTEL €€€
Map p388 (01 42 60 31 70; www.lepradey.com; 5 rue Saint Roch, 1er; d from €220; ; Tuileries) Enviably secreted behind the Louvre and Jardin des Tuileries on smart rue St-Honoré, this exclusive new address is the last word in luxury hotel design. Guests linger over glossy art books in the understatedly chic, mezzanine lounge – if they can drag themselves away from whichever individually themed suite they are staying in. Exuberant Cabaret evokes the theatrical glamour of the Moulin Rouge with its frilly-skirt bedspread, deep red walls and heart-shaped doorframe; while Opéra, elegantly dressed in pretty pinks and greys, treats guests to a magical night at the ballet.

HÔTEL THÉRÈSE HOTEL €€
Map p388 (01 42 96 10 01; www.hoteltherese.com; 5-7 rue Thérèse, 1er; s €165-185, d €195-295; Pyramides) From the same people who brought you the Left Bank's lovely Hotel Verneuil, the Thérèse is ideal for those with a fetish for Japanese food – this chic address is steps from rue Ste-Anne and Japantown. Rooms are individually decorated, classical yet eclectic in design, with stylish linen panels on the windows and tubs in the bathroom (cheaper, smaller rooms – and they are small – have showers). Highlight: the clubby library lounge.

LE RELAIS DU LOUVRE BOUTIQUE HOTEL €€
Map p392 (01 40 41 96 42; www.relaisdulouvre.com; 19 rue des Prêtres St-Germain l'Auxerrois, 1er; s €135-170, d €195-220, tr €235-250; ; Pont Neuf) If you like style in a traditional sense, choose this lovely 21-room hotel just west of the Louvre and across the street from Église St-Germain l'Auxerrois with its melodious chime of bells. The nine rooms facing the street and church are petite.

Room 2 has access to the garden; and the top-floor apartment sleeps five, has a fully equipped kitchen and memorable views across the rooftops.

HÔTEL DE LA PLACE DU LOUVRE BOUTIQUE HOTEL **€€**

Map p392 (☎01 42 33 78 68; www.paris-hotel-place-du-louvre.com; 21 rue des Prêtres St-Germain l'Auxerrois, 1er; d €140-185; ❄☎; ⓂPont Neuf) Not to be confused with the Relais du Louvre next door, this fairly recent addition to the Parisian hotel scene is warmly welcomed. It has just 20 rooms split across five floors and a couple on each floor are lucky enough to ogle at the majestic Louvre across the street.

Decor is contemporary and stylish – lots of white and oyster grey to show off those enviable views to perfection – and the kettle with tea and coffee in each room is an appreciated, atypical-for-Paris perk. Check the hotel website for last-minute deals and special offers.

HÔTEL ST-MERRY HISTORIC HOTEL **€€**

Map p392 (☎01 42 78 14 15; www.hotelmarais.com; 78 rue de la Verrerie, 4e; d €160-230, tr €205-275; ❄☎; ⓂChâtelet) The interior of this 12-room hostelry, with beamed ceilings, church pews and wrought-iron candelabra, is a neo-Goth's wet dream; you have to see the architectural elements of room 9 (flying buttress over the bed) and the furnishings of room 12 (choir-stall bed board) to believe them. On the downside there is no lift connecting the postage-stamp lobby with the four upper floors, and not all rooms have air-conditioning.

BVJ PARIS-LOUVRE HOSTEL **€**

Map p392 (☎01 53 00 90 90; www.bvjhotel.com; 20 rue Jean-Jacques Rousseau, 1er; dm/d incl breakfast €30/70; @☎; ⓂLouvre Rivoli) This modern, 200-bed hostel run by the Bureau des Voyages de la Jeunesse (BVJ; Youth Travel Bureau) has doubles and bunks in a single-sex room for four to 10 people with showers down the corridor. Guests should be aged 18 to 35. Rooms are accessible from 2.30pm on the day you arrive. There are no kitchen facilities. Wi-fi costs €3/5 per two/four hours.

LA MAISON FAVART HISTORIC HOTEL **€€**

Map p388 (☎01 42 97 59 83; www.lamaisonfavart.fr; rue de Marivaux, 2e; d €160-350; ❄☎; ⓂRichelieu Drouot) This stylish art nouveau hotel facing the Opéra Comique feels like it never let go of the belle époque. It's an excellent choice if you're interested in shopping, being within easy walking distance of the *grands magasins* on bd Haussmann. Goya slept here in 1824.

HÔTEL VIVIENNE HOTEL **€**

Map p388 (☎01 42 33 13 26; www.hotel-vivienne.com; 40 rue de Marivaux, 2e; d €102-150, tr & q €150-190; @☎; ⓂGrands Boulevards) This stylish two-star hotel is amazingly good value for Paris. While the 45 rooms are not huge, they have all the mod cons; some even boast little balconies.

Montmartre & Northern Paris

HÔTEL AMOUR BOUTIQUE HOTEL **€€**

Map p394 (☎01 48 78 31 80; www.hotelamourparis.fr; 8 rue Navarin, 9e; s €105, d €155-215; ☎; ⓂSt-Georges or Pigalle) Planning a romantic escapade to Paris? Say no more. The inimitable black-clad Amour (formerly a love hotel by the hour) features original design and artwork in each of the rooms – you won't find a more original place to lay your head in Paris at these prices. Of course, you have to be willing to forgo television – but who needs TV when you're in love?

TOP CHOICE **LOFT** APARTMENT **€€**

Map p394 (☎06 14 48 47 48; www.loft-paris.fr; 7 cité Véron, 18e; apt €110-290; ☎; ⓂBlanche) Book months in advance to secure one of the stylish apartments in this gem, which offers an intimacy that simply cannot be

BACK TO THE FUTURE

Parisian boutique-hotel maestro **Elegancia** (www.elegancia-hotels.com) has two startling new design addresses on its drawing board: the ravishingly futuristic and curvaceous cocoon of **Hôtel O** (Map p392; ☎01 42 36 04 02; www.hotel-o-paris.com; 19 rue Hérold, 1er; ⓂSentier or Bourse) will open in late 2012, followed by the more exclusive and elusive **Pocket Palace** (Map p392; 42 rue de Croix des Petits Champs, 1er) a wine-themed hotel with a wine cellar, list and tastings par excellence, in 2013.

replicated in a hotel. Just around the corner from the Moulin Rouge, this apartment block offers choices ranging from a two-person studio to a loft that can fit a large family or group. The owner is a culture journalist and great resource.

AU SOURIRE DE MONTMARTRE — B&B €€

(☎06 64 64 72 86; www.sourire-de-montmartre.com; rue du Mont Cenis, 18e; r €125-170, apt €600 per week; MJules Joffrin) This charming B&B on the backside of Montmartre has four rooms and one studio, each individually decorated with either French antiques or Moroccan motifs. The surrounding neighbourhood is delightful, though slightly out of the way (directions are available upon confirmation of booking). The owners also rent out an apartment that sleeps up to four in a separate building.

HÔTEL PARTICULIER MONTMARTRE — BOUTIQUE HOTEL €€€

Map p394 (☎01 53 41 81 40; http://hotel-particulier-montmartre.com; 23 av Junot, 18e; ste €390-590; ; MLamarck-Caulaincourt) An 18th-century mansion hidden down a private alleyway, this VIP bijou sparkles from every angle. Much more than an exclusive hotel, it's the equivalent of staying in a modern art collector's personal residence, with rotating exhibitions, five imaginative suites designed by top French artists (Philippe Mayaux, Natacha Lesueur) and a lush garden landscaped by Louis Benech of Jardin des Tuileries fame.

TERRASS HÔTEL — HOTEL €€€

Map p394 (☎01 46 06 72 85; www.terrass-hotel.com; 12 rue Joseph de Maistre, 18e; s & d €285-345; ; MBlanche) This very sedate, stylish hotel has 98 spacious, well-designed rooms and some of the best views in town. For the ultimate Parisian experience, choose double room 608 for stunning views of the Eiffel Tower and Panthéon or room 802, which boasts its own private terrace. Some of the rooms on floors 4, 5 and 6 were designed by Kenzo.

HÔTEL DES ARTS — HOTEL €€

Map p394 (☎01 46 06 30 52; www.arts-hotel-paris.com; 5 rue Tholozé, 18e; s €105, d €140-165; ; MAbbesses or Blanche) The Hôtel des Arts is a friendly, attractive 50-room hotel, convenient to both place Pigalle and Montmartre. It has comfortable midrange rooms that are excellent value; consider spending an extra €25 for the superior rooms, which have nicer views. Just up the street is the old-style windmill Moulin de la Galette.

RELAIS MONTMARTRE — HOTEL €€

Map p394 (☎01 70 64 25 25; www.relaismontmartre.fr; 6 rue Constance, 18e; d €185-240; ; MAbbesses or Blanche) This popular choice is in an excellent location and has country-style decor, with matching floral prints and exposed rafters painted to match the colour scheme in each room. The service is excellent.

ERMITAGE HÔTEL — HISTORIC HOTEL €€

Map p394 (☎01 42 64 79 22; www.ermitagesacrecoeur.fr; 24 rue Lamarck, 18e; s €85-88, d €99-105, tr €130, q €155; @; MLamarck-Caulaincourt) Located in a 19th-century townhouse, the family-run Ermitage is a quaint 12-room B&B in the shadow of Sacré-Cœur. The traditional-style rooms are simple but attractive, with floral-patterned fabric on the walls and antique furnishings that convey a yesteryear charm. Like many hotels in this area, the upper floors have better views.

PLUG-INN HOSTEL — HOSTEL €

Map p394 (☎01 42 58 42 58; www.plug-inn.fr; 7 rue Aristide Bruant, 18e; dm €25, d €60, tr €90; @; MAbbesses or Blanche) This 2010 hostel has several things going for it, the first of which is its central Montmartre location. The four- to five-person rooms all have their own showers, there's a kitchen, free breakfast and the staff are even friendly (a rarity among Parisian hostels). No curfew at night.

WOODSTOCK HOSTEL — HOSTEL €

Map p394 (☎01 48 78 87 76; www.woodstock.fr; 48 rue Rodier, 9e; per person dm/d €25/28; @; MAnvers) This hostel is just down the hill from place Pigalle in a quiet residential quarter. Dorm beds are in rooms sleeping four to six people in bunk beds. Each room has washbasin only; showers and toilets are off the corridor. The eat-in kitchen, situated down the steps from the patio, has everything. Curfew is at 2am.

HÔTEL REGYN'S MONTMARTRE — HOTEL €€

Map p394 (☎01 42 54 45 21; www.hotel-regyns-paris.com; 18 place des Abbesses, 18e; s €101-111, d & tw €122-142; @; MAbbesses) This 22-room hotel is a good choice if you want to stay in Montmartre and not break the bank. Although the rooms are nothing to crow about, its location is unbeatable – it's just opposite the Abbesses metro station. Some of the rooms have views out over Paris.

HOTEL CAULAINCOURT SQUARE HOSTEL €
Map p394 (☎01 46 06 46 06; www.caulaincourt.com; 2 square Caulaincourt, 18e; dm €30, s €59-69, d €70-80, tr €97; @📶; MLamarck-Caulaincourt) This hotel with dorm rooms is perched on the backside of Montmartre, beyond the tourist hoopla in a real Parisian neighbourhood. The rooms are in decent condition, with parquet floors and a funky design, though there is no lift. Wi-fi in the reception area only.

HÔTEL ELDORADO HOTEL €
Map p401 (☎01 45 22 35 21; www.eldoradohotel.fr; 18 rue des Dames, 17e; s €39-65, d €58-85, tr €75-93; 📶; MPlace de Clichy) This bohemian place is one of Paris' greatest finds: a welcoming, reasonably well-run place with 23 colourfully decorated and (often) ethnically themed rooms, with a private garden at the back. Rooms 1 and 2 in the garden annexe and rooms 16 and 17 in the main building are the pick of the bunch. Cheaper-category singles have washbasin only.

NEW ORIENT HÔTEL HOTEL €€
Map p401 (☎01 45 22 21 64; www.hotelneworient.com; 16 rue de Constantinople, 8e; s €105-140, d €125-160, q €175; ❄📶; MEurope) This delightful place has lots of personality – several rooms have Second Empire furnishings and decorative busts – and its tasteful decor makes this one of the nicest midrange choices in western Paris. The only drawback is its location, which is somewhat off the beaten track.

TOP CHOICE **LE CITIZEN HOTEL** BOUTIQUE HOTEL €€
Map p398 (☎01 83 62 55 50; www.lecitizenhotel.com; 96 quai Jemmapes, 10e; d €177-275, q €450; 📶; MGare du Nord) Opened in 2011, the Citizen is a sign the times are a changin' on the Canal St-Martin. A team of forward-thinking creative types put their heads together for this one, and the result is 12 alluring rooms that are equipped with niceties such as iPads, filtered water and warm minimalist design. Artwork is from Oakland's Creative Growth Art Center for disabled artists.

HÔTEL DU NORD – LE PARI VÉLO HOTEL €
Map p398 (☎01 42 01 66 00; www.hoteldunord-leparivelo.com; 47 rue Albert Thomas, 10e; s/d/q €71/85/110; 📶; MRépublique) This particularly charming place has 24 personalised rooms decorated with flea-market antiques. Beyond the bric-a-brac charm (and the ever popular dog, Pluto), Hôtel du Nord's other winning attribute is its prized location near place République. Bikes are on loan for guests.

A ROOM IN PARIS B&B €€
Map p394 (☎06 33 10 25 78; www.aroominparis.com; 130 rue Lafayette, 10e; r €78-150; 📶; MGare du Nord) Stay in a Parisian apartment at this cosy B&B near the Gare du Nord. Six rooms (three of which sleep up to four people) are available in a Haussmann-era building with herringbone parquet floors, period moulding and a fireplace. Thierry and Peet can also provide home-cooked dinners.

MANOIR DE BEAUREGARD B&B €€
Map p400 (☎01 42 03 10 20; manoir-de-beauregard-paris.com; 43 rue des Lilas, 19e; r €135-250; 📶; MDanube) If you ever dreamt of staying in an 18th-century French townhouse, this would certainly be your pick. Rooms are luxurious and done up in period style, with beautiful linens, floral wallpaper and original parquet floors – and there's even a garden, a true rarity in Parisian homes. Breakfast comes with homemade jam.

RÉPUBLIQUE HÔTEL HOTEL €€
Map p398 (☎01 42 39 19 03; www.republiquehotel.com; 31 rue Albert Thomas, 10e; s €82, d €95-120, tr/q €120/169; 📶; MRépublique) This hip spot is heavy on pop art – local street artists did some of the paintings here – and features what is possibly the narrowest elevator in Paris, if not the world. Regardless of what you think about the garden gnomes in the breakfast room, you won't be able to fault the inexpensive rates and fantastic location off place République.

ST CHRISTOPHER'S INN HOSTEL €
Map p400 (☎01 40 34 34 40; www.st-christophers.co.uk/paris-hostels; 68-74 quai de la Seine, 19e; dm €22-40, d from €70; @📶; MRiquet or Jaurès) This is certainly one of Paris' best, biggest (300 beds) and most up-to-date hostels. It features a modern design, four types of dorms (12-bed, 10-bed, eight-bed, six-bed) as well as doubles with or without bathrooms. Other perks include a canal-side cafe, a bar

and a female-only floor. Seasonal prices vary wildly; check the website for an accurate quote. No kitchen.

A new **branch** (Map p398; rue de Dunkerque) across from the Gare du Nord should be open by the time you read this. Although larger than its sibling at La Villette, the rooms here were designed to accommodate fewer people and thus should be more private.

Le Marais & Ménilmontant

TOP CHOICE HÔTEL JEANNE D'ARC HOTEL €€

Map p404 (☎01 48 87 62 11; www.hoteljeannedarc.com; 3 rue de Jarente, 4e; s €65, d €81-96, tr/q €149/164; 📶; Ⓜ St-Paul) About the only thing wrong with this gorgeous address is that everyone knows about it, meaning you need to book well in advance to snag one of its cosy, excellent value rooms. Games to play, a painted rocking chair for tots in the bijou lounge, knick-knacks everywhere and the most extraordinary mirror in the breakfast room create a real 'family home' air to this 35-room house.

The *pièce de résistance*: the 6th-floor attic room with sweeping Paris rooftop view.

LE PAVILLON DE LA REINE HISTORIC HOTEL €€€

Map p404 (☎01 44 59 80 40; www.pavillondelareine.com; 28 place des Vosges, 3e; d from €330; Ⓜ Chemin Vert) Dreamily set on Paris' most beautiful and elegant square, place des Vosges, this sumptuous address loaded with history doesn't come cheap. But who cares when you can sleep like a queen (indeed the hotel is named after Anne of Austria, queen to Louis XIII from 1615, who stayed here).

Its cobbled stoned courtyard gardens are as pretty as a picture, especially in summer when they are a real country retreat from the hubbub of urban Paris. Its spa is equally revitalising.

HÔTEL LES JARDINS DU MARAIS HOTEL €€€

Map p404 (☎01 40 21 20 00; www.lesjardinsdumarais.com; 74 rue Amelot, 4e; d from €320; Ⓜ Chemin Vert) A real summer address, the Marais Gardens is just that – a handful of buildings designed by Gustave Eiffel (of tower fame) and ensnared by beautiful courtyard cobblestone gardens strung with flowers and tables and chairs. Interior design gives a nod to art deco – lots of blacks, whites, purples and straight lines – and the hotel is always busy despite its size (more than 200 rooms).

Connecting doubles make it a perfect family choice; look out for special offers on its website.

HÔTEL DU HAUT MARAIS B&B €€

Map p402 (☎01 42 77 65 52; www.hotelhautmarais.com; 7 rue des Vertus, 3e; d €120, ste €180, apt €190; 📶; Ⓜ Arts et Métiers) Otherwise known as Chez Didier et Marc, this lovely 15th-century town house tucked down a narrow Haut-Marais lane is just the ticket for those seeking a stylish 'home away from home' experience in Paris. Didier, Marc and their pet dog live at this boutique address with just eight rooms, each very different in design and comfortably spread out on five floors.

The apartment with handy *coin cuisine* (kitchen corner) sleeps four and breakfast, included in the rates, is served together around a shared table in the old stone *cave* (cellar).

COSMOS HÔTEL HOTEL €

Map p402 (☎01 43 57 25 88; www.cosmos-hotel-paris.com; 35 Jean-Pierre Timbaud, 11e; s/d/t €55/62/78; 📶; Ⓜ République) Cheap, brilliant value and just footsteps from the fun and happening bars, cafes and music clubs of increasingly trendy rue JPT, Cosmos is a shiny star with retro style on the budget-hotel scene. It has been around for 30-odd years but, unlike most other hotels in the same price bracket, Cosmos has been treated to a thoroughly modern makeover this century. Enjoy.

HÔTEL DE LA PLACE DES VOSGES HOTEL €€

Map p404 (☎01 42 72 60 46; www.hotelplacedesvosges.com; 12 rue de Birague, 1er; d €95-140, qdr €250; 📶; Ⓜ St-Paul) This superbly situated 17-room hotel – stables to the nearby Bastille in the 16th century – is an oasis of tranquillity, a hop and a skip from place des Vosges. Ancient wood beams and exposed stone inject character into the hotel, which has 16 rooms and a loft piled up on six floors.

The outlook from the loft suite (with some pull-out beds for families) is heavenly – Sacré-Cœur in one direction, the July Column on place de la Bastille the other.

HÔTEL BASTILLE DE LAUNAY HOTEL €€

Map p404 (☎01 47 00 88 11; www.bastillede launay-hotel-paris.com; 42 rue Amelot, 3e; s/d €110/140; Ⓜ Chemin Vert) Glitzy and glam, this smart hotel with 36 rooms in two buildings separated by a small courtyard is fantastic value. Large windows and a judicious use of mirrors create a bright (and very quiet) environment just steps from busy bd Beaumarchais and place de la Bastille.

HÔTEL DE LA HERSE D'OR HOTEL €

Map p404 (☎01 48 87 84 09; www.hotel-herse-dor.com; 20 rue St-Antoine, 4e; d with shared bathroom €65-79, d €79-109, tr/q €109/139; @ 📶; Ⓜ Bastille) This friendly place on a busy shopping street not far from place de la Bastille has 35 serviceable rooms off a long stone corridor lined with mirrors. It's basic and cheap, but some rooms still have original old stone fireplaces and breakfast is a bargain at €6. And no, *herse* is not 'hearse' in French but rather 'portcullis'. So let's call it the 'Golden Gate Hotel'.

HÔTEL DU 7E ART BOUTIQUE HOTEL €€

Map p404 (☎01 44 54 85 00; www.paris-hotel-7art.com; 20 rue St-Paul, 4e; s €75, d €100-180, tr/q €180/200; 📶; Ⓜ St-Paul) Just across the road from the Village St-Paul, *le septième art* (or seventh art, as the French know cinema) is a fun place for film buffs with its jaunty 1950s and '60s movie posters and cinematic black-and-white bathroom tiling. Ground-floor reception doubles as a cosy cafe-bar selling postcards and figurines.

Its 23 rooms stagger up five floors (no lift) to climax with a spacious duo in the attic – both rooms are great for families with their extra beds, fridge, sloping ceilings, beams and rooftop-view.

HÔTEL CARON HOTEL €€

Map p404 (☎01 40 29 02 94; www.hotelcaron.com; 3 rue Caron, 4e; d €245; ❄ 📶; Ⓜ St-Paul) Footsteps from delightful place du Marché Ste-Catherine, this is a solid midrange hotel with stark black façade and convivial cosmopolitan neighbours (Scottish pub, Italian grocery and so on). Soft natural hues give its 18 rooms instant appeal and the L'Occitane products in the bathroom add a sweet-smelling touch.

HÔTEL PRATIC HOTEL €€

Map p404 (☎01 48 87 80 47; www.hotelpratic.com; 9 rue d'Ormesson, 4e; s €98, d €117-137, tr €159; 📶; Ⓜ St-Paul) Well placed across the street from place du Marché Ste-Catherine, the Practic is a friendly and relaxed address with period features and decor – exposed beams, gilt frames, half-timbered or stone walls – that is almost too much. Its 23 rooms stagger up six floors (no lift) and cheaper doubles overlook an interior courtyard.

MAISON INTERNATIONALE DE LA JEUNESSE ET DES ÉTUDIANTS HOSTEL €

Map p404 (MIJE; ☎01 42 74 23 45; www.mije.com; 6 rue de Fourcy, 4e; dm incl breakfast €31; Ⓜ St-Paul) Sweep through the elegant front door with brass knob and pride yourself on finding such magnificent digs. The MIJE runs three hostels in attractively renovated 17th- and 18th-century *hôtels particuliers* in the heart of the Marais, and it's difficult to think of a better budget deal in Paris. Rooms are closed from noon to 3pm, and the curfew is 1am to 7am. Annual membership costs €2.50.

HÔTEL CARON DE BEAUMARCHAIS BOUTIQUE HOTEL €€

Map p404 (☎01 42 72 34 12; www.carondebeau marchais.com; 12 rue Vieille du Temple, 4e; d €165-195; Ⓜ St-Paul) The attention to detail at this unique themed hotel, decorated like an 18th-century private house, is impressive. From the period card-table set as if time stopped half-way through a game, to the harp and sheet music propped on the music stand, everything evokes the life and times of the 18th-century playwright after whom the hotel is named.

Beaumarchais wrote the play *Le Mariage de Figaro* (1778), subsequently turned into an opera by Mozart.

HÔTEL DU PETIT MOULIN BOUTIQUE HOTEL €€€

Map p404 (☎01 42 74 10 10; www.hoteldupetit moulin.com; 29-31 rue du Poitou, 3e; d €190-350; Ⓜ Filles du Calvaire) This scrumptious 17-room hotel, a bakery at the time of Henri IV, was designed from head to toe by Christian Lacroix. Pick from medieval and rococo Marais (rooms sporting exposed beams and dressed in toile de Jouy wallpaper), to more modern surrounds with contemporary murals and heart-shaped mirrors just this side of kitsch.

CASTEX HÔTEL HOTEL €€

Map p404 (☎01 42 72 31 52; www.castexhotel.com; 5 rue Castex, 4e; s/d €145/175; Ⓜ Bastille) Equidistant from the Bastille and the

Marais, the 30-room Castex retains a certain 17th-century charm with its vaulted stone cellar used as a breakfast room, terracotta floor tiles and toile de Jouy wallpaper. Try to get one of the independent rooms (1 and 2) off the lovely patio; No 3 is a two-room suite or family room.

HÔTEL DU VIEUX SAULE HOTEL €€

Map p402 (☎01 42 72 01 14; www.hotelvieuxsaule.com; 6 rue de Picardie, 3e; s €90-140, d €110-160, tr €170-220; wi-fi; MFilles du Calvaire) This flower-bedecked 27-room hostelry in the northern Marais is something of a find because of its slightly off-the-beaten-track location. Breakfast is a 16th-century vaulted cellar affair.

HÔTEL BEAUMARCHAIS DESIGN HOTEL €€

Map p402 (☎01 53 36 86 86; www.hotelbeaumarchais.com; 3 rue Oberkampf, 11e; s/d/t from €75/90/160; MFilles du Calvaire) This brighter-than-bright 31-room design hotel, with its emphasis on sunbursts and bold primary colours, is just this side of kitsch. But it makes for a different Paris experience. There are monthly art exhibitions and guests are invited to the *vernissage* (opening night).

HÔTEL DE NICE HOTEL €

Map p404 (☎01 42 78 55 29; www.hoteldenice.com; 42bis rue de Rivoli, 4e; s/d/tr €80/110/135-170; MHôtel de Ville) This is an especially warm, family-run place with 23 comfy rooms full of Second Empire style furniture, oriental carpets and lamps with fringed shades. Some have balconies high above busy rue de Rivoli.

HÔTEL RIVOLI HOTEL €

Map p404 (☎01 42 72 08 41; 4 rue de Rivoli & 2 rue des Mauvais Garçons, 4e; s with washbasin €37, d/tr with shower €49/75, d with bathroom €60; MHôtel de Ville) Long a Lonely Planet favourite, the Rivoli is forever cheap and cheery, with 20 basic if noisy rooms. The cheapest rooms share a bathroom, but use of the shower room in the hallway is free. Annoyingly – given that it is in the heart of the Marais nightlife area – the front door is locked from 2am to 7am. Reception is on the 1st floor.

AUBERGE DE JEUNESSE JULES FERRY HOSTEL €

Map p402 (☎01 43 57 55 60; www.fuaj.fr; 8 bd Jules Ferry, 11e; dm incl breakfast €26; @; MRépublique or Goncourt) Somewhat institutional, this official hostel could use a refit ('certain parts are old and wait for works – we ask you to be indulgent', says a note on the wall to guests), but the atmosphere is relaxed and a night's sleep in a two- to six-person room comes cheap. Dorms are locked between 11am and 2pm for housekeeping; no curfew.

GRAND HÔTEL DU LOIRET HOTEL €

Map p404 (☎01 48 87 77 00; www.hotel-du-loiret.fr; 8 rue des Mauvais Garçons, 4e; s/d/tr €70/80/120; MHôtel de Ville or St-Paul) This 27-room budget hotel on the 'Street of the Bad Boys' in the heart of gay Marais is popular with young male travellers.

Bastille & Eastern Paris

TOP CHOICE **MAMA SHELTER** DESIGN HOTEL €

(☎01 43 48 48 48; www.mamashelter.com; 109 rue de Bagnolet, 20e; r €80-200; air-con @ wi-fi; bus 76, MAlexandre Dumas or Gambetta) Coaxed into its zany new incarnation by uberdesigner Philippe Starck, this former car park offers what is surely the best-value accommodation in the city. Its 170 super-comfortable rooms feature iMacs, trademark Starck details (like a chocolate-and-fuchsia colour scheme), cool concrete walls and even microwave ovens, while a rooftop terrace and cool pizzeria add to its street cred.

The only drawback? Mama Shelter is a hike from both central Paris and the nearest metro stop.

HÔTEL PARIS BASTILLE HOTEL €€

Map p408 (☎01 40 01 07 17; www.hotelparisbastille.com; 67 rue de Lyon, 12e; s €188, d €200-247, tr €247, q €263; air-con wi-fi; MBastille) A haven of serenity near busy Bastille, this comfortable midrange hotel has a range of modern rooms. Although it feels slightly chain-like, it's nonetheless one of the nicest and most dependable options in the neighbourhood.

HI MATIC HOTEL €€

Map p408 (☎01 43 67 56 56; www.hi-matic.net; 71 rue de Charonne, 11e; r €110-160; air-con @ wi-fi; MBastille) This unusual place has staked its claim as the 'urban hotel of the future', though there is both good and bad in that statement. The plus side is that it has some ecofriendly aspects (LED energy-saving lights, natural pigments instead of paint) and a colourful, Japanese-style space-saving design (mattresses are rolled out onto tatamis at night) that some will find kind of fun.

The drawback is that service is kept to a minimum – check-in is via computer, and the organic breakfast comes out of a vending machine. There is a manager on the premises to help with any problems, but it's safe to say this is definitely a spot that caters to independent personalities.

HÔTEL DU PRINTEMPS HOTEL €
(☎01 43 43 62 31; www.hotel-paris-printemps.com; 80 bd de Picpus, 12e; s €73-90, d €80-110, tr €103-125; ❄📶; Ⓜ Picpus) It may not be in the centre of the action, but the 38-room Spring Hotel offers excellent value for its standard of comfort. Located just off place de la Nation, central Paris is fewer than ten minutes away via the RER A.

HÔTEL DAVAL HOTEL €
Map p408 (☎01 47 00 51 23; www.hoteldaval.com; 21 rue Daval, 11e; s/d/tr/q €86/92/112/131; ❄📶; Ⓜ Bastille) This 23-room hotel is a very central option if you're looking for budget accommodation just off place de la Bastille. Rooms and bathrooms are on the small side; to ensure peace and quiet, choose a back room (eg room 13).

BLC DESIGN HOTEL DESIGN HOTEL €€€
Map p408 (☎01 40 09 60 16; www.blcdesign-hotel-paris.com; 4 rue Richard Lenoir, 11e; r €200-225; ❄📶; Ⓜ Charonne) Cobbled from what was an ordinary hotel, the very trendy BLC has 29 all-white rooms, as comfortable as they are 'Zen' cool.

HÔTEL CANDIDE HOTEL €€
Map p408 (☎01 43 79 02 33; www.new-hotel.com; 3 rue Pétion, 11e; s/d €130/170; Ⓜ Voltaire) This simple 48-room hotel is within easy striking distance of the Bastille and the Marais.

The Islands

TOP CHOICE HÔTEL ST-LOUIS EN L'ÎLE BOUTIQUE HOTEL €€
Map p412 (☎01 46 34 04 80; www.saintlouisenlisle.com; 75 rue St-Louis en l'Île, 4e; d €169-199, with balcony €239-259, tr €279; ❄@📶; Ⓜ Pont Marie) One of several hotels lining posh rue St-Louis en l'Île, this elegant abode brandishes a pristine taupe façade and a perfectly polished interior to match. Spot-on home comforts like the kettle with complimentary tea and coffee in each room or the iPod docking station next to the bed make St-Louis stand out from the crowd.

Room 52 on the 5th floor with beams and balcony is a dream come true, and the stone-cellar breakfast room with open kitchen is an early 17th-century gem.

HÔTEL DU JEU DE PAUME BOUTIQUE HOTEL €€€
Map p412 (☎01 43 26 14 18; www.hotel-saint-louis.com; 54 rue St-Louis en l'Île, 4e; s/d €185/285; ❄@📶; Ⓜ Pont Marie) Romantically set in a courtyard off the main street on Île St-Louis, this four-star hotel in what was a 17th-century royal tennis court is a perfect place to woo. Contemporary chic is its vibe and each of its 30 rooms are inspired by a different modern artist. Panton chairs add a design edge to the historic beamed house, and its leafy patio garden is simply divine, darling.

HÔTEL DE LUTÈCE HOTEL €€
Map p412 (☎01 43 26 23 52; www.paris-hotel-lutece.com; 65 rue St-Louis en l'Île, 4e; d €165-179; ❄📶; Ⓜ Pont Marie) A reception with ancient fireplace, wood panelling, antique furnishings and terracotta tiles set the inviting tone of the lovely Lutèce, an exquisite hotel with tastefully decorated rooms and one of the city's most desirable locations.

Latin Quarter

FIVE HOTEL DESIGN HOTEL €€€
Map p416 (☎01 43 31 74 21; www.thefivehotel-paris.com; 3 rue Flatters, 5e; d €202-342; ❄📶; Ⓜ Les Gobelins) Choose from one of five perfumes to scent your room at this contemporary romantic sanctum (the cheapest 'standard' rooms are especially conducive for romance, ie small). Its private apartment, One by The Five, has a phenomenal 'suspended' bed.

SELECT HÔTEL BOUTIQUE HOTEL €€€
Map p414 (☎01 46 34 14 80; www.selecthotel.fr; 1 place de la Sorbonne, 5e; s €165, d €215-299, tr €309-320; ❄@📶; Ⓜ Cluny-La Sorbonne) In the heart of the studenty Sorbonne area, the Select is a very Parisian art deco minipalace, with an atrium and cactus-strewn winter garden, an 18th-century vaulted breakfast room and 67 small but stylish bedrooms with ingenious design solutions to maximise their limited space. The 1920s-

style cocktail bar with an attached 'library' just off the lobby is a delight.

HÔTEL MINERVE HOTEL €€

Map p414 (☎01 43 26 26 04; www.parishotelminerve.com; 13 rue des Écoles, 5e; s €99, d €129-165, tr €165; ❄@📶; Ⓜ Cardinal Lemoine) Oriental carpets, antique books, frescoes of French monuments and reproduction 18th-century wallpaper make this family-run hotel a charming place to stay. Some rooms have small balconies with views of Notre Dame, and two have tiny courtyards that are swooningly romantic.

HÔTEL LES DEGRÉS DE NOTRE DAME HOTEL €€

Map p414 (☎01 55 42 88 88; www.lesdegreshotel.com; 10 rue des Grands-Degrés, 5e; d €115-170; 📶; Ⓜ Maubert-Mutualité) Wonderfully old-school, with a winding timber staircase (no lift), and charming staff, the value is unbeatable at this hotel a block from the Seine. Breakfast (included in the rate) comes with fresh-squeezed OJ. Rooms 47 and the spacious 501 have romantic views of Notre Dame.

HÔTEL RÉSIDENCE HENRI IV HOTEL €€€

Map p414 (☎01 44 41 31 81; www.residencehenri4.com; 50 rue des Bernadins, 5e; d €260-330; ❄@📶; Ⓜ Maubert-Mutualité) This exquisite late 19th-century cul-de-sac hotel has eight generously sized rooms (minimum 17 sq metres) and five two-room apartments (minimum 25 sq metres). All are equipped with kitchenettes (hot plates, fridge, microwave and dishes), making them particularly handy for families.

HÔTEL HENRI IV RIVE GAUCHE HOTEL €€

Map p414 (☎01 46 33 20 20; www.henri-paris-hotel.com; 9-11 rue St-Jacques, 5e; s/d/tr €169/195/230; ❄@📶; Ⓜ Cluny–La Sorbonne or RER St-Michel Notre Dame) Reminiscent of a Normandy manor house, from its 18th-century fireplace, terracotta tiles and portraits in the lobby to its 23 rooms awash with antiques, old prints and fresh flowers, this three-star hotel is a Latin Quarter oasis just steps from Notre Dame and the Seine. Front rooms have stunning views of the Église St-Séverin and its buttresses.

HÔTEL ST-JACQUES HOTEL €€

Map p414 (☎01 44 07 45 45; www.hotel-saintjacques.com; 35 rue des Écoles, 5e; s €131, d €152-263, tr €200; ❄@📶; Ⓜ Maubert-Mutualité) Audrey Hepburn and Cary Grant filmed some scenes of *Charade* here in the 1960s, and it still retains original 19th-century details such as trompe l'œil ceilings that look like cloud-filled skies, an iron staircase and balconies overlooking the Panthéon (but alas no lift). Welcome touches include a cabaret-themed breakfast room and bowl of jelly beans in the lobby.

HÔTEL DES GRANDES ÉCOLES HOTEL €€

Map p416 (☎01 43 26 79 23; www.hotel-grandes-ecoles.com; 75 rue du Cardinal Lemoine, 5e; d €118-195; @📶; Ⓜ Cardinal Lemoine or Place Monge) Spanning three buildings, this welcoming hotel just north of place de la Contrescarpe has one of the loveliest situations in the Latin Quarter, tucked away in a courtyard off a medieval street with its own private garden.

HÔTEL DU LEVANT HOTEL €€

Map p414 (☎01 46 34 11 00; www.hoteldulevant.com; 18 rue de la Harpe, 5e; s €142, d €175, tr €185, q €258-278; ❄@📶; Ⓜ Cluny–La Sorbonne or St-Michel) It's hard to imagine anything more central than this 47-room, heart-of-the-Latin Quarter hotel. The breakfast room is decorated with a large mural and lots of 19th-century fashion engravings, and decent-size rooms come with modern bathrooms. A five-person room is available for €350.

FAMILIA HÔTEL HOTEL €€

Map p414 (☎01 43 54 55 27; www.familiahotel.com; 11 rue des Écoles, 5e; s €88, d €89-120, tr €130; ❄@📶; Ⓜ Cardinal Lemoine) Sepia murals of Parisian landmarks, a flower-bedecked window and parquet floors make this friendly family-run hotel one of the most attractive 'almost budget' options on this side of the Seine. Eight rooms have little balconies, from which you can catch a glimpse of Notre Dame.

HÔTEL ESMERALDA HOTEL €

Map p414 (☎01 43 54 19 20; www.hotel-esmeralda.fr; 4 rue St-Julien le Pauvre, 5e; s €75, d €100-115, tr/q €130/150; Ⓜ St-Michel) Tucked away in a quiet street with million-dollar views of Notre Dame (choose room 12!), this no-frills place is about as central to the Latin Quarter as it gets. At these prices, the 19 rooms – the cheapest singles have wash basin only – are no great shakes, but they're popular – book well ahead by phone (no online bookings).

HÔTEL DE L'ESPÉRANCE — HOTEL €

Map p416 (☎01 47 07 10 99; www.hoteldelesperance.fr; 15 rue Pascal, 5e; s/d €80/85; ; Censier Daubenton) Furnishings in this immaculately kept 38-room hotel near lively rue Mouffetard are *faux* antique: picture floral canopy beds with drapes to match. The couple who run it are an absolute charm and very service oriented; grab ice for drinks in your room from the downstairs ice-machine.

YOUNG & HAPPY — HOSTEL €

Map p416 (☎01 47 07 47 07; www.youngandhappy.fr; 80 rue Mouffetard, 5e; dm €20-33, d €70-90; ; Place Monge) This friendly if frayed Latin Quarter favourite was Paris' first independent hostel. The self-catering kitchen gets a workout from guests trawling rue Mouffetard's markets and food shops; rates include breakfast in the dark stone-vaulted cellar. Beds are in cramped rooms with washbasins, but girls are in luck with an en suite female dorm (€29 to €38).

St-Germain & Les Invalides

TOP CHOICE L'HÔTEL — BOUTIQUE HOTEL €€€

Map p418 (☎01 44 41 99 00; www.l-hotel.com; 13 rue des Beaux Arts, 6e; d €285-795; ; St-Germain des Prés) In a quiet quayside street, this award-winning hostelry is the stuff of romance, Parisian myths and urban legends. Rock- and film-star patrons fight to sleep in room 16 where Oscar Wilde died in 1900 and that is now decorated with a peacock motif, or in the art deco room 36 of entertainer Mistinguett, with its huge mirrored bed.

A stunning, modern swimming pool occupies the ancient cellar. Guests and nonguests can soak up the atmosphere of the fantastic bar (often with live music by up-and-coming new talent) and restaurant under a glass canopy.

TOP CHOICE L'APOSTROPHE — DESIGN HOTEL €€

Map p418 (☎01 56 54 31 31; www.apostrophe-hotel.com; 3 rue de Chevreuse, 6e; d €150-350; ; Vavin) A street work-of-art with its stencilled façade, this art hotel's 16 dramatically different rooms pay homage to the written word. Spray-painted graffiti tags cover one wall of room U (for '*urbain*') which has a ceiling shaped like a skateboard ramp. Room P (for 'Paris parody') sits in the clouds overlooking Paris' rooftops.

Inspired design features include double sets of imprinted curtains (one for day, one for night) and a 'bar table' on wheels that slots over the bed.

TOP CHOICE LE BELLECHASSE — DESIGN HOTEL €€

Map p422 (☎01 45 50 22 31; www.lebellechasse.com; 8 rue de Bellechasse, 7e; d from €161; ; Solférino) Fashion and, increasingly, interior designer Christian Lacroix's entrancing room themes – including 'St-Germain', with brocades, zebra striping and faux-gold leafing, 'Tuileries' with trompe l'oeil and palms, and 'Jeu de Paume' with giant playing-card motifs – make you feel like you've stepped into a larger-than-life oil painting. Mod cons include iPod docks and 200 TV channels.

HÔTEL PERREYVE — HOTEL €€

Map p418 (☎01 45 48 35 01; www.hotel-perreyve.com; 63 rue Madame, 6e; d €145-165; ; Rennes) In close proximity to Jardin du Luxembourg, this warmly welcoming 1920s hotel is superb value given its coveted location, with cosy, carpeted rooms with patterned wallpaper and sleek furniture, and an elegant breakfast room in gold hues.

HÔTEL D'ANGLETERRE — HISTORIC HOTEL €€€

Map p418 (☎01 42 60 34 72; www.hotel-dangleterre.com; 44 rue Jacob, 6e; s €160, d €220-260; ; St-Germain des Prés) If the walls could talk... The garden of the beautiful 27-room England Hotel (a former British embassy) is where the Treaty of Paris ending the American Revolution was prepared in 1783. Hemingway lodged here in 1921, as did Charles Lindbergh in 1927 after completing the world's first solo nonstop flight from New York to Paris.

Rooms are individually and exquisitely decorated; rates include breakfast.

HÔTEL ST-ANDRÉ DES ARTS — HOTEL €

Map p418 (☎01 43 26 96 16; 66 rue St-André des Arts, 6e; s/d/tr/q €75/95/119/132; ; Odéon) Located on a lively, restaurant-lined thoroughfare, this 31-room hotel is a veritable bargain in the centre of the action. The rooms are basic, and there's no lift, but the public areas are very evocative of *vieux Paris* (old Paris), with beamed ceilings and ancient stone walls. Room rates include breakfast.

RELAIS CHRISTINE HOTEL €€€

Map p418 (☎01 40 51 60 80; www.relais-christine.com; 3 rue Christine, 6e; d from €395; ❄@📶; Ⓜ Odéon) Part of the Small Luxury Hotels (SLH) association, this exquisite property is entered by a cobbled courtyard entrance, and there is an enchanting rear garden. The spa and fitness centre, built in and around an original 13th-century cellar, as well as some of its spacious rooms, have beamed ceilings. Unusually for a hotel of this category, the decor is more modern than classic.

HÔTEL DES ACADÉMIES ET DES ARTS DESIGN HOTEL €€€

Map p418 (☎01 43 26 66 44; www.hoteldesacadelies.com; 15 rue de la Grande Chaumiére, 6e; d €189-314; ❄@📶; Ⓜ Vavin) Inspired by 1920s Montparnasse, a five-minute walk away, this avant-garde address features the distinctive signature of French street artist Jérôme Mesnager whose impish white figures back-flip up walls, scale stairs and dance above fireplaces – ride the lift to the 5th floor for the ultimate acrobatic performance.

HÔTEL LINDBERGH BOUTIQUE HOTEL €€

Map p418 (☎01 45 48 35 53; www.hotellindbergh.com; 5 rue Chomel, 7e; d €146-166, tr €186; @📶; Ⓜ Sèvres-Babylone) This *hôtel de charme* is totally kitted out in Charles Lindbergh photos and memorabilia. Behind the room-number plates with Parisian landmarks, the 26 guestrooms have silk fabric on the walls, rush matting on the floors and ample-sized bathrooms.

HÔTEL DE L'ABBAYE SAINT GERMAIN HOTEL €€€

Map p418 (☎01 45 44 38 11; www.hotelabbayeparis.com; 10 rue Cassette, 6e; d €260-380; ❄@📶; Ⓜ St-Sulpice) It's the delightfully romantic outside areas that set this abode apart from the four-star crowd. Swing through the wrought-iron gates and enjoy a moment in the plant- and flower-filled front courtyard, and linger over breakfast served beneath ivy-clad walls on one of the city's prettiest patios.

LE SIX BOUTIQUE HOTEL €€€

Map p418 (☎01 42 22 00 75; www.hotel-le-six.com; 14 rue Stanislas, 6e; s & d €249-309; 📶; Ⓜ Notre Dame des Champs) From the funky red-leather reception bar to rotating art exhibitions, glass-topped courtyard salon and ultracool spa bar, this four-star hotel defines contemporary design.

LA VILLA BOUTIQUE HOTEL €€€

Map p418 (☎01 43 26 60 00; www.villa-saintgermain.com; 29 rue Jacob, 6e; d €280-410; ❄📶; Ⓜ St-Germain des Prés) This 31-room hotel helped set Paris' small, minimalist boutique standard. Fabrics, lighting and soft furnishings are all of the utmost quality and taste. Subtly designed rooms are refreshingly modern (with a preference for chocolate browns, purples and burgundies), bathrooms are small but shimmering, and the lobby has a popular bar.

HÔTEL ST-GERMAIN DES PRÉS HOTEL €€€

Map p418 (☎01 43 26 00 19; www.hotel-paris-saint-germain.com; 36 rue Bonaparte, 6e; d €205-290; ❄@; Ⓜ St-Germain des Prés) Many guests come to lay their head where Henry Miller did at this tapestry-adorned, period-furnished hotel. Its location, just up from the cafes and hubbub of place St-Germain des Prés, couldn't be handier.

HÔTEL LE PLACIDE BOUTIQUE HOTEL €€€

Map p422 (☎01 42 84 34 60; www.leplacidehotel.com; 6 rue St-Placide, 6e; d €180-462, tr €242-510; ❄@📶; Ⓜ St-Placide) Understatedly chic, this white-shuttered townhouse pampers guests with just two rooms per floor, each coolly dressed in white Moroccan leather, luxurious linens and chrome. It was one of the first Parisian hotels to blog (at www.ruesaintplacide.com).

HÔTEL DES MARRONNIERS HOTEL €€

Map p418 (☎01 43 25 30 60; www.hotel-marronniers.com; 21 rue Jacob, 6e; s €139, d €180-195, tr €230, q €340; ❄@📶; Ⓜ St-Germain des Prés) At the end of a small courtyard 30m from the main street, this 37-room hotel has a delightful conservatory leading on to a magical garden. From the 3rd floor up, rooms ending in 1, 2 or 3 look on to the garden; the rooms on the 5th and 6th floors have views over Paris' rooftops.

HÔTEL AVIATIC HOTEL €€

Map p422 (☎01 53 63 25 50; www.aviatichotel.com; 105 rue de Vaugirard, 6e; d €250-300, tr €360; ❄@📶; Ⓜ Montparnasse-Bienvenüe) This 43-room hotel with a delightful canopied art deco entrance has been around since 1856, so it must be doing something right. The tiny 'winter garden' is a breath of fresh air. For more space choose a 'superior' or 'deluxe' room.

HÔTEL MUGUET HOTEL €€

Map p422 (☎01 47 05 05 93; www.hotelmuguet.com; 11 rue Chevert, 7e; s/d/tr €95/115-195/180; ❄@📶; MLa Tour Maubourg) This is a great family choice: generous-sized triples and an armchair-bed, which can convert the separate lounge area into a kid's bedroom. From the 4th floor up, the Eiffel Tower starts to sneak into view and several rooms stare at the equally arresting Église du Dôme. Back down on ground level, a trio of rooms open onto a delightful courtyard garden.

HÔTEL LE CLÉMENT HOTEL €€

Map p418 (☎01 43 26 53 60; www.clement-moliere-paris-hotel.com; 6 rue Clément, 6e; d €129-152; ❄@📶; MSt-Germain des Prés) Excellent value for the style and tranquillity it offers, the Clément has 28 stylish rooms, some of which overlook the Marché St-Germain (eg room 100). Rooms on the very top floor have sloping ceilings. The proprietors clearly know what they're doing – it's been in the same family for over a century.

HÔTEL DE SÈVRES HOTEL €€

Map p422 (☎01 45 48 84 07; www.hoteldesevres.com; 22 rue de l'Abbé Grégoire, 6e; s €185, d €195-215, tr €255, q €395; ❄@📶; MSt-Placide) The library area in reception makes you feel at home as soon as you walk in the door of this 31-room townhouse. Carpeted rooms are decently sized, and some have a balcony peeping onto a quiet street or courtyard. You can loll in the state-of-the-art basement spa from 3pm daily (treatments from €99).

HÔTEL DANEMARK BOUTIQUE HOTEL €€

Map p418 (☎01 43 26 93 78; www.hoteldanemark.com; 21 rue Vavin, 6e; d €125-188; ❄@📶; MVavin) This stone-walled hotel has 15 scrumptious, eclectically furnished rooms. All are well soundproofed and at least 20 sq metres, which is bigger than many Parisians' apartments and, also unlike many residential apartments, all have bathtubs.

GRAND HÔTEL LÉVÈQUE HOTEL €€

Map p422 (☎01 47 05 49 15; www.hotel-leveque.com; 29 rue Cler, 7e; s/d/tr €85/170/190; ❄📶; MÉcole Militaire) Quieter rooms are dark and small, and singles miniscule but this 50-room hotel is recommended less for its charms than its *bon rapport qualité prix* (good value for money) and excellent location. Choose any room ending in 1, 2 or 3, all of which have two windows overlooking rue Cler's market.

HÔTEL DU CHAMP-DE-MARS HOTEL €€

Map p422 (☎01 45 51 52 30; www.hotelduchampdemars.com; 7 rue du Champ de Mars, 7e; s/d €95/115; @📶; MÉcole Militaire) This charming 25-room cheapie (relatively speaking) in the shadow of the Eiffel Tower is on everyone's wish list – book a month or two ahead.

HÔTEL DE NESLE HOTEL €

Map p418 (☎01 43 54 62 41; www.hoteldenesleparis.com; 7 rue de Nesle, 6e; s €55-65, d €75-100; MOdéon or Mabillon) Most of the Nesle's 20 rooms are painted with brightly coloured naïve murals inspired by French literature. But its greatest asset is the huge (by Parisian standards) garden – a back yard really – accessible from the 1st floor, with pathways, trelliswork and even a small fountain.

Montparnasse & Southern Paris

LA MAISON BOUTIQUE HOTEL €€

Map p428 (☎01 45 42 11 39; www.lamaisonmontparnasse.com; 53 rue de Gergovie, 14e; s/d/tr €110/130/160; ❄@📶; MPernety) The House goes all out to recreate home, with homemade cakes and jams for breakfast in the open-plan kitchen-lounge or little courtyard garden. A candy-striped staircase leads to its 36 rooms (there's a box-sized lift too) with bold pinks, violets and soft neutral tones. Ask for an Eiffel Tower-view room. Rates tumble into budget range on weekends.

HÔTEL DE LA PAIX DESIGN HOTEL €€

Map p428 (☎01 43 20 35 82; www.hotelparispaix.com; 225 bd Raspail, 14e; s €105-125, d €140-150, tr €190-210; ❄@📶; MMontparnasse Bienvenüe) A hip mix of industrial workshop and *côte maison* (home-like), this restyled hotel is stacked on seven floors of a 1970s building. Its 39 light-filled modern rooms have at least one vintage feature in each – old pegs to hang coats on, an old-fashioned school desk, wooden-slat house shutters recycled as a bed head... Cheaper rooms are simply smaller than dearer ones.

HÔTEL DELAMBRE HOTEL €€

Map p428 (☎01 43 20 66 31; www.delambre-paris-hotel.com; 35 rue Delambre, 14e; s €95, d €140-160; ❄@📶; Ⓜ Montparnasse Bienvenüe) Wrought iron is used functionally (bed frames, lamps, shelving) and decoratively throughout this 30-room hotel, where writer André Breton (1896–1966) lived in the 1920s. Room 7 has its own little terrace while rooms 1 and 2 look onto a small private courtyard.

HÔTEL CARLADEZ CAMBRONNE HOTEL €

Map p430 (☎01 47 34 07 12; www.hotelcarladez.com; 3 place du Général Beuret, 15e; s/d/tr/q €94/97/167/180; @📶; Ⓜ Vaugirard) On a quintessential cafe-clad square, this accommodating hotel rents coffee- and tea-making facilities for you to make yourself at home. Room No 11 opens onto a tiny courtyard with a table for two.

CELTIC HÔTEL HOTEL €

Map p428 (☎01 43 20 93 53; hotelceltic@wanadoo.fr; 15 rue d'Odessa, 14e; s €59-65, d €74-80; 📶; Ⓜ Edgar Quinet) A cheapie of the old school, this 29-room hotel is an old-fashioned place with a small lift. The cheaper singles are pretty bare and even the en suite doubles and triples are not exactly *tout confort* (with all the mod cons), but Gare Montparnasse is only 200m away.

ALOHA HOSTEL HOSTEL €

Map p430 (☎01 42 73 03 03; www.aloha.fr; 1 rue Borromée, 15e; per person dm/d €28/32 incl breakfast; @📶; Ⓜ Volontaires) An aubergine staircase is among the rainbow of colours brightening this laid-back crash pad, with opera music in the hybrid reception-lounge, and a stone-walled self-catering kitchen. You'll need a credit card to reserve four- to eight-bed dorms (reservations for doubles aren't guaranteed) but must pay cash on arrival. Rooms are locked from 11am to 5pm, curfew is at 2am.

HÔTEL LA DEMEURE BOUTIQUE HOTEL €€

Map p426 (☎01 43 37 81 25; www.hotelladameureparis.com; 51 bd St-Marcel, 13e; d €180-250; ❄@📶; Ⓜ Gobelins) Jet showers, iPod docks, wine glasses for guests who like to BYO and art to buy on the walls are just some of the touches that make this small family-run hotel a pleasure.

HÔTEL LA MANUFACTURE BOUTIQUE HOTEL €€

Map p426 (☎01 45 35 45 25; www.hotel-la-manufacture.com; 8 rue Philippe de Champagne, 13e; d €165-175; ❄@📶; Ⓜ Place d'Italie) On the fringe of the Latin Quarter, minimalist La Manufacture has 57 individually – and minimalistically – decorated rooms. Those on the top (7th) floor are the most spacious and coveted; room 71 boasts a view of the Panthéon while room 74 glimpses the Eiffel Tower.

OOPS HOSTEL €

Map p426 (☎01 47 07 47 00; www.oops-paris.com; 50 av des Gobelins, 13e; dm €30, d €70; @📶; Ⓜ Gobelins) A lurid candyfloss-pink lift scales the six floors of Paris' first 'design hostel', each painted a different bold colour. Well-sized doubles and modern but lockerless four- to six-bed dorms are all en suite and some have Eiffel Tower views, though they're off-limits from 11am to 4pm. Breakfast is included but there's no kitchen. No credit cards, no alcohol allowed.

Understand Paris

Paris Today

While the elegance, depth and extraordinary spirit of the Paris of Haussmann, Hugo and Toulouse Lautrec will never disappear, Europe's mythical 'City of Light' is on the brink of redefining itself big-time. Reinvention and innovation is the name of the game for urban planners, and the arts scene has never been more exciting. Parisians themselves, moreover, are in the mood for change: 2012 presidential elections ushered in France's first Socialist president in 17 years.

Best on Film

Midnight in Paris (2011) Woody Allen tale about one family's trip to Paris.
La Môme (La Vie en Rose; 2007) Édith Piaf, from Paris waif to New York superstar.
The Da Vinci Code (2006) Popular film based on the blockbuster novel.
Le Fabuleux Destin d'Amélie Poulain (Amélie; 2001) Feel-good story of a winsome young Parisian do-gooder in Pigalle and Montmartre.
Last Tango in Paris (1972) Marlon Brando as a grief-stricken American in Paris searching for salvation with anonymous, sadomasochistic sex.

Best in Print

Paris in Colour (Nichole Robertson; 2012) No photographic title better captures the city's extraordinary colours and hues than this.
Stuff Parisians Like (Olivier Magny; 2011) Witty vignettes about (and how to be) Parisian.
The Paris Wife (Paula McLain; 2011) Hemingway in Jazz Age Paris.
The Ladies' Delight (Émile Zola; 1883) Nineteenth-century shopping at Le Bon Marché.
Paris in Mind (Jennifer Lee; 2003) Anthology of Paris-related pieces by 29 American writers.

A Left-Wing President

Presidential elections in May 2012 pitted incumbent right-wing president Nicolas Sarkozy against left-wing candidate François Hollande, only for France to walk away with its first Socialist president since 1988. Hollande had campaigned to reduce unemployment (which was at a 12-year high), clear the country's debts by 2017, raise income tax on top-end salaries and steer France though Europe's biggest economic crisis in decades. The French, fed up with austerity and desperate for change, welcomed this approach. Legislative elections held a month later sealed the left's comfortable grip on power: the Socialists won a comfortable majority (273 seats) in France's 577-seat lower-house National Assembly, paving the way for the new president to preside unfettered over a troubled France from his new Parisian home at the Élysée Palace.

Reinvention & Innovation

The city today is about reinvention and innovation. From community actions, like turning an art nouveau covered market to a sports centre in the Haut-Marais, to gargantuan projects affecting thousands of commuters every day, such as the overhaul of the Forum des Halles, Paris is not sitting on its laurels. The French capital is an architectural reference accustomed to looking good, and faded grandeur or a glamorous history is simply not sufficient: so out with the tired 1970s concrete at Les Halles, and in with designer garden crowned with a futuristic, rainforest-inspired canopy in glass (by 2016). Same goes for historic Gare d'Austerlitz and the Seine-side *quartier* around the train station where builders are beavering away on yet another renaissance in the city fashioned out of glass (and lurid lime-green in the case of the fashionable Docks en Seine). Paris-based Jean Nouvel is the architect.

At the Musée du Louvre meanwhile, the opening of brand new Islamic art galleries in Cour Visconti – a splendid piece of 21st-century architecture – only furthers the musuem's iconic standing as a pilgrimage for art lovers worldwide. In September 2012 some 900 of its art works (including Delacroix's rousing *Liberty Leading the People*) were moved from Paris to the new Louvre-Lens museum in northern France.

Growing Green Space

Creating more green space for Parisians to promenade in peace is the big driver for urban planners. Enter Île Seguin, an inventive project in Boulogne-Billancourt on Paris' western fringe, which will see Jean Nouvel morph an abandoned Renault car factory on an island into a visionary eco-city with a cultural centre, artist residences, waterside gardens, walkways, tree-lined esplanades, restaurants and play spaces (a 'modern Babylon' is his pitch). Work started in 2012 and continues until 2023.

In central Paris, place de la République will be a dramatically different place to be once the car-jammed roundabout is dumped on the scrapheap of history and replaced with a nonmotorised zone. Same goes for the 2.3km-long stretch of riverbank on the Left Bank, which will be pedestrianised to create a riverside footpath between the Musée d'Orsay and Eiffel Tower. Floating gardens on the Seine will complete the picturesque ensemble, part of the larger Berges de Seine initiative aimed at greening-up the riverbanks. Work started in 2012.

When the Paris Council adopted a new Plan de Biodiversité at the end of 2011, it did not ignore its urban rooftops. Doubling the 3.7 hectares currently planted green with vegetal roofs and roof gardens by 2020 is the goal.

A Boost to Morale

Unemployment in the Paris region remained at a disconcerting 8.1% in early 2012. Yet cultural morale runs high. Art lovers are bursting with excitement over the reopening, after months of painstaking renovation, of the Picasso museum in the Marais and the Comédie Française where Molière trod the boards at Palais Royal; building work on Paris' new €336 million philharmonic concert hall, to open in 2014, is back on track (after being stalled in 2010 for lack of national funding); and then there's Frank Gehry's dazzling glass crystal of a contemporary art gallery in the Bois de Bologne, an architectural redefinition of style. Cinema goers are celebrating Oscar wins by favourite Parisian actors and directors, and promised new restaurant openings by Guy Savoy (inside the Seine-side Hôtel de la Monnaie next to the Academie Française) and Anne-Sophie Pic (next to the Louvre on rue du Louvre) are titillating tastebuds of Parisian gourmets. *Bon appétit!*

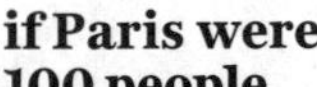

if Paris were 100 people

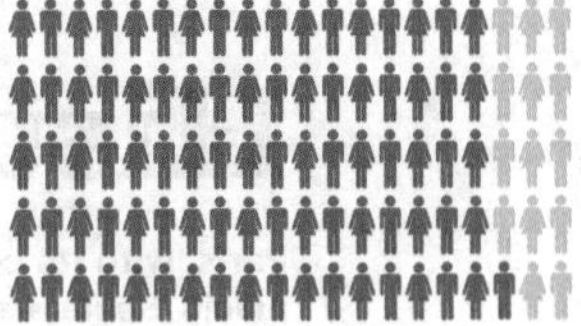

86 would be French
14 would be foreign

living in Paris

(% of population by area)

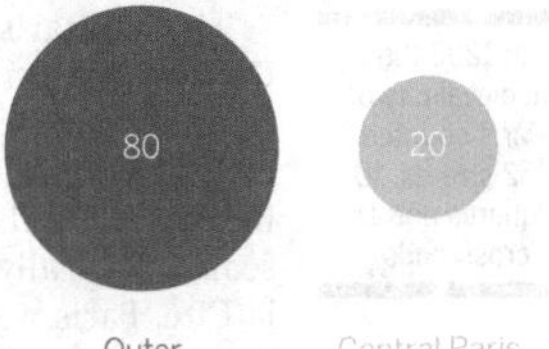

population per sq km

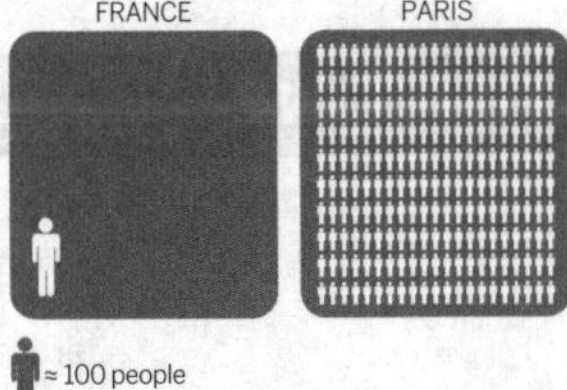

≈ 100 people

History

Paris, with its cobbled streets, terraced cafes, iconic landmarks and placid Seine waters, really does evoke a certain timelessness. Yet a quick dip into its elaborate history quickly reveals a city that has changed and evolved dramatically over the centuries.

DYNASTY

The Romans occupied what would become known as Paris from AD 212 to the late 5th century, a period which also saw Franks and other Germanic tribes from the north and northeast overrun the territory. In 508 Clovis I converted to Christianity and made Paris his seat, while his son and successor, Childeric II, founded the Abbey of St-Germain des Prés half a century later. The dynasty's most productive ruler, Dagobert, established an abbey at St-Denis that would became the richest, most important monastery in France and the final resting place of its kings.

The militaristic rulers of the Carolingian dynasty, beginning with Charles 'the Hammer' Martel (688–741), were almost permanently away fighting wars in the east, and Paris languished, controlled mostly by its counts. When Charles Martel's grandson, Charlemagne (768–814), moved his capital to Aix-la-Chapelle (today's Aachen in Germany), Paris' fate was sealed. Basically a group of separate villages with its centre on the Île de la Cité, Paris was badly defended throughout the second half of the 9th century and was raided incessantly by Vikings.

STATS

In 1292 the medieval city of Paris counted 352 streets, 10 squares and 11 crossroads.

MUD-HUT ISLAND TO TRAFFIC-CLOGGED CITY

The Paris counts, whose powers had grown as the Carolingians feuded among themselves, elected one of their own, Hugh Capet, as king at Senlis in 987. He made Paris the royal seat and lived in the renovated palace of the Roman governor on the Île de la Cité (site of the present Palais de Justice). Under the 800 years of Capetian rule that followed, Paris prospered as a centre of politics, commerce, trade, religion and culture.

TIMELINE

3rd century BC

Celtic Gauls called Parisii – believed to mean 'boat men' – arrive in the Paris area and set up a few wattle-and-daub huts on what is now the Île de la Cité.

52 BC

Roman legions under Julius Caesar crush a Celtic revolt on Mons Lutetius (site of today's Panthéon) and establish the town of Lutetia ('midwater dwelling' in Latin; Lutèce in French).

AD 845–86

Paris is repeatedly raided by Vikings for more than four decades, including the siege of 885–86 by Siegfried the Saxon, which lasts 10 months but ends in victory for the French.

Indeed, the city's strategic riverside position ensured its importance throughout the Middle Ages. The first guilds were created in the 11th century, and in the mid-12th century the ship merchants' guild bought the principal river port, by today's Hôtel de Ville (City Hall), from the crown. Frenetic building marked the 12th and 13th centuries. The Basilique de St-Denis was commissioned in 1136 and less than three decades later, work started on Notre Dame. During the reign of Philippe-Auguste (r 1180–1223), the city wall was expanded and fortified with 25 gates and hundreds of protective towers.

The swampy Marais was drained for agricultural use and settlement across the Seine to its right bank, prompting the eventual need for the food markets at Les Halles in 1183 and the Louvre as a riverside fortress in the 13th century. In a bid to resolve ghastly traffic congestion and stinking excrement (by 1200 the city had a population of 200,000), Philippe-Auguste paved four of Paris' main streets with metre-square sandstone blocks. Meanwhile, the Left Bank – particularly in the Latin Quarter – developed as a centre of European learning and erudition. Ill-fated lovers Pierre Abélard and Héloïse penned the finest poetry of the age and treatises on philosophy, Thomas Aquinas taught at the newly founded University of Paris, and the Sorbonne opened its doors.

Paris in the Middle Ages was Île de la Cité: the *Rive Gauche* (Left Bank) was a carpet of fields and vineyards; the Marais area on the *Rive Droite* (Right Bank) a boggy, waterlogged marsh.

MIDDLE AGES

BLACK TIMES: WAR & DEATH

The Hundred Years' War (1337–1453), the Black Death (1348–49) that killed more than a third of Paris' population, and the development of free, independent cities elsewhere in Europe, brought political tension and open insurrection to Paris. In 1420 the dukes of Burgundy, allied with the English, occupied the capital and two years later John Plantagenet, duke of Bedford, was installed as regent of France for the English king, Henry VI, then an infant. Henry was crowned king of France at Notre Dame less than 10 years later, but Paris was almost continuously under siege from the French.

Around that time a 17-year-old peasant girl known to history as Jeanne d'Arc (Joan of Arc) persuaded the French pretender to the throne that she'd received a divine mission from God to expel the English from France and bring about his coronation as Charles VII. She rallied French troops and defeated the English north of Orléans, and Charles was crowned at Reims. But Joan of Arc failed to take Paris. In 1430 she was captured, convicted of witchcraft and heresy by a tribunal of French ecclesiastics and burned at the stake. Charles VII returned to Paris in 1436, ending more than 16 years of occupation, but the English were not entirely driven from French territory for another 17 years.

987

Five centuries of Merovingian and Carolingian rule ends with the crowning of Hugh Capet; a dynasty that will rule for the next eight centuries is born.

1066

The so-called Norman Conquest of England ignites almost 300 years of conflict between the Normans in western and northern France and the Capetians in Paris.

1163

Two centuries of nonstop building reaches its zenith with the start of Notre Dame Cathedral under Maurice de Sully, the bishop of Paris, continuing for over a century and a half.

1358

The Hundred Years' War (1337–1453) between France and England and the devastation and poverty caused by the plague lead to the ill-fated peasants' revolt led by Étienne Marcel.

THE RISE OF THE ROYAL COURT

Under Louis XI (r 1461–83) the city's first printing press was installed at the Sorbonne and churches built around the city in the Flamboyant Gothic style. But it was during the reign of François I in the early 16th century that Renaissance ideas of scientific and geographic scholarship and discovery really assumed a new importance, as did the value of secular matters over religious life. Writers such as Rabelais, Marot and Ronsard of La Pléiade were influential, as were artist and architect disciples of Michelangelo and Raphael who worked towards a new architectural style designed to reflect the splendour of the monarchy (which was fast moving towards absolutism) and of Paris as the capital of a powerful centralised state. At François I's chateau superb artisans, many brought over from Italy, blended Italian and French styles to create what is known as the First School of Fontainebleau.

The population of Paris at the start of François' reign in 1515 was 170,000 – still almost 20% less than it had been some three centuries before, when the Black Death had decimated the city population.

But all this grandeur and show of strength was not enough to stem the tide of Protestant Reformation sweeping across Europe in the 1530s, strengthened in France by the ideas of John Calvin. Following the Edict of January 1562, which afforded the Protestants certain rights, the Wars of Religion, which lasted three dozen years, broke out between the Huguenots (French Protestants who received help from the English), the Catholic League (led by the House of Guise) and the Catholic monarchy. On 7 May 1588, on the 'Day of the Barricades', Henri

STAR-CROSSED LOVERS

He was a brilliant 39-year-old philosopher and logician with a reputation for his controversial ideas. She was the beautiful niece of a canon at Notre Dame. And like Bogart and Bergman in *Casablanca* and Romeo and Juliet in Verona, they had to fall in love in medieval Paris of all damned times and places.

In 1118, the wandering scholar Pierre Abélard (1079–1142) found his way to Paris, having clashed with yet another theologian in the provinces. There he was employed by Canon Fulbert of Notre Dame to tutor his niece Héloïse (1101–64). One thing led to another and a son, Astrolabe, was born. Abélard married his sweetheart in secret and when Fulbert found out, he was outraged. He had Abélard castrated and sent Héloïse off to a convent where she eventually became abbess. Abélard took monastic vows at the abbey in St-Denis and continued his studies and controversial writings.

Yet all the while, the star-crossed lovers corresponded: he sending tender advice on how to run the convent and she writing passionate, poetic letters to her lost lover. The two were reunited only in death; in 1817 their remains were disinterred and brought to Pére Lachaise cemetery (p154) in the 20e, where they lie together beneath a neo-Gothic tombstone in Division 7.

1572

Some 3000 Huguenots in Paris to celebrate the wedding of the Protestant Henri of Navarre (the future Henri IV) are slaughtered on 23 and 24 August.

1589

Henry IV, the first Bourbon king, ascends the throne after renouncing Protestantism; '*Paris vaut bien une messe*' (Paris is well worth a Mass), he is reputed to have said.

1643

'Sun King' Louis XIV ascends the throne aged five but only assumes absolute power in 1661.

1756-63

The Seven Years' War sees France lose flourishing colonies in Canada, the West Indies and India.

III, who had granted many concessions to the Huguenots, was forced to flee from the Louvre when the Catholic League rose up against him. He was assassinated the following year.

Henri IV, founder of the Bourbon dynasty, issued the controversial Edict of Nantes in 1598, guaranteeing the Huguenots many civil and political rights, notably freedom of conscience. Ultra-Catholic Paris refused to allow the new Protestant king to enter the city, and a siege of the capital continued for almost five years. Only when Henri IV embraced Catholicism at the cathedral in St-Denis did the capital submit to him. Henri's rule ended abruptly in 1610 when he was assassinated by a Catholic fanatic when his coach became stuck in traffic along rue de la Ferronnerie, south of Les Halles.

Arguably France's best known king of this or any other century, Louis XIV (r 1643–1715) aka 'Le Roi Soleil' (the Sun King), ascended the throne at the tender age of five. He involved the kingdom in a series of costly, almost continuous wars with Holland, Austria and England, which gained France territory but nearly bankrupted the treasury. State taxation, imposed to refill the coffers, caused widespread poverty and vagrancy, especially in cities. In Versailles, Louis XIV built an extravagant palace and made his courtiers compete with each other for royal favour, thereby quashing the ambitious, feuding aristocracy and creating the first centralised French state. In 1685 he revoked the Edict of Nantes.

ÎLE DE ST-LOUIS

During Louis XIII's reign (1610–43) two uninhabited islets in the Seine – Île Notre Dame and Île aux Vaches – were joined to form the Île de St-Louis.

FROM REVOLUTION TO REPUBLIC

During the so-called Age of Enlightenment, the royal court moved back to Paris from Versailles and the city effectively became the centre of Europe. Yet as the 18th century progressed, new economic and social circumstances rendered the *ancien régime* dangerously out of step with the needs of the country.

By the late 1780s, the indecisive Louis XVI and his dominating Vienna-born queen, Marie Antoinette, had alienated virtually every segment of society. When they tried to neutralise the power of more reform-minded delegates at a meeting of the États-Généraux (States-General) in Versailles from May to June 1789, the masses – spurred on by the oratory and inflammatory tracts circulating at places like the Café de Foy at Palais Royal – took to the streets of Paris. On 14 July, a mob raided the armoury at the Hôtel des Invalides for rifles, seized 32,000 muskets, and stormed the prison at Bastille. Enter the French Revolution.

14 July 1789

The French Revolution begins when a mob arms itself with weapons taken from the Hôtel des Invalides and storms the prison at Bastille, freeing a total of just seven prisoners.

KEN KAMINESKY / CORBIS ©

Hôtel des Invalides (p228)

1793

Louis XVI is tried and convicted as citizen 'Louis Capet' (all kings since Hugh Capet were said to have ruled illegally) and executed; Marie Antoinette's turn is nine months later.

At first, the Revolution was in the hands of moderate republicans, the Girondins. France was declared a constitutional monarchy and reforms were introduced, including the adoption of the Déclaration des Droits de l'Homme and du Citoyen (Declaration of the Rights of Man and of the Citizen). But as the masses armed themselves against the external threat to the new government – posed by Austria, Prussia and the exiled French nobles – patriotism and nationalism mixed with extreme fervour and then popularised and radicalised the Revolution. It was not long before the Girondins lost out to the extremist Jacobins, who abolished the monarchy and declared the First Republic. The Assemblée Nationale was replaced by an elected Revolutionary Convention.

Most historians agree that the overall military effectiveness of the Resistance was limited. But it served as an enormous boost to French morale and has impacted French literature and cinema right up till today.

Louis XVI was convicted of 'conspiring against the liberty of the nation' in January 1793 and guillotined at place de la Révolution, today's place de la Concorde. Two months later the Jacobins set up the notorious Committee of Public Safety to deal with national defence and try 'traitors'. The subsequent Reign of Terror (September 1793 to July 1794) saw religious freedoms revoked, churches closed and desecrated, cathedrals turned into 'Temples of Reason' and thousands incarcerated in dungeons in La Conciergerie before being beheaded.

After the Reign of Terror faded, a five-man delegation of moderate republicans set itself up to rule the republic as the Directory.

LITTLE BIG MAN & EMPIRE

The post-Revolutionary government was far from stable and when Napoleon returned to Paris in 1799 he found a chaotic republic in which few citizens had any faith. In November, when it appeared that the Jacobins were again on the ascendancy in the legislature, Napoleon tricked the delegates into leaving Paris for St-Cloud to the southwest ('for their own protection'), overthrew the discredited Directory and assumed power himself.

History Museums

Musée Carnavale (Le Marais & Ménilmontant)

Musée National du Moyen Âge (Latin Quarter)

Musée National d'Histoire de France (Latin Quarter)

Mémorial de la Shoah (Le Marais & Ménilmontant)

At first, Napoleon took the post of First Consul. In a referendum three years later he was named 'Consul for Life' and his birthday became a national holiday. By December 1804, when he crowned himself 'Emperor of the French' in the presence of Pope Pius VII at Notre Dame, the scope and nature of Napoleon's ambitions were obvious to all. But to consolidate and legitimise his authority, Napoleon needed more victories on the battlefield. So began a seemingly endless series of wars and victories by which France would come to control most of Europe.

In 1812 Napoleon invaded Russia and captured Moscow, only for his army to be quickly wiped out by the brutal Russian winter. Two years later, Allied armies entered Paris, exiled Napoléon to Elba and restored

1799

Napoleon overthrows the Directory and seizes control of the government in a *coup d'état*, opening the doors to 16 years of despotic rule, victory and then defeat on the battlefield.

1815

British and Prussian forces under the Duke of Wellington defeat Napoleon at Waterloo; he is sent into exile for the second time, this time to a remote island in the South Atlantic.

1830

During the July Revolution revolutionaries seize Hôtel de Ville and overthrow Charles X (r 1824–30). Place de la Bastille's Colonne de Juillet honours those killed.

1848

After more than three decades of monarchy, King Louis-Philippe is ousted and the short-lived Second Republic is established with Napoleon's incompetent nephew at the helm.

the House of Bourbon to the French throne at the Congress of Vienna (1814–15).

But in early 1815 Napoleon escaped from the Mediterranean island, landed in southern France and gathered a large army as he marched towards Paris. On 1 June he reclaimed the throne at celebrations held at the Champs de Mars. But his reign came to an end just three weeks later when his forces were defeated at Waterloo in Belgium. Napoleon was exiled again, this time to St Helena in the South Atlantic, where he died in 1821. In 1840 his remains were moved to Paris' Église du Dôme.

The Second Republic was established and elections in 1848 brought in Napoléon's inept nephew, the German-reared (and accented) Louis Napoleon Bonaparte, as president. But in 1851 he staged a coup d'état and proclaimed himself Emperor Napoléon III of the Second Empire, which lasted until 1870.

France enjoyed significant economic growth at this time, and Paris was transformed by town planner Baron Haussmann (1809–91) into the modern city it is today. Huge swaths of Paris were completely rebuilt (demolishing much of medieval Paris in the process), and its chaotic narrow streets replaced with the handsome, arrow-straight and wide thoroughfares for which the city is now celebrated.

HAUSSMANN'S INFLUENCE

Haussmann revolutionised Paris' water-supply and sewerage systems, and landscaped some of the city's loveliest parks. The city's first department stores were built, as were Paris' delightful shop-shrewn *passages couverts*.

THE BELLE ÉPOQUE

Though it would usher in the glittering belle époque (beautiful age), there was nothing particularly attractive about the start of the Third Republic. Born as a provisional government of national defence in September 1870, it was quickly besieged by the Prussians, who laid siege to Paris and demanded National Assembly elections be held. Unfortunately, the first move made by the resultant monarchist-controlled assembly was to ratify the Treaty of Frankfurt, the harsh terms of which – a huge war indemnity and surrender of the provinces of Alsace and Lorraine – prompted an immediate revolt known as the Paris Commune during which several thousand Communards were killed and another 20,000 executed. The Wall of the Federalists in Cimetière du Père Lachaise (p154) is as a deathly reminder of the bloodshed.

The belle époque launched art nouveau architecture, a whole field of artistic 'isms' from impressionism onwards, and advances in science and engineering, including the construction of the first metro line (1900). World Fairs were held in the capital in 1889 (showcased by the Eiffel Tower and again in 1900 in the purpose-built Grand and Petit Palais). The Paris of nightclubs and artistic cafes made its first

1852–70

Paris enjoys economic growth during the Second Empire of Napoleon III and much of the city is redesigned or rebuilt by Baron Haussmann as the Paris we know today.

1870–1

Harsh terms inflicted on France by victor Prussia in the Franco-Prussian War leads to open revolt and the establishment of the insurrectionary Paris Commune.

1880s

The Third Republic ushers in the bloody-then-beautiful belle époque, a creative era that among other things conceives Bohemian Paris, with its raunchy nightclubs and artistic cafes.

1889

The Eiffel Tower is completed in time for the opening of the Exposition Universelle (World Fair) but is vilified in the press and on the street as the 'metal asparagus' – or worse.

appearance around this time, and Montmartre became a magnet for artists, writers, pimps and prostitutes.

But all was not well in the republic. France was consumed with a desire for revenge after its defeat by Germany, and looking for scapegoats. The so-called Dreyfus Affair began in 1894 when a Jewish army captain named Alfred Dreyfus was accused of betraying military secrets to Germany; he was then court-martialled and sentenced to life imprisonment on Devil's Island. Liberal politicians and writers succeeded in having the case reopened despite bitter opposition from the army command, right-wing politicians and many Catholic groups – and Dreyfus was vindicated in 1900. This resulted in more rigorous civilian control of the military and, in 1905, the legal separation of the church and the state. When he died in 1935 Dreyfus was laid to rest in the Cimetière de Montparnasse.

DIVINE KINGS

Paintings by Jules Hardouin-Mansart in the Royal Chapel at Versailles evoke the idea that the French king was chosen by God and is thus his lieutenant on earth – a divinity the 'Sun King' believed in devoutly.

WWII & OCCUPATION

Two days after the German invasion of Poland on 1 September 1939, Britain and France declared war on Germany. For the first nine months Parisians joked about *le drôle de guerre* – what Britons called 'the phoney war' – in which nothing happened. But the battle for France began in earnest in May 1940 and by 14 June France had capitulated. Paris was occupied, and almost half the population fled the city by car, by bicycle or on foot. The British expeditionary force sent to help the French barely managed to avoid capture by retreating to Dunkirk, described so vividly in Ian McEwan's *Atonement* (2001), and crossing the English Channel in small boats. The Maginot Line, a supposedly impregnable wall of fortifications along the Franco–German border, had proved useless – the German armoured divisions simply outflanked it by going through Belgium.

The Germans divided France into a zone under direct German rule (along the western coast and the north, including Paris), and into a puppet-state based in the spa town of Vichy and led by General Philippe Pétain, the ageing WWI hero of the Battle of Verdun. Pétain's collaborationist government and French police forces in German-occupied areas (including Paris), helped the Nazis round up 160,000 French Jews and others for deportation to concentration and extermination camps in Germany and Poland.

After the fall of Paris, General Charles de Gaulle, France's undersecretary of war, fled to London. He set up a French government-in-exile and established the Forces Françaises Libres (Free French Forces), a military force dedicated to fighting the Germans alongside the Allies.

1914

Germany and Austria-Hungary declare war on Russia and France. German troops reach the River Marne 15km east of Paris and the government moves to Bordeaux.

1918

Armistice ending WWI signed northeast of Paris sees the return of Alsace and Lorraine; of the eight million French men called to arms, 1.3 million die and another million are crippled.

1920s

Paris sparkles as the centre of the avant-garde with its newfound liberalism, cutting-edge nightlife and painters pushing into new fields of art like cubism and surrealism.

1940

After more than 10 months of *le drôle de guerre* (phoney war), Germany launches the battle for France, and the four-year occupation of Paris under direct German rule begins.

The liberation of France started with the Allied landings in Normandy on D-day (Jour-J in French): 6 June 1944. On 15 August that same year, Allied forces also landed in southern France. After a brief insurrection by the Résistance and general strikes by the metro and police, Paris was liberated on 25 August by an Allied force spearheaded by Free French units – these units were sent in ahead of the Americans so that the French would have the honour of liberating the capital the following day. Hitler, who visited Paris in June 1940 and loved it, demanded that the city be burned towards the end of the war. It was an order that, thankfully, was not obeyed.

POSTWAR INSTABILITY

De Gaulle returned to Paris and established a provisional government. But in January 1946 he resigned as president, wrongly believing the move would provoke a popular outcry for his return. A few months later, a new constitution was approved by referendum. De Gaulle formed his own party, Rassemblement du Peuple Français (RPF; Rally of the French People) and spent the next 13 years in opposition.

The Fourth Republic saw unstable coalition cabinets follow one another with bewildering speed (on average, one every six months), and economic recovery, helped immeasurably by massive American aid. France's disastrous defeat in Vietnam in 1954 ended its colonial supremacy in Indochina. France also tried to suppress an uprising by Arab nationalists in Algeria, where over a million French settlers lived.

The Fourth Republic came to an end in 1958, when extreme right-wingers, furious at what they saw as defeatism as opposed to tough action in dealing with the uprising in Algeria, began conspiring in an effort to overthrow the government. De Gaulle was brought back to power to prevent a military coup and possible civil war. He drafted a new constitution that handed considerable powers to the president, at the expense of the National Assembly.

Essential Historical Encounters

Arènes de Lutèce (Latin Quarter)

Hôtel des Invalides (St-Germain & Les Invalides)

Les Catacombes (Montparnasse & Southern Paris)

CHARLES DE GAULLE & THE FIFTH REPUBLIC

The Fifth Republic was rocked in 1961 by an attempted coup staged in Algiers by a group of right-wing military officers. When it failed, the Organisation de l'Armée Secrète (OAS) – a group of French *colons* (colonists) and sympathisers opposed to Algerian independence – turned to terrorism, trying several times to assassinate de Gaulle and nearly succeeding in August 1962 in the town of Clamart just southwest of Paris.

25 August 1944

Spearheaded by Free French units, Allied forces liberate Paris and the city escapes destruction, despite Hitler's orders that it be torched; the war in Europe will end nine months later.

1949

Simone de Beauvoir publishes her ground-breaking and very influential study *Le Deuxième Sexe* (The Second Sex) just four years after French women win the right to vote.

1958

De Gaulle returns to power after more than a dozen years in the opposition to form the Fifth Republic.

1962

War in Algeria is brought to an end after claiming the lives of more than 12,000 people; three-quarters of a million Algerian-born French citizens arrive in France.

In 1962, after more than 12,000 had died as a result of this 'civil war', de Gaulle negotiated an end to the war in Algeria. Some 750,000 *pied-noir* (black feet), as Algerian-born French people are known in France, came to France and the capital. Meanwhile, almost all of the other French colonies and protectorates in Africa had demanded and achieved independence. Shrewdly, the French government began a program of economic and military aid to its former colonies to bolster France's waning importance internationally and to create a bloc of French-speaking nations – *la francophonie* – in the developing world.

Paris retained its position as a creative and intellectual centre, particularly in philosophy and film-making, and the 1960s saw large parts of the Marais beautifully restored.

PARIS COUNCIL

Paris is run from the Hôtel de Ville (City Hall) by the *maire* (mayor) with help from 18 *adjoints* (deputy mayors), elected by 163 members of the Conseil de Paris (Council of Paris) and serving terms of six years.

A PIVOTAL YEAR

The year 1968 was a watershed year. In March a large demonstration in Paris against the war in Vietnam gave impetus to the student movement and protests by students of the University of Paris peppered the capital for most of spring. In May police broke up yet another demonstration, prompting angry students to occupy the Sorbonne and erect barricades in the Latin Quarter. Workers joined in very quickly with six million people across France participating in a general strike that virtually paralysed the country. It was a period of creativity and new ideas with slogans like '*L'Imagination au Pouvoir*' (Put Imagination in Power) and '*Sous les Pavés, la Plage*' (Under the Cobblestones, the Beach) – a reference to Parisians' favoured material for building barricades and what they could expect to find beneath them – popping up everywhere.

But such an alliance between workers and students couldn't last long. While the former wanted to reap greater benefits from the consumer market, the latter supposedly wanted to destroy it. De Gaulle took advantage of this division and appealed to people's fear of anarchy. And just as Paris and the rest of France seemed on the verge on revolution, a mighty 100,000-strong crowd of Gaullists came out on the streets of Paris to show their support for the government, and so squash any idea of revolution. Stability was restored.

MODERN SOCIETY

Once stability was restored the government immediately decentralised the higher education system, and implemented a series of reforms (including lowering the voting age to 18, and enacting an abortion law) throughout the 1970s to create the modern society France is today.

1968

Paris is rocked by student-led riots that bring the nation and the city to the brink of civil war; as a result de Gaulle is forced to resign the following year.

1977

Jacques Chirac, the first Paris mayor to be elected with real power, assumes office. He later becomes France's president in 1995.

1978

The Centre Pompidou, the first of a string of *grands projets*, huge public edifices through which French leaders seek to immortalise themselves, opens to great controversy.

Centre Pompidou (p111)

President Charles de Gaulle resigned in 1969 and was succeeded by the Gaullist leader Georges Pompidou and later Valéry Giscard d'Estaing. Socialist François Mitterrand became president in 1981 and immediately nationalised privately owned banks, large industrial groups and other parts of the economy. A more moderate economic policy in the mid-1980s ensured a second term in office for the now 69-year-old Mitterrand.

The book and film, *The Day of the Jackal*, portrays a fictional attempt by the OAS on de Gaulle's life.

Jacques Chirac, mayor of Paris since 1977, took over the presidential baton in 1995 and received high marks in his first few months for his direct words and actions in European Union (EU) matters and the war in Bosnia. But his decision to resume nuclear testing on the French Polynesian island of Mururoa and a nearby atoll was met with outrage in France and abroad and when, in 1997, Chirac gambled with an early parliamentary election for June, the move backfired. Chirac remained president but his party, the Rassemblement Pour la République (RPR; Rally for the Republic), lost support, and a coalition of Socialists, Communists and Greens came to power – under whom France's infamous 35-hour working week was introduced.

Chirac's second term in office, starting in 2002, was marred by some of the worst violence seen in Paris since WWII. In autumn 2005, following the death of two teenage boys of North African origin hiding in an electrical substation while on the run from the police, riots broke out in Paris' *cités,* the enormous housing estates encircling the capital where a dispossessed population lives. The violence quickly spread to other cities in France and the government called a state of emergency. Only 9000 burnt cars and buildings later was peace in Paris was restored.

FIRST GAY MAYOR

Bertrand Delanoë, a Socialist backed by the Green Party, became the first openly gay mayor of Paris (and any European capital) in 2001. He was re-elected for a second term in 2008.

A NEW BREED OF PRESIDENT

Presidential elections in 2007 ushered old-school Jacques Chirac out and the dynamic, ambitious and media-savvy Nicolas Sarkozy (b 1955) in. The former interior minister and chairman of centre-right party UMP (Union pour un Mouvement Populaire) wooed voters with promises of reducing unemployment, job creation, lower income tax, a crackdown on crime and help for France's substantial immigrant population – something that had particular pulling power coming straight from the son of a Hungarian immigrant and Greek Jewish-French mother. Female Socialist Party candidate Ségolène Royal (b 1953) put up a grand fight. But the French, fed up with an economically stagnant, socially discontented France, wanted change. And this charismatic politican seemed to be the man to do it. A new breed of French president was born. See the Paris Today chapter (p300) for more information.

1989

President Mitterrand's *grand projet*, Opéra de Paris Bastille, opens to mark the bicentennial of the French Revolution; IM Pei's Grande Pyramide is unveiled at the Louvre.

1998

France beats Brazil to win the World Cup at the spanking-new Stade de France (Stadium of France) in St-Denis north of central Paris.

2001

Socialist Bertrand Delanoë becomes the first openly gay mayor of Paris (and of any European capital) but is wounded in a knife attack by a homophobic assailant the following year.

2002

The French franc is thrown onto the scrap heap of history as the country adopts the euro as its official currency, along with 14 other EU member-states.

Contrary to the rigorous economic reform platform on which he'd been elected on, Sarkozy struggled to keep the French economy buoyant. Unemployment fluctuated from 8.7% in 2007, to 7.6% during the 2008 global banking crisis (when the government injected €10.5 billion into France's six major banks), to 9.1% in 2010 – all to the horror of the French who traditionally have great expectations of their economy. For a few months of 2009, as economic growth shrank, France joined much of the rest of Europe in recession.

Hard-line attempts meanwhile to reform a pension system, unchanged since 1982, which entitles 1.6 million workers in the rail, metro, energy-supply and fishing industries to draw a full state pension after 37.5 working years (and everyone else after 40) merely provoked widespread horror and a series of national strikes and protests. In mid-2010 when the French government unveiled concrete plans to push the retirement age back to 62 by 2018 there were widespread strikes across the country

As a result Sarkozy's party suffered badly in the regional elections, Alsace in northeast France being the only region his centre-right UMP held onto. The left scooped 54% of votes and control of 21 out of 22 regions on mainland France and Corsica, pre-empting the devastating lack of support Sarkozy would subsequently encounter in the country's 2012 presidential elections.

QUALITY OF LIFE

The French are accustomed to receiving free education and health care, state-subsidised child care, travel concessions for families, ample leisure time and a 35-hour working week – all at great cost to state coffers.

2002

President Jacques Chirac overwhelmingly defeats Front National leader Jean-Marie Le Pen to win a second term.

2007

Pro-American pragmatist Nicolas Sarkozy, Interior Minister under Chirac, beats Socialist candidate Ségolène Royal to become France's new president.

2012

France loses its top AAA credit rating. Economic policy becomes a campaign issue in the run-up to the 2012 presidential elections in late April.

2012

Socialist candidate François Hollande beats Nicolas Sarkozy to become France's new president.

Fashion

'Fashion is a way of life,' Yves St Laurent once pronounced, and most Parisians would agree. They live, breathe and consume fashion. After all, to their reckoning, fashion is French - like gastronomy - and the competition from Milan, Tokyo or New York simply doesn't cut the mustard. But what few Parisians know (or want to admit) is that an Englishman created Parisian *haute couture* (literally 'high sewing') as it exists today.

REVOLUTION & DRAMA

Known as 'the Napoleon of costumers', Charles Frederick Worth (1825–95) arrived in Paris at the age of 20 and revolutionised fashion by banishing the crinoline (stiffened petticoat), lifting hemlines up to the oh-so-shocking ankle length and presenting his creations on live models. The House of Worth stayed in the family for four generations until the 1950s.

In the early 1990s the Brits-abroad baton in Paris was taken over by highly creative British designers, such as Alexander McQueen (1969–2010) and John Galliano (b. 1960). One of the industry's most influential designers until his dramatic fall from grace, the Gibraltar-born London-raised Galliano moved to Paris in 1991, became chief designer at Givenchy in 1995 and a year later moved to the house of Dior. His first women's collection for the mythical French fashion house, responsible for re-establishing Paris as world fashion capital after WWII, was nothing short of spectacular – models waltzed down a catwalk framed by 500 gold chairs and 4000 roses perfectly arranged to recreate the post-war glamour of Christian Dior's 1946 showroom on av Montaigne, 8e, in the Triangle d'Or (Golden Triangle).

The downfall of this talented, *enfant terrible* of fashion was as dramatic. In 2011 Galliano was dismissed by the House of Dior after being caught on camera casting public insults to punters at his local neighbourhood cafe-bar La Perle in the Marais, and subsequently being found guilty of racist and anti-Semitic abuse.

Fashion Museums & Exhibitions

Fondation Pierre Bergé–Yves Saint Laurent (16e)

Musée Galliera de la Mode de la Ville de Paris (16e)

Cité de la Mode et du Design (Docks en Seine, 13e)

NOSTALGIA & RECYCLING

Outlandish designs by 'wild child' couturiers, such as punk-influenced Parisian Jean Paul Gaultier, known for dressing men in skirts and Madonna in her signature conical bra, might well appear on the catwalk during fashion week. But the chances are you won't encounter Gaultier-clad women rubbing shoulders in the metro: Parisian style is too classical for that.

Vintage

Many Parisian women prefer to play safe (and often slightly sexy) in classic designs, monotones and perhaps a scarf or other simple accessory thrown in for good luck – inspired by Coco Chanel (1883–1971), creator of the 'little black dress' in the 1920s! Indeed, nostalgia for Chanel – known for her practical designs and modern simplicity – as well as Givenchy, Féraud and other designers from the 1950s Parisian fashion heyday, has contributed to

Louis Vuitton (p99)

big demand in the capital today for vintage clothing. Twice a year Paris' mythical auction house Hôtel Drouot hosts *haute-couture* auctions, while collector Didier Ludot – in the designer trade since 1975 – sells the city's finest couture creations of yesteryear in an exclusive twinset of boutiques at Palais Royal. Utterly irresistible is La Petite Robe Noir, his legendary boutique, showcasing dozens of little black dresses by designers from the 1920s to the 1990s. No address is more chic or Parisian.

Post-Vintage

Post-vintage fashion is all about recycling. Art and fashion studio Andrea Crews, starting out in 2002 between sex shops in the red light district of Pigalle and now at home in Belleville, was among the first to reinvent grandpa's discarded shirts and daughter's has-beens into new hip garments. Love child of French designer Maroussia Rebecq (b. 1975), the groundbreaking label turns the conventional distinction between fashion, art and performance ('activism') on its head.

Ethical, sustainable and reasonably priced to boot, recycled fashion is flourishing in contemporary Paris: Made in Used in the Haut Marais and Room Service near Les Halles are boutiques to look for.

> No movie better captures the compelling life story of orphan Coco Chanel than Anne Fontaine's *Coco Avant Chanel* (Coco Before Chanel; 2009), starring Audrey Tautou of *Le Fabuleux Destin d'Amélie Poulain* fame. The film won four BAFTAs and a clutch of other awards.

CONTEMPORARY FASHION

Parisian style is not only about yesterday. Other contemporary 'Parisian styles' have their grass roots in particular neighbourhoods and social classes. The funky street-wear style, heavily inspired by London, jumps off the shelves in the shops around rue Étienne Marcel (Louvre & Les Halles) and the Marais. The Haut Marais in the 3e is known for its up-and-coming young designers and their boutiques that double as studios and workshops: names to watch include Moon Young Hee, Valentine Gauthier and Yukiko. Anne Elisabeth is another favourite.

BCBG & Intello

Meanwhile the more upper-crust 'BCBG' (*bon chic bon genre*) Parisian shops at Le Bon Marché or Chanel, and rarely ventures outside her preferred districts: the 7e, 8e and 16e. The chic Left Bank *intello* (intellectual) meanwhile struts her Agnès b (created in Paris in 1975 by Versailles designer Agnès Troublé – the 'b' gives a nod to her husband) and APC (an abbreviation for Atelier de Production et de Création), known for its trendy but highly wearable fashion.

Paris coined the expression *lèche-vitrine* (literally 'window-licker') for window-shopping; 'tasting' without buying is an art like any other so don't be shy. The fancy couture houses on av Montaigne may seem daunting but, in most, no appointment is necessary and you can simply walk in.

Bobo

The eastern districts of Oberkampf, Bastille, the area of the 10e around Canal St-Martin and the Batignolles section of Clichy in the 17e tend to be the stomping ground of the *bobo* (bourgeois bohemian) whose take on style is doused in nostalgia for her voyage to India, Tibet or Senegal and her commitment to free trade and beads. The wildest ones wear Kate Mack and dress their kids in chic and romantic prints and patterns by Liza Korn, shopped for with love in the designer's sweet boutique near Canal St-Martin.

Younger professional *bobos* frequent concept store Colette, Kabuki Femme and Isabel Marant (the current darling of the Paris fashion scene with boutiques in the Marais, Bastille and St-Germain des Prés). In recent years the design from Boulogne-Billancourt near Paris has attained something akin to cult worship among Parisian hipsters, thanks to an easy style that translates as deliciously wearable-year-round floral dresses, suede fringed boots, denim miniskirts, loose knits and lush scarves. The other big name is Vanessa Bruno, a Parisian brand again known for its wearable fashion, if masculine-edged.

Ready to Wear

Céline, prided for its stylish and clever minimalism, is a popular luxury label. Founded in 1945, it has only really been since 2008 when British fashion designer Phoebe Philo joined as creative director that Céline has been up with the best in the premier league. Prior to Céline, Philo was with Chloé, another Parisian fashion house, dating to 1952, and known as being the first *haute-couture* label to introduce, in 1956, a designer ready-to-wear collection. Paris' prêt-à-porter industry was born.

TRENDS OF TOMORROW

Each year the Ville de Paris honours its rising stars in fashion with the Grand Prix Création de la Ville de Paris – a prize awarded to the best new designer working in the trade for fewer than three years, and the best confirmed designer (at least three years in the fashion biz). The published list of prize laureates, past and present, is tantamount to a who's who of tomorrow's fashion scene. Names to watch out for include the bold and unconventional 2008 winner, Sakina M'sa, who staged her fashion show in 2011 in a Parisian prison; Marion Vidal whose showroom in the 9e showcases bold, funky jewellery; and duo Marion Lalanne and Pierre-Alexis Heret whose increasingly popular label, IRM Design, features bold, often hand-painted fabrics and cuts.

Then there is the loud and lurid-lime Cité de la Mode et du Design (City of Fashion & Design; Docks en Seine) in the rejuvenated Gare d'Austerlitz area in the 13e. Home to the French Fashion Institute, the cultural centre is intended to celebrate and showcase fashion and design in the city, and serves as a cutting-edge venue for a growing program of fashion exhibitions and events in Paris. Watch this space.

With their fondness for a neutral palette of black, grey, beige, brown and white, Parisians do accessories exceptionally well. Parisian handbag designers include Nat & Nin, Clarisse (Pauline Pin), Kasia Dietz and Jamin Puech.

Architecture

It took disease, clogged streets, an antiquated sewerage system, a lack of open spaces and Baron Georges-Eugène Haussmann to drag architectural Paris out of the Middle Ages and into the modern world. Few town planners anywhere in the world have had as great an effect on the city of their birth as Haussmann did on his. His 19th-century transformation of Paris was gargantuan. Parisians endured years of 'flying dust, noise, and falling plaster and beams', as one contemporary observer wrote. Entire areas of the city (such as the labyrinthine Île de la Cité) were razed, and hundreds of thousands of (mostly poor) people displaced. But Paris has never looked back.

GALLO-ROMAN

Traces of Roman Paris can be seen in the residential foundations and dwellings in the Crypte Archéologique under the square in front of Notre Dame; in the partially reconstructed Arènes de Lutèce; and in the *frigidarium* (cooling room) and other remains of Roman baths dating from around AD 200 at the Musée National du Moyen Âge.

The Musée National du Moyen Âge also contains the so-called Pillier des Nautes (Boatsmen's Pillar), one of the most valuable legacies of the Gallo-Roman period. It is a 2.5m-high monument dedicated to Jupiter and was erected by the boatmen's guild during the reign of Tiberius (AD 14-37) on the Île de la Cité. The boat has become the symbol of Paris, and the city's Latin motto is '*Fluctuat Nec Mergitur*' (Tossed by Waves but does not Sink).

Architectural Pilgrimages

- *Eiffel Tower (Eiffel Tower & Western Paris)*
- *Louvre pyramid (Louvre & Les Halles)*
- *Arc de Triomphe (Louvre & Les Halles)*
- *Basilique de Sacré-Cœur (Montmartre & Northern Paris)*
- *Centre Pompidou (Louvre & Les Halles)*
- *Cité de l'Architecture et du Patrimoine (Eiffel Tower & Western Paris)*

MEROVINGIAN & CAROLINGIAN

Although quite a few churches were built in Paris during the Merovingian and Carolingian periods (6th to 10th centuries), very little of them remain.

When the Merovingian ruler Clovis I made Paris his seat in the early 6th century, he established an abbey dedicated to Sts Peter and Paul on the south bank of the Seine. All that remains of this once-great abbey (later named in honour of Paris' patron, Ste Geneviève, and demolished in 1802) is the Tour Clovis, a heavily restored Romanesque tower within the grounds of the prestigious Lycée Henri IV just east of the Panthéon.

Archaeological excavations in the crypt of the 12th-century Basilique de St-Denis have uncovered extensive tombs from both the Merovingian and Carolingian periods. The oldest of these dates from around AD 570.

ROMANESQUE

A religious revival in the 11th century led to the construction of a large number of *roman* (Romanesque) churches, so-called because their architects adopted many architectural elements (eg vaulting) from Gallo-Roman buildings still standing at the time. Romanesque buildings typically have round arches, heavy walls, few (and small) windows that let in very little light, and a lack of ornamentation that borders on the austere.

No building or church in Paris is entirely Romanesque, but several have important representative elements. Église St-Germain des Prés, built in the 11th century on the site of the Merovingian ruler Childeric's 6th-century abbey, has been altered many times over the centuries, but the Romanesque bell tower over the west entrance has changed little since AD 1000. The choir, apse and truncated bell tower of Église St-Nicolas des Champs, now part of the Musée des Arts et Métiers, are Romanesque, dating from about 1130. Église St-Germain l'Auxerrois was built in a mixture of Gothic and Renaissance styles between the 13th and 16th centuries on a site used for Christian worship since about AD 500.

As new as tomorrow, the richly illustrated coffee-table book *Paris 2000+: New Architecture* by Sam Lubell focuses on 30 buildings that have been created this millennium. For DIY architectural walking tours of the city, pick up Hervé Martin's *Guide to Modern Architecture in Paris.*

GOTHIC

The world's first Gothic building was Basilique de St-Denis, which combined various late-Romanesque elements to create a new kind of structural support in which each arch counteracted and complemented the next. Begun in around 1135, the basilica served as a model for many 12th-century French cathedrals, including Notre Dame de Paris and Chartres cathedral.

In the 14th century, the Rayonnant – or Radiant – Gothic style, named after the radiating tracery of the rose windows, developed, with interiors becoming even lighter, thanks to broader windows and more translucent stained glass. One of the most influential Rayonnant buildings was Ste-Chapelle, whose stained glass forms a curtain of glazing on the 1st floor. The two transept façades of Cathédrale de Notre Dame de Paris and the vaulted Salle des Gens d'Armes (Cavalrymen's Hall) in the Conciergerie, the largest surviving medieval hall in Europe, are other fine examples of Rayonnant Gothic style.

By the 15th century, decorative extravagance led to Flamboyant Gothic, so named because the wavy stone carving made the towers appear to be blazing or flaming *(flamboyant)*. Beautifully lacy examples of Flamboyant architecture include the Clocher Neuf (New Bell Tower; located at Chartres' cathedral), Église St-Séverin and Tour St-Jacques, a 52m tower which is all that remains of an early 16th-century church. Inside Église St-Eustache, there's some outstanding Flamboyant Gothic arch work holding up the ceiling of the chancel. Several *hôtels particuliers* (private mansions) were also built in this style, including Hôtel de Cluny, now the Musée National du Moyen Âge.

RENAISSANCE

The Renaissance set out to realise a 'rebirth' of classical Greek and Roman culture and first affected France at the end of the 15th century, when Charles VIII began a series of invasions of Italy, returning with some new ideas.

The Early Renaissance style, in which a variety of classical components and decorative motifs (columns, tunnel vaults, round arches, domes etc) were blended with the rich decoration of Flamboyant Gothic, is best exemplified in Paris by Église St-Eustache on the Right Bank and Église St-Étienne du Mont on the Left Bank.

Mannerism was introduced by Italian architects and artists brought to France around 1530 by François I. In 1546 Pierre Lescot designed the richly decorated southwestern corner of the Cour Carrée at the Musée du Louvre.

Architecture

From Roman arenas and Gothic cathedrals to postmodernist cubes and shimmering skyscrapers, the Paris skyline is far from dull. Laced with the whole gambit of architectural styles, it excites, it inspires, it demands to be admired – and never more so than at sunset with its extraordinary light.

Grand Palais

1 One of the skyline's most recognisable landmarks, thanks to the gargantuan glass dome that tops it, this romantic exhibition hall from 1900 is art nouveau perfection – and the world's largest glass and iron structure to boot.

Palais Garnier

2 Neoclassicism in Paris was grand and it was fitting that the climax to this great 19th-century movement should be the city's opera house, designed by Charles Garnier to showcase the splendour of Napoleon III's France.

Institute of the Arab World

3 One of Paris' most beautiful, late-20th-century modern buildings, this stunner by Jean Nouvel mixes modern and traditional Arab and Western elements. France's leading and arguably most talented architect is likewise the creative force behind Paris' long-awaited Philharmonie de Paris, set to open in 2014.

Centre Pompidou

4 The 'bad boy' of exhibition spaces when it opened in 1977, Paris' once reviled but now beloved Centre Pompidou saw its creators Renzo Piano and Richard Rogers – in a bold attempt to keep gallery space uncluttered – turn the entire building inside-out.

Clockwise from top left

1 Grand Palais (p93), Paris, detail. © ADAGP Paris & DB, Photo/Corbis **2** Palais Garnier (p97) **3** Institute of the Arab World (p210) **4** Centre Pompidou (p111), designed by R Piano, R Rogers and G Franchini

2

YANG LIU / CORBIS ©

3

JEAN-BERNARD CARILLET / GETTY IMAGES ©

The Marais remains the best area for Renaissance reminders in Paris proper, displaying as it does some fine *hôtels particuliers* like Hôtel Carnavalet, which houses part of the Musée Carnavalet.

Designer Rooftops

Grand Palais (Champs-Élysées & Grands Boulevards)

Cathédrale de Notre Dame (The Islands)

Galeries Lafayette (Champs-Élysées & Grands Boulevards)

BAROQUE

During the baroque period – which lasted from the tail end of the 16th to the late 18th centuries – painting, sculpture and classical architecture were integrated to create structures and interiors of great subtlety, refinement and elegance. With the advent of the baroque, architecture became more pictorial, with painted church ceilings illustrating the Passion of Christ to the faithful, and palaces invoking the power and order of the state.

Salomon de Brosse, who designed Paris' Palais du Luxembourg in the Jardin du Luxembourg in 1615, set the stage for two of France's most prominent early baroque architects: François Mansart, designer of Église Notre Dame du Val-de-Grâce, and his young rival Louis Le Vau, architect of Château de Vaux-le-Vicomte, which served as a model for Louis XIV's palace at Versailles.

Other fine French-baroque examples are: Église St-Louis en l'Île, Chapelle de la Sorbonne, Palais Royal, and Hôtel de Sully with its inner courtyard decorated with allegorical figures.

A zany structure if ever there was one is auction house Hôtel Drouat, in business since 1852. In the late 1970s it was given a complete facelift by architects Jean-Jacques Fernier and André Biro. Their surrealist interpretation of the 19th-century Hausmann building was instantly hailed as a modern architectural gem when unveiled in 1980.

NEOCLASSICISM

Neoclassical architecture emerged about 1740 and had its roots in the renewed interest in classical forms – a search for order, reason and serenity through the adoption of forms and conventions of Graeco-Roman antiquity: columns, geometric forms and traditional ornamentation.

Among the earliest examples of this style are the Italianate façade of Église St-Sulpice; and the Petit Trianon at Versailles, designed by Jacques-Ange Gabriel for Louis XV in 1761. The domed building in Paris housing the Institut de France is a masterpiece of early French neoclassical architecture, but France's greatest neoclassical architect of the 18th century was Jacques-Germain Soufflot, creator of the Panthéon in the Latin Quarter.

Neoclassicism really came into its own, however, under Napoleon, who used it extensively for monumental architecture intended to embody the grandeur of imperial France and its capital. Well-known Paris sights designed during the First Empire (1804-14) include the Arc de Triomphe, the Arc de Triomphe du Carrousel, Église de Ste-Marie Madeleine, the Bourse de Commerce, the Assemblée Nationale in the Palais Bourbon, and the Palais Garnier.

ART NOUVEAU

Art nouveau, which emerged in Europe and the USA in the second half of the 19th century under various names (Jugendstil, Sezessionstil, Stile Liberty) caught on quickly in Paris, and its influence lasted until about 1910. It was characterised by sinuous curves and flowing, asymmetrical forms reminiscent of creeping vines, water lilies, the patterns on insect wings and the flowering boughs of trees. Influenced by the arrival of exotic *objets d'art* from Japan, art nouveau's French name came from a Paris gallery that featured works in the 'new art' style.

A lush and photogenic architectural style, art nouveau is expressed to perfection in Paris by Hector Guimard's graceful metro entrances and Marais synagogue, and parts of the interiors in the Musée d'Orsay and the city's main department stores, Le Bon Marché and Galeries Lafayette.

MODERN

France's best-known 20th-century architect, Charles-Édouard Jeanneret (better known as Le Corbusier), was born in Switzerland but settled in Paris in 1917 at the age of 30. A radical modernist, he tried to adapt buildings to their functions in industrialised society without ignoring the human element. Most of Le Corbusier's work was done outside Paris, though he did design several private residences and the Pavillon Suisse, a dormitory for Swiss students at the Cité Internationale Universitaire in the 14e.

But until 1968, French architects were still being trained almost exclusively at the conformist École de Beaux-Arts, and that is reflected in most of the early impersonal and forgettable 'lipstick tube' and 'upended shoeboxe' structures erected in the skyscraper district of La Défense; the Unesco building (1958) in the 7e; and the unspeakable, 210m-tall Tour Montparnasse (1973).

Interesting and frightening were Le Corbusier's plans for Paris that never left the drawing board. Called Plan Voisin (Neighbour Project; 1925), it envisaged wide boulevards linking the Gare Montparnasse with the Seine and lined with skyscrapers. The project would have required the bulldozing of much of the Latin Quarter.

CONTEMPORARY

For centuries France's leaders have sought to immortalise themselves by erecting huge public edifices – known as *grands projets* – in Paris, and the recent past has been no different. Georges Pompidou commissioned the Centre Pompidou and his successor, Valéry Giscard d'Estaing, was instrumental in transforming the derelict Gare d'Orsay train station into the glorious Musée d'Orsay, a design carried out by the Italian architect Gaeltana Aulenti in 1986. François Mitterrand surpassed all of the postwar presidents with monumental projects costing taxpayers a whopping €4.6 billion, and Jacques Chirac orchestrated the magnificent Musée du Quai Branly, a glass, wood and sod structure by Jean Nouvel with 3-hectare experimental garden.

1980s Grand Designs

Since the early 1980s, Paris has seen the construction of IM Pei's glass-pyramid entrance at the hitherto sacrosanct and untouchable Musée du Louvre, an architectural cause célèbre that paved the way for Mario Bellini and Rudy Ricciotti's magnificent 'flying carpet' roof atop the museum's Cour Visconti in 2012; the city's second opera house, the tile-clad Opéra de Paris Bastille designed by Uruguayan architect Carlos Ott in 1989; the monumental Grande Arche de la Défense by Danish architect Johan-Otto von Sprekelsen, which opened the same year; the delightful Conservatoire National Supérieur de Musique et de Danse (1990) and Cité de la Musique (1994), designed by Christian de Portzamparc and serving as a sort of gateway from the city to the whimsical Parc de la Villette; the four glass towers of the €2 billion Bibliothèque Nationale de France (Dominique Perrault, 1995) and neighbouring M2K Bibliothèque pleasure palace (Wilmotte & Namur, 2003) in a glass shoebox that glimmers at night.

On a more human scale is the redeveloped warehouse district known as Masséna Nord, where narrow streets and open blocks link conversions such as the Grands Moulins (an old mill now the hub of the new Paris Diderot University), the former SNCF cold-storage warehouse of Les Frigos (now a colourful artists' community) and an old factory complete with smokestack (a new architecture school).

Tomorrow's Paris

Right in the heart of Right-Bank Paris, in the 1er, the thoroughly unattractive Forum des Halles shopping centre is currently being transformed from 1970s eyesore to contemporary creation – a curvaceous, curvilinear and glass-topped construction by architects Patrick Berger and Jacques Anziutti, to be completed 2016.

Exciting architectural projects of tomorrow include the sizeable, beautiful and sustainable Tour Phare (Lighthouse Tower; www.tour-phare.com) at La Défense, a 297m-tall office and retail tower with 69 floors that will torque like a human torso and, through awnings that are raised and lowered when the sun hits them, use light as a building material when it is completed in 2017. In the Parc des Expositions at Porte de Versailles in the 15e, Swiss architectural firm Herzog & de Meuron (creators of London's Tate Modern) have drawn up the plans for a 200m-tall glass structure in the shape of a triangle to be built, red tape pending, by 2017.

A signature architectural feature of Paris is the vertical garden or *mur végétal* (vegetation wall). Seeming to defy gravity, these vertical gardens cling to walls in chic boutique interiors, outside museums and within spas. The Seine-facing garden at the Musée du Quai Branly by Patrick Blanc is Paris' most famous.

Literary Paris

Whether reading a book, attending a poetry recital or browsing shelf-loads of novels in a hip wine bar in the Marais, Parisians have always had a deep appreciation for the written word and literature remains an important focus in their sense of identity.

MEDIEVAL

Paris does not figure largely in early medieval French literature, although the misadventures of Pierre Abélard and Héloïse took place in the capital as did their mutual correspondence, which ended only with their deaths.

François Villon, considered the finest poet of the late Middle Ages, received the equivalent of a Master of Arts degree from the Sorbonne before he turned 20. Involved in a series of brawls, robberies and generally illicit escapades, 'Master Villon' (as he became known) was sentenced to be hanged in 1462 supposedly for stabbing a lawyer. However, the sentence was commuted to banishment from Paris for 10 years, and he disappeared forever. As well as a long police record, Villon left behind a body of poems charged with a highly personal lyricism, among them the *Ballade des Pendus* (Ballad of the Hanged Men), in which he writes his own epitaph, and the *Ballade des Dames du Temps Jadis,* which was translated by the English poet and painter Dante Gabriel Rossetti as the 'Ballad of Dead Ladies'.

Contemporary Literary Venues

La Bellevilloise (Le Marais & Ménilmontant)

Drouant (Louvre & Les Halles)

Shakespeare & Company (Latin Quarter)

Café des Phares (Le Marais & Ménilmontant)

RENAISSANCE

The great landmarks of French Renaissance literature are the works of François Rabelais, Pierre de Ronsard (and other poets of the Renaissance group known as La Pléiade) and Michel de Montaigne. The exuberant narratives of the erstwhile monk Rabelais blend coarse humour with erudition in a vast *œuvre* that seems to include every kind of person, occupation and jargon to be found in the France of the early 16th century. Rabelais had friends in high places in Paris, including Archbishop Jean du Bellay, whom he accompanied to Rome on two occasions. But some of Rabelais' friends and associates fell afoul of the clergy, including his publisher Étienne Dolet. After being convicted of heresy and blasphemy in 1546, Dolet was hanged and then burned at place Maubert in the 5e arrondissement.

CLASSICAL

During the 17th century, François de Malherbe, court poet under Henri IV, brought a new rigour to the treatment of rhythm in literature. One of his better-known works is his sycophantic *Ode* (1600) to Marie de Médici. Transported by the perfection of Malherbe's verses, Jean de La Fontaine went on to write his charming *Fables* (1668) in the manner of Aesop – though he fell out with the Académie Française (French Academy) in the process. The mood of classical tragedy permeates *La Princesse de Clèves* (1678) by Marie de La Fayette, which is widely regarded as the precursor of the modern character novel.

18TH CENTURY

The literature of the 18th century is dominated by philosophers, among them Voltaire (François-Marie Arouet) and Jean-Jacques Rousseau. Voltaire's political writings, arguing that society is fundamentally opposed to nature, had a profound and lasting influence on the century, and he is buried in the Panthéon. Rousseau's sensitivity to landscape and its moods anticipate romanticism, and the insistence on his own singularity in *Les Confessions* (1782) made it the first modern autobiography. He, too, is buried in the Panthéon.

Literary Sights

Maison de Victor Hugo (Le Marais & Ménilmontant)

Maison de Balzac (Eiffel Tower & Western Paris)

Musée de la Vie Romantique (Montmartre & Northern Paris)

FRENCH ROMANTICISM

The 19th century produced Victor Hugo, as much acclaimed for his poetry as for his novels, who lived on the place des Vosges before fleeing to the Channel Islands during the Second Empire. *Les Misérables* (1862) describes life among the poor and marginalised of Paris during the first half of the 19th century; the 20-page flight of the central character, Jean Valjean, through the sewers of the capital is memorable. *Notre Dame de Paris* (The Hunchback of Notre Dame; 1831), a medieval romance and tragedy revolving around the life of the celebrated cathedral, made Hugo the key figure of French romanticism.

Other influential 19th-century novelists include Stendhal (Marie-Henri Beyle), Honoré de Balzac, Amandine Aurore Lucile Dupin (better known as George Sand) and, of course, Alexandre Dumas, who wrote the swashbuckling adventures *Le Compte de Monte Cristo* (The Count of Monte Cristo; 1844) and *Les Trois Mousquetaires* (The Three Musketeers; 1844). The latter tells the story of d'Artagnan, based on the historical personage Charles de Batz d'Artagnan (c 1611–73), who arrives in Paris as a young Gascon determined to become one of the guardsmen of Louis XIII.

FOREIGN LITERATURE: STRANGERS IN PARIS

Foreigners (*étrangers*, or strangers, to the French) have found inspiration in Paris since Charles Dickens used the city alongside London as the backdrop to *A Tale of Two Cities* in 1859. But the glory days of Paris as a literary setting were the interwar years.

Both Ernest Hemingway's *The Sun Also Rises* (1926) and the posthumous *A Moveable Feast* (1964) portray bohemian life in Paris between the wars. So many vignettes in the latter – dissing Ford Maddox Ford in a cafe, 'sizing up' F Scott Fitzgerald in a toilet in the Latin Quarter and overhearing Gertrude Stein and her lover, Alice B Toklas, bitchin' at one another from the sitting room of their salon near the Jardin du Luxembourg – are classic and *très parisien*.

Language guru Stein, who could be so tiresome with her wordplay and endless repetitions in books like *The Making of Americans* (1925), was able to let her hair down by assuming her lover's identity in *The Autobiography of Alice B Toklas*. It's a fascinating account of the author's many years in Paris, her salon on rue de Fleurus, 6e, and her friendships with Matisse, Picasso, Braque, Hemingway and others.

Down and Out in Paris and London (1933) is George Orwell's account of the time he spent working as a *plongeur* (dishwasher) in Paris and living with tramps in the 1930s. Henry Miller's *Tropic of Cancer* (1934) and *Quiet Days in Clichy* (1956) are steamy novels set partly in the French capital. Then there are Anaïs Nin's diaries and fiction; her published correspondence with Miller is particularly evocative of 1930s Paris.

For 1950s Paris read *Giovanni's Room* (1956), James Baldwin's poignant account of a young American in Paris who falls in love with an Italian bartender, and his struggle with his sexuality. *Satori in Paris* (1966) by Jack Kerouac is the sometimes entertaining (eg the scene in the Montparnasse gangster bar) but often irritating account of the American Beat writer's last trip to France.

STUART DEE / ROBERT HARDING WORLD IMAGERY / CORBIS©

Café de Flore (p243)

In 1857 two landmarks of French literature were published in book form: *Madame Bovary* by Gustave Flaubert and *Les Fleurs du Mal* by Charles Baudelaire. Both writers were tried for the supposed immorality of their works. Flaubert won his case, and his novel was distributed without censorship. Baudelaire, who moonlighted as a translator in Paris (he introduced the works of the American writer Edgar Allan Poe to Europe in editions that have since become classics of English-to-French translation), was obliged to cut half a dozen poems from his work and was fined 300 francs. He died an early and painful death, practically unknown. Flaubert's second-most popular novel, *L'Éducation Sentimentale* (Sentimental Education; 1869), presents a vivid picture of life among Parisian dilettantes, intellectuals and revolutionaries during the decline and fall of Louis-Philippe's monarchy and the February Revolution of 1848.

Histoire d'O (Story of O; 1954), Dominique Aury's erotic, sadomasochistic novel written under a pseudonym, has sold more copies outside France than any other contemporary French novel. Most believed it to be the work of a man; it was only 40 years after publication than the female author revealed her identity.

The aim of Émile Zola, who came to Paris with his close friend, the artist Paul Cézanne, in 1858, was to transform novel-writing from an art to a science by the application of experimentation. His theory may now seem naive, but his work influenced most significant French writers of the late 19th century and is reflected in much 20th-century fiction as well. His novel *Nana* (1880) tells the decadent tale of a young woman who resorts to prostitution to survive the Paris of the Second Empire.

SYMBOLISM & SURREALISM

Paul Verlaine and Stéphane Mallarmé created the symbolist movement, which strove to express states of mind rather than simply to detail daily reality. Arthur Rimbaud, apart from crowding an extraordinary amount of exotic travel into his 37 years and having a tempestuous sexual relationship with Verlaine, produced two enduring pieces of work: *Une Saison en Enfer* (A Season in Hell; 1873) and *Illuminations* (1874). Verlaine died at 39 rue Descartes, 5e, in 1896.

Marcel Proust dominated the early 20th century with his giant seven-volume novel *À la Recherche du Temps Perdu* (Remembrance of Things Past; 1913–27), which explores in evocative detail the true meaning of past experience recovered from the unconscious by 'involuntary memory'. In 1907 Proust moved from the family home near av des Champs-Élysées to the apartment on blvd Haussmann that was famous for its cork-lined bedroom (now in the Musée Carnavalet) from which he almost never stirred. André Gide found his voice in the celebration of gay sensuality and, later, left-wing politics. His novel *Les Faux-Monnayeurs* (The Counterfeiters; 1925) exposes the hypocrisy and self-deception to which people resort in order to fit in with others or deceive themselves.

André Breton led the French surrealists and wrote their three manifestos, although the first use of the word 'surrealist' is attributed to the poet Guillaume Apollinaire, a fellow traveller of surrealism who was killed in action in WWI. As a poet, Breton was overshadowed by Paul Éluard and by Louis Aragon, whose most famous surrealist novel was *Le Paysan de Paris* (Nightwalker; 1926). Colette (Sidonie-Gabrielle Colette) enjoyed tweaking the noses of conventionally moral readers with titillating novels that detailed the amorous exploits of such heroines as the schoolgirl Claudine. Her best-known work is *Gigi* (1945) but far more interesting is *Paris de Ma Fenêtre* (Paris from My Window; 1944), dealing with the German occupation of Paris. Her view, by the way, was from 9 rue de Beaujolais in the 1er, overlooking the Jardin du Palais Royal.

Literary Cafes

Café de Flore & Les Deux Magots (St-Germain & Les Invalides)

La Belle Hortense & L'Autre Café (Le Marais & Ménilmontant)

Café des Phares (Le Marais & Ménilmontant)

EXISTENTIALISM

After WWII, existentialism developed as a significant literary movement around Jean-Paul Sartre, Simone de Beauvoir and Albert Camus, who worked and conversed in the cafes of blvd St-Germain, 6e, in St-German des Prés. All three stressed the importance of the writer's political engagement. De Beauvoir, author of *Le Deuxième Sexe* (The Second Sex; 1949), had a profound influence on feminist thinking. Camus' novel *L'Étranger* (The Stranger; 1942) reveals that the absurd is the condition of modern man, who feels himself a stranger – more accurately translated as 'outsider' in English – in his world.

SARTRE'S TRILOGY

L'Âge de Raison (The Age of Reason; 1945), the first volume of Jean-Paul Sartre's trilogy *Les Chemins de la Liberté* (The Roads to Freedom), is a superb Parisian novel; his subsequent volumes recall Paris immediately before and during WWII.

MODERN LITERATURE

In the late 1950s certain novelists began to look for new ways of organising narrative. The so-called *nouveau roman* (new novel) refers to the works of Nathalie Sarraute, Alain Robbe-Grillet, Boris Vian, Julien Gracq, Michel Butor and others. But these writers never formed a close-knit group, and their experiments took them in divergent directions. Today the *nouveau roman* is very much out of favour in France, though the authors' names often appear in print and conversation.

In 1980 Marguerite Yourcenar, best known for her memorable historical novels such as *Mémoires d'Hadrien* (Hadrian's Memoirs; 1951), became the first woman to be elected to the Académie Française. Several years later Marguerite Duras came to the notice of a larger public when she won the Prix Goncourt for *L'Amant* (The Lover) in 1984.

Philippe Sollers was one of the editors of *Tel Quel*, a highbrow and left-wing Paris-based review, very influential in the 1960s and early 1970s. His 1960s novels were highly experimental, but with *Femmes* (Women; 1983) he returned to a conventional narrative style. Another editor of *Tel Quel* was Julia Kristeva, best known for her theoretical writings on literature and psychoanalysis. In recent years she has turned her hand to fiction, and *Les Samuraï* (The Samurai; 1990), a fictionalised account

READING LIST

One way of ensuring your city-break reading is right up to the minute is to plump for the latest winner of the **Prix Goncourt**, France's most prestigious literary prize awarded annually since 1903. Marcel Proust won it in 1919 for *À l'Ombre des Jeunes Filles en Fleurs* (Within a Budding Grove, translation published 1924); Simon de Beauvoir in 1954 for *Les Mandarins* (The Mandarins, 1957); and Franco-Senelagese writer Marie NDiaye in 2009 with *Trois Femmes Puissantes* (Three Powerful Women; 2012). The first black woman to win the award, NDiaye stunned the literary world at age 21 with *Comédie Classique* (1988), a 200-page novel containing just one single sentence.

The choice of 2011 Prix Goncourt victor reflects a preoccupation in French literature with issues of race, multiculturalism and immigration. Lyonnais biology teacher Alexis Jenni's *L'Art Français de la Guerre* (The French Art of War) portrays 50 years of French military history and colonial wars in southeast Asia and Algeria. The winning Prix Goncourt works are usually translated pretty swiftly into English.

Once you add the laureate of France's other big literary award, the **Grand Prix du Roman de l'Académie Française** (around since 1918) to your holiday reading list then you're sorted. The 2011 winner, *Retour à Killybegs* by Sorj Chalandon, was inspired by the French journalist's time spent reporting from Northern Ireland in the 1970s for French daily newspaper *Libération*. It was the sequel to Chalandon's earlier novel, *Mon Traître* (2008), translated into English as *My Traitor* (2011), about a French violinmaker's 25-year friendship with an Irish man ultimately exposed as an IRA traitor.

The 2009 Grand Prix winner, *Les Onze* by French novelist Pierre Michon, published in English as *The Eleven* (2013), portrays a humble Parisian painter who decorates the homes of Louis XIV's mistresses and goes on to create a Mona Lisa–type masterpiece. Michon's earlier novels, *Small Lives* (2008) and *Masters & Servants* (1997), come equally recommended.

of the heady days of *Tel Quel,* is an interesting document on the life of the Paris intelligentsia. Roland Barthes and Michel Foucault are other notable 1960s and '70s authors and philosophers.

CONTEMPORARY

Serious contemporary French writers include Jean Echenoz, Nina Bouraoui, Jean-Philippe Toussaint, Annie Ernaux and Erik Orsenna. Christine Angot is known as '*la reine de l'autofiction*' ('the queen of autobiography'), while Yasmina Khadra is actually a man – a former colonel in the Algerian army who adopted his wife's name as a nom de plume.

No contemporary French writer better delves into the mind, mood and politics of the capital's ethnic population than Faïza Guène, who writes in a notable 'urban slang' style. Born and bred on a housing estate outside Paris, she stunned critics with her debut novel, *Kiffe Kiffe Demain* (2004), sold in 27 countries and published in English as *Just Like Tomorrow* (2006). Faïza Guène's father moved from a village in western Algeria to northern France in 1952, aged 17, to work in the mines. Only in the 1980s could he return to Algeria where he met his wife, whom he brought back to France – to Les Courtillières housing estate in Seine-St-Denis where 6000-odd immigrants live like sardines in five-storey high-rise blocks stretching for 1.5km. Such is the setting for Guène's first book and her second semi-autobiographical novel, *Du Rêve pour les Oeufs* (2006), published in English as *Dreams from the Endz* (2008). Her third novel, *Les Gens du Balto* (2008), published in English as *Bar Balto* (2011), is a series of colloquial, first-person monologues by various characters who live on a street in a Parisian suburb 'at the end of the RER line, somewhere you'll never set foot'.

French writing in the 1990s focused in a nihilistic way on what France had lost as a nation (identity, international prestige, etc), and never more so than in the work of controversial writer Michel Houellebecq who rose to national prominence in 1998 with his *Les Particules Élémentaires* (Atomised).

Painting & Visual Arts

While art in Paris today means anything and everything – wacky installations in the metro, monumental wall frescoes, mechanical sculpture, suburban tags and bicycles strung as art on bistro walls – the city's rich art heritage has its roots firmly embedded in the traditional genres of painting and sculpture.

Painting Meccas

Musée du Louvre (Louvre & Les Halles)

Musée d'Orsay (St-Germain & Les Invalides)

Musée Picasso (Le Marais & Ménilmontant)

BAROQUE TO NEOCLASSICISM

According to philosopher Voltaire, French painting proper began with baroque painter Nicolas Poussin (1594–1665), the greatest representative of 17th-century classicism who frequently set scenes from ancient Rome, mythology and the Bible in ordered landscapes bathed in golden light.

In the field of sculpture, extravagant and monumental tombs had been commissioned by the nobility from the 14th century, and in Renaissance Paris Pierre Bontemps (c 1507–68) decorated the beautiful tomb of François I at Basilique de St-Denis, and Jean Goujon (c 1510–67) created the Fontaine des Innocents near the Forum des Halles, 1er. No sculpture better evokes baroque than the magnificent *Horses of Marly* of Guillaume Coustou (1677-1746), smart at the entrance to the av des Champs-Élysées.

Modern still life pops up on canvas with Jean-Baptiste Chardin (1699–1779) who brought the domesticity of the Dutch masters to French art. In 1785, neoclassical artist Jacques Louis David (1748–1825) wooed the public with his vast portraits with clear republican messages: *The Oath of the Horatii* and *The Lictors Bring to Brutus the Bodies of His Sons.* David became one of the leaders of the French Revolution, and a virtual dictator in matters of art, where he advocated a precise, severe classicism. He was made official state painter by Napoleon Bonaparte, glorifying Napoleon as general, first consul and then emperor. David is best remembered for his *Death of Marat,* depicting the Jacobin propagandist lying dead in his bath.

Jean-Auguste-Dominique Ingres (1780–1867), David's most gifted pupil in Paris, continued in the neoclassical tradition. The historical pictures to which he devoted most of his life (eg *Oedipus and the Sphinx*, the 1808 version of which is in the Louvre) are now generally regarded as inferior to his portraits. The name of Ingres, who played the violin for enjoyment, lives on in the phrase *violon d'Ingres,* which means 'hobby' in French.

ROMANTICISM

One of the gripping paintings in the Musée du Louvre, the *Raft of the Medusa* by Théodore Géricault (1791–1824), hovers on the threshold of romanticism; if Géricault had not died early (33) he probably would have become a leader of the movement, along with his friend Eugène Delacroix (1798–1863; find him in the Cimetière du Père Lachaise), best known for his masterpiece commemorating the July Revolution of 1830, *Liberty Leading the People.*

While romantics essentially revamped the subject picture, the Barbizon School effected a parallel transformation of landscape painting. The school derived its name from a village near the Forêt de Fontainebleau (Forest of Fontainebleau), where Jean-Baptiste Camille Corot (1796–1875) and Jean-François Millet (1814–75), among others, gathered to paint *en plein air* (in the open air). The son of a peasant farmer from Normandy, Millet took many of his subjects from peasant life, and reproductions of his *L'Angélus* (The Angelus; 1857) – the best-known French painting after the *Mona Lisa* – are strung above mantelpieces all over rural France. The original hangs in Paris' Musée d'Orsay.

In sculpture, the work of Paris-born Auguste Rodin (1840–1917), at the end of the 19th century, overcame the conflict between neoclassicism and romanticism. One of Rodin's most gifted pupils was his lover Camille Claudel (1864–1943), whose work can be seen along with that of Rodin in the Musée Rodin.

Sculpture Studios

Musée Rodin (St-Germain & Les Invalides)

Musée Atelier Zadkine (St Germain & Les Invalides)

Atelier Brancusi (Louvre & Les Halles)

Musée Bourdelle (Montparnasse & Southern Paris)

REALISM

The realists were all about social comment: Millet anticipated the realist program of Gustave Courbet (1819–77), a prominent member of the Paris Commune who was accused of, and imprisoned for, destroying the Vendôme Column. Courbet's paintings depicted the drudgery and dignity of working-class lives and were often a study on the human figure. In 1850 he broke new ground with *A Burial at Ornans* (now in the Musée d'Orsay), painted on a canvas of monumental size reserved until then exclusively for historical paintings.

Édouard Manet (1832–83) used realism to depict the life of the Parisian middle classes, yet he included in his pictures numerous references to the Old Masters. His *Déjeuner sur l'Herbe* and *Olympia* were both considered scandalous, largely because they broke with the traditional treatment of their subject matter. He was a pivotal figure in the transition from realism to impressionism.

One of the best sculptors from this period was François Rude (1784–1855), creator of the Maréchal Ney statue, *Maréchal under Napoleon,* outside La Closerie des Lilas in Montparnasse; and the relief on the Arc de Triomphe. Several of his pieces can also be seen in the Musée d'Orsay. By the mid-19th century, memorial statues in public places had replaced sculpted tombs, making such statues all the rage.

Another sculptor, Jean-Baptiste Carpeaux (1827–75), began as a romantic but his work in Paris – such as *The Dance* on the Palais Garnier and his fountain in the Jardin du Luxembourg – recalls the gaiety and flamboyance of the baroque era.

With the decentralisation of the Louvre collection and opening of a new Louvre museum in Lens (northern France) in September 2012, some 900 works from the Louvre in Paris now have a new home – including Delacroix's *Liberty Leading the People*.

IMPRESSIONISM

The Musée d'Orsay in Paris is the crown jewel of impressionism, with every worthy artistic palette represented in the Seine-side gallery on the Left Bank. Impressionism, initially a term of derision, was taken from the title of an 1874 experimental painting, *Impression: Soleil Levant* (Impression: Sunrise) by Claude Monet (1840–1926). Monet was the leading figure of the school and a visit to the Musée d'Orsay unveils a rash of other members, among them Alfred Sisley (1839–99), Camille Pissarro (1830–1903), Pierre-Auguste Renoir (1841–1919), Berthe Morisot (1841–95) and so on. The impressionists' aim was to capture the effects of fleeting light. They painted almost universally in the open air.

Edgar Degas (1834–1917) was a fellow traveller of the impressionists, but he preferred painting cafe life *(Absinthe)* and in ballet studios *(The*

Countryside Departure by Henri de Toulouse-Lautrec

Dance Class) than the great outdoors – several beautiful examples hang in the Musée d'Orsay.

Henri de Toulouse-Lautrec (1864–1901) was a great admirer of Degas, but chose subjects one or two notches below: people in the bistros, brothels and music halls of Montmartre (eg *Au Moulin Rouge*). He is best known for his posters and lithographs, in which the distortion of the figures is both satirical and decorative.

Paul Cézanne (1839–1906) celebrated for his still lifes and landscapes depicting the south of France, spent many years in Paris after breaking with the impressionists. The name of Paul Gauguin (1848–1903) immediately conjures up studies of Tahitian and Breton women. Both Cézanne and Gauguin are usually referred to as postimpressionists, something of a catch-all term for the diverse styles that flowed from impressionism.

In the late 19th century Gauguin worked for a time in Arles in Provence with the Dutch-born Vincent Van Gogh (1853–90), who spent most of his painting life in France and died in the town of Auvers-sur-Oise north of Paris. A brilliant, innovative artist, Van Gogh produced haunting self-portraits and landscapes in which bold colour assumes an expressive and emotive quality.

Trend-setting Galleries

Maison Rouge (Bastille & Eastern Paris)

Palais de Tokyo (Eiffel Tower & Western Paris)

Fondation Cartier pour l'Art Contemporain (Montparnasse & Southern Paris)

POINTILLISM & SYMBOLISM

Pointillism was a technique anticipated by Van Gogh and later developed by Georges Seurat (1859–91) who applied paint in small dots or uniform brush strokes of unmixed colour to produce fine 'mosaics' of warm and cool tones. His tableaux *Une Baignade, Asnières* (Bathers at Asnières) is a perfect example.

Henri Rousseau (1844–1910) was a contemporary of the postimpressionists but his 'naive' art was totally unaffected by them. His dreamlike pictures of the Paris suburbs and of jungle and desert scenes (eg *The*

Snake Charmer) – again in Musée d'Orsay – have influenced art right up to this century. Gustave Moreau (1826–98) was a member of the symbolist school. His eerie treatment of mythological subjects can be seen in his old studio, which is now the Musée Gustave-Moreau in the 9e.

20TH CENTURY

Twentieth-century French painting is notable for a diversity of styles, including **fauvism**, named after the slur of a critic who compared the exhibitors at the 1905 Salon d'Automne (Autumn Salon) in Paris with *fauves* (wild animals) because of their wild brushstrokes and radical colours. Among these 'beastly' painters was André Derain (1890–1954), Maurice de Vlaminck (1876–1958) and Henri Matisse (1869-1954).

Cubism was effectively launched in 1907 with *Les Demoiselles d'Avignon* by the Spanish prodigy Pablo Picasso (1881–1973). Cubism, as developed by Picasso, Georges Braque (1882–1963) and Juan Gris (1887–1927), deconstructed the subject into a system of intersecting planes and presented various aspects simultaneously. Good examples are Braque's *Houses at l'Estaque* and *Woman Playing the Mandolin* by Picasso.

In the 1920s and '30s the so-called **École de Paris** (School of Paris) was formed by a group of expressionists, mostly foreign born, including Amedeo Modigliani (1884–1920) from Italy, Foujita (1886–1968) from Japan and Marc Chagall (1887–1985) from Russia, whose works combined fantasy and folklore.

No piece of French art better captures the rebellious, iconoclastic spirit of **Dadaism** – a Swiss-born literary and artistic movement of revolt – than *Mona Lisa* by Marcel Duchamp (1887–1968) complete with moustache and goatee. In 1922 German Dadaist Max Ernst (1891–1976) moved to Paris and worked on **surrealism**, a Dada offshoot that flourished between the wars. Drawing on the theories of Sigmund Freud, it attempted to reunite the conscious and unconscious realms. Among the most important proponents of this style were Chagall, as well as René Magritte (1989–1967), André Masson (1896–1987), Max Ernst, André Breton (1896–1966) and Piet Mondrian (1872–1944). The most influential was the Spanish-born artist Salvador Dalí (1904–89), who arrived in Paris in 1929 and painted some of his most seminal works (eg *Sleep*, *Paranoia*) while residing here. To see his work, visit the Dalí Espace Montmartre.

One of the most influential sculptors to emerge in Paris before WWII was the Romanian-born Constantin Brancusi (1876–1957), whose work

EXPERIMENTAL SCULPTURE

Both Braque and Picasso experimented with sculpture, and in the spirit of Dada, Marcel Duchamp exhibited 'found objects', one of which was a urinal, which he mounted, signed and dubbed *Fountain* in 1917.

BOLD & BRAZEN: 1990S ART

Artists in the 1990s turned to the minutiae of everyday urban life to express social and political angst, using media other than paint to let rip. Conceptual artist Daniel Buren (b. 1938) reduced his painting to a signature series of vertical 8.7cm-wide stripes that he applies to every surface imaginable – white marble columns in the courtyard of Paris' Palais Royal included. The painter (who in 1967, as part of the radical *groupe BMPT*, signed a manifesto declaring he was not a painter) was the *enfant terrible* of French art in the 1980s. Partner-in-crime Michel Parmentier (1938–2000) insisted on monochrome painting – blue in 1966, grey in 1967 and red in 1968.

Paris-born conceptual artist Sophie Calle (b. 1953) brazenly exposes her private life in public with her eye-catching installations, which most recently involved 107 women (including Carla Bruni before she became First Lady) reading and commenting on an email she received from her French lover, dumping her. The resultant work of art – compelling and addictive – is published in the artist's book *Take Care of Yourself*.

can be seen in the Atelier Brancusi, part of the Centre Pompidou. After the war César Baldaccini (1921–98) used iron and scrap metal to create his imaginary insects and animals, later using pliable plastics. Among his best-known works are the *Centaur* statue in the 6e and the statuette handed out at the Césars (France's version of the Oscars). Two sculptors who each have a museum devoted to their work are Ossip Zadkine (1890–1967) and Antoine Bourdelle (1861–1929).

WWII ended Paris' role as the world's artistic capital. Many artists left during the occupation, and while some returned after the war, the city never regained its old attractiveness, with New York and then London exerting more magnetism.

A CREATIVE BILL

A bill in 1936 provided for 'the creation of monumental decorations in public buildings' by allotting 1% of building costs to art. The concept mushroomed half a century later (with Daniel Buren) and now there's artwork everywhere: in the Jardin des Tuileries, La Défense, Parc de la Villette, the metro ....

METRO ART

Almost half of the city's 300-plus metro stations were given a facelift to mark the centenary of the world-famous Métropolitain at the turn of the millennium, many being assigned themes relating to the *quartier* (neighbourhood) or name of the station. Montparnasse Bienvenüe, for example, evokes the creation of the metro – it was an engineer named Fulgence Bienvenüe (1852–1936) who oversaw the building of the first 91km from 1886; while Carrefour Pleyel, named in honour of the 18th-century composer and piano-maker Ignace Joseph Pleyel (1757–1831), focuses on classical music.

The following list is a sample of the most artistic stations.

➡ **Abbesses** (line 12 metro entrance) The noodle-like pale-green metalwork and glass canopy of the station entrance is one of the finest examples of Hector Guimard (1867–1942), the French art nouveau architect whose signature style once graced most metro stations. For a list of the stations that retain *édicules* (shrine-like entranceways) designed by Guimard, see www.parisinconnu.com.

➡ **Arts et Métiers** (line 11 platform) The copper panelling, portholes and mechanisms of this station recall Jules Verne, Captain Nemo and collections of the nearby Musée des Arts et Métiers.

➡ **Assemblée Nationale** (line 12 platform) Huge posters of silhouettes in red, white and blue by artist Jean-Charles Blais (b. 1956) represent current MPs.

➡ **Bastille** (line 5 platform) A 180-sq-m ceramic fresco features scenes taken from newspaper engravings published during the Revolution, with illustrations of the destruction of the infamous prison.

➡ **Chaussée d'Antin-Lafayette** (line 7 platform) Large allegorical painting on the vaulted ceiling recalls the Marquis de Lafayette (1757–1834) and his role as general in the American Revolution.

➡ **Cluny–La Sorbonne** (line 10 platform) A big ceramic mosaic replicates the signatures of intellectuals, artists and scientists from the Latin Quarter including Molière (1622–73), Rabelais (c 1483–1553) and Robespierre (1758–96).

➡ **Concorde** (line 12 platform) What look like kids' building blocks in white-and-blue ceramic on the station walls are 45,000 tiles spelling the text of the *Déclaration des Droits de l'Homme et du Citoyen* (Declaration of the Rights of Man and of the Citizen), the paper setting out the principles of the French Revolution.

➡ **Javel-André Citroën** (line 10 platform) Photographs and display cases examine the life and work of inventor and automobile manufacturer André Citroën (1878–1935).

➡ **Louvre Rivoli** (line 1 platform & corridor) Statues, bas-reliefs and photographs offer a small taste of what to expect at the Musée du Louvre above ground.

➡ **Palais Royal–Musée du Louvre** (line 1 metro entrance) The entrance on the place du Palais by Jean-Michel Othoniel (b. 1964) is composed of two crown-shaped cupolas (one representing day, the other night) consisting of 800 red, blue, amber and violet glass balls threaded on an aluminium structure.

Music & Cinema

From organ recitals bathed in Gothic architectural splendour to some of the world's best rap, music is embedded deep in the Parisian soul. To understand the capital's musical heritage is to enrich your experience of a city where talented musicians audition to perform in the metro and silent movies with little or no dialogue – simply an extraordinary musical soundtrack – scoop Oscars.

CLASSICAL

French baroque music influenced European musical output in the 17th and 18th centuries. Composers François Couperin (1668–1733) and Jean-Philippe Rameau (1683–1764) were two luminaries of this period.

French musical luminaries – Charles Gounod (1818–93), César Franck (1822–90) and *Carmen*-creator Georges Bizet (1838–75) among them – were a dime a dozen in the 19th century. Modern orchestration was founded by French romantic Hector Berlioz (1803–69). He demanded gargantuan forces: his ideal orchestra included 240 stringed instruments, 30 grand pianos and 30 harps.

Claude Debussy (1862–1918) revolutionised classical music with *Prélude à l'Après-Midi d'un Faune* (Prelude to the Afternoon of a Fawn), creating a light, almost Asian musical impressionism. Impressionist comrade Maurice Ravel (1875–1937) peppered his work, including *Boléro,* with sensuousness and tonal colour. For decades the chief organist at Église de la Trinité in the 9e, composer Olivier Messiaen (1908–92) combined modern almost mystical music with natural sounds, such as birdsong. Unsurprisingly, his student Pierre Boulez (b. 1925) works with computer-generated sound.

JAZZ & FRENCH CHANSONS

Jazz hit Paris in the 1920s with a bang in the banana-clad form of Josephine Baker, an African-American cabaret dancer. The years after WWII ushered in a much-appreciated bunch of musicians – Sidney Bechet, Kenny Clarke, Bud Powell and Dexter Gordon among them. In 1934 a chance meeting between Parisian jazz violinist Stéphane Grappelli (1908–97) and three-fingered Roma guitarist Django Reinhardt

FRENCH CINEMA

1895

The world's first paying public film-screening is held in Paris' Grand Café on blvd des Capucines, 9e, in December 1895 by the Lumière brothers, inventors of 'moving pictures'.

1920s

French film flourishes. Sound ushers in René Clair's (1898–1981) world of fantasy and satirical surrealism. Watch Abel Gance's antiwar blockbuster *J'Accuse!* (I Accuse!; 1919), filmed on actual WWI battlefields.

1930s

WWI inspires a new realism: portraits of ordinary lives dominate film. Watch *La Grande Illusion* (The Great Illusion; 1937), based on the trench warfare experience of director Jean Renoir.

1940s

Surrealists eschew realism. Watch Jean Cocteau's *La Belle et la Bête* (Beauty and the Beast; 1946) and *Orphée* (Orpheus; 1950). WWII saps the film industry of both talent and money.

1950s

Nouvelle Vague (New Wave): small budgets, no stars and real-life subject matter produce uniquely personal films. Watch Jean-Luc Goddard's carefree, B&W celebration of Paris *À Bout de Souffle* (Breathless; 1959).

Single record sleeve of Édith Piaf and Theo Sarapo

APIC / GETTY IMAGES ©

(1910–53; whose birth centenary was feted nationwide in 2010) in a Montparnasse nightclub led to the formation of the Hot Club of France quintet. Claude Luter and his Dixieland band were hip in the 1950s.

The *chanson française,* a tradition dating from the troubadours of the Middle Ages, was eclipsed by the music halls and burlesque of the early 20th century, but was revived in the 1930s by Édith Piaf (1915–63) and Charles Trenet (1913–2001). In the 1950s Paris' Left Bank cabarets nurtured *chansonniers* (cabaret singers) such as Léo Ferré (1916–63), Georges Brassens (1921–81), Claude Nougaro (1929–2004), Jacques Brel (1929–78) and the very charming, very sexy, very Parisian Serge Gainsbourg (1928–91) whose music remains enormously popular more than two decades after his death.

The turn of the new millennium saw a revival of this genre called *la nouvelle chanson française.* Among the most exciting performers of this old-fashioned, slightly wordy genre are Vincent Delerm (b. 1976), Bénabar (b 1969; www.benabar.com), Jeanne Cherhal (b. 1978; www.jeannecherhal.net), Camille (b. 1978), Soha and a group called Les Têtes Raides. Another hip crooner on the scene is Arnaud Fleurent-Didier (b. 1974; www.arnaudfleurentdidier.com).

Top Five Albums

- *Histoire de Melody Nelson, Serge Gainsbourg*
- *Moon Safari, AIR*
- *Made in Medina, Rachid Taha*
- *L'Absente, Yann Tiersen*
- *Dante, Abd al Malik*

ROCK & POP

One could be forgiven for thinking that French pop is becoming dynastic. The very distinctive M (for Mathieu) is the son of singer Louis Chédid; Arthur H (b. 1966) is the progeny of pop-rock musician Jacques Higelin; and Thomas Dutronc (b. 1973; www.thomasdutronc.fr) is the offspring of 1960s idols *père* Jacques Dutronc and Françoise Hardy. And the Gainsbourg dynasty doesn't look like ending any time soon. Serge's daughter with Jane Birkin, songwriter/singer and actress Charlotte (b. 1971, www.charlotte-gainsbourg.blogspot.com)

and released her fourth album, *Stage Whisper,* with great success at the end of 2011.

Noir Désir was *the* sound of French rock until its lead singer, Bertrand Cantat (b. 1964), was imprisoned in 2003 for the murder of his girlfriend and it disbanded. Worth noting are Louise Attaque (http://louiseattaque.com) and the very funky Nosfell (www.nosfell.com) who sings in his very own invented language. The hottest group to emerge in recent years, electro-dance rock-pop Pony Pony Run Run (www.ponyponyrunrun.net), sing in English – a long way from the *yéyé* (imitative rock) of the 1960s as sung by Johnny Hallyday, otherwise known as 'Johnny National'. Pony Pony Run Run released a much-awaited second album, simply titled *Pony Pony Run Run,* in early 2012.

In recent years a distinctly urban and highly exportable Parisian sound has developed, often mixing computer-enhanced Chicago blues and Detroit techno with 1960s lounge music and vintage tracks from the likes of Serge Gainsbourg and Brassens. Among those playing now are Parisian electro-dance duo and hip-hop duo Daft Punk (www.daftalive.com), a band originally from Versailles that adapts first-wave acid house and techno to their younger roots in pop, indie rock. Daft Punk's debut album *Homework* (1997) fused disco, house, funk and techno, and at the start of 2012 the internet was abuzz with excitement over rumours that Daft Punk would soon release their next album, *Sky Dive.*

1960s

France – land of romance: Watch Claude Lelouch's *Un Homme et une Femme* (A Man and a Woman; 1966) and Jacques Demy's *Les Parapluies de Cherbourg* (The Umbrellas of Cherbourg; 1964).

1980s

Big-name stars, slick production values and nostalgia: generous state subsidies see filmmakers switch to costume dramas and comedies in the face of growing competition from the USA.

1990s

Box-office hits starring France's best-known actor, Gérard Depardieu, win over huge audiences in France and abroad. Watch *Cyrano de Bergerac* (1990) & *Astérix et Obélix: Mission Cléopâtre* (2002).

WORLD

From Algerian raï to other North African music (artists include Cheb Khaled, Natacha Atlas, Jamel and Cheb Mami) and Senegalese *mbalax* (Youssou N'Dour), West Indian zouk (Kassav', Zouk Machine) and Cuban salsa, the world beat in Paris is strong. One musician who uses world elements to stunning effect is Manu Chao (b. 1961; formerly frontman for Mano Negra; www.manuchao.net), the Paris-born son of Spanish parents, whose albums are international best sellers.

In the late 1980s, bands Mano Negra and Les Négresses Vertes combined many of these elements with brilliant results. Magic System from Côte d'Ivoire popularised *zouglou* (a kind of West African rap and dance music) with its album *Premier Gaou,* and Congolese Koffi Olomide (b. 1956) still packs the halls. Also try to catch the blind singing couple, Amadou and Mariam, and Rokia Traoré (www.rokiatraore.net) from Mali.

Also from Versailles, electronica duo Air (an acronym for *'Amour, Imagination, Rêve'* meaning 'Love, Imagination, Dream') bagged a massive loyal following with their sensational album *Moon Safari* (1998) and didn't disappoint with their seventh, *Le Voyage dans la Lune* (2012). Then there is Rachid Taha (www.rachidtaha.fr), a Franco-Algerian DJ-turned-singer whose music mixes Arab and Western musical styles to create an extraordinarily rich fusion of rock, punk, afro-pop, Algerian raï, salsa and pretty much you-name-it-it's-there. To add extra appeal there are song lyrics in English and Berber as well as French.

Musical Pilgrimages

Serge Gainsbourg's grave (Montparnasse & Southern Paris)

Jim Morrison's grave (Le Marais & Ménilmontant)

La Cigale (Montmartre & Northern Paris)

CINEMA

Never have the French been so euphoric about film. At the 2012 Oscars, French film *The Artist* (2011), a silent B&W romantic comedy set in 1920s Hollywood, scooped five awards, including 'Best Picture', 'Best Director' for Parisian director Michel Hazanavicius (b. 1967), and 'Best Original Score' for French composer and pianist Ludovic Bource (b. 1970) who wrote the film's extraordinary soundtrack. 'Best Actor' went to charismatic Jean Dujardin (b. 1972), a born-and-bred Parisian suburbs lad who started with one-man shows in city bars and cabarets, and made his name with roles as varied as surfer Brice waiting for his wave in *Brice de Nice* (2005), James Bond in *OSS 117: Le Caire, Nid d'Espions* (OSS 117: Cairo, Nest of Spies; 2006) and the sexiest cowboy around in *Lucky Luke* (2009). Watch out for Dujardin in Michel Hazanavicius' latest cinematic creation, *Les Infidèles* (The Players; 2012), a series of comic sketches on marriage, infidelity and adultery.

The Artist is the most awarded film in French history, but it is not the only contemporary French film to excite: accolades have been showered on Olivier Nakache and Éric Toledano's *Intouchables* (Untouchables; 2011), a comic drama set in Paris about a rich quadriplegic in Paris and his live-in Senegalese carer. France's leading lady, the sexy, dark-haired Marion Cotillard (b. 1975), was the first French woman since 1959 to win an Oscar for her role as Édith Piaf in Olivier Dahan's *La Môme* (La Vie en Rose; 2007); while waifish French actress Audrey Tautou (b. 1976) conquered stardom with her role as Parisian do-gooder Amélie in Jean-Pierre Jeunet's *Le Fabuleux Destin d'Amélie Poulain* (2001). Celebrated French composer Yann Tiersen (b. 1970; www.yanntiersen.com) wrote the compelling soundtrack.

Then there was Dany Boon's (b. 1966; www.bienvenuechezdanyboon.com) French comedy *Bienvenue Chez Les Ch'tis* (Welcome to the Sticks; 2008), watched in France by 17 million cinema spectators. For decades 'Most Watched French Film' kudos went to *La Grand Vadrouille* (The Great Ramble; 1966), a French comedy in which five British airmen are shot down over German-occupied France in 1942. One is catapulted into Paris' Bois de Vincennes zoo, another into the orchestra pit of its opera house and so the comic tale unfurls.

RAP

France is known for its rap, an original 1990s sound spearheaded by Senegal-born, Paris-reared rapper MC Solaar and Suprême NTM (NTM being an acronym for a French expression far too offensive to print). Most big-name rappers are French twenty-somethings of Arabic or African origin whose prime preoccupation is the frustrations and fury of fed-up immigrants in the French *banlieues* (suburbs). Take hot-shot rapper Disiz La Peste (b. 1978), born in Amiens to a Senegalese father and Belgian mother: his third album *Histoires Extra-Ordinaires d'un Jeune de Banlieue* (The Extraordinary Stories of a Youth in the Suburbs; 2005) portrayed just what its title suggested, as did his 'last' album *Disiz The End* (2009) following which he morphed into Peter Punk and created a very different rock-punk-electro sound with *Dans La Ventre du Crocodile* (In the Crocodile's Stomach; 2010). In December 2011 the artist announced on Twitter his 2012 return to rap as Disiz La Peste, with the release of the much-vaunted album *Lucide*.

Honoured with the Palme d'Or at Cannes, Laurent Cantet's *Entre Les Murs* (The Class; 2008) is based on the autobiographical novel of teacher François Begaudeau. The documentary-drama is a brilliant reflection of contemporary multi-ethnic society.

One of France's few female rappers, Cyprus-born Diam's (short for *'diamant'* meaning 'diamond'; www.diams-lesite.com), arrived in Paris aged seven and was MTV's French Artist of the Year in 2007.

No artist has cemented France's reputation in world music more than Paris-born, Franco-Congolese rapper, slam poet and three-time Victoire de la Musique–award winner, Abd al Malik (www.abdalmalik.fr). His albums *Gibraltar* (2006), *Dante* (2008) and *Château Rouge* (2010) are classics.

Survival Guide

Transport

GETTING TO PARIS

Few roads *don't* lead to Paris, one of the most visited destinations on earth. Practically every major airline flies though one of its three airports, and most European train and bus routes cross it.

Paris is the central point in the French rail network, Société Nationale des Chemins de Fer Français (SNCF), which has six train stations that handle passenger traffic to different parts of France and Europe. Each is well connected to the Paris public transportation system, the Régie Autonome des Transports Parisiens (RATP). To buy onward tickets from Paris, visit a station or go to **Voyages SNCF** (www.voyages-sncf.com). Most trains – and certainly all Trains à Grande Vitesse (TGV) – require advance reservations. As with most tickets, the earlier you book, the better your chances of securing a discounted fare. Mainline stations in Paris have left-luggage offices and/or *consignes* (lockers).

On public transport, children under four travel free and those aged between four and nine (inclusive) pay half-price; exceptions are noted.

Flights, tours and rail tickets can be booked online at www.lonelyplanet.com/bookings.

Charles de Gaulle Airport

Most international airlines fly to **Charles de Gaulle** (CDG; www.aeroportsdeparis.fr), located 28km northeast of central Paris; in French the airport is commonly referred to as 'Roissy', after the suburb in which it is located.

Metro & RER Networks

CDG is served by the RER B line (€9.10, approx 35 minutes, every 10 to 15 minutes), which serves the Gare du Nord, Châtelet–Les Halles and St-Michel–Notre Dame stations in the city centre. Trains run from 5am to 11pm; there are fewer trains on weekends.

Taxi

A taxi to the city centre takes approximately 40 minutes, assuming no traffic jams. During the day, expect to pay around €50; the fare increases 15% between 5pm and 10am and on Sundays. Only take taxis at a clearly marked rank. Never follow anyone who approaches you at the airport and claims to be a driver.

Bus

There are six main bus lines.

➡ **Air France bus 2** (€15, 45 minutes, every 20 minutes, 6am to 11pm) Links the airport with the Arc de Triomphe. Children aged two to 11 pay half price.

➡ **Air France bus 4** (€16.50, every 30 minutes, 6am-10pm from CDG, 6am-9.30pm from Paris) Links the airport with Gare de Lyon (50 minutes) in eastern Paris and Gare Montparnasse (55 minutes) in southern Paris. Children aged two to 11 pay half price.

➡ **Roissybus** (€10, 45 to 60 minutes, every 15 minutes, 5.30am-11pm) Links the airport with the Opéra.

➡ **RATP bus 350** (€5.10 or 3 metro tickets, one hour, every 30 minutes, 5.30am-11pm) Links the airport with Gare de l'Est in northern Paris.

➡ **RATP bus 351** (€5.10 or 3 metro tickets, 50 minutes, every 30 minutes, 5.30am-11pm) Links the airport with place de la Nation in eastern Paris.

➡ **Noctilien bus 140 & 143** (€7.60, hourly, 12.30am-5.30pm) Part of the RATP night service, Noctilien has two buses that go to CDG: bus 140 from Gare de l'Est, and 143 from Gare de l'Est and Gare du Nord.

Gare du Nord

Eurostar (www.eurostar.com) The London–Paris line runs from St-Pancras International to Gare du Nord. Voyages take 2¼ hours.

Thalys (www.thalys.com) Thalys trains pull into Paris' Gare du Nord from Brussels, Amsterdam and Cologne.

CLIMATE CHANGE & TRAVEL

Every form of transport that relies on carbon-based fuel generates CO_2, the main cause of human-induced climate change. Modern travel is dependent on aeroplanes, which might use less fuel per kilometre per person than most cars but travel much greater distances. The altitude at which aircraft emit gases (including CO_2) and particles also contributes to their climate change impact. Many websites offer 'carbon calculators' that allow people to estimate the carbon emissions generated by their journey and, for those who wish to do so, to offset the impact of the greenhouse gases emitted with contributions to portfolios of climate-friendly initiatives throughout the world. Lonely Planet offsets the carbon footprint of all staff and author travel.

Orly Airport

Orly (ORY; ☎01 70 36 39 50; www.aeroportsdeparis.fr) is located 19km south of central Paris but, despite being closer than CDG, it is not as frequently used by international airlines and public transportation options aren't quite as straightforward. If you have heavy luggage or young kids in tow, consider a taxi.

Taxi

A taxi to the city centre takes roughly 30 minutes, assuming no traffic jams. During the day, expect to pay around €45; the fare increases 15% between 5pm and 10am and on Sundays. Only take taxis at a clearly marked rank. Never follow anyone who approaches you at the airport and claims to be a driver.

Metro & RER Networks

There is no direct train to/from Orly; you'll need to change transport halfway. Note that while it is possible to take a shuttle to the RER C line, this service is quite slow and not recommended.

➡ **RER B** (€10.75, 35 minutes, every four to 12 minutes) This line connects Orly with the St-Michel–Notre Dame, Châtelet–Les Halles and Gare du Nord stations in the city centre. In order to get from Orly to the RER station (Antony), you must first take the Orlyval automatic train. The service runs from 6am to 11pm; there are fewer trains on weekends. You only need one ticket to take the two trains.

Bus

There are several bus lines that serve Orly; only the most practical are listed here.

➡ **Air France bus 1** (€11.50, every 20 minutes, 5am-10.20pm from Orly, 6am-11.20pm from Invalides) This bus runs to/from the Gare Montparnasse (35 minutes) in southern Paris, Invalides in the 7e, and the Arc de Triomphe. Children aged two to 11 pay half price.

➡ **Orlybus** (€6.90, 30 minutes, every 15 minutes, 6am-11.20pm from Orly, 5.35am-11.05pm from Paris) This bus runs to/from the metro station Denfert Rochereau in southern Paris, making several stops en route.

Beauvais Airport

Beauvais (BVA; ☎08 92 68 20 66; www.aeroportbeauvais.com) is located 75km north of Paris and a few low-cost flights go through here – but before you snap up what may appear to be a bargain, consider if the time and expense of the post-arrival journey to the city is worth it.

Bus

Beauvais Shuttle (€15, 1¼ hours) links the airport with the metro station Porte de Maillot in western Paris. See the airport website for exact details.

Gare d'Austerlitz

Gare d'Austerlitz is the terminus for a handful of trains from the south, including services from Orléans and Limoges. There are currently no TGV services, although renovations are underway so it's an option for the future. Gare d'Austerlitz is located on the Left Bank.

Gare de l'Est

Gare de l'Est is the terminus for trains from Strasbourg, Berlin and Vienna. It's located in northern Paris.

Gare de Lyon

Gare de Lyon is the terminus for trains from Provence, the Alps, the Riviera and Italy. Also serves Geneva. It's located in eastern Paris.

Gare Montparnasse

Gare Montparnasse is the terminus for trains from the southwest and west, including services from Bretagne, the Loire, Bordeaux, Toulouse and Spain and Portugal. It's located in southern Paris.

Gare St-Lazare

Gare St-Lazare is the terminus for trains from Normandy. Located in Clichy (western Paris).

Gare Routière Internationale de Paris-Galliéni

Eurolines (www.eurolines.fr) connects all major European capitals to Paris' international bus terminal, **Gare Routière Internationale de Paris-Galliéni** (☎08 92 89 90 91; 28 av du Général de Gaulle; Ⓜ Galliéni). The terminal is in the eastern suburb of Bagnolet; it's about a 15-minute metro ride to the more central République station.

GETTING AROUND

Getting around Paris is comparatively easy a big city. Most visitors combine the vast and efficient metro with walking – few cities can match Paris for scenic strolls. Buses offer a good view of the city, but can be hard to figure out and slowed by traffic. More tempting is the city's communal bike-share scheme, Vélib'.

Underground Rail

Paris' underground network is run by RATP and consists of two separate but linked systems: the metro and the RER suburban train line. The metro has 14 numbered lines; the Réseau Express Régional (RER) has five main lines (but you'll probably only need to use A, B and C). When giving the names of stations in this book, the term 'metro' is used to cover both the metro and the RER within Paris proper. At the time of writing, there were five concentric transportation zones rippling out from Paris (five being the furthest); if you travel from Charles de Gaulle airport to Paris, for instance, you will have to buy a zone 1–5 ticket. But a 2012 initiative proposed eliminating the zones altogether. If this happens, expect regular ticket and pass prices to increase significantly.

For information on the metro, RER and bus systems, visit www.ratp.fr. Metro maps of various sizes and degrees of detail are available for free at metro ticket windows; several can also be downloaded for free from the RATP website.

Metro

➡ Metro lines are identified by both their number (eg ligne 1; line 1) and their colour, listed on official metro signs and maps.

➡ Signs in metro and RER stations indicate the way to the correct platform for your line. The *direction* signs on each platform indicate the terminus. On lines that split into several branches (such as lines 7 and 13), the terminus of each train is indicated on the cars and on signs on each platform giving the number of minutes until the next and subsequent train.

➡ Signs marked *correspondance* (transfer) show how to reach connecting trains. At stations with many intersecting lines, like Châtelet and Montparnasse Bienvenüe, walking from one platform to the next can take a very long time.

➡ Different station exits are indicated by white-on-blue *sortie* (exit) signs. You can get your bearings by checking the *plan du quartier* (neighbourhood maps) posted at exits.

➡ Each line has its own schedule, but trains usually start at around 5.30am, with the last train beginning its run between 12.35am and 1.15am (2.15am on Friday and Saturday).

RER

➡ The RER is faster than the metro but the stops are much farther apart. Some attractions, particularly those on the Left Bank (eg the Musée d'Orsay, Eiffel Tower and Panthéon), can be reached far more conveniently by the RER than by the metro.

➡ If you're making a trip out to the suburbs (eg Versailles, Disneyland), ask for help on the platform – finding the right train can be confusing. Also ensure your ticket is for the correct zone.

Tickets & Fares

➡ The same RATP tickets are valid on the metro, the RER (for travel within the city limits), buses, trams and the Montmartre funicular.

➡ A ticket – white in colour and called *Le Ticket t+* – costs €1.70 (half price for children aged four to nine years) if bought individually and €12.70 for adults for a *carnet* (book) of 10.

➡ Tickets are sold at all metro stations: ticket windows accept most credit cards; however, automated machines *do not* accept North American credit cards.

➡ One ticket lets you travel between any two metro stations (no return journeys) for a period of 1½ hours, no matter how many transfers are required. You can also use it on the RER for travel within zone 1, which encompasses all of central Paris.

➡ A single ticket can be used to transfer between buses, but not to transfer from the metro to bus or vice-versa. Transfers are not allowed on Noctilien buses.

➡ Always keep your ticket until you exit from your station; if you are stopped by a ticket inspector, you will have to pay a fine if you don't have a valid ticket.

Tourist Passes

The Mobilis and Paris Visite passes are valid on the metro, RER, SNCF's suburban lines, buses, night buses, trams and Montmartre funicular railway. No photo is needed, but write your card number on the ticket. Passes are sold at larger metro and RER stations, SNCF offices in Paris, and the airports.

The **Mobilis card** allows unlimited travel for one day and costs €6.40 (two zones) to €14.20 (five zones). Buy it at any metro, RER or SNCF station in the Paris region. Depending on how many times you plan to hop on/off the metro in a day, a *carnet* might work out cheaper.

Paris Visite allows unlimited travel (including to/from airports) as well as discounted entry to certain museums and other discounts and bonuses. Passes are valid for either three or five zones. The zone 1 to 3 pass costs €9.75/15.85/21.60/31.15 for one/two/three/five days. Children aged four to 11 years pay half price.

NAVIGO PASS

If you're staying in Paris longer than a few days, the cheapest and easiest way to use public transport in Paris is to get a combined travel pass that allows unlimited travel on the metro, RER and buses for a week, a month or even a year. You can get passes for travel in two to five zones but, unless you'll be using the suburban commuter lines extensively, the basic ticket valid for zones 1 and 2 should be sufficient.

Navigo (www.navigo.fr), like London's Oyster or Hong Kong's Octopus cards, is a system that provides you with a refillable weekly, monthly or yearly unlimited pass that you can recharge at machines in most metro stations; to pass through the station barrier swipe the card across the electronic panel as you go through the turnstiles. Standard Navigo passes, available to anyone with an address in Île de France, are free but take up to three weeks to be issued; ask at the ticket counter for a form or visit the Navigo website. Otherwise pay €5 for a Navigo Découverte (Navigo Discovery) card, which is issued on the spot but (unlike the standard Navigo pass) not replaceable if lost or stolen. Both passes require a passport photo and can be recharged for periods of one week or more.

A weekly pass costs €19.15 for zones 1 and 2 and is valid from Monday to Sunday. It can be purchased from the previous Friday until Thursday; from the next day weekly tickets are available for the following week only. Even if you're in Paris for three or four days, it may work out cheaper than buying *carnets* and will certainly cost less than buying a daily Mobilis or Paris Visite pass. The monthly pass (€62.90 for zones 1 and 2) begins on the first day of each calendar month; you can buy one from the 20th of the preceding month. Both are sold in metro and RER stations from 6.30am to 10pm and at some bus terminals.

Bicycle

Vélib'

The **Vélib' bike share** (http://en.velib.paris.fr) scheme has revolutionised how Parisians get around. There are some 1800 stations throughout the city, each with anywhere from 20 to 70 bike stands. The bikes are accessible around the clock.

➡ To get a bike, you first need to purchase a one-/seven-day subscription (€1.70/8). There are two ways to do this: either at the terminals found at docking stations or online.

➡ The terminals require a credit card with an embedded smartchip – this means the majority of North Americans cannot subscribe here. But, fret not, because you can purchase a subscription online. Just be sure to do this before you leave your hotel.

➡ After you authorise a deposit (€150) to pay for the bike should it go missing, you'll receive an ID number and PIN and you're ready to go.

➡ Bikes are rented in 30-minute intervals: the 1st half-hour is free, the 2nd is €2, the 3rd and each additional half-hour are €4. If you return a bike before a half-hour is up and then take a new one, you will not be charged.

➡ If the station you want to return your bike to is full, log in to the terminal to get 15 minutes for free to find another station.

➡ Bikes are geared to cyclists aged 14 and over, and are fitted with gears, an antitheft lock with key, reflective strips and front/rear lights. Bring your own helmet, though!

Rentals

Most rental places will require a deposit. Take ID and bank card/credit card.

Au Point Vélo Hollandais (☎01 43 45 85 36; www.pointvelo.com; 83 bd St-Michel, 5e; per day €15; ⏰10am-7.30pm Mon-Sat; Ⓜ Cluny–La Sorbonne or RER Luxembourg)

Bike About Tours (☎06 18 80 84 92; www.bikeabouttours.com; inside the Vinci Car Parking, rue de Lobau, 4e; per day €15; ⏰9am-6.30pm Mon-Sat, to 4pm Sun; Ⓜ Hôtel de Ville)

Freescoot (☎01 44 07 06 72; www.freescoot.com; 63 quai de la Tournelle, 5e; bike/tandem per day €20/45; ⏰9am-1pm & 2-7pm Mon-Sat, Sun mid-Apr–mid-Sep; Ⓜ Maubert-Mutualité)

Gepetto et Vélos (☎01 43 54 19 95; www.gepetto-et-velos.com; 59 rue du Cardinal Lemoine, 5e; per day €15; ⏰9am-1pm & 2-7.30pm Tue-Sat; Ⓜ Cardinal Lemoine)

Paris à Vélo, C'est Sympa (☎01 48 87 60 01; www.parisvelosympa.com; 22 rue Alphonse Baudin, 11e; per day €20; ⏰9.30am-1pm & 2-6pm Mon-Fri, 9am-1pm & 2-7pm Sat & Sun Apr-Oct, shorter hr winter; Ⓜ St-Sébastien Froissart)

Bus

Buses can be a fun way to get around – and there are no stairs to climb – but they're slower and less intuitive to figure out than the metro.

Local Buses

Paris' bus system, operated by RATP, runs from 5.30am to 8.30pm Monday to Saturday; after that, certain evening-service lines continue until between midnight and 12.30am. Services are drastically reduced on Sunday and public holidays, when buses run from 7am to 8.30pm.

Night Buses

The RATP runs 47 night bus lines known as **Noctilien** (www.noctilien.fr), which depart hourly from 12.30am to 5.30am. The services pass through the main *gares* (train stations) and cross the major axes of the city before heading out to the suburbs. Look for navy-blue N or Noctilien signs at bus stops. There are two circular lines within Paris (the N01 and N02) that link four main train stations – St-Lazare, Gare de l'Est, Gare de Lyon and Gare Montparnasse – as well as popular nightlife areas (Bastille, Champs-Elysées, Pigalle, St-Germain).

Noctilien services are included on your Mobilis or Paris Visite pass for the zones in which you are travelling. Otherwise you pay a certain number of standard €1.70 metro/bus tickets, depending on the length of your journey.

Tickets & Fares

Normal bus rides embracing one or two bus zones cost one metro ticket; longer rides require two or even three tickets. Transfers to other buses – but not the metro – are allowed on the same ticket as long as the change takes place 1½ hours between the first and last validation. This does not apply to Noctilien services.

Whatever kind of single-journey ticket you have, you must validate it in the ticket machine near the driver. If you don't have a ticket, the driver can sell you one for €1.90. If you have a Mobilis or Paris Visite pass, flash it at the driver when you board.

Boat

Batobus (www.batobus.com; adult 1-/2-/5-day pass €15/18/21; ⏰10am-9.30pm Apr-Aug, to 7pm rest of year) runs a ferry down the Seine, docking at eight stops: Eiffel Tower, Champs-Élysées, Musée d'Orsay, Musée du Louvre, St-Germain des Prés, Hôtel de Ville, Notre Dame and Jardin des Plantes.

Buy tickets online, at ferry stops or at tourist offices. You can also buy a 2-/3-day ticket in conjunction with the L'Open Tour buses for €43/46.

Taxi

- ➡ The *prise en charge* (flagfall) is €2.40. Within the city limits, it costs €0.96 per kilometre for travel between 10am and 5pm Monday to Saturday (*Tarif A;* white light on taxi roof and meter).
- ➡ At night (5pm to 10am), on Sunday from 7am to midnight, and in the inner suburbs the rate is €1.21 per km (*Tarif B;* orange light).
- ➡ Travel in the outer suburbs is at *Tarif C*, €1.47 per kilometre (blue light).
- ➡ There's a €2.95 surcharge for taking a fourth passenger, but drivers sometimes refuse for insurance reasons. The first piece of baggage is free; additional pieces over 5kg cost €1 extra. When tipping, round up to the nearest €1 or so.
- ➡ Flagging down a taxi in Paris can be difficult; it's best to find an official taxi stand.
- ➡ To order a taxi, call or reserve online with **Taxis G7** (☎01 41 27 66 99; www.taxisg7.fr), **Taxis Bleus** (☎01 49 36 10 10; www.taxis-bleus.com) or **Alpha Taxis** (☎01 45 85 85 85; www.alphataxis.com).

Car & Motorcycle

Driving in Paris is defined by the triple hassle of navigation, heavy traffic and parking. It doesn't make sense to use a car to get around, but if you're heading out of the city on an excursion, then your own set of wheels can certainly be useful. If you plan on hiring a car, it's best to do it online and in advance.

Autolib'

In December 2011 Paris launched the world's first electric-car-share program,

Autolib' (www.autolib.eu). The premise is quite similar to Vélib' (the bike-share scheme): you pay a subscription (day/week €10/15) and then rent a GPS-equipped car in 30-minute intervals and drop it off at one of the 1000 available stations when you're done. Unfortunately, it's really only good for short hops, because renting a car overnight would be exorbitant – the rates are €7 for the 1st half hour, €6 for the 2nd half-hour and €8 for subsequent intervals. The car battery is good for 250km, which means you can take it into the surrounding countryside (eg Fontainebleau), but no further. You'll need a driver's license and photo ID.

Scooters

Freescoot (☎01 44 07 06 72; www.freescoot.com) Rents 50/125cc scooters in various intervals (per 24hr €40/55). Prices include third-party insurance as well as helmets, locks, rain gear and gloves. To rent a 50/125cc scooter you must be at least 21/23 and leave a credit card deposit of €1300/1600. No license required for smaller scooters.

Left Bank Scooters (☎06 82 70 13 82; www.leftbankscooters.com) Run by a young Australian-British couple, this outfit rents pastel-coloured Vespa XLV 50/125cc scooters for 24 hours at €70/80, including insurance, helmet and wet-weather gear. To rent a 50/125cc scooter, you must be at least 18/20 years old and have a car/motorcycle licence. Credit-card deposit is €1000.

Parking

Parking meters in Paris do not accept coins but require either a chip-enabled credit card or a Paris Carte, available at any *tabac* (tobacconist) for €10 to €30. The machine will issue you a ticket for the allotted time. You should place it on the dashboard behind the windscreen. Municipal public car parks, of which there are more than 200 in Paris, charge between €2 and €3.50 an hour or €20 to €25 per 24 hours. Most open 24 hours.

TOURS

Bicycle & Scooter

Fat Tire Bike Tours (Map p382; ☎01 56 58 10 54; www.fattirebiketours.com) Daytime bike tours of the city (€28; four hours) start at 11am daily from mid-February to early January, with an additional departure at 3pm from April to October. Night bicycle tours depart at 7pm from April to October and 6pm (not always daily) in low season. Other tours go to Versailles, Monet's garden in Giverny and the Normandy beaches. Participants generally meet opposite the Eiffel Tower's South Pillar at the start of the Champ de Mars; look for the yellow signs. Reserve in advance.

Bike About Tours (Map p404; ☎06 18 80 84 92; www.bikeabouttours.com; 4 rue de Lobau, 4e; ⌚office 10am-7pm; Ⓜ Hôtel de Ville) This expat-run tour group offers daytime tours (€30; 3.5 hours). They begin at 10am and run from mid-February to November, with an extra tour at 3pm also scheduled from May through September. They leave from in front of Notre Dame; reservations are recommended. Another tour to Versailles (€75) leaves at 9am. Private family and group tours are also available.

Paris à Vélo, C'est Sympa! (☎01 48 87 60 01; www.parisvelosympa.com; ⌚Apr-Oct) Four guided bike tours (€34; three hours), including an evening cycle and a sunrise tour. Reserve ahead.

Left Bank Scooters (☎06 82 70 13 82; www.leftbankscooters.com) If you'd rather not pedal, sign up for a scooter tour around Paris or Versailles (€150/250).

Yellow Pedicab This new pedicab company runs tours from most of Paris' major tourist sights.

Boat

A boat cruise down the Seine is the most relaxing way to watch the city glide by. If it's your first time in Paris, it's also a good way to get a quick introduction to the city's main monuments.

Bateaux-Mouches (Map p384; ☎01 42 25 96 10; www.bateauxmouches.com; Port de la Conférence, 8e; adult/4-12yr €11/5.50; ⌚Apr-Dec; Ⓜ Alma Marceau) The largest river cruise company in Paris and a favourite with tour groups. Cruises (70 minutes) run regularly from 10.15am to 11pm April to September and 13 times a day between 11am and 9pm the rest of the year. Commentary is in French and English. It's located on the Right Bank, just east of the Pont de l'Alma.

Bateaux Parisiens (Map p382; www.bateauxparisiens.com; Port de la Bourdonnais, 7e; adult/3-11yr €12/6; ⌚every 30min 10am-10.30pm Apr-Sep, hourly 10am-10pm Oct-Mar; Ⓜ Pont de l'Alma) Runs smaller boats that do one-hour river circuits with recorded commentary in 13 different languages. There are two locations: one northwest of the Eiffel Tower, the other south of Notre Dame.

Vedettes du Pont Neuf (Map p412; ☎01 46 33 98 38; www.vedettesdupontneuf.fr;

Pont Neuf, 1er; adult/4-12yr €13/7; Ⓜ Pont Neuf) This company has a centrally located dock at the western tip of Île de la Cité and offers 1hr cruises year-round. Tours run (almost) half-hourly from 10.30am to 10.30pm from mid-March to November, and less regularly the rest of the year.

Bus

L'Open Tour (Map p386; www.pariscityrama.com; 2-day pass adult/child €32/15) This hop-on, hop-off bus tour runs open-deck buses along four circuits (central Paris; Montmartre–Grands Boulevards; Bastille–Bercy; and Montparnasse–St-Germain) daily year-round. You can jump on and off at main sites, making them very convenient for whirlwind tours of the city. Cityrama, which owns the buses, has a host of other packages as well.

Les Cars Rouges (www.carsrouges.fr; 2 days adult/4-12yr €26/13) These red double-decker buses run to nine major sites around Paris, from roughly 10am to 6pm. In total, the tours last two hours and 15 minutes, and various audio-guides can be downloaded as MP3s from its website.

Walking

Ça Se Visite (www.ca-se-visite.fr; €12) Meet local artists and craftspeople on resident-led 'urban discovery tours' of the northeast.

Context Paris (www.contexttravel.com; €55-75) Small group walks led by specialists; interesting range of topics, from the popular foodie walks to art history.

Eye Prefer Paris (www.eyepreferparistours.com; €195 for 3 people) New Yorker turned Parisian leads offbeat tours of the city.

Free Tour (neweuropetours.eu; donation) A group tour of the city's main highlights, it takes 3½ hours with two departures a day. It also runs daily two-hour tours of Montmartre for €12.

Paris Greeter (www.parisiendunjour.fr; donation) See Paris through local eyes with these two- to three-hour city tours. Volunteers lead groups (max six people) to their favourite spots in the city. Minimum two weeks' advance notice needed.

Paris Walks (www.paris-walks.com; adult/child €12/8) Long established and highly rated by our readers, Paris Walks offers thematic tours (fashion, chocolate, the French Revolution).

Sightseeker's Delight (www.sightseekersdelight.com; €30) Four popular walks from expat guides with a background in theatre.

Directory A–Z

Business Hours

The following list shows *approximate* standard opening hours for businesses. Reviews throughout this book show specific hours only if they vary from these standards. Note, too, that hours can vary significantly by season. Our listings only depict peak-season operating hours. It's worth remembering that many businesses close for the entire month of August for summer holidays.

Banks 9am–1pm and 2–5pm Monday to Friday, some Saturday morning

Bars & cafes 7am–2am

Museums 10am–6pm, closed Monday or Tuesday

Post offices 8am–7pm Monday–Friday and Saturday till noon

Restaurants Lunch noon–2pm, dinner 7.30–10.30pm

Shops (clothing) 10am–7pm Monday to Saturday. Occasionally close in the early afternoon for lunch.

Shops (food) 8am–1pm and 4–7.30pm, closed Sunday afternoon & sometimes Monday.

Customs Regulations

For visitors from EU countries, limits only apply for excessive amounts. Log onto www.douane.gouv.fr for details.

Residents of non-EU countries are limited to the following:

- **Alcohol** 4L of wine and 1L of spirits
- **Perfume** 50g of perfume and 250cc of eau de toilette
- **Tobacco** 200 cigarettes, 50 cigars or 250g of loose tobacco

Discount Cards

Almost all museums and monuments in Paris have discounted tickets *(tarif réduit)* for students and seniors (generally those aged over 60 years), provided you have a valid ID. Children often get in for free, though the cut-off age for 'child' can be anywhere between six and 18 years.

EU citizens under 26 years get free admission at national monuments and museums; see p36 for exact details.

Paris Museum Pass (www.parismuseumpass.fr; 2/4/6 days €39/54/69) Gets you into some 38 venues in the city and 22 more outside the city; also allows you to bypass long ticket queues. See p38 for more.

La Colline des Musées Pass (www.lacollinedesmusees.com; free) Reduced rates for four major museums near the Eiffel Tower during a five-day stretch. See p82 for more.

Electricity

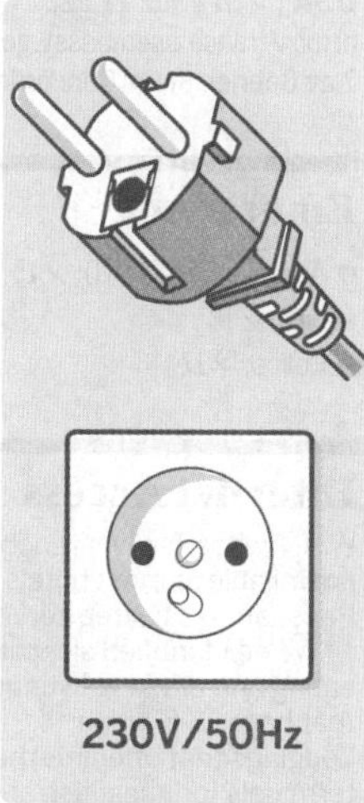

Embassies

The following is a list of selected embassies in Paris.

Australia (☎01 40 59 33 00; www.france.embassy.gov.au; 4 rue Jean Rey, 15e; Ⓜ Bir Hakeim)

Canada (☎01 44 43 29 00; www.amb-canada.fr; 35 av Montaigne, 8e; Ⓜ Franklin D Roosevelt)

Germany (☎01 53 83 45 00; www.paris.diplo.de; 13 av Franklin D Roosevelt, 8e; Ⓜ Franklin D Roosevelt)

Ireland (☎01 44 17 67 00; www.embassyofireland.fr; 4 rue Rude, 16e; Ⓜ Argentine)

Netherlands (☎01 40 62 33 00; www.amb-pays-bas.fr; 7 rue Eblé, 7e; Ⓜ St-François Xavier)

New Zealand (☎01 45 01 43 43; www.nzembassy.com/france; 7ter rue Léonard de Vinci, 16e; Ⓜ Victor Hugo)

South Africa (☎01 53 59 23 23; www.afriquesud.net; 59 quai d'Orsay, 7e; Ⓜ Invalides)

UK (☎01 44 51 31 00; http://ukinfrance.fco.gov.uk; 35 rue du Faubourg St Honoré, 8e; Ⓜ Concorde)

USA (☎01 43 12 22 22; http://france.usembassy.gov; 2 av Gabriel, 8e; Ⓜ Concorde)

Emergency

➡ Ambulance (SAMU): ☎15

➡ Fire: ☎18

➡ Police: ☎17

Internet Access

Wi-fi ('whee-fee' in French) is available at most hotels in Paris, often as a free service.

We've identified sleeping, eating and drinking listings that have wi-fi with a 📶. Lodgings that offer internet terminals for guest use are denoted with a @.

Wi-fi is available at 400 public hot spots: mainly parks, but also libraries and municipal buildings. Participating parks will have a purple 'Zone Wi-Fi' sign near the gate. To connect, look for the Orange network and log in. You'll have two hours of consecutive use.

Some museums, particularly ones that offer audio guides as smartphone apps, also offer free wi-fi.

If you don't have a laptop or internet access in your hotel, you should find an internet cafe nearby. Expect to pay about €4 for one hour.

Legal Matters

Police

Police in France are here are to maintain order, not mingle and smile. If asked a direct question, a French policeman or policewoman will be correct and helpful but not much more; assisting tourists is not part of their job description.

If the police stop you for any reason, be polite and remain calm. They have wide powers of search and seizure and, if they take a dislike to you, they may choose to use them all.

Be aware that the police can, without any particular reason, decide to examine your passport, visa, *carte de séjour* (residence permit) and so on. (You are expected to have photo ID on you at *all* times.) Do *not* challenge them.

French police are very strict about security. Do not leave baggage unattended; they are quite serious when they say that suspicious objects will be summarily blown up.

Medical Services

EU passport holders have access to the French social security system, which can reimburse up to a reasonable amount of medical costs.

Hospitals

There are some 50 hospitals in Paris, including the following:

American Hospital of Paris (☎01 46 41 25 25; www.american-hospital.org; 63 bd Victor Hugo, Neuilly-sur-Seine; Ⓜ Pont de Levallois) Private hospital offering emergency 24-hour medical and dental care.

Hertford British Hospital (☎01 47 59 59 59; www.ihfb.org; 3 rue Barbès, Levallois; Ⓜ Anatole France) A less expensive private English-speaking option than the American Hospital.

Hôpital Hôtel Dieu (☎01 42 34 82 34; www.aphp.fr; 1 place du Parvis Notre Dame, 4e; Ⓜ Cité) One of the city's main government-run public hospitals; after 8pm use the emergency entrance on rue de la Cité.

Pharmacies

There will always be at least one *pharmacie* in your neighbourhood with extended hours.

Pharmacie Bader (☎01 43 26 92 66; 12 bd St-Michel, 5e; ⊙9am-9pm; Ⓜ St-Michel)

Pharmacie de la Mairie (☎01 43 54 23 99; 9 rue des Archives, 4e; ⊙9am-8pm; Ⓜ Hôtel de Ville)

Pharmacie les Champs (☎01 45 62 02 41; 84 av des Champs-Élysées, 8e; ⊙24hr; Ⓜ George V)

Money

France uses the euro (€). Denominations of the currency are €5, €10, €20, €50, €100, €200 and €500 notes, and €0.01, €0.02, €0.05, €0.10, €0.20, €0.50, €1 and €2 coins (amounts under €1 are called centimes).

French vendors can be very ornery when it comes to breaking a €50 note – don't even bother with bills larger than this (most won't take them unless you'll receive less than €20 in change).

To check the latest exchange rates, visit websites such as www.oanda.com or www.xe.com.

ATMs

You'll find an automated teller machine (ATM), which is known here as a *distributeur automatique de billets*,or *distributeur* for short, on many corners. Most French banks don't charge transaction fees to use their ATMs; however, check with your own bank before you travel to know if and how much you will be charged for international cash withdrawals. Unless you have particularly high transaction fees, ATMs are usually the best and easiest way to deal with currency exchange.

Changing Money

In general, cash is not a very good way to carry money. Not only can it be stolen, but in France it doesn't usually offer the best exchange rates.

In Paris, *bureaux de change* are usually more efficient, open longer hours and give better rates than most banks – in fact, many banks don't offer exchange services at all.

Bureaux de change charge anything from 6% to 13% plus €3 or €4 on cash transactions, and 6% to just under 10% (plus €3) to change travellers cheques.

Some of the better *bureaux de change* include:

Best Change (21 rue du Roule, 1er; ⌚9.30am-7.30pm Mon-Sat; Ⓜ Louvre Rivoli) Three blocks southwest of Forum des Halles.

CCO (9 rue Scribe, 9e; ⌚9am-6pm Mon-Fri, 9.30am-5pm Sat; Ⓜ Opéra)

European Exchange Office (6 rue Yvonne Le Tac, 18e; ⌚10am-noon & 2-6pm Mon-Sat; Ⓜ Abbesses) A few steps from the Abbesses metro station.

Kanoo (11 rue Scribe, 9e; ⌚9am-6.30pm Mon-Sat; Ⓜ Auber or Opéra)

Le Change du Louvre (151 rue St-Honoré, 1e; ⌚10am-6pm Mon-Fri; Ⓜ Palais Royal-Musée du Louvre) This moneychanger is on the northern side of Le Louvre des Antiquaires.

Multi Change (180 bd St-Germain, 6e; ⌚9.30am-6.30pm Mon-Sat; Ⓜ St-Germain des Prés) West of Église St-Germain des Prés.

Société Touristique de Services (2 place St-Michel, 6e; ⌚9am-8pm Mon-Fri, 10am-8pm Sat; Ⓜ St-Michel) A *bureau de change* in the heart of the Latin Quarter.

Credit Cards

In Paris, Visa/Carte Bleue is the most widely accepted credit card, followed by MasterCard (Eurocard). Amex cards can be useful at more upmarket establishments. In general, all three cards can be used to pay for train travel and restaurant meals and for cash advances. Note that France uses a smartcard with an embedded microchip and PIN. North Americans will not be able to use their credit cards at automated machines (such as at a metro station or museum) – you'll have to buy from the ticket window.

Travellers Cheques

The most flexible travellers cheques are issued by Amex (in US dollars or euros) and Visa, as they can be changed at many post offices.

Post

Most post offices *(bureaux de poste)* in Paris are open from 8am to 7pm weekdays and 8am or 9am till noon on Saturday. *Tabacs* (tobacconists) usually sell postage stamps.

The main **post office** (www.laposte.fr; 52 rue du Louvre, 1er; ⌚24hr; Ⓜ Sentier or Les Halles), five blocks north of the eastern end of the Musée du Louvre, is open round the clock, but only for basic services such as sending letters. Other services, including currency exchange, are available only during regular opening hours. Be prepared for long queues.

Each arrondissement has its own five-digit postcode, formed by prefixing the number of the arrondissement with '750' or '7500' (eg 75001 for the 1er arrondissement, 75019 for the 19e). The only exception is the 16e, which has two postcodes: 75016 and 75116. All mail to addresses in France *must* include the postcode.

Public Holidays

There is close to one public holiday a month in France and, in some years, up to four in May alone. Be aware, though, that unlike in the USA or UK, where public holidays usually fall on (or are shifted to) a Monday, in France a *jour férié* (public holiday) is celebrated strictly on the day on which it falls. Thus if May Day falls on a Saturday or Sunday, no provision is made for an extra day off.

The following holidays are observed in Paris:

New Year's Day (Jour de l'An) 1 January

Easter Sunday & Monday (Pâques & Lundi de Pâques) Late March/April

May Day (Fête du Travail) 1 May

Victory in Europe Day (Victoire 1945) 8 May

Ascension Thursday (L'Ascension) May (celebrated on the 40th day after Easter)

Whit Monday (Lundi de Pentecôte) Mid-May to mid-June (seventh Monday after Easter)

Bastille Day/National Day (Fête Nationale) 14 July

Assumption Day (L'Assomption) 15 August

All Saints' Day (La Toussaint) 1 November

Armistice Day/Remembrance Day (Le 11 Novembre) 11 November

Christmas (Noël) 25 December

Safe Travel

In general, Paris is a safe city and random street assaults are rare. The city is generally well lit and there's no reason not to use the metro until it stops running at some time between 12.30am and just past 1am. As you'll notice, women *do* travel alone on the metro late at night in most areas, though not all who do so report feeling 100% comfortable.

Metro stations that are best avoided late at night include Châtelet–Les Halles and its seemingly endless corridors, Château Rouge in Montmartre, Gare du Nord, Strasbourg St-Denis, Réaumur Sébastopol and Montparnasse Bienvenüe. *Bornes d'alarme* (alarm boxes) are located in the centre of each metro/RER platform and in some station corridors.

Nonviolent crime such as pickpocketing and thefts from handbags and packs is a problem wherever there are crowds, especially packs of tourists. Places to be particularly careful include Montmartre (especially around Sacré Cœur); Pigalle; the areas around Forum des Halles and the Centre Pompidou; the Latin Quarter (especially the rectangle bounded by rue St-Jacques, bd St-Germain, bd St-Michel and quai St-Michel); below the Eiffel Tower; and anywhere on the metro during rush hour (particularly on line 4 and the western part of line 1).

Take the usual precautions: don't carry more money than you need, and keep your credit cards, passport and other documents in a concealed pouch, a hotel safe or a safe-deposit box.

Vigipirate is a security plan devised by the Paris city council to combat terrorism. Both citizens and visitors are asked to report any abandoned luggage or package at all times. When the full Vigipirate scheme is put into action, public litter bins are sealed, left-luggage services in train stations and at airports are unavailable, checks at the entrances to public buildings and tourist sites are increased, and cloakrooms and lockers in museums and at monuments are closed.

Taxes & Refunds

France's value-added tax (VAT) is known as TVA *(taxe sur la valeur ajoutée)* and is 19.6% on most goods except medicine and books, for which it's 5.5%. Prices that include TVA are often marked TTC (*toutes taxes comprises;* literally 'all taxes included').

If you're not an EU resident, you can get a TVA refund provided that: you're aged over 15; you'll be spending less than six months in France; you purchase goods worth at least €175 at a single shop on the same day (not more than 10 of the same item); the goods fit into your luggage; you are taking the goods out of France within three months after purchase; and the shop offers *vente en détaxe* (duty-free sales).

Present a passport at the time of purchase and ask for a *bordereau de vente à l'exportation* (export sales invoice) to be signed by the retailer and yourself. Most shops will refund less than the full amount (about 14%) to which you are entitled, in order to cover the time and expense involved in the refund procedure.

As you leave France or another EU country, have all three pages of the *bordereau* validated by the country's customs officials at the airport or at the border. Customs officials will take one sheet and hand you two. You must post one copy (the pink one) back to the shop and retain the other (green) sheet for your records in case there is any dispute. Once the shop where you made your purchase receives its stamped copy, it will send you a *virement* (fund transfer) in the form you have requested. Be prepared for a wait of up to three months.

If you're flying out of Orly or Charles de Gaulle, certain shops can arrange for you to receive your refund as you're leaving the country, though you must complete the steps outlined above. You must make such arrangements at the time of purchase.

For more information contact the **customs information centre** (☎08 11 20 44 44; www.douane.minefi.gouv.fr; ⌚8.30am-6pm Mon-Fri).

Telephone

There are no area codes in France – you always dial the 10-digit number.

Telephone numbers in Paris always start with 01, unless the number is provided by an internet service provider (ISP), in which case it begins with 09.

Mobile phone numbers throughout France commence with either 06 or 07.

France's country code is 33.

To call abroad from Paris, dial France's international access code (00), the country code, the area code (usually without the initial '0', if there is one) and the local number. International Direct Dial (IDD) calls to almost anywhere in the world can be placed from public telephones. The international reduced rate applies from 7pm to 8am weekdays and all day at the weekend.

Note that while numbers beginning with 0 800, 0 804, 0 805 and 0 809 are toll-free in France, other numbers beginning with '08' are not (costs range from €0.078 to €1.35).

Customer service numbers are generally more expensive than local rates.

Most four-digit numbers starting with 10, 30 or 31 are free of charge.

If you can read basic French, directory enquiries are best done via the *Yellow Pages* (www.pagesjaunes.fr; click on Pages Blanches for the *White Pages*), which will provide more information, including maps, for free. From a mobile phone, use the site http://mobile.pagesjaunes.fr.

Mobile Phones

You can use your smartphone or mobile phone *(portable)* in France provided it is GSM (the standard in Europe, which is becoming increasingly common elsewhere) and tri-band or quad-band. If you meet the requirements, you can check with your service provider about using it in France, but beware of roaming costs, especially for data.

Rather than staying on your home network, it is usually more convenient to buy a local SIM card from a French provider such as **Orange** (www.orange.fr), which will give you a local phone number. In order for this to work, however, you'll need to ensure your phone is 'unlocked', which means you can use another service provider while abroad. A SIM card with €5 calling time (nine minutes) plus a €5 recharge card costs €7.90. Throw a phone into the deal and it costs €15. The company www.callineurope.com offers good mobile phone packages for North American travellers to France and Europe.

For more time, buy a prepaid Mobicarte recharge card (€5 to €100) from *tabacs* (tobacconists), mobile phone outlets, supermarkets etc. Mobicartes from €25 upward offer extra talk time. One major outlet is **La Boutique Orange** (16 place de la Madeleine, 8e; ⏲10am-7pm Mon-Sat; Madeleine). Other major service providers include **Free Moblie** (http://mobile.free.fr), **SFR** (www.sfr.fr) and **Bouygues** (www.bouyguestelecom.fr).

Phonecards

Although mobile phones and **Skype** (www.skype.com) may have killed off the need for public phones, they do still exist. In France they are all phonecard-operated, but in the event of an emergency you can use your credit card to call.

Public telephones in Paris usually require a *télécarte* (phonecard; €7.50/15 for 50/120 calling units), which can be purchased at post offices, *tabacs*, supermarkets, SNCF ticket windows, metro stations and anywhere you see a blue sticker reading *'télécarte en vente ici'* (phonecard for sale here).

You can buy prepaid phonecards in France such as **Allomundo** (www.allomundo.com). These cards can be up to 60% cheaper for calling overseas than the standard *télécarte*. They're usually available in denominations of up to €15 from *tabacs*, newsagents, phone shops and other sales points, especially rue du Faubourg St-Denis (10e), Chinatown (13e) and Belleville (19e and 20e). In general they're valid for two months, but the ones offering the most minutes for the least euros can expire in just a week.

All public phones can receive both domestic and international calls. If you want someone to call you back, just give them France's country code and the 10-digit number, usually written after the words *'Ici le...'* or *'No d'appel'* on the tariff sheet or on a little sign inside the phone box. Remind them to drop the '0' from the initial '01' of the number. When there's an incoming call, the words *'décrochez – appel arrive'* (pick up receiver – incoming call) will appear in the LCD window.

Time

France uses the 24-hour clock in most cases, with the hours usually separated from the minutes by a lowercase 'h'. Thus, 15h30 is 3.30pm, 00h30 is 12.30am and so on.

France is on Central European Time (like Berlin and Rome), which is one hour ahead of GMT. When it's noon in Paris it's 11am in London, 3am in San Francisco, 6am in New York and and 9pm in Sydney.

Daylight-saving time runs from the last Sunday in March to the last Sunday in October.

Tipping

French law requires that restaurant, cafe and hotel bills include a service charge (usually between 12% and 15%). Taxi drivers expect small tips of between 5% and 10% of the fare, though the usual procedure is to round up to the nearest €1 regardless of the fare.

Toilets

Public toilets in Paris are signposted *toilettes* or *WC*. The self-cleaning cylindrical toilets you see on Parisian pavements are open 24 hours, reasonably clean and free of charge, though, of course, they never seem to be around when you need them. Look for the words *libre* ('available'; green-coloured) or *occupé* ('occupied'; red-coloured).

Cafe owners do not appreciate you using their facilities if you are not a paying customer; however, if you have young children they may make an exception (ask first!). When desperate, try a fast-food chain, major department store or even a big hotel.

There are free public toilets in front of Notre Dame

cathedral, near the Arc de Triomphe, east down the steps at Sacré Cœur and at the northwestern entrance to the Jardins des Tuileries.

Tourist Information

The main branch of the **Paris Convention & Visitors Bureau** (Office de Tourisme et de Congrès de Paris; ☎08 92 68 30 00; www.parisinfo.com; 25-27 rue des Pyramides, 1er; ⌚9am-7pm Jun-Oct, shorter hours rest of year; ⓂPyramides) is about 500m northwest of the Louvre.

The bureau maintains a handful of centres elsewhere in Paris, most of which are listed here (telephone numbers and websites are the same as for the main office). There are also information desks at Charles de Gaulle Airport, where you can pick up maps and brochures. For details of the area around Paris, check out **Paris Île de France** (www.nouveau-paris-ile-de-france.fr).

Paris Convention & Visitors Bureau (opp 72 blvd Rochechouart, 18e; ⌚10am-6pm; ⓂAnvers) At the foot of Montmartre.

Paris Convention & Visitors Bureau (Place du 11 Novembre 1918, 10e; ⌚8am-7pm Mon-Sat; ⓂGare de l'Est) In the arrivals hall for TGV trains.

Paris Convention & Visitors Bureau (Hall d'Arrivée, 20 blvd Diderot, 12e; ⌚8am-6pm Mon-Sat; ⓂGare de Lyon) In the arrivals hall for mainline trains.

Paris Convention & Visitors Bureau (18 rue de Dunkerque, 10e; ⌚8am-6pm; ⓂGare du Nord) Under the glass roof of the Île de France departure and arrival area at the eastern end of the station.

Syndicate d'Initiative de Montmartre (☎01 42 62 21 21; 21 place du Tertre, 18e; ⌚10am-7pm; ⓂAbbesses) This locally run tourist office and shop is in Montmartre's most picturesque square and is open year-round. It sells maps of Montmartre and organises tours in July and August.

Travellers with Disabilities

Paris is an ancient city and therefore not particularly well equipped for *les handicapés* (disabled people): kerb ramps are few and far between, older public facilities and budget hotels usually lack lifts, and the metro, dating back more than a century, is mostly inaccessible for those in a wheelchair *(fauteuil roulant)*. But, pleasingly, efforts are being made and early in the new millennium the tourist office launched its 'Tourisme & Handicap' initiative in which museums, cultural attractions, hotels and restaurants that provided access or special assistance or facilities for those with physical, mental, visual and/or hearing disabilities would display a special logo at their entrances. For a list of the places qualifying, visit the tourist office's website (www.parisinfo.com) and click on 'Practical Paris'.

Information & Organisations

The SNCF has made many of its train carriages more accessible to people with disabilities. A traveller in a wheelchair can travel in both the TGV (*train à grande vitesse;* high-speed train) and in the 1st-class carriage with a 2nd-class ticket on mainline trains provided they make a reservation by phone or at a train station at least a few hours before departure. Details are available in the SNCF booklet *Le Mémento du Voyageur Handicapé* (Handicapped Traveller Summary) available at all train stations. For advice on planning your journey from station to station, contact the SNCF service **Acces Plus** (☎0 890 640 650; www.accessibilite.sncf.com).

For information on accessibility on all forms of public transport in the Paris region, get a copy of the *Guide Practique à l'Usage des Personnes à Mobilité Réduite* (Practical Usage Guide for People with Reduced Mobility) from the **Syndicate des Transports d'Île de France** (☎0 810 646 464; www.stif-idf.fr). Its **Info Mobi** (www.infomobi.com) is useful.

For information about what cultural venues in Paris are accessible to people with disabilities, visit the website of **Accès Culture** (www.accesculture.org).

Access in Paris, a 245-page guide to the French capital for the disabled, is available online from **Access Project** (www.accessinparis.org; 39 Bradley Gardens, West Ealing, London).

The following organisations can provide information to disabled travellers:

Association des Paralysées de France (APF; ☎01 40 78 69 00; www.apf.asso.fr; 17 bd Blanqui, 13e) Brochures on wheelchair access and accommodation throughout France, including Paris.

Groupement pour l'Insertion des Personnes Handicapées Physiques (GIHP; ☎01 43 95 66 36; www.gihpnational.org; 32 rue de Paradis, 10e) Provides special vehicles outfitted for people in wheelchairs for use within the city.

Mobile en Ville (☎09 52 29 60 51; www.mobile-en-ville.asso.fr; 8 rue des Mariniers, 14e) Association set up in 1998 by students and researchers with the aim of making independent travel within the city easier for people in wheelchairs.

Visas

There are no entry requirements for nationals of EU countries. Citizens of Australia, the USA, Canada and New Zealand do not need visas to visit France for up to 90 days. Except for people from a handful of other European countries (including Switzerland), everyone, including citizens of South Africa, needs a so-called Schengen Visa, named after the Schengen Agreement that has abolished passport controls among 22 EU countries and has also been ratified by the non-EU governments of Iceland, Norway and Switzerland. A visa for any of these countries should be valid throughout the Schengen area, but it pays to double-check with the embassy or consulate of each country you intend to visit. Note that the UK and Ireland are not Schengen countries.

Visa fees depend on the current exchange rate, but transit and the various types of short-stay (up to 90 days) visas all cost €60, while a long-stay visa allowing stays of more than 90 days costs €99. You will need: your passport (valid for a period of three months beyond the date of your departure from France); a return ticket; proof of sufficient funds to support yourself; supporting documents explaining your stay in France for an extended period; recent passport-sized photos; a completed visa form; and the visa fee. Check www.france.diplomatie.fr for the latest visa regulations and the closest French embassy to your current residence.

Titre de Séjour

If you are issued a long-stay visa valid for six months or longer, you may need to apply for a *titre de séjour* (residence permit; also called a *carte de séjour*) after arrival in France. Regulations have been relaxed in recent years; if you are only staying in France for up to 12 months you probably won't need it, but you will need to register with the French Office of Immigration and Integration. Check the website of the Préfecture de Police first for instructions for all possible situations: go to www.prefecturedepolice.interieur.gouv.fr, then select Vos démarches/Ressortissants étrangers (the instructions are in French, though an English pdf is available for students by clicking on 'Médiathèque' on the page given above).

Those holding a passport from one of 31 European countries and seeking to take up residence in France no longer need to acquire a *titre de séjour;* their passport or national ID card is sufficient. Check the website given above to see which countries are included.

Foreigners with non-European passports should check the website of the Préfecture de Police or call 01 58 80 80 58.

Long-Stay & Student Visas

If you would like to work, study or stay in France for longer than three months, apply to the French embassy or consulate nearest to you for the appropriate *long séjour* (long-stay) visa. Au pairs are granted student visas: they must be arranged *before* you leave home (unless you're an EU resident); the same goes for the year-long working holiday visa *(permis vacances travail)*.

Unless you hold an EU passport or are married to a French national, it's extremely difficult to get a visa that will allow you to work in France. For any sort of long-stay visa, begin the paperwork in your home country several months before you plan to leave. Applications usually cannot be made in a third country nor can tourist visas be turned into student visas after you arrive in France. People with student visas can apply for permission to work part-time; enquire at your place of study.

Visa Extensions

Tourist visas *cannot* be extended except in emergencies (such as medical problems). If you have an urgent problem, you should call the Service Étranger (Foreigner Service) at the **Préfecture de Police** (☎08 91 01 22 22, 01 58 80 80 58) for guidance. If you entered France on the 90-day visa-waiver program (ie you are Australian or American) and you have stayed for 90 days, you must leave the Schengen area for an additional 90 days before you can re-enter.

Women Travellers

In 1923 French women obtained the right to – wait for it – open their own mail. The right to vote didn't come until 1945 during De Gaulle's short-lived postwar government, and a woman still needed her husband's permission to open a bank account or get a passport until 1964. It was in such an environment that Simone de Beauvoir wrote *Le Deuxième Sexe* (The Second Sex) in 1949.

Younger French women are quite outspoken and emancipated but self-confidence has yet to translate into equality in the workplace, where women are often passed over for senior and management positions in favour of their male colleagues. Women attract more unwanted attention than men, but female travellers need not walk around Paris in fear: people are rarely assaulted on the street. However, the French seem to have given relatively little thought to sexual harassment *(harcèlement sexuel)*, and many men still think that to stare suavely at a passing woman is to pay her a compliment.

Information & Organisations

France's women's movement flourished as in other countries in the late 1960s and early '70s, but by the mid-'80s had become moribund. For reasons that have more to do with French society than anything else, few women's groups function as the kind of supportive social institutions that exist in English-speaking countries.

France's rape crisis hotline (Viols Femmes Informations; ☎08 00 05 95 95; 10am-7pm Mon-Fri) can be reached toll-free from any telephone, without using a phonecard. It's run by a group called **Collectif Féministe contre le Viol** (CFCV; Feminist Collective Against Rape; www.cfcv.asso.fr).

In an emergency, you can always call the police (17). Medical, psychological and legal services are available to people referred by the police at the **Service Médico-Judiciaire** (☎01 42 34 86 78; ⏲24hr) of the Hôtel Dieu.

Recommended organisations follow:

La Maison des Femmes de Paris (☎01 43 43 41 13; http://maisondesfemmes.free.fr; 163 rue de Charenton, 12e; ⏲office 11am-7pm Mon, Thu & Fri, 9am-5pm Tue & Wed; MReuilly Diderot) A meeting place for women of all ages and nationalities, with events, workshops and exhibitions scheduled throughout the week.

Paris Woman (www.pariswoman.com) A useful resource that deals with news, issues and events affecting expat twomen in Paris.

Language

The sounds used in spoken French can almost all be found in English. If you read our pronunciation guides as if they were English, you'll be understood just fine. There are a couple of sounds to take note of: nasal vowels (represented in our guides by o or u followed by an almost inaudible nasal consonant sound m, n or ng), the 'funny' *u* (ew in our guides) and the deep-in-the-throat *r*. Syllables in French words are, for the most part, equally stressed. As English speakers tend to stress the first syllable, try adding a light stress on the final syllable of French words to compensate.

BASICS

Hello.	*Bonjour.*	bon·zhoor
Goodbye.	*Au revoir.*	o·rer·vwa
Excuse me.	*Excusez-moi.*	ek·skew·zay·mwa
Sorry.	*Pardon.*	par·don
Yes./No.	*Oui./Non.*	wee/non
Please.	*S'il vous plaît.*	seel voo play
Thank you.	*Merci.*	mair·see
You're welcome.	*De rien.*	der ree·en

How are you?
Comment allez-vous? ko·mon ta·lay·voo

Fine, and you?
Bien, merci. Et vous? byun mair·see ay voo

What's your name?
Comment vous appelez-vous? ko·mon voo·za·play voo

WANT MORE?

For in-depth language information and handy phrases, check out Lonely Planet's *French Phrasebook*. You'll find it at **shop.lonelyplanet.com**, or you can buy Lonely Planet's iPhone phrasebooks at the Apple App Store.

My name is ...
Je m'appelle ... zher ma·pel ...

Do you speak English?
Parlez-vous anglais? par·lay·voo ong·glay

I don't understand.
Je ne comprends pas. zher ner kom·pron pa

ACCOMMODATION

Do you have any rooms available?
Est-ce que vous avez des chambres libres? es·ker voo za·vay day shom·brer lee·brer

How much is it per night/person?
Quel est le prix par nuit/personne? kel ay ler pree par nwee/per·son

Is breakfast included?
Est-ce que le petit déjeuner est inclus? es·ker ler per·tee day·zher·nay ayt en·klew

dorm	*dortoir*	dor·twar
guesthouse	*pension*	pon·syon
hotel	*hôtel*	o·tel
youth hostel	*auberge de jeunesse*	o·berzh der zher·nes

a ... room	*une chambre ...*	ewn shom·brer ...
single	*à un lit*	a un lee
double	*avec un grand lit*	a·vek un gron lee

with (a) ...	*avec ...*	a·vek ...
air-con	*climatiseur*	klee·ma·tee·zer
bathroom	*une salle de bains*	ewn sal der bun
window	*fenêtre*	fer·nay·trer

DIRECTIONS

Where's ...?	*Où est ...?*	oo ay ...
What's the address?	*Quelle est l'adresse?*	kel ay la·dres

Signs

Entrée	Entrance
Femmes	Women
Fermé	Closed
Hommes	Men
Interdit	Prohibited
Ouvert	Open
Renseignements	Information
Sortie	Exit
Toilettes/WC	Toilets

Can you write down the address, please?

Est-ce que vous pourriez écrire l'adresse, s'il vous plaît?	es·ker voo poo·ryay ay·kreer la·dres seel voo play

Can you show me (on the map)?

Pouvez-vous m'indiquer (sur la carte)?	poo·vay·voo mun·dee·kay (sewr la kart)

at the corner	*au coin*	o kwun
at the traffic lights	*aux feux*	o fer
behind	*derrière*	dair·ryair
in front of	*devant*	der·von
far (from ...)	*loin (de ...)*	lwun (der ...)
left	*gauche*	gosh
near (to ...)	*près (de ...)*	pray (der ...)
next to ...	*à côté de ...*	a ko·tay der ...
opposite ...	*en face de ...*	on fas der ...
right	*droite*	drwat
straight ahead	*tout droit*	too drwa

EATING & DRINKING

What would you recommend?

Qu'est-ce que vous conseillez?	kes·ker voo kon·say·yay

What's in that dish?

Quels sont les ingrédients?	kel son lay zun·gray·dyon

I'm a vegetarian.

Je suis végétarien/ végétarienne.	zher swee vay·zhay·ta·ryun/ vay·zhay·ta·ryen (m/f)

I don't eat ...

Je ne mange pas ...	zher ner monzh pa ...

Cheers!

Santé!	son·tay

That was delicious.

C'était délicieux!	say·tay day·lee·syer

Please bring the bill.

Apportez-moi l'addition, s'il vous plaît.	a·por·tay·mwa la·dee·syon seel voo play

I'd like to reserve a table for ...	*Je voudrais réserver une table pour ...*	zher voo·dray ray·zair·vay ewn ta·bler poor ...
(eight) o'clock	*(vingt) heures*	(vungt) er
(two) people	*(deux) personnes*	(der) pair·son

Key Words

appetiser	*entrée*	on·tray
bottle	*bouteille*	boo·tay
breakfast	*petit déjeuner*	per·tee day·zher·nay
cold	*froid*	frwa
delicatessen	*traiteur*	tray·ter
dinner	*dîner*	dee·nay
fork	*fourchette*	foor·shet
glass	*verre*	vair
grocery store	*épicerie*	ay·pees·ree
hot	*chaud*	sho
knife	*couteau*	koo·to
lunch	*déjeuner*	day·zher·nay
market	*marché*	mar·shay
menu	*carte*	kart
plate	*assiette*	a·syet
spoon	*cuillère*	kwee·yair
wine list	*carte des vins*	kart day vun
with/without	*avec/sans*	a·vek/son

Meat & Fish

beef	*bœuf*	berf
chicken	*poulet*	poo·lay
crab	*crabe*	krab
lamb	*agneau*	a·nyo
oyster	*huître*	wee·trer
pork	*porc*	por
snail	*escargot*	es·kar·go
squid	*calmar*	kal·mar
turkey	*dinde*	dund
veal	*veau*	vo

Fruit & Vegetables

apple	*pomme*	pom
apricot	*abricot*	ab·ree·ko
asparagus	*asperge*	a·spairzh
beans	*haricots*	a·ree·ko
beetroot	*betterave*	be·trav

cabbage	*chou*	shoo
celery	*céleri*	sel·ree
cherry	*cerise*	ser·reez
corn	*maïs*	ma·ees
cucumber	*concombre*	kong·kom·brer
gherkin (pickle)	*cornichon*	kor·nee·shon
grape	*raisin*	ray·zun
leek	*poireau*	pwa·ro
lemon	*citron*	see·tron
lettuce	*laitue*	lay·tew
mushroom	*champignon*	shom·pee·nyon
peach	*pêche*	pesh
peas	*petit pois*	per·tee pwa
(red/green) pepper	*poivron (rouge/vert)*	pwa·vron (roozh/vair)
pineapple	*ananas*	a·na·nas
plum	*prune*	prewn
potato	*pomme de terre*	pom der tair
prune	*pruneau*	prew·no
pumpkin	*citrouille*	see·troo·yer
shallot	*échalote*	eh·sha·lot
spinach	*épinards*	eh·pee·nar
strawberry	*fraise*	frez
tomato	*tomate*	to·mat
turnip	*navet*	na·vay
vegetable	*légume*	lay·gewm

Other

bread	*pain*	pun
butter	*beurre*	ber
cheese	*fromage*	fro·mazh
egg	*œuf*	erf
honey	*miel*	myel
jam	*confiture*	kon·fee·tewr
oil	*huile*	weel
pepper	*poivre*	pwa·vrer
rice	*riz*	ree
salt	*sel*	sel
sugar	*sucre*	sew·krer
vinegar	*vinaigre*	vee·nay·grer

Drinks

beer	*bière*	bee·yair
coffee	*café*	ka·fay
(orange) juice	*jus (d'orange)*	zhew (do·ronzh)
milk	*lait*	lay
red wine	*vin rouge*	vun roozh
tea	*thé*	tay
(mineral) water	*eau (minérale)*	o (mee·nay·ral)
white wine	*vin blanc*	vun blong

EMERGENCIES

Help!
Au secours! — o skoor

Leave me alone!
Fichez-moi la paix! — fee·shay·mwa la pay

I'm lost.
Je suis perdu/perdue. — zhe swee·pair·dew (m/f)

Call a doctor.
Appelez un médecin. — a·play un mayd·sun

Call the police.
Appelez la police. — a·play la po·lees

I'm ill.
Je suis malade. — zher swee ma·lad

It hurts here.
J'ai une douleur ici. — zhay ewn doo·ler ee·see

I'm allergic (to ...).
Je suis allergique (à ...). — zher swee za·lair·zheek (a ...)

SHOPPING & SERVICES

I'd like to buy ...
Je voudrais acheter ... — zher voo·dray ash·tay ...

Can I look at it?
Est-ce que je peux le voir? — es·ker zher per ler vwar

I'm just looking.
Je regarde. — zher rer·gard

I don't like it.
Cela ne me plaît pas. — ser·la ner mer play pa

How much is it?
C'est combien? — say kom·byun

It's too expensive.
C'est trop cher. — say tro shair

There's a mistake in the bill.
Il y a une erreur dans la note. — eel ya ewn ay·rer don la not

bank	*banque*	bonk
internet cafe	*cybercafé*	see·bair·ka·fay
tourist office	*office de tourisme*	o·fees der too·rees·mer

Question Words

What?	*Quoi?*	kwa
When?	*Quand?*	kon
Where?	*Où?*	oo
Who?	*Qui?*	kee
Why?	*Pourquoi?*	poor·kwa

Numbers

1	*un*	un
2	*deux*	der
3	*trois*	trwa
4	*quatre*	ka·trer
5	*cinq*	sungk
6	*six*	sees
7	*sept*	set
8	*huit*	weet
9	*neuf*	nerf
10	*dix*	dees
20	*vingt*	vung
30	*trente*	tront
40	*quarante*	ka·ront
50	*cinquante*	sung·kont
60	*soixante*	swa·sont
70	*soixante-dix*	swa·son·dees
80	*quatre-vingts*	ka·trer·vung
90	*quatre-vingt-dix*	ka·trer·vung·dees
100	*cent*	son
1000	*mille*	meel

TIME & DATES

What time is it?
Quelle heure est-il? kel er ay til

It's (eight) o'clock.
Il est (huit) heures. il ay (weet) er

Half past (10).
(Dix) heures et demie. (deez) er ay day·mee

morning	*matin*	ma·tun
afternoon	*après-midi*	a·pray·mee·dee
evening	*soir*	swar
yesterday	*hier*	yair
today	*aujourd'hui*	o·zhoor·dwee
tomorrow	*demain*	der·mun

Monday	*lundi*	lun·dee
Tuesday	*mardi*	mar·dee
Wednesday	*mercredi*	mair·krer·dee
Thursday	*jeudi*	zher·dee
Friday	*vendredi*	von·drer·dee
Saturday	*samedi*	sam·dee
Sunday	*dimanche*	dee·monsh

TRANSPORT

I want to go to ...
Je voudrais aller à ... zher voo·dray a·lay a ...

Does it stop at ...?
Est-ce qu'il s'arrête à ...? es·kil sa·ret a ...

At what time does it leave/arrive?
À quelle heure est-ce qu'il part/arrive? a kel er es kil par/a·reev

I want to get off here.
Je veux descendre ici. zher ver day·son·drer ee·see

a ... ticket	*un billet ...*	un bee·yay ...
1st-class	*de première classe*	der prem·yair klas
2nd-class	*de deuxième classe*	der der·zyem klas
one-way	*simple*	sum·pler
return	*aller et retour*	a·lay ay rer·toor

aisle seat	*côté couloir*	ko·tay kool·war
boat	*bateau*	ba·to
bus	*bus*	bews
cancelled	*annulé*	a·new·lay
delayed	*en retard*	on rer·tar
first	*premier*	prer·myay
last	*dernier*	dair·nyay
plane	*avion*	a·vyon
platform	*quai*	kay
ticket office	*guichet*	gee·shay
timetable	*horaire*	o·rair
train	*train*	trun
window seat	*côté fenêtre*	ko·tay fe·ne·trer

I'd like to hire a ...	*Je voudrais louer ...*	zher voo·dray loo·way ...
car	*une voiture*	ewn vwa·tewr
bicycle	*un vélo*	un vay·lo
motorcycle	*une moto*	ewn mo·to

child seat	*siège-enfant*	syezh·on·fon
helmet	*casque*	kask
mechanic	*mécanicien*	may·ka·nee·syun
petrol/gas	*essence*	ay·sons
service station	*station-service*	sta·syon·ser·vees

Can I park here?
Est-ce que je peux stationner ici? es·ker zher per sta·syo·nay ee·see

I have a flat tyre.
Mon pneu est à plat. mom pner ay ta pla

I've run out of petrol.
Je suis en panne d'essence. zher swee zon pan day·sons

GLOSSARY

(m) indicates masculine gender, (f) feminine gender, (pl) plural and (adj) adjective

adjoint (m) – deputy mayor

ancien régime (m) – 'old order'; France under the monarchy before the Revolution

apéritif (m) – a drink taken before dinner

arrondissement (m) – one of 20 administrative divisions in Paris; abbreviated on street signs as 1er (1st arrondissement), 2e or 2ème (2nd) etc

auberge (de jeunesse) (f) – (youth) hostel

avenue (f) – avenue (abbreviated av)

banlieues (f pl) – suburbs

belle époque (f) – 'beautiful age'; era of elegance and gaiety characterising fashionable Parisian life roughly from 1870 to 1914

billet (m) – ticket

billeterie (f) – ticket office or window

biologique or **bio** (adj) – organic

boucherie (f) – butcher

boulangerie (f) – bakery

boules (f pl) – a game played with heavy metal balls on a sandy pitch; also called *pétanque*

brasserie (f) – 'brewery'; a restaurant that usually serves food all day long

brioche (f) – small roll or cake, sometimes made with nuts, currants or candied fruit

bureau de change (m) – currency exchange bureau

café du quartier (m) – neighbourhood café

carnet (m) – a book of (usually) 10 bus, tram, metro or other tickets sold at a reduced rate

carrefour (m) – crossroads, intersection

carte (f) – card; menu; map

carte de séjour (f) – residence permit

cave (f) – (wine) cellar

chambre (f) – room

chanson française (f) – 'French song'; traditional musical genre where lyrics are paramount

chansonnier (m) – cabaret singer

charcuterie (f) – a variety of meat products that are cured, smoked or processed, including sausages, hams, pâtés and rillettes; shop selling these products

cimetière (m) – cemetery

consigne (f) – left-luggage office

correspondance (f) – linking tunnel or walkway, eg in the metro; rail or bus connection

cour (f) – courtyard

couvert (m) – covered shopping arcade (also called *galerie*)

dégustation (f) – tasting, sampling

demi (m) – half; 330mL glass of beer

département (m) – administrative division of France

dessert (m) – dessert

eau (f) – water

église (f) – church

entrée (f) – entrance; first course or starter

épicerie (f) – small grocery store

espace (f) – space; outlet

exposition universelle (f) – world exhibition

fête (f) – festival; holiday

ficelle (f) – string; a thinner, crustier 200g version of the baguette not unlike a very thick breadstick

fin de siècle (adj) – 'end of the century'; characteristic of the last years of the 19th century and generally used to indicate decadence

forêt (f) – forest

formule (f) – similar to a *menu* but allows choice of whichever two of three courses you want (eg starter and main course or main course and dessert)

fromagerie (f) – cheese shop

galerie (f) – gallery; covered shopping arcade (also called passage)

galette (f) – a pancake or flat pastry, with a variety of (usually savoury) fillings

gare (f) – railway station

gare routière (f) – bus station

gendarmerie (f) – police station; police force

grand projet (m) – huge, public edifice erected by a government or politician generally in a bid to immortalise themselves

Grands Boulevards (m pl) – 'Great Boulevards'; the eight contiguous broad thoroughfares that stretch from place de la Madeleine eastwards to the place de la République

halles (f pl) – covered food market

hameau (m) – hamlet

hammam (m) – steam room, Turkish bath

haute couture (f) – literally 'high sewing'; the creations of leading designers

haute cuisine (f) – 'high cuisine'; classic French cooking style typified by elaborately prepared multicourse meals

hôtel de ville (m) – city or town hall

hôtel particulier (m) – private mansion

jardin (m) – garden

kir (m) – white wine sweetened with a blackcurrant (or other) liqueur

lycée (m) – secondary school

mairie (f) – city or town hall
marché (m) – market
marché aux puces (m) – flea market
menu (m) – fixed-price meal with two or more courses; see *formule*
musée (m) – museum
musette (f) – accordion music
nocturne (f) – late night opening at a museum, department store etc
orangerie (f) – conservatory for growing citrus fruit
pain (m) – bread
palais de justice (m) – law courts
parc (m) – park
parvis (m) – square in front of a church or public building passage
pastis (m) – an aniseed-flavoured aperitif mixed with water
pâté (m) – potted meat; a thickish paste, often of pork, cooked in a ceramic dish and served cold (similar to terrine)
pâtisserie (f) – cakes and pastries; shop selling these products
pelouse (f) – lawn
pétanque (f) – see boules
pied-noir (m) – 'black foot'; French colonial born in Algeria
place (f) – square or plaza
plan (m) – city map
plan du quartier (m) – map of nearby streets (hung on the wall near metro exits)
plat du jour (m) – daily special in a restaurant
poissonnerie (f) – fishmonger, fish shop
pont (m) – bridge
port (m) – harbour, port
port de plaisance (m) – boat harbour or marina
porte (f) – door; gate in a city wall
poste (f) – post office
préfecture (f) – prefecture; capital city of a département
produits biologique – organic food
quai (m) – quay
quartier (m) – quarter, district, neighbourhood
raï – a type of Algerian popular music
RATP – Régie Autonome des Transports Parisiens; Paris' public transport system
RER – Réseau Express Régional; Paris' suburban train network
résidence (f) – residence; hotel usually intended for longterm stays
rillettes (f pl) – shredded potted meat or fish
rive (f) – bank of a river
rond point (m) – roundabout
rue (f) – street or road
salle (f) – hall; room
salon de thé (m) – tearoom
SNCF – Société Nationale de Chemins de Fer; France's national railway organisation
soldes (m pl) – sale, the sales
sono mondiale (f) – world music
sortie (f) – exit
spectacle (m) – performance, play or theatrical show
square (m) – public garden
syndicat d'initiative (m) – tourist office
tabac (m) – tobacconist (which also sells bus tickets, phonecards etc)
tarif réduit (m) – reduced price (for students, seniors, children etc)
tartine (f) – a slice of bread with any topping or garnish
taxe de séjour (f) – municipal tourist tax
télécarte (f) – phonecard
TGV – train à grande vitesse; high-speed train
tour (f) – tower
tous les jours – every day (eg on timetables)
traiteur (m) – caterer, delicatessen
Vélib' (m) – communal bicycle rental scheme in Paris
vélo (m) – bicycle
version française (m) – literally 'French version': a film dubbed in French
version originale – literally 'original version': a nondubbed film in its original language with French subtitles

Behind the Scenes

SEND US YOUR FEEDBACK

We love to hear from travellers – your comments keep us on our toes and help make our books better. Our well-travelled team reads every word on what you loved or loathed about this book. Although we cannot reply individually to postal submissions, we always guarantee that your feedback goes straight to the appropriate authors, in time for the next edition. Each person who sends us information is thanked in the next edition – the most useful submissions are rewarded with a selection of digital PDF chapters.

Visit **lonelyplanet.com/contact** to submit your updates and suggestions or to ask for help. Our award-winning website also features inspirational travel stories, news and discussions.

Note: We may edit, reproduce and incorporate your comments in Lonely Planet products such as guidebooks, websites and digital products, so let us know if you don't want your comments reproduced or your name acknowledged. For a copy of our privacy policy visit lonelyplanet.com/privacy.

OUR READERS

Many thanks to the travellers who used the last edition and wrote to us with helpful hints, useful advice and interesting anecdotes:

Jonathan Brach, Kim Laidlaw, Myriam Lépine, Kate Mcginley, Margarita Perez, Paul White, Stefanie Wojciech

AUTHOR THANKS

Catherine Le Nevez

Un grand merci to my co-authors Chris and Nicola – it was a pleasure working with you both on this book. *Merci mille fois* to Julian, and to all of the innumerable Parisians who offered insights and inspiration. Thanks too to Jo Cooke, Annelies Mertens, Mandy Sierp, and everyone at LP. And *merci encore* to my parents, brother and *belle-sœur* for instilling in me and sustaining my lifelong love of Paris.

Christopher Pitts

Special thanks to my two great co-authors for their advice and input; to Jo, Annelies and the rest of the in-house staff who have put much hard work into making this book what it is; and to Perrine, Elliot and Celeste, for sharing with me the everyday adventure of exploring our city.

Nicola Williams

Un grand merci to the many in Paris who aided and abetted in tracking down the next best place to be in the capital, especially Lindsey Tramuta, Kasia Dietz, Nicolas Paradis, Nelly Girault, Romée de goriainoff, Ada Laferrère and Ciara Browne. Kudos to this book's original Right Bank author, Steve Fallon, whose exceptional insights and words inspired, entertained and form a large part of the current text.

ACKNOWLEDGMENTS

Cover photograph: The Eiffel Tower viewed over roof tops, JLImages/Alamy.
Illustrations pp106-7, pp198-9, pp268-9 by Javier Zarracina.

THIS BOOK

This 9th edition of Lonely Planet's *Paris* guidebook was written by Catherine Le Nevez, Chris Pitts and Nicola Williams. The 1st edition was researched and written by Daniel Robinson and Tony Wheeler. The 2nd, 3rd, 4th and 5th editions were updated by Steve Fallon. The 6th edition was updated by Steve Fallon and Annabel Hart and the 7th by Steve Fallon and Nicola Williams. The 8th edition was written by Steve Fallon, Nicola Williams and Chris Pitts. This guidebook was commissioned in Lonely Planet's London office, and produced by the following:

Commissioning Editor Joanna Cooke
Coordinating Editor Karyn Noble
Coordinating Cartographer Xavier di Toro
Coordinating Layout Designer Mazzy Prinsep
Managing Editors Barbara Delissen, Annelies Mertens
Managing Cartographer Shahara Ahmed
Managing Layout Designer Jane Hart
Assisting Editors Kate Daly, Samantha Forge, Laura Gibb, Carly Hall, Kellie Langdon, Kate Mathews, Kristin Odijk, Charlotte Orr, Alison Ridgway, Gina Tsarouhas, Luna Soo, Jeanette Wall
Assisting Cartographer Alex Leung
Cover Research Naomi Parker
Internal Image Research Aude Vauconsant
Illustrator Javier Zarracina
Language Content Branislava Vladisavljevic
Thanks to Dan Austin, Anita Banh, Imogen Bannister, Sasha Baskett, David Carroll, Nicholas Colicchia, Laura Crawford, Brigitte Ellemor, Ryan Evans, Larissa Frost, Tobias Gattineau, Chris Girdler, Jouve India, Asha Ioculari, Kate McDonell, Katie O'Connell, Trent Paton, Kirsten Rawlings, Averil Robertson, Amanda Sierp, Fiona Siseman, Gerard Walker

See also separate subindexes for:
EATING P373
DRINKING & NIGHTLIFE P375
ENTERTAINMENT P375
SHOPPING P376
SPORTS & ACTIVITIES P377
SLEEPING P377

Index

Sights 000
Map Pages **p000**
Photo Pages **p000**

C

D

Sights 000
Map Pages **p000**
Photo Pages **p000**

Sights 000
Map Pages **p000**
Photo Pages **p000**

Sights 000
Map Pages **p000**
Photo Pages **p000**

Sights 000
Map Pages **p000**
Photo Pages **p000**

EATING

Sights 000
Map Pages **p000**
Photo Pages **p000**

DRINKING & NIGHTLIFE

ENTERTAINMENT

Sights 000
Map Pages **p000**
Photo Pages **p000**

SHOPPING

SPORTS & ACTIVITIES

SLEEPING

Sights 000
Map Pages **p000**
Photo Pages **p000**

Paris Maps

Map Legend

Sights
- Beach
- Buddhist
- Castle
- Christian
- Hindu
- Islamic
- Jewish
- Monument
- Museum/Gallery
- Ruin
- Winery/Vineyard
- Zoo
- Other Sight

Eating
- Eating

Drinking & Nightlife
- Drinking & Nightlife
- Cafe

Entertainment
- Entertainment

Shopping
- Shopping

Sleeping
- Sleeping
- Camping

Sports & Activities
- Diving/Snorkelling
- Canoeing/Kayaking
- Skiing
- Surfing
- Swimming/Pool
- Walking
- Windsurfing
- Other Sports & Activities

Information
- Post Office
- Tourist Information

Transport
- Airport
- Border Crossing
- Bus
- Cable Car/ Funicular
- Cycling
- Ferry
- Metro
- Monorail
- Parking
- S-Bahn
- Taxi
- Train/Railway
- Tram
- Tube Station
- U-Bahn
- Other Transport

Routes
- Tollway
- Freeway
- Primary
- Secondary
- Tertiary
- Lane
- Unsealed Road
- Plaza/Mall
- Steps
- Tunnel
- Pedestrian Overpass
- Walking Tour
- Walking Tour Detour
- Path

Boundaries
- International
- State/Province
- Disputed
- Regional/Suburb
- Marine Park
- Cliff
- Wall

Geographic
- Hut/Shelter
- Lighthouse
- Lookout
- Mountain/Volcano
- Oasis
- Park
- Pass
- Picnic Area
- Waterfall

Hydrography
- River/Creek
- Intermittent River
- Swamp/Mangrove
- Reef
- Canal
- Water
- Dry/Salt/ Intermittent Lake
- Glacier

Areas
- Beach/Desert
- Cemetery (Christian)
- Cemetery (Other)
- Park/Forest
- Sportsground
- Sight (Building)
- Top Sight (Building)

MAP INDEX

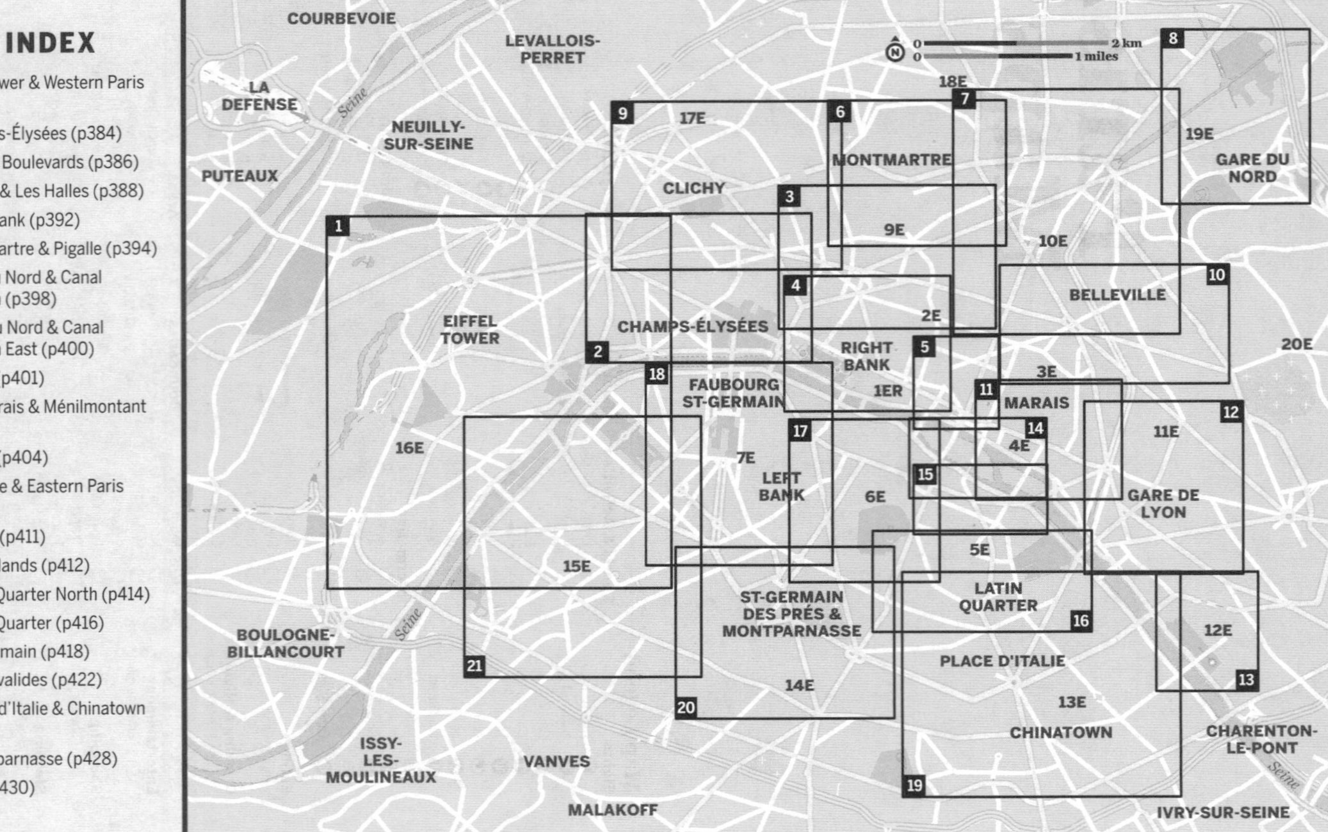

COURBEVOIE
LEVALLOIS-PERRET
N
0 2 km
0 1 miles
18E
LA DEFENSE
Seine
NEUILLY-SUR-SEINE
PUTEAUX
9
17E
6
7
8
19E
GARE DU NORD
MONTMARTRE
CLICHY
3
9E
1
10E
4
2E
EIFFEL TOWER
CHAMPS-ÉLYSÉES
BELLEVILLE
10
2
RIGHT BANK
5
20E
18
FAUBOURG ST-GERMAIN
1ER
3E
11
MARAIS
12
14
4E
11E
16E
17
7E
LEFT BANK
15
6E
GARE DE LYON
5E
15E
ST-GERMAIN DES PRÉS & MONTPARNASSE
LATIN QUARTER
16
12E
BOULOGNE-BILLANCOURT
PLACE D'ITALIE
21
14E
13
13E
20
CHINATOWN
CHARENTON-LE-PONT
ISSY-LES-MOULINEAUX
VANVES
19
MALAKOFF
IVRY-SUR-SEINE

EIFFEL TOWER & WESTERN PARIS *Map on p382*

Top Sights (p78)

- Cité de l'Architecture et du Patrimoine ... E4
- Eiffel Tower ... F5
- Musée du Quai Branly ... F4
- Musée Guimet des Arts Asiatiques ... F3
- Musée Marmottan Monet ... B5

Sights (p81)

- **1** Cinéaqua ... F4
- **2** École Militaire ... G6
- **3** Flame of Liberty Memorial ... G4
- **4** Fondation Louis Vuitton pour la Création ... B1
- **5** Fondation Pierre Bergé-Yves Saint Laurent ... G3
- **6** Galerie-Musée Baccarat ... F3
- **7** Galeries du Panthéon Bouddhique du Japon et de la Chine ... F3
- **8** Jardin d'Acclimatation ... B1
- **9** Maison de Balzac ... D5
- **10** Musée Dapper ... E2
- **11** Musée d'Art Moderne de la Ville de Paris ... F4
- **12** Musée de la Marine ... E4
- Musée de l'Homme ... (see 12)
- **13** Musée du Vin ... E5
- **14** Musée Galliera de la Mode de la Ville de Paris ... F3
- **15** Palais de Tokyo ... F4
- **16** Parc du Champ de Mars ... G5

Eating (p84)

- 58 Tour Eiffel ... (see 21)
- **17** Bert's ... G3
- **18** Café Branly ... G4
- **19** Firmin Le Barbier ... G5
- **20** L'Astrance ... E5
- Le Cristal Room ... (see 6)
- **21** Le Jules Verne ... F5
- **22** Le Petit Rétro ... E3
- **23** Les Ombres ... F4
- **24** Marché Président Wilson ... F3
- Tokyo Eat ... (see 15)

Entertainment (p87)

- **25** Marionnettes du Champ de Mars ... F5

Sports & Activities (p87)

- **26** Bateaux Parisiens ... F5
- **27** Fat Tire Bike Tours ... F5
- **28** Hippodrome d'Auteuil ... A6
- **29** Paris Cycles ... B3
- **30** Rowing Boats ... B3

Sleeping (p285)

- **31** Gentle Gourmet ... E1
- **32** Hôtel Sezz ... E5
- **33** Mon Hôtel ... E1

EIFFEL TOWER & WESTERN PARIS

Key on p381

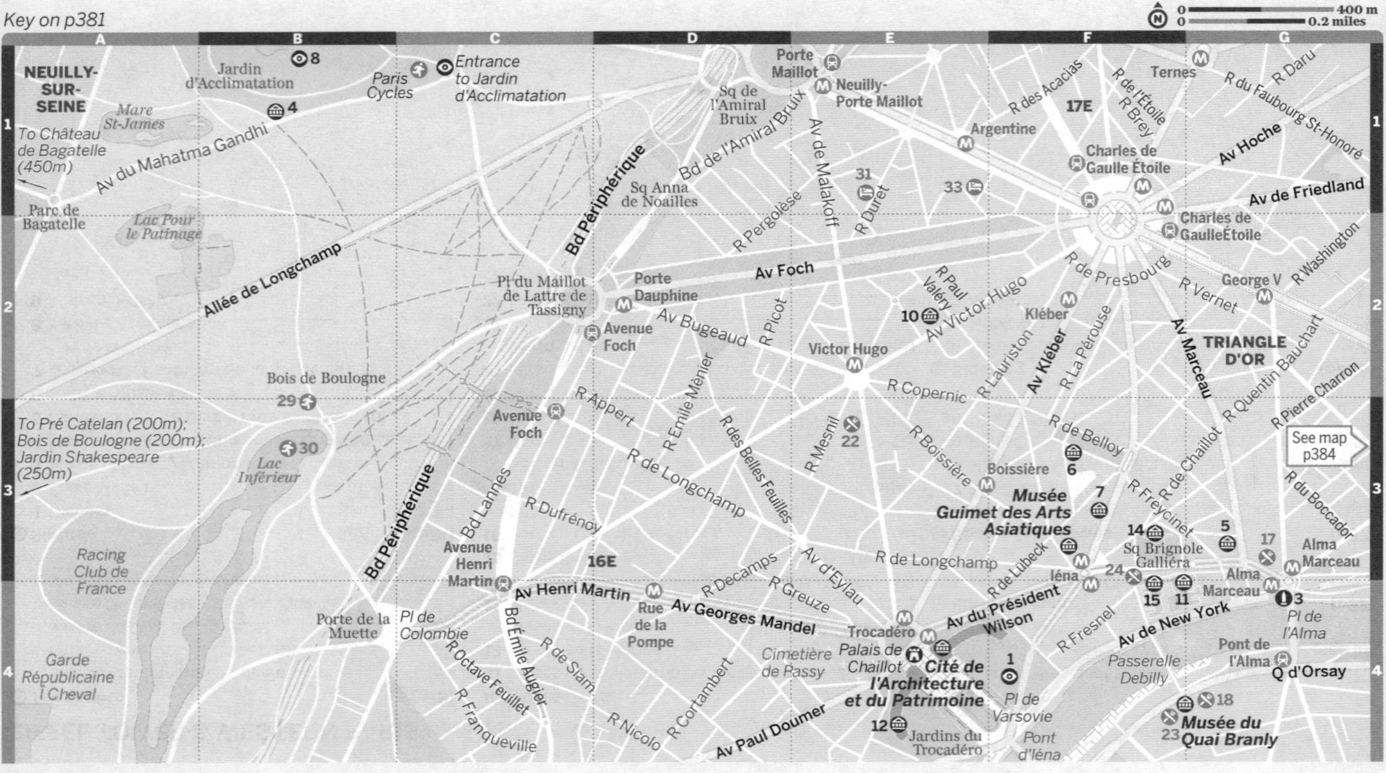

EIFFEL TOWER & WESTERN PARIS

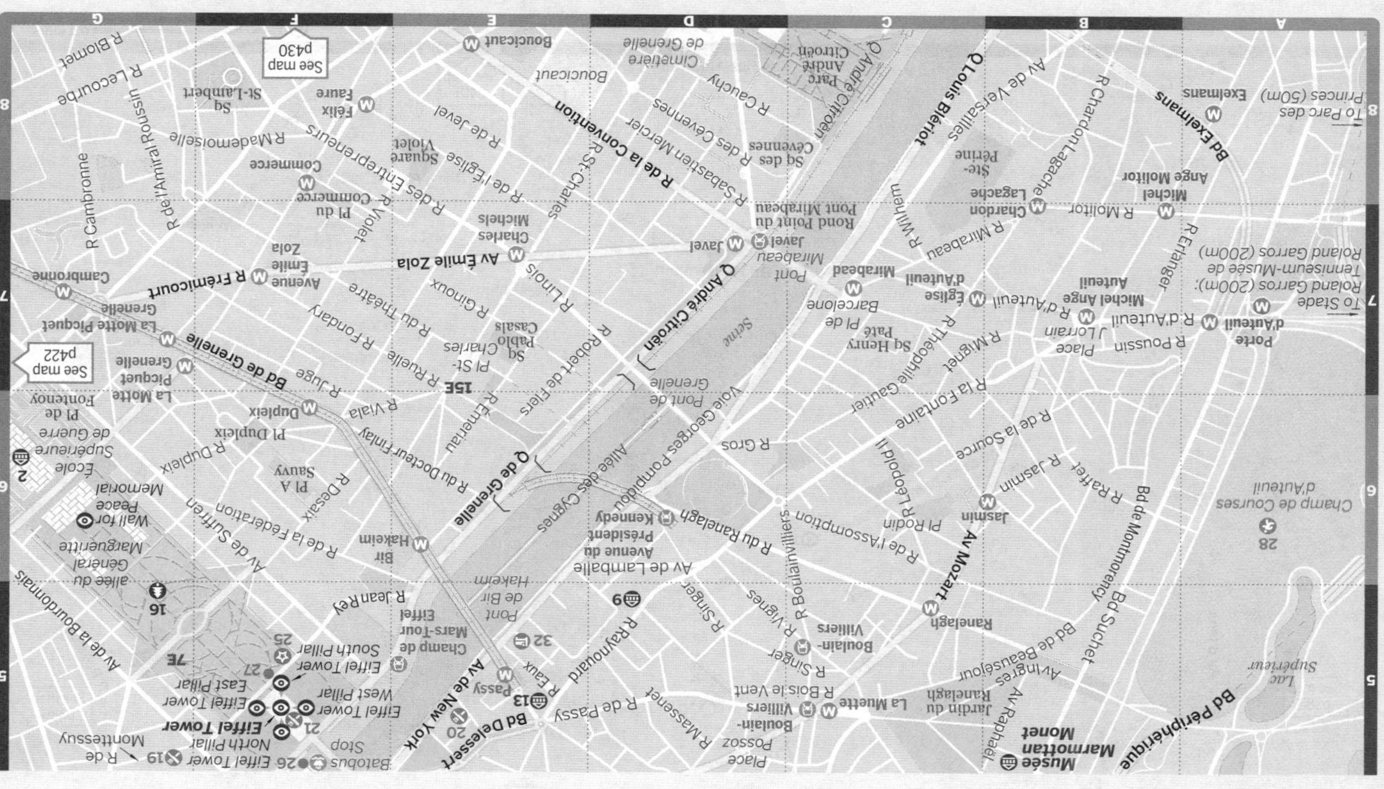

CHAMPS-ÉLYSÉES

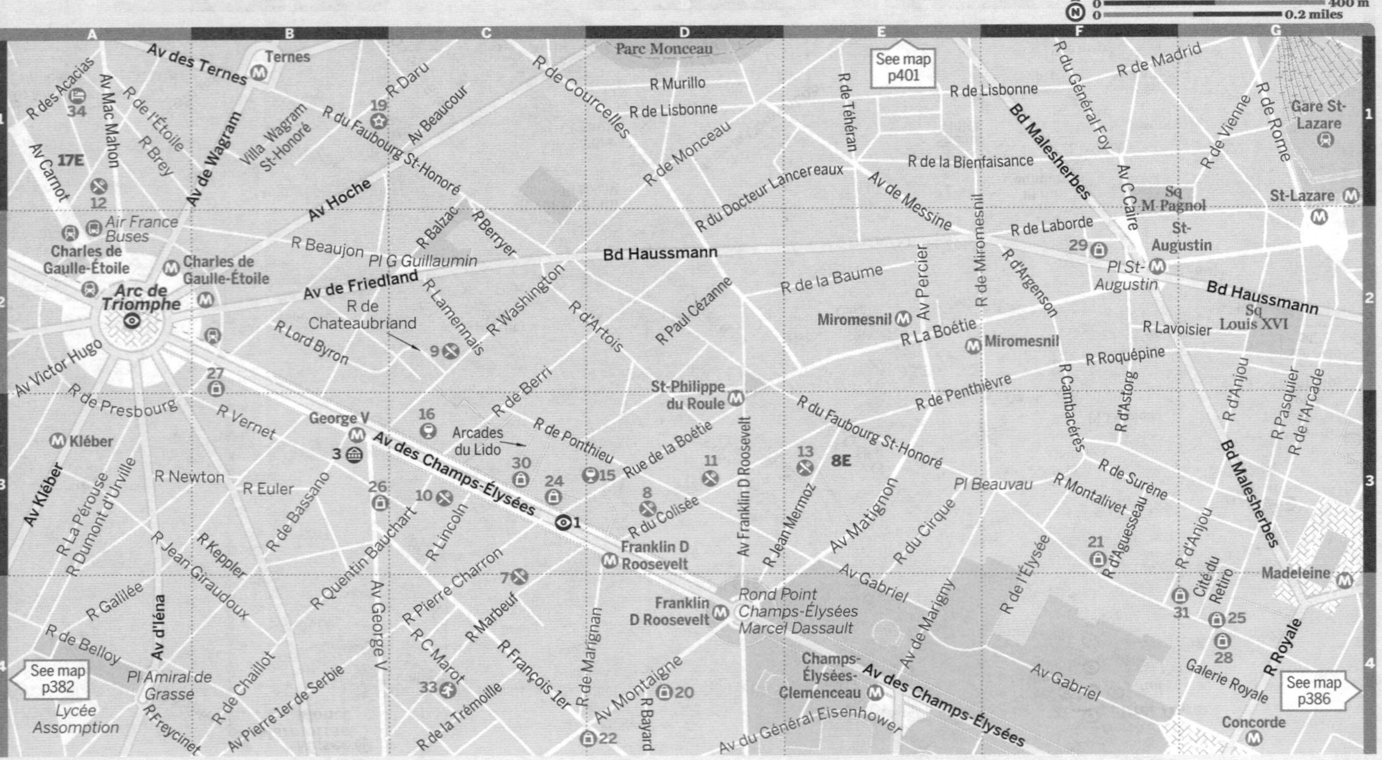

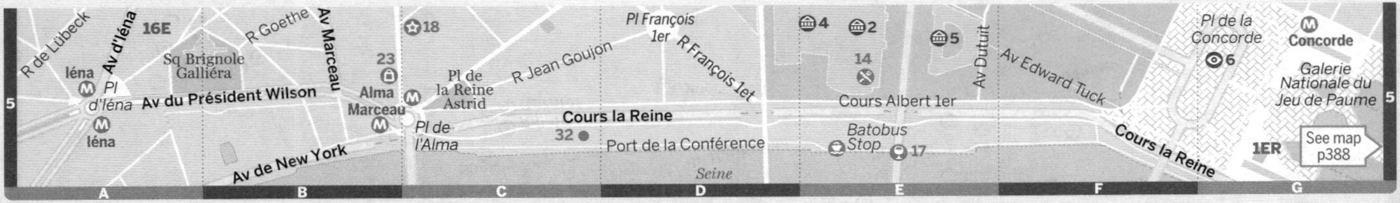

Top Sights **(p90)**
Arc de Triomphe ... A2

Sights **(p92)**
1 Avenue des Champs-Élysées ... C3
2 Grand Palais ... E5
3 Louis Vuitton Espace Culturel ... B3
4 Palais de la Découverte ... E5
5 Petit Palais ... E5
6 Place de la Concorde ... G5

Eating **(p94)**
7 Aubrac Corner ... C4
8 Caffè ... D3
9 Cojean ... C2
10 Ladurée ... C3
11 Le Boudoir ... D3
12 Le Hide ... A1
13 Makoto Aoki ... E3
14 Minipalais ... E5

Drinking & Nightlife **(p97)**
15 Charlie Birdy ... D3
16 Queen ... C3
17 ShowCase ... E5

Entertainment **(p97)**
18 Crazy Horse ... C5
19 Salle Pleyel ... B1

Shopping **(p98)**
20 Chanel ... D4
21 Chloé ... F3
22 Christian Dior ... D4
23 Givenchy ... B5
24 Guerlain ... C3
25 Hermès ... G4
26 Jean-Paul Gaultier ... B3
27 Lancel ... B2
28 Lanvin ... G4
29 Les Caves Augé ... F2
Louis Vuitton ... (see 3)
30 Séphora ... C3
31 Yves Saint Laurent ... G4

Sports & Activities **(p100)**
32 Bateaux-Mouches ... C5
33 Russie Blanche ... C4

Sleeping **(p285)**
34 Hidden Hotel ... A1

GRANDS BOULEVARDS

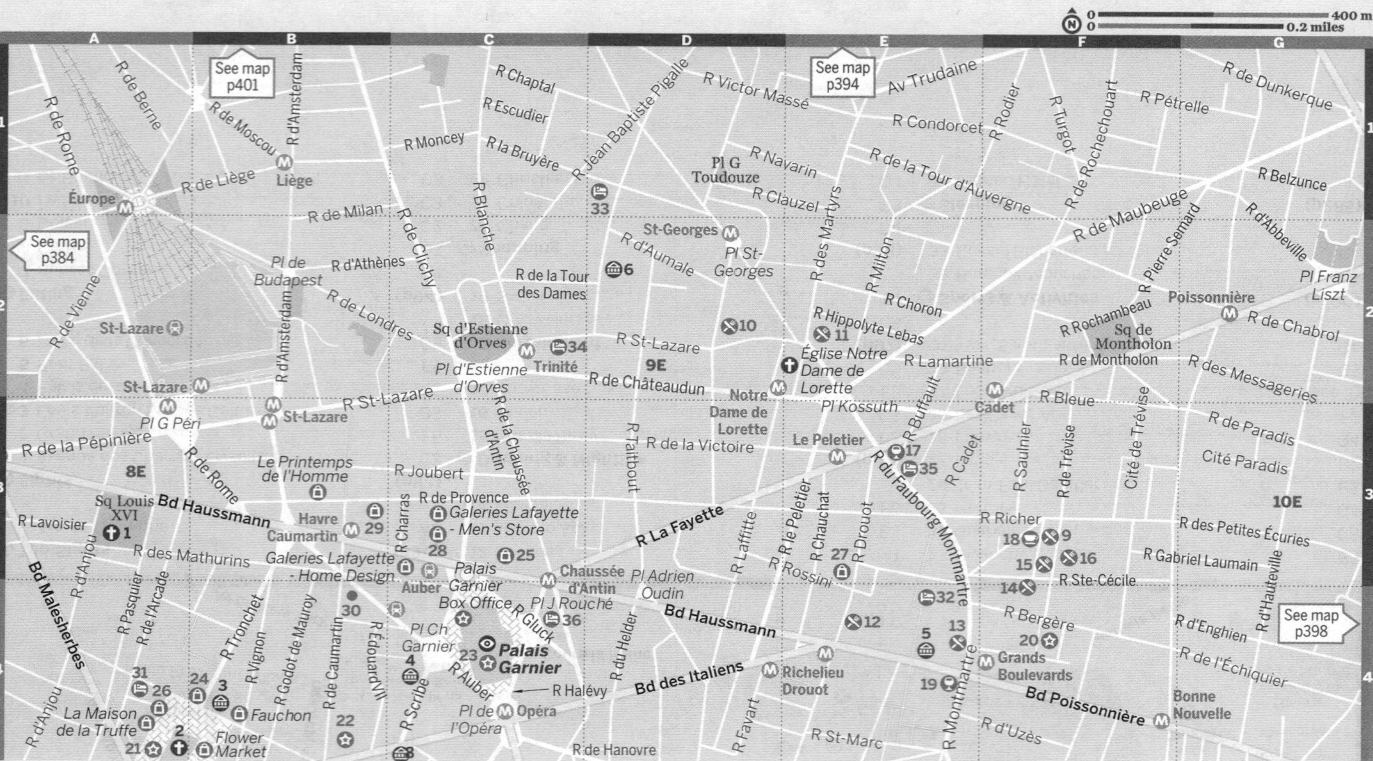

Top Sights **(p92)**
Palais Garnier C4

Sights **(p93)**
1 Chapelle Expiatoire A3
2 Église de la Madeleine A4
3 La Pinacothèque B4
4 Musée du Parfum C4
5 Musée Grévin E4
6 Musée National Gustave Moreau D2
7 Place de la Madeleine A5
8 Théâtre-Musée des Capucines C4

Eating **(p96)**
9 Autour d'un Verre F3
10 Casa Olympe D2
11 Chez Plume E2
Cojean .... (see 28)
Galeries Lafayette .... (see 25)
12 Le J'Go E4
13 Le Zinc des Cavistes E4
Les Pâtes Vivantes .... (see 35)
14 Nouveau Paris-Dakar F4
15 Prego F3
16 SuperNature F3

Drinking & Nightlife **(p97)**
17 Au Général La Fayette E3
18 Folie's Café F3
19 O'Sullivan's E4

Entertainment **(p97)**
20 Au Limonaire F4
21 Kiosque Théâtre Madeleine A4
22 L'Olympia B4
23 Palais Garnier C4

Shopping **(p98)**
24 ERES B4
25 Galeries Lafayette C3
26 Hédiard A4
27 Hôtel Drouot E3
28 Lafayette Gourmet C3
29 Le Printemps B3
Place de la Madeleine .... (see 7)

Sports & Activities **(p344)**
30 L'Open Tour B4

Sleeping **(p285)**
31 Hôtel Amarante Beau Manoir A4
32 Hôtel Chopin E4
33 Hôtel Joyce D1
34 Hôtel Langlois C2
35 Hôtel Monte Carlo E3
36 W Paris - Opéra C4

Key on p390

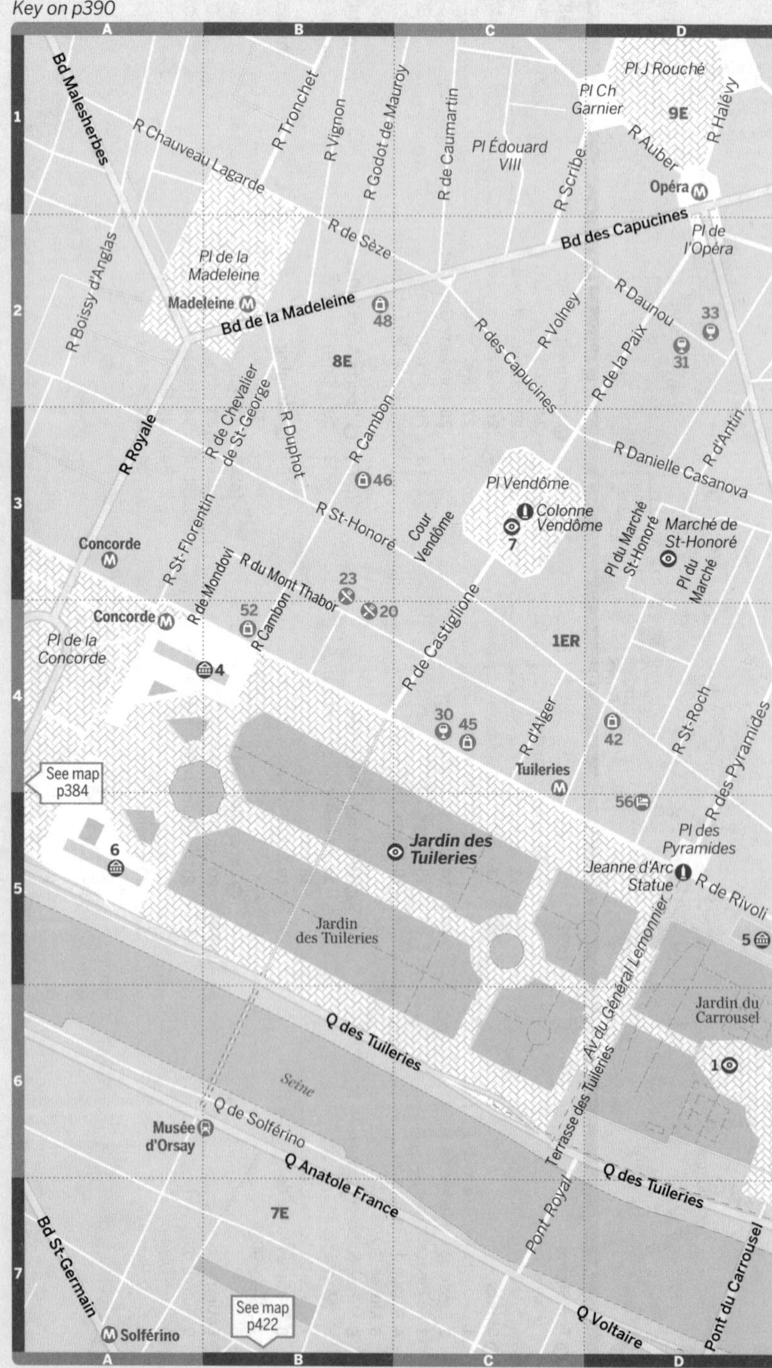
A
B
C
D
1
2
3
4
5
6
7
Bd Malesherbes
R Tronchet
R Vignon
R Godot de Mauroy
R de Caumartin
Pl Édouard VIII
Pl J Rouché
Pl Ch Garnier
9E
R Halévy
R Auber
R Scribe
Opéra
R Chauveau Lagarde
R de Sèze
Bd des Capucines
Pl de l'Opéra
R Boissy d'Anglas
Pl de la Madeleine
Madeleine
Bd de la Madeleine
48
8E
R Volney
R Daunou
33
31
R des Capucines
R de la Paix
R Royale
R de Chevalier de St-George
R Duphot
R Cambon
46
R Danielle Casanova
R d'Antin
Pl Vendôme
Colonne Vendôme
7
Marché de St-Honoré
Pl du Marché St-Honoré
Pl du Marché
R St-Honoré
Cour Vendôme
Concorde
R St-Florentin
R de Mondovi
R du Mont Thabor
23
20
52
R Cambon
Concorde
Pl de la Concorde
4
R de Castiglione
1ER
30
45
R d'Alger
42
R St-Roch
R des Pyramides
Tuileries
See map p384
56
Pl des Pyramides
6
Jardin des Tuileries
Jeanne d'Arc Statue
R de Rivoli
5
Jardin des Tuileries
Av du Général Lemonnier
Jardin du Carrousel
Q des Tuileries
1
Seine
Terrasse des Tuileries
Musée d'Orsay
Q de Solférino
Q Anatole France
Pont Royal
Q des Tuileries
7E
Pont du Carrousel
Bd St-Germain
Q Voltaire
See map p422
Solférino

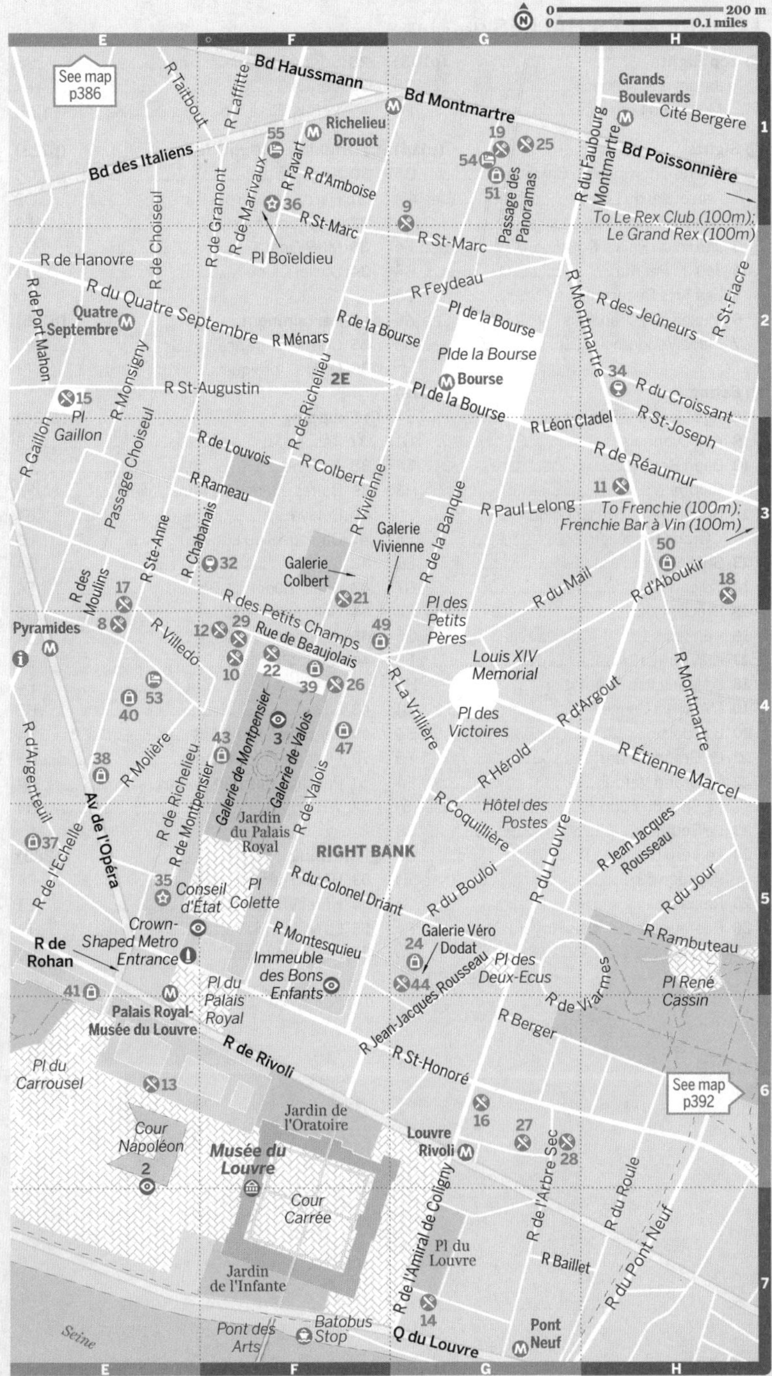
0 200 m
0 0.1 miles
E
F
G
H
See map p386
See map p392
Bd Haussmann
Bd Montmartre
Bd des Italiens
Bd Poissonnière
Grands Boulevards
Cité Bergère
Richelieu Drouot
R Taitbout
R Laffitte
R de Gramont
R de Marivaux
R Favart
R d'Amboise
R St-Marc
Pl Boïeldieu
Passage des Panoramas
R du Faubourg Montmartre
To Le Rex Club (100m); Le Grand Rex (100m)
R de Hanovre
R de Choiseul
R du Quatre Septembre
Quatre Septembre
R de Port Mahon
R Monsigny
R Ménars
R de la Bourse
R Feydeau
Pl de la Bourse
Bourse
2E
R Montmartre
R des Jeûneurs
R St-Fiacre
R du Croissant
R St-Joseph
R Léon Cladel
R de Réaumur
R St-Augustin
Pl Gaillon
R Gaillon
Passage Choiseul
R de Louvois
R Rameau
R de Richelieu
R Colbert
R Vivienne
R Paul Lelong
To Frenchie (100m); Frenchie Bar à Vin (100m)
R de la Banque
Galerie Vivienne
Galerie Colbert
R Ste-Anne
R Chabanais
R des Moulins
R des Petits Champs
Rue de Beaujolais
Pl des Petits Pères
R du Mail
R d'Aboukir
Pyramides
R Villedo
R La Vrillière
Louis XIV Memorial
Pl des Victoires
R d'Argout
R Montmartre
R Étienne Marcel
R d'Argenteuil
R Molière
Galerie de Montpensier
Galerie de Valois
R de Valois
R de Montpensier
R Hérold
Hôtel des Postes
R Coquillière
R Jean Jacques Rousseau
Av de l'Opéra
R de l'Echelle
Jardin du Palais Royal
RIGHT BANK
R du Colonel Driant
R du Bouloi
R du Louvre
R du Jour
Conseil d'État
Pl Colette
Crown-Shaped Metro Entrance
R de Rohan
R Montesquieu
Immeuble des Bons Enfants
Galerie Véro Dodat
Pl des Deux-Ecus
R Rambuteau
Pl René Cassin
R de Viarmes
R Jean-Jacques Rousseau
R Berger
Palais Royal-Musée du Louvre
Pl du Palais Royal
R de Rivoli
R St-Honoré
Pl du Carrousel
Cour Napoléon
Jardin de l'Oratoire
Musée du Louvre
Louvre Rivoli
Cour Carrée
R de l'Amiral de Coligny
Pl du Louvre
R de l'Arbre Sec
R du Roule
R du Pont Neuf
R Baillet
Jardin de l'Infante
Pont des Arts
Batobus Stop
Q du Louvre
Pont Neuf
Seine
1
2
3
4
5
6
7

LOUVRE & LES HALLES *Map on p388*

Top Sights **(p103)**

Jardin des Tuileries C5
Musée du Louvre F6

Sights **(p114)**

1 Arc de Triomphe du Carrousel D6
Carrousel du Louvre .... (see 41)
2 Grande Pyramide E6
3 Jardin du Palais Royal F4
4 Jeu de Paume B4
5 Les Arts Décoratifs D5
6 Musée de l'Orangerie A5
7 Place Vendôme C3

Eating **(p118)**

8 Ace Gourmet Bento E4
9 Aux Lyonnais G1
10 Baan Boran F4
11 Bioboa H3
12 Boulangerie Pâtisserie du Grand Richelieu F4
13 Café Marly E6
14 Cojean G7
15 Drouant E2
16 Kaï G6
17 Kunitoraya E3
18 La Mauvaise Réputation H3
19 L'Arbre à Cannelle G1
20 L'Ardoise B4
21 Le Grand Colbert F3
22 Le Grand Véfour F4
Le Saut du Loup .... (see 5)
23 Le Soufflé B3
24 Le Véro Dodat G5
Passage 53 .... (see 51)
25 Racines G1
26 Restaurant du Palais Royal F4
27 Spring G6
28 Spring Épicerie G6
29 Verjus F4
Verjus Bar à Vin .... (see 29)

Drinking & Nightlife **(p123)**

30 Angelina C4
31 Harry's New York Bar D2
32 La Champmeslé F3
33 MKP Opéra D2
34 Social Club H2

Entertainment **(p125)**

35 Comédie Française E5
36 Opéra Comique F1

Shopping **(p126)**

37 Aesop E5
38 Antoine E4
39 Boîtes à Musique Anna Joliet F4
40 Bukiya E4
41 Carrousel du Louvre E5
42 Colette D4
43 Didier Ludot F4
44 Galerie Véro Dodat G5
45 Galignani C4
46 Jamin Puech B3
47 La Petite Robe Noire F4
48 Lavinia B2
49 Legrand Filles & Fils F4
50 Librairie Gourmande H3
51 Passage des Panoramas G1
52 WH Smith B4

Sleeping **(p286)**

53 Hôtel Thérèse E4
54 Hôtel Vivienne G1
55 La Maison Favart F1
56 Le Pradey D5

RIGHT BANK AREA *Map on p392*

Top Sights (p111)
- Centre Pompidou ... G6
- Église St-Eustache ... C3

Sights (p114)
- 1 59 Rivoli ... D7
- 2 Atelier Brancusi ... G5
- 3 Bibliothèque Publique d'Information ... G5
- 4 Bourse de Commerce ... B4
- 5 Église St-Germain l'Auxerrois ... A6
- 6 Forum des Halles ... D4
- 7 Musée en Herbe ... A2
- 8 Musée National d'Art Moderne ... G6
- 9 Tour Jean sans Peur ... E2
- 10 Tour St-Jacques ... E8

Eating (p118)
- 11 Adèle's Family ... C1
- 12 Au Pied de Cochon ... B3
- 13 Beef Club ... B3
- 14 Blend ... B1
- Café Beaubourg ... (see 26)
- Café La Fusée ... (see 27)
- 15 Claus ... A4
- 16 Djakarta Bali ... B4
- Fée Nature ... (see 11)
- 17 Georges ... G6
- 18 Joe Allen ... E3
- 19 Khatag ... F4
- 20 La Bague de Kenza ... A4
- 21 Lina's Beautiful Sandwich ... B1
- 22 Racines (2) ... B5
- 23 Saveurs Végét'Halles ... C5
- 24 Ta Sushi ... F3
- 25 Yam'Tcha ... B4

Drinking & Nightlife (p123)
- 26 Café Beaubourg ... F6
- 27 Café La Fusée ... G4
- 28 Christ Inn's Bistrot ... C1
- 29 Depur ... F1
- 30 Experimental Cocktail Club ... E1
- 31 Jefrey's ... E1
- 32 Kong ... B6
- 33 Le Cœur Fou ... C1
- 34 Le Fumoir ... A6
- 35 Le Tambour ... C1
- 36 Le Troisème Lieu ... F5
- 37 Ô Chateau ... C2

Entertainment (p125)
- 38 Forum des Images ... D4
- 39 Le Baiser Salé ... E6
- 40 Sunset & Sunside ... E6
- 41 Théâtre de la Ville ... E8
- 42 Théâtre du Châtelet ... D8

Shopping (p126)
- 43 2WS ... C2
- 44 AllSaints Spitalfields ... B1
- 45 Comptoir de la Gastronomie ... C2
- 46 E Dehillerin ... B3
- 47 Kabuki Femme ... E3
- 48 Kiliwatch ... C2
- 49 Marithé & François Girbaud ... C2
- 50 Room Service ... C1

Sleeping (p286)
- 51 BVJ Paris-Louvre ... A4
- 52 Hôtel Crayon ... A3
- 53 Hôtel de la Place du Louvre ... A7
- 54 Hôtel O ... A2
- 55 Hôtel St-Merry ... F7
- 56 Hôtel Tiquetonne ... F2
- 57 Le Relais du Louvre ... A7
- 58 Pocket Palace ... A2

RIGHT BANK

Key on p391

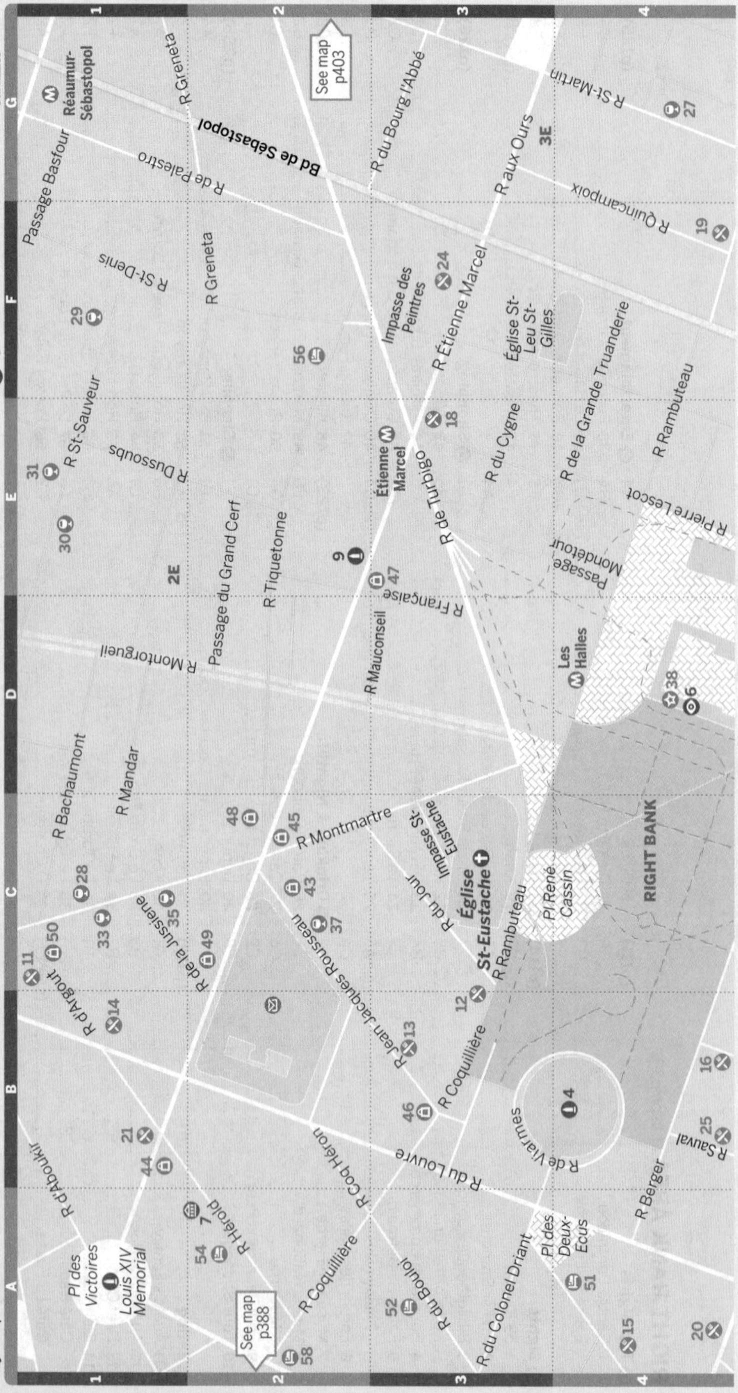

0 200 m
0 0.1 miles

A B C D E F G
1 2 3 4

Pl des Victoires
Louis XIV Memorial
R d'Aboukir
R d'Argout
R Bachaumont
R Mandar
R de la Jussiene
R Hérold
R Coquillière
R Coq Héron
R Jean Jacques Rousseau
R Montmartre
R Montorgueil
Passage du Grand Cerf
R Tiquetonne
R Mauconseil
R Française
R St-Sauveur
R Dussoubs
R St-Denis
Passage Basfour
Réaumur-Sébastopol
R de Palestro
Bd de Sébastopol
R Greneta
R Greneta
2E
Étienne Marcel
R de Turbigo
Impasse des Peintres
R Étienne Marcel
R du Bourg l'Abbé
R du Bouloi
R du Louvre
R du Jour
Impasse St-Eustache
Église St-Eustache
R Rambuteau
R du Colonel Driant
Pl des Deux-Ecus
R de Viarmes
Pl René Cassin
Les Halles
Passage Mondétour
R Pierre Lescot
R du Cygne
Église St-Leu St-Gilles
R de la Grande Truanderie
R aux Ours
3E
R Quincampoix
R St-Martin
R Rambuteau
R Berger
R Sauval
RIGHT BANK

See map p388
See map p403

1 2 4 6 7 9 11 12 13 14 15 16 18 19 20 21 24 25 27 28 29 30 31 33 35 37 38 43 44 45 46 47 48 49 50 51 52 54 56 58

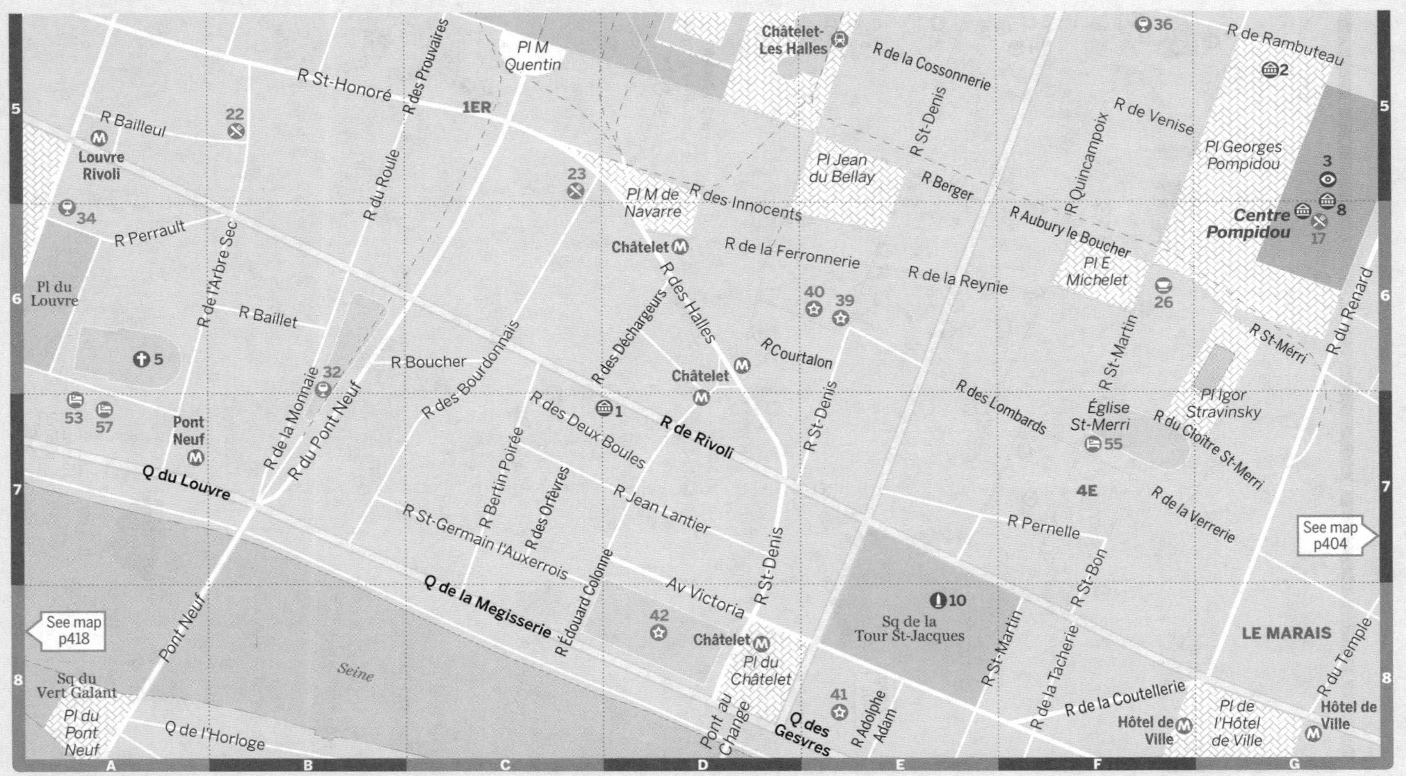
RIGHT BANK
R St-Honoré
R des Prouvaires
Pl M Quentin
1ER
Châtelet-Les Halles
R de la Cossonnerie
R de Rambuteau
R Bailleul
Louvre Rivoli
R du Roule
R St-Denis
R de Venise
Pl Georges Pompidou
Pl Jean du Bellay
R Quincampoix
R Berger
Pl M de Navarre
R des Innocents
Centre Pompidou
R Perrault
R de l'Arbre Sec
Châtelet
R de la Ferronnerie
R Aubury le Boucher
Pl E Michelet
R de la Reynie
Pl du Louvre
R Baillet
R des Déchargeurs
R des Halles
R Courtalon
R St-Martin
R du Renard
R St-Merri
R Boucher
R des Bourdonnais
Pl Igor Stravinsky
R des Lombards
Église St-Merri
R du Cloître St-Merri
R de la Monnaie
R du Pont Neuf
R des Deux Boules
R de Rivoli
Pont Neuf
Q du Louvre
R Bertin Poirée
R des Orfèvres
R Jean Lantier
4E
R de la Verrerie
R St-Germain l'Auxerrois
R Pernelle
See map p404
R Édouard Colonne
Av Victoria
R St-Bon
Q de la Megisserie
Sq de la Tour St-Jacques
See map p418
LE MARAIS
R du Temple
Pl du Châtelet
R de la Tacherie
Seine
Sq du Vert Galant
R de la Coutellerie
Pl du Pont Neuf
Q de l'Horloge
Pont au Change
Q des Gesvres
R Adolphe Adam
Hôtel de Ville
Pl de l'Hôtel de Ville

Key on p396

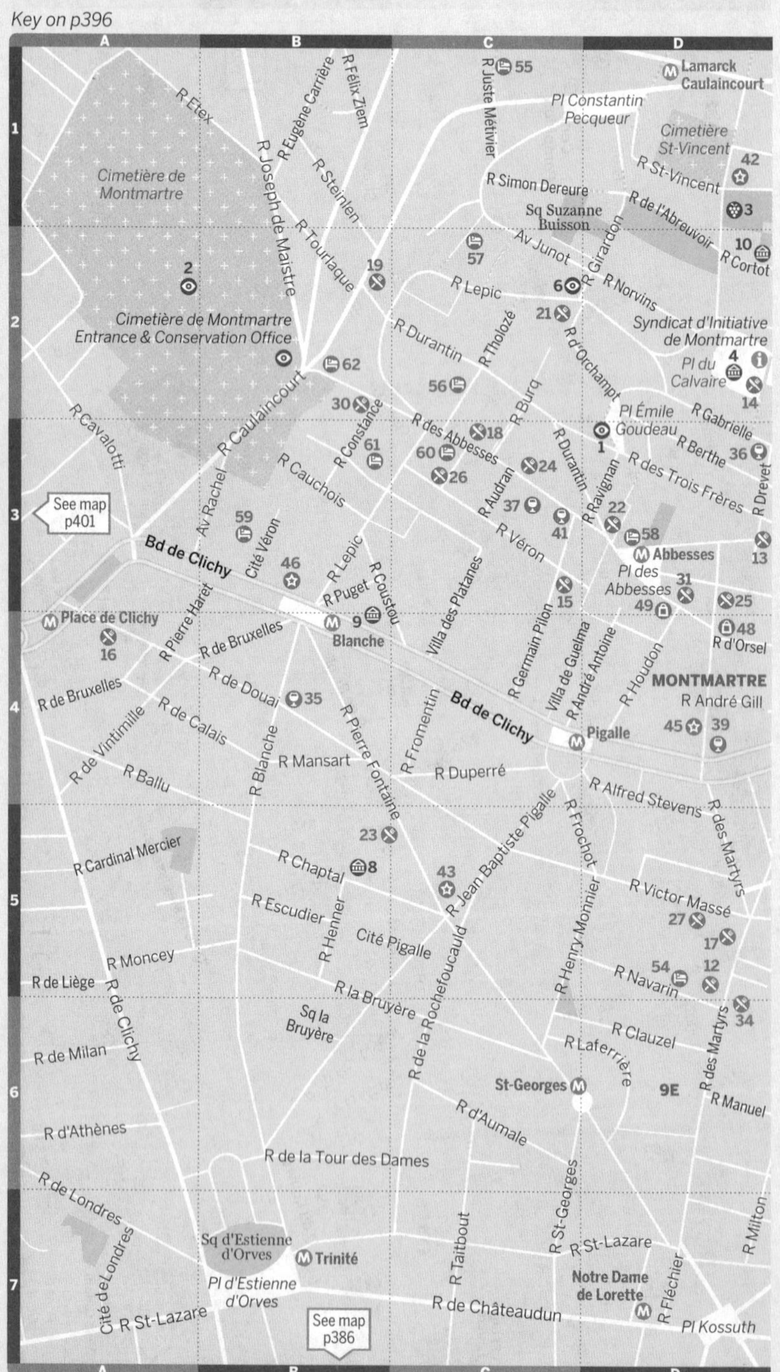

Cimetière de Montmartre
Cimetière de Montmartre Entrance & Conservation Office
R Etex
R Eugène Carrière
R Félix Ziem
R Joseph de Maistre
R Steinlen
R Tourlaque
R Caulaincourt
R Cavalotti
See map p401
Av Rachel
Bd de Clichy
Cité Véron
R Lepic
R Puget
R Coustou
Blanche
Place de Clichy
R Pierre Haret
R de Bruxelles
R de Douai
R de Calais
R de Vintimille
R Ballu
R Blanche
R Mansart
R Pierre Fontaine
R Fromentin
R Duperré
R Cardinal Mercier
R Chaptal
R Escudier
R Henner
Cité Pigalle
R Moncey
R de Liège
R de Clichy
R la Bruyère
Sq la Bruyère
R de Milan
R d'Athènes
R de la Tour des Dames
R de Londres
Cité de Londres
Sq d'Estienne d'Orves
Trinité
Pl d'Estienne d'Orves
R St-Lazare
See map p386
R Juste Métivier
Pl Constantin Pecqueur
Lamarck Caulaincourt
Cimetière St-Vincent
R St-Vincent
R Simon Dereure
Sq Suzanne Buisson
R de l'Abreuvoir
R Cortot
Av Junot
R Girardon
R Norvins
R Lepic
Syndicat d'Initiative de Montmartre
R Tholozé
R Durantin
R d'Orchampt
Pl du Calvaire
R Burq
Pl Émile Goudeau
R Gabrielle
R Berthe
R des Abbesses
R Constance
R Cauchois
R Audran
R Durantin
R Ravignan
R des Trois Frères
R Drevet
R Véron
Abbesses
Pl des Abbesses
Villa des Platanes
R d'Orsel
R Germain Pilon
Villa de Guelma
R André Antoine
R Houdon
MONTMARTRE
R André Gill
Pigalle
R Alfred Stevens
R des Martyrs
R Jean Baptiste Pigalle
R Frochot
R Victor Massé
R de la Rochefoucauld
R Henry Monnier
R Navarin
R Clauzel
R Laferrière
St-Georges
9E
R Manuel
R d'Aumale
R St-Georges
R Taitbout
R Milton
Notre Dame de Lorette
R Fléchier
R de Châteaudun
Pl Kossuth

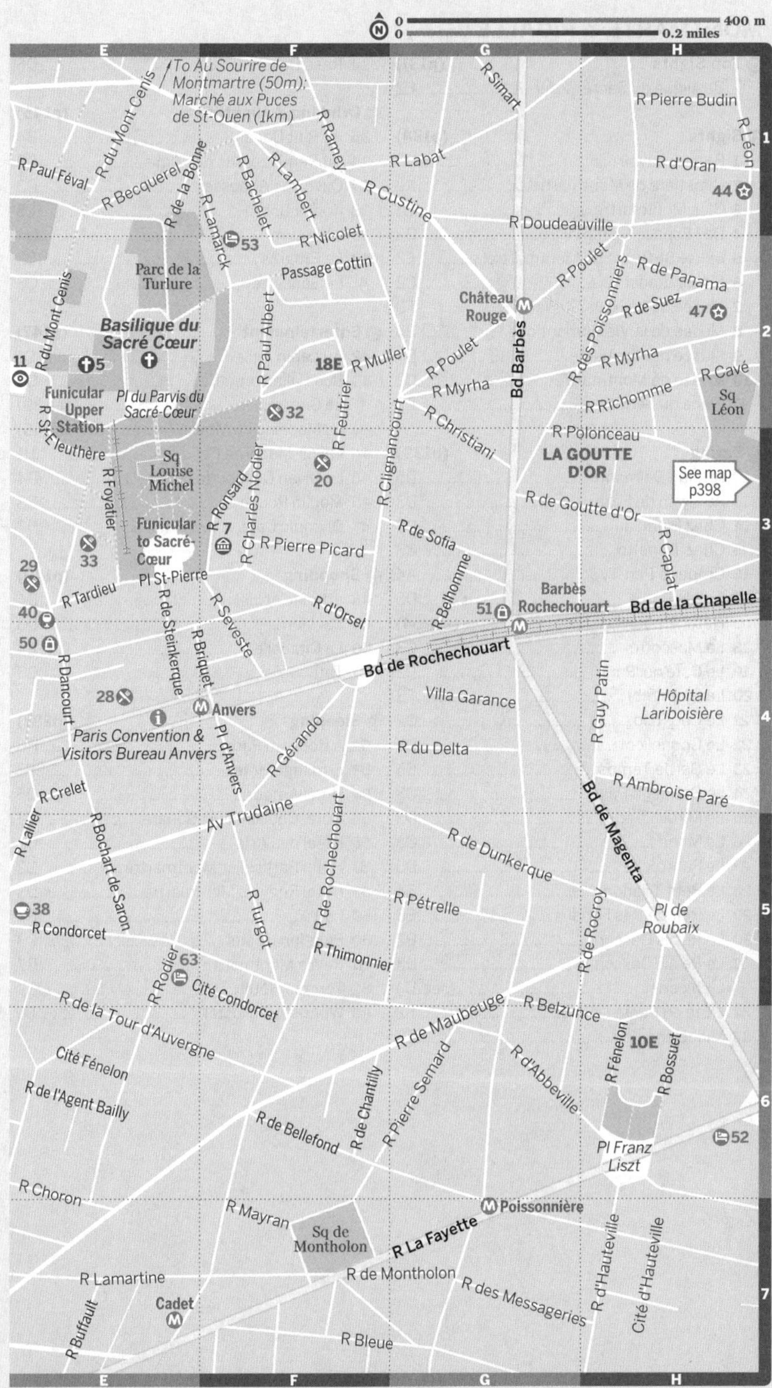
MONTMARTRE & PIGALLE
0
400 m
0
0.2 miles
To Au Sourire de Montmartre (50m); Marché aux Puces de St-Ouen (1km)
R du Mont Cenis
R Paul Féval
R Becquerel
R de la Bonne
R Lamarck
R Bachelet
R Lambert
R Ramey
R Labat
R Custine
R Simart
R Pierre Budin
R Léon
R d'Oran
R Doudeauville
R Nicolet
Parc de la Turlure
Passage Cottin
R Poulet
R des Poissonniers
R de Panama
R de Suez
Château Rouge
Basilique du Sacré Cœur
R Paul Albert
18E
R Muller
Bd Barbès
R Myrha
R Cavé
Sq Léon
Funicular Upper Station
Pl du Parvis du Sacré-Cœur
R Feutrier
R Clignancourt
R Christiani
R Richomme
R Polonceau
LA GOUTTE D'OR
R St-Eleuthère
Sq Louise Michel
R Foyatier
R Charles Nodier
R Ronsard
R de Goutte d'Or
See map p398
Funicular to Sacré-Cœur
R Pierre Picard
R de Sofia
R Caplat
Pl St-Pierre
R Tardieu
R de Steinkerque
R Seveste
R d'Orsel
R Belhomme
Barbès Rochechouart
Bd de la Chapelle
R Briquet
Bd de Rochechouart
R Dancourt
Villa Garance
R Guy Patin
Hôpital Lariboisière
Anvers
Paris Convention & Visitors Bureau Anvers
Pl d'Anvers
R Gérando
R du Delta
R Crelet
R Lallier
R Bochart de Saron
Av Trudaine
R de Rochechouart
Bd de Magenta
R Ambroise Paré
R de Dunkerque
R Turgot
R Pétrelle
Pl de Roubaix
R Condorcet
R Thimonnier
R de Rocroy
R Rodier
Cité Condorcet
R de la Tour d'Auvergne
R de Maubeuge
R Belzunce
R d'Abbeville
R Fénelon
10E
R Bossuet
Cité Fénelon
R de l'Agent Bailly
R Pierre Semard
R de Chantilly
R de Bellefond
Pl Franz Liszt
R Choron
R Mayran
Sq de Montholon
R La Fayette
Poissonnière
R Lamartine
R de Montholon
R des Messageries
R d'Hauteville
Cité d'Hauteville
Cadet
R Buffault
R Bleue
E
F
G
H
1
2
3
4
5
6
7
5
7
11
20
28
29
32
33
38
40
44
47
50
51
52
53
63

MONTMARTE & PIGALLE *Map on p394*

Top Sights (p131)

Basilique du Sacré-Cœur E2

Sights (p134)

1 Bateau Lavoir D3
2 Cimetière de Montmartre A2
3 Clos Montmartre D1
4 Dalí Espace Montmartre D2
5 Église St-Pierre de Montmartre E2
6 Moulin Radet C2
7 Musée de La Halle St-Pierre F3
8 Musée de la Vie Romantique B5
9 Musée de l'Érotisme B4
10 Musée de Montmartre D2
11 Place du Tertre E2

Eating (p139)

12 Arnaud Delmontel D5
13 Au Grain de Folie D3
14 Chez Plumeau D2
15 Chez Toinette C3
16 Crêperie Pen-Ty A4
17 Cul de Poule D5
Hôtel Amour .... (see 54)
18 La Mascotte C3
19 Le Café qui Parle B2
20 Le Chéri Bibi F3
21 Le Coq Rico C2
22 Le Coquelicot D3
23 Le Garde Temps B5
24 Le Grenier à Pain C3
25 Le Miroir D3
26 Le Mono C3
27 Le Pantruche D5
28 Le Petit Trianon E4
29 Le Refuge Des Fondus E3
30 Le Relais Gascon B2
31 Le Relais Gascon D3
L'Épicerie .... (see 17)
32 L'Été en Pente Douce F2
33 Michelangelo E3
34 Rose Bakery D6

Drinking & Nightlife (p145)

35 Au P'tit Douai B4
36 Au Rendez-Vous des Amis D3
37 Cave des Abbesses C3
38 Kooka Boora E5
39 La Fourmi D4
40 Le Progrès E3
41 Le Sancerre C3

Entertainment (p147)

42 Au Lapin Agile D1
43 Bus Palladium C5
La Cigale .... (see 39)
La Machine du Moulin Rouge .... (see 46)
44 Lavoir Moderne Parisien H1
45 Le Divan Du Monde D4
46 Moulin Rouge B3
47 Olympic Café H2

Shopping (p149)

48 Antoine et Lili D4
49 Ets Lion D3
50 La Citadelle E4
51 Tati G3

Sleeping (p287)

52 A Room in Paris H6
53 Ermitage Hôtel F2
54 Hôtel Amour D5
55 Hotel Caulaincourt Square C1
56 Hôtel des Arts C2
57 Hôtel Particulier Montmartre C2
58 Hôtel Regyn's Montmartre D3
59 Loft B3
60 Plug-Inn Hostel C3
61 Relais Montmartre B3
62 Terrass Hôtel B2
63 Woodstock Hostel E5

GARE DU NORD & CANAL ST-MARTIN *Map on p398*

Map on p398

Sights (p136)
1 Canal St-Martin ... D6
2 Le 104 ... F1
3 Musée de l'Évantail ... B8
4 Porte St-Denis & Porte St-Martin ... B7

Eating (p142)
5 Albion ... A5
6 Bistrot des Faubourgs ... C6
7 Bob's Juice Bar ... D7
Chez Casimir ... (see 8)
8 Chez Michel ... B4
9 Dishny ... C3
10 Du Pain et des Idées ... D7
11 Jambo ... F6
12 Jardin des Voluptés ... B7
13 Krishna Bhavan ... C3
14 La Cantine de Quentin ... D6
15 La Marine ... D7
16 La Rotonde ... F3
17 La Sardine ... F6
18 Le Cambodge ... E7
19 Le Chansonnier ... D5
20 Le Grenier à Pain ... A5
21 Le Réveil Du Xe ... C7
22 Le Verre Volé ... D6
23 L'Office ... A6
24 Madame Shawn ... D7
25 Marché St-Quentin ... B5
Philou ... (see 18)
26 Pink Flamingo ... D6
27 Terminus Nord ... B4
28 Vivant ... A6
Zuzu's Petals ... (see 18)

Drinking & Nightlife (p146)
29 Café Chéri(e) ... G6
30 Chez Jeanette ... B7
31 Chez Prune ... D7
32 DeLaVille Café ... A7
33 Hôtel du Nord ... D6
34 L'Atmosphère ... D6
35 Le Jemmapes ... E7
36 Swinging Londress ... B6

Entertainment (p148)
37 Alhambra ... D7
Le 104 ... (see 2)
38 New Morning ... B6
39 Point Éphémère ... E4

Shopping (p150)
40 Antoine et Lili ... D6
Bazar Éthic ... (see 41)
41 Liza Korn ... D7
42 Maje ... D7

Sports & Activities (p151)
43 Canauxrama ... F3
44 Cook'n With Class ... A1
45 Vélib' ... A3

Sleeping (p287)
46 Hôtel du Nord – Le Pari Vélo ... D7
47 Le Citizen Hotel ... D6
48 République Hôtel ... D8
49 St Christopher's Inn ... C4

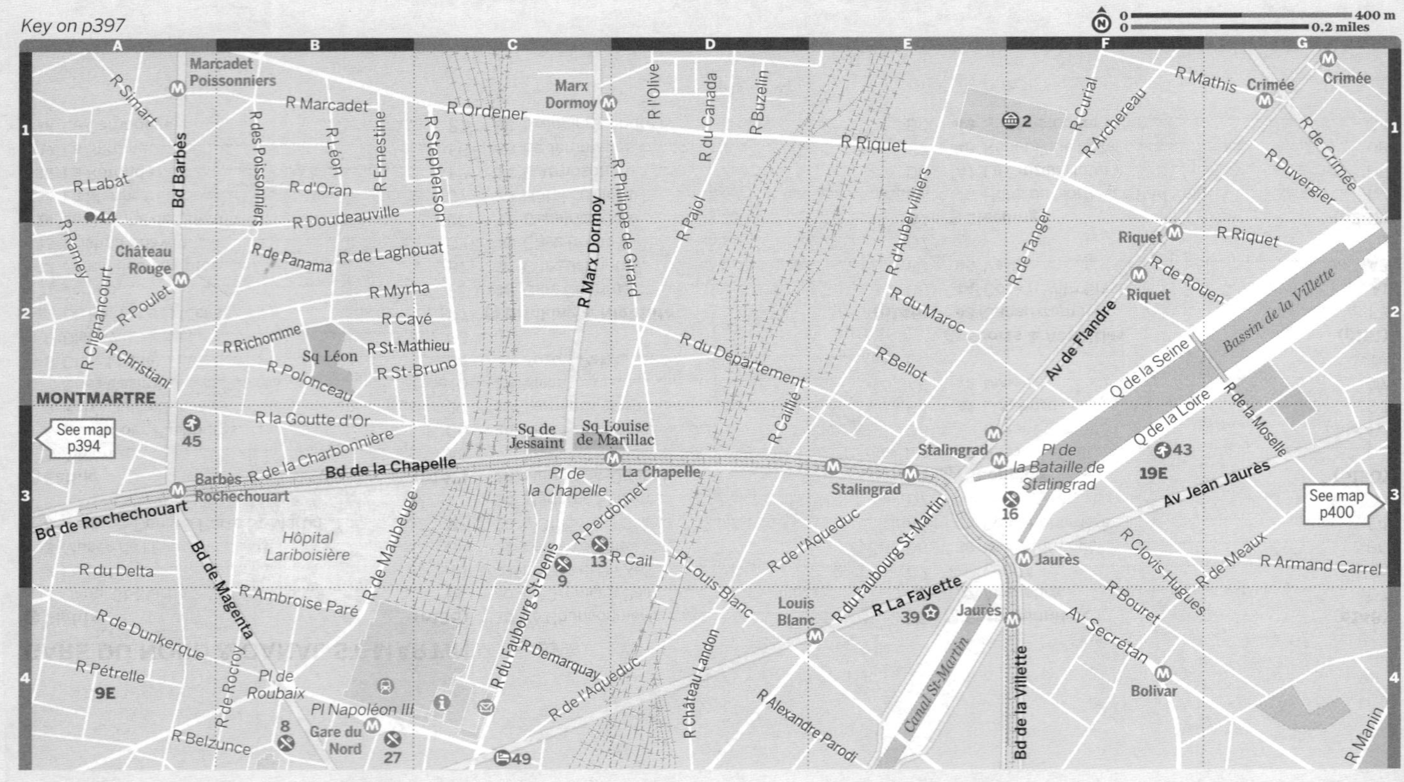
GARE DU NORD & CANAL ST-MARTIN
Key on p397
400 m
0.2 miles
See map p394
See map p400
MONTMARTRE
19E
9E
Marcadet Poissonniers
R Simart
R Marcadet
R Ordener
Marx Dormoy
R l'Olive
R du Canada
R Buzelin
R Riquet
R Curial
R Archereau
R Mathis
Crimée
R de Crimée
R Duvergier
R Labat
Bd Barbès
R des Poissonniers
R Léon
R Ernestine
R Stephenson
R d'Oran
R Doudeauville
R Marx Dormoy
R Philippe de Girard
R Pajol
R d'Aubervilliers
R de Tanger
Riquet
R de Rouen
R Ramey
Château Rouge
R de Panama
R de Laghouat
R Myrha
R Cavé
R Clignancourt
R Poulet
R Richomme
Sq Léon
R St-Mathieu
R St-Bruno
R Christiani
R Polonceau
R du Département
R du Maroc
R Bellot
Av de Flandre
Bassin de la Villette
Q de la Seine
Q de la Loire
R de la Moselle
R la Goutte d'Or
Sq de Jessaint
Sq Louise de Marillac
R Caillié
Stalingrad
Pl de la Bataille de Stalingrad
R de la Charbonnière
Bd de la Chapelle
Pl de la Chapelle
La Chapelle
Barbès Rochechouart
Bd de Rochechouart
Av Jean Jaurès
Hôpital Lariboisière
R de Maubeuge
R Perdonnet
R Cail
R de l'Aqueduc
R du Faubourg St-Martin
R Clovis Hugues
R de Meaux
R Armand Carrel
R du Delta
Bd de Magenta
R du Faubourg St-Denis
R Louis Blanc
Jaurès
R Ambroise Paré
Louis Blanc
R La Fayette
R Bouret
R de Dunkerque
Av Secrétan
R Pétrelle
R de Rocroy
Pl de Roubaix
R Demarquay
R Château Landon
Canal St-Martin
Bd de la Villette
Bolivar
Pl Napoléon III
R Alexandre Parodi
R Belzunce
Gare du Nord
R Manin
2
8
9
13
16
27
39
43
44
45
49

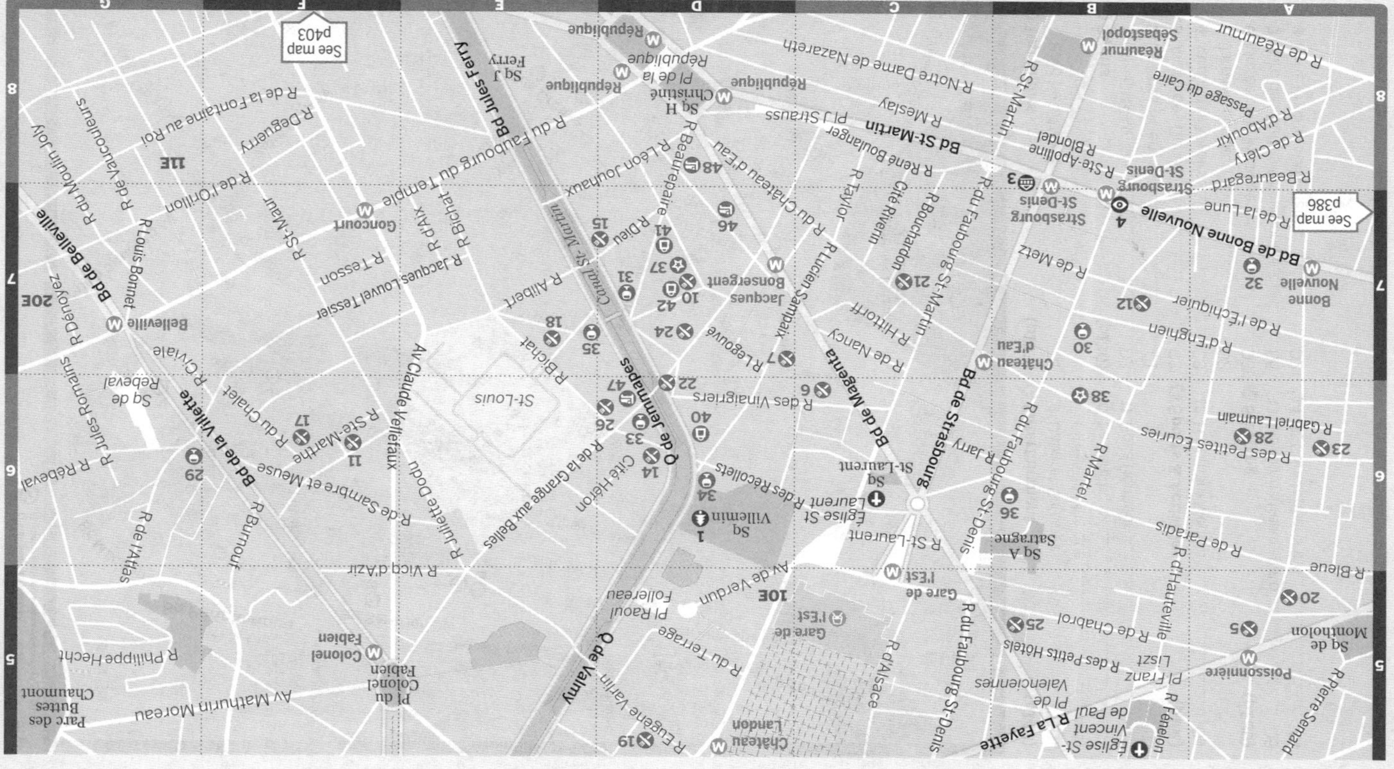
Parc des Buttes Chaumont
R Philippe Hecht
Av Mathurin Moreau
Pl du Colonel Fabien
Colonel Fabien
R Rébeval
R Jules Romains
R Dénoyez
Bd de Belleville
R du Moulin Joly
R de Vaucouleurs
R Louis Bonnet
Belleville
20E
11E
Sq de Rebeval
R de l'Atlas
R Burnouf
Bd de la Villette
R Civiale
R du Chalet
R de l'Orillon
R de la Fontaine au Roi
R Deguerry
R St-Maur
R Ste-Marthe
R de Sambre et Meuse
R Vicq d'Azir
R Juliette Dodu
Av Claude Vellefaux
R Tesson
R Jacques Louvel Tessier
Goncourt
R d'Aix
R Bichat
R du Faubourg du Temple
Bd Jules Ferry
Sq J Ferry
St-Louis
R de la Grange aux Belles
R Alibert
Canal St-Martin
R Bichat
Cité Héron
Q de Jemmapes
R Dieu
R Léon Jouhaux
République
Pl de la République
Sq H Christiné
R Beaurepaire
Q de Valmy
R Eugène Varlin
Pl Raoul Follereau
R du Terrage
Av de Verdun
Sq Villemin
R des Récollets
R des Vinaigriers
R Legouvé
Jacques Bonsergent
R Lucien Sampaix
R du Château d'Eau
Château Landon
Gare de l'Est
10E
Église St Laurent
Sq St-Laurent
Bd de Magenta
R de Nancy
R Hittorff
R Taylor
Cité Riverin
R René Boulanger
Pl J Strauss
R d'Alsace
R St-Laurent
Bd de Strasbourg
R du Faubourg St-Martin
R Bouchardon
Bd St-Martin
R Meslay
R Notre Dame de Nazareth
R du Faubourg St-Denis
R Jarry
Château d'Eau
R St-Martin
Église St-Vincent de Paul
R La Fayette
Pl de Valenciennes
R des Petits Hôtels
R de Chabrol
Sq A Satragne
R Martel
R de Metz
Strasbourg St-Denis
R Ste-Apolline
R Blondel
Réaumur Sébastopol
R Fénelon
Pl Franz Liszt
R d'Hauteville
R de Paradis
R des Petites Écuries
R Gabriel Laumain
R d'Enghien
R de l'Échiquier
Bd de Bonne Nouvelle
R de la Lune
R Beauregard
R de Cléry
R d'Aboukir
Passage du Caire
R de Réaumur
Poissonnière
Sq de Montholon
R Pierre Semard
R Bleue
Bonne Nouvelle
See map p386
See map p403
1
3
4
5
6
7
10
11
12
14
15
17
18
19
20
21
22
23
24
25
26
28
29
30
31
32
33
34
35
36
37
38
40
41
42
46
47
48
A
B
C
D
E
F
G

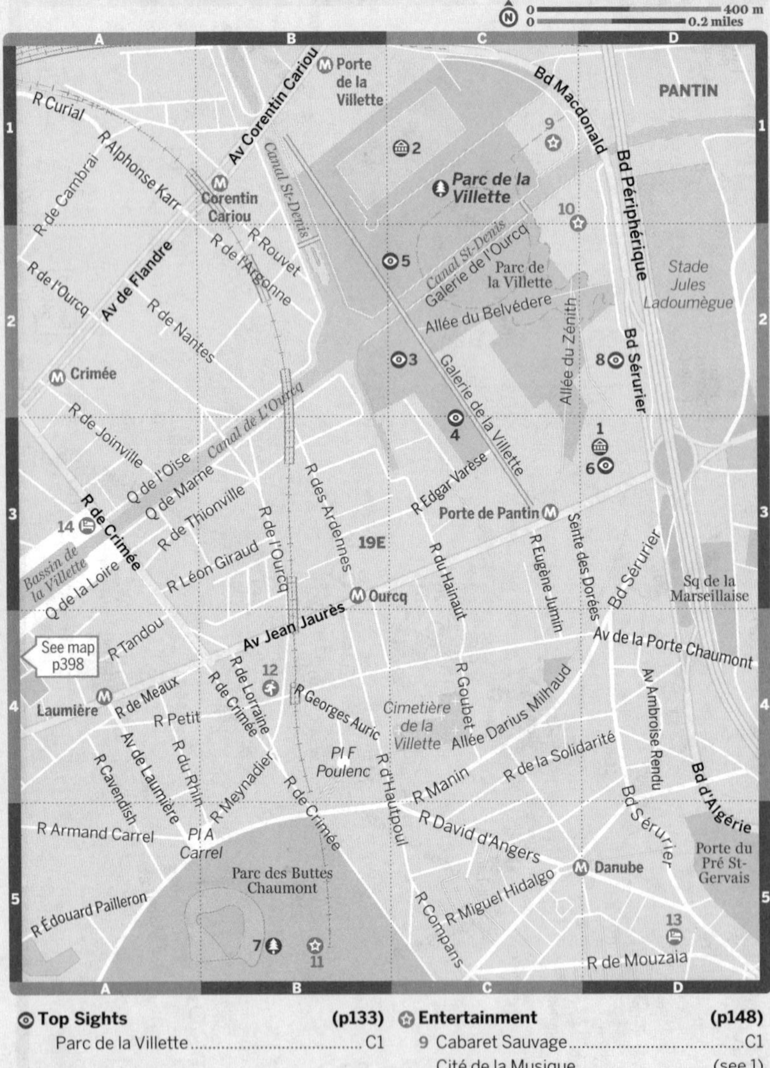

Top Sights (p133)
Parc de la Villette ... C1

Sights (p136)
1 Cité de la Musique ... D3
2 Cité des Sciences ... C1
3 Jardin des Dunes ... C2
4 Jardin des Miroirs ... C3
5 Jardin du Dragon ... C2
6 Musée de la Musique ... D3
7 Parc des Buttes-Chaumont ... B5
8 Paris Philharmonic hall ... D2

Entertainment (p148)
9 Cabaret Sauvage ... C1
Cité de la Musique ... (see 1)
10 Le Zénith ... C1
11 Rosa Bonheur ... B5

Sports & Activities (p151)
12 Hammam Medina ... B4

Sleeping (p289)
13 Manoir de Beauregard ... D5
14 St Christopher's Inn ... A3

CLICHY

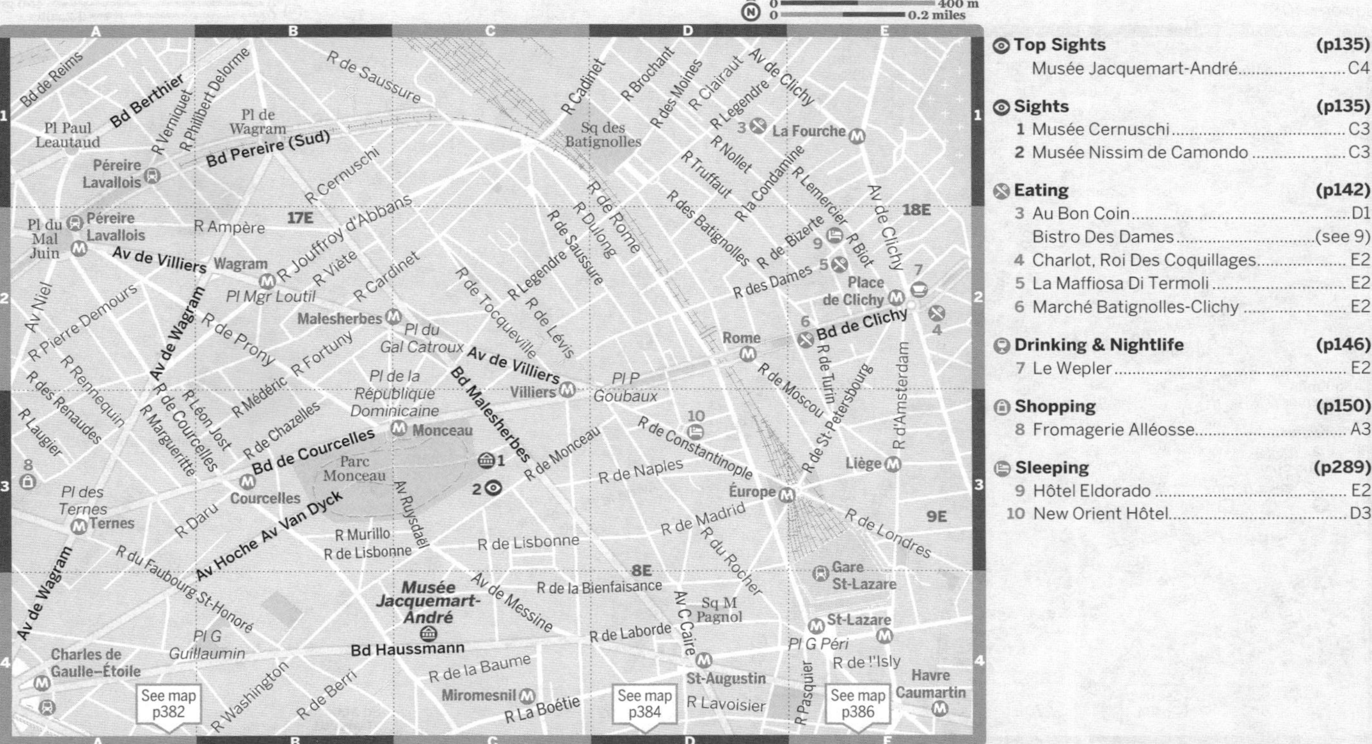

Top Sights (p135)

Musée Jacquemart-André C4

Sights (p135)

1 Musée Cernuschi C3
2 Musée Nissim de Camondo C3

Eating (p142)

3 Au Bon Coin D1
Bistro Des Dames .... (see 9)
4 Charlot, Roi Des Coquillages E2
5 La Maffiosa Di Termoli E2
6 Marché Batignolles-Clichy E2

Drinking & Nightlife (p146)

7 Le Wepler E2

Shopping (p150)

8 Fromagerie Alléosse A3

Sleeping (p289)

9 Hôtel Eldorado E2
10 New Orient Hôtel D3

LE MARAIS & MÉNILMONTANT

Key on p403

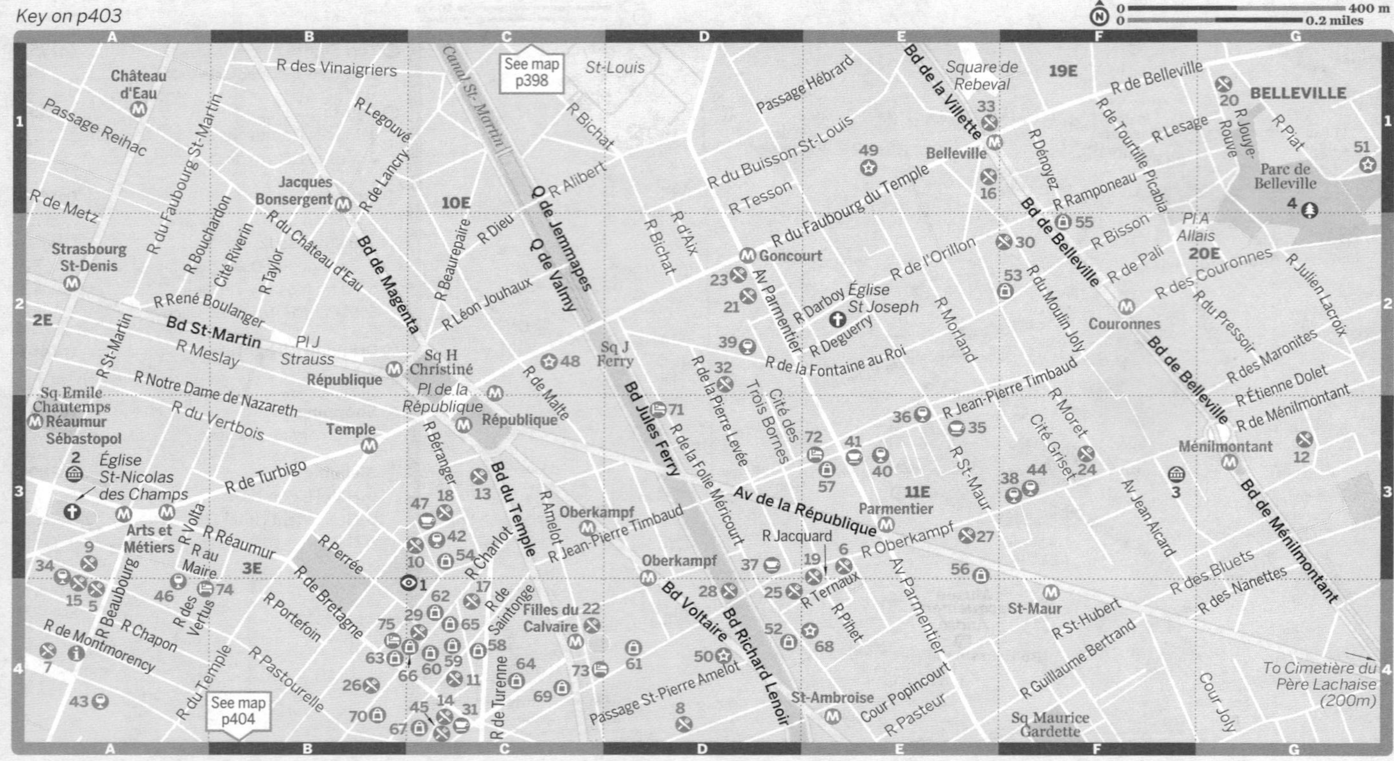

LE MARAIS & MÉNILMONTANT *Map on p402*

Sights (p157)
1 Marché du Temple ... C4
2 Musée des Arts et Métiers ... A3
3 Musée Édith Piaf ... F3
4 Parc de Belleville ... G1

Eating (p161)
5 404 ... A4
6 Al Taglio ... E3
7 Ambassade d'Auvergne ... A4
8 Au Passage ... D4
9 Bob's Kitchen ... A3
10 Café Crème ... C3
11 Candelaria ... C4
12 Chatomat ... G3
13 Chez Jenny ... C3
14 Cuisine de Bar ... C4
15 Derrière ... A4
16 Dong Huong ... E1
17 La Briciola ... C4
18 L'Aller-Retour ... C3
19 L'Ave Maria ... E3
20 Le Baratin ... G1
21 Le Chateaubriand ... D2
22 Le Clown Bar ... C4
23 Le Dauphin ... D2
24 Le Porokhane ... F3
25 Le Villaret ... D4
26 Marché aux Enfants Rouges ... B4
27 Marche ou Crêpe ... E3
28 Marché Popincourt ... D4
29 Nanashi ... C4
30 Reuan Thai ... F2
31 Rose Bakery ... C4
32 Soya Cantine BIO ... D2
33 Tai Yien ... E1

Drinking & Nightlife (p168)
34 Andy Walhoo ... A3
35 Au Chat Noir ... E3
36 Au P'tit Garage ... E3
37 Aux Deux Amis ... D3
38 Café Charbon ... F3
Café Charlot ... (see 63)
39 La Caravane ... D2
40 L'Alimentation Générale ... E3
41 L'Autre Café ... E3
42 Le Barav ... C3
43 Le Duplex ... A4
44 Le Nouveau Casino ... F3
45 Le Progrès ... C4
46 Le Tango ... A4
47 Merce and the Muse ... C3
Scream Club ... (see 48)

Entertainment (p173)
48 La Favela Chic ... C2
49 La Java ... E1
50 Le Bataclan ... D4
51 Le Vieux Belleville ... G1
52 Satellit Café ... E4

Shopping (p174)
53 Andrea Crews ... F2
54 Anne Elisabeth ... C3
55 Belleville Market ... F2
56 Boutique Obut ... E3
57 By Sophie ... E3
58 Finger In the Nose ... C4
59 Isabel Marant ... C4
60 Julien Caviste ... C4
61 Kate Mack ... D4
62 La Boutique Extraordinaire ... C4
63 Le Repaire de Bacchus ... B4
64 Lieu Commun ... C4
65 Moon Young Hee ... C4
66 Pauline Pin ... C4
67 Popelini ... C4
68 Puzzle Michèle Wilson ... D4
69 Rougier & Plé ... C4
70 Valentine Gauthier ... B4

Sleeping (p290)
71 Auberge de Jeunesse Jules Ferry ... D3
72 Cosmos Hôtel ... E3
73 Hôtel Beaumarchais ... C4
74 Hôtel du Haut Marais ... A4
75 Hôtel du Vieux Saule ... B4

Key on p406

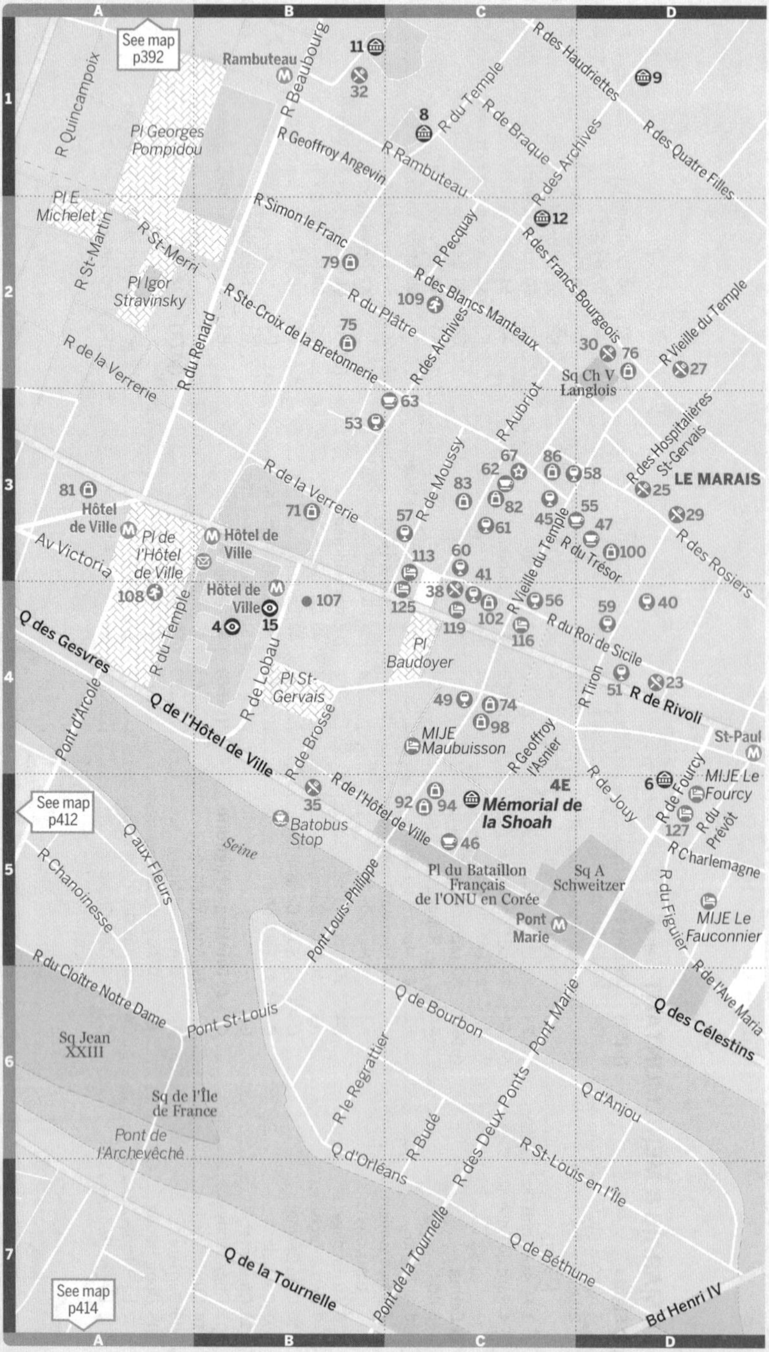

See map p392

A B C D
1 2 3 4 5 6 7

Rambuteau
R Beaubourg
R Quincampoix
Pl Georges Pompidou
R Geoffroy Angevin
R Rambuteau
R du Temple
R de Braque
R des Haudriettes
R des Quatre Filles
R des Archives
Pl E Michelet
R St-Martin
R St-Merri
R Simon le Franc
R Pecquay
R des Francs Bourgeois
Pl Igor Stravinsky
R Ste-Croix de la Bretonnerie
R du Plâtre
R des Blancs Manteaux
R des Archives
R du Renard
R de la Verrerie
Sq Ch V Langlois
R Vieille du Temple
R Aubriot
R des Hospitalières St-Gervais
LE MARAIS
R de Moussy
R de la Verrerie
Hôtel de Ville
Pl de l'Hôtel de Ville
Av Victoria
R Vieille du Temple
R du Trésor
R des Rosiers
Hôtel de Ville
R du Temple
R du Roi de Sicile
Q des Gesvres
R de Lobau
Pl St-Gervais
Pl Baudoyer
R Tiron
R de Rivoli
Pont d'Arcole
Q de l'Hôtel de Ville
R de Brosse
MIJE Maubuisson
R Geoffroy l'Asnier
St-Paul
R de Jouy
R de Fourcy
MIJE Le Fourcy
R du Prévôt
R de l'Hôtel de Ville
Mémorial de la Shoah
Batobus Stop
Seine
Q aux Fleurs
R Chanoinesse
Pont Louis-Philippe
Pl du Bataillon Français de l'ONU en Corée
Sq A Schweitzer
R Charlemagne
R du Figuier
MIJE Le Fauconnier
Pont Marie
R de l'Ave Maria
Q des Célestins
R du Cloître Notre Dame
Pont St-Louis
Q de Bourbon
Pont Marie
Sq Jean XXIII
R le Regrattier
R des Deux Ponts
Q d'Anjou
Sq de l'Île de France
Pont de l'Archevêché
R Budé
Q d'Orléans
R St-Louis en l'Île
Q de Béthune
Q de la Tournelle
Pont de la Tournelle
Bd Henri IV

11 32 9 8 12 79 109 75 30 76 27 63 53 67 86 62 58 25 81 83 82 55 47 57 61 45 29 71 60 113 41 100 108 38 125 119 102 56 59 40 4 15 107 116 51 23 49 74 98 6 35 92 94 4E 127 46

See map p412

See map p414

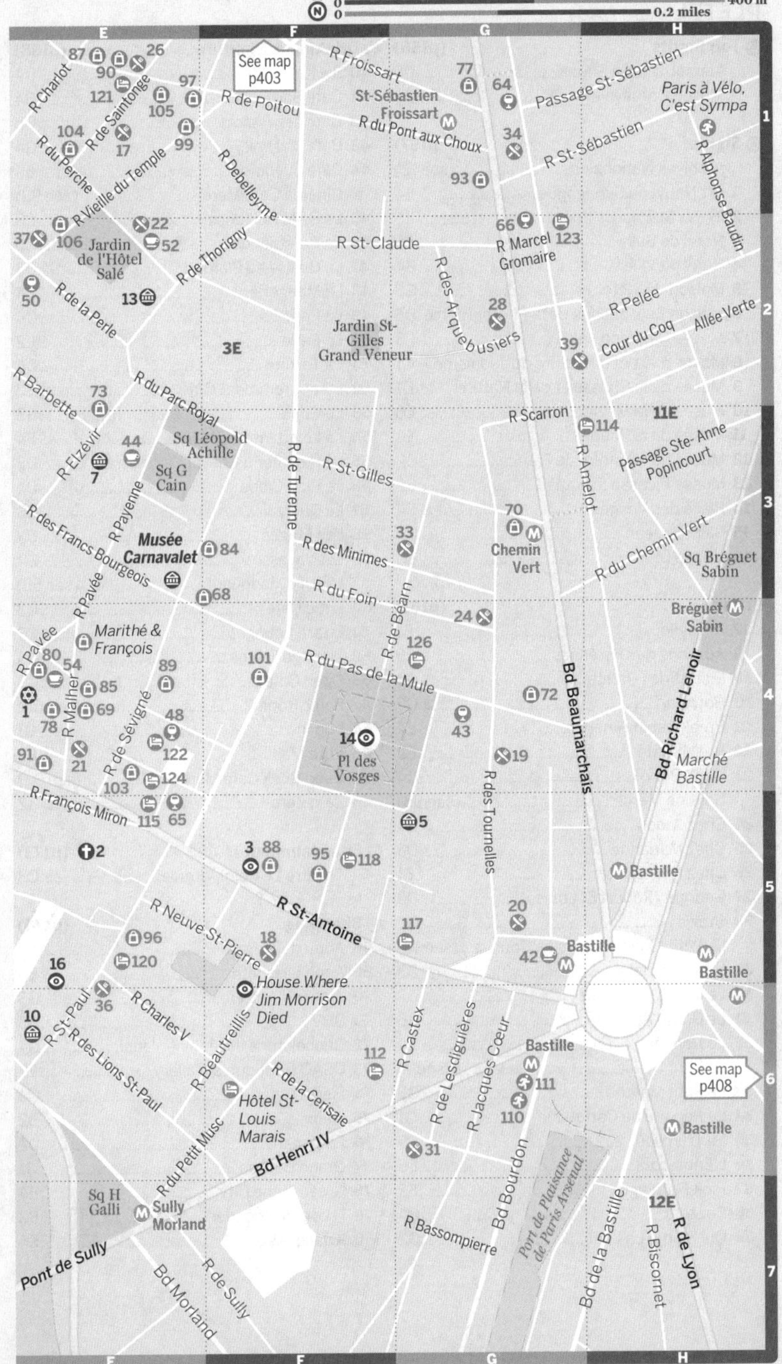
PLETZL
See map p403
See map p408
R Froissart
R de Poitou
St-Sébastien Froissart
R du Pont aux Choux
Passage St-Sébastien
R St-Sébastien
Paris à Vélo, C'est Sympa
R Alphonse Baudin
R Charlot
R de Saintonge
R du Perche
R Vieille du Temple
R Debelleyme
R St-Claude
R Marcel Gromaire
R des Arquebusiers
R de Thorigny
Jardin de l'Hôtel Salé
R de la Perle
Jardin St-Gilles Grand Veneur
R Pelée
Cour du Coq
Allée Verte
3E
11E
R Barbette
R du Parc Royal
Sq Léopold Achille
Sq G Cain
R Elzévir
R Scarron
Passage Ste-Anne Popincourt
R Amelot
R de Turenne
R St-Gilles
R Payenne
R des Francs Bourgeois
Musée Carnavalet
R des Minimes
Chemin Vert
R du Chemin Vert
Sq Bréguet Sabin
Bréguet Sabin
R Pavée
R du Foin
R de Béarn
Marithé & François
R du Pas de la Mule
R Malher
R de Sévigné
Pl des Vosges
Bd Beaumarchais
Bd Richard Lenoir
Marché Bastille
R des Tournelles
R François Miron
R St-Antoine
Bastille
R Neuve St-Pierre
House Where Jim Morrison Died
R St-Paul
R Charles V
R des Lions St-Paul
R Beautreillis
R Castex
R de Lesdiguières
R Jacques Cœur
Hôtel St-Louis Marais
R de la Cerisaie
Bd Henri IV
Bd Bourdon
Port de Plaisance de Paris Arsenal
Bd de la Bastille
12E
R de Lyon
R Biscornet
R Bassompierre
Sq H Galli
Sully Morland
R du Petit Musc
Pont de Sully
Bd Morland
R de Sully
400 m
0.2 miles

PLETZL *Map on p404*

Top Sights (p156)

Mémorial de la Shoah ... C5
Musée Carnavalet ... E3

Sights (p157)

Archives Nationales ... (see 12)
1 Art Nouveau Synagogue ... E4
2 Église St-Paul St-Louis ... E5
3 Hôtel de Sully ... F5
4 Hôtel de Ville ... B4
5 Maison de Victor Hugo ... G5
6 Maison Européenne de la Photographie ... D5
7 Musée Cognacq-Jay ... E3
8 Musée d'Art et d'Histoire du Judaïsme ... C1
9 Musée de la Chasse et de la Nature ... D1
10 Musée de la Magie ... E6
11 Musée de la Poupée ... B1
12 Musée de l'Histoire de France ... C2
13 Musée Picasso ... E2
14 Place des Vosges ... F4
15 Salle St-Jean ... B4
16 Village St-Paul ... E5

Eating (p161)

17 Al Taglio ... E1
18 Aux Vins des Pyrénées ... F5
19 Bistrot de l'Oulette ... G4
20 Bofinger ... G5
21 Breakfast in America ... E4
22 Breizh Café ... E2
23 Caffé Boboli ... D4
Cantine Merci ... (see 93)
24 Chez Janou ... G4
25 Chez Marianne ... D3
26 Chez Nénesse ... E1
27 Georget (Robert Et Louise) ... D2
28 Grazie ... G2
La Petite Maison dans La Cour ... (see 16)
29 L'As du Felafel ... D3
30 Le Dôme du Marais ... D2
31 Le Grand Appétit ... G6
32 Le Hangar ... B1
Le Petit Dakar ... (see 7)
33 Le Petit Marché ... G3
34 Le Repaire de Cartouche ... G1
35 Le Trumilou ... B5
36 L'Enoteca ... E6
37 Pink Flamingo ... E2
38 Pozzetto ... C4
39 Qui Plume La Lune ... G2

Drinking & Nightlife (p168)

40 3w Kafé ... D4
41 Café Baroc ... C4
42 Café des Phares ... G5
43 Café Martini ... G4
44 Café Suédois ... E3
Cinéma Café Merci ... (see 93)
45 La Belle Hortense ... C3
46 La Caféthèque ... C5
47 La Chaise au Plafond ... D3
48 La Mangerie ... E4
49 La Perla ... C4
50 La Perle ... E2
51 La Tartine ... D4
52 L'Apparemment Café ... E2
53 Le Cox ... B3
54 Le Loir dans La Théière ... E4
55 Le Petit Fer à Cheval ... D3
56 Le Pick-Clops ... C4
57 Le Quetzal ... C3
58 Les Étages ... C3
59 Les Jacasses ... D4
L'Étoile Manquante ... (see 55)
60 Little Café ... C3
61 Lizard Lounge ... C3
62 Mariage Frères ... C3
63 Open Café ... C3
Panic Room ... (see 64)
64 Pop In ... G1
65 Pure Malt ... E5
Used Book Café Merci ... (see 93)
66 Zéro Zéro ... G2

Entertainment (p173)

67 Théâtre Le Point Virgule ... C3

Shopping (p174)

68 Abou d'Abi Bazar ... F3
69 Anne Elisabeth ... E4
70 Atelier d'Autrefois ... G3
71 BHV ... B3
72 Chocolaterie Joséphine Vannier ... G4
73 CSAO Boutique & Gallery ... E2
74 Fiesta Galerie ... C4
75 Fleux ... B2
76 Fragonard ... D2
77 Grand Bonton ... G1
78 Green in the City ... E4
79 I Love my Blender ... B2
80 K Jacques ... E4

81 La Maison de l'Astronomie......A3
82 L'Artisan Parfumeur......C3
83 Le Studio des Parfums......C3
84 L'Éclaireur......F3
85 L'Éclaireur (Menswear)......E4
86 Les Mots à la Bouche......C3
87 L'Habilleur......E1
88 Librairie de l'Hôtel de Sully......F5
89 Losco......E4
90 Made in Used......E1
91 Maison Georges Larnicol......E4
92 Mélodies Graphiques......C5
93 Merci......G1
94 Mi Amor......C5
95 My E-Case......F5
96 Red Wheelbarrow Bookstore......E5
97 Shine......E1
98 Sic Amor......C4
99 Surface to Air......E1
100 Trésor......D3
101 Tumbleweed......F4
102 Un Chien dans le Marais......C4
103 Vert d'Absinthe......E4
104 Violette et Léonie......E1
105 Violette et Léonie......E1
106 Yukiko......E2

Sports & Activities **(p180)**

107 Bike About Tours......B4
108 Hôtel de Ville Ice-Skating Rink......A4
109 Les Bains du Marais......C2
110 Nomades......G6
111 Rollers & Coquillages......G6

Sleeping **(p290)**

112 Castex Hôtel......F6
113 Grand Hôtel du Loiret......C3
114 Hôtel Bastille de Launay......H3
115 Hôtel Caron......E5
116 Hôtel Caron de Beaumarchais......C4
117 Hôtel de la Herse d'Or......G5
118 Hôtel de la Place des Vosges......F5
119 Hôtel de Nice......C4
120 Hôtel du 7e Art......E5
121 Hôtel du Petit Moulin......E1
122 Hôtel Jeanne d'Arc......E4
123 Hôtel Les Jardins du Marais......G2
124 Hôtel Pratic......E4
125 Hôtel Rivoli......C4
126 Le Pavillon de la Reine......G4
127 Maison Internationale de la Jeunesse et des Étudiants......D5

BASTILLE & EASTERN PARIS

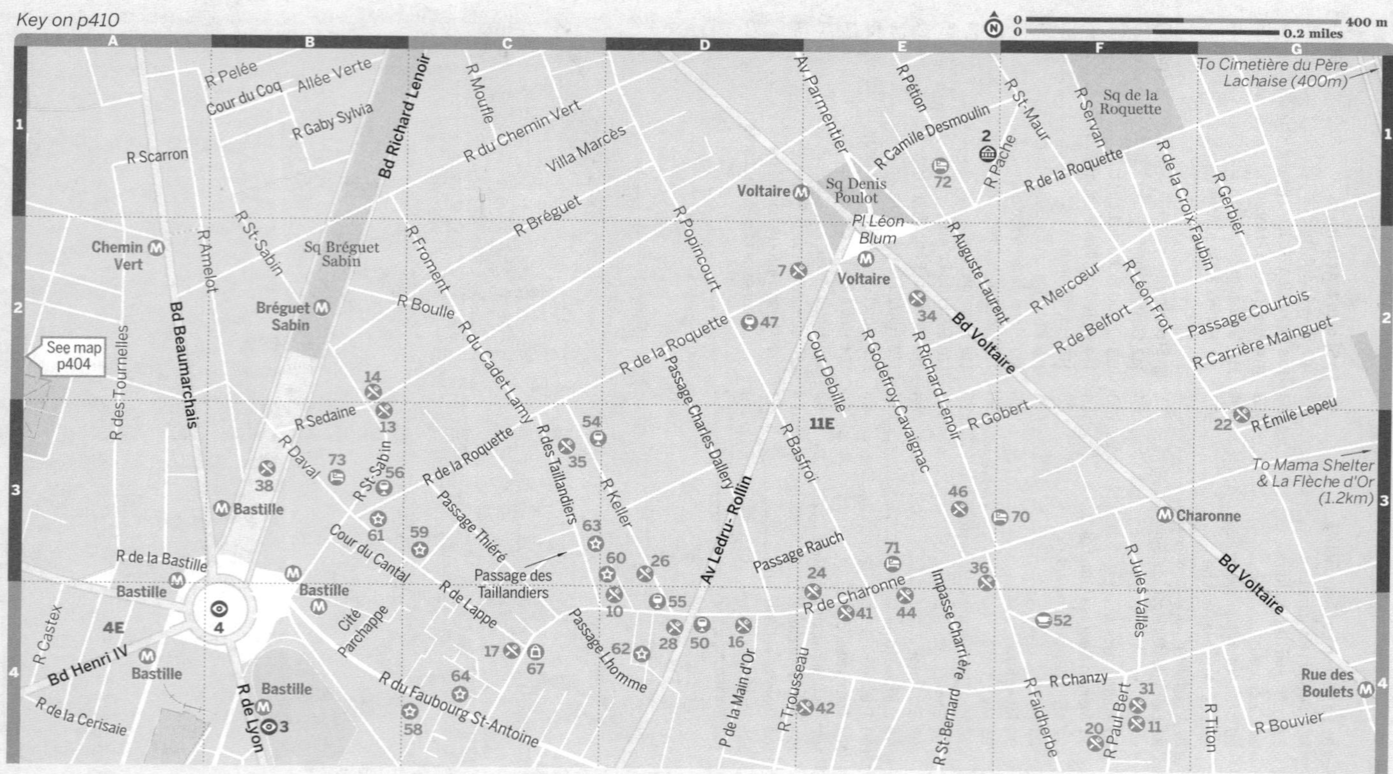

BASTILLE & EASTERN PARIS

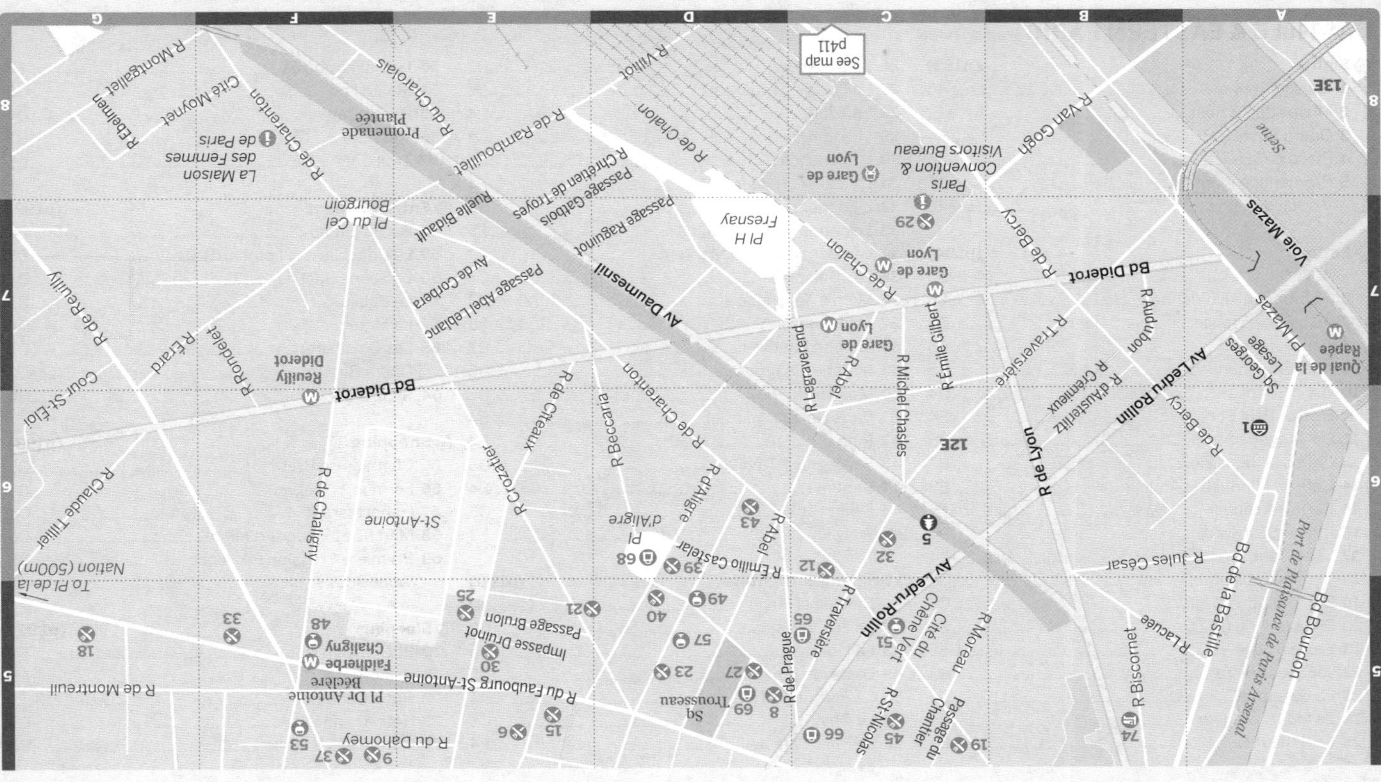

BASTILLE & EASTERN PARIS *Map on p408*

Sights **(p183)**
1 Maison Rouge A6
2 Musée du Fumeur E1
3 Opéra Bastille B4
4 Place de la Bastille B4
5 Promenade Plantée C6
Viaduc des Arts (see 5)

Eating **(p184)**
40/60 (see 42)
6 À La Banane Ivoirienne E5
7 À La Renaissance D2
8 Agua Limón D5
9 Au Vieux Chêne F5
10 Bar à Soupes D4
11 Bistrot Paul Bert F4
12 Boulangerie Bazin C6
13 Café de l'Industrie B3
14 Café de L'Industrie Annexe B2
15 Caffè dei Cioppi E5
16 Chalet Savoyard D4
17 Chez Paul C4
18 Chez Ramulaud G5
19 Eat Intuition C5
20 El Galpon de Unico F4
21 Étoile Rouge E5
22 Jacques Mélac G3
23 La Gazzetta D5
24 Le Mouton Noir E4
25 Le Siffleur de Ballons E5
26 Le Souk D3
27 Le Square Trousseau D5
28 Le Tiffin D4
29 Le Train Bleu C7
30 L'Ébauchoir E5
31 L'Écailler du Bistrot F4
32 L'Encrier C6
33 Les Amis de Messina F5
34 Les Domaines Qui Montent E2
35 Les Galopins C3
36 Mamie Tevennec E3
37 Mansouria F5
38 Marché Bastille B3
39 Marché d'Aligre D6
40 Moisan D5
41 Paris Hanoi E4
42 Rino E4
43 Sardegna A Tavola D6
44 Septime E4
45 Swann et Vincent C5
46 Waly Fay E3

Drinking & Nightlife **(p190)**
Café de la Plage (see 24)
47 La Fée Verte D2
48 La Liberté F5
49 Le Baron Rouge D5
50 Le Bistrot du Peintre D4
51 Le China C5
52 Le Pure Café F4
53 Les Funambules F5
54 Mojito Lab C3
55 Pause Café D4
56 Tape Bar B3
57 Troll Café D5

Entertainment **(p192)**
58 Barrio Latino C4
59 La Chapelle des Lombards C3
60 La Scène Bastille D3
61 Le Balajo B3
62 Le Motel D4
63 Les Disquaires C3
Opéra Bastille (see 3)
64 Sanz Sans C4

Shopping **(p193)**
65 Chemins de Bretagne C5
66 Fermob C5
67 Isabel Marant C4
68 Marché aux Puces d'Aligre D6
69 Première Pression Provence D5
Viaduc des Arts (see 5)

Sleeping **(p292)**
70 BLC Design Hotel F3
71 Hi Matic E3
72 Hôtel Candide E1
73 Hôtel Daval B3
74 Hôtel Paris Bastille B5

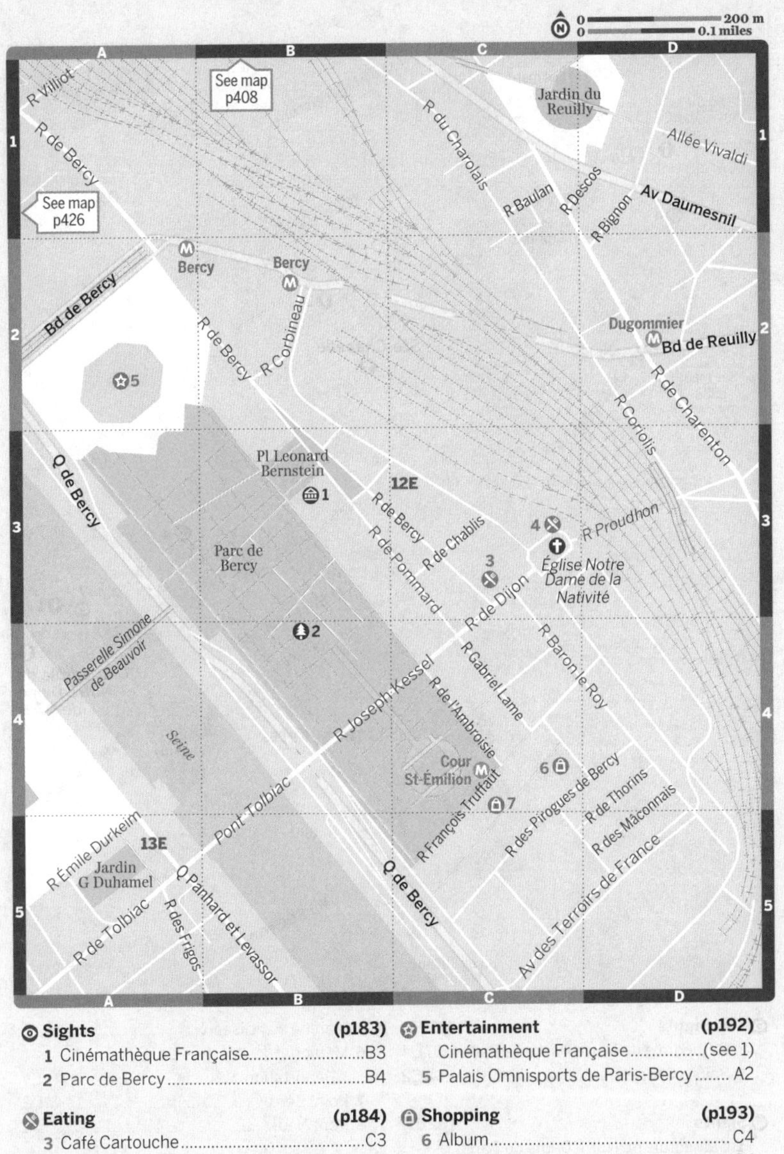

Sights (p183)

1 Cinémathèque Française B3
2 Parc de Bercy B4

Eating (p184)

3 Café Cartouche C3
4 L'Oulette C3

Entertainment (p192)

Cinémathèque Française .... (see 1)
5 Palais Omnisports de Paris-Bercy A2

Shopping (p193)

6 Album C4
7 Bercy Village C4

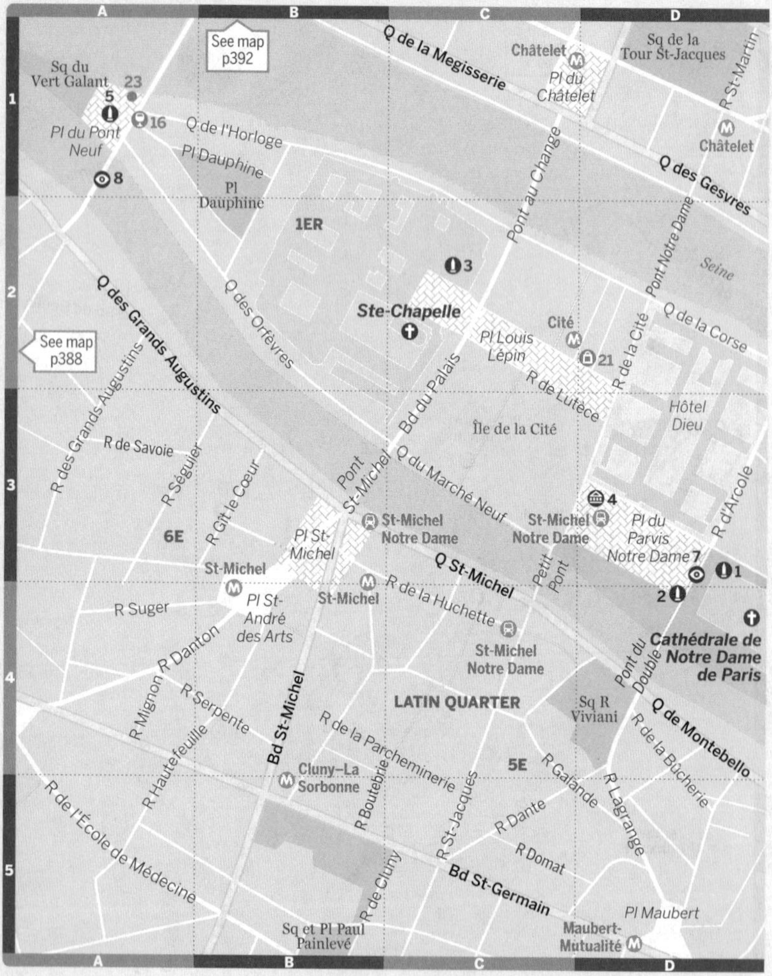

Top Sights **(p196)**

Cathédrale de Notre Dame de Paris D4
Sainte Chapelle C2

Sights **(p201)**

1 Cathédrale de Notre Dame de Paris North Tower D3
2 Charlemagne Memorial D4
3 Conciergerie C2
4 Crypte Archéologique D3
5 Henri IV Statue A1
Marché aux Oiseaux ....(see 21)
6 Mémorial des Martyrs de la Déportation E4
7 Point Zéro D3
8 Pont Neuf A1

Eating **(p202)**

9 Berthillon G4
10 Café Saint Regis F4
11 Le Tastevin G4
12 Les Fous de l'Île G4

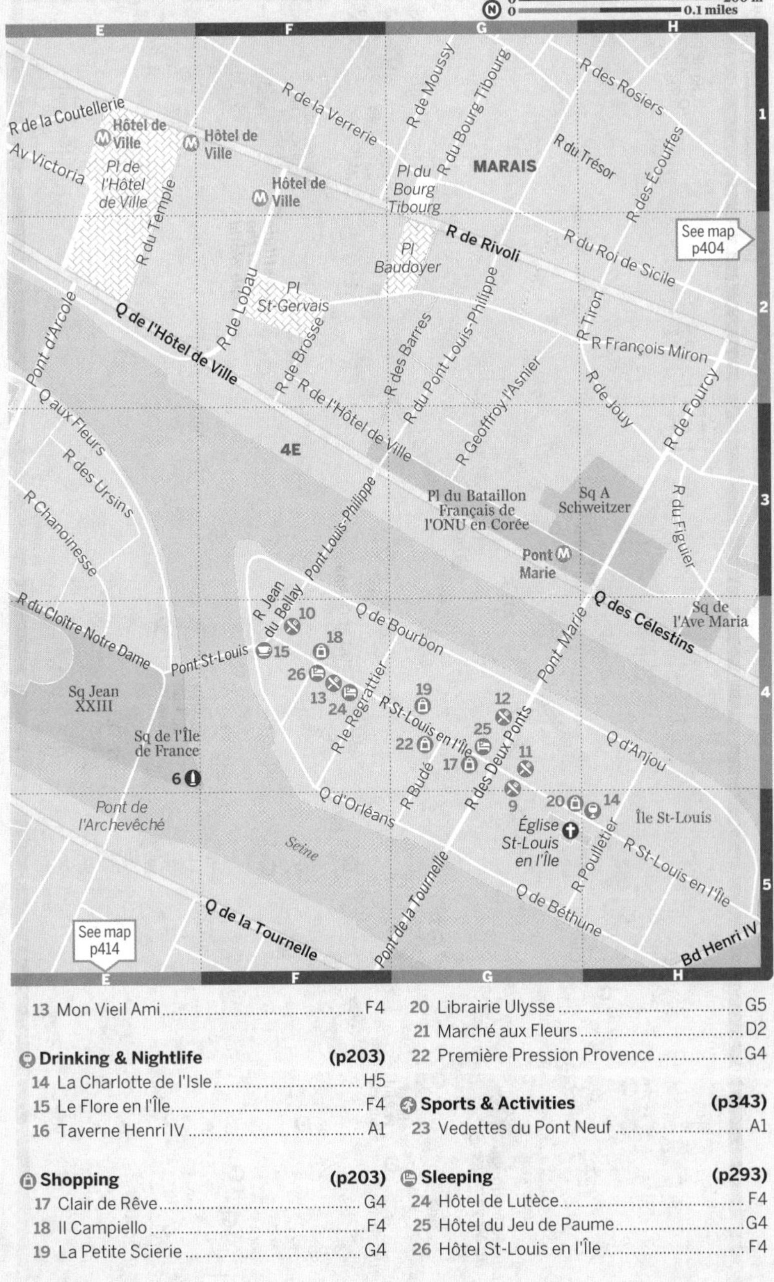

13 Mon Vieil Ami F4

Drinking & Nightlife (p203)

14 La Charlotte de l'Isle H5
15 Le Flore en l'Île F4
16 Taverne Henri IV A1

Shopping (p203)

17 Clair de Rêve G4
18 Il Campiello F4
19 La Petite Scierie G4
20 Librairie Ulysse G5
21 Marché aux Fleurs D2
22 Première Pression Provence G4

Sports & Activities (p343)

23 Vedettes du Pont Neuf A1

Sleeping (p293)

24 Hôtel de Lutèce F4
25 Hôtel du Jeu de Paume G4
26 Hôtel St-Louis en l'Île F4

LATIN QUARTER NORTH

Key on p415

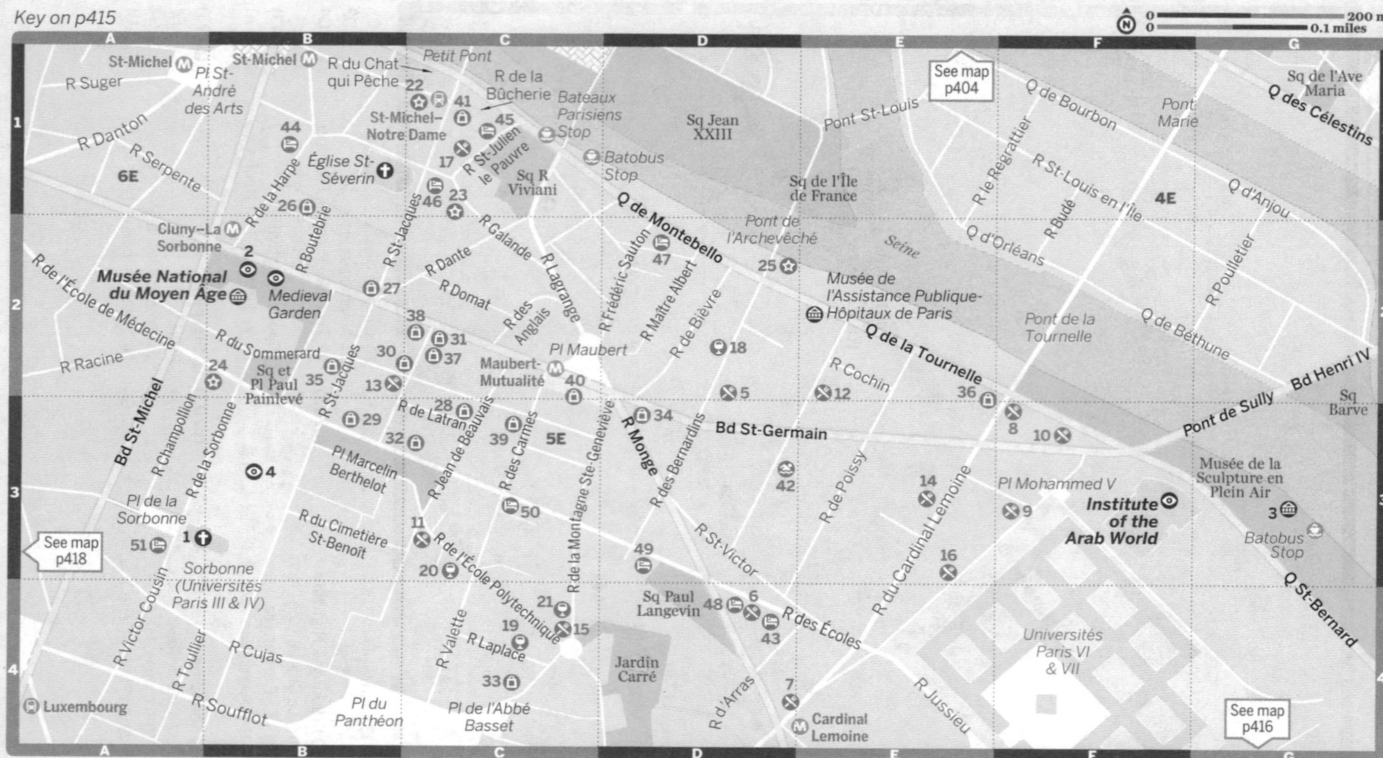

LATIN QUARTER NORTH *Map on p414*

Top Sights **(p206)**
Institute of the Arab World F3
Musée National du Moyen Âge B2

Sights **(p207)**
1 Chapelle de la Sorbonne A3
2 Forêt de la Licorne B2
3 Musée de la Sculpture en Plein Air G3
4 Sorbonne B3

Eating **(p209)**
5 Anahuacalli D2
6 Breakfast in America D4
7 Kootchi D4
8 La Tour d'Argent F3
9 L'AOC F3
10 Le Baba Bourgeois F3
11 Le Coupe-Chou C3
12 Le Petit Pontoise E2
13 Le Pré Verre B2
14 Le Puits de Légumes E3
15 Les Pipos C4
16 Moissonnier E3
17 Tea Caddy C1

Drinking & Nightlife **(p214)**
18 Curio Parlor Cocktail Club D2
19 Le Piano Vache C4
20 Le Pub St-Hilaire C3
21 Le Violon Dingue C4

Entertainment **(p215)**
22 Caveau de la Huchette C1
23 Le Caveau des Oubliettes C1
24 Le Champo B2
25 Métamorphosis D2

Shopping **(p216)**
26 Abbey Bookshop B1
27 Album B2
28 Au Vieux Campeur C3
29 Au Vieux Campeur B3
30 Au Vieux Campeur C2
31 Au Vieux Campeur C2
32 Crocodisc C3
33 Crocojazz C4
34 Fromagerie Laurent Dubois D3
35 La Boutique du Créateur de Jeux B2
36 La Tour d'Argent Boutique E2
37 Librairie de Voyage C2
38 Librairie Eyrolles C2
39 Magie C3
40 Marché Maubert C2
41 Shakespeare & Company C1

Sports & Activities **(p218)**
42 Piscine Pontoise D3

Sleeping **(p293)**
43 Familia Hôtel D4
44 Hôtel du Levant B1
45 Hôtel Esmeralda C1
46 Hôtel Henri IV Rive Gauche C1
47 Hôtel les Degrés de Notre Dame D2
48 Hôtel Minerve D4
49 Hôtel Résidence Henri IV D3
50 Hôtel St-Jacques C3
51 Select Hôtel A3

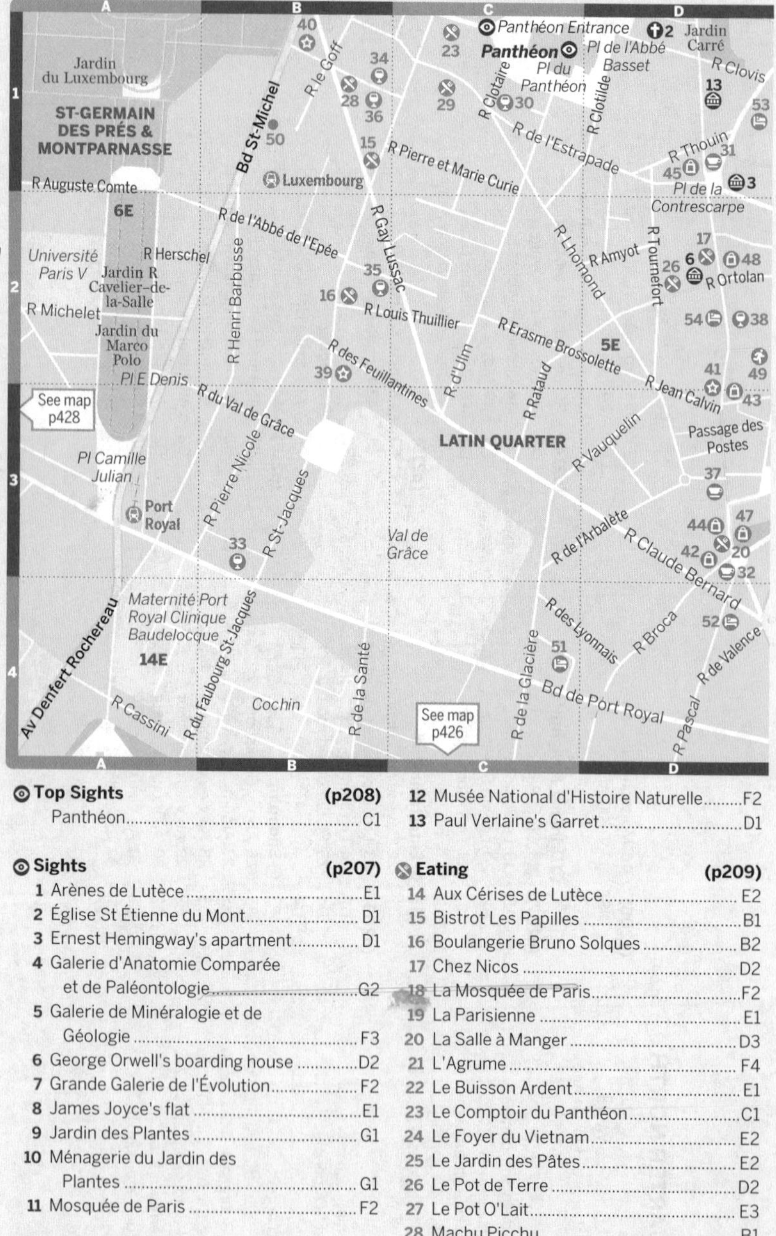

Top Sights (p208)

Panthéon ... C1

Sights (p207)

1 Arènes de Lutèce ... E1
2 Église St Étienne du Mont ... D1
3 Ernest Hemingway's apartment ... D1
4 Galerie d'Anatomie Comparée et de Paléontologie ... G2
5 Galerie de Minéralogie et de Géologie ... F3
6 George Orwell's boarding house ... D2
7 Grande Galerie de l'Évolution ... F2
8 James Joyce's flat ... E1
9 Jardin des Plantes ... G1
10 Ménagerie du Jardin des Plantes ... G1
11 Mosquée de Paris ... F2
12 Musée National d'Histoire Naturelle ... F2
13 Paul Verlaine's Garret ... D1

Eating (p209)

14 Aux Cérises de Lutèce ... E2
15 Bistrot Les Papilles ... B1
16 Boulangerie Bruno Solques ... B2
17 Chez Nicos ... D2
18 La Mosquée de Paris ... F2
19 La Parisienne ... E1
20 La Salle à Manger ... D3
21 L'Agrume ... F4
22 Le Buisson Ardent ... E1
23 Le Comptoir du Panthéon ... C1
24 Le Foyer du Vietnam ... E2
25 Le Jardin des Pâtes ... E2
26 Le Pot de Terre ... D2
27 Le Pot O'Lait ... E3
28 Machu Picchu ... B1

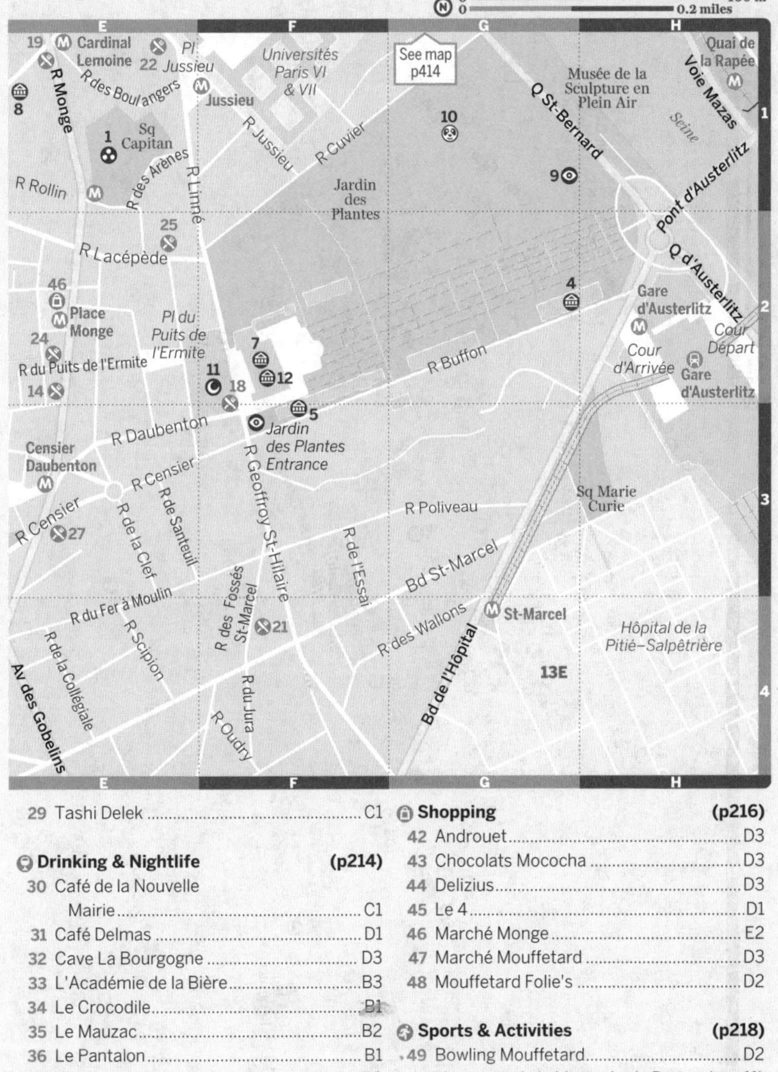

29 Tashi Delek C1

Drinking & Nightlife (p214)

30 Café de la Nouvelle Mairie C1
31 Café Delmas D1
32 Cave La Bourgogne D3
33 L'Académie de la Bière B3
34 Le Crocodile B1
35 Le Mauzac B2
36 Le Pantalon B1
37 Le Verre à Pied D3
38 Le Vieux Chêne D2

Entertainment (p215)

39 Café Universel B2
40 Le Petit Journal St-Michel B1
41 L'Epée de Bois D2

Shopping (p216)

42 Androuet D3
43 Chocolats Mococha D3
44 Delizius D3
45 Le 4 .... D1
46 Marché Monge E2
47 Marché Mouffetard D3
48 Mouffetard Folie's D2

Sports & Activities (p218)

49 Bowling Mouffetard D2
Hammam de la Mosquée de Paris .. (see 11)
50 La Cuisine Paris B1

Sleeping (p293)

51 Five Hotel C4
52 Hôtel de l'Espérance D4
53 Hôtel des Grandes Écoles D1
54 Young & Happy D2

ST-GERMAIN

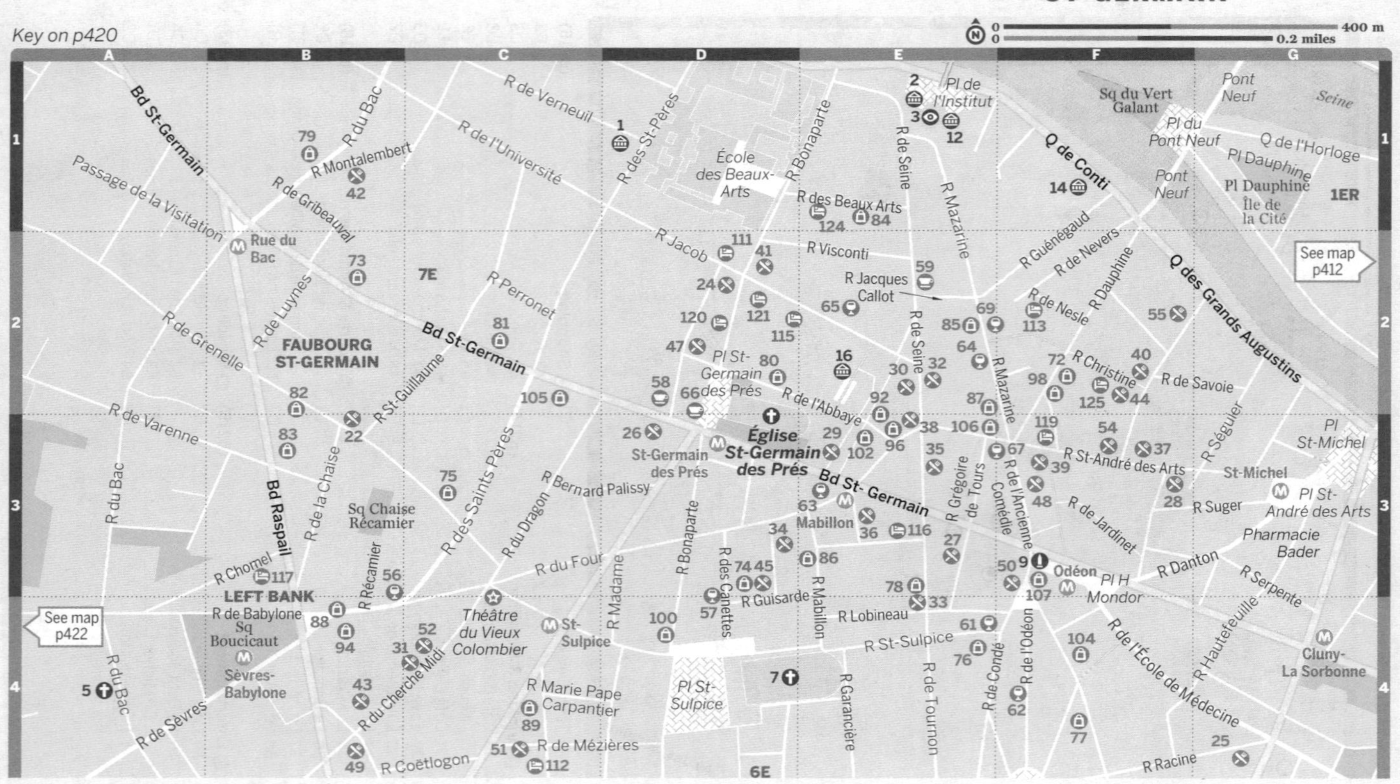
Key on p420
0 400 m
0 0.2 miles
See map p412
See map p422
Bd St-Germain
Passage de la Visitation
R du Bac
R Montalembert
R de Gribeauval
Rue du Bac
R de Luynes
R de Grenelle
FAUBOURG ST-GERMAIN
7E
R de Varenne
R St-Guillaume
R de la Chaise
Bd Raspail
R Chomel
LEFT BANK
R de Babylone
Sq Boucicaut
Sèvres-Babylone
R de Sèvres
R du Cherche Midi
R Coëtlogon
R Récamier
Sq Chaise Récamier
R de Verneuil
R de l'Université
R Perronet
R des Saints Pères
R du Dragon
R Bernard Palissy
Théâtre du Vieux Colombier
St-Sulpice
R Marie Pape Carpantier
R de Mézières
R du Four
R Madame
R des St-Pères
École des Beaux-Arts
R Bonaparte
R Jacob
R des Beaux Arts
R Visconti
R Jacques Callot
Pl St-Germain des Prés
R de l'Abbaye
Église St-Germain des Prés
St-Germain des Prés
Bd St-Germain
Mabillon
R des Canettes
R Guisarde
R Mabillon
Pl St-Sulpice
R Garancière
R Lobineau
R St-Sulpice
R de Tournon
6E
Pl de l'Institut
R de Seine
R Mazarine
Q de Conti
R Guénégaud
R de Nevers
R Dauphine
R de Nesle
R Christine
R de Savoie
R Grégoire de Tours
R de l'Ancienne Comédie
R St-André des Arts
R de Jardinet
Odéon
Pl H Mondor
R de Condé
R de l'Odéon
R de l'École de Médecine
R Racine
Sq du Vert Galant
Pont Neuf
Pl du Pont Neuf
Q de l'Horloge
Pl Dauphine
Île de la Cité
1ER
Seine
Q des Grands Augustins
R Séguier
Pl St-Michel
St-Michel
Pl St-André des Arts
R Suger
Pharmacie Bader
R Danton
R Serpente
R Hautefeuille
Cluny-La Sorbonne

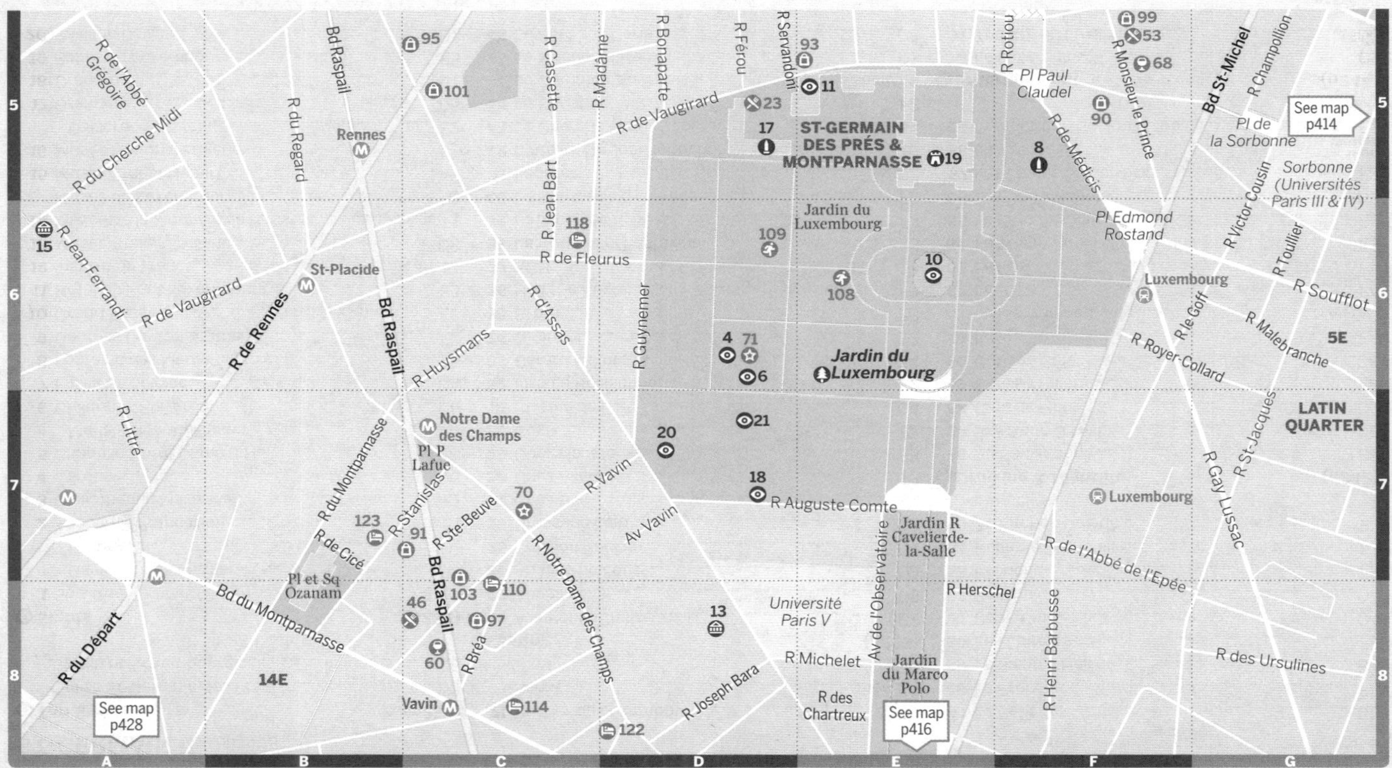
ST-GERMAIN
See map p414
See map p416
See map p428
LATIN QUARTER
5E
14E
ST-GERMAIN DES PRÉS & MONTPARNASSE
Jardin du Luxembourg
Jardin du Luxembourg
Sorbonne (Universités Paris III & IV)
Pl de la Sorbonne
Pl Edmond Rostand
Pl Paul Claudel
Université Paris V
Jardin R Cavelierde-la-Salle
Jardin du Marco Polo
Pl et Sq Ozanam
Pl P Lafue
Notre Dame des Champs
Luxembourg
Luxembourg
Vavin
Rennes
St-Placide
Bd St-Michel
R Champollion
R Monsieur le Prince
R Victor Cousin
R Toullier
R Soufflot
R Malebranche
R le Goff
R Royer-Collard
R St-Jacques
R Gay Lussac
R des Ursulines
R de l'Abbé de l'Epée
R Henri Barbusse
R Herschel
Av de l'Observatoire
R Michelet
R des Chartreux
R Auguste Comte
R Joseph Bara
Av Vavin
R Vavin
R Notre Dame des Champs
R Bréa
Bd Raspail
R Ste-Beuve
R Stanislas
R de Cicé
R du Montparnasse
Bd du Montparnasse
R du Départ
R de Médicis
R Rotiou
R Servandoni
R Férou
R de Vaugirard
R Bonaparte
R Guynemer
R de Fleurus
R Madame
R Jean Bart
R Cassette
R d'Assas
R Huysmans
R de Rennes
R du Regard
R Littré
R Jean Ferrandi
R du Cherche Midi
R de l'Abbé Grégoire
A
B
C
D
E
F
G
5
6
7
8
99
53
68
90
8
93
11
23
17
19
10
108
109
4
71
6
21
18
20
13
122
118
70
110
97
103
91
46
60
123
114
95
101
15

ST-GERMAIN *Map on p418*

Top Sights **(p228)**
Église St-Germain des Prés ... D3
Jardin du Luxembourg ... E6

Sights **(p232)**
1 5bis Rue Verneuil (Serge Gainsbourg's Former Home) ... D1
2 Académie Française ... E1
3 Bibliothèque Mazarine ... E1
4 Carousel ... D6
5 Chapelle Notre Dame de la Medaille Miraculeuse ... A4
6 Children's Playground ... D6
7 Église St-Sulpice ... D4
8 Fontaine des Médici ... F5
9 Georges Danton Statue ... F3
10 Grand Bassin ... E6
11 Hôtel du Petit Luxembourg ... E5
12 Institut de France ... E1
13 Musée Atelier Zadkine ... D8
14 Musée de la Monnaie de Paris ... F1
Musée du Luxembourg ... (see 11)
15 Musée Ernest Hébert ... A6
16 Musée National Eugène Delacroix ... E2
17 Orangery ... D5
18 Orchards ... D7
19 Palais du Luxembourg ... E5
20 Pavillon Davioud ... D7
21 Rucher du Luxembourg ... D7
Sénat ... (see 19)

Eating **(p235)**
22 À la Petite Chaise ... B3
23 Angelina ... D5
24 Au Pied de Fouet ... D2
25 Bouillon Racine ... G4
26 Brasserie Lipp ... D3
27 Casa Bini ... E3
28 Chez Allard ... F3
29 Chez Hanafousa ... E3
30 Cosi ... E2
31 Cuisine de Bar ... C4
32 Fish La Boissonnerie ... E2
33 Gérard Mulot ... E4
34 Giraudet ... D3
35 Grom ... E3
36 Huîterie Regis ... E3
37 KGB ... F3
38 La Bottega di Pastavino ... E3
39 La Jacobine ... F3
40 La Rôtisserie d'en Face ... F2
41 Ladurée ... D2
42 L'Atelier De Joël Robuchon ... B1
43 Le Cherche Midi ... B4
44 Le Christine ... F2
Le Comptoir du Relais ... (see 107)
45 Le Mâchon d'Henri ... D3
46 Le Parc aux Cerfs ... C8
47 Le Petit Zinc ... D2
48 Le Procope ... F3
49 Le Salon d'Hélène ... B4
50 Les Éditeurs ... F3
51 Pizza Chic ... C4
52 Poilâne ... C4
53 Polidor ... F5
54 Roger la Grenouille ... F3
55 Ze Kitchen Galerie ... F2

Drinking & Nightlife **(p242)**
56 Au Sauvignon ... B3
57 Brasserie O'Neil ... D3
58 Café de Flore ... D2
59 Café La Palette ... E2
60 Cubana Café ... C8
61 Kilàli ... E4
La Mezzanine ... (see 64)
62 Le 10 ... F4
63 Le Pré ... E3
64 Le Wagg ... E2
65 Le Zéro De Conduite ... E2
66 Les Deux Magots ... D2
67 Les Etages St-Germain ... F3
68 L'Urgence Bar ... F5
69 Prescription Cocktail Club ... E2

Entertainment **(p244)**
70 Le Lucernaire ... C7
71 Théâtre du Luxembourg ... D6

Shopping (p244)

72 A La Recherche De Jane F2
73 Alexandra Sojfer B2
74 Au Plat d'Étain D3
75 Carine Gilson C3
76 Cave St-Sulpice E4
77 Ciné Reflet F4
78 Cire Trudon E3
79 Deyrolle B1
80 Flamant Home Interiors D2
81 Fragonard Boutique C2
82 Frédéric Malle B2
83 Galerie François Rénier B3
84 Galerie Loft E1
85 Galerie Onega E2
86 Giraudet Boutique E3
87 Hapart E2
88 Hermès B4
89 JB Guanti C4
90 La Chaumière à la Musique F5
91 La Clef des Marques C7
92 La Dernière Goutte E3
La Galerie Moderne (see 85)
93 La Maison de Poupée E5
94 La Maison du Chocolat B4
95 Le Bain Rose C5
96 Le Dépôt-Vente de Buci E3
97 Lin et Cie C8
98 Max Maroquinerie Bagagerie et Accessoires F2
99 Pâtisserie Sadaharu Aoki F5
100 Pierre Hermé D4
101 Plastiques C5
102 Ragtime E3
103 Rouge et Noir C7
104 San Francisco Book Company F4
105 Sonia Rykiel C2
106 Taschen E3
107 Theatr'Hall F3

Sports & Activities (p228)

108 Shetland Ponies for Hire E6
109 Tennis Courts D6

Sleeping (p295)

110 Hôtel Danemark C8
111 Hôtel d'Angleterre D2
112 Hôtel de l'Abbaye Saint Germain C4
113 Hôtel de Nesle F2
114 Hôtel des Académies et des Arts C8
115 Hôtel des Marronniers D2
116 Hôtel Le Clément E3
117 Hôtel Lindbergh B3
118 Hôtel Perreyve C6
119 Hôtel St-André des Arts F3
120 Hôtel St-Germain des Prés D2
121 La Villa D2
122 L'Apostrophe D8
123 Le Six B7
124 L'Hôtel E1
125 Relais Christine F2

LES INVALIDES

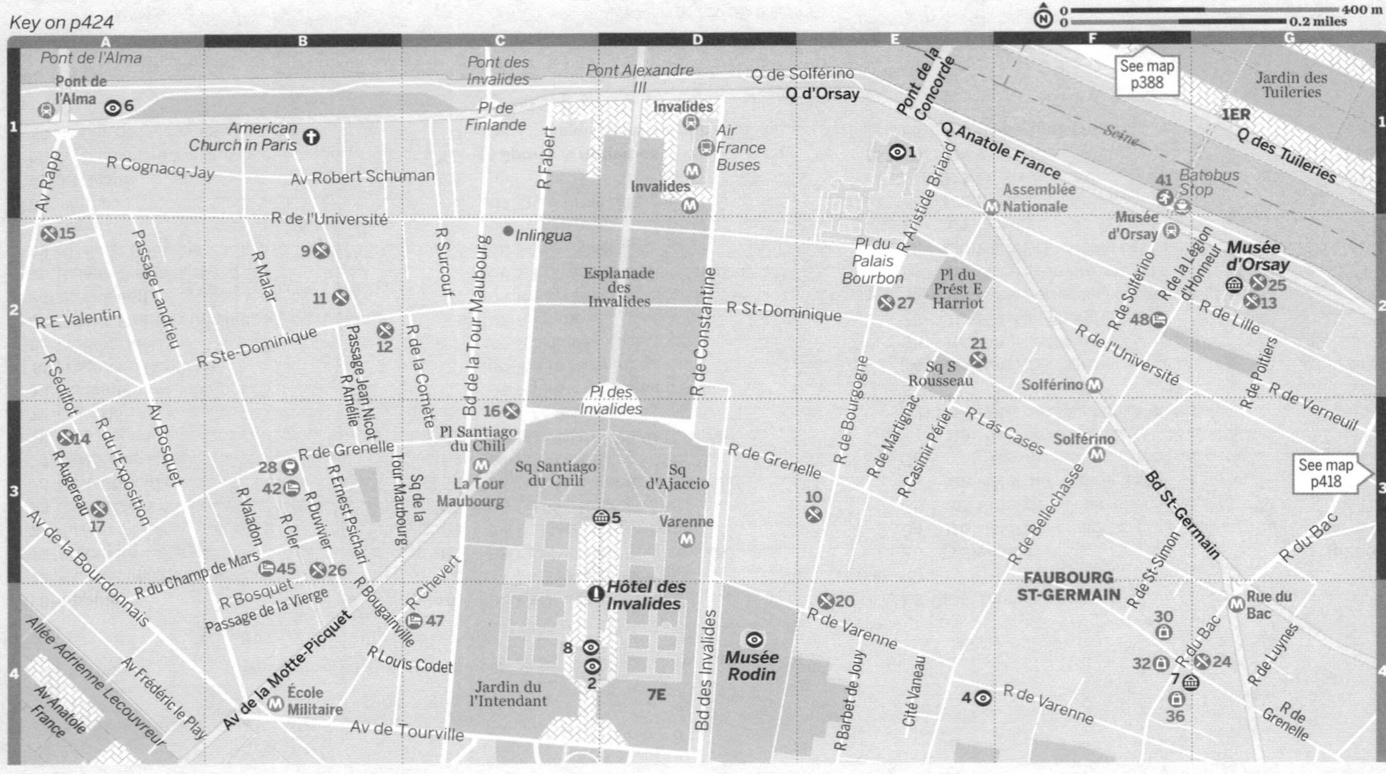

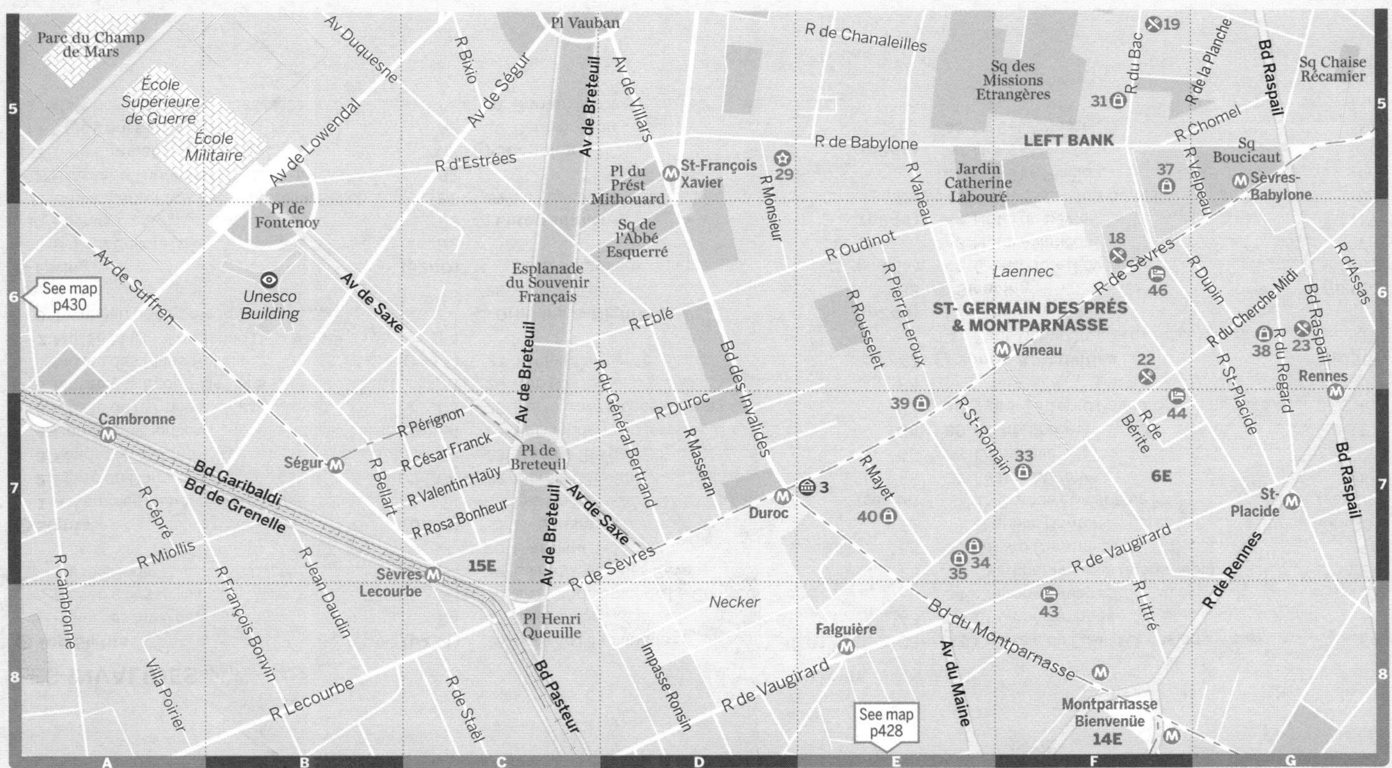
Parc du Champ de Mars
École Supérieure de Guerre
École Militaire
Av Duquesne
Av de Lowendal
Pl de Fontenoy
Unesco Building
Av de Suffren
See map p430
R Bixio
Av de Ségur
Pl Vauban
Av de Breteuil
Av de Villars
R d'Estrées
Pl du Prést Mithouard
St-François Xavier
Sq de l'Abbé Esquerré
Esplanade du Souvenir Français
Av de Saxe
R de Chanaleilles
R de Babylone
R Monsieur
R Vaneau
Jardin Catherine Labouré
Sq des Missions Etrangères
LEFT BANK
R du Bac
R de la Planche
R Chomel
R Velpeau
Sq Boucicaut
Sèvres-Babylone
Bd Raspail
Sq Chaise Récamier
R Oudinot
R Eblé
Laennec
R de Sèvres
R Dupin
R d'Assas
R du Cherche Midi
R du Regard
Rennes
ST- GERMAIN DES PRÉS & MONTPARNASSE
Vaneau
R Rousselet
R Pierre Leroux
R St-Placide
R de Bérite
R St-Romain
R du Général Bertrand
R Masseran
R Duroc
Bd des Invalides
Cambronne
Ségur
R Pérignon
R César Franck
R Valentin Haüy
R Rosa Bonheur
R Bellart
Pl de Breteuil
Bd Garibaldi
Bd de Grenelle
R Cépré
R Miollis
R Cambronne
Sèvres Lecourbe
15E
Duroc
R Mayet
6E
St-Placide
R de Vaugirard
R de Rennes
R Littré
R François Bonvin
R Jean Daudin
Villa Poirier
R Lecourbe
R de Staël
Bd Pasteur
Pl Henri Queuille
Necker
Impasse Ronsin
Falguière
See map p428
Av du Maine
Bd du Montparnasse
Montparnasse Bienvenüe
14E
3
18
19
22
23
29
31
33
34
35
37
38
39
40
43
44
46
5
6
7
8
A
B
C
D
E
F
G

LES INVALIDES *Map on p422*

Top Sights **(p224)**
Hôtel des Invalides C4
Musée d'Orsay G2
Musée Rodin D4

Sights **(p232)**
1 Assemblée Nationale E1
2 Église du Dôme C4
3 Fondation Dubuffet E7
4 Hôtel Matignon E4
5 Musée de l'Armée D3
6 Musée des Égouts de Paris A1
Musée des Plans-Reliefs (see 2)
7 Musée Maillol-Fondation Dina Vierny F4
8 Tombeau de Napoléon 1er C4

Eating **(p240)**
9 Bellota Bellota B2
10 Besnier E3
11 Boulangerie-Pâtisserie Stéphane Secco B2
12 Brasserie Thoumieux B2
13 Café Campana G2
14 Café Constant A3
15 Café de l'Alma A2
16 Café de l'Esplanade C3
17 Chez Lucie A3
18 La Grande Épicerie Le Comptoir Picnic F6
19 La Pâtisserie des Rêves F5
20 L'Arpège E4
21 Le Square E2
Les Cocottes (see 14)
22 Mamie Gâteaux F6
23 Marché Raspail G6
24 Poissonnerie du Bac G4
25 Restaurant Musée d'Orsay G2
26 Rue Cler B3
27 Tante Marguerite E2

Drinking & Nightlife **(p244)**
28 Alain Milliart B3
Café Thoumieux (see 12)

Entertainment **(p244)**
29 La Pagode Cinema D5

Shopping **(p244)**
30 Bébé Bonton F4
31 Bonton Bazar F5
32 Centrale du Fusil d'Occasion F4
33 Chercheminippes F7
34 Chercheminippes E7
35 Chercheminippes (Menswear) E7
36 Gérard Durand F4
Grenelle Bonton (see 30)
La Grande Épicerie de Paris (see 18)
37 Le Bon Marché F5
38 L'Embellie G6
39 Quatrehomme E7
40 Tea & Tattered Pages E7

Sports & Activities **(p136)**
41 Paris Canal Croisières F1

Sleeping **(p295)**
42 Grand Hôtel Lévèque B3
43 Hôtel Aviatic F8
44 Hôtel de Sèvres F7
45 Hôtel du Champ-de-Mars B3
46 Hôtel Le Placide F6
47 Hôtel Muguet C4
48 Le Bellechasse F2

PLACE D'ITALIE & CHINATOWN *Map on p426*

Sights (p254)

1 Bibliothèque Nationale de France ... H3
2 Docks en Seine ... G1
3 Galerie Itinerrance ... H4
4 Les Frigos ... H4
5 Manufacture des Gobelins ... C3
6 Musée National du Sport ... H5
7 Parc Montsouris ... A7
8 Wanderlust ... G1

Eating (p258)

9 Chez Gladines ... C5
10 Chez Nathalie ... C5
11 Chez Paul ... C5
12 Entoto ... A3
13 Hao Hao ... D7
14 La Chine Masséna ... E7
15 La Tropicale ... D4
16 L'Auberge du 15 ... A2
17 L'Avant Goût ... C5
18 L'Avant-Goût Coté Cellier ... C5
19 Le Petit Marguery ... C2
20 Le Temps des Cérises ... C5
21 Les Cailloux ... B5
22 L'Ourcine ... B3
23 Pho 14 ... D5

Drinking & Nightlife (p261)

24 Frog & British Library ... H4
25 La Dame de Canton ... H3
26 La Folie en Tête ... B5
La Taverne de la Butte ... (see 29)
27 Le Batofar ... H3
28 Le Djoon ... G2
29 Le Merle Moqueur ... C5
30 Peniche El Alamein ... H3
31 Sputnik ... C5
Tandem ... (see 31)

Entertainment (p262)

32 MK2 Bibliothèque ... G4
Studio Harcourt ... (see 32)

Shopping (p263)

33 Tang Frères ... F6

Sports & Activities (p264)

34 Piscine de la Butte Aux Cailles ... C5
35 Piscine Joséphine Baker ... H2

Sleeping (p297)

36 Hôtel La Demeure ... D2
37 Hôtel La Manufacture ... D3
38 Oops ... C3

Key on p425

A B C D

1 2 3 4 5 6 7

See map p416

R Mouffetard
R Monge
R Larrey
Jardin des Plantes
R d'Ulm
R Lhomond
R Daubenton
R St-Jacques
R Vauquelin
Censier Daubenton
R Mirbel
R Censier
R Geoffroy St-Hilaire
R Claude Bernard
Pl B Halpern
Sq St-Médard
R Censier
5E
R de l'Essai
Val de Grâce
R Berthollet
R du Fer à Moulin
R Broca
R Pascal
36
R Duméril
16
Bd de Port Royal
Bd St-Marcel
Cochin
R Lebrun
R Pirandello
LATIN QUARTER
19
Les Gobelins
R St-Hippolyte
R Méchain
22
R du Banquier
R Berbier du Mets
Les Gobelins
Campo Formio
Bd Arago
R de la Santé
5
38
R Pinel
R Léon Maurice Nordmann
R Pascal
R de Cordelière
Av des Gobelins
R Rubens
12
R Corvisart
Sq René Le Gall
Villa des Gobelins
37
R de la Glacière
R de Croulebarbe
R Fagon
Bd St-Jacques
Pl d'Italie
15
R Vulpian
Glacière
Place d'Italie
R Ferrus
Place d'Italie
Bd Auguste Blanqui
Corvisart
R des Cinq Diamants
R Samson
14E
17
Ste-Anne
9
20
31
18
21
11
R de la Butte aux Cailles
10
R Vendrezanne
26
29
R Buot
34
R du Moulinet
R d'Alésia
23
Tolbiac
R de Tolbiac
R Bobillot
Av d'Italie
R du Moulin des Près
Pl de l'Abbé G Henocque
Pl de Rungis
R de Choisy
7
13
Jardin du Moulin de la Pointe
Maison Blanche
Av d'Italie
Parc Kellerman

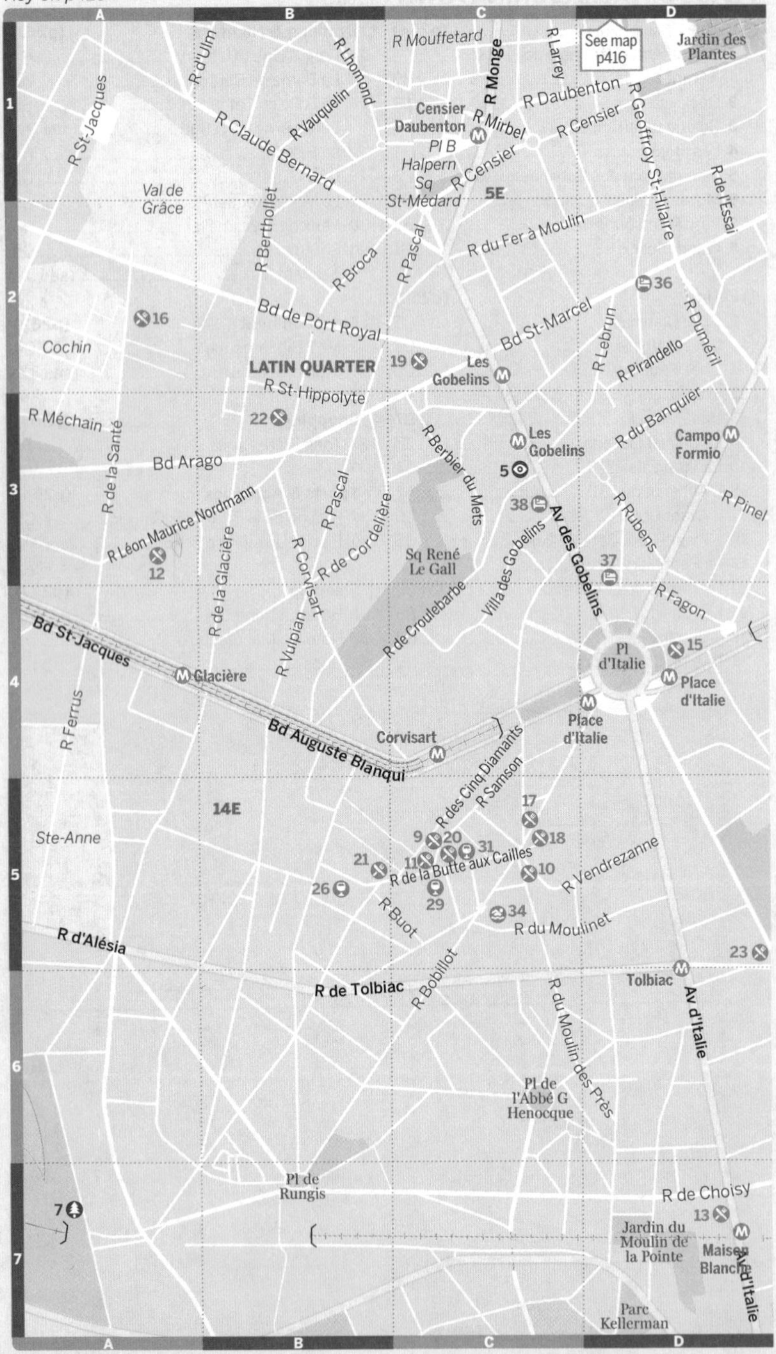

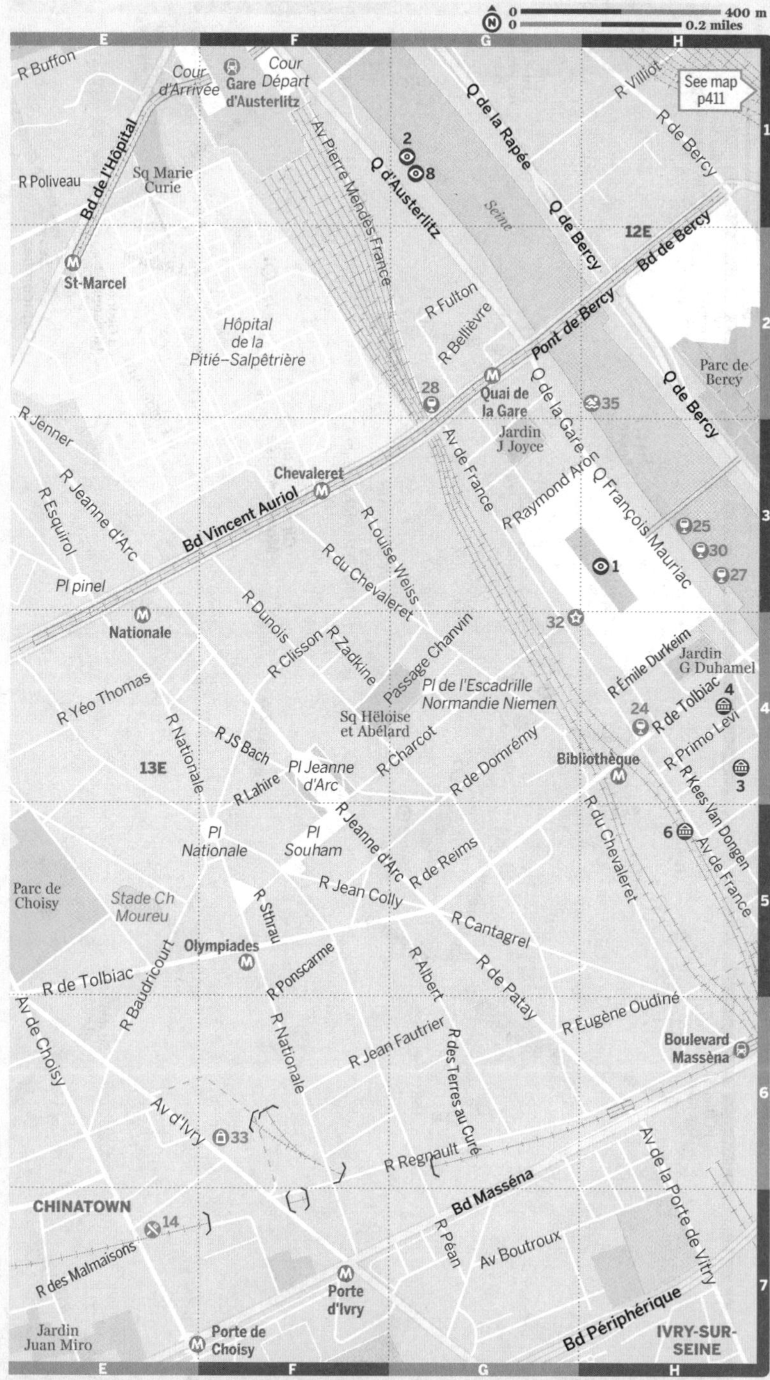
PLACE D'ITALIE & CHINATOWN
See map p411
0 400 m
0 0.2 miles
Gare d'Austerlitz
Cour d'Arrivée
Cour Départ
R Buffon
R Poliveau
Bd de l'Hôpital
Sq Marie Curie
St-Marcel
Hôpital de la Pitié–Salpêtrière
Av Pierre Mendès France
Q d'Austerlitz
Q de la Rapée
Seine
Q de Bercy
R Villiot
R de Bercy
12E
Bd de Bercy
Pont de Bercy
R Fulton
R Bellièvre
Quai de la Gare
Q de la Gare
Parc de Bercy
Jardin J Joyce
Av de France
R Jenner
R Jeanne d'Arc
R Esquirol
Chevaleret
Bd Vincent Auriol
R Louise Weiss
R du Chevaleret
R Raymond Aron
Q François Mauriac
Pl pinel
Nationale
R Dunois
R Clisson
R Zadkine
Passage Chanvin
Pl de l'Escadrille Normandie Niemen
R Émile Durkeim
Jardin G Duhamel
R de Tolbiac
R Primo Levi
R Yéo Thomas
R Nationale
R JS Bach
Sq Héloïse et Abélard
R Charcot
R de Domrémy
Bibliothèque
R Kees Van Dongen
13E
Pl Jeanne d'Arc
R Lahire
Pl Nationale
Pl Souham
R de Reims
R du Chevaleret
Parc de Choisy
Stade Ch Moureu
R Sthrau
R Jean Colly
R Cantagrel
Olympiades
R Ponscarme
R Albert
R de Patay
R de Tolbiac
R Baudricourt
Av de Choisy
R Jean Fautrier
R des Terres au Curé
R Eugène Oudiné
Boulevard Massèna
Av d'Ivry
R Regnault
Av de la Porte de Vitry
CHINATOWN
Bd Masséna
R Péan
R des Malmaisons
Av Boutroux
Porte d'Ivry
Bd Périphérique
Jardin Juan Miro
Porte de Choisy
IVRY-SUR-SEINE

MONTPARNASSE

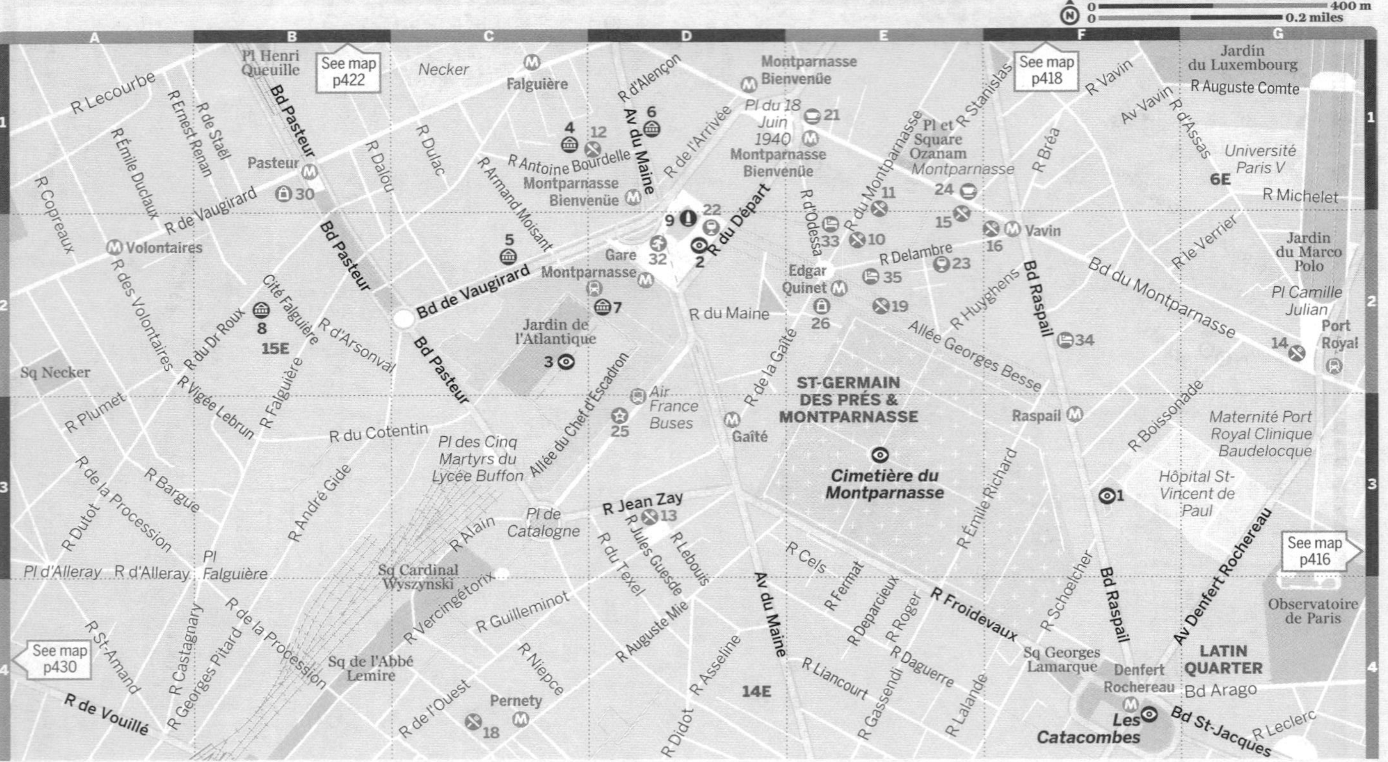

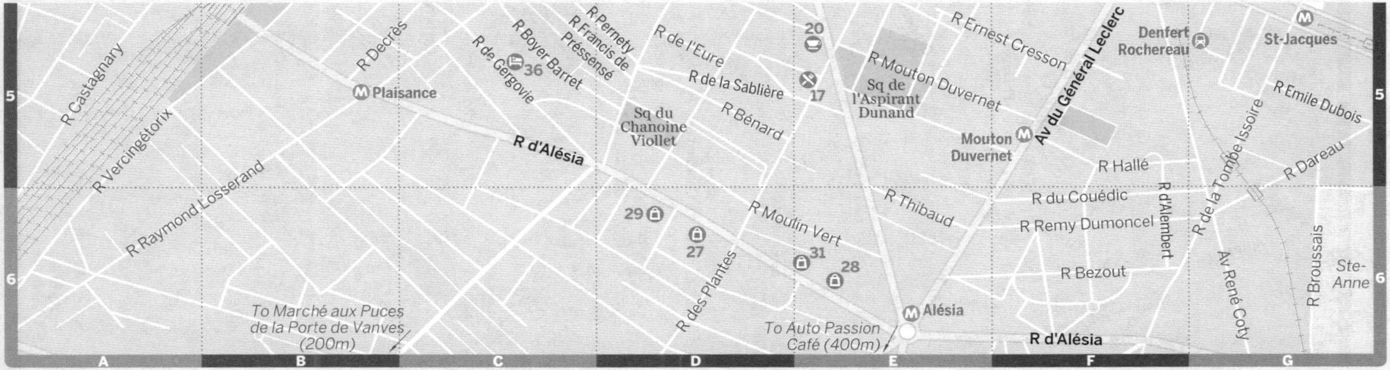

Top Sights (p253)

Cimetière du Montparnasse ... E3
Les Catacombes ... F4

Sights (p252)

1 Fondation Cartier pour l'Art Contemporain ... F3
2 Gare Montparnasse ... D2
3 Jardin de l'Atlantique ... C2
4 Musée Bourdelle ... C1
5 Musée de la Poste ... C2
6 Musée du Montparnasse ... D1
7 Musée Jean Moulin ... D2
8 Musée Pasteur ... B2
9 Tour Montparnasse ... D2

Eating (p256)

10 Crêperie Josselin ... E2
11 Crêperie Plougastel ... E1
12 La Cabane à Huîtres ... D1
13 La Cagouille ... D3
14 La Closerie des Lilas ... G2
15 La Coupole ... E2
Le Ciel de Paris ... (see 9)
16 Le Dôme ... F2
17 Le Sévéro ... E5
18 L'Entrepôt ... C4
Marché Brancusi ... (see 15)
19 Marché Edgar Quinet ... E2

Drinking & Nightlife (p261)

20 Félicie ... E5
21 La Ruche ... E1
22 Le Redlight ... D2
23 Le Rosebud ... E2
24 Le Select ... E1

Entertainment (p262)

Dancing La Coupole ... (see 15)
25 Le Petit Journal Montparnasse ... D3
L'Entrepôt ... (see 18)

Shopping (p263)

26 Adam Montparnasse ... E2
27 Cacharel ... D6
28 Dorotennis ... E6
29 Naf Naf Stock ... D6
30 Pierre Hermé ... B1
31 SR Store ... E6

Sports & Activities (p264)

32 Pari Roller ... D2

Sleeping (p297)

33 Celtic Hôtel ... E2
34 Hôtel de la Paix ... F2
35 Hôtel Delambre ... E2
36 La Maison ... C5

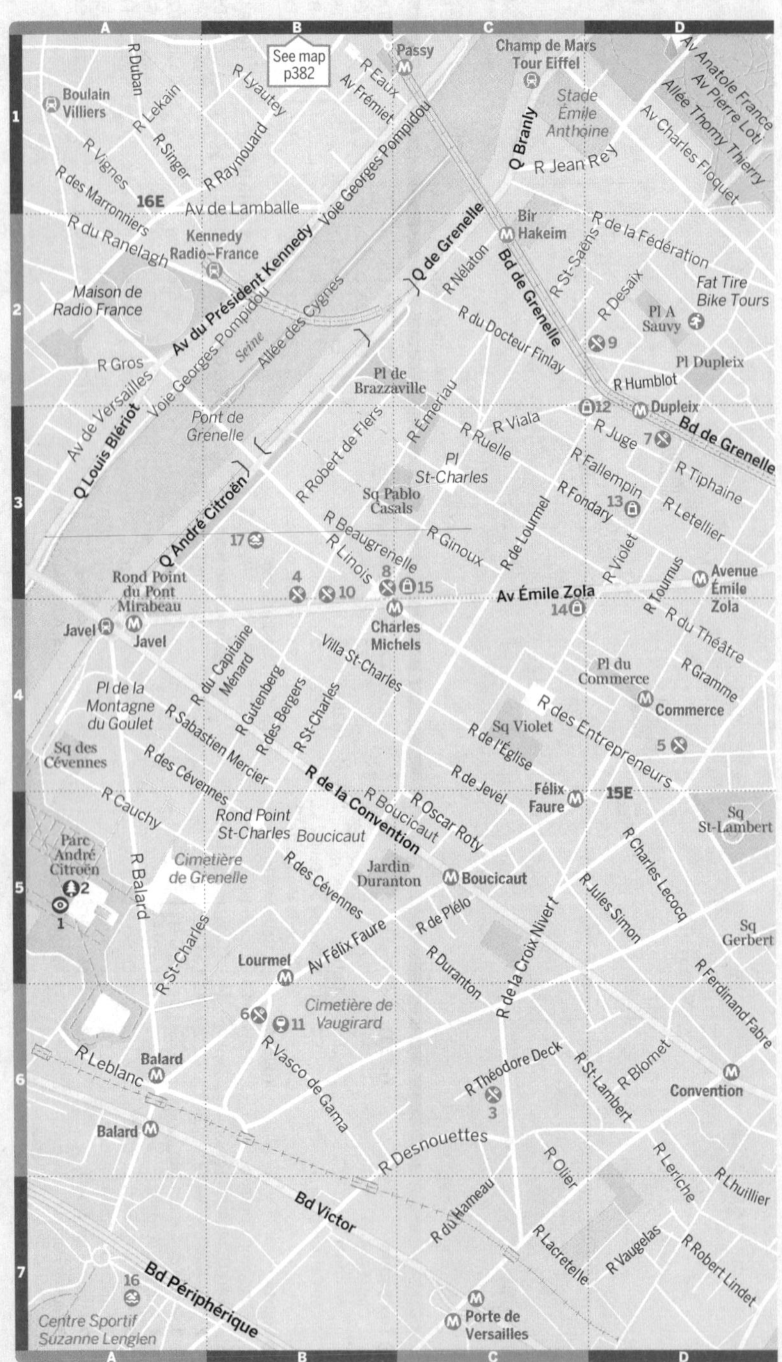

15E
See map p382
Passy
Champ de Mars Tour Eiffel
Stade Émile Anthoine
Boulain Villiers
R Duban
R Lekain
R Lyautey
R Eaux
Av Frémiet
Av Anatole France
Av Pierre Loti
Allée Thomy Thierry
Av Charles Floquet
R Vignes
R Singer
R Raynouard
Voie Georges Pompidou
Q Branly
R Jean Rey
R des Marronniers
16E
Av de Lamballe
Bir Hakeim
R de la Fédération
R du Ranelagh
Kennedy Radio-France
Av du Président Kennedy
Q de Grenelle
R Nélaton
Bd de Grenelle
R St-Saëns
R Desaix
Fat Tire Bike Tours
Maison de Radio France
Seine
Allée des Cygnes
Pl A Sauvy
R du Docteur Finlay
9
R Gros
Av de Versailles
Pl de Brazzaville
R Émeriau
Pl Dupleix
R Humblot
Q Louis Blériot
Pont de Grenelle
R Robert de Flers
R Viala
12
Dupleix
Bd de Grenelle
R Ruelle
R Juge
7
Pl St-Charles
R Fallempin
R Tiphaine
Q André Citroën
Sq Pablo Casals
R Fondary
13
R Letellier
17
R Beaugrenelle
R Ginoux
R de Lourmel
R Violet
R Linois
R Tournus
Avenue Émile Zola
Rond Point du Pont Mirabeau
4
10
8
15
Av Émile Zola
14
Javel
Javel
Charles Michels
R du Théâtre
R du Capitaine Ménard
Villa St-Charles
Pl du Commerce
R Gramme
Pl de la Montagne du Goulet
R Gutenberg
R des Bergers
R St-Charles
Commerce
R Sabastien Mercier
R des Entrepreneurs
Sq des Cévennes
Sq Violet
R de l'Église
5
R des Cévennes
R de la Convention
R de Javel
Félix Faure
15E
R Cauchy
R Boucicaut
R Oscar Roty
Sq St-Lambert
Rond Point St-Charles
Boucicaut
Parc André Citroën
2
1
R Balard
Cimetière de Grenelle
R des Cévennes
Jardin Duranton
Boucicaut
R Charles Lecocq
R Jules Simon
Sq Gerbert
R de Plélo
R de la Croix Nivert
Av Félix Faure
R St-Charles
Lourmel
R Duranton
R Ferdinand Fabre
6
11
Cimetière de Vaugirard
R Vasco de Gama
R Leblanc
Balard
R Théodore Deck
R St-Lambert
R Blomet
Convention
3
Balard
R Desnouettes
R Olier
R Leriche
R Lhuillier
Bd Victor
R du Hameau
R Lacretelle
R Vaugelas
R Robert Lindet
16
Bd Périphérique
Centre Sportif Suzanne Lenglen
Porte de Versailles

See map p422

See map p428

Sights (p252)

1 Le Ballon Air de Paris A5
2 Parc André-Citroën A5

Eating (p256)

3 Jadis C6
4 Kim Anh B3
5 Le Cristal De Sel D4
6 L'Os à Moëlle B6
7 Marché Grenelle D3
8 Marché St-Charles B3
9 Poilâne D2
10 Sawadee B3

Drinking & Nightlife (p261)

11 La Cave de l'Os à Moëlle B6

Shopping (p263)

12 Fromagerie Laurent Dubois D3
13 L'Arbre à Beurre D3
14 Le Petit Bazar C4
15 Mistigriff C3

Sports & Activities (p264)

16 Forest Hill Aquaboulevard A7
17 Piscine Keller B3

Sleeping (p297)

18 Aloha Hostel F5
19 Hôtel Carladez Cambronne E5

Our Story

A beat-up old car, a few dollars in the pocket and a sense of adventure. In 1972 that's all Tony and Maureen Wheeler needed for the trip of a lifetime – across Europe and Asia overland to Australia. It took several months, and at the end – broke but inspired – they sat at their kitchen table writing and stapling together their first travel guide, *Across Asia on the Cheap*. Within a week they'd sold 1500 copies. Lonely Planet was born.

Today, Lonely Planet has offices in Melbourne, London and Oakland, with more than 600 staff and writers. We share Tony's belief that 'a great guidebook should do three things: inform, educate and amuse'.

Our Writers

Catherine Le Nevez

Coordinating Author, Latin Quarter, St-Germain & Les Invalides, Montparnasse & Southern Paris, Day Trips from Paris Catherine first lived in Paris aged four and she's been returning here at every opportunity since, completing her Doctorate of Creative Arts in Writing, Masters in Professional Writing, and post-grad qualifications in Editing and Publishing along the way.

Catherine's writing on Paris includes numerous Lonely Planet guides to the city. Revisiting her favourite Parisian haunts and uncovering new ones is a highlight of this (and every) book. As well as newspaper and radio reportage covering Paris' literary scene, Catherine has authored, co-authored and contributed to dozens of Lonely Planet guidebooks throughout France, Europe and beyond. Wanderlust aside, Paris remains her favourite city on earth. Catherine also wrote the Welcome to Paris, Paris' Top 16, What's New, Need to Know, Top Itineraries, If You Like, Month by Month, Like a Local and For Free chapters, and the Drinking & Nightlife, Shopping, Entertainment, and Gay & Lesbian overviews.

Christopher Pitts

Eiffel Tower & Western Paris, Champs Élysées & Grands Boulevards, Montmartre & Northern Paris, Bastille & Eastern Paris Christopher Pitts has lived in Paris since 2001. He first started writing about the city as a means to buy baguettes – and to impress a certain Parisian (it worked, they're now married with two kids). Over the past decade he has written for various publications, in addition to working as a translator and editor. Chris also wrote the Museums & Galleries, Eating, and Sports & Activities overviews, and the Transport and Directory chapters.

Nicola Williams

Louvre & Les Halles, Le Marais & Ménilmontant, The Islands British writer and editorial consultant Nicola Williams has lived in France and written about it for more than a decade. From her hillside house on the southern shore of Lake Geneva, it's an easy hop to Paris where she has spent endless years revelling in its extraordinary art, architecture and cuisine. Resisting the urge to splurge in every boutique she passed while walking the streets of the Marais was this trip's challenge. Nicola also wrote the With Kids chapter and the Understand section.

Published by Lonely Planet Publications Pty Ltd
ABN 36 005 607 983
9th edition – Jan 2013
ISBN 978 1 74220 035 4

10 9 8 7 6 5 4 3 2 1
Printed in China